National Income Analysis & Forecasting

Critical Readers

Lucille G. Ford, *Ashland College*

Thomas G. Gies, *University of Michigan*

Bruce T. McKim, *University of California, Riverside*

Lawrence F. Mansfield, *University of Miami*

Lawrence Southwick, *State University of New York at Buffalo*

Paul Wachtel, *New York University*

National Income Analysis & Forecasting

Edward J. Chambers
University of Alberta

Robert Haney Scott
University of Washington

Roger S. Smith
International Monetary Fund
and
University of Alberta

Scott, Foresman and Company

Glenview, Illinois

Dallas, Tex. Oakland, N.J. Palo Alto, Cal. Tucker, Ga. Brighton, England

To Elizabeth, Joy, and Libby

Library of Congress Catalog Card Number: 73-93332
ISBN: 0-673-05134-x

Printed in the United States of America.

PREFACE

The national economic environment concerns decision-making units in both the public and the private sectors of the economy. Under the Employment Act of 1946, the federal government is committed to the adoption and implementation of policies that maintain a stable and growing economy with maximum purchasing power and employment opportunities. The fortunes of business reflect the impact of external forces, and the costs and revenues of firms of all sizes in many industries are sensitive—in all degrees—to the level and rate of change of total economic activity. Sales and net profits move with fluctuations in the aggregate economy.

The interaction of governmental authorities, domestic consumers and businessmen, and foreign consumers and investors is what this book is about. A basic understanding of the interdependence of these groups is essential for an intelligent evaluation of the more fundamental economic policy actions. The major portion of the book is devoted to a development of the interdependence of the various groups in the economy. This is done with the help of an algebraic tool—a simultaneous equation model. The model developed is a standard macroeconomic model. It is not a simple model, since there are many interacting variables in every economy, but the student of business administration or economics who masters the material from Chapter 1 through Chapter 14 should be well equipped to understand and analyze many of the economic policy issues which will confront him daily. We try to help him do this by integrating our discussions of policy issues and instruments throughout the book, rather than in a separate section.

The first part of the book, through Chapter 14, concentrates on factors influencing the level of employment. Since World War II, full employment has been the primary objective of economic policy makers. Achieving balance of payments objectives, stable prices, a low rate of inflation, and rapid growth has usually been secondary to the employment goal, although recent history suggests that problems in these areas may soon become critical. Whatever the objective, however, all macroeconomic variables have been, and are, analyzed in order to gain a basic understanding of how the control of factors such as the money supply, government spending, and taxes enables policy makers to achieve their objectives.

Chapter 15, using the tools developed in the earlier chapters, carefully analyzes the policy options available for achieving and maintaining a "desirable" balance between exports and imports. During the last two decades, while the total value of world imports in monetary terms more than tripled, that of U.S. imports increased by 267 percent, but that of U.S. exports only increased by 171 percent. To accommodate such a growing imbalance, domestic interest rates may be increased to produce an inflow of investment capital from other countries. To correct this imbalance, an export subsidy may be used to stimulate production for foreign markets, or the dollar may be devalued. Economic theory indicates when certain actions are appropriate, but this book will not have achieved its end if it does not reveal the limitations of policy options. The choices open to those who have the responsibility for guiding our economy are rarely simple ones.

Chapter 16 analyzes the obstacles to achieving the objective of stable prices. Organizational structures and rigidities, psychological factors, and the distribution of political power, all increase the difficulty of achieving stable prices, but none of these factors is easily manipulable by economic policy makers in the legislative or executive branches of government. Nevertheless, an understanding of economic variables, as developed in the first part of the book, enables us to see what can be achieved by conventional monetary and fiscal policies. An appreciation of the limitations of the more conventional policy options helps us understand what additional benefits might be derived by the assertion of direct control over wages and prices—such as President Nixon introduced in Phases I through IV under the authority of the Economic Stabilization Act of 1970.

Rapid economic growth has been and continues to be a national objective—if not for itself, then for the support it lends to full employment and price stability. It is, however, clear that increases in output cannot be equated with increases in welfare. The rate of growth of output depends upon many things, among them the demand for the additional goods produced, the increase in the volume of resources used in production, and improvements in technology and the rate at which improved techniques are implemented. Building from the earlier chapters, Chapter 17 analyzes the potential contribution of each of the above factors to the rate of growth and examines the effects of specific economic policies upon the rate of growth.

Because the state of the national economy is so important to those who make decisions in both the public and private sectors, in the final part of the book we have found it essential to introduce the student of macroeconomics to prediction, or forecasting. Prediction cannot really be separated from life. Human activity inevitably reflects forecasts of the future blended with current pressures and past commitments. This part of the book presents a few short-run forecasting models based on the functional relationships established in Chapters 3 through 14. Input-output as a forecasting technique is also described in a special chapter written by Philip Bourque.

Greater equity in the distribution of income has received increasing attention as an objective of macroeconomic policy.[1] We do not, and cannot, specify the optimum distribution of wealth and income within the economy. We do, however, continually recognize that while income distribution is important in itself, it also plays a crucial role in determining the level of income and employment, the rate of change in prices, and the rate of growth.

During the time that this book was in process the authors have had much assistance from their students and colleagues. Students in our macro classes at the University of Washington and the University of Alberta have worked their way through the teaching notes and thereby materially contributed to the evolution of the manuscript. Besides encouragement, they offered many helpful comments whose incorporation has, we believe, increased pedagogic effectiveness. We wish also to acknowledge the assistance of reviewers and colleagues who examined the manuscript in part or in its entirety. Special thanks to Philip Bourque, Lucille Ford, Tom Gies, Dudley Johnson, Bruce McKim, L. F. Mansfield, Ed Mills, Rolf Mirus, William Pigott, Gil Reschenthaler, Lawrence Southwick, and Paul Wachtel. Our thanks also to our editor, Tom Easton, for his precision and efficiency.

Last, but hardly least, we wish to express our appreciation to those persons who carried the typing of the manuscript through numerous drafts, including Doreen Fletcher, Beverley Frangos, Merle Lobo, and Joy Osgood.

Edward J. Chambers
R. Haney Scott
Roger S. Smith

[1] See Joan Robinson, "The second crisis of economic theory," pp. 1–9, and Gunnar Myrdal, "Response to introduction," pp. 456–63, *American Economics Review*, 62 (May 1972).

TABLE OF CONTENTS

PART I
MEASUREMENT 1

1. **Transactions and the Measurement of Output** 3

Grouping units according to their roles 3 Personal and disposable income 12 The gross savings and investment account 14 Intertemporal comparisons of GNP 17
Conclusion 21 Appendix: National income accounts 22 Additional readings 27 Questions 27

2. **The Money Supply** 30

What is money? 30 Credit money and the monetary system 31
Conclusion 46 Appendix: The relations of reserves to the money supply 47 Additional readings 50 Questions 50

PART II
FROM MEASUREMENT TO THEORY 52

3. **Household Behavior: Basic Theory** 54

Consumption and income 54 The theory and measurement of consumption 69
Conclusion 70 Additional readings 70 Questions 70

4. **Household Behavior: Theory and Evidence** 72

Long-run implications of APC > MPC 72 Short-run and long-run consumption functions—Empirical evidence from time series 74 The absolute income hypothesis 75 The relative income hypothesis 76 The permanent income hypothesis 79 Empirical evidence concerning the relative and permanent income hypotheses 81
Conclusion 82 Additional readings 83 Questions 84

5. **Investment Demand** 85

Classic analysis of investment demand 85 Income and investment 95
Conclusion 98 Additional readings 99 Questions 100

6. **The Public Sector and the Foreign Sector** 101

Government expenditures 101 Incorporating a lump-sum tax into the commodity market model 105 Equilibrium conditions in a three-sector commodity market model 108 Adding transfer payments to the commodity market model 112 Introducing automatic stabilizers into the commodity market model 113 The relation of budget positions to output levels 117 Introducing the foreign sector 120
Conclusion 122 Additional readings 123 Questions 124

7. **Equilibrium in Commodity Markets** 126

A revised multiplier matrix 126 Income determination in commodity markets 127 Graphs relating Y to R in commodity markets 128
The *IS* curve: A linear and numerical model 130
Conclusion 136 Additional readings 136 Questions 136

8. **Money in a Portfolio of Assets** 138

The balance sheets of decision-making units 138
Conclusion 145 Additional readings 146 Questions 146

9. **The Demand for Money** 148

The demand for a medium of exchange 148 The capital certainty or asset demand for money 152 Adding the transactions and asset demands for money 153 Shifts in the M_D function 154 The money supply 155 Model of the monetary sector 155
Conclusion 160 Additional readings 161 Questions 162

10. **Bringing the Commodity Market and Money Market Together** 164

The linear and numerical model 164 The portfolio balance effect 175
Conclusion 176 Appendix: Empirical estimates of *IS* and *LM* curves 177 Additional readings 179 Questions 180

11. **Aggregate Supply: Output and the Price Level** 182

Derivation of the model 183 Predicting with the model 193
Conclusion 197 Additional readings 197 Questions 198

12. **The Labor Market** 200

The aggregate demand for labor 200 The supply of labor 202 Equilibrium level of employment 203 Negotiated wage levels 204 Bringing together the supply of and demand for labor in money wage terms 211 The asymmetry of price level behavior 214
Conclusion 214 Appendix: Measuring employment, unemployment, and wages 215 Additional readings 222 Questions 223

13. **Labor, Commodity, and Money Markets Combined** 224

Putting the model together 224 Summary of the model 229
Conclusion 235 Additional readings 236 Questions 236

14. **Further Complications: A Variable Wage Rate and Wealth Effects** 237

The money wage rate as a function of employment 237 The wealth effect 247
Additional readings 249 Questions 250

15. **Income and the Balance of Payments** 251

The foreign sector: Effect on aggregate supply 251 The foreign sector: Feedback effects on aggregate demand 252 The balance of international payments 253 Some key functional relationships 258 Flexible exchange rates 270 Fiscal and monetary policy for stabilization under fixed and flexible exchange rates 271
Conclusion 275 Additional readings 276 Questions 277

PART III
INFLATION AND GROWTH 278

16. **Inflation** 280

The trade-off between the rate of change in the price level and the rate of unemployment 282 Theories of inflation 286 Price-incomes policy 300
Conclusion 311 Additional readings 311 Questions 313

17. Economic Growth 315

Domar's theory of economic growth 317 A neoclassical model of economic growth 325 Empirical evidence 330 Policy implications 334
Conclusion 338 Additional readings 338 Questions 339

PART IV
PREDICTION 341

18. Business Fluctuations 345

Business cycle theories 346 Cycle forecasting and measurement 350
Conclusion 359 Additional readings 359 Questions 360

19. Forecasting with Econometric Models 361

Econometric models 362 Alternative projections and model reliability 369
Conclusion 370 Additional readings 371 Questions 371

20. Forecasting with Input-Output Tables 372

The input-output accounting framework 373 Input-output coefficients 375 Industrial multipliers and Keynesian income multipliers 384 Use of input-output in impact analysis 385 The economic impact of disarmament 386 Input-output projections 387 Applications of input-output at the firm level 391 Applications in regional analysis 393
Concluding comments 393 Additional readings 394 Questions 394

Index 396

I
Part

MEASUREMENT

Generally accepted principles of social accounting have some shortcomings (such as a failure to cost fully some noxious by-products of output), but they do provide a systematic basis for measuring output over time. In a highly interdependent exchange economy like our own, it is desirable to divide the economy into groups of similar transactors, such as the four main sectors considered in this book: households; business firms; government; and the rest of the world (nonresidents). Although we recognize that the motivations and behavior of these designated sectors of the economy differ significantly, transactions between and within these sectors can be combined and summarized into meaningful classes in terms of the kinds of goods produced and the factors of production employed. The purpose of Part I is to describe briefly the network of transactions that underlies the production and distribution of goods in a country. Concepts that explain sectoral behavior, the rate at which factors of production are used, and the level of national output will be developed in Part II.

Part I also deals specifically with the supply of money—the medium through which transactions occur. In the discussion of money, we emphasize that transactions require *both* a unit of account in which their value can be measured *and* a generally accepted asset that facilitates the process of exchange.

Transactions and the Measurement of Output

1
Chapter

The task of this book may be described as developing a model that will relate the variations in economic output, employment, income, exports, imports, government spending, and other economic variables. Our first concern must therefore be with defining these variables in such a way that they can later be incorporated into the model. And this may perhaps be best done by examining the measurement of economic output during some specified period of time, such as a year, for in our money-using exchange economy, most decisions about how much and what to produce are made in the marketplace. Privately owned producing units respond to the demands of consumers by organizing productive factors. Yet, even in an economy relying primarily on the market mechanism to allocate resources, certain goods and services, called "public goods," are provided collectively; education, national defense, public safety, and similar services provided by federal, state, or local governments are examples. Consumers, business firms, and government each add to the flow of output and receive income in exchange. In our economy, countless transactions occur between these economic units. Therefore it is on transactions that attention must be centered.

GROUPING UNITS ACCORDING TO THEIR ROLES

Our task is to set up a social accounting system capable of measuring the flow of output and the income received through its exchange. As in any accounting system, the first necessity is to group economic units in a logical manner. We will establish three producing groups: business firms; government; and households. With the accounts of a double-entry accounting system one can show the interdependence of output and income flows between each of these three different types of decision-making units. In addition we take explicit account of the foreign-trade and the capital goods—or investment—sectors of the economy and integrate them with the three producing sectors.

Producing Units: (1) Business Firms

In a market economy the basic responsibilities for production fall on business firms. A measurement of the output of the private business sector of the economy can be obtained by "aggregating," or adjusting and adding up selected elements of, the income and product statements of all private producing units. To see this, we can start with a representative producing unit and show the derivation of its income and product statements.

The difference between an income statement and a production statement arises because a firm may produce either more or less than it sells. Thus production will differ from sales by the change in inventories. Below (Table 1–1) is a production statement for a representative business firm, the Black Corporation, which buys and sells in a number of markets. Each of its transactions may be labeled as either a "use" or a "source" of "payments" by and to the firm, with the value of output, both in the form of production for sale and production for stock (inventory), appearing on the "sources" side of payments to the firm. The use of the terms "uses," "sources," and "payments" is somewhat arbitrary because in the case of inventories there is no transaction with another party.

On the "sources" side of this table, all sales are entered according to the type of transaction involved, together with the net change in inventories. Sales to consumers, to government, and to other business firms on capital account (such as sales of long-lived machinery) are all sales for "final" use; they differ from total sales by sales to other business firms on current account (for example, sales of materials to be used by the other firms in production in the current accounting period). The numerical value of sales revenue is the

Table 1–1. Black Corporation Production Statement for the Calendar Year.

Uses (Income)	Sources (Product)
Purchases from other domestic firms for current use	Total Sales:
Plus purchases from abroad	Sales to households
Plus depreciation	Sales to government
Plus indirect business taxes	Sales to other business firms on capital account
Plus business transfer payments	Sales to foreigners
Plus factor payments:	Net inventory change
Wages and salaries	Sales to other domestic business firms on current account for further production
Social Security payments	
Net interest paid	
Corporate income taxes	
Dividends paid out	
Retained earnings	
Less subsidies	
Equals: Total uses (essentially costs of inputs)	Equals: Total sources (essentially revenues from output)

product of quantity and market price per unit. Inventories are also valued at market price. Hence, a *market valuation* is placed on Black Corporation's production.

On the "uses" side appear all of the charges against production. These include purchases of current inputs from other firms (which appear again as receipts, or sources, for those firms), depreciation charges, indirect business taxes (property taxes, excise taxes, and customs duties), and transfer payments (bad debts and charitable contributions). These are "costs" of production but do not constitute payments to the factors of production. Factor payments are those charges against output necessary to bring forth the required factors of production: labor, capital, and enterprise. The inclusion of employer Social Security contributions and corporate income taxes can be viewed as charges against product arising from the imposition of institutional and legal constraints upon the production process.

It should be stressed that all transactions are reciprocal affairs. Every sale appears in two production statements, in one as a source, in the other as a use. What is cost to Black is revenue to its suppliers. What is cost to Black's customers is revenue to Black.

A word about direct subsidies. They are deducted from the income side because, although they are received and used to defray charges against product, they do not appear on the sources side of the statement. That is, they do not come from the sale of output but are a direct payment to the Black Corporation by government. Since they are not included in the market value of a firm's production, they must be deducted from charges against that product.[1]

Deriving an Income and Product Statement for the Representative Corporation: The Concept of Value-Added

The production statement requires further alteration, however, if it is to measure accurately the net contribution of Black Corporation to the economy. This adjustment is reflected in the "value added" by Black, i.e., the value created when Black combines the services of labor and capital with inputs purchased from domestic and foreign suppliers. Value-added is the effective or net contribution to the output of the economy; alternatively, it can be thought of as the income created by Black. It is arrived at by deducting from the "uses" side of the production statement the sum of (a) Black's purchases from other firms for current use, and (b) Black's purchases from foreign producers for current use.

Corresponding deductions from Black's product side give the income and product statement (Table 1–2), where the product side shows Black's net contribution to the output of the economy, while the income side shows the value added in production by Black.

[1] "Indirect" subsidies, arising from such measures as protective tariffs, tax credits, depletion allowances, etc., are difficult to account for inasmuch as they alter the market value of the product.

Table 1–2. Income and Product Statement for the Black Corporation.

Uses (Income)	Sources (Product)
Depreciation	Sales to households
Plus indirect business taxes	Plus sales to government
Plus business transfer payments	Plus sales to business on capital account
Plus factor payments:	Plus sales to foreigners
Wages and salaries	Plus net inventory change
Social Security contributions	Plus sales to other domestic firms for current inputs
Net interest paid	
Corporate income taxes	Less purchases from other domestic firms for current use
Dividends paid	
Retained earnings	Less purchases from abroad
Less subsidies received	
Equals: Value added by Black	Equals: Black's product

The Aggregate Business Income and Product Account

To find business income, we need not only the income generated by Black, but also the income generated by other business firms. The income and product account of the business sector as a whole can be derived (Table 1–3) by aggregating the income and product statements of *all* business producing units. Table 1–3 differs from Table 1–2 only in that all sales between businesses for current use do not appear: They sum to zero. Similarly, all purchases from foreign businesses are deducted from exports to foreigners to derive a "net sales to foreigners" figure for the business sector.

Table 1–3 shows the *gross* income and product of the business sector. Because the machinery and equipment used in producing this product have depreciated in value, however, we can subtract depreciation allowances from both sides of the statement to give us a measure of net income and product.

Table 1–3. Income and Product Account of the Business Sector.

Uses (Income)	Sources (Product)
Depreciation	Sales to households
Plus indirect business taxes	Plus sales to business on capital account
Plus business transfer payments	Plus sales to government
Plus factor payments:	Plus net sales to foreigners
Wages and salaries	Plus net inventory change
Social Security payments	
Net interest paid	
Corporate income taxes	
Dividends paid	
Retained earnings	
Less subsidies received	
Equals: Gross income originating in business	Equals: Gross business product

Table 1–4. Sources and Uses of Government Receipts.

Uses (Income)	Sources (Product)
Wages and salaries	Indirect business taxes
Plus purchases from business	Plus Social Security receipts
Plus interest paid	Plus corporate income taxes
Plus transfer payments to households	Plus personal tax receipts
Plus transfer payments to foreigners	Plus direct sales
Plus grants to other government units	Plus current surplus of government enterprise
Plus subsidies	Plus grants from other governmental units
Plus surplus	
Equals: Total uses	Equals: Total sources

Producing Units: (2) Governments

In measuring the product of the second producing unit of the economy, government, there arises a complication not found in the measurement of activity in the business sector. Government does not serve only to produce goods, in particular those that are collectively consumed; it also exists as an institution for redistributing the income and wealth of society in the light of generally accepted social norms. Our social accounting system must therefore carefully distinguish activities concerned with production from those designed to redistribute income.

If we consider a representative government, we can see both the function of producing collective goods and the function of redistributing income in its sources and uses statement (Table 1–4). On the sources side are all revenues available to our representative unit, largely consisting of different forms of tax payments; in the example, it is assumed that our representative unit has a diversified tax base including indirect business taxes, corporate and personal income taxes, and employment security levies. A small portion of receipts comes from direct sales by government to the public (one may assume, for example, that our unit operates a water company). A final source of revenue is "grants-in-aid" from other governmental units (such as grants by the federal government to state government for specific programs). One important contrast with the representative business firm appears on the sources side of this statement; namely, no market valuation is placed on the output of the collective goods that tax receipts are used to produce. Only "direct sales" are evident, and to these a market valuation may be assigned.

On the uses side appear all of the categories of charges against government revenues. These include wage, salary, and interest payments; transfer payments; grants by our representative unit to other government units; purchases from business firms; subsidies; and a balancing item (surplus) representing the budgetary position.

Aggregation of All Government Sources and Uses Statements

In aggregating across the receipt and expenditure statements of all government units, one change takes place in the composition of the government account. While "grants from other government units" appears on the sources side and "grants to other government units" appears on the uses side, consolidation across all governments will obviously cancel out these items, leaving a picture of the impact of both government provision of collective goods and the redistributive effects of government on the economy.

The Special Problem of Measuring Government Production

The redistributive effects of government may be removed from the revenue and expenditure statement by returning to the revenue and expenditure statement of our representative government unit and deducting, from the sources side, "grants from other government units," and, from the uses side, "transfer payments," "subsidies," and "grants to other government units." What is left then is the government product, a difficult thing to value. The government's sources consist, in the main, of compulsory tax payments rather than revenues derived from sales of commodities that are voluntarily purchased in the marketplace. Hence some alternative to market valuation must be adopted. To convert to a production statement, the convention is to remove from the sources side all items that cannot be directly related to the cost of government production, for there is no reason to assume that personal tax payments represent the cost of producing the public goods and services consumed by households; nor should we assume that the sum of indirect business taxes and corporate profit taxes measures the cost of producing the collective goods used by business. Thus we eliminate all tax payments, leaving only direct sales. (This in our case might be cubic feet of water sold by our government unit times the price per cubic foot.)

A money value may then be attributed to those goods and services provided collectively. On the uses side are three eligible items: wages and salaries; purchases from business; and interest paid. These uses may be regarded as the *costs* of production of government services, and we could therefore value these services *not* at market value (as we do in the business sector), *but at cost*. However, it is now necessary to introduce the convention, followed by national income accountants, that interest paid by government should *not* be treated as a cost of providing current government services. The underlying logic is that almost all government interest payments stem from past activity (such as wars) and have nothing to do with the provision of current government services. Accordingly, they are treated in the same manner as a transfer payment (i.e., as a redistributive payment). On the uses side of our government production statement we are then left with (a) wages and salaries, and (b) purchases from business. The production statement of our representative government unit will then be as follows:

Table 1–5. Production Statement of a Representative Government Unit.

Uses (Income)	Sources (Product)
Wages and salaries	Direct sales
Plus purchases from business	Plus imputed sales
Total: ———	Total: ———

Conversion to a Government Income and Product Statement

Table 1–5 may be very simply converted to a statement of the product and income originating in government by deducting from both the sources and uses sides "purchases from business." The value added by government is then wages and salaries on the uses side, and the sum of direct and imputed sales minus purchases from business on the product side, as shown in Table 1–6. To repeat, by "imputed sales" is meant the monetary value attached to those goods and services provided by the government that do not involve market transactions.

As before, aggregating across all government units in the economy will provide a measure of the total income originating in government and of total government product.

Producing Units: (3) Households

Finally, how should we treat households as producers? We have seen that selected members of households engage in production by selling their services either to business or government. Normally, we think of households as consuming units, but to do so surely represents a very narrow view of household activity. The extent of enjoyment derived from acts of consumption depends upon the quality of life in the households. In fact, there is a lot of work in the household that requires learning and technical skill in application. The raising of children, the preparing of meals, the planning of consumption, and the organization and execution of numerous other tasks are all examples of productive effort within the household. The value of these activities—all *internal* to the households—could all be considered as *product* and *income originating* in households. The products are not sold in the marketplace nor are hours of labor inputs acquired by paying the prevailing wage and salary rate. How then do we value these services, provided in the main by those adult members of the household who are not employed for monetary gain by other producing units? We were faced in the case of government with measuring an output that did

Table 1–6. Income and Product Statement of a Representative Government Unit.

Uses (Income)	Sources (Product)
Wages and salaries	Direct sales
	Plus imputed sales
	Less government purchases from business
Equals: Income originating in government	Equals: Gross government product

not go through the marketplace, and we solved the problem by attributing to it a value based upon the difference between total wage and salary payments and that portion of these payments assignable to direct sales by government. In the case of households, however, we would have to attribute values to both the income and the product sides of the table. This might be done by estimating the sum that would have to be paid in wages and salaries to acquire the household management necessary to carry out the tasks already identified; for example, the person to provide child care, the shopper to make purchases, the manager to take care of household administration, the cook to prepare the meals, and the domestic help to do the housekeeping "dirties." When one considers that there are about 70 million households in the United States, it is readily apparent that we are dealing with a significant amount of activity.

The prevailing social accounting convention is, however, to bypass the difficulties of assigning value to the activities just described. Only where households employ servants and domestic help is there held to be any such income or product. On the sources side of such a household's income and product statement (Table 1–7) are expenditures for domestic servants, deemed to be a sale by the household (as the organizer and manager of this activity) to itself. On the uses side appear the charges against that product in the form of wages, wage supplements (board and room provided to domestic help), and Social Security contributions. If the services of housewives were counted as part of household product, an imputed value of sales would appear on the product side, and an imputed wage value would appear on the income side. Housewives could be placed on the Social Security program through a payroll tax remitted by the household on the imputed value of wages.

Finally, this sector also includes the case of the household that owns and occupies its own home. In this instance the household can be viewed as renting the house to itself, and a value can be imputed to the stream of services flowing from the asset.[2] Conceptually the imputed rent would be equal in value to the cost of renting equivalent facilities. In Table 1–7 we then add to the product side a further item, "imputed sales of rental services to households," and to the income side a similar "rental payment in kind."

Table 1–7. Income and Product Statement of a Representative Household Using Domestic Help.

Uses (Income)	Sources (Product)
Wages paid	Sales of domestic services to households
Plus employer Social Security contributions	Plus imputed sales of rental services to households
Plus wage supplements	
Plus rental payments in kind	
Equals: Total income originating in households	Equals: Total household product

[2] Someone who owns dwelling units and derives income from their rent would be included as a producing unit in the business sector.

The reader may feel some legitimate concern at the apparent illogic in the conventional accounting treatment of the household as a producing unit. The inclusion of an imputed rental value for owner-occupied dwellings and the exclusion of an imputed value for the labor services rendered by houseworkers lacks a certain internal consistency.

Deriving Measures of Aggregate Product and Income Originating from Our Three Producing Units

Having a measure of income and product for each of three types of producing units, we can now develop measures of the gross output, the net output after depreciation allowances, and income payments to the factors of production. One measure of the first of these is called "gross national product," and it may be derived by aggregating across either the sources (product) side or the uses (income) side of the income and product statements. Considering the product side first:

Gross National Product (GNP) = Sales to households
+ Sales to business on capital account
+ Net inventory change
+ Sales to government (including gross government product valued at cost)
+ Net sales to foreigners

This measurement of GNP, as in the sources side of Table 1–3, shows expenditures or purchases of output for final use. Table 1–14 in the appendix to this chapter contains a breakdown of actual data estimates prepared by the U.S. Department of Commerce.

GNP may also be derived from the income payment or "value-added" side as follows:

Gross National Product (GNP) = Non-factor charges
- **Depreciation**
- **Indirect business taxes**
- **Business transfer payments**

+ Factor payments
- **Wages and salaries**
- **Wage supplements**
- **Employer Social Security contributions**
- **Interest**
- **Rent**
- **Dividends**
- **Income of unincorporated enterprises**
- **Retained earnings**
- **Corporate income taxes**

− Subsidies

Two other measures of special interest, net national product and national income, may be derived from the income side of the aggregated income and product statements. The first is the difference between gross national product and capital consumption allowances (depreciation). This measure tells us the output of the economy after allowing for that portion of the capital stock used up in producing output over the specified period. The second, also known as national income at factor cost, is a measure of the rewards paid to the factors of production in the creation of output. If we adjust net national product for all of the other non-factor charges against output, we are left with the sum of income payments to the factors. To find national income, then, we subtract indirect taxes from net national product and add subsidies. Indirect taxes are subtracted out because they reflect a flow of funds directly to the government and not payments to factors of production. Subsidies are added back in to the net national product since it is assumed that they represent payments to the factors for services rendered in producing output. The sum of these charges represents the value added in production, and it is also referred to as gross national product. Table 1–15 in the appendix to this chapter contains examples of these calculations as published by the Department of Commerce.

PERSONAL AND DISPOSABLE INCOME

Two further widely used measures of income flows can be derived from a full statement of sources and uses in the household sector. First, on the sources side of Table 1–8, are income flows (including supplements) representing the contribution by members of all households to current production. These represent payments necessary to employ factors of production—payments that accrue to household units. In arriving at personal income, however, it is necessary to add payments by both government and business which effect income redistribution. Government transfer payments are Social Security payments, Veterans Administration allotments, aid to dependent children, etc., which are made independently of any contribution to current output. Business transfer payments (bad debts and charitable contributions) also represent income transfers. Deducting employee contributions to Social Security as well then provides a measure of *personal income*, as in Table 1–17 in the appendix to this chapter.

The uses side provides information about the disposition of income. Personal consumption expenditures reflect (a) services purchased directly from producing households, (b) purchases from business, and (c) net purchases from abroad, primarily reflecting foreign travel. Item (a) would include expenditures on domestic help, child care services provided for a fee in the home, and similar kinds of direct purchases. Item (b) is in fact by far the largest dollar sum covering all marketplace purchases of goods and services for final consumption. Item (c) mainly represents the services provided by foreigners to tourists (lodging and travel accommodations) and purchases by tourists while traveling abroad. Note that there is no account for purchase of

Table 1–8. Income and Product Statement of the Household Sector.

Uses	Sources
Personal consumption expenditures:	Wages and salaries and wage supplements received
Purchases of direct service	—from households
Net business purchases	—from business
Net purchases from abroad	—from government
Plus personal taxes and non-tax payments	Plus income of unincorporated business enterprises
Plus personal savings	Plus rental income of persons
	Plus dividends
	Plus personal interest income
	Plus government transfer payments
	Plus business transfer payments
	Less employee contributions to Social Security
Equals: Total personal expenditures and savings	Equals: Total personal income

government output. It may bear repeating that government, as a producing unit, provides collectively consumed goods and services, and it is therefore not possible to distinguish consumption of these goods in the household from their contribution as inputs in the business sector.

Personal tax and non-tax payments—license fees and fines of various kinds—are the second major claim against income. The final item in Table 1–8, personal savings, is a residual or balancing item in the account. *Disposable income*, not shown in the table, is the most appropriate measure to use when describing consuming purchasing power. It is, simply, personal income less personal tax and non-tax payments. Tables 1–16 and 1–17 in the appendix to this chapter contain examples of the breakdown of the published data on personal disposable income, etc.

The Foreign Sector

The business, government, and household consuming and producing units have a definite combined effect upon the foreign sector, whose account is presented in Table 1–9. The foreign sector, or "the rest of the world," receives payments when U.S. citizens pay for imported goods—sources from the point of view of foreigners. Foreigners then use these receipts to purchase goods from the U.S.—U.S. exports. Foreign account "uses" are therefore made up of payments by foreigners for our sales to foreigners and these payments are the equivalent of the sales receipts of U.S. exporters. Foreigners are able to finance these payments with funds arising from three sources: U.S. imports of goods and services from the rest of the world; net cash transfers from the U.S. government to the rest of the world; and net foreign investment.

Table 1–9. Income and Product Statement of the Foreign Sector.

Uses	Sources
Exports of goods and services	Imports of goods and services by business, households, and government
	Plus net transfer payments from government
	Plus net foreign investment (investment by Americans in foreign countries minus investment by foreigners in the U.S.)

THE GROSS SAVINGS AND INVESTMENT ACCOUNT

The last account needed to close our social accounting system is the gross savings and investment account. In the analysis in succeeding chapters of this book concerning cause-and-effect relations between the elements of the economic system, this account is of great importance. Almost every item in the four basic accounts (business as producer, government as producer and redistributor, households as consumers and producers, and the foreign sector) has appeared twice, as when sales to foreigners in the business sector accounts appear also as exports of goods and services in the foreign sector accounts. There are, however, some notable exceptions, as noted in the gross savings and investment account in Table 1–10. By setting up an account to accommodate these exceptions, the system becomes completely self-contained.

Table 1–10 shows the sources and disposition of what is currently produced but not currently consumed. On the sources, or savings, side are retained corporate earnings and depreciation allowances from the business sector, personal savings from the household sector, and the government surplus or deficit. These charges against product, or residual items, become sources of product not used up in the current accounting period. Disposition may be in the form of capital formation and net inventory change in the business sector, or in the form of net investment in the foreign sector.

The gross savings and investment account is important because it provides a major connecting link between income flows and changes in the wealth (or

Table 1–10. The Gross Savings and Investment Account.

Uses	Sources
Business purchases on capital account	Retained corporate earnings
Plus net inventory change	Plus depreciation allowances
Plus net foreign investment	Plus personal savings
	Plus government surplus or deficit
Equals: Gross investment	Equals: Gross savings

Table 1–11. Black Corporation, Initial Income Statement.

Assets		Liabilities	
Plant and equipment	$1,000,000	Net worth	$750,000
		Bonded indebtedness	$250,000

balance sheet) positions of transactor units, as may be seen by considering a typical producing unit such as the Black Corporation at the beginning of the accounting period for which an income statement is to be generated. Suppose that during the year plant and equipment expenditures amount to $200,000, of which half is for replacement of worn-out equipment and half is for net additions to the stock of capital. The former is financed by depreciation, a cost item in the income statement of the business. It is internal savings (internal to the firm) and is used in this instance to replace old machinery. The latter may be financed in several ways, such as half by the sale of bonds to households and half by the use of retained earnings. At the end of the accounting period, Black's balance sheet would have changed as shown in Table 1–12.

The example reflects the fact that the sources of finance for business purchases on capital account are both internal and external to the firm. Internal sources are depreciation allowances and retained corporate earnings. Internal transfers pose no special problems. Savings are both generated and utilized by the Black Corporation. But the example also reflects the fact that firms raise funds externally in order to finance capital expenditures. In this case personal savings in the amount of $50,000 are transferred either directly or through financial intermediaries (banks, savings and loan societies, insurance companies, mutual funds, etc.). Such transfers in a complex exchange economy, in which the corporate legal form is employed, require a willingness on the part of those who have an excess of income over expenditure to augment their wealth by acceptance of debt (or equity) instruments in exchange for their savings.

The change in household wealth positions over the year, resulting from the simple example in which no financial intermediaries are involved, amounts to an increase of $50,000, representing personal savings converted into fixed assets with a fixed claim on the future income stream of the corporation. Savers have accepted bonds, though they may wish to increase their net wealth in other ways, as by holding equities, debentures, or real assets.

Table 1–12. Black Corporation, Final Income Statement.

Assets		Liabilities	
Plant and equipment	$1,100,000	Net worth	$800,000
		Bonded indebtedness	$300,000
Net change	+$100,000	Net change	+$100,000

Table 1–13. Change in Household Wealth Positions over the Income Statement Accounting Period.

Assets		Liabilities	
Bonds	+$50,000	Net wealth	+$50,000
Equals savings from income		Equals savings from income	

In the above simple example, a financial intermediary is not involved. Most probably, however, a financial institution will be involved in the savings-investment process. In this instance, savings accrue initially to the financial intermediary as it accepts savings deposits and issues its own liabilities (i.e., a claim on these funds) to the saver in exchange. The intermediary is the agency through which funds are transferred to ultimate users. In the above example, the financial institution would accept the debt or equity instrument of the corporation, thereby placing savings at the disposition of the enterprise.

A moment's reflection makes it apparent that such transfers raise a number of important questions bearing on the savings decision itself and on the terms and conditions under which the savings-investment conversion is made. In developing a set of social accounts, personal savings, that is, the savings of households, are treated as a residual. After taxes have been paid and expenditures on goods and services have been added up, then the difference between household income and these outlays is personal savings. Alternatively, as has already been indicated, savings could be treated as a change in the net wealth position of the transactor unit that occurs between the commencement and the termination dates of the accounting period. We take the total increase in assets in whatever form, subtract from it the total increase in liabilities, and the remainder (in fact, the change in net worth) is savings.

These techniques of measuring savings are suggestive of the conceptual approach to be taken in this book. Our task is to develop rules for economic actions. Economic behavior concerning household purchases of goods and services, spending by business on capital goods, the holding of securities, the holding of cash, and borrowing by transactor units will be examined. Attention, then, will focus on selected components of both income statements and balance sheets. This will be necessary in order to construct an internally consistent macroeconomic model of the national economy. Employing this approach helps us to deduce certain conclusions about saving. Exclusive concern either with income flows, on the one hand, or with net wealth positions, on the other, would be inadequate. Attention to both is necessary if the interdependence between the producing sectors and the financial system is to be understood.

The links between measures of output and financial variables and between income statements and balance sheets are suggested by business purchases of plant and equipment and the financial instruments used to finance these transactions. We need a decision rule, however, for capital spending by business, for the profitability of an investment in machinery depends upon financial considerations. Are bonds or equities to be used if external funds are required to purchase the machines? The business firm and the household will weigh the issuance and the acceptance of bonds as against equities. Such an evaluation involves many factors. Consideration must be given to prices in financial and commodity markets, to the stability of dividend payments, to opportunities for capital gain, to the degree of risk attaching to the alternatives, and so on. These topics will be discussed in later chapters.

INTERTEMPORAL COMPARISONS OF GNP

For many purposes it is necessary to compare the value of the GNP in one year with that in another (see Table 1–18 in the appendix for annual data since 1929). Such comparisons would be relatively straightforward if the dollar itself were not an elastic measuring rod subject to changes in value in response to changes in the level of prices. Because of such changes, however, it is necessary to construct a measure of GNP standardized for the value of the unit of account, the dollar.

In the framework of social accounts this can be done, operationally, on the sources side rather than on the uses side. The reason is that on the uses side inputs are expressed in value-added terms, and certain difficulties arise when changes in value-added are used as the basis for constructing an index to measure changes in the purchasing power of the dollar over time. To illustrate this we can consider a simple wage and salary index:

$$\frac{W_1}{W_0} \times 100 = W_1^* \tag{1.1}$$

where W_1 is an average of wage and salary rates per period in period 1;
W_0 is an average of wage and salary rates in the base period;
W_1^* is an index showing the level of wages and salaries in period 1 relative to that in the base period.

If, in the base year, the average weekly wage rate were \$200, and in the current year the average weekly wage were \$250, then the index of the wage rate for the current year would be $(250/200) \times 100 = 125$, indicating that a 25 percent increase in the wage rate has occurred since the base year. The difficulty with this index is that increases in efficiency or productivity may have occurred during the year. The wage and salary rate per period worked will rise as a result of increases in labor productivity captured by the factor of production. This is quite distinct from an increase in wages and salaries that arises as a result of general increases in the price level. We would want to know what part of the 25 percent increase in the wage rate reflected productivity improvements and what part merely reflected the reduced purchasing power of the dollar.

Because of this difficulty, attempts to derive "constant dollar" GNP are almost always made on the sources side of the accounts, which reflects the dollar values of the commodities produced—the dollar values of the expenditures made by the public for the output of the producing sectors. Price indices may be constructed for *each* of the several components of expenditure: consumers' durable goods; nondurable goods; services; business plant and equipment; government purchases; inventories; and exports and imports. For example, the one formula (among many) most frequently used in constructing a price index for consumers' purchases is often somewhat imprecisely referred to as a "cost of living" index. It is derived by assuming, first, that there are n different goods being consumed routinely by consumers. By sampling, the quantity of each good contained in the typical consumer's "basket" of purchases in a given "base" year can be observed. Then, letting the subscript 0 represent the base year and the subscript 1 refer to the given year for which the index number is being constructed, we have:

$$P_1 = \frac{\sum_{i=1}^{n} P_{1,i}Q_{0,i}}{\sum_{i=1}^{n} P_{0,i}Q_{0,i}} \times 100, \qquad i = 1, 2, \ldots n \tag{1.2}$$

$P_{1,i}$ refers to the price of the ith good in period 1, $P_{0,i}$ was the price of the ith good in the base period and $Q_{0,i}$ was the quantity of the ith good found in the typical consumer's basket of goods in the base year. In the denominator of the fraction we have the sum representing the dollar value of the consumer's basket of goods in the base period; in the numerator we have observed the current prices of the n commodities and found the dollar amount that is now required to purchase the *same* basket of goods at the new prices existing in the given period. Statisticians say that this index is weighted by base period quantities. By multiplying by 100 we express the index as a percentage.

After constructing a similar price index for each of the components of spending that enters the GNP, these indices are used to "deflate" each component. The deflated components are then added together to arrive at a "constant dollar" GNP.

After having estimated current dollar GNP, and having deflated each component to arrive at "constant dollar" GNP, we may take the ratio of current dollar GNP to "constant dollar" GNP. This ratio is called the implicit price deflator. In a sense it is an "average" of the price indices that are relevant to each of the principle components of GNP. As such, it is often applied in aggregate economic analysis and in forecasting.

Implicit price deflators, being price indices, suffer from the difficulties of all such measures. The two main biases in the construction of a price index are: (a) In our example, expenditures are standardized by base-year quantities, but base-year quantities do *not* allow for the effect that changes in prices have in inducing changes in the composition of the given year's market basket, for an optimal bundle in the base year will be suboptimal in year 1 if prices change; (b) an additional bias arises because it is impossible to adjust fully for quality changes, for some improvements in productivity may appear in the form of increased quality of products; implicit price deflators do not make formal allowance for this factor, although an attempt is made to maintain the quality of the basket of goods being represented at a constant level.

The Concept of Gross National Cost: The GNC

The social accounts developed above have come under increased scrutiny in recent years. Their adequacy has been questioned because they do not include the concept of gross national *cost*, a deficiency that arises in part because of the uses to which national accounts have been put. Economists have used them to measure the level and the rate of increase in the "material" means of existence, both for the nation as a whole and on a per capita, or per capita employed, basis, and it has been suggested that the potential to produce GNP can be expected to continue to grow at a rate of between 3 and 4 percent per year. Indeed, the GNP, or GNP per capita, has been used as an index for the growth of economic welfare, but this it clearly is not. There is, at present, no measure of gross national cost that one can find in the data compiled and released by the Department of Commerce. Measurements of GNC are lacking, but this does not mean that the issue of national costs can be politely ignored.

The accounts we have constructed are called national social accounts. Such labeling implies adequate measurement of the social costs and social benefits of what is produced. In constructing the accounts, goods and services were valued at their market price wherever possible. In the case of the government sector, valuation was at cost of production. However, it is now very apparent to us that market values, reflecting as they do only *private* costs and benefits, are not an adequate measure of *social* costs and benefits. Hence the entire concept of GNP is constructed on a relatively shaky foundation.

The problem of accounting for GNC has two dimensions, one of which has proven to be more important than the other. The less important matter is that GNP, based as it is primarily on market values, may understate output in a social sense. There may be useful by-products, not fully recognized in market prices, that accompany production or use of output, and these social benefits may contribute to material satisfactions. The second, and more important, difficulty is that social costs may in some cases exceed the market cost (value added in production) measurement of output. Apparent to everyone is the fact that there are noxious by-products as the result of the production and use of marketable commodities. These by-products are not costs in a private sense, i.e., those who create by-products do not compensate those who are adversely affected by their production. Examples are legion: the paper producer who discharges sulphide wastes into a river and thereby helps destroy its recreational use; the auto whose Hollywood muffler creates noise pollution; the thermoelectric plant that discharges smoke into the atmosphere of a metropolitan area. Nor need we limit our examples to the private sector of the economy. We have seen that government production was valued as the cost of input, but this valuation may be inadequate from a social point of view. The actions of a government agency may create a noxious by-product in the same manner as private actions; for example, bureaucratic red tape and the invasion of privacy accompanying security checks.

These conditions illustrate why demands for an accounting system based on social costs and social benefits have arisen. The need becomes exceedingly critical as a result of the uses to which measures of the gross national product have been put. Emphasis has been placed upon the fact that, with continuous full employment, the economy's level of output should increase by about 3.5 percent per year. But this siren song of growth, when based on the conventional measures of cost and valuation, can too easily lull people into ignoring the effects of the by-products of growth on the well-being of the individual. If the last decade has shown us anything, it has shown us the dangers that growth poses for ecological balance.

The problem of measuring gross national cost is critical, and it therefore warrants a concerted effort to translate that cost into quantitative terms in ways similar to the Measure of Economic Welfare recently proposed by James Tobin and William Nordhaus. Such an effort is essential if we are to obtain a more accurate assessment of the impact of economic activity on our environment.

Some Additional Problems in the Measurement of GNP

The value of most goods included in GNP is determined by market forces. There exists, however, a flow of goods and services over the year that does not enter the market place and whose value, since it cannot be established by the market, must be imputed for inclusion in GNP. Three important types of goods and services have a value imputed to them: the rental value of owner-occupied houses; the value of goods produced and consumed on the farm; and the value of services provided by financial intermediaries to their customers. The reasons for imputing value in the first two cases seem obvious, but the third needs additional explanation. Service charges by financial intermediaries are usually far below the cost of providing the service. For example, the cost incurred by a bank when clearing a check is often above the service charge levied by it. Rather than raise service charges, financial intermediaries simply pay lower interest rates on certain types of deposits. This causes the market value of services provided by the financial intermediaries to be undervalued.

An unclear line divides those services which are included in GNP from those excluded. No value, as we have seen, is imputed to the services of housewives, yet if these services are provided by domestic servants, wages, wage supplements, and employer contributions to Social Security are included in

GNP. The classic case would be that of a man reducing GNP by marrying his housekeeper. It is similarly true that if a man does his own carpentry, house-painting, plumbing, or wiring GNP does not rise, but if he hires professionals to do the tasks this will be reflected in a higher GNP. The value of the service he provides in driving himself to work is excluded, though the value of the gas, oil, tires, etc., is included. National income accounting is a complex task, and it is not surprising that the distinction between the goods included in GNP and those excluded is sometimes arbitrary.

Three additional problems arise in the use of GNP estimates. First, the market value of goods and services may not adequately reflect the change in quality that has occurred over the years. This has been mentioned earlier in our discussion of the problems of intertemporal comparisons. Second, GNP figures may not accurately reflect economic welfare, since they fail to reflect the distribution of income within a society. Third, the fact that a value is not imputed to leisure time distorts the use of GNP as a measure of welfare. A choice of increased leisure over increased production, and the consequent increase in general economic well-being, will be reflected in a lower GNP.

The following sections of this book indicate that national income accounts can be used for assorted valuable purposes. It is precisely because they are so heavily relied upon in the development of theory and the formulation of policy that their limitations should be clearly understood.

CONCLUSION

In this chapter we have described the conceptual basis for the compilation of national income accounts. Whenever possible, valuation of production is based upon the monetary exchange values that open markets generate with competitive prices. Peculiar problems arise, however, in attributing values to production of public goods by government, and to valuation of goods produced within the household which do not enter the marketplace.

Concepts are one thing; measurement another. The practical methods of arriving at estimates by collecting data are complex, and it is beyond the scope of this book to discuss them. There are problems not only in data collection, but also in the omission of any allowance for certain social costs that arise as output increases. We have hence concluded that, by itself, GNP is not likely to be a satisfactory basis for measuring economic welfare.

APPENDIX

National Income Accounts

Table 1–14. Gross National Product for 1971 and 1972 (in billions of dollars).

Item	1971	1972
Gross national product	1050.4	1151.8
Final purchases	1046.7	1145.9
Personal consumption expenditures	664.9	721.0
Durable goods	103.5	116.1
Nondurable goods	278.1	299.5
Services	283.3	305.4
Gross private domestic investment	152.0	180.4
Fixed investment	148.3	174.5
Nonresidential	105.8	120.6
Structures	38.4	42.2
Producers' durable equipment	67.4	78.3
Residential structures	42.6	54.0
Nonfarm	42.0	53.2
Change in business inventories	3.6	5.9
Nonfarm	2.4	5.6
Net exports of goods and services	.7	—4.2
Exports	66.1	73.7
Imports	65.4	77.9
Government purchases of goods and services	232.8	254.6
Federal	97.8	105.8
National defense	71.4	75.9
Other	26.3	29.9
State and local	135.0	148.8
Gross national product in constant (1958) dollars	741.7	789.5

Note—Dept. of Commerce estimates.

Table 1–15. Relation of GNP, National Income and Personal Income and Saving for 1971 and 1972 (in billions of dollars)

Item		1971	1972
Gross national product		1050.4	1151.8
Less:	Capital consumption allowances	93.8	103.7
	Indirect business tax and non-tax liability	101.9	110.1
	Business transfer payments	4.6	4.9
	Statistical discrepancy	—4.8	.1
Plus:	Subsidies less current surplus of government enterprises	.9	1.7
Equals:	National income	855.7	934.7
Less:	Corporate profits and inventory valuation adjustment	78.6	87.3
	Contributions for social insurance	65.3	74.0
	Excess of wage accruals over disbursements	.6	—.5
Plus:	Government transfer payments	89.0	99.1
	Net interest paid by government and consumers	31.1	31.6
	Dividends	25.4	26.4
	Business transfer payments	4.6	4.9
Equals:	Personal income	861.4	935.9
Less:	Personal tax and non-tax payments	117.0	140.8
Equals:	Disposable personal income	744.4	795.1
Less:	Personal outlays	683.4	740.2
	Personal consumption expenditures	664.9	721.0
	Consumer interest payments	17.6	18.2
	Personal transfer payments to foreigners	1.0	1.1
Equals:	Personal saving	60.9	54.8
Disposable personal income in constant (1958) dollars		554.7	578.5

Note.—Dept. of Commerce estimates.

Table 1–16. National Income for 1971 and 1972 (in billions of dollars).

Item	1971	1972
National income	855.7	934.7
Compensation of employees	644.1	705.3
Wages and salaries	573.5	626.5
Private	449.7	491.9
Military	19.4	20.6
Government civilian	104.4	114.0
Supplements to wages and salaries	70.7	78.8
Employer contributions for social insurance	34.1	38.5
Other labor income	36.5	40.3
Proprietors' income	70.0	75.2
Business and professional	52.6	55.6
Farm	17.3	19.6
Rental income of persons	24.5	25.6
Corporate profits and inventory valuation adjustment	78.6	87.3
Profits before tax	83.3	93.3
Profits tax liability	37.3	40.8
Profits after tax	45.9	52.5
Dividends	25.4	26.4
Undistributed profits	20.5	26.1
Inventory valuation adjustment	−4.7	−6.0
Net interest	38.5	41.3

Note—Dept. of Commerce estimates.

Table 1–17. Personal Income for 1971 and 1972 (in billions of dollars).

Item	1971	1972
Total personal income	861.4	935.9
Wage and salary disbursements	572.9	627.0
Commodity-producing industries	206.1	224.6
Manufacturing only	160.3	175.8
Distributive industries	138.2	151.5
Service industries	105.0	116.1
Government	123.5	134.8
Other labor income	36.5	40.3
Proprietors' income	69.9	75.2
Business and professional	52.6	55.6
Farm	17.3	19.6
Rental income	24.5	25.6
Dividends	25.4	26.4
Personal interest income	69.6	72.9
Transfer payments	93.6	104.0
Less: Personal contributions for social insurance	31.2	35.5
Nonagricultural income	837.2	909.3
Agricultural income	24.2	26.6

Note—Dept. of Commerce estimates.

Table 1–18. Composition of Gross National Product or Expenditure in the United States, 1929–1972 (in billions of dollars, 1958 prices).

	$GNP =$	C $+$	I_g $+$	G $+$	E_x $-$	I_m
Year	GNP	Consumption	Gross Investment	Government Purchases of Goods & Services	Exports	Imports
1929	203.6	139.6	40.4	22.0	11.8	10.3
1930	183.5	130.4	27.4	24.3	10.4	9.0
1931	169.3	126.1	16.8	25.4	8.9	7.9
1932	144.2	114.8	4.7	24.2	7.1	6.6
1933	141.5	112.8	5.3	23.3	7.1	7.1
1934	154.3	118.1	9.4	26.6	7.3	7.1
1935	169.5	125.5	18.0	27.0	7.7	8.7
1936	193.0	138.4	24.0	31.8	8.2	9.3
1937	203.2	143.1	29.9	30.8	9.8	10.5
1938	192.9	140.2	17.0	33.9	9.9	8.0
1939	209.4	148.2	24.7	35.2	10.0	8.7
1940	227.2	155.7	33.0	36.4	11.0	8.9
1941	263.7	165.4	41.6	56.3	11.2	10.8
1942	297.8	161.4	21.4	117.1	7.8	9.9
1943	337.1	165.8	12.7	164.4	6.8	12.6
1944	361.3	171.4	14.0	181.7	7.6	13.4
1945	355.2	183.0	19.6	156.4	10.2	13.9
1946	312.6	203.5	52.3	48.4	19.6	11.2
1947	309.9	206.3	51.5	39.9	22.6	10.3
1948	323.7	210.8	60.4	46.3	18.1	12.0
1949	324.1	216.5	48.0	53.3	18.1	11.7
1950	355.3	230.5	69.3	52.8	16.3	13.6
1951	383.4	232.8	70.0	75.4	19.3	14.1
1952	395.1	239.4	60.5	92.1	18.2	15.2
1953	412.8	250.8	61.2	99.8	17.8	16.7
1954	407.0	255.7	59.4	88.9	18.8	15.8
1955	438.0	274.2	75.4	85.2	20.9	17.7
1956	446.1	281.4	74.3	85.3	24.2	19.1
1957	452.5	288.2	68.8	89.3	26.2	19.9
1958	447.3	290.1	60.9	94.2	23.1	20.9
1959	475.9	307.3	73.6	94.7	23.8	23.5
1960	487.7	316.1	72.4	94.9	27.3	23.0
1961	497.2	322.5	69.0	100.5	28.0	22.9
1962	529.8	338.4	79.4	107.5	30.0	25.5
1963	551.0	353.3	82.5	109.6	32.1	26.6
1964	581.1	373.7	87.8	111.2	36.5	28.2
1965	617.8	397.7	99.2	114.7	37.4	31.2
1966	658.1	418.1	109.3	126.5	40.2	36.1
1967	675.2	430.1	101.2	140.2	42.1	38.5
1968	706.6	452.7	105.2	147.7	45.7	44.7
1969	725.6	469.1	110.5	145.9	48.4	48.3
1970	722.1	477.0	104.0	139.0	52.2	50.0
1971	741.7	495.4	108.6	137.6	52.6	52.5
1972^p	789.5	524.8	123.8	142.9	56.9	58.7

Source: Economic Report of the President, 1972 **(Washington, D.C.: U.S. Government Printing Office, 1972). (*p* = preliminary estimates).**

ADDITIONAL READINGS

For a clear and thorough treatment of national income accounting in textbook form see either Richard and Nancy Ruggles, *National Income Accounts and Income Analysis* (New York: McGraw-Hill, 1956), or Gardner Ackley, *Macroeconomic Theory* (New York: Macmillan, 1961), Chapters 2–4. A more critical and detailed statement of difficulties encountered by national income accountants may be found in the National Bureau of Economic Research's *Studies in Income and Wealth*, Vol. 22, *A Critique of the United States Income and Product Accounts* (Princeton, N.J.: Princeton University Press, 1958). Another thorough examination of national income accounting is Paul Studenski's *The Income of Nations, Theory, Measurement and Analysis, Past and Present* (New York: New York University Press, 1958). In 1958 the Office of Business Economics published a supplement to the *Survey of Current Business*, entitled *U.S. Income and Output* (Washington: Department of Commerce, 1958), on the methodology and data sources of the U.S. accounts.

For two recent discussions of what social accounts do and do not measure, see Edward F. Denison, "Welfare measurement and the GNP," *Survey of Current Business*, 51 (January 1971): 13–16; and F. Thomas Juster, "On the measurement of economic and social performance," 50th Annual Report, National Bureau of Economic Research, 1970, pp. 8–24. A useful treatment of the effects of growth by-products on individual well-being is E. J. Mishan's *Growth: The Price We Pay* (London: Staples Press, 1969). A recent attempt to quantify social cost is that of W. Nordhaus and J. Tobin in "Is growth obsolete?" in *Fiftieth Anniversary Colloquium V* (New York: National Bureau of Economic Research, Columbia University Press, 1972).

QUESTIONS

1. Construct a national income and product statement and a set of sector accounts for Happyland, where there are the following economic units: 3 business corporations, the Black, White, and Yellow Corporations; 1 government body; and 1000 households. Some trade occurs internationally.

   You are given below production statements for the 3 business corporations and a revenue and expenditure statement for the government. In Happyland we assume there is no income originating in households. Hence there are 3 private producing units and the government.

   (a) Construct a national income and product statement for Happyland, i.e., on the sources side, show gross national product, and on the uses side, show gross national product on a value-added basis.

   (b) Construct sector accounts for the business sector; government; and the household sector; and a gross savings and investment account. What is the size of the business gross product? What is the size of income originating in the government sector? Does income originating in government measure redistributional activities of government?

(c) Does the information provided permit a full construction of sources and uses in the foreign sector? Why? What further information is required?

(d) What is the size of personal income? Of personal income per household? Of disposable personal income? Of disposable personal income per household? Is the government budget in balance, surplus, or deficit?

(e) What is the size of net national product? Of net national income at factor cost?

(f) Construct an intra-business sector, sales-purchase matrix for the 3 corporations showing how intermediate transactions cancel out for the economy.

Black Corporation

Uses		Sources	
Purchases from other firms		Sales to consumers (households)	$900,000
from White	$30,000		
from Yellow	100,000	Sales to government	450,000
Indirect business taxes	162,000	Sales on capital account to business	263,000
Depreciation	164,000		
Business transfer payments	1800	Net inventory change	15,000
Subsidies received	1800	Net foreign sales	10,000
Wages and salaries	846,000	Sales to other firms on current account	
Social Security taxes	72,000		
Interest paid	54,000	to White	100,000
Corporate profits tax	180,000	to Yellow	70,000
Net dividends	90,000		
Retained earnings	110,000		

White Corporation

Uses		Sources	
Purchases from other firms		Sales to consumers	
from Black	$100,000	(households)	$2,690,000
from Yellow	100,000	Net inventory change	30,000
Depreciation	185,000	Net foreign sales	10,000
Indirect business taxes	270,000	Sales to other firms on current account	
Business transfer payments	3000		
Wages and salaries	1,410,000	to Black	30,000
Social Security taxes	120,000	to Yellow	60,000
Interest paid	90,000		
Corporate profits tax	300,000		
Dividends paid	150,000		
Retained earnings	95,000		
Subsidies received	3000		

Yellow Corporation

Uses		Sources	
Purchases from other firms		Sales to consumers	$310,000
from Black	$70,000	Sales to government	210,000
from White	60,000	Sales on capital account	
Depreciation	131,000	to business	547,000
Indirect business taxes	108,000		
Business transfer payments	1200	Net inventory change	15,000
Social Security taxes	48,000	Net foreign sales	10,000
Wages and salaries	564,000	Sales to other firms on	
Interest paid	36,000	current account	
Corporate profits tax	120,000	to Black	100,000
Dividends paid	60,000	to White	100,000
Retained earnings	95,000		
Subsidies received	1200		

Sources & Uses of Government Receipts

Uses		Sources	
Purchases from non-government		Indirect business taxes	$540,000
sellers	$660,000	Social Security receipts	240,000
Wages and salaries	540,000	Corporate profits taxes	600,000
Transfer payments	194,000	Personal tax payments	100,000
Net interest paid	60,000		
Subsidies	6000		
Surplus	20,000		

The Money Supply

2
Chapter

In the previous chapter a technique was developed for measuring income and activity levels in the commodity-producing sectors of the economy. We now turn to the measurement of money and to an examination of transactions between monetary institutions and the public, which bring about changes in the money supply, and transactions between the monetary institutions alone.

We will see in later chapters that the supply of money significantly influences, among other things, the levels of output, employment, and prices. Through the effective control of the money supply, policy makers are able to increase the likelihood of achieving national objectives such as full employment and stable prices. Later chapters will help us determine whether a rapid, slow, zero, or negative rate of growth in the money supply is appropriate for achieving certain national objectives. But first we must study the ways in which the monetary authorities can affect the rate of growth in the money supply.

WHAT IS MONEY?

Money is any property which its owner may use to pay off a given amount of debt with certainty and without delay. Today in the United States two means of holding wealth are generally agreed upon as being "money": (a) coin and paper currency; and (b) demand deposits. Both are forms of what is called "credit money."

Money has general "acceptability." Coin and paper currency are accepted because they are designated by law as "legal tender." This means that an offer of legal tender must be accepted by a creditor in discharge of a debtor's obligation. Demand deposits are a liability of the commercial banking system, and though no creditor must by law accept a check drawn on a demand deposit in a commercial bank, more than 90 percent of transactions are settled by checks drawn on demand deposits. Transactors have confidence in the ability of commercial banks to exchange demand deposits for currency.

Differences in the measures of money do, however, exist. Some economists include savings and time deposits in the "money supply." Others include certificates of deposit. But time and savings deposits and certificates of deposit cannot, in general, be used directly to purchase something. Instead, they must first be exchanged for money and that money used in the purchase. The conceptual problems that arise in measuring the money supply are discussed at the end of this chapter, but since all economists agree that currency and demand deposits are money, the money supply referred to as we describe the monetary system consists of these two types of assets. The following pages concentrate on the way in which activities of the general public and monetary institutions affect the size of a money supply measured in terms of currency and demand deposits.

CREDIT MONEY AND THE MONETARY SYSTEM

The money supply of the United States consists of credit money arising from the creation of debt (or credit) by three monetary institutions: (a) the Treasury; (b) the Federal Reserve System; and (c) the commercial banking system. These three monetary institutions are associated with types of money as noted in Table 2–1.

A three-fold classification of the money supply based on the distinction between coins, paper currency, and demand deposits would reveal the following:

Coins	3%
Paper currency	22%
Demand deposits	75%
	100%

These figures illustrate the dominant importance of demand deposits in the total money supply. Three quarters of it is in this form.

Table 2–1. U.S. Credit Money, 1973.

Type of Credit Money	Percent of Total Credit Money	Average Amount as of June 30, 1973 (in billions of dollars)
A. Issued by the Treasury		
1. Token coins and representative token money	2.8	7.50
2. Circulating promissory notes (United States notes)	.1	.32
B. Issued by banks		
1. Circulating promissory notes issued by the Federal Reserve System	22.2	59.81
2. Demand deposit liabilities of commercial banks subject to check	74.8	201.80
	99.9*	269.43

*The percentages do not add to 100% due to rounding.
Source: Federal Reserve Bulletin (August 1973).

How Is Credit Money Expanded and Contracted?

In examining the process by which the quantity of credit money is expanded and contracted it is necessary to consider the various operations of our monetary institutions: the Treasury; the Federal Reserve System; and the commercial banks. Let us first consider the nature of a fractional reserve banking system.

A Fractional Reserve Banking System

An important attribute of the American banking system is its fractional reserve base. It is, in fact, the need for commercial banks to maintain reserves against their demand deposit liabilities that limits the ability of commercial banks to expand their demand deposits.

By law, the Board of Governors of the Federal Reserve System (America's "central bank") is authorized to require member banks to hold between 7 and 22 percent of their demand deposits in the form of reserves. Reserves, as legally defined, may consist of (a) cash in the vault and (b) deposits in Federal Reserve Banks. The precise reserve ratio set by the Board formerly depended upon a bank's geographical location—higher ratios were required for large city banks than for smaller country banks. But in November 1972 regulations governing reserves were changed so that required reserves now depend upon the amount of deposits held by the individual banks rather than upon the banks' locations. For example, in July 1973 the required reserves were 8 percent on the first $2 million of deposits, 10.5 percent from $2–$10 million, 12.5 percent from $10–$100 million, 13.5 percent from $100–400 million and 18 percent for deposits over $400 million. The net effect of this schedule of ratios is to assist the smaller bank by not requiring it to have so large a part of its assets tied up in non-interest-bearing reserves.[1]

The existence of a reserve ratio means that if the sum of cash in the vault and deposits at the central bank is just sufficient to satisfy the legal requirements, then the individual bank is unable to expand its loans and deposits any further. While the volume of reserves is of special interest to us because of its relationship to the money supply, reserves serve other purposes as well. For example, they serve also as clearing accounts. Thus banks may use these accounts by writing checks on them or by authorizing the central bank to debit them in payment of customers' checks. But it is essentially by controlling the volume of reserves that the Federal Reserve exercises its control over the money supply.

[1] On June 30, 1973, there were 14,048 commercial banks of which only 5707 were members of the Federal Reserve System. The tendency for the larger banks to be members of the Federal Reserve System means that the proportion of banking assets under control of the Federal Reserve is not reflected in these figures. Nonmember banks are regulated by state authorities and reserve requirements vary widely from state to state although several states simply impose the same reserve requirements as the Federal Reserve.

In our analysis of the creation of money, we assume that *all* banks are members of the Federal Reserve. We do this in order not to complicate the picture of the way the system works with excessive detail. Our results hold in general in spite of this abstraction.

We can now consider a series of transactions, involving monetary institutions and the general public, which change the volume of reserves available to the commercial banking system. Once this is done, we will be able to show how changes in the volume of reserves will lead to changes in the money supply.

The relevant transactions fall into three categories:

(1) actions initiated by the general public;

(2) Treasury and foreign operations; and

(3) Federal Reserve operations, both policy and nonpolicy.

The T-account, so called because of its form, is useful in permitting us to trace the effect of each transaction on the assets and liabilities (balance sheets) of monetary institutions and, more particularly, on the reserves of the banking system. Changes in assets appear on the left-hand side of the T-account, and changes in liabilities appear on the right-hand side.

For simplicity in the examples, all transactions will be based on the suppositions that the legally required reserve ratio is 20 percent and that, prior to the transaction, the actual reserves of the banking system equal the required reserves, that is, that the system is "fully loaned." For simplicity, we have also chosen to consider, in each case, a $100 transaction.

Actions Initiated by the General Public

By definition, the money supply includes coin and paper currency and demand deposits held by the public. Therefore, the currency ratio, the proportion of the money supply which the public wishes to hold in the form of currency, will affect the available volume of bank reserves. The currency ratio at any time depends upon the preferences of the general public for demand deposits relative to currency. If the public decides to reduce the ratio, currency will flow into commercial banks and will provide reserves that will enable banks to expand their loans and deposits, thus increasing the money supply. If currency is withdrawn from banks the opposite effect will occur. To see this more clearly we can note the following numerical examples.

(i) An increase in the currency holdings of the public.

When a member of the general public exchanges some of his demand deposits for currency by cashing a check for $100, the total reserves held by the commercial banking system then decline by $100, while the required reserves decline by $20 because deposits have also fallen by $100. The consequent deficiency in reserves amounts to $80.

Commercial Banking System

Assets		Liabilities
Vault cash reserves		**Demand deposits**
−100		**−100**
required	**−20**	
deficiency	**−80**	

(ii) A decrease in the currency holdings of the public.

In this case, $100 in currency is deposited in exchange for demand deposits, resulting in a $20 increase in required reserves and a $100 increase in actual reserves, or an increase of $80 in the bank's lending capacity.

Commercial Banking System

Vault cash reserves		Demand deposits
+100		+ 100
[required	+20]	
[excess	+80]	

The effect of these two transactions on the reserves of the commercial banking system is summarized in the first part of Table 2–2.

Actions Initiated by the Treasury

There are a number of ways in which Treasury actions influence the reserves available to the commercial banking system.

(i) An increase in Treasury deposits at the Federal Reserve Banks.

An increase in Treasury deposits at the Federal Reserve Banks occurs because of transfers of Treasury deposits in commercial banks to the central banks. When tax remittances are made by check to the Internal Revenue Service, the IRS deposits the checks in the commercial banks against which they are written. Such deposits are recorded in accounts known as "tax and loan" accounts; they are Treasury deposits in commercial banks. The Treasury

Table 2–2. Summary of the Effects of Transactions on Reserves.

	Effect on Commercial Bank Reserves
Public's Action	
Increase in currency holdings	Decrease
Decrease in currency holdings	Increase
Treasury Action	
Increase in Treasury balances at the Federal Reserve Bank	Decrease
Decrease in Treasury balances at the FRB	Increase
Sale of gold	Decrease
Purchase of gold	Increase
Federal Reserve Action	
Purchase of government securities	Increase
Sale of government securities	Decrease
Loans to commercial banks	Increase
Repayment of loans by commercial banks	Decrease
Reduction in reserve ratio	Increase
Increase in reserve ratio	Decrease

writes checks against its "tax and loan" accounts in the commercial banks for deposit at the Federal Reserve Banks. The effect of this transaction is to reduce commercial bank reserves by the transfer of an equal amount of Federal Reserve liabilities to the Treasury.

Commercial Banking System		Federal Reserve Banks	
Reserve deposits at the FRB −100 [required −20, deficiency −80]	Treasury tax and loan accounts −100		Treasury deposits +100 Deposits of commercial banking system −100

(ii) A decrease in Treasury deposits at the Federal Reserve Banks.

Treasury balances are drawn down when checks are written by the government on its account at the central bank. Such checks are used to pay for government purchases of goods, to pay government employees, etc. The recipient of the check will deposit it in his account at the commercial bank. The commercial bank will then send it to the Federal Reserve for collection.

Commercial Banking System		Federal Reserve Banks	
Reserve deposits at FRB +100 [required +20, excess +80]	Demand deposits +100		Deposits of commercial banking system +100 Treasury deposits −100

(iii) Treasury sales of gold.

When the Treasury sells monetary gold, as it will if jewelers buy gold or if foreigners decide to exchange dollars for gold, the available reserves of the commercial banking system are decreased. This can be illustrated by the following two stages.

Treasury		Commercial Banking System		Federal Reserve Banks	
Gold −100 Deposits in FRB +100		Reserve deposits at FRB −100 [required −20, deficiency −80]	Demand deposits −100		Deposits of commercial banking system −100 Treasury deposits +100

In the first stage gold is paid for by, say, a jeweler's check drawn on his commercial bank. When this check is deposited in the Federal Reserve by the Treasury the reserves of the commercial banking system decline and Treasury deposits rise.

While the first stage of the transaction is of interest to us because of its potential effect on the money supply, a second stage involving the Treasury and the Federal Reserve Banks is necessary to complete the analysis of balance sheet changes. Gold certificates (non-interest-bearing receipts) which are originally issued by the Treasury to the Federal Reserve Banks when the Treasury purchases gold, are now cancelled, and Treasury balances at the central bank are correspondingly reduced. Thus the initial rise in Treasury deposits in the first stage is offset by the decline in deposits in the second stage and the net effect is principally on commercial bank deposits and reserves, both of which have declined.

Treasury		Federal Reserve Banks	
Deposits at FRB −100	Gold certificates −100	Gold certificates −100	Treasury deposits −100

(iv) Treasury purchases of gold.

When the Treasury purchases monetary gold, the effect is to increase commercial bank reserves. The accounts change in precisely the opposite direction to that seen when the Treasury sells its gold. Again there are two stages to this transaction.

Treasury		Commercial Banking System		Federal Reserve Banks	
Gold +100 Deposits in FRB −100		Reserve deposits at FRB +100 [required +20] [excess +80]	Demand deposits +100		Deposits of commercial banking system +100 Treasury deposits −100

When the Treasury buys gold, it issues a check to the seller drawn on its account at the Federal Reserve Bank. When the seller deposits the check in his bank, the reserves of the commercial banking system rise and Treasury deposits fall. In the second stage, the Treasury issues non-interest-bearing gold certificates against its acquisition of monetary gold and assigns these to the central bank, thereby recouping its deposits. The net effect remaining is the increase in the deposits and reserves of the commercial banks.

Treasury	
Deposits at FRB +100	Gold certificates +100

Federal Reserve Banks	
Gold certificates +100	Treasury deposits +100

A summary of the effects of the above Treasury transactions on commercial bank reserves is shown in the second part of Table 2–2.

Federal Reserve Operations

Finally, since it is the purpose of the central bank to control the reserves of commercial banks, and therefore the money supply, we must consider the effect of central bank operations on the availability of bank reserves. The most important of these central bank operations are *discretionary;* these are transactions deliberately undertaken by the central bank for the purpose of influencing the quantity of reserves available to the commercial banking system. These are called "open market operations."

(i) Purchases and sales of government securities by the Federal Reserve.

The major earning assets of the Federal Reserve Banks are their holdings of U.S. government securities. When holdings are increased by purchases in the securities market, the reserves of the commercial banking system increase.

Commercial Banking System	
Reserve deposits at FRB +100 [required +20, excess +80]	Demand deposits +100

Federal Reserve Banks	
U.S. Government securities +100	Deposits of commercial banking system +100

The above T-accounts summarize the effect of a purchase. When the Federal Reserve purchases securities (as through the bond market from an insurance company or other holder, whose balance sheet we do not show) it issues a check drawn on itself in payment. The seller of the securities deposits this check with his commercial bank and receives a demand deposit in exchange. The commercial bank, in turn, presents the check to the Federal Reserve and receives payment in the form of a credit to its reserve deposit account. The principal effect to observe is the increase in deposits and reserves of the commercial bank.

In the opposite case, in which the Federal Reserve wishes to reduce the volume of commercial bank reserves, it will dispose of some of its holdings of government securities by selling them in the open market. The purchaser will issue a check drawn on his account in a commercial bank. Upon receipt of the check, the Federal Reserve collects by charging the deposit account of the commercial bank. The commercial bank in turn charges the demand account of its customer, and the result is a decline in bank deposits and reserves.

Commercial Banking System		Federal Reserve Banks	
Reserve deposits at FRB −100 [required −20 deficiency −80]	Demand deposits −100	U.S. government securities −100	Deposits of commercial banking system −100

(ii) Loans by the Federal Reserve Banks to the commercial banking system, or repayment of these loans.

One of the functions of a central bank is to serve as a "lender of last resort." This means that it stands ready, on special terms and conditions set by it, to provide credit to commercial banks. The effect of central bank lending is to increase the reserve availability of commercial banks.

Commercial Banking System		Federal Reserve Banks	
Reserve deposits at FRB +100 [required 0 excess +100]	Loans payable to FRB +100	Loans receivable from commercial banking system +100	Deposits of commercial banking system +100

When the latter borrow, they receive a deposit credit at the Federal Reserve equal to the face value of the loan, although, in this particular instance, there is no increase in required reserves since no demand deposit liabilities to the public have been created.

The effect of repayment of the loan is to reduce the reserves of commercial banks.

Commercial Banking System		Federal Reserve Banks	
Reserve deposits at FRB −100 [required 0 deficiency −100]	Loans payable to FRB −100	Loans receivable from commercial banking system −100	Deposits of commercial banking system −100

When the commercial bank redeems its note, reserve deposits are correspondingly reduced at the Federal Reserve. In this instance there is a reserve decline equal to the full amount of the transaction.

(iii) A change in reserve requirements.

The Federal Reserve may also manipulate the money supply by changing the required reserve ratio. If the required reserve ratio is reduced, as from 20 to 15 percent, previously required reserves become excess reserves. Commercial banks will then increase their loans and deposits until there are $100 of deposits for every $15 of reserves instead of for every $20 of reserves as before, and excess reserves will no longer be excess. There would be no change in the balance sheet position of the central bank.

If the required ratio is increased from, say, 20 to 22 percent, the effect is to force commercial banks to reduce the volume of loans and deposits that can be created on a given volume of reserves. Again, although the balance sheet of the commercial banks must change to reflect the reduction in deposits, there will be no change in the balance sheet of the Federal Reserve.

The effect of these discretionary transactions involving the central bank is summarized in the third part of Table 2–2.

There are several other miscellaneous transactions involving the Federal Reserve Banks and the Treasury which influence reserve availability. These are generally minor in their impact compared with the operations described above.

From Changes in Reserve Availability to Changes in Demand Deposits

Why do changes in reserve availability lead to changes in demand deposits and, therefore, in the money supply? Here we must adopt a rule respecting the behavior of commercial banks. The change in reserves coupled with the reserve requirement gives us the information necessary to compute the maximum increase possible in demand deposits. If the reserve requirement is 20 percent, then an additional $20 of reserves will support an added $100 in deposits—a 5-fold expansion of deposits. Thus the expansion of deposits will be some multiple of the change in the volume of reserves if the system remains fully loaned and if other things remain unchanged. In this example the deposit multiplier of 5 is simply the reciprocal of the required reserve ratio under our restricted assumptions. The actual amount of the increase in deposits may, however, be less than the potential increase because of the reactions of commercial banks or because of certain feedback effects of deposit expansion on commercial bank reserves, that is, the actual value of the deposit multiplier is likely to be less than the 5 we gave in our example.

If the commercial banking system acquires excess reserves, it can permit them to remain unused and the system would not be fully loaned or, alternatively, it can put them to work by acquiring earning assets, as when it makes loans and investments and receives promises to pay in exchange for demand deposit liabilities. If the banking system possesses $800 in excess reserves and the required reserve ratio is 20 percent, it is then possible for commercial banks as a whole to expand their deposits by $800/.2, or by $4000. How does this expansion occur? One way is by creating deposits through loans, in which case the balance sheet of the commercial banking system will change as follows:

Commercial Banking System

Loans to the public	Demand deposits
+4000	+4000
[$800 of excess reserves have become required reserves]	

Excess reserves have become required reserves through the creation of demand deposits in exchange for an earning asset, loans to the public.

Alternatively, excess reserves may be used to expand deposits as a result of increases in bank investments, that is, in holdings of government, municipal, and other securities that banks are authorized to purchase. In this case, the changes in the balance sheet of the commercial banking system would be as follows:

Commercial Banking System

Investments	Demand deposits
+4000	+4000
[$800 of excess reserves have become required reserves]	

The response of the commercial banking system to changes in reserve availability obviously has a time dimension. In the above examples nothing is said about the time required for excess reserves to be absorbed through the creation of derivative demand deposits in exchange for earning assets—loans and investments. Further, we assumed that excess reserves are fully absorbed. Whether in fact they are depends upon the decision criteria that bankers employ, but for purposes of exposition we assume that the banking system does not wish to hold excess reserves.

Finally, are there any "leakages" that would limit the expansion in the reserve base to something less than the increase in reserves divided by the required reserve ratio? Such leakages could arise for two reasons. (a) When demand deposits are increased, there could be some increase in the amount of currency that the public wishes to hold. This can be described as a "cash drain" accompanying deposit expansion. As suggested at the beginning of this chapter, demand deposits, on the one hand, and currency, on the other, are not perfectly substitutable from the point of view of individual convenience. Some transactions are more conveniently completed by direct transfer of coin and paper currency while demand deposits are more practical for others. With the growth in deposits, it is certain that the public will wish to hold some of the expanded money supply in currency. (b) It is also likely that when demand deposits increase the public will prefer to hold some portion of this in the form of time deposits. For example, as demand deposits are transferred from one economic unit to another in settlement of transactions, some recipients may prefer to put them in time deposits. Whenever this occurs a further drain on demand deposit expansion arises. These two conditions will lead to a reduction in reserves available for expansion of demand deposits.

In spite of these leakages, the Federal Reserve System has the ability to control the money supply by using open market operations to offset them. There is some time lag in implementing offsets, however, because it takes time to compile the data and provide the information to those in charge. The appendix to this chapter provides a formal statement of the relations between bank reserves and the money supply which makes explicit allowance for the leakages that have been described and their impact on the deposit multiplier.

Difficulties in Measuring the Money Supply

Used analytically, "money" is defined in terms of its functions, and its primary function is to act as a universally acceptable means for individuals either to engage in current transactions (discharge their debts) or to store their wealth so they can engage in future transactions. Sometimes things other than currency and demand deposits can perform these same functions. A poker chip used to buy a meal in Las Vegas could be counted as part of the money supply, as could food stamps used to buy groceries in a supermarket, but neither food stamps nor poker chips, though they are used in the exchange or purchase of economic goods, are *universally* acceptable. However, personal checks drawn on demand deposits are not universally acceptable either. It is clear that the measurement of money requires some arbitrary choices.

Money is immediately spendable—therefore, it is sometimes called the most "liquid" of all assets that people hold. The "liquidity" of any asset is measured by the ease and certainty with which it can be exchanged for money, that is, the ease and certainty with which it can be converted into spendable form.

Having described the way in which money is created and controlled under a legally instituted fractional reserve banking system, the way monetary officials *measure* the amount of money outstanding at any time can now be considered. Actual measurements, however, tend to be mechanistic, and they are not always entirely appropriate for all analytical uses. Such is the case with the measurement of the money supply as reported by the Federal Reserve System. Convention, rather than theory, often rules the measurement of money.

As reported by the Federal Reserve, the money supply consists of the currency in circulation and the demand deposits in commercial banks. Adding these together, we have what is often called the *narrow* definition of the money supply. If time and savings deposits in commercial banks are included too, we have what is called the *broad* definition of the money supply.

Currency in Circulation

Currency, of course, consists of coins and paper money. The paper money of today is no longer redeemable in the form of gold or silver, but its appearance reflects the past when it consisted of negotiable non-interest-bearing notes or certificates of indebtedness. But not *all* currency issued is considered part of the money supply—only that part held outside of the vaults of commercial banks. To estimate "currency in circulation," the Federal Reserve staff takes figures on all currency issued and then subtracts figures on vault cash in commercial banks. Whatever is left over is called the amount of currency in circulation. Commercial banks that are not members of the Federal Reserve System only report data on vault cash twice each year—so-called bench-mark figures—and during other periods such data are estimated. Member banks, of course, report daily figures from their balance sheets, and money supply figures are prepared by the Federal Reserve and regularly reported as weekly or monthly averages of the daily figures. Reported data on the money supply are adjusted to eliminate the typical seasonal variations to which the series of raw data is subject.

Cash in the vaults of commercial banks is not part of "currency in circulation" because it must be withdrawn before it can be spent or because most cash being held follows from a deposit which is itself spendable. To include it would therefore allow the money supply to increase whenever people decided to deposit their cash and hold demand deposits instead. But, of course, the amount of spendable money held by the public does not change when cash deposits are made in commercial banks and exchanged for checking accounts.

By contrast, cash in the vaults of savings banks *is* included as part of currency in circulation. This cash is presumably spendable, even though the savings deposit itself is not. A savings deposit must be withdrawn before it can be spent, except in limited instances.[2]

Thus a savings deposit is not considered to be money—although it is a very liquid asset—but the cash in the vault of a savings bank *is* considered to be money. Therefore, "currency in circulation" does not change when one deposits cash in a savings bank. If one wished to consider savings bank deposits as part of the money supply, it would be necessary to deduct the volume of vault cash held by savings banks from the measure of currency in circulation. But this is not done by the Federal Reserve when they report their figures on the very broadest definition of money which includes savings deposits in savings and loan associations.

[2] The Queen City Savings and Loan in Seattle, Washington, began issuing nonnegotiable PaCHEK's to their depositors in July 1971. Customers can use these to pay bills and they are redeemed by Queen City either in cash or with a check drawn on a commercial bank. Savings banks have, in recent years, pursued their efforts to become more and more competitive with commercial banks and have tried to make their deposits as similar to commercial bank deposits as possible. See the lead article in *Savings and Loan News* (September 1971): 36–43. Also Mutual Savings Banks in the State of Massachusetts, under recent legislation, are allowed to issue NOW accounts (Negotiable Orders of Withdrawal).

Table 2–3. The Adjustment of Demand Deposits and the Money Supply.

Demand deposits in domestic commercial banks		
Individuals	____	
Companies	____	
Foreign owned deposits	____	
U.S. government deposits (tax and loan accounts)	____	
State and local government deposits	____	
Deposits of other domestic commercial banks	____	
		+____
Total demand deposits		
Subtract:		
U.S. government deposits	____	
Deposits of other domestic commercial banks	____	
Cash items in the process of collection	____	
Federal Reserve float	____	
Total subtracted		−____
Equals:		____
Demand deposits "adjusted"		
Add:		
Foreign and international demand deposits held in the Federal Reserve Banks	____	
Currency in circulation (outside of the Treasury, Federal Reserve, and vaults of commercial banks)	____	
		+____
The "narrow" money supply (sometimes called M_1)		____

Demand Deposits "Adjusted"

Table 2–3 lists the adjustments that Federal Reserve staff members make to total demand deposits in order to arrive at that part of all demand deposits considered to be part of the money supply. Commercial banks must hold reserves against all types of demand deposits except for the item "deposits of other domestic commercial banks"—known as interbank deposits.[3] If a commercial bank deposits funds in another commercial bank, the depositing bank loses either cash or reserves while the receiving bank gains cash or reserves. Therefore, if banks were required to hold reserves against deposits of other banks, an increase in the volume of interbank deposits would increase the volume of required reserves in the system as a whole and contract the lending capacity of the banking system. For this reason those demand deposits owned by other commercial banks are not subject to reserve requirements.

[3] In the actual computation process, deposits of other commercial banks *and* deposits of mutual savings banks (a kind of bank found in only some states and differing from other banks principally in the form of their charter and in that they invest chiefly in real estate) are included in the reporting of "interbank deposits," then the deposits of mutual savings banks are added back in with total deposits to become part of the money supply so that only *commercial* bank interbank deposits are finally eliminated in the money supply calculations. Thus, in the final treatment for money supply measurement, mutual savings banks are treated like other savings institutions and not like commercial banks which provide demand deposit accounts.

Also, the volume of demand deposits subject to reserve requirements is reduced by the value of the asset account, "cash items in the process of collection." If a check is drawn on commercial bank *A* and deposited in commercial bank *B*, then commercial bank *B* has to maintain reserves against this deposit. But if the check has not yet cleared, commercial bank *A* is still required to hold reserves against the deposit represented by this outstanding check as well. Thus to require that both commercial banks hold reserves against these items would mean that *both* banks would be holding reserves against the "same" deposit, and an increase in cash items resulting from, say, a transportation failure would lead to an increase in required reserves and would again contract the lending capacity of the system as a whole.[4]

In Table 2–3, both "deposits of other domestic commercial banks" and "cash items in the process of collection" are subtracted not only from deposits against which banks must hold reserves but also from total demand deposits in computing the money supply in the hands of the public. Interbank deposits exist primarily to effect transfers of funds and are generally not spendable by citizens for goods and services until after such transfers occur. Cash items in the process of collection are also excluded because, presumably, those citizens who wrote the checks that are being cleared have reduced their own checkbook stubs by the amount involved and "know" that their deposits have fallen (or will fall). Thus, although banks still hold deposits in their names, these deposits are not thought of as spendable. On the other hand, those who have just deposited the checks do feel that their newly acquired deposits are spendable. Therefore, such deposits should presumably be counted only once, rather than twice, and to accomplish this, cash items in the process of collection are subtracted from the total of demand deposits in estimating the money supply.

However, most citizens know that it takes time for checks to clear and will often write checks over the weekend and run down to "cover" them with a deposit on Monday morning. They "spend money they don't have." To the extent that this happens with any regularity, the amount of money that citizens "feel" they have in spendable form is larger than that reported in the official statistics. Just how much larger, of course, can probably never be known. But in periods of high interest rates even corporation treasurers have been known to "kite" large checks over the weekend. Tight money conditions tend to stimulate such behavior. Credit cards now frequently carry with them an auto-

[4] The *Federal Reserve Bulletin* for October 1969 contains a revision of the money supply series (the record of money supply behavior over time) which became necessary principally because of a correction needed to account for the "Euro-dollar float." When a U.S. bank borrows funds from a European bank or a branch office of a U.S. bank, the transfer of funds gives rise to an increase in the account "cash items in the process of collection." But there is no demand deposit outstanding to counterbalance the cash item. Hence, subtracting cash items leads to an understatement of the money supply. In the revised series, these cash items are added back into the demand deposit component of the money supply. Where, according to the old series, the money supply grew at an annual rate of 2.2 percent in the first half of 1969, the revised series corrected for the Euro-dollar float grew at an annual rate of 3.8 percent. Thus this item had generated a sizable distortion in the analyst's picture of what had been happening to the money supply. Also see the *Federal Reserve Bulletin* (February 1973): 61–79 for revision details and back data on the money supply.

matic "line of credit" that can be tapped by a customer at any time. With this credit source do people feel as if they have more money? Perhaps not, but surely they feel more free to kite checks than they would without a line of credit.

Business firms that borrow money are often required to hold "compensating balances." These are not available for spending but *are* included as part of the money supply.[5]

The Federal Reserve "float" is also subtracted from total demand deposits in arriving at an estimate of the money supply. It represents the cash items in the process of collection that have cleared in favor of the original depository bank and are now in the hands of the Federal Reserve, although they have not yet cleared the bank on which they are drawn.

U.S. government deposits are also subtracted from total demand deposits in estimating the money supply. Economists have questioned the appropriateness of this treatment in recent years, arguing that governments as well as citizens and firms have a demand for spendable funds. Therefore, perhaps, the supply of these available even to the U.S. government—the ultimate source of such funds—should be included as part of the money supply.[6]

To "demand deposits 'adjusted,' " we add the deposits of foreigners (including foreign governments) in the Federal Reserve (which are considered to be spendable even though the deposits of our own federal government are not). Finally, we add currency in circulation to arrive at the "narrow" definition of money, sometimes called M_1.

The *Federal Reserve Bulletin* also contains data on the broader definitions of money, M_2 and M_3. M_2 includes M_1 and time and savings deposits in commercial banks (adjusted in a fashion similar to the adjustment of demand deposits), but not large (over $100,000) negotiable certificates of time deposits. M_3 includes M_2 and the deposits of mutual savings banks and savings and loan companies. In recent years, some banks have issued "notes payable" in order to raise additional funds for lending. These liabilities differ from time certificates of deposit in only superficial ways, yet they are not always subject to reserve requirements. Bank holding companies sometimes sell notes pay-

[5] See Tilford C. Gaines, "Some inadequacies of financial data and theory," National Westminister Bank, *Quarterly Review* (November 1969): 35–44. Dr. Gaines notes the problems posed by both compensating balances and checkbook float. He states: "Debits to demand deposits at metropolitan centres outside New York have been averaging $230 billion daily while gross demand deposits have averaged in the neighborhood of $200 billion. If one assumes only a one-day average life for 'cheque-book float,' one is driven to conclude that not only are there no net demand deposits in the true money supply but that there is a lot of check-kiting going on" (p. 38). Dr. Gaines is sympathetic to the proposal that a demand deposit ownership sample survey be used to replace demand deposits on bank ledgers in estimating this part of the money supply.

[6] ". . . Treasury deposits should be included in the money supply both because they perform the function of money in the economy and because without them the conventional money supply often behaves in a manner which gives misleading indications as to the impact of money and monetary policy." See Paul S. Anderson and Frank E. Morris, "Defining the money supply: The case of government deposits," Federal Reserve Bank of Boston, *New England Economic Review* (March-April 1969): 21–31. Also see "A complicating factor for money supply watchers," *Morgan Guaranty Survey* (March 1969): 3–7; and C. W. Hall, "The influence of government deposits on the money supply," Federal Reserve Bank of Cleveland, *Economic Commentary* (June 28, 1971).

able in the market for commercial paper and then transfer the funds acquired into the capital account of the subsidiary bank. Again, no reserve requirements exist for funds acquired in this fashion. Perhaps, if one includes time deposits as part of the money supply, one ought also to include notes payable.

In England, economists now use a technique called Domestic Credit Expansion (DCE), wherein the change in Domestic Credit is said to equal the change in the money supply plus the balance of payments deficit. Its application can be seen best if we suppose that the money supply increases and that imports increase. Domestic residents write checks against their demand deposits to pay foreigners. Foreigners turn in these funds at the central bank and the levels of both domestic demand deposits and foreign exchange reserves immediately fall as a consequence. In retrospect, it would appear from the data that the money supply had not, in fact, increased greatly, but that would be an erroneous observation. To account for this spurious fall in the money supply the value of the balance of payments deficit is added to it to form the DCE, which is supposedly a better measure to use in analysis than the measured money supply itself. Thus the DCE is merely the money supply adjusted for changes in the balance of payments. It should be noted, however, that measures of the balance of payments deficit and surplus are themselves subject to disagreeable controversy over definition and this technique of adjusting money supply figures carries with it its own pitfalls.[7]

How much money exists in the economy at any time? Convention largely rules the answer to this question. Different measures of the money supply often give remarkably different impressions of what is happening to the volume of money over a period of time. The volume of liquid assets can change even though the officially measured money supply does not, and vice versa. Perhaps some sort of weighted average of the volume of different liquid assets existing at a point in time would give a better picture of the "correct" money supply. In any case, the measurement question will doubtless be the subject of continuing concern and debate.[8]

CONCLUSION

At a Conference of University Professors sponsored by the American Bankers Association with the cooperation of the London Banking Community, Ditchley Park, Oxfordshire, England in September 1968, Professor Kenneth Boulding composed a verse concerning the measurement of money.[9]

[7] See P. G. Gschwindt de Gyor, "The money supply question," National Westminister Bank, *Quarterly Review* (August 1969): 61–68; David Kern, "The implications of DCE," National Westminister Bank, *Quarterly Review* (November 1970): 29–44; and Geoffrey Bell, "Recent issues in monetary policy in United States and United Kingdom," *Financial Analysts Journal* (March-April 1970): 1–6.

[8] Milton Friedman devoted several sections of his book, *A Program for Monetary Stability* (Bronx, N.Y.: Fordham University Press, 1959), to the subject of "liquidity" and suggested that large changes in the volume of liquid assets outstanding will affect the demand for money. For an extensive discussion of the problems of measuring money, see Milton Friedman and Anna Jacobson Schwartz, *Monetary Statistics of the United States, Estimates, Sources, Methods* (New York: National Bureau of Economic Research, 1970).

We must have a good definition of Money,
For if we do not, then what have we got,
But a Quantity Theory of no-one-knows-what,
And this would be almost too true to be funny.
Now, Banks secrete something, as bees secrete honey;
(It sticks to their fingers some, even when hot!)
But what things are liquid and what things are not,
Rests on whether the climate of business is sunny.
For both Stores of Value and Means of Exchange
Include, among Assets, a very wide range,
So your definition's no better than mine.
Still, with credit-card-clever computers, it's clear
That money as such will one day disappear;
Then what isn't there we won't have to define.

The truth to be found in his humor is that as payment mechanisms change with technological development and with changing laws and customs, what is to be included in a measurement of money will also change. Thus the problem of measuring the money supply is not likely ever to be resolved in any permanent way.

In this chapter we have concentrated on money—coin, paper currency, and demand deposits—as a means of exchange. In the fractional reserve system of the United States, changes in the money supply can be initiated by the general public—including foreigners—the commercial banks, the Treasury, and the Federal Reserve System. From a policy standpoint, the most important changes are those initiated by the monetary authorities in the U.S.—the Federal Reserve System. The main types of actions undertaken by the Federal Reserve System to control the money supply are (a) the purchase and sale of government securities, (b) the increase or decrease in loans from the Federal Reserve Banks to commercial banks, and (c) the change of reserve requirements.

While this chapter has concentrated on factors affecting the money supply and measurement of the money supply, it is important to remember that control of the money supply is not an end in itself, but a tool whose effective use is likely to increase the chance of achieving the important objectives of full employment output and greater stability in the economy.

APPENDIX

The Relations of Reserves to the Money Supply: A Formal Statement

We have now described the mechanics of money control over the money supply and pointed out that certain leakages might occur so that an addition

[9] *Journal of Money Credit and Banking,* 1 (August 1969): 555. Also see David Laidler, "The definition of money: Theoretical and empirical problems," the comments by C. M. Sprenkle and R. L. Teigen, and other papers, pp. 508 ff.

of reserves to the banking system might not have the full multiple effect that the required reserve ratio by itself would imply. In this appendix we take explicit account of certain leakages by assuming that the public desires to hold a certain portion of its money in currency and that it desires to hold time deposits in a fixed ratio to demand deposits. With these assumptions, we examine the general effect of a change in reserves on money.

The approach we have chosen is only one of several possible alternatives. After working through the following equations the reader will appreciate that other assumptions might be introduced, but that the method of approach in attempting to pool the variety of factors at work into one statement of relationship would nevertheless remain the same.[10]

To begin, we define the following terms:

ΔM is the change in the money supply;
ΔD_p is the initial change in a primary deposit entering the banking system;
ΔD_d is the change in derivative deposits created by the commercial banking system as loans are expanded;
ΔC is the change in the public's holdings of currency;
ΔR_i is the initial change in the volume of reserves held by the commercial banking system;
ΔR_q is the change in the required reserves of the commercial banking system;
ΔT is the change in the volume of time deposits of the commercial banking system;
ΔL is the change in commercial banking system loans and investments.

We also assume the following relations:

$$\Delta M = \Delta D_p + \Delta D_d + \Delta C \tag{2.1}$$

an equation relating the changes in the money supply to changes in demand deposits and currency which is derived from our definition of money;

$$\Delta C = c\Delta D_d \tag{2.2}$$

an equation stating the assumption that the public has a preference for holding currency in a certain proportion, $c = C/D_d$, to demand deposits;

$$\Delta R_q = r\Delta D_p + r\Delta D_d + t\Delta T \tag{2.3}$$

an equation showing the reserve requirements of the banking system, where r is the ratio of required reserves to demand deposits and t is the ratio of required reserves to time deposits;

[10] Another way to formalize the relation between Treasury and Federal Reserve actions and the money supply rests on the concept of the monetary "base" consisting of bank reserves and currency in circulation. By changing the base, and by assuming certain currency and time deposit ratios, one can estimate the change in the money supply that would follow. For detailed descriptions of the mechanics of this approach, see J. L. Jordan, "Elements of money stock determination," Federal Reserve Bank of St. Louis, *Review*, 51 (October 1969): 10–19; and J. Anderson and T. M. Humphrey, "Determinants of change in the money stock: 1960–1970," Federal Reserve Bank of Richmond, *Monthly Review* (March 1972): 1–8.

$$\Delta R_i = \Delta C + \Delta R_q \tag{2.4}$$

an equation showing that an initial increase in reserves will be used either to supply additional currency to the public or to provide required reserves against deposits;

$$\Delta L = \Delta D_d + \Delta T + \Delta C \tag{2.5}$$

an equation expressing the equality of a change in bank earning assets (loans and investments) to changes in derivative demand deposits, time deposits, and currency in circulation;

$$\Delta D_P = \Delta R_i \tag{2.6}$$

an equation showing that any increase in primary deposits will equal the increase in reserve availability; such an increase in deposits might occur, for example, if the Federal Reserve were to purchase a government security from an individual who in turn deposits the check he receives into his account at his bank; and

$$\Delta T = n\Delta D_d \tag{2.7}$$

an equation expressing the public's preference for holding time deposits as a certain proportion, $n = T/D_d$, of their holdings of demand deposits.

The initial change in reserves, ΔR_i, is determined outside the commercial banking system and is subject to manipulation by the central bank.

General Solution for ΔM

A general solution for ΔM may now be derived by substituting equation (2.2) into equation (2.1):

$$\Delta M = \Delta D_P + \Delta D_d\,(1 + c) \tag{2.8}$$

and, using equations (2.2)–(2.4), (2.6), and (2.7) to express ΔD_d in terms of r, t, n, and c and the exogenous variable ΔR_i:

$$\Delta R_q = r\Delta D_P + r\Delta D_d + t\Delta T \tag{2.3}$$

$$\Delta R_q = \Delta R_i - \Delta C \tag{2.4}$$

$$\Delta C = c\Delta D_d \tag{2.2}$$

$$\Delta D_P = \Delta R_i \tag{2.6}$$

$$\Delta T = n\Delta D_d \tag{2.7}$$

we have: $$r\Delta R_i - \Delta R_i + (r + c + tn)\Delta D_d = 0$$

or: $$\Delta D_d = \Delta R_i(1 - r)\frac{1}{(r + c + tn)} \tag{2.9}$$

Substituting equation (2.9) into equation (2.8), we then have the general solution:

$$\Delta M = \Delta R_i \left(1 + \frac{1 + c}{r + c + tn} [1 - r] \right) \tag{2.10}$$

We thus see that the change in the money supply resulting from a change in reserves created by the central bank depends upon the several coefficients expressing public preferences, etc. These coefficients, of course, are not necessarily constant, for public preferences do change over time, and equation (2.10) should not be interpreted as the rigid mechanical relation that any equation appears to be. For example, if an increase in reserves leads to an increase in the money supply and lower interest rates, and these lower rates induce the public to shift their holdings out of time deposits, then the coefficient n will change and affect the final extent to which money is created.

The student is left to derive general solutions for ΔL and ΔD_d himself to see how loans and deposits might expand in the wake of an increase in bank reserves. The technique is similar.

ADDITIONAL READINGS

Thorough treatment of the fractional reserve banking system and factors affecting the money supply can be found in any of the standard text books on money and banking, five of which are: L. V. Chandler, *The Economics of Money and Banking,* 4th ed. (New York: Harper & Row, 1964); A. G. Hart, P. Kenen, and A. D. Entine, *Money, Debt and Economic Activity,* 4th ed. (Englewood Cliffs, N.J.: Prentice-Hall, 1968); B. P. Pesek and T. R. Saving, *The Foundations of Money and Banking* (New York: Macmillan, 1968); E. Shapiro, E. Solomon, and W. L. White, *Money and Banking* (San Francisco: Holt, Rinehart and Winston, 1968); and H. M. Smith, *The Essentials of Money and Banking* (New York: Random House, 1968).

The derivation of three alternative definitions of money is explained in: "What is money?" Federal Reserve Bank of Chicago, *Business Conditions* (June 1971).

QUESTIONS

1. Write an essay showing how the stock of money is determined in a fractional reserve banking system.
2. Does each of the following changes increase or decrease the size of the money supply multiplier, taking the money supply as demand deposits and currency held by the public?
   (a) an increase in the reserve requirement against demand deposits;
   (b) an increase in the desire to hold time rather than demand deposits;

(c) a decrease in the public's desire to hold cash;
(d) the insistence of some commercial banks on holding excess reserves.

3. While law prevents the Treasury from simply printing the new money it needs if it is short of tax receipts, printing-press money can, in effect, be created. How?

4. With a required reserve ratio of 20 percent and excess reserves of $100, the potential expansion of demand deposits is $500. However, people prefer to hold not only demand deposits, but time deposits as well. How do these preferences affect the potential expansion of demand deposits?

5. How is each of the following actions likely to affect the money supply?

   (a) an increase in the currency holdings of the public;
   (b) a decrease in Treasury deposits at Federal Reserve Banks;
   (c) sale of gold to the Treasury by the public;
   (d) sale of government securities by the Federal Reserve Banks;
   (e) repayment of loans by the commercial banking systems to the Federal Reserve Banks;
   (f) a fall in reserve requirements.

   Describe the process of adjustment that occurs.

6. What seasonal movements might you expect with regard to the amount of currency compared to the total money supply? How would these movements affect the availability of credit and the extent of excess reserves?

7. (a) Suppose that it is desirable to include time deposits as a part of the money supply together with currency and demand deposits. Work out a general solution for ΔM, modifying in whatever way necessary the system of equations found in the appendix to this chapter.
   (b) Still considering the model in the appendix, what reasoning can you develop for and against the inclusion of time deposits as part of the money supply?
   (c) Suppose $r = .15$; $c = .25$; $n = .20$; $t = .04$.
   Solve for ΔM, ΔD_d, and ΔL, letting $\Delta R_i = \$1$ million.
   (d) Draw a diagram relating ΔR_i to ΔM, where the values of the coefficients are those found in question 7(c).
   (e) How would the slope of the line through the origin connecting values for ΔR_i and ΔM change if r became .10 and c became .20?

II
Part

FROM MEASUREMENT TO THEORY

We have seen how measures of income and output are calculated, and we have examined the nature of the money supply. Our task is now to develop a model of the commodity and money markets of the economy that will explain the linkages between them.

We will begin by considering the commodity-producing sector, where our transactor units will be households, business firms, governments, and foreigners. Our first step will be to develop a statement of the demands for output by these transactors under conditions of a stable price level up to the point of full employment. This will permit a statement of the simplest kind of income determination model in which there is no monetary sector and no statement of production conditions in the economy.

Next, we will develop the monetary sector, particularly the nature of demands for money by transactor units. It will then be possible to relate the commodity-producing to the monetary sector and to show how output and employment levels, together with the interest rate, are simultaneously determined.

The final step in developing the full model will be to introduce the conditions under which output is produced and income payments are generated. This will necessitate a description of businessmen's behavior in employing labor and an explanation of wage rate determination. Once labor market conditions are combined with commodity and money markets, then the determination of the price level can be fully integrated with that of output and interest rates.

Our model will use the *method of comparative statics*. This means that it will explain movements in the dependent variables from one equilibrium position to another, but it will not follow the true path of change. For example, it will be possible to see the change in output and the general price level accompanying shifts in the behavior of transactor units, but it will not be possible to examine the time phasing of the change. For many purposes, particularly those of economic policy, it is enough to know only the direction and the magnitude of change in the relevant variables.

Household Behavior: Basic Theory

3

Chapter

Since household purchases are by far the most important component of the total demand for goods and services in an economy and are hence a crucial determinant of the levels of output and employment, it is essential to understand what factors determine them. Is the level of real consumption expenditure related to real income in the economy? If it is, what is the nature of the relationship? What other factors influence the decisions that households must make about the allocation of their income between current consumption and future consumption (or savings)? This chapter addresses these questions.

One warning: Initially we shall assume a constant price level, for this permits us to describe consumer behavior under conditions of stable prices. Later, however, in Chapters 13, 14, and 16, this restrictive condition will be dropped so that the influence of price level change on household behavior can be explicitly considered.

CONSUMPTION AND INCOME

Within the framework of the social accounting system, it is apparent that over the past several decades there has been a close relationship between "real" consumption (C) and "real" income (Y). This is evident in Figure 3–1, which shows the appropriate data for 1929–1970. (In the years 1942–1945, consumption was held low even though income increased because military production was given priority over production of consumer's goods during World War II. After the war, consumption returned to its "normal" relation with income.) The measure of income used here is real disposable income (Y_d). Suitable alternatives would be real gross output (GNP) and real personal income, but since our measure of consumption is of privately consumed goods and services (it excludes goods collectively consumed), it is more appropriate to use income received by households from wages, salaries, dividends, interest, business profits (noncorporate), welfare payments, etc., after deducting personal tax

Figure 3–1. "Real" Consumption and "Real" Disposable Income 1929–1970 (in 1958 constant dollars).

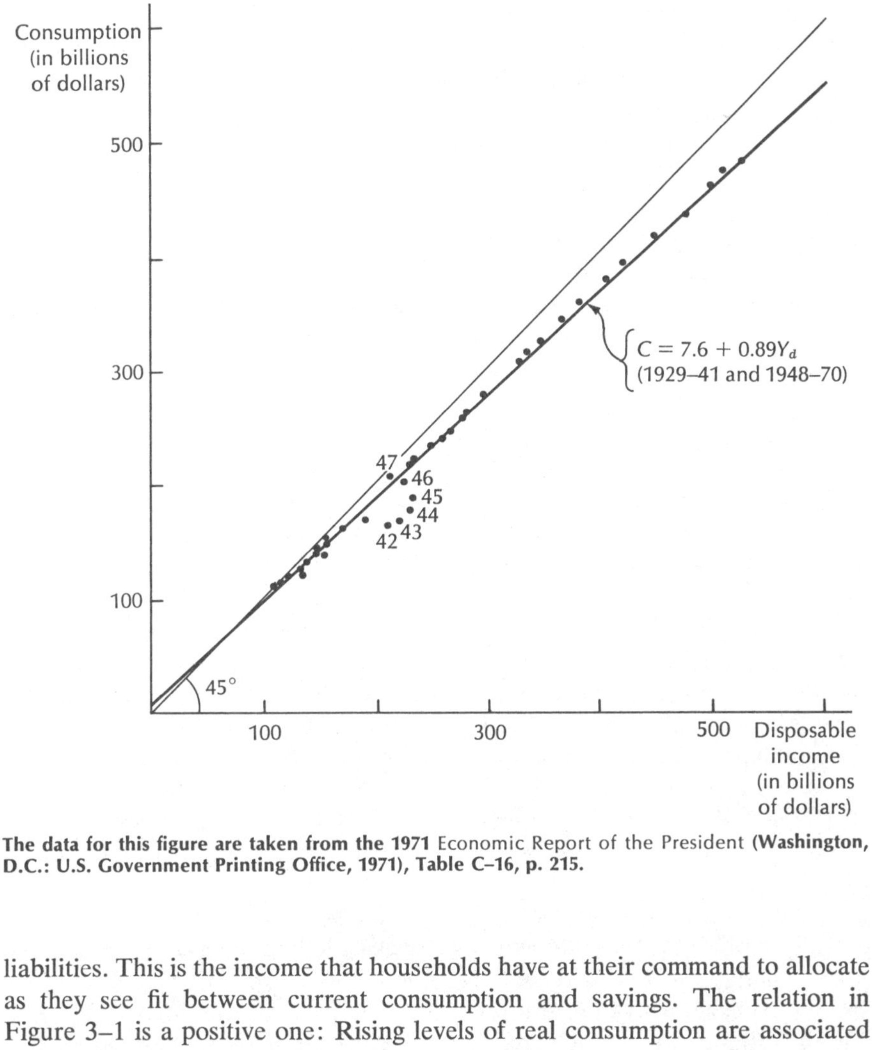

The data for this figure are taken from the 1971 Economic Report of the President **(Washington, D.C.: U.S. Government Printing Office, 1971), Table C–16, p. 215.**

liabilities. This is the income that households have at their command to allocate as they see fit between current consumption and savings. The relation in Figure 3–1 is a positive one: Rising levels of real consumption are associated with rising levels of real income.

In the graph, real consumption of each year is related to real disposable income of the *same* year. Current consumption is made dependent upon current income. This is an important statement of household behavior. An alternative might be to assume that current consumption reflects the response of households to their income in the recent past as they plan current expenditures by extrapolating their past income experience. In this case lagged income, rather than current income, would be the variable on which consumption depended. Still another explanation of current consumption would have it dependent upon a household's estimate of normal income over some much longer period. A change in current income would then be expected to influence personal consumption of a household only through its effect on "expectations" of what "normal" or "permanent" income might be. These alternative formulations of the consumption function raise important, and as yet unresolved, issues in theory and policy (which will be discussed in some detail in the following chapter). But, in developing the basic comparative static model, we assume that current consumption is a function of current income.

The Consumption Function

The consumption-income relation of Figure 3–1 is one of the principal functions in an income determination model. John Maynard Keynes predicted that we would find this relation in the data when he wrote:

> "The fundamental psychological law, upon which we are entitled to depend with great confidence both *a priori* from our knowledge of human nature and from the detailed facts of experience, is that men are disposed, as a rule and on the average, to increase their consumption as their income increases, but not by as much as the increase in their income." [1]

As Keynes noted, households will not choose to allocate an increase in income entirely to current consumption. Figure 3–1 clearly supports his hypothesis. Since households do not consume all of their income, what they have left over is savings. To save is to accumulate wealth in the form of both real and financial assets. This desire to save is expected to increase along with increases in income. Empirically, the evidence of the past two decades indicates that household savings have amounted to between 5 and 8 percent of real disposable income, while the remaining 92 to 95 percent of income is consumed.

We can set the stage for analysing the consumption function in greater depth by briefly reviewing our analytical tools with the help of the equations and graphs that appear in Figure 3–2. The consumption function, $C = C(Y)$ may be approximated by the linear form of the equation and be written as $C = a + bY$. An example of this relation appears in Figure 3–2(a). Consumption is the dependent variable and is measured on the vertical axis. Income is the independent variable and is measured on the horizontal axis.

The coefficient a in the equation is the value of the intercept of the function with the vertical axis. It is the value taken by consumption when income is zero; it is not itself zero because in any society, even if income is zero, there will be some consumption as inventories accumulated in previous periods of production are drawn upon. The coefficient of Y in the equation, b,

[1] J. M. Keynes, *The General Theory of Employment, Interest, and Money* (New York: Harcourt Brace Jovanovich, Inc., 1936), p. 96.

Figure 3–2.

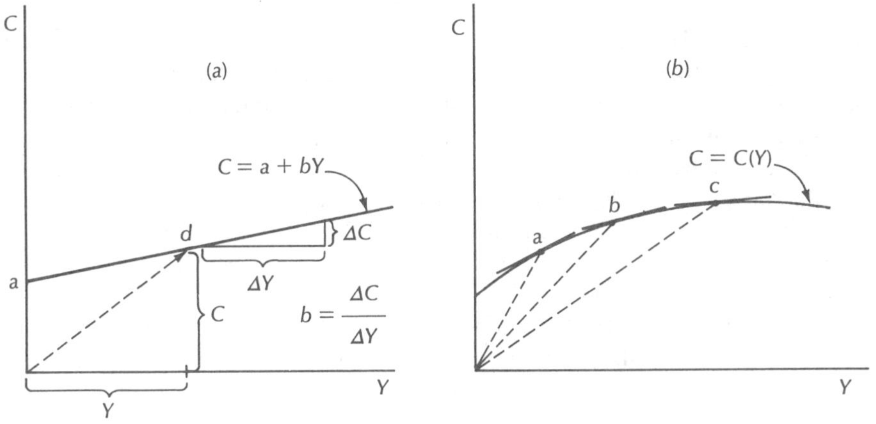

is the slope of the function. This slope is the same at every point on a linear function and can be measured by the ratio $\Delta C/\Delta Y$. We define the *marginal propensity to consume* as the slope of the consumption function at any point, hence $MPC = \Delta C/\Delta Y$. In a linear function, $MPC = b$ and is the same for every point on the function. We define the *average propensity to consume* as the ratio C/Y. This ratio can also be described as the slope of a radius vector (a line drawn from the origin to any point in the graph). Such a vector appears as the dashed line in Figure 3–2(a). It is clear that the ratio of C to Y is the slope of the radius vector from the origin to point d on the consumption function. If the radius vector were drawn to a point on the consumption function further to the right of point d, its slope would be less. Thus in this example the average propensity to consume declines as income increases, while the marginal propensity to consume remains unchanged as income increases. Also, as depicted, it will always be true, for any point on the function, that the marginal propensity to consume will be less than the average propensity to consume, $MPC < APC$. This can easily be verified by comparing the respective slopes at any point on the function.

A nonlinear consumption function, $C(Y)$, appears in Figure 3–2(b). Slopes of this function at points a, b, and c are indicated by the slopes of the short lines of tangency drawn to touch the function at those points. As the function is drawn, it is clear that the marginal propensity to consume declines as income rises, as does the average propensity to consume. Finally, as in Figure 3–2(a), the marginal propensity to consume remains less than the average propensity to consume at every point on this function.

These two shapes taken by consumption functions play important roles in the analysis that follows, and the reader should keep the concepts of the average and marginal propensities to consume and the relation between them carefully in mind.

The Simple Theory of Income Determination: The Multiplier and Consumption-Income Interdependence

Consumption expenditures account for between ⅔ and ¾ of total output. We have said that consumption depends upon income. But income (output) levels also depend upon consumption; that is, consumption and income are interdependent, for if there is some factor operating in the economy that gives rise to an increase in income, this will lead to an increase in consumption in an amount somewhat less than the initial increase in income. But the increase in consumption will in its own turn lead to a further increase in income. And this will lead to another increase in consumption. Thus, in the economic system, consumption and income are simultaneously determined.

We can illustrate this interdependence with a very simple algebraic model in which there are only two groups of transactors: business and households. A simple numerical example which some students may find helpful is also provided.

We can take:

$Y =$ income
$C =$ household expenditures
$I =$ investment expenditures
$a =$ a constant specifying the level of consumption when income (Y) is zero
$b =$ the slope of the consumption function

Our consumption function is $C = a+bY$, and, by definition, $Y = C + I$, where I is given. Substituting the consumption function for Y into $Y = C + I$ we obtain:

	Numerical Example
	$C = 10 + .6Y$, where $a = 10$, $b = .6$
	$I = 20$
$Y = a + bY + I$	$Y = 10 + .6Y + 20$
$Y(1 - b) = a + I$	$Y(1 - .6) = 10 + 20$
$Y = \frac{1}{1 - b}(a + I)$	$Y = \frac{1}{1 - .6}(10 + 20) = 2.5\,(30) = 75$

Given the level of investment spending, income is then determined by the values of a and b in the consumption function.

C is determined simultaneously with Y. Substituting $C + I$ for Y in the consumption function, we obtain:

	Numerical Example
$C = a + b(C + I)$	$C = 10 + .6(C + 20)$
$C(I - \mathrm{b}) = a + bI$	$C(1 - .6) = 10 + .6(20)$
$C = \frac{a}{1 - b} + \frac{b}{1 - b} I$	$C = \frac{10}{1 - .6} + \frac{.6}{1 - .6}(20) = 25 + 30 = 55$

The solution values for Y and C can be shown graphically as in Figure 3–3, where the curves are drawn to fit the numerical example. On the vertical axis we now measure both consumption and investment. A guideline is drawn through the origin at a 45-degree angle to show all the points in the quadrant for which the numerical value on the horizontal axis equals the value on the vertical axis.

To the consumption function, $C = 10 + .6Y$, we add an amount of investment, $I = 20$. This shifts the curve upward vertically by 20 to form a new curve $C + I = 30 + .6Y$. The point at which this new curve intersects the guide line, point a, indicates the solution values of Y on the horizontal axis and $C + I$ on the vertical axis.

Now, if investment spending, the independent variable, increases by ΔI, the effect on income and consumption will be given by the equations:

$$\Delta Y = \Delta C + \Delta I$$
$$\Delta C = b\Delta Y$$
$$\Delta I \text{ is given}$$

By substitution:

	Numerical Example
	$b = .6;\ \Delta I = 10$
$\Delta Y = b\Delta Y + \Delta I$	$\Delta Y = .6\Delta Y + 10$
$\Delta Y(1 - b) = \Delta I$	$\Delta Y(1 - .6) = 10$
$\Delta Y = \dfrac{1}{1-b}\Delta I$	$\Delta Y = \dfrac{1}{1-.6}(10) = 2.5(10) = 25$

Figure 3–3.

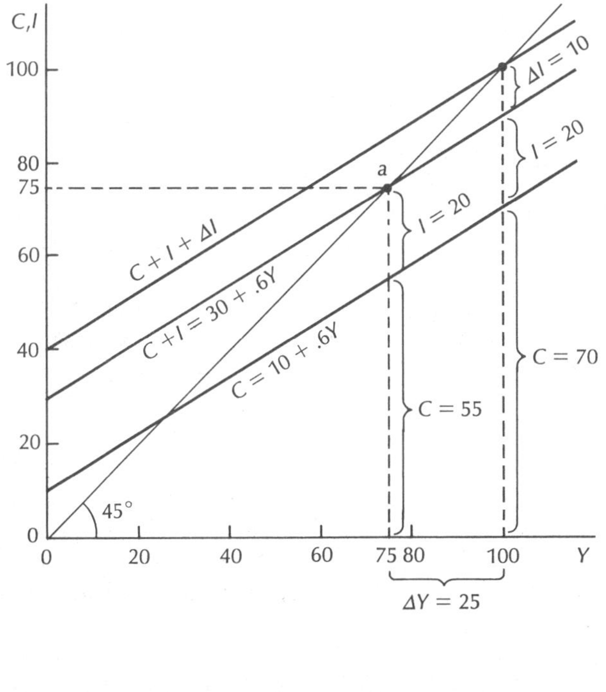

The expression $1/1 - b$ is called a "multiplier," in this case the "investment multiplier." In the numerical example the multiplier equals 2.5. Its size determines the ultimate change in income associated with a given change in investment spending. Note that its size depends upon b, which must take a value between zero and one, $0 < b < 1$. The nearer b is to unity, the larger the effect upon income as a result of a change in investment outlays.

An example will help make this clear. If I increases by ΔI, the initial rise in I will lead to an increase in income to the suppliers of investment goods. The proportion of the increase in income that is spent by these suppliers depends on the marginal propensity to consume, b. An amount $b\Delta I$ will be consumed, and $(1 - b)\Delta I$ will be saved. The increase in consumption will increase the income of others who produce consumers' goods and, again, part of this income, $b(b\Delta I)$, will be consumed. As the process is repeated n times, the stream of expenditures attributable to ΔI becomes $\Delta I + b\Delta I + b^2\Delta I + \ldots + b^n\Delta I$. This is a geometric series which approaches $1/(1 - b)\Delta I$ as n approaches infinity. Figure 3–3 also shows that ΔY is 25 when ΔI is 10. The equilibrium level of income associated with the higher level of investment spending is now 100.

The investment spending multiplier can be applied not only to income, but also to consumption:

	Numerical Example
$\Delta Y = \Delta C + \Delta I$	$\Delta Y = \Delta C + 10$
$\Delta C = b\Delta Y$	$\Delta C = .6\Delta Y$
$\Delta C = b(\Delta C + \Delta I)$	$\Delta C = .6(\Delta C + 10)$
$\Delta C(1 - b) = b\Delta I$	$\Delta C(1 - .6) = .6(10)$
$\Delta C = \dfrac{b}{1 - b}\Delta I.$	$\Delta C = \dfrac{.6}{1 - .6}(10) = (1.5)(10) = 15$

With a specified increase in investment, consumption will increase by a factor of $b/1 - b$, or 1.5 in the numerical example. In Figure 3–3 we see that C has increased from 55 to 70 as a result of the increase in investment of 10.

Household Savings

In this model investment expenditure is undertaken by business firms. All income earned is paid to households. The difference between consumption expenditure and total income or output is investment expenditure; that is, $Y - C = I$. However, from the viewpoint of the allocation of income by households, what is not consumed out of current income is savings, or the claim on future consumption; that is, $Y - C = S$. Hence, savings and investment are always, by definition, equal.

The savings-investment-income relationship is expressed in Figure 3–4, where, since investment is assumed to be independent of income, the given levels of investment are represented by lines parallel to the income axis. Savings, like consumption, is a function of income, $S(Y)$. Y_1 is an equilibrium level of income, where the capital expenditure plans of business coincide with the savings plans of households. At any income level below Y_1, savings are

Figure 3–4.

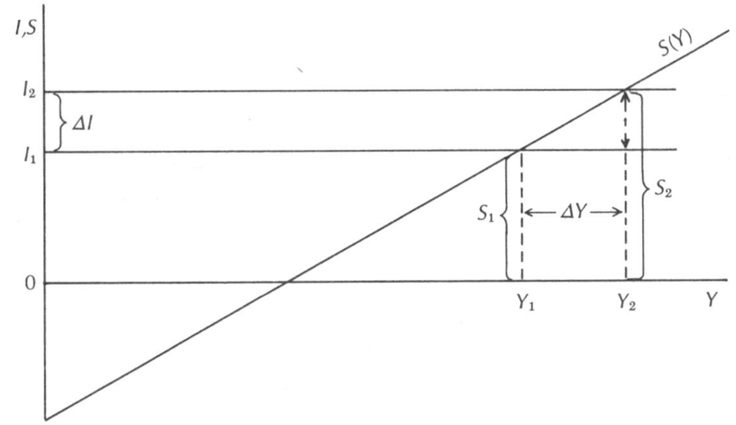

less than investment and total demand for output exceeds the total supply. This will lead to a depletion in inventories and a rise in production and income. When the expenditures of businesses rise by ΔI to I_2, income increases to Y_2 and savings will rise to equal investment.

The savings function intersects the vertical axis *below* the origin. Thus the intercept of $S(Y)$ is negative, and its slope is the difference between unity and the marginal propensity to consume. This can be shown as follows:

$$S = Y - C$$
$$C = a + bY$$

By substitution:

$$S = Y - (a + bY)$$
$$S = -a + (1 - b)Y$$

Thus the slope of the savings function is the coefficient of Y in this equation, or $(1 - b)$. This slope is also called the marginal propensity to save, where b is the marginal propensity to consume. Therefore, $MPS = 1 - MPC$. Since $0 < b < 1$, the expression $(1 - b)$ is positive, and the savings function has a positive slope. If income increases, savings will also increase, but not by the full amount of the increase in income.

The average propensity to save is S/Y at a specified level of income. The average propensity to save plus the average propensity to consume equals unity.

A word of warning is desirable here. This model of savings behavior is very useful pedagogically, but at the same time it is also simplistic. Here savings is a residual, what is left over after all current consumption expenditures have been taken care of. The actual behavior of households with respect to future consumption is a good deal more complicated than this. Decisions to save are conscious, and they cannot be isolated from the form in which the savings are to be held. Of greatest significance is the fact that households save because they desire to accumulate assets. And what households want in the way of assets is part of the package of all household expenditures. It is not a residual; it is rather the result of deliberate choice.

Factors Affecting Consumption

Our analysis has concentrated upon income as the principal determinant of consumption and savings, but other factors also affect them. Someone once said, only half jokingly, that "consumption is determined by income—and everything else," and income is indeed the most important determinant of consumption by far. There are, however, a large number of factors influencing the intercept and slope of the consumption function. Some of these additional factors are:

(1) volume of wealth and liquid assets;
(2) interest rates and the availability of consumer credit;
(3) consumer attitudes and expectations;
(4) demographic composition;
(5) income distribution;
(6) the existing stock of consumer durables; and
(7) sales effort and the availability of new products.

Volume of Wealth and Liquid Assets

Next to income, wealth has perhaps been given the most consideration as a determinant of consumption. For a given level of income it seems reasonable to believe that the greater the stock of wealth held by individuals, the greater their consumption will be. In fact, this belief is the basis for the "wealth effect" (discussed in other parts of this text, particularly Chapter 14), which, according to A. C. Pigou, would ensure the automatic achievement of full employment as long as prices were flexible.[2] Pigou argued that as prices fall during periods of unemployment, the stock of wealth will increase in real terms as the real values of cash holdings and government securities, which are fixed in dollar amounts, increase. Prices will eventually fall enough so that the increase in wealth will be sufficient to shift the consumption function upward enough to achieve full employment.

This argument may be theoretically sound, but it is not practical.[3] Fluctuations in the stock of wealth in an economy will be small, and as a result the importance of wealth for both short-term and medium-term movements in the consumption function is likely to be strictly limited. After surveying the available empirical studies concerning the influence of wealth on consumption, Michael K. Evans states that:

> "In particular, it was found that the stock of household wealth was not an additional determinant of consumption. Thus various asset effects

[2] A. C. Pigou, "The classical stationary state," *Economic Journal,* 52 (1943): 343–351; and "Economic progress in a stable environment," *Economica,* 14 (1947): 180–190.
[3] Don Patinkin, "Price flexibility and full employment," in *Readings in Monetary Theory,* selected by the American Economic Association (Homewood, Ill.: Irwin, 1951), pp. 252–283, and reprinted in M. G. Mueller (Ed.), *Readings in Macroeconomics,* 2nd ed. (New York: Holt, Rinehart and Winston, 1972).

> which have suggested that the C/Y ratio increases when prices fall because of the greater real value of wealth have been found to have virtually no empirical support." [4]

Despite Evans' findings, however, wealth may still be a significant determinant of consumption. The empirical evidence indicates only that the *fluctuations* in wealth that have occurred over the periods studied have apparently been insufficient to have influenced the position or slope of the consumption function significantly.

Not only the volume of wealth, but also the form in which wealth is held may have an effect upon consumption. For a given level of income and stock of wealth, some economists have claimed that consumption increases as the share of wealth held in liquid assets (money and near-monies) increases. In other words, *liquidity* is a determinant of consumption.[5] The argument is that, as liquidity increases, the actual holdings of liquid assets are more likely to exceed desired holdings, and households can be expected to adjust their wealth positions. They may move from liquid assets into other forms of wealth, either tangible assets (durable consumer goods or housing) or financial assets. There is here what may be called an element of *portfolio adjustment* (developed at length in Chapter 8) in the household's wealth position, but though this argument appears sound, the empirical work has not yet proved convincing on this point. In fact, Evans has concluded that:

> "Since the more stringent tests show no effect of liquid assets on consumption, we believe that the weight of the evidence would argue against their inclusion in consumption functions." [6]

To conclude, it appears logical that both wealth and liquidity should influence the level of consumption. However, in neither case is the empirical evidence entirely clear. More empirical work is needed to further clarify the effects of both.

Interest Rates and the Availability of Consumer Credit

Before Keynes developed the consumption function presented in the earlier sections of this chapter, many economists held that interest rates were an important determinant of consumption. Savings was thought to be a function of interest rates, and it was thought that as interest rates rose savings would also rise and consumption would fall. Keynes pointed out that savings and consumption would be determined primarily by the level of income—interest rates would have little effect. The empirical evidence to date has been overwhelmingly in support of Keynes' position, but of course further evidence to be

[4] Michael K. Evans, *Macroeconomic Activity* (New York: Harper & Row, 1969), p. 69.

[5] Two studies indicating that liquid assets are of some importance in determining consumption are L. R. Klein and A. S. Goldberger, *An Econometric Model of the United States, 1929–1952* (Amsterdam: North-Holland, 1955), p. 90; and A. Zellner, "The short-run consumption function," *Econometrica,* 25 (October 1957): 552–567.

[6] Evans, *Macroeconomic Activity,* p. 42.

collected in future periods in which interest rates fluctuate more widely might reveal an influence.

Although it is now generally accepted that consumers are little affected by the effect of interest rates on consumer credit terms, those aspects of consumer credit which do appreciably affect willingness to buy are the availability of credit, the size of the down payment, and the amount of time allowed to repay. Credit permits households to enjoy future income in the present. Consumption need not be deferred until the income is actually earned and received. Making consumer installment credit more available through improved terms and a lowering of credit standards should thus serve to raise the consumption function, but an important question is whether the net effect of such a change is not merely to bring consumption expenditures forward from future periods to the present. If it is, then the net effect is to create a temporary bulge in consumption, that is, to lift the function only temporarily. If consumer credit terms are eased, automobiles and other consumer durables may be purchased this year which would, in the normal course of things, be acquired next year.[7] Next year's outlays for these items might be somewhat reduced, so that the time phasing of consumption as well as the total amount may be affected.

In contrast, a worsening of the terms of credit and a raising of standards could be expected to have opposite effects.

Consumer Attitudes and Expectations

A more favorable set of attitudes and expectations about current and future income prospects could be expected to raise the consumption function, for household planning would then be predicated on the basis of larger revenue streams than originally anticipated. Studies have increasingly shown that, by incorporating an attitudinal variable into the consumption function, changes in consumption can be predicted more effectively than if income alone is relied upon.[8] Perhaps the Korean War presents the clearest case of how changes in expectations can affect consumer behavior. As the likelihood of a major conflict increased, consumption spending rose rapidly as consumers stockpiled goods in anticipation of rationing similar to that experienced during World War II. Though expectations rarely change so radically as in this case, it does indicate that changing expectations affect the level of consumption.

Expectations of either once-and-for-all or continuous unidirectional changes in the price level may also be expected to influence consumer behavior, although the direction of the influence remains unclear. Some have argued that expectations of continually rising prices will lead consumers to buy now rather

[7] For the importance of credit terms on automobile demand, see Daniel B. Suits, "The demand for new automobiles in the United States, 1929–1956," *Review of Economics and Statistics,* 40 (August 1958): 273–280.

[8] In particular, see G. Katona, *Psychological Analysis of Consumer Behavior* (New York: McGraw-Hill, 1951); Eva Mueller, "Ten years of consumer attitude surveys: Their forecasting record," *Journal of the American Statistical Association,* 58 (December 1963): 899–917, and "Effects of consumer attitudes on purchases," *American Economic Review,* 47 (December 1957): 946–965; and H. T. Shapiro and G. E. Angevine, "Consumer attitudes, buying intentions and expenditures: An analysis of the Canadian data," *Canadian Journal of Economics,* 2 (May 1969): 230–249.

than wait and pay the higher prices. This desire to buy now to beat the rise in prices, of course, contributes to the inflationary pressures. In conflict with this position, however, is one study that shows that periods of more rapidly rising prices in the 1950s caused consumption expenditures, out of a given level of income, to be lower than they otherwise would have been,[9] and that consumption thus played a stabilizing role. This behavior is attributed to resentment of higher prices and a consequent unwillingness to buy. Where the likely effect on consumption of attitudes and expectations concerning income and employment is clear, evidence concerning the influence of price expectation on consumption is far from conclusive.

Demographic Composition

In the short run, little change is likely to occur in demographic factors such as age and family size distribution, urban-rural balance, and racial mix. Changes in these factors are unlikely to lead to sudden significant shifts in the consumption function, but they can and do influence the position of the consumption function over relatively long periods of time.

(a) *Age distribution.* Individuals who have recently entered the labor force for the first time and who may be establishing a household consume a relatively large part of their income. Their average propensity to consume is greater than that of either middle-aged persons, who already possess a stock of durable goods and are now saving for retirement, or retired individuals, who have already purchased many of the durable and nondurable goods they need. Therefore, as the percentage of the population composed of young working people increases, relative to these other two groups, one might expect a shift upward in the consumption function.

(b) *Family size distribution.* Large families consume a larger amount of a given income than do small families. This point is subject to little argument. Therefore, a trend toward smaller average family size will lead to a downward shift in the consumption function, other things being equal.

(c) *Urban-rural balance.* Farmers and small businessmen have traditionally saved a relatively large percentage of their income. As the rural percentage of the population decreases, this will cause upward shifts in the consumption function. A decrease in the importance of small businessmen would have the same effect.

(d) *Racial mix.* Some existing evidence indicates that racial minorities consume less than whites out of a given level of income.[10] This may be due to a difference in their wealth position or in the availability of credit. It may also be explained, at least in part, by the relative income hypothesis developed in the following chapter. Other things being equal, as racial minorities increase as a percentage of the population, the consumption function may shift downward.

[9] Eva Mueller, "Consumer reactions to inflation," *Quarterly Journal of Economics*, 73 (May 1959): 246–262.

[10] James S. Duesenberry, *Income, Savings and the Theory of Consumer Behavior* (Cambridge, Mass.: Harvard University Press, 1949), pp. 50–52.

As earlier mentioned, the above factors, though each of them may be important in determining the position of the consumption function in the long run, are each unlikely to lead to significant shifts in the consumption function over relatively short periods.

Income Distribution

There are several possible classifications of income distribution by function, age, and size. Each classification has its unique effect upon the relation between consumption and income, as may be seen by considering a change in the functional distribution of income away from *rentiers* (those whose income is principally from rent, interest, and dividends) and toward wage earners and profit recipients. The effect on the aggregate consumption function depends upon the existence of differences in the propensity to consume of the three groups of income recipients and in how these groups are affected by an income redistribution.

A change in the age distribution of income from, say, the middle-aged toward the older members of society will have an effect on the aggregate consumption function dependent upon whether the propensity to consume differs by age groups. One might expect, for example, that older persons would have a higher propensity to consume than the middle-aged who are saving for retirement, thus raising the aggregate consumption function.

In the case of the size distribution of income, our concern is with differing propensities by income class. It is generally believed that if income were to become more equally distributed, as it might, for example, if income tax schedules were more steeply graduated, the aggregate consumption function would be raised and the savings function lowered. If individual *A* receives an income of $100,000 per year and consumes $50,000, his average propensity to consume is 0.5. If individual *B* receives $10,000 per year and consumes $9000, his average propensity to consume is 0.9. The total amount of consumption is $59,000 out of $110,000 income. If we take $1000 from *A* and give it to *B, and if* both *A* and *B* continue to consume the *same* proportions of their income as before (that is, if *A* and *B* keep the same *APC and* the same *MPC*), then *A* will reduce his consumption by $500, but *B* will increase his by $900. The net increase in consumption will be $400, for of a total income of $110,000 consumption will amount to $59,400 instead of only $59,000. The consumption function will shift upward since total consumption out of income will be higher than it was earlier for the same total income.

Cross-sectional data on the distribution of income and its uses do verify that the ratio S/Y_d increases while the ratio C/Y_d falls as income rises. Freely translated, the rich save more and consume less than the poor, *if* we measure savings and consumption *proportionally* with income. This result is, of course, consistent with the linear consumption function we drew in Figure 3–2(a). There, as income rose, the average propensity to consume, C/Y, fell; but the marginal propensity to consume, $\Delta C/\Delta Y$, remained constant.

In our numerical example, we implicitly assumed that the marginal propensity to consume was *different* for the rich and the poor. This assumption was imposed when we required the two individuals to continue to consume the same proportion of their income after the transfer as before it. We could have made the different assumption that the rich individual who gave up $1000 reduced his consumption by $500 as before, but the poor individual, receiving $1000 more income, increased his consumption by only $500, so that there would be no net increase in consumption; here, *MPC* is the *same* for the rich and the poor. This result, showing *no* upward shift in the consumption function, would result if the consumption function were linear, as in Figure 3–2(a). Only if the function were nonlinear, as in Figure 3–2(b), would the *marginal* propensity to consume actually become lower as income rose. If a redistribution of income away from the rich in favor of the poor (the Robin Hood effect) is to shift the consumption function upward, that function must have the curvilinear shape of Figure 3–2(b).

We can also examine this behavior of the consumption function for *income classes.* In Figure 3–5 we have measured income classes in $5000-per-year intervals along the horizontal axis; the dots represent the average consumption expenditure by families in the designated classes, and the hypothetical overall consumption function $C^*(Y)$ is drawn by connecting these dots (of course, this is not the same consumption function as that in earlier figures). The short, thin lines through the dots represent the consumption-income relations *within* each class; in the $10–$15,000 range, for example, the marginal propensity to consume is 0.9, and since this line is straight and would intersect the origin if it were extended down and to the left, the average and marginal propensities to consume are equal *within* the class. The slopes of the thin lines show equal *APC* and *MPC* for *each* income class, and they show that these diminish as income rises.

With this graph in mind, we can see that if income is taken from someone in a higher bracket and given to someone in a lower bracket, they will each

Figure 3–5.

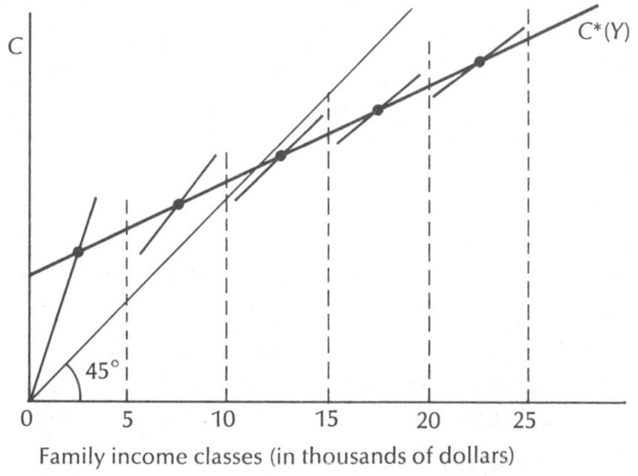

retain the same *MPC* and *APC* as before the redistribution and the consumption function will shift upward only so long as the amount transferred is insufficient to change the donor's or the recipient's income bracket. If the redistribution is so extensive as to move the high income receiver into a lower bracket and the low income receiver into a higher one, and if these families now adopt the consumption-to-income ratios characteristic of their new income classes, then the consumption function will not shift upward. That it is reasonable to expect a shift from class to class becomes clear if we view the lowest income class, whose *APC* and *MPC* are both greater than one: It is hardly likely that an increase in income of $1000 will lead to an increase in consumption of, say, $1500. We would in general, therefore, not expect persons whose incomes have increased to remain in their same income class, but rather to adopt the consumption patterns of those others whose income levels they have just attained. It may thus be that changing the distribution of income will have little overall effect on the height of the consumption function.

Existing empirical evidence on the variety of possible effects of income redistribution on consumption is unclear. This is, in all likelihood, primarily because changes in income distribution that have actually occurred in the United States over the past few decades have been quite small. As a result, the effects of these changes on the consumption function have been difficult to detect in empirical studies. If we can go on past evidence, patterns of income distribution in the U.S. are likely to change significantly only over quite long periods. Therefore, as with demographic factors, the position and slope of the short-run consumption function are unlikely to be altered markedly by changes in income distribution.

The Stock of Consumer Durables

As in the case of liquid assets, a portfolio adjustment approach reveals the effect that changes in the stock of consumer durables might have upon consumption. If household stocks of durable goods are less than desired, then an optimum position will be sought by wealth adjustments as well as through expenditures of income. Such portfolio adjustments produce shifts in the consumption function. It was this type of adjustment that many felt occurred at the end of World War II. The dearth of consumer goods during the war had led to a deferral of demand and a depletion in the stock of durable goods held by households. This depletion was accompanied by an increase in the wealth position of households as rationing resulted in forced savings. With the end of the war and the increased availability of consumer goods, portfolio adjustment led to an upward shift in the consumption function. However, two factors other than the small existing stock of durable goods could have accounted at least in part for the increase in consumption at the end of the war—the previously mentioned increases in household wealth and the increased holdings of liquid assets. Sorting out the relative importances of the roles of these three factors in the rise in consumption has so far proved an impossible task. In theory each of these factors would be expected to alter the position of the consumption function, and some evidence that the stock of durables is a determinant of consumer expenditures has been found by Professor D. B. Suits in his study of the demand for automobiles.

Availability of New Products and Sales Effort

Though empirical evidence is lacking, there has been increasing recognition that sales efforts and new products can influence the position of the consumption function. This point has been pressed hardest—and most polemically—by Professor J. K. Galbraith, who has argued that in their desire for security the managers of today's large enterprises need to control demand; an extensive sales effort is one way in which they achieve this end.[11] Marxists and others have argued that built-in obsolescence has been an important factor in ensuring adequately high consumption demand.[12] Through the development of new or purportedly new products and the accompanying sales effort, the consumer comes to feel that the goods currently in his possession must be replaced.

The amount of money spent on advertising has been growing steadily, but fluctuations in these expenditures tend to be fairly small. Fluctuations in the rate of appearance of new products also do not seem to be great. Therefore, though sales effort and new product development may both influence the position of the consumption function in the long run, these factors are likely to have relatively little impact on the consumption function over a short period, although exceptions may exist upon occasion. For example, the development of a new product equal in importance to the automobile would certainly lead to an immediate and marked shift in the consumption function.

THE THEORY AND MEASUREMENT OF CONSUMPTION

In the household sector account, personal consumption expenditures are defined as including purchases of direct services, purchases from businesses, and purchases from abroad. Empirically, consumption is equal to household purchases. However, there is a sizable component of household purchases which is not consumed during the time period covered by the accounts. For example, to consider two extreme cases, a household purchase of either food or a new automobile is considered as consumption in the year of the purchase. The automobile, however, being a household capital good, yields a stream of services that are enjoyed over its useful life and that are not restricted to the year in which the purchase was made.

The example permits us to distinguish between consumption as it is now measured empirically by the Department of Commerce and consumption as

[11] J. K. Galbraith, *The New Industrial State* (Boston: Houghton Mifflin, 1967), Chapters 18 and 19.

[12] Paul A. Baaran and Paul M. Sweezy, *Monopoly Capital* (New York: Monthly Review Press, 1966), Chapter 5.

we define it for analytical use. Analytically, consumption should include all consumption of income yielded by the wealth that the consumer acquired in the past. The consumption represented by a new car should be spread across all the years in which the car is used (much as is done in practice when the car is bought on time).

This difficulty exists for all consumer capital goods except houses. In the case of houses, expenditures on newly constructed houses are regarded for social accounting purposes as part of investment expenditure; that is, they are contained in the business sector account. The stream of income off the existing stock of houses is included in the accounts in the form of cash and imputed rental payments.

An obvious difficulty exists in reconciling empirical and analytical consumption. Casual observation does not permit us to know whether the analytical concept of consumption is even roughly equivalent to the empirical measurement found in the national accounts.

CONCLUSION

In this chapter, we have seen that household consumption expenditures are related to income, wealth, interest rates, credit terms, attitudes and expectations, demography, income distribution, sales effort, and new products. Income appears to be by far the most important of the determinants of consumption expenditures, and it is therefore important to understand the relationship between consumption and income thoroughly. Several theories which attempt to define this relationship are discussed in the following chapter.

ADDITIONAL READINGS

R. F. Kahn, in "The relation of home investment to unemployment," *Economic Journal*, 41 (June 1931): 173–198, was the first to deal fully with the multiplier concept. J. M. Keynes developed his concept of the consumption function and multiplier in Chapters 8–10 of *The General Theory of Employment, Interest and Money* (New York: Harcourt Brace Jovanovich, Inc., 1936). Gardner Ackley devoted himself to the matter of lags accompanying the working of the multiplier in "The multiplier time period: Money, inventories, and flexibility," *American Economic Review*, 41 (1951): 350–368.

For a discussion of the effect of consumer attitudes on consumption, see George Katona, *Psychological Analysis of Economic Behavior* (New York: McGraw-Hill, 1951), Part II.

QUESTIONS

1. If $C = 100 + 0.8Y$, and $I = 20$, the equilibrium level of income is 600.

(a) If the marginal propensity to consume rises to 0.9, what is the new equilibrium level of income?
(b) What is the new multiplier?

2. This chapter has concentrated on the way in which the multiplier works with respect to a change in the level of investment expenditures. Explain how the multiplier process will work with respect to an upward shift in the savings function.

3. Explain how each of the following will affect the multiplier:

   (a) an increase in the marginal propensity to save;
   (b) an increase in the marginal propensity to consume;
   (c) an increase in the average propensity to save;
   (d) an increase in the average propensity to consume.

   Is it possible to have an increase in the average propensity to consume without an increase in the marginal propensity to consume?

4. If in our two-sector model, $C = a + bY$, specify the relationship between savings and income. How would a decrease in the marginal propensity to save affect the multiplier?

5. Consumer expenditure is 600, total gross investment is 200, and gross national product is 800 in a simple two-sector economy. Is gross national product at an equilibrium level? Explain.

6. Explain how you think the increasing importance of contractual savings such as life insurance policies would affect the consumption function. Would it cause it to vary more or less from year to year? Would it be flatter or steeper?

7. If household purchases of automobiles and other consumer durables were to be considered as investments and added to consumption only as services are used over time,

   (a) how would this affect the aggregate average propensity to consume?
   (b) how would this affect the aggregate marginal propensity to consume?
   (c) how would this affect the stability of the relationship between consumption and income?

8. Do you think that increased equality in the distribution of income would lower the aggregate average propensity to consume? Explain your reasoning. What kinds of evidence would you have to collect to verify your reasoning?

Household Behavior: Theory and Evidence

4 Chapter

Consumption is by far the largest component of aggregate demand. Small changes in consumption may therefore lead to sizable changes in employment and output in the economy. For this reason it is particularly important to gain a sounder understanding of consumer behavior than could be obtained from the simple, linear model of Chapter 3.

Keynes believed that income is the primary determinant of consumption, and that the marginal propensity to consume (MPC) is less than the average propensity to consume (APC). In addition he argued that MPC falls as income rises. These characteristics hold for the two consumption functions drawn earlier in Figure 3–2.

As income increases, does the slope of the consumption function decrease, indicating that less and less is consumed out of each additional dollar of income and that MPC falls? Does existing empirical evidence lend support to this view of the consumption function? Is it important to establish that APC is or is not greater than MPC? These are the questions that we will attempt to answer in this chapter.

LONG-RUN IMPLICATIONS OF $APC > MPC$

In Figure 4–1 the consumption function is drawn in such a way that $APC > MPC$. This means that as income increases APC decreases and the average propensity to save, APS, increases. As income increases, the gap between the consumption function and the 45-degree line becomes larger relative to income. This can be seen in Figure 4–1, where DE/DF exceeds AB/AO. If consumption falls as a proportion of income, higher levels of income can be maintained in a growing economy only if investment grows as a proportion of income.

Figure 4–1.

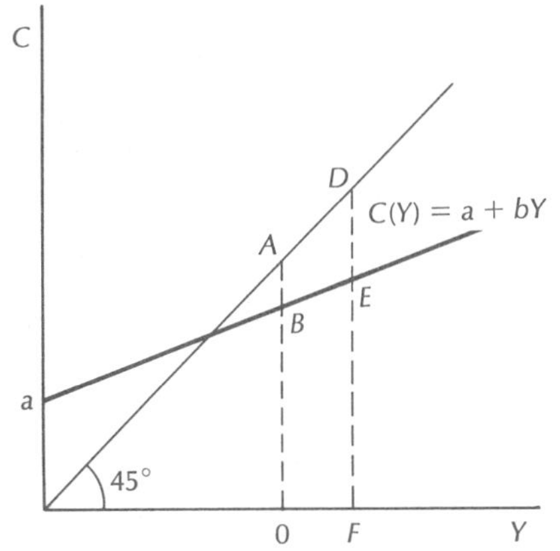

Figure 4–2.

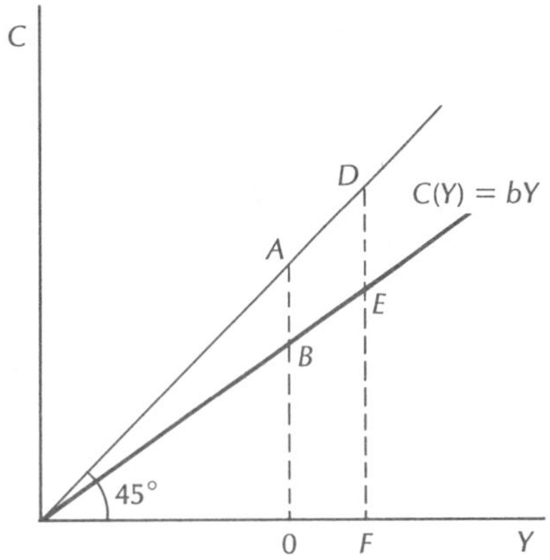

As before, our consumption function is $C = a + bY$, where a is the intercept and b the slope of $C(Y)$. Then, since $Y = C + S$:

$$S = -a + (1 - b)Y \tag{4.1}$$

And, because $S = I$ at equilibrium:

$$I = -a + (1 - b)\ Y$$

$$\text{or:} \quad I/Y = -a/Y + (1 - b) \tag{4.2}$$

$(1 - b)$ is a constant greater than zero and a is positive, so a/Y becomes smaller as Y grows. Therefore, I/Y, or the proportion of income that must be invested, will grow as income grows. This means that investment must grow at a faster rate than income. This condition might temporarily exist in a nation passing through the industrialization stage of development or through a capital intensification process. However, it seems unlikely that such a situation would exist in a developed economy in which the service sector is growing more rapidly than other sectors of the economy. If the consumption function is in fact linear, there is a probability that developed countries will find that investment will not grow rapidly enough to sustain high levels of income and employment.

If, on the other hand, *APC* = *MPC*, the consumption function can be represented by a straight line through the origin. This situation is represented by the consumption function in Figure 4–2, where $a = 0$ and $C = bY$. Here DE/DF is equal to AB/AO, and investment grows at the same rate as income. Since $C = bY$ and $Y = C + S$:

$$S = (1 - b)Y \tag{4.3}$$

And, because $S = I$ at equilibrium:

$$I = (1 - b)\ Y$$

$$\text{or:} \quad I/Y = (1 - b) \tag{4.4}$$

In this case, as income grows the higher levels can be maintained if investment grows at the same rate as income.

In the case of Figure 4–1, where $APC > MPC$, consumption will grow less rapidly than income. This view of consumption, put forward by Keynes in 1936, was a matter of concern to economists long before then. For example, over a hundred years ago, Karl Marx believed that as income grew and capitalists' profits (surplus) rose, they would want to spend a smaller proportion of their income on consumption.[1] This would lead to a fall in consumption as a proportion of total output. For this reason, among others, Marx believed that the capitalist system would collapse. The capitalist system has, however, proved in the *long run* to be more viable than Marx predicted. This may, in part, be attributed to the fact that the long-run *MPC* has been approximately equal to the long-run *APC*—a point to which we will return shortly.

SHORT-RUN AND LONG-RUN CONSUMPTION FUNCTIONS—EMPIRICAL EVIDENCE FROM TIME SERIES

Much of the debate concerning the difference or equality between *APC* and *MPC* stems from time series analysis. With the advent of the first official U.S. national income accounts in 1934, it became possible to examine more closely the relationship between consumption and income and to test the hypotheses which had been presented by Lord Keynes. Using U.S. data from the period 1929 to 1941, the regression of aggregate consumption on aggregate disposable income yielded an equation of the form $C = a + bY_d$, where C is consumption and Y_d is disposable income:

$$C = 31.4 + .926\ Y_d$$

The regressions for the more recent periods of 1948 to 1958, and 1959 to 1970 yielded:

$$C = 10.0 + .880\ Y_d$$
$$C = 20.4 + .865\ Y_d$$

The consumption function for each of these periods indicates that $MPC < 1$ and that $APC > MPC$ since $a > 0$. The time series data for these years support the consumption function in Figure 4–1. As income grows, it appears that the proportion of income being consumed decreases.

When viewed over a longer period of time, the relationship between consumption and income appears somewhat different, as can be seen in the consumption-to-income ratios compiled from data developed by Simon Kuznets for the United States from 1869 to 1959. For selected periods, it appears from the figures in Table 4–1 that consumption ranged between .861 and .885 of net national product (*NNP*) for the 1869 to 1928 period. As might have been expected, the proportion of income being consumed during the depression years rose significantly to .975.

[1] See Paul M. Sweezy, *The Theory of Capitalist Development* (New York: Monthly Review Press, 1942).

Table 4–1. Ratio of Consumption to Net National Product for the United States (averages of annual figures—selected periods).

Period	C/NNP
1869–1888	.869
1889–1908	.861
1909–1928	.885
1929–1938	.975
1946–1955	.902
1950–1959	.902

Source: Compiled from estimates provided by Simon Kuznets, *Modern Economic Growth: Rate, Structure, and Spread* (New Haven: Yale University Press, 1966), p. 249.

These findings strongly suggest that *APC* does not fall in the long run, and they support the consumption function represented in Figure 4–2, where $C = bY$. From the time series evidence, it would appear that the long-run consumption function, describing the relationship between income and consumption over a period of decades, may differ significantly from the consumption-income relationship viewed over a period of a single decade or less. Consumption may be relatively stable in the short run in the sense that $APC > MPC$. This means that given percentage changes in income result in smaller percentage changes in consumption. However, in the long run we may expect consumption and income to grow at approximately equal rates. In the long run, investment spending need not grow more rapidly than income in order to achieve higher levels of income.

The following sections of this chapter offer some insight as to why the long- and short-run consumption functions might be expected to differ.

THE ABSOLUTE INCOME HYPOTHESIS

Keynes' position, *the absolute income hypothesis*, that consumption is dependent upon the absolute level of income and that the average propensity to consume will fall as income rises, therefore appears consistent with time series data for shorter periods, but not for longer periods. Arthur Smithies attempted to bridge this gap between the short- and long-run consumption functions by explaining that continual upward shifts in the short-run consumption function had been occurring.[2] In Figure 4–3, $C(Y)_1$ through $C(Y)_4$ represent the short-run consumption functions at different points in time over several decades. Points *A* through *D* represent the *levels* of consumption and income for four points in time. By drawing a line through these points, the long-run consumption function is discovered, and the long-run *APC* equals the long-run *MPC*. Smithies offered several explanations as to why the continual upward shifts in the short-run consumption function had been occurring, including a movement

[2] Arthur Smithies, "Forecasting postwar demand: I," *Econometrica*, 13 (January 1945): 1–14.

Figure 4–3.

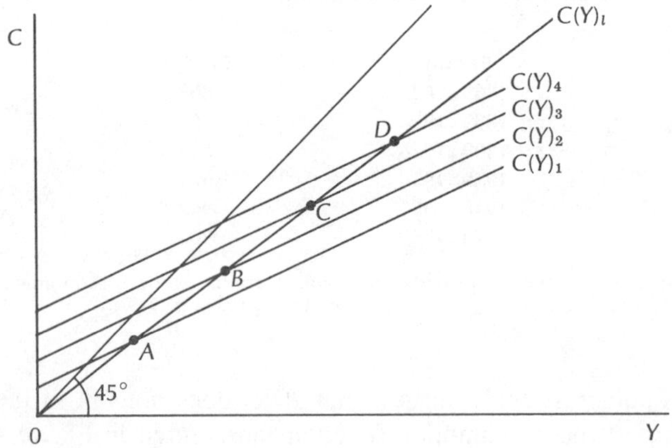

from farms to cities that would cause the consumption function to shift upward since city dwellers have a higher propensity to spend than those living on farms. Smithies also felt that the upward shifts might be due to a trend toward a more equal distribution of income, which we discussed in Chapter 3, and to rising living standards, which had increased the minimum costs of living. This factor, the rising "minimum cost of living," would follow from the arrival of new products on the market. Goods that were at one time considered luxuries would become essentials, and as a result consumption would rise. Others have since added to the list of factors which might lead to upward shifts in the consumption function. Among these are changes in the age distribution of the population, increasing amounts of leisure, and increasing availability of consumer credit. As indicated in Chapter 3, young households have a relatively high propensity to consume, and as they increase as a percentage of the population this will cause a rise in the average propensity to consume. Increased leisure provides additional opportunities to consume, and the increased availability of consumer credit makes it easier to consume.

A serious weakness, however, exists in Smithies' attempt to reconcile the differences between the long-run and short-run consumption functions: During the period of his study, consumption may have grown at as rapid a rate as income only, for instance, because of unique trends in population. If consumption were going to continue to grow at as fast a rate in the future, we would have to rely on similar trends.

THE RELATIVE INCOME HYPOTHESIS

Professor James Duesenberry of Harvard University was among those who were not satisfied by Smithies' explanation and attempted to offer a better one.

Figure 4–4.

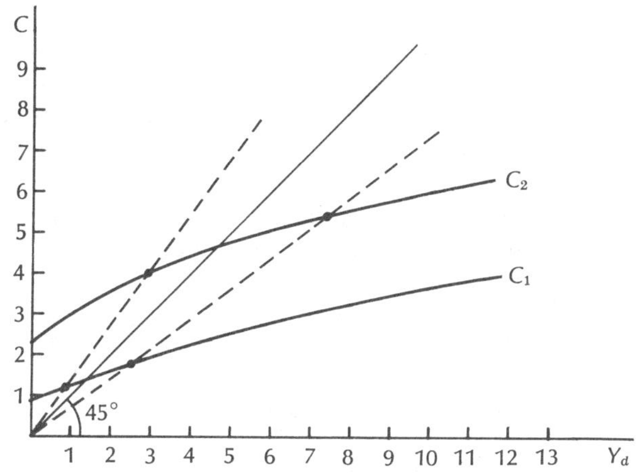

He claimed that consumption was not dependent upon absolute income, but rather on relative income, and that the percentage of income that an individual family consumes depends upon the family's *relative* position in the income scale.[3] If \$2500 and \$7500 are respectively the median levels of family income in 1920 and 1970, families with \$2500 in 1920 would consume the same proportion as families with \$7500 in 1970. Likewise, families with different levels of income in the two periods, but at the same percentile on the income scale in both periods, will consume the same percentage of their income. This is illustrated in the two budget study curves in Figure 4–4. C_1 represents the budget study curve for 1920 and C_2 represents the budget study curve for 1970. In 1920, \$2500 was at the same percentile on the income scale as \$7500 in 1970. Similarly, in 1920 \$1000 was at the same percentile as \$3000 in 1970. Therefore, we should expect the *APC* of the family receiving \$2500 in 1920 to equal that of the family receiving \$7500 in 1970. The *APC*s of the respective groups are shown by the slopes of the dashed lines in the diagram.[4]

As incomes increase, so long as everyone remains in the same relative position on the income scale, their average propensity to consume will not change and the average propensity to consume for the nation as a whole will not change.

Duesenberry's relative income hypothesis is based to a large degree upon what he labeled the *demonstration effect*. People will attempt to emulate those around them. Even though one's income may be increasing, so long as he remains in the same position on the income scale he will continue to spend the

[3] James S. Duesenberry, *Income, Savings and the Theory of Consumer Behavior* (Cambridge, Mass.: Harvard University Press, 1949).

[4] The consumption functions in Figure 4-4 are *not* reletad to aggregate consumption but are from family budget data, and the horizontal axis measures family income levels, not national income.

same percentage of his income in an attempt (a) to keep up with those earning like amounts, (b) to emulate those earning more, and (c) to impress those lower on the income scale.

The part of the relative income hypothesis so far discussed explains why, in the long run, the *APC* is constant and equal to the *MPC*. A second part of Duesenberry's hypothesis explains why the short-run *MPC* is less than the short-run *APC*, and less than both the long-run *APC* and the long-run *MPC*.

Duesenberry believed that consumption was not dependent solely upon the current level of income, but also upon the highest level of income experienced in the past. This consumption function may be written:

$$C_t = aY_t + b(Y_t^2/Y^*)$$
$$\text{or: } C_t/Y_t = a + b(Y_t/Y^*) \tag{4.5}$$

where Y^* is the previous peak level of income and $b < 0$.

So long as income grows at a constant rate, Y_t/Y^* will be a constant equal to one, and the average propensity to consume, C_t/Y_t, will remain a constant equal to $a + b$, as suggested by the long-run consumption function. However, if income in year t grows at an unusually rapid, and apparently unsustainable, rate, C_t/Y_t will temporarily fall below its normal level since $b < 0$. In Figure 4–5 this is represented by a movement along the C_s curve rather than the C_l curve, from A to E rather than from A to F. Similarly, if income falls or grows less rapidly than normal, Y_t/Y^* will be less than normal and *APC* will rise. Hence a fall in income from Y_1 to Y_2 would lead to a movement from point A to point B on the C_s curve rather than along the C_l curve to point D. This tendency for consumption to fall back to B rather than to D has been referred to as the *ratchet effect*.

There exist at least two reasons why we might expect a change in income to move us along C_s rather than along C_l. First, if past experience has generally been one of rising incomes, people will believe that a decrease in income is only temporary. They will be unwilling to forego standards of living to which they have grown accustomed, and they will attempt to maintain past consumption levels even though income has fallen. Second, as income recovers from Y_2, rather than move up along C_l' the *MPC* will remain lower than in normal times as households attempt to rebuild the stock of wealth depleted by their attempts to maintain previous peak standards of living. Once Y_1 is again reached, a normal and steady rate of growth will cause consumption to move along C_l.

The ratchet effect goes far toward explaining the stabilizing role consumption plays in the economy by helping us understand why sizable shifts in *APC* may occur from year to year. These shifts do occur in fact, but, as Figure 4–6 demonstrates, we may expect *APC* to remain relatively constant in the long run. The two parts of the relative income hypothesis help explain both this and why statistical estimates of the short-run consumption function will show an *MPC* less than *APC*, and a short-run *MPC* less than the long-run *MPC*.

Figure 4–5.

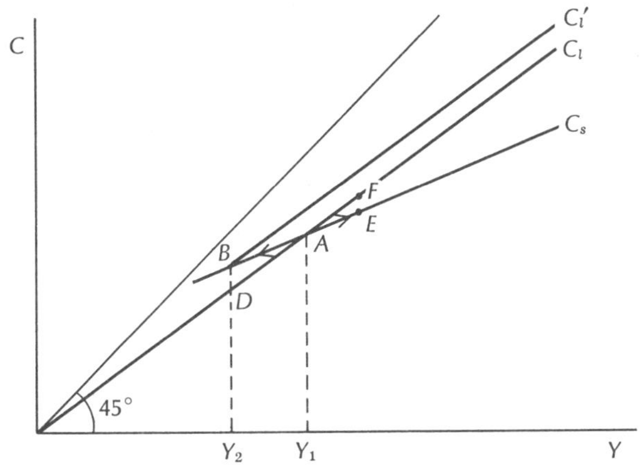

THE PERMANENT INCOME HYPOTHESIS

In 1957 Milton Friedman of the University of Chicago published a monograph[5] in which he argued that a family's consumption in a year is not dependent upon income realized in that year, but rather on what the family considers to be its *permanent income*. According to Friedman, permanent income is that income level to which consumers adapt their behavior. It will depend very much on what consumers would expect their income levels to be throughout their life under normal circumstances. Friedman asserts that for any year the *measured income* of a family consists of two components, permanent income and *transitory income*. The latter may be either positive or negative, depending on whether the household unit has experienced a windfall gain or a windfall loss during the given year.

According to the permanent income hypothesis, the primary reason for saving is to even out consumption over one's lifetime. Friedman thus argues that, if one receives a large element of transitory income in a year due to, say, a once-in-a-lifetime lottery win, most of that windfall will be saved in the year received and spent gradually over one's lifetime. Similarly, a sizable loss will not lead to a great fall in consumption; its effect on consumption will also be spread out over one's lifetime.

If, in fact, the motive behind saving is to distribute consumption, then it follows that those with low permanent incomes will save the same percentage as those with high permanent incomes. This is the heart of the permanent income hypothesis—that the ratio of consumption to permanent income is

[5] Milton Friedman, *A Theory of the Consumption Function* (Princeton, N.J.: Princeton University Press, 1957).

Figure 4–6. Average Propensity to Consume out of Disposable Income in the U.S.

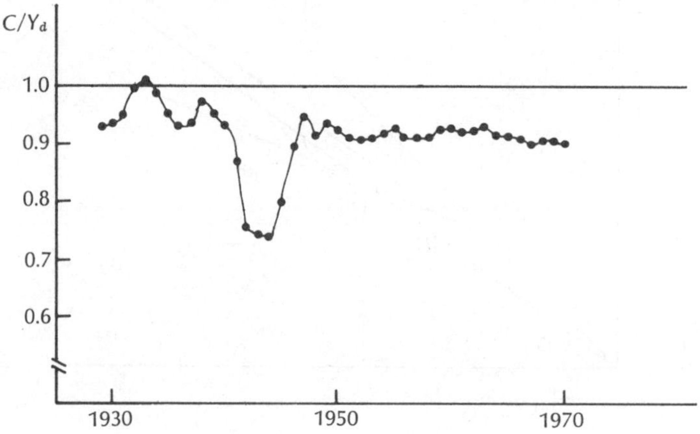

Source: U.S. Department of Commerce data.

independent of the level of permanent income. This is to say that the average propensity to consume out of different levels of permanent income should be about the same. How can this be reconciled with the earlier budget study data that appeared to indicate that the *APC* for low-income families was much higher than that for high-income families? Friedman argues that a large percentage of the families that are in area *A* in Figure 4–7 are experiencing windfall losses, and if permanent income were measured along the horizontal axis they would shift to area *B*. Similarly, a sizable percentage of the high-income individuals during the budget study year are experiencing a windfall gain and they would shift from area *D* to area *E* if consumption were measured in terms of permanent income. The modified budget study data should now indicate that the *APC* is approximately the same for families at all income levels.

So long as the motivation for saving is to spread out consumption evenly over a lifetime, then as family incomes rise in general, average propensities to consume will remain unchanged, and the aggregate average propensity to consume will be constant. This is consistent with Kuznets' findings that the long-run *APC* has been constant.

The permanent income hypothesis can also help explain the differences between the short- and long-run consumption functions. If a fall in aggregate income that is expected to be only temporary occurs, its impact will be felt almost entirely in terms of transitory income and will have very little impact on the permanent income of individual families. The permanent income hypothesis would therefore predict a slight fall in measured consumption relative to measured income. This can be pictured as moving down along C_s

Figure 4–7.

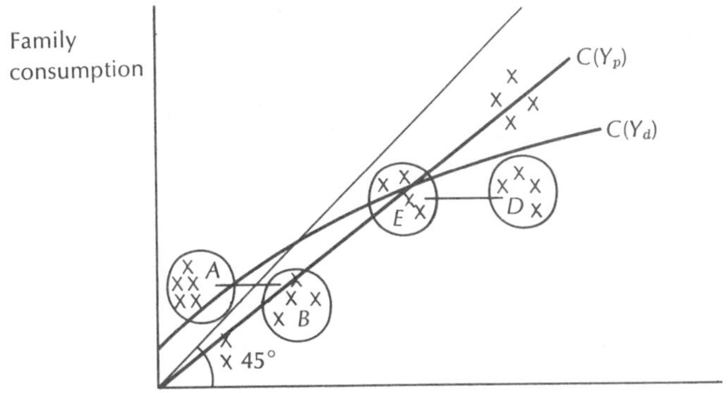

from *A* to *B* in Figure 4–5 rather than along C_l from *A* to *D*. Consumption out of measured income might be expected to have a lower *MPC* in the short run than in the long run.

EMPIRICAL EVIDENCE CONCERNING THE RELATIVE AND PERMANENT INCOME HYPOTHESES

In his original work on the relative income hypothesis, Duesenberry examined the savings behavior of the white and black communities in the two cities of Columbus, Ohio, and New York City.[6] The relative income hypothesis would suggest that a black family would save more than a white family at the same income level. This would be true because the black family would be at a higher percentile on the income scale in the ghetto community, and Duesenberry indeed found that the black families saved more than white families at the same income levels. Professor James Tobin, however, does not find this evidence convincing.[7] Tobin points out that white families may have saved less because of greater financial resources available to them in the form of a greater stock of wealth or better credit facilities, and not because they were at a lower point on their relative income scale.

Empirical evidence developed by Dorothy Brady and Rose Friedman has also been used to support the relative income hypothesis.[8] Brady and Friedman

[6] Duesenberry, *Income, Savings and the Theory of Consumer Behavior,* pp. 50–52.
[7] James Tobin, "Relative income, absolute income, and savings," in *Money, Trade, and Economic Growth: Essays in Honor of John H. Williams* (New York: Macmillan, 1951), pp. 135–156.
[8] Dorothy S. Brady and Rose D. Friedman, "Savings and the income distribution," *Studies in Income and Wealth,* Vol. 10 (New York: National Bureau of Economic Research. 1947), pp. 247–265.

found that savings rates in village and city families varied for the same income level. The higher rate of savings in the villages could be explained by the relative income hypothesis. Similar evidence developed by Modigliani and Ando in support of the permanent income hypothesis can also be used to support the relative income hypothesis.[9] In an examination of small and large cities and suburbs in various sections of the country, they found that there existed no close relationship between the aggregate *APC* of the community and the per capita income of the community.

Some empirical evidence supports the permanent income hypothesis, and some does not. Modigliani and Ando, using housing expenditures as a proxy for permanent income, and dividing their sample into groups according to the amount spent on housing, assumed that the transitory income element for each group should be about the same. They expected to find that the average propensity to consume for each group was about the same, and this they did find. In another discussion they noted the near constancy of the aggregate wealth-to-income ratio among rich people. This implies that over their lifetimes the rich have not been saving proportionately more than any other income group. As pointed out earlier, the similar propensities to save in both rich and poor communities also lend support to the permanent income hypothesis.

A number of findings contrary to the permanent income hypothesis do exist. Ronald Bodkin found that World War II veterans exhibited a very high propensity to consume out of a once-and-for-all windfall gain received in the form of an unexpected dividend from National Service Life Insurance,[10] although the permanent income hypothesis indicates that little consumption should have occurred out of this transitory income. A second piece of evidence casting doubt on the permanent income hypothesis was provided by Thomas Mayer in his study of high-income and low-income occupations in various countries.[11] Taking the average income of a broad occupational group as a proxy for permanent income, Mayer found that in general the low-income occupations had higher average propensities to consume than the higher-income occupations. The permanent income hypothesis would lead us to expect, other things being the same, that the *APC*s for the low and high occupations would be about the same.

CONCLUSION

The Great Depression made clear the possibility of inadequate aggregate demand, for as output increases, consumption, investment, government spending, and net exports must also grow to absorb the increased output. Keynes believed that consumption cannot grow as rapidly as output and that the *APC*

[9] F. Modigliani and A. Ando, "The 'permanent income' and the 'life cycle' hypothesis of savings behaviour: Comparison and tests," in I. Friend and R. Jones (Eds.), *Consumption and Saving,* Vol. 2 (Philadelphia: University of Pennsylvania Press, 1960), pp. 49–174.

[10] Ronald Bodkin, "Windfall income and consumption," *American Economic Review,* 49 (September 1959): 602–614.

[11] Thomas Mayer, "The propensity to consume permanent income," *American Economic Review,* 56 (December 1966): 1158–1177.

must fall. And since it is unlikely that investment would grow more rapidly than output for a protracted period of time, to many it has appeared likely that the relative size of the government sector of the economy must grow.

The historical data produced in the 1940s by Simon Kuznets disagreed with Keynes' hypothesis that the *APC* must fall as incomes rise, and the possibility of a constant long-run *APC* made the specter of a constantly growing government sector, one that would control a larger and larger share of total output, less visible. Economists were left to try to determine why Keynes' hypothesis concerning a falling *APC* was invalid. Smithies, Duesenberry, Friedman, and Modigliani and Ando have all made important contributions to the theory of household behavior in their attempts to explain a constant long-run *APC*. Opinion remains divided as to whether the absolute, relative, or permanent income hypothesis best explains household behavior. Much room for further research remains in this area.

ADDITIONAL READINGS

Smithies' original brief discussion of upward shifts in the short-run consumption function may be found in "Forecasting postwar demand: I," *Econometrica*, 13 (January 1945): 1–14. James S. Duesenberry's original work concerning the relative income hypothesis appeared in *Income, Saving and the Theory of Consumer Behavior* (Cambridge, Mass.: Harvard University Press, 1949). The relative merits of the absolute and relative income hypotheses are discussed by James Tobin in "Relative income, absolute income, and savings," in *Money, Trade, and Economic Growth: Essays in Honor of John H. Williams* (New York: Macmillan, 1951), pp. 135–136. Milton Friedman's thorough treatment of his permanent income hypothesis appears in *A Theory of the Consumption Function* (Princeton, N.J.: Princeton University Press, 1957). Independently of Friedman, F. Modigliani and R. Brumberg and later F. Modigliani and A. Ando developed a theory of consumption quite similar to Friedman's permanent income hypothesis. Their two papers are "Utility analysis and the consumption function: An interpretation of cross-section data," in K. Kurihara (Ed.), *Post-Keynesian Economics* (New Brunswick, N.J.: Rutgers University Press, 1954), and "The 'life cycle' hypothesis of saving: Aggregate implications and tests," *American Economic Review*, 53 (March 1963): 55–84.

Three general surveys of consumption function literature should prove of value to the interested student. In Chapters 2 and 3 of *Macroeconomic Activity* (New York: Harper & Row, 1969), Michael K. Evans reviews consumption theories and empirical evidence relevant to each. E. E. Hagen's "The consumption function: A review article," *Review of Economics and Statistics*, 37 (February 1966): 48–54, and Robert Ferber's "Research on household behavior," *American Economic Review*, 52 (March 1962): 19–63, and "Consumer economics, a survey," *Journal of Economic Literature*, 11 (December 1973): 1303–1342; are useful surveys.

Three studies which deal with empirical testing of the validity of the permanent income hypothesis are I. Friend and I. Kravis, "Consumption patterns and permanent income," *American Economic Review*, 47 (May 1957): 536–555; R. Bodkin, "Windfall income and consumption," *American Economic Review*, 49 (September 1959): 602–614; and T. Mayer, "The propensity to consume permanent income," *American Economic Review*, 56 (December 1966): 1158–1177.

QUESTIONS

1. Carefully explain the ratchet effect and its stabilization role. Can you think of times during the past few decades when the ratchet effect may have been important?
2. How do the absolute income, relative income, and permanent income hypotheses reconcile budget data and time series data?
3. Suppose that new research were to show conclusively that Kuznets was wrong, that the average propensity to consume has been falling over time. What difference would this make to your thinking about the various theories of the consumption function?
4. Economists have devoted considerable time and effort to establishing the fact that the long-run *MPC* is equal to the long-run *APC*. Develop the main hypotheses used to explain why *APC* equals *MPC* in the long run. Why have economists felt that it is important to establish the fact that consumption will grow in proportion to income in the long run?
5. If the permanent income hypothesis is valid we should expect a sudden major shift in investment expenditures to have a lesser effect through the multiplier on our economy than our previous analysis might suggest. Explain.
6. Suppose that consumption in any period is a function of past living standards as well as of current income so that $C_t/Y_t = a + bY_t/Y^*$, where Y^* is the highest income level achieved in the past. Show that with historical data this model helps explain cyclical movements in the ratio of consumption to income as well as the long-run constancy of this ratio.
7. Professor Robert Eisner argued in 1969 that a temporary income tax surcharge would do little to stem inflation. Relying upon the permanent income hypothesis, explain why this is likely to be true. On the other hand, a temporary excise tax on all investment goods may temporarily do much to help reduce inflation pressures. Explain.

Investment Demand

5
Chapter

As indicated in Chapter 3, investment in new plant and equipment is the second major component of aggregate demand. Changes in investment demand can also have an important impact on output, employment, and prices, and thus on the rate of capital formation by business enterprises. Gross spending on plant and equipment by business amounts to about 15 percent of GNP, or, after allowance for depreciation, for about 6 percent of the net national product, during years of full employment. In the national accounts the components of capital formation also include residential construction and net inventory change, but the model of investment demand developed here is of special relevance to plant and equipment spending in the business sector.

CLASSIC ANALYSIS OF INVESTMENT DEMAND

Beginning our discussion with a single firm, we can assume (a) that conditions of pure competition prevail, and (b) that its investment alternatives are mutually exclusive. This means that, because the return from the acquisition of any tangible or financial asset will be an income stream over the expected life of the asset, the value of this stream must be compared with the cost (or supply price) of the asset before an investment demand function can be derived for the firm. Summing across the demand functions for all firms and for all capital goods then yields an aggregate investment demand function. In developing this approach it will be necessary to consider (a) the definition of income, (b) the discount formula, (c) the choice of a discount rate, and (d) the incorporation of risk.

The Definition of Income

If our single firm, operating in pure competition when no externalities are present, considers whether it should expand its "gadget" producing capacity, it must compare the *present value* of expected net income with the capital costs of expansion. It must then, as a first step, estimate its expected revenues and the anticipated operating costs over the life of the project.

Table 5–1 shows the expected gross revenues during the 10-year life of a sample project.

Table 5–1.

Year	Quantity Sold	Price Per Unit	Gross Revenues	Total Operating Costs	Net Revenues
1	1 million units	$14	$14 million	$9 million	$5 million
2	"	14	"	"	"
3	"	14	"	"	"
4	"	14	"	"	"
5	"	14	"	"	"
6	"	14	"	"	"
7	"	14	"	"	"
8	"	14	"	"	"
9	"	12	$12 million	"	$3 million
10	"	12	"	"	"

It is estimated that one million units of a certain gadget can be sold each year, and that the market price will be $14 per unit for the first eight years and $12 for the final two years.

Because it is net revenues with which we are ultimately concerned, the firm must also estimate the operating costs of producing this gadget. These costs include the costs of labor and material inputs (those complementary to capital inputs), as well as other direct and indirect operating costs. Table 5–1, column 5, shows these complementary inputs necessary to produce one million gadgets per year. It is assumed that the best estimate of these costs amounts to $9 million each year.

Now we are in a position to calculate the net revenues, defined here in the conventional economic sense, as the difference between gross revenues and total operating costs. For the first eight years of the project annual net revenues amount to $5 million, while for the final two years they are estimated at $3 million.

We must, however, be careful in our calculation of operating costs. These do not include direct taxes, such as corporate profits taxes, although the costs of license fees and other government requirements relating to production would be included. Also, we do not deduct depreciation as a cost of production in the particular formula we will describe immediately below. When depreciation is deducted the firm allows for replacement of the equipment at the end of its life; the firm thus works on the assumption that production will be continued indefinitely into the future. In our example we choose a formula that allows the firm to view the project for a given life and a given period of future years, therefore excluding depreciation. Finally, we do not include as operating costs any interest charges on borrowed funds that might be used to finance the purchase of the equipment. Because these interest charges become the focus of our attention as managers of the firm consider whether they are too high to warrant undertaking the project, we will consider them explicitly.

The Discount Formula

In calculations of net revenue, monetary values applicable to transactions during different years must be referred to some base year. For such monetary values to be comparable, they must be "homogenized" with respect to time; otherwise income and expenditure undertaken at different periods of time cannot be considered as equivalent. In the analysis of investment demand, the usual technique is to discount projections of net revenues to their "present value" for ease of comparison with the cost of investment goods (the price that must be paid for the plant and equipment to be used, often called the "supply price" of the capital goods).

The process of computing present value may be illustrated by assuming that net revenues for the years 1 to n are NR_1, NR_2, . . . NR_n. If we let V_1 stand for the present value of NR_1, V_2 stand for the present value of NR_2, etc., then at the beginning of the n-year life of the project there are n equations relating present value to net revenue. For the first year, $NR_1 = V_1\ (1 + i)$, where i is the rate of discount—a market-determined rate of interest. For example, if $i = 6$ percent, then \$106.00 = \$100 (1 + .06); the present value of \$106.00 to be received one year from today is \$100.00 if the interest rate is 6 percent. Thus \$100.00 is today's discounted value of 106 future dollars.

For the second year, $NR_2 = V_2\ (1 + i)^2$; for the third year $NR_3 = V_3\ (1 + i)^3$; and so forth. These equations may thus be rewritten as:

$$V_n = NR_n/(1 + i)^n$$

If the sum of the present values for all future years of the project is V, then $V = V_1 + V_2 + \ldots + V_n$ for an n-year project, or:

$$V = \sum_{j=1}^{n} \frac{NR_j}{(1 + i)^j} \tag{5.1}$$

In terms of the example of the gadget producer above, the present value of net revenues, V, would be:

$$V = \frac{\$5 \text{ million}}{(1 + i)} + \frac{\$5 \text{ million}}{(1 + i)^2} + \ldots + \frac{\$5 \text{ million}}{(1 + i)^8} + \frac{\$3 \text{ million}}{(1 + i)^9} + \frac{\$3 \text{ million}}{(1 + i)^{10}}$$

The Choice of a Discount Rate

Before the firm's managers can proceed further, they must choose a discount rate—a value of i to use in the formula. This choice may be approached through a series of approximations.

First Approximation

The firm's managers may use the current market interest rate or yield on a ten-year government bond as i in the discount formula. Government bonds are, for the most part, risk-free because they are free of the risk of default.[1] They therefore represent an alternative opportunity for the investment of funds; the firm could buy bonds or it could choose to pass up the bonds' "opportunity earnings" to purchase plant and equipment and obtain income from either source. The question the managers of the firm must ask themselves is, which investment is the more profitable?

If the firm's managers take the net revenues they estimated, NR_1, NR_2, etc., and use the interest rate on government bonds, i_b, as the discount rate in the discount formula, then they can calculate V_b, the dollar amount of government bonds that must be purchased at a yield of i_b in order to provide an income stream with the value of NR_1, NR_2, etc. If P_K is the supply price of the capital equipment (the purchase cost of machinery, etc.), then P_K may be compared with V_b to provide a decision rule. If $P_K > V_b$, the cost of the plant and machinery is greater than the cost of an amount of government bonds that would yield equivalent revenues, and therefore the project should be abandoned. If, however, $P_K < V_b$, the investment project would cost less than the government bonds would cost, and managers might proceed with the project.

Second Approximation

A moment's reflection will show why this first approximation must be modified. For the businessman himself and any investors who provide him with financial capital (loans) there will be a risk element accompanying the production of gadgets. There will be internal risks inherent in organization and management; these reflect the probabilities of less than optimum performance, and, in the extreme case, of outright failure or default. There will also be external risks present in the socioeconomic environment; these are risks associated with technical change, with economic instability, with changes in relative prices and the general price level, and the like. Such risks are relevant whether the firm employs its own funds or uses externally generated funds.

The businessman or investor will want a return for assuming this risk. It will be added to the opportunity earnings from investment in a relatively risk-free financial asset. The appropriate discount rate, then, will be the minimum prospective yield that will make it a worthwhile project from his viewpoint. If such a yield is 10 percent, then the rate of discount to apply will be 10 percent rather than, say, the 6 percent that might be earned on default-free government bonds. In this case the present value of the net revenues discounted at 10 percent must be equal to or greater than the supply price of the capital goods, P_K, if the investment expenditure is to be undertaken.

[1] There are other risks, such as the risk of possible capital loss in case of sale before maturity, accepted with the purchase of a government bond, but we will not examine them here. They are treated extensively in courses in financial managment.

The higher the discount rate used, the lower will be the value of V calculated from the discount formula. Thus the higher the discount rate, the lower P_K must be if the investment is to be undertaken.

Third Approximation

A third approximation involved in approaching the choice of an appropriate discount rate concerns the possibility that the discount rate will vary with the size of the investment project the managers have in mind. If the project costs \$10 million and if the firm can save this sum out of its earnings (retained earnings), then the discount rate can be estimated by the rate on other financial assets with equivalent risk premiums, but if the project costs \$20 million retained earnings of \$10 million will have to be supplemented with funds borrowed from others in the financial markets. The larger the volume of borrowing required for the project, the higher the interest rate that the firm must pay the lender. Thus the extent of external, as opposed to internal, financing required will affect the appropriate choice of a discount rate.[2]

In Figure 5–1 the horizontal line labeled "internal finance" shows the basic default-free rate plus the risk premium that represents the opportunity earnings from financial securities that the firm might purchase with its retained earnings. But, if the cost of the investment project exceeds \$10 million, this 10 percent figure is no longer appropriate. The discount rate to be used in the formula will rise.

Debt and equity financing costs come to exceed internal financing costs for three principal reasons. First, there is a "transaction" cost of issuing debt. Second, greater reliance on debt financing causes fixed costs to rise as a per-

Figure 5–1.

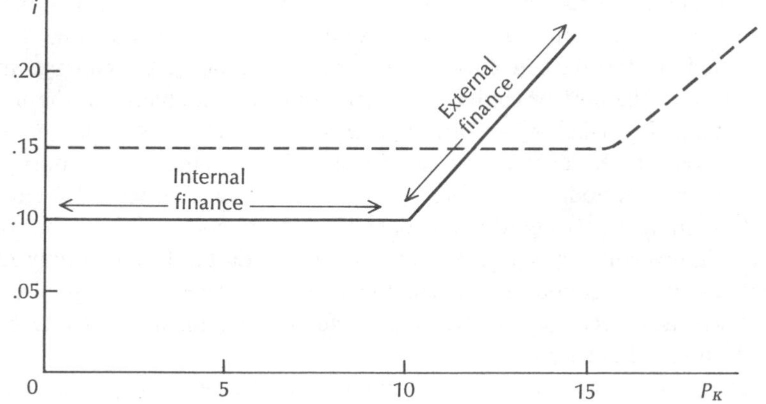

[2] James S. Duesenberry, *Business Cycles and Economic Growth,* (New York: McGraw-Hill, 1958), Chapter 5; J. Robert Lindsay and Arnold W. Sametz, *Financial Management: An Analytical Approach,* revised ed. (Homewood, Ill.: Irwin, 1967), Chapters 16–19; Glen A. Mumey, *Theory of Financial Structure,* (New York: Holt, Rinehart, and Winston, 1969), Chapters 6–8; and Michael K. Evans, *Macroeconomic Activity* (New York: Harper & Row, 1969), Chapter 4.

centage of total costs. Hence small fluctuations in earnings may lead to larger fluctuations in profits available for distribution to shareholders. Third, increased reliance on debt may lead to demands by creditors for positions on the board of directors.

The cost of equity financing may exceed that of debt financing since interest payments on debt are tax deductible, whereas dividend payments to shareholders are not. If the corporate tax rate is 50 percent, in order to pay $5 in dividends to shareholders the corporation must earn $10 on its investment. But, in order to pay $5 to bondholders the corporation need only earn $5. Greater dispersion of control and the cost of issuing equity may also be viewed as costs accompanying the acquisition of equity capital.

Therefore, rather than being horizontal, the cost schedule of funds used by the firm, as shown in Figure 5–1, slopes upward as soon as spending becomes large enough to make necessary the raising of funds externally. We now see that the appropriate i to be chosen as the discount rate in the formula can be called the "cost of capital," or the interest rate that must be paid for borrowing funds to use to purchase the capital equipment. This interest rate is what the firm's managers must pay if they are to have available the services of the capital goods. Using the firm's own financial resources is less costly (in terms of opportunity earnings) than using externally borrowed funds. And the curve in Figure 5–1 can now be called the supply schedule of funds faced by the firm. It is from such a supply schedule that the appropriate discount rate must be chosen.

A second view of the supply of funds is that many firms will, over a period of time, attempt to maintain a fairly stable financial structure.[3] This means that in choosing among alternatives for incremental financing they will wish to maintain the same relative mix of internally raised funds, debt financing, and equity financing. For this reason, when new investment is being considered, the appropriate cost of capital is the weighted average of the existing capital structure, where capital structure refers to the existing mix between internal financing, debt financing, and equity financing. This average may be represented by the dashed curve in Figure 5–1. Since the financing mix is held constant, the cost of capital does not rise due to a change in the method of financing. Nevertheless, according to this view, there exists another reason why the cost of capital may rise as the quantity demanded rises during any particular time period. This is because some time may be needed for a company to demonstrate to equity and debt holders its ability to generate profits on existing investments. Therefore, in any one period the firm can only raise a limited amount of capital at the same cost. In this case the marginal cost of capital will also increase as investment expands, again, as indicated by the dashed curve in Figure 5–1.

Based on a set of stringent assumptions, it has been shown that changes in the financing mix will not change the cost of capital.[4] However, consistent

[3] See James C. Van Horn, *Financial Management and Policy*, 2nd ed. (Englewood Cliffs, N. J.: Prentice-Hall, 1971), Chapter 4.

[4] F. Modigliani and M. H. Miller, "The cost of capital, corporation finance and the theory of investment," *American Economic Review*, 68 (June 1958): 261–297.

with this view is the idea that during any given short-run period a firm may be able to raise only a limited quantity of funds at the same cost. Again, the firm may need time to prove to investors and creditors that it can make intelligent investments. Thus the cost of capital to the firm doubtless increases in the short run, as depicted in Figure 5–1, even though the financing mix itself has little effect.

The Investment Decision

If the additional machinery needed for an expansion of gadget production costs \$26 million and the proper discount rate is 10 percent, and if the latter is taken to represent *i*, the present value of the revenue stream depicted in Table 5–1 is \$29.1 million. Since the present value, *V*, exceeds the supply price, P_K, the gadget producer should increase his production. However, if the cost of capital rises in the attempt to obtain the necessary funds, the proper rate of discount may be 15 percent. In this case the present value of the investment would be only \$24 million. This is \$2 million below the supply price of the machinery and the investment would not be profitable.

The decision rule, therefore, is that if $P_K < V$, the project is expected to be profitable and should be initiated—assuming that the proper discount rate was chosen in calculating *V*.

An alternative, and equivalent, way of stating the decision rule is in terms of a comparison of the cost of capital, *i*, with the "internal rate of return," *r*. To find *r*, we can then let the series of *NR*s be given, let P_K be the present value of the capital goods, and then solve the discount formula $P_K = NR_1/(1 + r) + \ldots + NR_n/(1 + r)^n$ for the value of *r*.

In this way we find the value of *r* as the interest rate or yield obtainable from the investment of P_K dollars in a project that is expected to provide an income (net revenue) stream of $NR_1, NR_2, \ldots, NR_n$ over the coming *n* years. The decision rule now is that if $r > i$, the investment in capital goods will provide a return greater than the cost of retained earnings and borrowings from financial markets, *i;* therefore, the investment project should be undertaken.[5]

The equilibrium condition exists for the firm when $r = i$. That is, so long as $r > i$, the particular project under consideration will be undertaken and plant and equipment will be enlarged, while if *r* remains greater than *i*, further expansion of plant and equipment will also be warranted. From microeconomics we know that the law of diminishing returns applies to capital expansion, so that, as plant expansion continues, the expected net revenues will fall and therefore *r* will fall. This will bring *r* into equality with *i*.

[5] Courses in finance are devoted to examining these relationships in detail. Our treatment is cursory, but adequate for our purpose, though there are many complications the student may wish to examine in finance texts.

Aggregating Investment Projects

Our example has shown the process by which a representative firm evaluates an investment project. We must now aggregate across all firms in an industry and then across all industries to derive an investment demand schedule for the economy as a whole.

In aggregating across an industry, we can consider gadget production as requiring a particular type of capital asset. By summing across the projects of all gadget producers, an investment demand schedule for the capital assets required in the production of gadgets is derived. This is illustrated in Figure 5–2, in which the internal rate of return, r, diminishes as the volume of investment undertaken increases. On a priori grounds we could expect the schedule to have a negative slope for the following reasons:

(1) As the demand for particular plant and equipment necessary to the production of gadgets increases, the supply price of these assets will rise. This is because the costs of capital goods producers increase with rising output demands. At the very least there will be a backlogging of orders by capital goods producers and a lengthening of the delivery period; therefore, the uncertainties of the gadget producer increase. The latter is, in turn, reflected in diminished present value of the expected net revenues and in a lower r.

(2) The larger the volume of investment undertaken, the greater the addition to the production capacity of the gadget-producing industry. As the industry expands, the additional gadgets can be sold only at lower prices. The expected returns from sales of gadgets will fall.

Therefore, as the volume of investment, I, expands, the value of r will fall, and the function $I = I(r)$ can be formed. We expect the relation between I and r to be negative, as depicted in Figure 5–2. (Mathematical convention places the independent variable on the horizontal axis and the dependent variable on the vertical axis. Economists often violate that convention, especially when describing demand curves. Here, although we write the quantity of investment demanded as a function of r, the axes in the graph are reversed from the conventional mathematical treatment. This is the conventional form of presentation by economists.)

In aggregating across all industries, the investment demand function in each instance will resemble that in Figure 5–2; that is, if each firm has a negatively sloped investment demand function and if these are added together horizontally, then the investment demand function for the industry itself will also be negatively sloped.

For the economy as a whole the aggregate investment demand function will also be negatively sloped as we add together the investment demand functions for all industries. Thus, in Figure 5–2, $I = I(r)$ represents the investment demand function for the economy. If some weighted average cost of capital for all firms in the economy is i_1, then the aggregate volume of investment, I_1, would be undertaken, and if the lower cost of capital i_2 were to hold,

Figure 5–2.

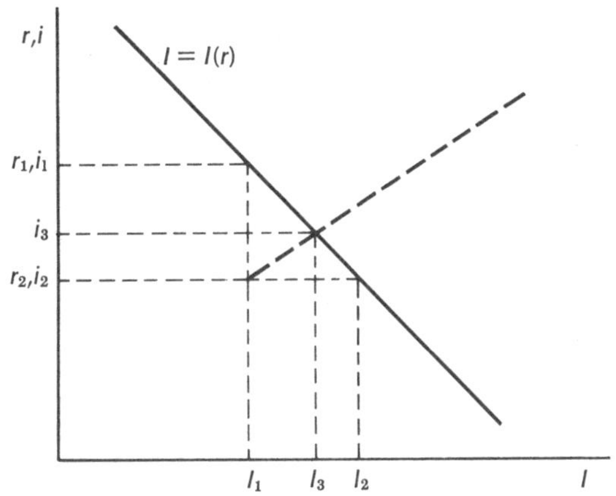

then there would be a movement down the investment demand schedule to I_2. (This aggregate investment demand function is also frequently referred to as the marginal efficiency of investment [*MEI*] curve. The term *MEI* stems from the fact that as we move down along the curve each point represents the rate of return to the last, or marginal, dollar invested.)

If, at the volume of investment associated with I_2, it is necessary for business firms to raise part of their funds externally, the firms might then confront an upward sloping supply of funds schedule. In Figure 5–2 this is illustrated by the positively sloped dashed line—which intersects the investment demand schedule at an expenditure level equal to I_3. The difference between I_2 and I_3 represents a reduction in investment spending due to the rising cost of capital as the volume of investment expands. Therefore i_3 and I_3 may represent the final equilibrium values.

Factors Determining the Position of the Investment Demand Function

The function in Figure 5–3 may be written $I = I(r)$, or in linear form, $I = c + dr$, where we expect $d < 0$. The values assumed by the coefficients c and d specify the shape and position of this function, and they are determined by such factors as the existing stock of capital, the state of technology, and the state of expectations. These factors, through their effect on I, strongly influence net revenues—the differences between gross revenues and operating costs.

The Stock of Capital

If there exists an excess of capital due to overinvestment in the past or to current low levels of consumption, new investment will merely create further

Figure 5–3.

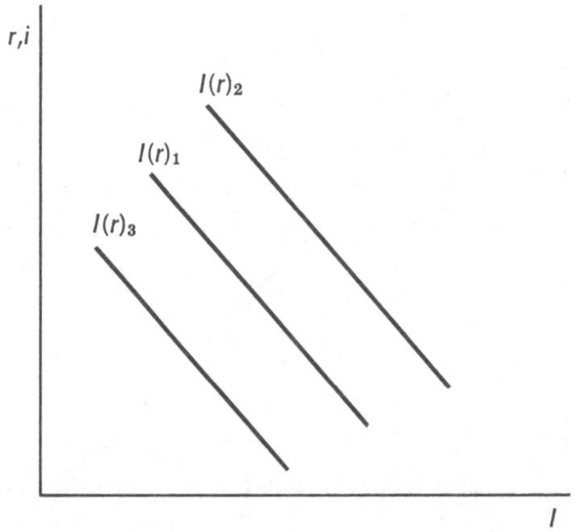

redundancy in the stock of capital. The newly created capital stock will be little utilized and the rate of return on the additional units of investment will be low. On the other hand, if, as after World War II, the nation's capital stock has been depleted and serious shortages exist, new investment will enable highly desired additional goods to be produced, and the aggregate investment demand (*MEI*) curve will be much further to the right than in the first case. In Figure 5–3 $I(r)_1$ may be said to represent the investment demand when the capital stock is considered nearly sufficient or redundant, and $I(r)_2$ to represent the investment demand when there is a shortage of capital.

As the economy's stock of capital increases through new investment and approaches the desired level, new investment becomes less necessary to meet existing and expected demand, and the aggregate investment demand (*MEI*) curve shifts down to the left. This is shown as the curve shifts from $I(r)_2$ to $I(r)_1$ and then to $I(r)_3$. In this way it can be seen how the level of the stock of capital affects the position of the investment demand curve. Capital stock effects will be further discussed in the following section.

Technology

Technological change may be called "neutral" with respect to the mix of capital and labor; that is, changes in techniques may not alter the rate of the substitution of capital for labor. Thus an improvement in technique will serve either to increase the physical quantity of output that can be produced with specified quantities of inputs or to reduce the costs of producing a given quantity of output. In the one case, gross revenues will increase; in the other, costs will decline. In both instances the present value of net revenues will increase, and $I(r)$ will shift to the right. Projects that may have been outside the margin of acceptability will now be eligible.

It is not difficult to cite major technological breakthroughs that have led to sizable shifts in the investment demand function: (a) technological changes reducing the cost of transportation—the steam engine and the internal combustion engine—(b) technological changes reducing the costs of production—the power loom and electricity—and (c) technological changes reducing the costs of raw or semifinished materials—the cotton gin and the reaper. It is, of course, possible for some technological change to be non-neutral and to lead to the introduction of capital saving techniques that would reduce investment demand, but this has not been typical of most technological change. Most change has led to the introduction of labor-saving devices that increase the demand for capital relative to the demand for labor.

Expectations

Expectations are the sets of beliefs held about the magnitude of economic variables over some future period. Obviously, in projecting gross revenues businessmen make an estimate of the size of their future markets based upon a set of income and price-level assumptions. If expectations change, it means that they have come to hold as more relevant an alternative set of prospective income and price levels. Again, projections of net revenues are affected. As an example, we can cite the following three factors which may alter market expectations: (a) expected changes in foreign trade opportunities; (b) expected changes in population growth or composition; and (c) changes in the political climate. If a devaluation of the domestic currency is anticipated, this may lead to a desire to increase investment as both new domestic markets and new foreign markets may open up to domestic producers. Decreased investment may also accompany an expected decrease in population growth, for a shrinking population decreases the market and provides a smaller labor force with which to combine the new capital equipment. The political climate may also affect investment, for unstable governments may lead to fear that the return on investment will not materialize; in such a case, businessmen will abandon their investment plans and $I(r)$ will shift to the left. The opposite will occur if the political climate is stable.

INCOME AND INVESTMENT

The classical analysis of investment specifies that investment expenditure is negatively related to the cost of capital, but it does not consider whether there are other important variables that help determine the level of investment spending and that should be explicit in a model. The model builder must use discretion in choosing among factors that determine values for those parameters that affect the position and shape of a function and for those other variables that may also help determine the level of investment. As a working rule, we consider as parameters all those factors that change only in an unpredictable fashion, such as technology and expectations, and we include as variables all other factors that have a systematic effect on investment, such as income. If expectations or technological improvements were to become predictable, then these factors would become variables in the function and would no longer be listed as factors determining the value of parameters in the function.

Before looking at the effect of income on investment, it is important to emphasize again the distinction between gross investment, net investment, and capital stock. By gross investment is meant the flow of expenditures on capital goods during some time interval. Net investment represents that portion of gross investment which changes the stock of capital and may therefore be either positive or negative. When both gross and net investment are positive, the difference represents the amount of spending necessary to sustain the capital stock at its existing level. Hence gross investment minus capital consumption allowances equals net investment. If at time $t-1$ the stock of capital is K_{t-1} then at time t the capital stock will be K_t, and:

$$K_t = K_{t-1} + I_t - \phi K_{t-1} \qquad (5.2)$$

where I_t is gross investment;

ϕ is a capital consumption coefficient applied to the capital stock.

If I_{nt} is net investment, then:

$$I_{nt} = I_t - \phi K_{t-1} \qquad (5.3)$$

It is evident that when net investment is positive, the capital stock grows and there is an increase in the productive capacity of the economy.

What forces create demands by businessmen to expand their production capabilities? The answer to this question gives an added insight into the nature of investment demand. If we consider a production function in which output depends upon factor inputs of labor and capital, with capital the fixed factor determining the scale of operations, we can designate some quantity of capital as optimal or "desirable." A desirable capital stock may be thought of in terms of the scale at which the firm operates. If, at a given scale, the firm can operate at the minimum point on its average cost curve, then its actual capital stock may be considered optimal, that is, equal to what is desired. In long-run equilibrium under pure competition, normal profits will be enjoyed by producers with the return on capital exactly equal to opportunity earnings. The desired relationship between capital stock and output can only be understood in terms of the profitability criterion. It should *not* be interpreted in strictly technological terms.

When the typical firm is faced with an increased demand for output, as would be the case if national income increased, it can no longer operate at its lowest average cost, and therefore its desired capital stock and output levels will rise. Returns to capital employed will exceed opportunity earnings, and the profit incentive will lead to increases in capacity and net investment. Hence, increased national income should lead to increases in the level of investment demand for each level of r. That is, the investment demand function should shift to the right.

This effect is the "capital stock adjustment" principle of investment demand. To rephrase its nature, business firms are regarded as having some desired quantity of tangible assets for given levels of output and sales. This quantity is determined by technology, relative factor prices (which lead to a choice of production technique), market forces (which affect the level of and variations in output demands and the opportunity earnings on capital), and risk factors (which are incorporated in the minimum acceptable rate of return on capital). Investment behavior is then represented as the effort by businessmen to adjust the actual stock of capital to the desired stock.

Of great importance in such a specification of investment demand is the rapidity with which actual stocks are adjusted to desired levels. Time therefore has to be introduced as an explicit variable in the analysis of net investment. Adjustment may be very rapid, it may occur at a moderate pace, or it may be extremely sluggish. Considered below are the two polar cases. In the first, the adjustment occurs within a single period. In the second, adjustment is very slow, and investment can then be regarded as a function of the level of income.

Case I: Rapid Capital Stock Adjustment

The first case may be illustrated by a linear system that ignores all variables other than income and capital stock: If K_t^* is the desired capital stock at the end of period t, Y_t is income in the period t, K_{t-1} is actual capital stock at the end of period $t - 1$, and I_{nt} is net investment in period t, then net investment demand is:

$$I_{nt} = \gamma(K_t^* - K_{t-1}) \tag{5.4}$$

In addition, desired capital stock may be expressed as:

$$K_t^* = \beta + \alpha Y_t \tag{5.5}$$

In this equation, α is a positive coefficient expressing the desired capital stock output ratio. $\gamma = 1$ when the capital stock adjustment is completed within the period t. Therefore:

$$I_{nt} = K_t^* - K_{t-1} \tag{5.6}$$

and substituting equation (5.5) into equation (5.6) gives us:

$$I_{nt} = \beta + \alpha Y_t - K_{t-1}^* \tag{5.7}$$

If adjustment is always completed in the current period, then at the beginning and at the end of each period, K will equal K^*. Hence:

$$K_{t-1} = K_{t-1}^* \tag{5.8}$$

By application of equation (5.5), we then obtain:

$$K_{t-1}^* = \beta + \alpha Y_{t-1} \tag{5.9}$$

and, by substitution of equation (5.9) into equation (5.7), we get:

$$I_{nt} = \alpha(Y_t - Y_{t-1}) \tag{5.10}$$

In this case of rapid adjustment, investment demand in period t is determined by the *change* in income during the interval from $t - 1$ to t.

Case II: Slow Adjustment

In the polar case of no adjustment, that is, where $\gamma = 0$, we may simply relate investment spending to the *level* of income. In this case there is no response of actual to desired stocks. It is therefore no longer appropriate to formulate net investment as in equation (5.4). Net investment, specified in terms of levels of income, and showing the response of firms to a change in aggregate demand, can then be written as:

$$I_{nt} = I(r, Y) \tag{5.11}$$

where we expect the relation between I and Y to be positive. Hence, as Y increases, the investment demand function of Figure 5–3 will shift to the right.

Again, it is necessary to emphasize the economic logic behind this "financial availability" statement of investment demand. The higher the level of output and income, the larger the level of retained earnings, for if internally generated funds, that is, corporate savings, are the major source of finance for capital consumption allowances (replacement investment) and net investment, then equation (5.11) is a usable specification of investment behavior. Implied here is a reluctance on the part of firms to engage in external financing. The issuance of new equities is not likely to be favored by stockholders because of its effect on share appreciation, while extensive amounts of debt financing may be precluded by the existence of a relatively stable debt-to-total asset ratio.

CONCLUSION

Gross investment, though a somewhat volatile factor, is a major component of aggregate demand. It accounts for 14 to 17 percent of GNP. Since small shifts in investment may lead to sizable changes in the level of output because of the multiplier, this chapter has focused on those factors that may cause the level of investment to change.

One factor affecting the level of investment is the rate of interest, although its importance as a determinant of investment demand has been subject to some debate. The empirical evidence has not been conclusive on this point, but it does suggest that other factors may be equally important. These other factors include the level of income, changes in technology, and changes in expectations. Changes in expectations have been used here to encompass a wide variety of factors—demographic, political, economic, scientific, social, etc.

The emphasis of this chapter indicates that, even though other factors are frequently as important in determining the level of investment, the rate of interest continues to receive the most attention. There is good reason for this. The interest rate is a variable which can, within limits, be controlled by the monetary authorities in their efforts to achieve certain economic objectives. And on some occasions the existence of links between interest rate changes and expectations may make changing the interest rate the most effective way of altering the level of investment.

ADDITIONAL READINGS

For a thorough survey of factors affecting investment decisions, see R. Eisner and R. Strotz, "Determinants of business investment," in the Commission on Money and Credit's *Impacts of Monetary Policy* (Englewood Cliffs, N.J.: Prentice-Hall, 1963). Chapters 4 through 8 of Michael K. Evans' *Macroeconomic Activity* (New York: Harper & Row, 1969) contain a valuable systematic review and interpretation of the empirical evidence concerning investment in inventories, consumer durables, residential construction, and business fixed investment.

Another lengthy study of investment is John R. Meyer and Edwin Kuh, *The Investment Decision* (Cambridge, Mass: Harvard University Press, 1957). Several shorter studies have concentrated upon particular aspects of the investment decision. William H. White examined the role of the cost of funds in his "Interest inelasticity of investment demand—The case from business attitude surveys re-examined," *American Economic Review,* 46 (September 1956): 565–877. Jack Hirshliefer was concerned with the proper choice of a discount rate in his "Risk, the discount rate, and investment decisions," *American Economic Review,* 51 (May 1961): 112–120, and in his *Investment, Interest and Capital,* (Englewood Cliffs, N.J.: Prentice-Hall, 1970). J. G. Witte, Jr., critically analyzed the derivation of the aggregate investment demand schedule in "The microfoundations of the social investment function," *Journal of Political Economy,* 71 (October 1963): 441–456.

The early classic article dealing with the capital stock adjustment process is John M. Clark's "Business acceleration and the law of demand: A technical factor in economic cycles," reprinted in the American Economic Association's *Readings in Business Cycle Theory* (Philadelphia: Blakiston, 1944). For a discussion of the possible destabilizing effects of the accelerator and the multiplier see Paul A. Samuelson, "Interaction between the multiplier analysis and the principle of acceleration," *Review of Economics and Statistics,* 21 (1939): 75–78.

Discussions of factors affecting the cost of investment funds may be found in Evans' *Macroeconomic Activity,* Chapter 4; in J. S. Duesenberry's *Business Cycles and Economic Growth* (New York: McGraw-Hill, 1958), Chapters 4 and 5; and in G. A. Mumey's *Theory of Financial Structure* (New York: Holt, Rinehart and Winston, 1969), Chapters 6–8.

QUESTIONS

1. If interest rates were low enough, would there be sufficient private investment for full employment? Explain.

2. In periods of voluminous business investment, interest rates go up. How can we say that high interest rates inhibit investment? What is the shape of the investment demand function?

3. Describe how an increase in the corporate profits tax would be expected to affect the position of the investment demand function.

4. Distinguish between the various types of financing, external and internal, and explain how heavy reliance on internal financing can influence the effectiveness of monetary policy. Are changes in interest rates likely to affect all firms equally? Explain.

5. Why might we expect the cost of external funds to be greater than the cost of internal funds? Throughout the 1960s American corporations increasingly (both in absolute and relative terms) relied upon external funds for their financing needs. Can you think of reasons why this occurred?

6. Why do you think that investment might be affected by the level of income? How do you think the multiplier would be affected if our model in Chapter 3 incorporated the fact that investment is directly related to the level of income as in equation (5.11)?

7. Thoroughly discuss the role played by expectations in the investment decision. How does a businessman normally compensate for increasing risk?

8. Fully explain the impact of technological change, innovation, market structures, and finance on the level of investment spending.

9. Thoroughly describe the procedure that you would suggest a large corporation use in making its investment decisions. Include all factors which you believe should be given consideration and explain how changes in these factors could affect the investment decision.

10. What are the implications of the rapid capital stock adjustment model for the stability of the economy? How will a decrease in the capital stock-to-output ratio (α) affect the stability of the economy? Review the conditions which must hold if this model is to represent an accurate picture of the U.S. economy. Which of these conditions is unlikely to hold?

11. Show that the present value of the dollar to be received at the end of n periods when the interest rate is i percent is $1/(1 + i)^n$.

The Public Sector and the Foreign Sector

6
Chapter

Having examined in some detail those factors influencing household consumption of goods and services and business demand for capital goods, there remain two additional important sources of demand for domestically produced goods: (a) demand by the public sector for goods and services; and (b) demand by foreigners for U.S. goods and services. Government expenditures on goods and services and exports of goods and services account for roughly 20 and 7 percent of the GNP, respectively.

When viewing the public sector and the foreign sector of the economy, we find two factors that lead to a reduction in the demand for domestically produced goods and services. First, taxes used to finance (at least in part) public expenditures reduce the ability of both households and businesses to consume and invest. Second, the more that households and businesses spend on goods produced abroad (imports), the less they have to spend on domestically produced goods.

The purpose of this chapter is to make clear the role that government expenditures, taxation, exports, and imports have upon the levels of aggregate demand, output, and employment. We will consider in turn public expenditures, lump-sum taxation, transfer payments, income taxation, exports, and imports. Policy implications will be considered as they arise.

GOVERNMENT EXPENDITURES

As noted in our study of the national accounts, the government pays both the costs of the goods and services it uses and the wages and salaries of the civil and military services. These expenditures cover all those activities that may be performed more efficiently when carried out collectively than when carried out individually. What activities to undertake collectively and the amount of total resources to be devoted to these activities are decided in democratic societies as the result of an extended and continuing political process in which the ultimate sanction rests at the ballot box. Since the level of government expenditures (G) is determined primarily by sociopolitical considerations, it is generally treated as exogenous in an income determination model. We will assume, then, that it is given.

Incorporating Government Expenditures on Goods and Services into Our Commodity Market Model

If G is treated as an exogenous variable then the commodity market model may be expanded as follows:

$$\text{Income: } Y = C + I + G \tag{6.1}$$

$$\text{Consumption: } C = a + bY \tag{6.2}$$

$$\text{Investment: } I \text{ is given}$$

$$\text{Government: } G \text{ is given}$$

The preceding chapter was devoted to factors determining investment, but here, to focus on the impacts of government spending and taxation, we will temporarily assume that the level of investment is fixed. Later on we will relax this assumption.

In this equation system there are two equations with two givens, G and I, and two unknowns, C and Y. The only difference between this model and that described in Chapter 3 is that G has been added as an independent variable. The first step to take in solving the equations for equilibrium values of Y and C is to put the equations into "reduced form." We do this by substituting equation (6.2) in place of C in equation (6.1) and by then substituting equation (6.1) in place of Y in equation (6.2). In this way C and Y are each expressed only in terms of parameters and givens (independent variables). Thus:

$$Y = C + I + G$$

$$Y = a + bY + I + G$$

$$Y(1 - b) = a + I + G$$

$$Y = \frac{1}{1 - b}a + \frac{1}{1 - b}I + \frac{1}{1 - b}G \tag{6.3}$$

Equation (6.3) is the reduced form expression for Y.

The reduced form expression for consumption may be derived similarly:

$$C = a + bY$$

$$C = a + b(C + I + G)$$

$$C(1 - b) = a + b(I + G)$$

$$C = \frac{1}{1 - b}a + \frac{b}{1 - b}I + \frac{b}{1 - b}G \tag{6.4}$$

Derivation of Government Spending Multipliers

In Chapter 3 we derived income and consumption multipliers for a change in investment. Multipliers also accompany changes in government spending, for if G increases, there must be a higher level of income payments to government contractors and public servants. The recipients of this added income can be expected to add to their consumption expenditures, which will in turn increase income, and so on. With a given propensity to consume, the government spending multiplier will equal the investment spending multiplier. There is no a priori reason to expect recipients of increased government expenditure to have consumption-income patterns significantly different from those of the recipients of increased private investment spending by business firms.

Algebraically, the government spending multiplier applied to income may be derived as follows:

Because we are assuming that I is constant, $\Delta I = 0$, and:

$$\Delta Y = \Delta C + \Delta G$$

$$\Delta C = b\Delta Y$$

$$\Delta Y = b\Delta Y + \Delta G$$

$$(1 - b)\Delta Y = \Delta G$$

$$\Delta Y = \Delta G \frac{1}{1 - b}$$

$$\frac{\Delta Y}{\Delta G} = \frac{1}{1 - b} \tag{6.5}$$

The government spending multiplier is $\Delta Y/\Delta G$ or $1/(1 - b)$. It is positive if $0 < b < 1$, and its size depends upon b, the marginal propensity to consume.[1]

A government spending multiplier can be developed for consumption similarly:

$$\Delta C = b\Delta Y$$

$$\Delta C = b(\Delta C + \Delta G)$$

$$(1 - b)\Delta C = b\Delta G$$

$$\Delta C = \frac{b}{1 - b}\Delta G$$

$$\frac{\Delta C}{\Delta G} = \frac{b}{1 - b} \tag{6.6}$$

[1] We should recognize that the multipliers are actually the partial derivatives of the dependent variables with respect to the independent variables in the reduced form equation. Thus, from equation (6.3), if $Y = [1/(1-b)](a+I+G)$, $\partial Y/\partial G = 1/(1-b)$. The consumption multiplier is derived from equation (6.4) by taking $\partial C/\partial G = b/(1-b)$.

Figure 6–1.

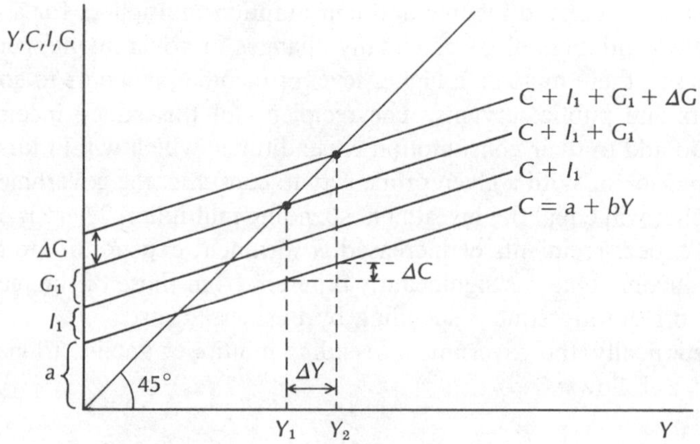

The government spending multiplier applied to consumption is $\Delta C/\Delta G$ or $b/(1 - b)$. It is positive if $0 < b < 1$ and its size in this instance depends also upon b.

Diagrammatic Illustration of the Government Spending Multiplier

The above algebraic example may also be illustrated graphically. In Figure 6–1, Y_1 represents an initial equilibrium level of income with government and investment spending of G_1 and I_1. If G_1 now increases by ΔG, then the increase in demand temporarily causes demand to exceed supply. As inventories are depleted production is stepped up, and income increases until output again equals aggregate effective demand $(C + I + G)$ and inventories are no longer being depleted. Y_1 rises by ΔY to Y_2 and C rises by ΔC. These new equilibrium levels of income and consumption are consistent with the original level of investment spending and a higher level of government purchases of goods and services.

Policy Implications

The most important policy implication of this simple model is that the level of aggregate demand can be changed by alterations in the level of government spending. Thus if we suppose that the maintenance of full employment is one of the objectives of public policy and that all the effective demands of the private and public sectors are insufficient to produce full employment, then one available option is to increase G to the level required to generate a full employment level of income. Of course, G is not the only policy instrument available. There are others, too, which we will examine. But we can see that if the consumption function remains stable, and if the increase in Y is not offset by some other change, then full employment may be attained by increasing G.

If G were deliberately increased to secure full employment, this would be an application of what is known as discretionary fiscal policy, involving (a) recognition of the existence of a gap between full employment output and actual output, (b) agreement by Congress and the administration on how much and for what purposes expenditures should be increased, and, of course, (c) the actual carrying out of the increased expenditures once they are authorized. The process of getting ΔG into the income stream is complicated and it may be very time consuming. Hence, because of the time involved, the chosen policy may be both too weak to accomplish its goal and too outdated by the time it is put into effect; it may even work against the achievement of that goal if the lag in implementation is sufficiently long. This is one reason why many economists regard it as a rather blunt and ineffective instrument for pursuing full employment goals.

INCORPORATING A LUMP-SUM TAX INTO THE COMMODITY MARKET MODEL

The next step in building the model is to include the tax revenue counterpart of government expenditures. This can be done by assuming that the government collects a lump-sum tax, that is, a specified amount of tax. In this case the amount of tax to be collected is a result of the sociopolitical process, and, as in the case of government expenditures, the ultimate sanction is at the ballot box. The concept of lump-sum taxation may seem unrealistic to the student, but it is very useful for pedagogical purposes, and it will be modified to a more realistic form later when we introduce a tax function dependent upon income.

One further necessary assumption is that the lump-sum tax is levied on the households to which all income is paid in our model. Thus, with the introduction of a revenue source for the public sector, household expenditures can now be written as a function of disposable household income:

$$Y_d = Y - T \tag{6.7}$$

where T is taxes.

Now our commodity market model may be written as follows in a linear system:

$$\begin{aligned} Y &= C + I + G \\ C &= a + b(Y - T) \\ C &= a + b(Y_d) \end{aligned} \tag{6.8}$$

where G, I, and T are given.

The reduced form expression for Y is derived as follows:

$$Y = a + b(Y - T) + I + G$$

$$(1 - b)Y = a - bT + I + G$$

$$Y = \frac{1}{1-b}a - \frac{b}{1-b}T + \frac{1}{1-b}I + \frac{1}{1-b}G \qquad (6.9)$$

And the reduced form expression for consumption is:

$$C = a + b(Y - T)$$

$$C = a + b(C + I + G - T)$$

$$(1 - b)C = a + b(I + G - T)$$

$$C = \frac{1}{1-b}a + \frac{b}{1-b}I + \frac{b}{1-b}G - \frac{b}{1-b}T \qquad (6.10)$$

Derivation of Lump-Sum Tax Multipliers

As with government spending and private investment, a multiplier for income and consumption may also be derived for taxes. The logic of a tax multiplier can be explained by realizing that the initial effect of an increase in the lump-sum tax is to reduce the income available for private consumption and savings by households (remember that the tax is levied on households and all income is paid to them). Unless the impact of the tax is totally on savings (householders save less by exactly the amount of the tax), then consumption expenditures will fall. This fall in consumption produces a decline in income payments, and the latter induces a further decline in consumption. The induced fall in consumption leads to a further decline in income, and so on.

Algebraically the tax multiplier applied to income may be derived by following the same procedure as used earlier. Holding I and G constant, ΔI and ΔG are both zero. Therefore:

$$\Delta Y = \Delta C$$

$$\Delta C = b\Delta(Y - T)$$

$$\Delta Y = b\Delta(Y - T)$$

$$\text{and: } (1 - b)\,\Delta Y = -b\Delta T$$

$$\Delta Y = -\frac{b}{1-b}\Delta T \qquad (6.11)$$

The tax multiplier is $\Delta Y/\Delta T$ or $-b/(1 - b)$; it is negative, and its size depends upon b, the marginal propensity to consume.

As before, the lump-sum tax multiplier can also be developed for consumption:[2]

[2]As earlier, calculus gives us $\partial Y / \partial T$ for equation (6.9) as $-b / (1-b)$, the tax multiplier for income; from equation (6.10) the tax multiplier for consumption is $\partial C / \partial T = -b / (1-b)$.

$$\Delta C = b\,\Delta(Y - T)$$

$$\Delta C = b\,\Delta(C - T)$$

$$(1 - b)\Delta C = -\,b\Delta T$$

$$\Delta C = -\frac{b}{1 - b}\Delta T \tag{6.12}$$

The lump-sum tax multiplier applied to consumption is $\Delta C/\Delta T$ or $-b/(1 - b)$; it too is negative and its size also depends upon b. Its value is the same as that of the multiplier applied to income because $\Delta Y = \Delta C$.

Having derived two sets of multipliers, it should now be clear that each multiplier corresponds to the respective coefficients of the independent variables in the reduced form equations. Thus, in equation (6.9) the coefficients of a, T, I, and G are their respective multipliers. If only G changes, the change in Y will be $1/(1 - b)$ times the change in G; if only T changes, the change in Y will be $-b/(1 - b)$ times the change in T; and so forth. Similarly, consumption multipliers are the coefficients of the respective independent variables in equation (6.10). These propositions hold whenever reduced form equations are linear.

Policy Implications

It is apparent from the examination of lump-sum tax multipliers that here is another policy instrument. If output is at less than full employment levels, it can be stimulated by a reduction in taxes. If it is desirable to restrict effective demand, then taxes can be increased. Such changes are another example of discretionary fiscal policy. The power to levy taxes and to alter tax rates on the national level is one reserved to the Congress. Hence Congressional action is necessary if taxes are to be used as a policy instrument.

But the policy implications are not quite so simple as this. The model does not rigorously represent the working of the real world. G represents collectively consumed goods and services and T is the compulsory levy to pay for the resources necessary to provide them, but only if the problem in the economy is one of underutilization will a reduction in T as a means of increasing output meet little resistance. The same quantity of G will then be available for a lower tax bill, because expansion will be generated in the private sector of the economy. If, however, the difficulty is one of excess aggregate demand (i.e., planned expenditures at the prevailing price level exceed full employment output), then the appropriate policy action—assuming taxes are the appropriate control instrument—is to increase the lump-sum tax, T. The result of such a decision will be that households in the society will have to pay more taxes for the same quantity of G. Hence, the tax bill will rise with no direct return in the form of an increase in public goods. Taxpayers are asked to accept an increase in the general tax burden without any change in the quantity or quality of public services. The benefit to the taxpayer of an increase in T is found in a reduction of upward pressures on the general price level, i.e., in a more stable price level at full employment output. The burden of adjustment is on the private sector through the decline in private consumption. The taxpayer is required to give up satisfactions from direct consumption for the indirect benefits of a less inflationary economic environment. Needless to say, this requires not only altruism, but also a substantial level of economic sophistication on the part of both taxpayers and their elected representatives.

Later we will construct a model covering supply conditions in the economy to show how taxpayers may try to compensate for increases in taxes by demanding higher monetary incomes.

EQUILIBRIUM CONDITIONS IN A THREE-SECTOR COMMODITY MARKET MODEL

In our two-sector—households and business—commodity market model, the equilibrium level of income was defined to exist when the investment intentions of businessmen matched the savings plans of households. That is:

$$\overbrace{C+I}^{\text{Sources of income}} \qquad = \qquad \overbrace{C+S}^{\text{Uses of income}}$$

and the equilibrium condition was $I = S$. Now that our model has been extended to include government as a third sector, G and T have been introduced and the equivalent equality is:

$$\overbrace{C+I+G}^{\text{Sources of income}} \qquad = \qquad \overbrace{C+S+T}^{\text{Uses of income}}$$

The equilibrium condition is now $I + G = S + T$.

An equilibrium level of income can be illustrated by Figure 6–2, where I, G, and T are all given. The pretax savings function is $S(Y_0)$. Taxes will affect both consumption and savings and will cause the savings function to be lower for each level of income since part of the tax will come out of consumption and part will come out of savings. With the introduction of a lump-sum tax, the savings function becomes $S(Y)$, showing the lower savings level for each level of income. To $S(Y)$ are added the revenues from the lump-sum tax, T, and the function shifts upward by the amount T. We also assume the realistic situation that the government finds a way to spend all the revenues it collects so that $G = T$. Y_1 then represents an equilibrium level of income after the tax in contrast with Y_0 which is the equilibrium level of income before the tax was introduced.

Figure 6–2.

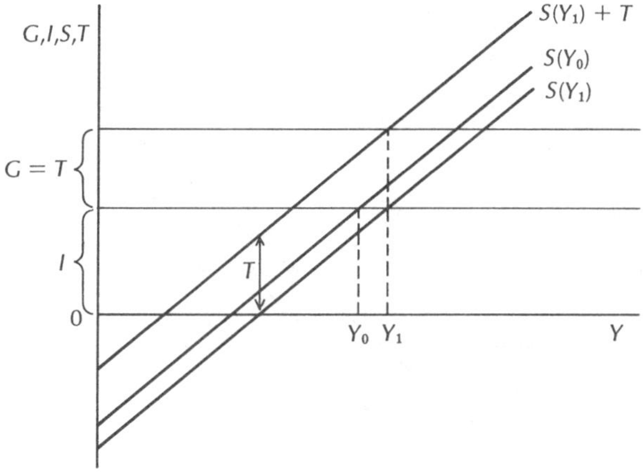

The government's budget position may be defined in terms of the difference $G - T$. If $G - T < 0$, there is a budget surplus; if $G - T = 0$, as in Figure 6–2, the budget is in balance; and if $G - T > 0$, there is a budget deficit. Given G and T, then, the resulting equilibrium level of Y is not necessarily one in which the budget is in balance. There may be a balanced budget, a budget surplus, or a budget deficit, and the question of which budgetary position may be preferred may be best answered by considering specific cases.

Figure 6–3 has been drawn to let $G = T$, Y_1 represent an income level below full employment, and Y_f represent a full employment level of income. If full employment is a prime objective of public policy, then in order to achieve full employment G could be raised by ΔG and equilibrium would be represented by a shift from point *a* to point *b*. Since G increases and T is held constant, $G > T$ at *b* and we have a deficit in the budget. Alternatively, T could be lowered, leaving G constant. A negative value for ΔT lowers the savings function and the equilibrium would shift from point *a* to point *c*. Again, with G constant and T lowered, $G > T$ at *c* and the budget is in deficit. It is possible, of course, to use any of a variety of combinations of increases in G and reductions in T to achieve Y_f as equilibrium income, but regardless of which combination is chosen, since we began with $G = T$, after raising G and lowering T it is certain that $G > T$ in the end. The net effect will inevitably be a deficit.

On the other hand, Y_1 might represent a level of income in excess of the full employment level, Y_f, as in Figure 6–4. At Y_1 the budget is balanced since $G = T$ at point *a*, and one way to reduce income from Y_1 to Y_f would be by an increase in taxes, causing the $S + T$ curve to shift to $S + T + \Delta T$, with equilibrium represented by point *b*. An alternative would be to reduce G

Figure 6–3.

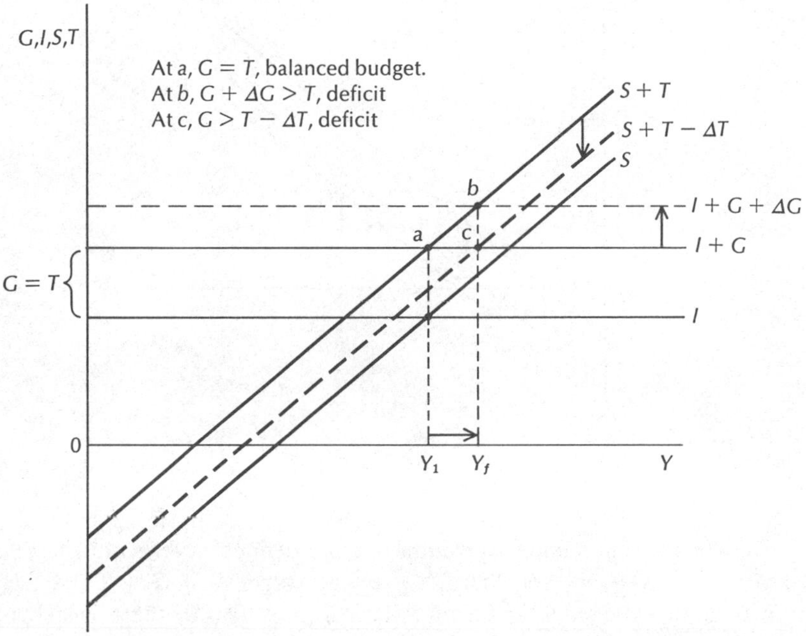

Figure 6–4.

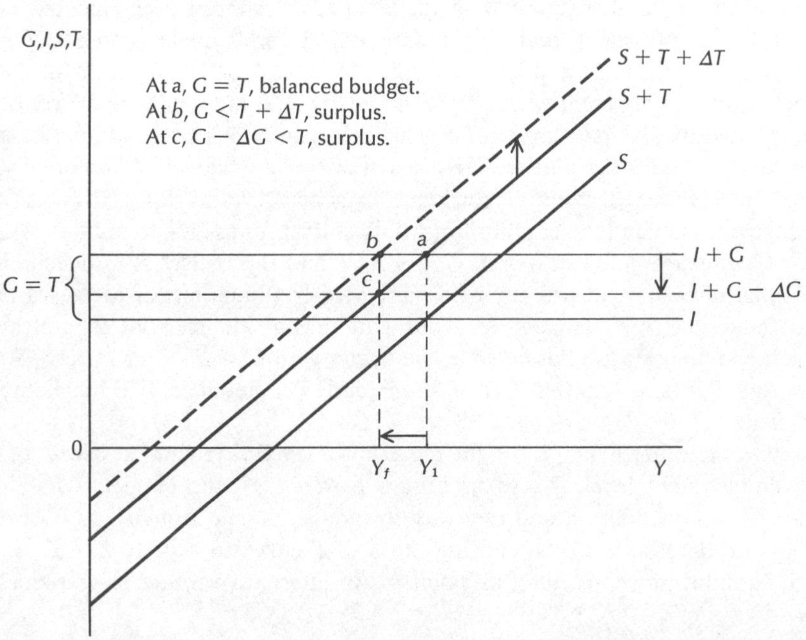

by ΔG and move from point *a* to point *c*. Or some combination of increases in T and decreases in G could be used; in all of these cases, a budget surplus is necessary to achieve full employment without inflationary pressures.

These brief examples emphasize that the budget is not likely to be perfectly balanced at full employment and that the rate of resource utilization should be the principal criterion for evaluating the government's budget position. As a result, any of the three possible budgetary positions may be consistent with full employment. What is optimal in specific circumstances depends upon the demands exhibited by the private sectors, business and households. If C and I are so great that, when coupled with a given level of G, they are sufficient to push the economy beyond its economic potential, then a budgetary surplus is optimal because it serves to restrain inflationary pressures. In contrast, if C and I are somewhat weak, a budgetary deficit to sustain full employment is called for. Changes in either G or T, or some combination of changes, can be used to adjust aggregate demand.

The Balanced Budget Multiplier

When tax rate changes were debated in Congress in 1964 and again in 1968, the willingness of Congressmen to vote changes in tax rates was linked to changes in government expenditures of an approximately equivalent dollar amount. In 1964, when taxes were cut to stimulate the economy, the argument was advanced that the budget should be kept in balance by reducing government expenditures by a similar amount.[3]

Our model, simple though it is, provides an analysis of the effects on the level of economic activity of efforts to balance the budget through simultaneous changes in G and T. We can suppose that $G = T$ but that the level of Y is less than the full employment level. To remedy unemployment a \$10 billion reduction in taxes (a lump-sum reduction) is proposed. However, this is to be accompanied by an equivalent reduction of \$10 billion in G in order to "keep the budget balanced." We can then ask if the combination of a tax reduction and a reduction in government expenditures would do the job.

To answer, we can refer to the government spending and tax multiplier developed previously. First, let us examine the effects of equal increases in government spending and taxes. For every \$1 *increase* in G, the *increase* in Y is $1/(1 - b)$, and for every \$1 *increase* in T, the decrease in Y is $-b/(1 - b)$. Adding these two multipliers together gives us a "balanced budget multiplier," $1/(1 - b) + -b/(1 - b) = 1$. This means that when G and T are increased simultaneously by \$1, the result is to increase Y by \$1. In fact, then, Y increases by just the amount of the increase in G when this increase is accompanied by an equal increase in T. The secondary effects upon consumption of

[3] In 1968, the problem was one of curtailing inflationary pressures by increasing taxes. At that time, some Congressmen said they would support a tax increase only if the administration proposed an expenditure reduction of a similar amount.

the increase in G are exactly offset by the countervailing increase in T, leaving only the initial effect of G itself to change Y.

In the question we have posed, where both G and T are reduced by \$10 billion, the net effect upon income is $-\$10$ billion $\times 1 = -\$10$ billion. If such a program to decrease *both* G and T were adopted, it would make more severe the unemployment it was meant to correct.

ADDING TRANSFER PAYMENTS TO THE COMMODITY MARKET MODEL

In discussing the role of government when explaining social accounting systems, we pointed out that one function of government is the redistribution of income and wealth in terms of some socially acceptable standard of equity. Transfer payments, such as unemployment and Social Security retirement benefits, represent redistribution through the fiscal machinery of government. They are not payments for personal services like wages, rent, interest, and profits, but nevertheless they are counted as part of personal disposable income.

Now we wish to allow for this redistributive mechanism in our income determination model. Since transfer payments go to households, it will be necessary to modify slightly our statement of household behavior. We do this by defining personal income, Y_d, as:

$$Y_d = Y - T + T_r \tag{6.13}$$

where T_r is transfer payments. Consumption can then be described as:

$$C = a + b(Y - T + T_r) \tag{6.14}$$

In the manner presented previously in this chapter, our target variables Y and C can now be fully expressed, in reduced form, as:

$$Y = \frac{1}{1-b}a + \frac{1}{1-b}I + \frac{1}{1-b}G - \frac{b}{1-b}T + \frac{b}{1-b}T_r \tag{6.15}$$

$$C = \frac{1}{1-b}a + \frac{b}{1-b}I + \frac{b}{1-b}G - \frac{b}{1-b}T + \frac{b}{1-b}T_r \tag{6.16}$$

As with investment, government spending, and taxes, a transfer payment multiplier for income and consumption can be derived whose logic can be seen by supposing that, for some reason, transfer payments are increased. The effect is to increase the disposable income of households. The increased consumption expenditures of these households will then lead to an increase in income payments, which will increase consumption further, and so on. This suggests that, as an additional tool of economic policy, transfer payments can be increased to raise income to full employment levels.

As earlier, the multipliers could be derived algebraically. But without repeating that derivation here it is sufficient that the coefficients of T_r in equations (6.15) and (6.16) provide the respective multipliers.

Table 6–1. A Matrix of Multipliers.

Target Variables	Independent Variables	a	I	G (Fiscal Policy Variables)	T (Fiscal Policy Variables)	T_r (Fiscal Policy Variables)
Y		$\frac{1}{1-b}$	$\frac{1}{1-b}$	$\frac{1}{1-b}$	$\frac{-b}{1-b}$	$\frac{b}{1-b}$
C		$\frac{1}{1-b}$	$\frac{b}{1-b}$	$\frac{b}{1-b}$	$\frac{-b}{1-b}$	$\frac{b}{1-b}$

A MULTIPLIER MATRIX

The incorporation of government spending, lump-sum taxation, and transfer payments into our model can be summarized in a multiplier matrix such as Table 6–1, whose rows contain the coefficients of the equations for income and consumption. The first two column headings refer to a, the autonomous component of consumption, and I. The final three are the variables that can be manipulated by fiscal policy—G, T, and T_r. The cells of the matrix show the amount by which the target variables, Y and C, change for every \$1 increase in a, I, G, T, and T_r.

INTRODUCING AUTOMATIC STABILIZERS INTO THE COMMODITY MARKET MODEL

In the preceding sections we examined a commodity market model for a closed economy with three types of transactor units, households, business, and government. In the government, or public, sector G was exogenously determined, T was a lump-sum tax, and T_r was, in effect, a lump-sum transfer payment. Changes in the level of any of these, under the conditions specified, would require discretionary action by the government. Now we can improve our model by functionally relating both taxes and transfer payments to income. This relation depends on "automatic stabilizers."

Automatic Stabilizers

An automatic stabilizer helps maintain Y at nearly constant levels without the necessity for discretionary action on the part of the executive and legislative branches of government. In other words, "automatic" refers to the fact that the program concerned is written into the statute books. Such stabilizers are among the parameters of the economic system particularly relevant to the objective of income maintenance. They include the legislatively defined income tax system, unemployment benefits, and retirement benefits.

An important contrast may be drawn with discretionary fiscal policy: Automatic stabilizers do not involve the lags commonly found in the forecasting of economic activity and in the development and implementation of programs. The very real difficulties in appraising economic prospects and in hammering out a legislative program to deal with the most probable situation are avoided.

What is meant by "stabilizer"? A stabilizer works against the direction of change in income. We regard the income tax and the unemployment insurance system as stabilizing rather than destabilizing because of the nature of their relationship to income payments: When income increases, as with an upsurge in effective demand, tax liabilities also increase; on the other hand, when income payments decline with a decrease in effective demand, tax liabilities also fall. In the first case, the increase in income is tempered by the increase in tax liabilities; in the second, the fall in income is cushioned by the fall in taxes.

In contrast with a tax system based on a lump-sum tax, the level of tax liabilities is not set independently of income levels. When income increases or decreases in response to a change in effective demand, lump-sum tax payments do not change; income tax payments do.

Unemployment compensation is also an automatic stabilizer. When output falls, compensation payments increase, thereby serving to moderate the fall in income. Some portion of the fall in personal income owing to unemployment is offset by the unemployment insurance programs. Of course, when employment is rising and the unemployment rolls are falling, compensation payments decline also.

An Amended Tax Function

In fact, taxes are functionally related to income. When Y changes, T also changes, as is bound to be the case when some 85 percent of federal revenues are raised from personal and corporate income taxes. Further, at the state level the major revenue producers, state income and retail sales taxes, are also related to income. T is not exogenous. Rather:

$$T = T(Y)$$

$$\text{or:} \quad T = tY$$

$$\text{where } t = \Delta T/\Delta Y > 0 \tag{6.17}$$

The tax function is illustrated in Figure 6–5, where $T(Y)$ represents the tax function and its slope represents the marginal propensity to tax, t.

Figure 6–5.

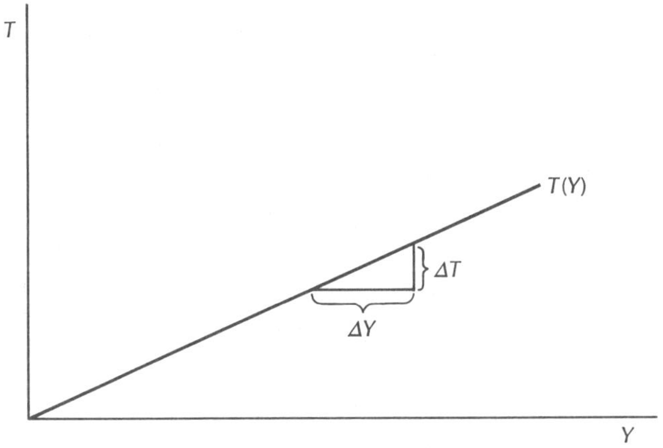

An Amended Transfer Payment Function

Transfer payments are also functionally related to income. Unemployment compensation payments are negatively related to output levels, and there is evidence that this is also true of the Old Age and Survivors' Insurance part of the Social Security program.[4] Transfer payments are not exogenous, but rather should be written as:

$$T_r = T_r(Y)$$

$$\text{or:} \quad T_r = g + hY$$

$$\text{where } h = \Delta T_r/\Delta Y < 0 \tag{6.18}$$

The transfer payments function is represented in Figure 6–6. It is negatively related to income. The intercept value, g, is the maximum level of transfer payments possible under existing programs. The slope of the function, h, may be interpreted as the marginal propensity to make transfer payments.

Effect on Income and Consumption Multipliers

Earlier in this chapter, when T and T_r were treated as given, tax and transfer payment multipliers were developed. But now we have reduced the number of exogenous variables in our model by making both taxes and transfer payments dependent upon income. Consumption, savings, taxes, transfer payments, and the government's budget position are now all functions of income. How will the income and consumption multipliers be altered?

[4] When labor market conditions are very good, as is the case when full employment is approached, there is a tendency for those over 65 to enter the job market and forego old-age benefits. On the other hand, when less than full employment is experienced, those over 65 withdraw from the labor force, and there is a tendency toward accelerated retirement, i.e., toward retiring before 65.

Figure 6–6.

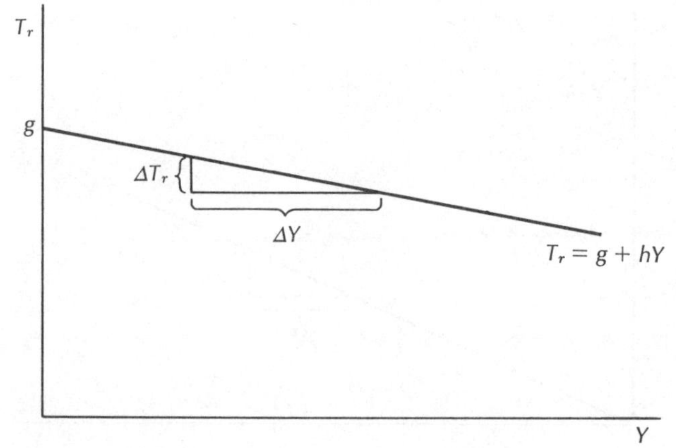

Previously, the size of the multiplier depended upon the marginal propensity to consume. Now, the propensities to tax and to pay transfer payments will be directly incorporated into our set of income and consumption multipliers. The need for this becomes obvious if we consider an increase in one of the exogenous types of spending. If, for example, G increases, this will produce an initial increase in income in response to the rise in effective demand. The recipients of this income will allocate it between current consumption, savings, and tax payments. In addition, for the society as a whole, transfer payments will fall as a result of the increase in output levels and decrease in unemployment. The net change in income payments received by households will therefore be the difference between the increase in income payments from increased output and the fall in transfer payments.

The multipliers themselves may be explained just as before: The increase in consumption resulting from the initial net increase in income will in turn give rise to further increases in income, and so on through additional rounds.

We can now consider our commodity market model in the following linear form:

$$Y = C + I + G$$
$$C = a + b(Y - T + T_r) \tag{6.19}$$
$$T = tY$$
$$T_r = g + hY$$
$$G \text{ and } I \text{ are given}$$

where a, b, g, h, and t are coefficients and $a > 0$; $0 < b < 1$; $g > 0$; $h < 0$ and $t > 0$. Of these coefficients, a and b are called *behavioral* because they are determined by the composite behavior of the multitude of economic units within society; g, h, and t are called *institutional* because they are determined by government policy decisions. The tax coefficient, t, is established by legislation; g is the maximum level of transfer payments, again set by statute; h reflects the effects of the statutory provisions of the Social Security and unemployment insurance programs.

By substitution:

$$Y = a + b(Y - tY + g + hY) + I + G$$

Shifting Y to the left yields:

$$(1 - b + bt - bh)\,Y = a + bg + I + G$$

And solving for Y gives the reduced form equation:

$$Y = \frac{1}{1 - b + bt - bh}\,a + \frac{1}{1 - b + bt - bh}\,bg + \frac{1}{1 - b + bt - bh}\,I + \frac{1}{1 - b + bt - bh}\,G \qquad (6.20)$$

In this expression, the denominator is greater than $1 - b$ because bt and, since the coefficient h is negative (the change in transfer payments is inversely related to income), $-bh$ are positive. bg represents consumption expenditures out of the maximum level of transfer payments.

The reduced form expression for C can be obtained in the same way as:

$$C = \frac{1}{1 - b + bt - bh}\,a + \frac{1}{1 - b + bt - bh}\,bg + \frac{b - bt + bh}{1 - b + bt - bh}\,I + \frac{b - bt + bh}{1 - b + bt - bh}\,G \qquad (6.21)$$

Contrasted with the earlier expressions, the coefficient of I and G has a smaller numerator and a larger denominator when taxes and transfer payments depend on income.

Again, in this set of linear equations, we know that the multipliers associated with the relevant policy variables are found to be the coefficients of the respective variables in equations (6.20) and (6.21). These multipliers now depend not only upon the marginal propensity to consume, but also upon the marginal tax rate and the marginal propensity to make transfer payments. By now it should be clear that there exists no single simple multiplier, but that multipliers are formed by the various parameters in the simultaneous equation model.

THE RELATION OF BUDGET POSITIONS TO OUTPUT LEVELS

In our consideration of the government sector, one further matter that needs attention is the relation of budget positions to output levels. The model's tax rate, t, helps determine the level of output through the multiplier. Thus, for

Figure 6–7.

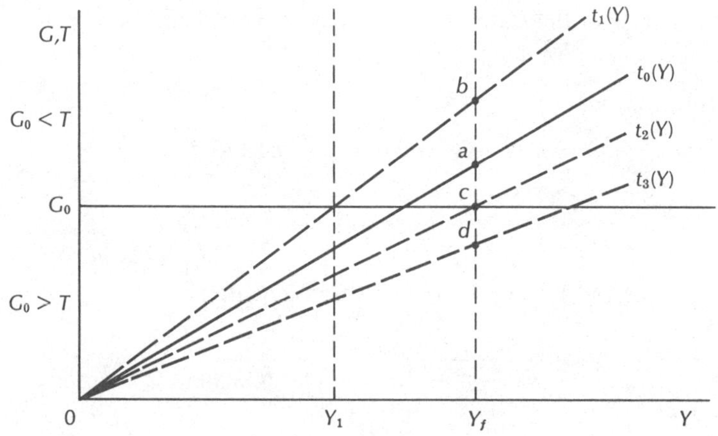

given I and G, $\Delta Y/\Delta t < 0$. An increase in t reduces the size of the income multiplier; a decrease in t raises it. But it is also clear that the tax revenues raised, T, depend upon the level of Y as well as the *tax rate*. Hence, for a *given* tax rate, $\Delta T/\Delta Y > 0$. This relation was illustrated in Figure 6–5. There the value of t is the slope of the curve and a larger t would make the slope steeper, showing a larger value of T for any given Y. But at the same time a larger t would reduce the value of Y, given I, G, and so forth, because a larger t leads to a larger T and a decline in Y.

It follows directly from the interdependence between the tax rate, t, tax revenues, T, and the level of output, Y, that special precautions must be taken in attaching significance to the budget position of the federal government. When we were dealing with a lump-sum tax, a movement from a budgetary surplus to a balanced budget, or from a balanced budget to a budgetary deficit, was unequivocally expansionary in its effect. But now, when tax revenues are dependent upon income, a movement from a balanced budget to a deficit can result from a fall in the level of output, *not* as a result of either a decrease in t or an increase in G.

Figure 6–7 summarizes the budgetary positions possible in this model under alternative tax rates. If under a given expenditure program, $G = G_0$ and Y_f represents a full employment level of output, then at Y_f a tax rate of t_0 produces a budget surplus of ac, because at point a, $G_0 < T$; a tax rate of t_1 yields even a greater surplus of bc; the rate t_2 results in a balanced budget; and the lowest rate of all, t_3, results in a deficit of cd since $G_0 > T$. No adequate assessment of the effect of a given fiscal program on the economy can be made at any other level of output. For example, all values of t yield budgetary deficits when Y is below Y_1. Yet to read these fiscal programs as expansionary just because a deficit prevails is completely misleading, for if output is below Y_1 and the actual tax rate is t_1, one reason for this budgetary deficit is the restricting effect on output of a tax rate as high as t_1.

This relationship between the budget position and the level of output was first stressed by the Council of Economic Advisors in its *Annual Report* for 1962. They emphasized that the "full-employment budget," measuring the difference between the full employment receipts and expenditures rather than between actual receipts and expenditures, is the proper measure of the direction and strength of the government's fiscal policy. The early 1960s, when unemployment persistently exceeded 5 percent, was a time when fiscal policy appeared to many to be appropriately expansionary. However, Table 6–2 indicates that if income had increased to the full employment level for the period 1961 through 1964, the fall in transfer payments and the rise in tax receipts accompanying this increase would have created surpluses in each of the four fiscal years, as indicated by the positive values for the full employment budget in these same years.[5] The full employment budget, therefore, indicates that fiscal policy was not having the desired effect in the attempt to achieve full employment. The data in Table 6–2 also indicate that fiscal 1970 and 1971

Table 6–2. Comparison of Surpluses and Deficits (−): The National Income Accounts Budget and the Full Employment Budget (in billions of dollars).

Fiscal Year	National Income Accounts Budget	Full Employment Budget on National Income Accounts Basis
1960	3.5	9.8
1961	−2.7	11.3
1962	−2.1	5.4
1963	−1.2	7.3
1964	−1.4	4.8
1965	2.0	4.3
1966	0.9	−2.8
1967	−7.2	−8.0
1968	−11.9	−10.2
1969	4.6	5.4
1970	0.8	10.1
1971	−18.4	7.5
1972 (est.)	−35.00	−3.0
1973 (est.)	−28.0	n.a.

Sources: U.S. Treasury Department; Office of Management and the Budget; U.S. Department of Commerce; and Council of Economic Advisors.
The data are presented by James R. McCabe in "The full-employment budget: A guide for fiscal policy," Federal Reserve Bank of Richmond, Monthly Review (May 1972).

[5] The full employment budget estimates presented here were prepared by the Council of Economic Advisors. The Federal Reserve Bank of St. Louis makes its own high-employment estimates which are found in its publications "Federal budget trends" and "Technical notes for estimates of the high-employment budget." Since the two sets of estimates are based on differing assumptions, they differ significantly upon occasion. See Arthur M. Okun and Nancy H. Teeters, "The full employment surplus revisited," *Brookings Papers on Economic Activity*, No. 1, 1970, and Michael J. Prell, "The full employment budget—Its uses and limitations," Federal Reserve Bank of Kansas City, *Monthly Review* (April 1972).

were periods when the actual and full employment budgets differed significantly. This was again a time when, given the trend in unemployment, the full employment budget indicated that fiscal policy was more restrictive than desirable.

We concluded when discussing budget positions under a lump-sum tax that the optimality of a deficit, a budget balance, or a surplus depends upon conditions in the private sector of the economy. When there is a weakness in private demand, one way to correct this is by reductions in taxes even though a deficit may result. Which tax program is optimal, and therefore whether a surplus, a balanced budget, or a deficit results, depends upon the strength of demand in the private sectors. What we want to achieve is a full employment level of output. Under conditions of extremely weak private demand this may be achieved only with a tax rate such as t_3 in Figure 6–7, and therefore with a large deficit. On the other hand, if demand in the private sector is very strong, then a budgetary surplus may be required. But only by standardizing for output in terms of the level we wish to attain is it possible to interpret the economic impact of a particular fiscal program and its appropriateness.

INTRODUCING THE FOREIGN SECTOR

One task remains before our working model of the commodity-producing sector is complete: Foreign accounts must be added to those of households, business, and government. We have already seen how the foreign sector enters into our social accounting system, and now we will add exports and imports to the model.

Exports

Exports represent the demands of foreigners for American goods and services, and the independent variables in the demand function for them, like those in any demand function, are the buyers' real income, relative prices, and tastes and preferences. Tastes and preferences we take as given, and since we are following the convention of holding the price level stable, exports will depend primarily upon the level of real income in America's major trading partners.

Output levels abroad are matters over which American influence is very small. For example, economic conditions in Japan or West Germany depend upon the strength of effective demands in those countries together with the appropriateness of the economic policies followed by their respective governments. Accordingly, we treat exports, which we will call E_x, as an exogenous variable in the model.

Imports

Imports represent the demands of Americans for foreign-produced goods and services of all types. These demands too are determined by tastes and preferences, relative prices, and real income. Again, if we assume that only the last varies, then the level of imports is a function of real income in the United States, and we will treat imports, I_m as dependent upon income.

$$I_m = I_m(Y)$$

$$\text{or: } I_m = mY \tag{6.22}$$

where m is the marginal propensity to import.

Net Foreign Investment

The difference between exports of goods and services and imports of goods and services is defined as net foreign investment, $E_x - I_m$. Net foreign investment may be positive, zero, or negative. If it is positive, it means that American sales of goods to foreigners for payment exceed foreigners' sales to Americans. Put otherwise, income payments to Americans in the production of exports exceed the money spent by Americans on imports. Net income payments are therefore injected into the domestic economy as a result of transactions with the foreign sector. Such expenditures can be expected to have a multiplier effect just like investment or government expenditures.

An Expanded Linear Model

We are now in a position to write our expanded linear model as follows:

$$Y = C + I + G + E_x - I_m \tag{6.23}$$

$$C = a + b(Y - T + T_r)$$

$$E_x, G, \text{ and } I \text{ are given}$$

$$T = tY$$

$$T_r = g + hY$$

$$I_m = mY$$

In this expanded model I, G, and E_x are exogenous, while C, T, T_r, and I_m are all functions of Y.

By following the usual procedure of substituting the functions and givens into $Y = C + I + G + E_x - I_m$ and collecting terms so as to leave Y as the dependent variable expressed only in terms of parameters and independent variables, we arrive at the reduced form equation:

$$Y = \frac{1}{1 - b + bt - bh + m}(a + bg + I + G + E_x), \tag{6.24}$$

The reduced form expression for C is:

$$C = \frac{1 + m}{1 - b + bt - bh + m}(a + bg) + \frac{b - bt + bh}{1 - b + bt - bh + m}(I + G + E_x) \qquad (6.25)$$

It is clear that these expressions differ from those described earlier in this chapter by the appearance of m, the propensity to import, in the coefficients. And we recall that these coefficients provide the respective multipliers for the independent variables.

There is a multiplier associated with exports just as there is with government spending and investment. So long as there is some degree of unemployment in the economy, an increase in any of the exogenous variables will lead to increases in effective demand. If exports rise, for instance, there will be an income payment increase in those industries producing for export. This in turn will lead to an increase in consumption which increases income which further increases consumption, and so on. The size of the multiplier now depends upon the marginal propensities to consume, b, to pay taxes, t, to pay transfer payments, h, and to import, m.

Since m appears in the denominator of the coefficient of I, G, and E_x, the value of the coefficient falls as m increases. This means that an increase in G, say, will not have as large an effect on Y as it would in an economy isolated from world trade. Payments for imports do not enter the domestic income stream but rather create effective demand abroad. To the extent that part of an increase in expenditure is used to purchase imports, therefore, the demand for domestically produced goods does not increase. Hence the expansion in demand for domestically produced goods is less than it would be without a foreign sector.

CONCLUSION

We have now concluded for the most part our detailed discussion of the major components of aggregate demand. In Chapter 15 we will return to examine the foreign sector more closely. By this time it should be clear to the student that there are a large number of factors that influence the level of aggregate demand, output, and employment in the economy, including, as we will see, the price level and the rate of interest.

The public sector, concerned with government spending, taxes, welfare payments, and budget deficits, is the focus of political forces—many of which fall beyond the range of this book. We do not wish to minimize the importance of these forces, but rather to emphasize the kind of macroeconomic impact one can expect from the variety of packages of public action likely to occur. And as international trade grows in importance, again a mixture of political and economic forces dominates the scene. We have, however, examined here only the broadest and most fundamental effects of imports and exports on the level of economic activity.

ADDITIONAL READINGS

The role that a budget deficit or surplus can play in balancing the economy is clearly spelled out by Abba P. Lerner in "Functional finance and the federal debt," *Social Research* (February 1943), reprinted in the American Economic Association's *Readings in Fiscal Policy*, edited by A. Smithies and J. K. Butters (Homewood, Ill.: Irwin, 1955). *Readings in Fiscal Policy* also contains other papers of interest, as well as a 30-page bibliography on fiscal policy at the end. Another comprehensive theoretical treatment of fiscal policy is Part IV of R. A. Musgrave's *The Theory of Public Finance* (New York: McGraw-Hill, 1959).

A useful view of the anticipated impact of the tax cut of 1964 is presented by the Council of Economic Advisors in the *1963 Annual Report of the Council of Economic Advisors* (Washington, D.C.: U.S. Government Printing Office, 1963), pp. 45–51. For an examination of the actual impact of the tax cut, see Arthur Okun, "Measuring the impact of the 1964 tax reduction," in Walter W. Heller (Ed.), *Perspectives on Economic Growth* (New York: Random House, 1968).

William A. Salant presents a concise but thorough treatment of the balanced budget multiplier in "Taxes, income determination, and the balanced budget theorem," *Review of Economics and Statistics*, 39 (May 1957): 152–161, reprinted in the American Economic Association's *Readings in Business Cycles*, edited by R. A. Gordon and L. R. Klein (Homewood, Ill: Irwin, 1965).

The issue of built-in flexibility is treated briefly but quite thoroughly in R. A. Musgrave's *The Theory of Public Finance* (New York: McGraw-Hill, 1959), pp. 501–517. Another general but brief discussion may be found in Herbert E. Newman's *An Introduction to Public Finance* (New York: John Wiley & Sons, 1968), pp. 95–101. The following three articles also deal with the issue of built-in stabilizers and their effectiveness: P. Eilbott, "The effectiveness of automatic stabilizers," *American Economic Review*, 56 (1966): 450–465; D. J. Smyth, "Built-in flexibility of taxation and automatic stabilization," *Journal of Political Economy*, 74 (1966): 396–400, reprinted in J. Lindauer's *Macroeconomic Readings* (New York: The Free Press, 1968); D. J. Smyth, "Tax changes linked to government expenditure changes and the magnitude of fluctuations in national income," *Journal of Political Economy*, 78 (1970): 60–67.

There exist several excellent treatments of the effect that international trade may have upon the multiplier. Two of the more comprehensive treatments may be found in Fritz Machlup's *International Trade and the National Income Multiplier* (Philadelphia: Blakiston, 1943) and in James E. Meade's

The Balance of Payments (London: Oxford University Press, 1951), pp. 125–148, and *Mathematical Supplement to the Balance of Payments* (London: Oxford University Press, 1951), Section VIII, (i)–(iii).

The foreign trade multiplier is also discussed in C. P. Kindleberger's *International Economics*, 4th ed. (Homewood, Ill.: Irwin, 1968), Chapter 16 and Appendix G, and in J. Vanek's *International Trade: Theory and Economic Policy* (Homewood, Ill.: Irwin, 1962), Chapter 7.

QUESTIONS

1. Explain the government spending multiplier, the tax multiplier, and the relation between the two forming the balanced budget multiplier.

2. What is meant by an "automatic stabilizer"? Using an algebraic model, show how transfer payments and income taxes contribute to the stability of an economy. Then explain it fully in words.

3. Increasing transfer payments will generally have a less expansionary impact on the economy than an equal increase in government purchases of goods and services. Why? Under what conditions might the impact of an increase in transfer payments be equally great?

4. In early 1964, Congress passed a tax measure to reduce taxes by $11 billion, a move designed to stimulate the nation's economy. Before the bill was passed, opponents of this tax cut said they would favor the bill only if government spending were cut by an equal amount. Members of the President's Council of Economic Advisors argued that to cut *both* taxes and government spending by this amount would not only fail to stimulate the economy, but would also precipitate a depression. Using the analysis of the impact of government fiscal activities presented in this chapter, explain the position taken by members of the Council of Economic Advisors.

5. "It is a simple inescapable fact that any government—like individuals and families—cannot continue to spend more than it takes in without inviting disaster. With government, continued deficit spending inevitably leads to debasement of the currency."

   "It is also true that increasing government debt places a burden on future generations, and by causing higher interest rates and higher tax rates the existence of government debt reduces investment, income, and growth."

   Explain why you agree or disagree with the above statements.

6. For the following two models the equilibrium level of income is the same.

$Y = C + I + G$	$Y = C + I + G$
$C = 20 + 0.5Y_d$	$C = 20 + 0.5Y_d$
$Y_d = Y - T$	$Y_d = Y - T$
$T = 20$	$T = -10 + .2Y$
$I = 25$	$I = 25$
$G = 40$	$G = 40$

   (a) Find the investment multiplier in each of the models.
   (b) Why is the investment multiplier less in one than in the other?
   (c) In which model is the built-in stability greatest? Why?

7. How is the investment multiplier affected by the explicit introduction into the simple Keynesian model of an "import function"?

8. In what sense might it be said that imports act as a built-in stabilizer for the economy?

9. Given the following model:

$$Y = C + I + G + E_x - I_m$$
$$C = 15 + 0.6Y_d$$
$$Y_d = Y - T$$
$$T = 15$$
$$I = 25$$
$$G = 30$$
$$E_x = 20$$
$$I_m = 10 + 0.1Y$$

   (a) Find the equilibrium level of income.
   (b) Explain clearly in words why income will rise if it is below the equilibrium level and fall if it is above the level.
   (c) Find the government expenditure multiplier and the tax multiplier.
   (d) Explain how the multiplier works.
   (e) Explain why the multiplier for a change in taxes is smaller than that for a change in government expenditures.
   (f) If the *MPC* rises to 0.7, what will happen to the equilibrium level of income?

Equilibrium in Commodity Markets

7
Chapter

In this chapter we draw together the behavioral and institutional relations developed earlier to show how equilibrium levels of income are determined in commodity markets. These pages, then, serve as a summary of the material in the last four chapters.

A REVISED MULTIPLIER MATRIX

Let us begin by revising the multiplier matrix presented in Chapter 6. We have made taxes and transfer payments dependent upon income, and we have added a foreign sector in which the volume of imports is also determined by income. It is therefore necessary to revise the multiplier matrix (as in Table 7–1) in order to show the relationship of the target variables to those

Table 7–1.

				Policy Instrument
	Autonomous Consumption	Investment	Exports	Government Expenditure
Y	$\frac{1}{1-b+bt-bh+m}$	$\frac{1}{1-b+bt-bh+m}$	$\frac{1}{1-b+bt-bh+m}$	$\frac{1}{1-b+bt-bh+m}$
C	$\frac{1}{1-b+bt-bh+m}$	$\frac{b-bt+bh}{1-b+bt-bh+m}$	$\frac{b-bt+bh}{1-b+bt-bh+m}$	$\frac{b-bt+bh}{1-b+bt-bh+m}$

Coefficients:
behavioral: **b, the marginal propensity to consume**
m, the marginal propensity to import
legal or institutional (and therefore subject to direct alteration to attain the stabilization objectives of economic policy):
t, the marginal propensity to tax
h, the marginal propensity to make transfer payments
Policy variable:
G, government expenditure on goods and services

that are now exogenous. Table 7–1 also shows which variables or coefficients are amenable to income and consumption alteration policies.

Two policy instruments, taxes and transfer payments, are automatic stabilizers. They are expressed as coefficients, t and h, and not as variables. If they are to be used as part of a discretionary program, the coefficients themselves must be altered. If it is desired to restrict demand, for example, then t can be raised. If the opposite effect on output is desired, then t must be lowered.[1]

INCOME DETERMINATION IN COMMODITY MARKETS

We can summarize the situation in commodity markets by saying that—with a given level of investment spending, government spending, exports, and autonomous consumption as represented by the constant, a, in the consumption function—the level of income and output is determined by the size of the multiplier. Paying particular attention, for the moment, to investment spending, we saw in Chapter 5 that one acceptable formulation of investment demand is to treat it as negatively related to the cost of capital, i, and the internal rate of return, r. In equilibrium, $i = r$, so that we may now speak of the rate of interest, R. We will use this capital letter to represent both i and r in equilibrium. A given level of investment spending, I_1, implies a specified rate of interest, R_1. If we add the effects of government spending, exports, and autonomous consumption to that of I_1, then through the operation of the multiplier the level of income will be determined. We can call this level of income Y_1, and we can plot the relationship between income levels and interest rates as in Figure 7–1, where a point (Y_1, R_1) indicates that if the interest rate is R_1, then investment demand will be I_1, and, when these factors are coupled with the exogenous components of spending and the multiplier, the level of income

Figure 7–1.

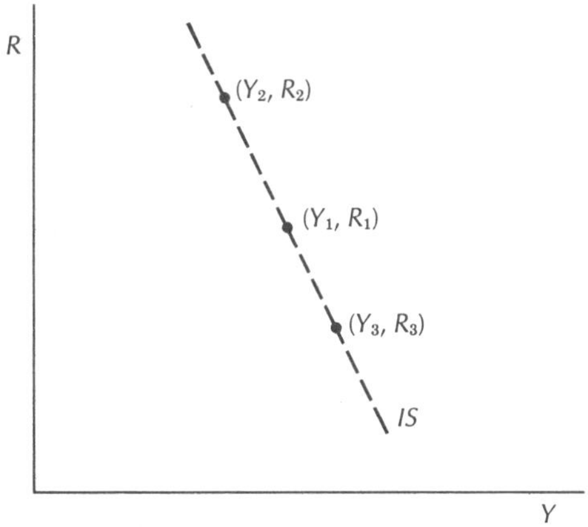

[1] Since h takes a negative sign, its absolute value can be raised or lowered to give similar effects.

will be Y_1. Given the autonomous components of spending, the investment demand function, and the marginal propensities reflected in the multiplier, only Y_1 is a sustainable level of income when investment demand is I_1. At any other level of Y there would be a discrepancy between the expenditure plans and production plans of transactor units.

If interest rates now rise to R_2, according to our analysis of investment spending, this should lead to a movement upwards and to the left *along* the investment demand function, say to I_2. I_2 will be less than I_1 since R_2 is greater than R_1. If the autonomous components of spending and the marginal propensities reflected in the multiplier remain unchanged, then Y will fall because in this instance ΔI, $I_2 - I_1$, is negative. The new position of Y, Y_2, is found in Figure 7–1. (Y_2, R_2) is above and to the left of (Y_1, R_1), and (Y_2, R_2) again represents an equilibrium level of income. Given the set of functional relationships in the model, any other Y associated with R_2 through I_2 would not be sustainable.

To take another illustration, we can let interest rates fall from R_1 to R_3. From our investment demand function, we know that this will mean a movement along the function downward and to the right, where I_3 will be greater than I_1 since R_3 is less than R_1. If, as before, the autonomous components of expenditures and the marginal propensities to consume, tax, import, and pay transfer payments remain unchanged, Y will rise, for ΔI, $I_3 - I_1$, is positive. Y will increase to Y_3 through the application of the multiplier to ΔI. (Y_3, R_3) represents a third equilibrium level of income.

GRAPHS RELATING *Y* TO *R* IN COMMODITY MARKETS

Case I

It is evident that a graph of equilibrium income levels can be constructed for commodity markets for a given investment demand schedule. At each interest rate there will be a unique level of income, as illustrated by the dashed line through the points in Figure 7–1 labeled *IS* and called the Hicksian *IS* curve.[2]

It should be borne in mind that this curve is derived from movements along a *given* investment demand function of the form $I = I(R)$. The parameters are G, E_x, autonomous consumption, and the behavioral and institutional coefficients that express the relevant marginal propensities and determine the size of the multiplier. The *position* of the *IS* curve is determined by the autonomous components of spending and the *slope* of the investment demand schedule.

[2] Sir John Hicks, of All Souls College, Oxford University, first formulated the Keynesian model in this fashion in, "Mr. Keynes and the 'classics': A suggested interpretation," *Econometrica,* 5 (1937): 147–159.

Figure 7–2.

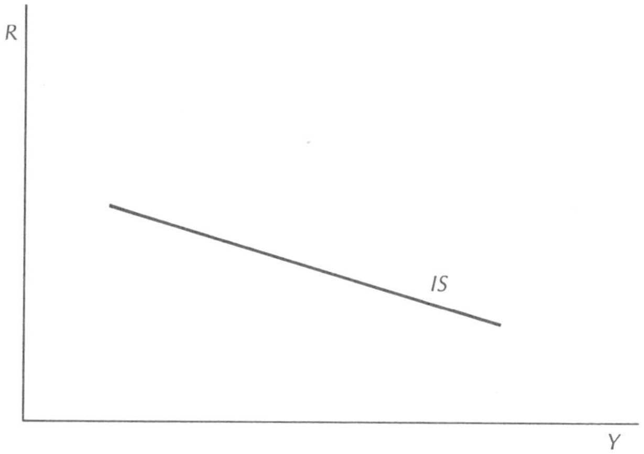

Case II

In Chapter 5 dealing with investment spending, we developed the acceleration (capital stock adjustment) principle, one version of which was consistent with comparative static analysis in that it made I dependent upon Y. This formulation is reasonable if investment spending is partly determined by the availability of funds to the enterprise.

It is now appropriate to ask what will happen to the set of income equilibria in commodity markets if we make investment dependent upon income as well as upon the rate of interest. The case is illustrated in Figure 7–2, where the position of *IS* depends upon the autonomous components of expenditure. The slope is drawn to be *less* negative (less steeply sloped) than that in Figure 7–1 because if investment is positively dependent upon income, the effect is to increase the size of the income multiplier. For every feasible R, there will be investment induced by some income. Thus if I is dependent upon R and Y and we assume for simplicity that the relationship is linear, then:

$$I = c + dR + eY$$
$$\text{where } c > 0,\ d < 0 \text{ and } e > 0$$

It is now evident that at every R there will be more investment spending than if I were dependent upon R alone, and hence the literature of macroeconomics generally applies the term "super-multiplier" to the multiplier coefficient when income is introduced as a determinant of investment along with R.

Case III

Of course, the possible nature of *IS* is not limited to that shown in Figure 7–2. In the function $I = c + dR + eY$, the coefficient e may have a value

Figure 7–3.

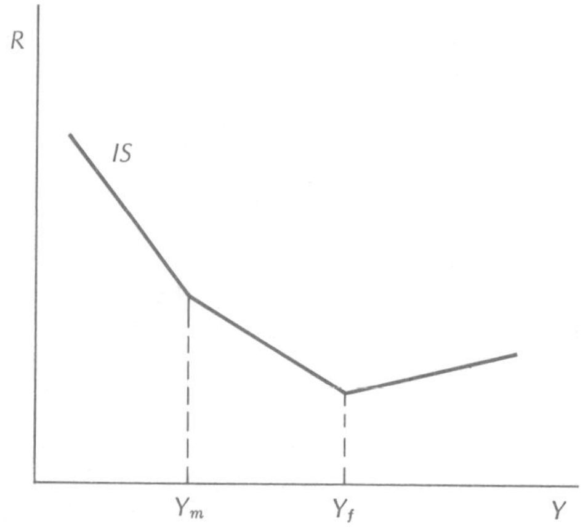

such that the *IS* function is positively sloping. If investment is quite sensitive to income levels this would be the case. We will see later in this chapter how changes in the values of other coefficients may also have the effect of rotating *IS* into a positive slope.

Alternatively, *IS* may not be a straight line. There is a good deal of economic sense in the proposition that income becomes a significant influence on investment only after some minimum level of output has been surpassed. Figure 7–3 illustrates this situation. The kink in the *IS* function at Y_m is meant to portray the level of output at which a relationship between investment and income becomes operative. For all output levels $\leq Y_m$, $\Delta I/\Delta Y = 0$; for all output levels $> Y_m$, then $\Delta I/\Delta Y > 0$. It is also kinked at Y_f, and, indeed, it even becomes positively sloped as the influence of changes in income or investment becomes sufficiently strong.

THE *IS* CURVE: A LINEAR AND NUMERICAL MODEL

The *IS* curve may be derived directly through the use of our algebraic model. The model presented below is identical to that in Chapter 6, except that investment is here taken to be a function of both the interest rate and income. In the following sections of this chapter, the position and slope of the *IS* curve will be discussed. Reference to the algebraic model may help clarify the manner in which different factors may be expected to affect the *IS* curve.

Our complete model of the commodity market may be stated as follows:

General Linear Model	*Numerical Model*	
Income:		
$Y = C + I + G + E_x - I_m$	$Y = C + I + G + E_x - I_m$	(7.1)
Consumption:		
$C = a + b\,(Y - T + T_r)$	$C = 25 + .5\,(Y - T + T_r)$	(7.2)
Investment:		
$I = c + dR + eY$	$I = 20 - 4R + .1Y$	(7.3)
Income tax:		
$T = tY$	$T = .3Y$	(7.4)
Transfer payments:		
$T_r = g + hY$	$T_r = 20 - .1Y$	(7.5)
Imports:		
$I_m = mY$	$I_m = .2Y$	(7.6)
Government spending:		
G is given	$G = 30$	(7.7)
Exports:		
E_x is given	$E_x = 15$	(7.8)

Substituting into equation (7.1):

$$Y = a + bY - btY + bg + bhY + c + dR + eY + G + E_x - mY$$

$$Y = 25 + .5Y - .15Y + 10 - .05Y + 20 - 4R + .1Y + 30 + 15 - .2Y$$

Solving for R, the *IS* curve can then be stated with R as a function of Y:

$$R = -\left[\frac{a + bg + c + G + E_x}{d}\right] + \left[\frac{1 - b + bt - bh - e + m}{d}\right] Y$$

$$R = -\left[\frac{25 + 10 + 20 + 30 + 15}{-4}\right] + \left[\frac{1 - .5 + .15 + .05 - .1 + .2}{-4}\right] Y \quad (7.9)$$

$$R = -\left[\frac{100}{-4}\right] + \left[\frac{.8}{-4}\right] Y$$

$$R = 25 - .2Y$$

The numerical example allows us to see how changes in e in the investment demand function could alter the slope of *IS* from negative to positive. If, for purposes of illustration, we let $e = .95$, then, in economic terms, this means that investment is much more sensitive to income levels. If we work out the numerical model with this new coefficient we find that the *IS* curve now has a positive slope. Of course, the slope could also be altered as a result of changes in other coefficients.

Figure 7–4.

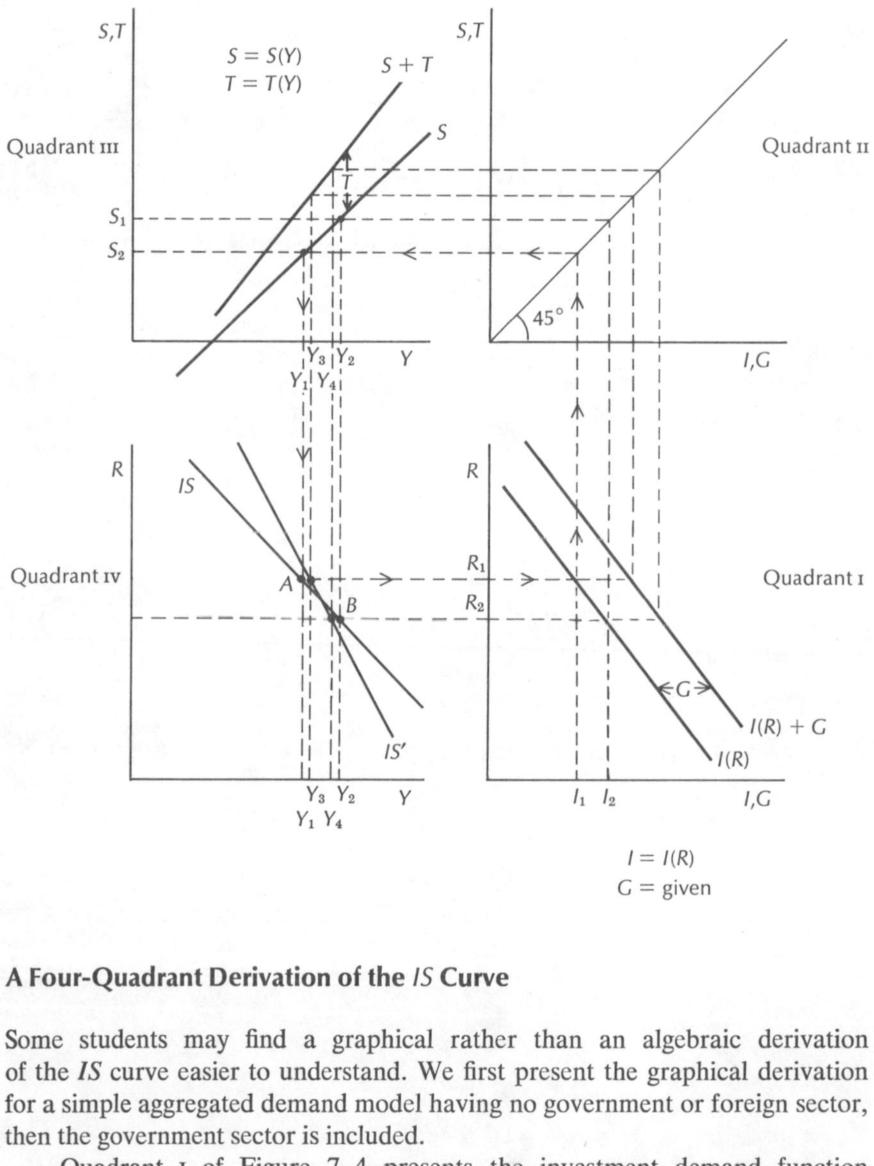

A Four-Quadrant Derivation of the *IS* Curve

Some students may find a graphical rather than an algebraic derivation of the *IS* curve easier to understand. We first present the graphical derivation for a simple aggregated demand model having no government or foreign sector, then the government sector is included.

Quadrant I of Figure 7–4 presents the investment demand function $I = I(R)$. In quadrant II is a 45-degree line depicting all points where investment equals savings and the economy is in equilibrium; it is used to connect quadrants I and III. Quadrant III depicts the savings function where savings is determined by the level of income, $S = S(Y)$. By working with these three quadrants we can in quadrant IV depict levels of income, Y, and interest, R, at which investment will equal savings. For the functions drawn here, for each interest rate level there is one level of income at which savings will equal investment. The set of points in quadrant IV that represents the interest rate and income level combinations at which investment is equal to savings forms the *IS* curve.

For example, if we assume the interest rate to be R_1 where investment is I_1, then investment, I_1, equals savings only when income equals Y_1 and savings equals S_1 in quadrant III. Therefore, if the interest rate is R_1, only at Y_1 will the economy be in equilibrium. Hence point A in quadrant IV represents one point where $I = S$ and the economy is in equilibrium. Similarly, if the interest rate is R_2, investment equals I_2 and only at Y_2 in quadrant III, where savings is equal to S_2, will the economy be in equilibrium. Point B also represents an interest rate and level of income combination at which the economy is in equilibrium. Other points along the *IS* curve can be derived in a similar manner.

Now if taxes and government spending are brought into the graphical model, with G given and $T = T(Y)$, the function in quadrant I shifts to the right by G to $I(R) + G$. An increase in government spending has the same type of effect on the economy as an increase in the investment demand function. In quadrant III a rise in taxes has an effect similar to a rise in savings. S shifts up to $S + T$, and $S + T$ is steeper than S since T increases with income. The equilibrium condition will be met when $S + T = I + G$. Now if the interest rate is at R_1, investment plus government spending equals $I_1 + G$. Working through quadrant II, we see that $S + T$ in quadrant III will equal $I_1 + G$ only if income equals Y_3. Hence (R_1, Y_3) is one point on the new *IS* curve. Similarly, if the rate of interest is R_2, the level of savings plus taxes connected through quadrant II equals $I_2 + G$ only if income is at Y_4. Other points along *IS′* represent similar combinations when the model includes taxes and government spending.

Remembering that imports have effects similar to taxes and saving, and that exports have effects similar to investment and government spending, the student may also incorporate the foreign sector into the graphical derivation.

Changes in the Position and Slope of the *IS* Curve

It is now time to ask what factors will bring about a shift in the *IS* curve's position and what factors will change its slope.

Positional Changes

Any of the following will bring about a shift in the curve's position:

(1) a change in investment demand reflecting technological change or altered business expectations;
(2) an exogenous change in G;
(3) an exogenous change in E_x;
(4) a shift in the consumption function, meaning a shift in the autonomous component of consumption, a;
(5) a shift in the transfer payments function, meaning a shift in the autonomous component of transfer payments, g.

A shift in the investment demand curve upwards and to the right means that more investment spending will be undertaken at each rate of interest. For every R there will be a higher level of real income and the *IS* curve will move right. Similarly if ΔG, ΔE_x, or the autonomous change in consumption or transfer payments is positive, then the *IS* schedule will move up and/or to the right.

Seen in terms of discretionary fiscal policy, a change in G will alter the position of the entire *IS* curve to bring about a socially acceptable rate of resource utilization. A positive ΔG will stimulate the economy; a negative ΔG will restrain inflationary pressures.

Shifts in the *IS* curve are illustrated in Figure 7–5, where the original curve is *IS*. The reasons for a rightward shift to *IS′* have been detailed. Should the schedule shift in the opposite direction to *IS″* it would reflect the presence of some combination of the following:

(1) a downward shift in the investment demand schedule, $I(R)$;
(2) a negative ΔG;
(3) a negative ΔE_x;
(4) a downward shift in $C(Y)$, i.e., a decrease in a;
(5) a downward shift in the transfer payments schedule, $T_r = g + hY$, i.e., a decrease in g.

The horizontal distance between *IS* and *IS″*, ΔY, at each rate of interest, R, reflects the fall in Y resulting from any of these changes, together with the multiplier effect on income of such changes.

Slope Changes

The slope of the curve is determined by the coefficients b, d, e, h, m, and t. Therefore any change in the value of these coefficients will make the slope either more or less negative, i.e., it will rotate *IS* in a clockwise or a counter-

Figure 7–5.

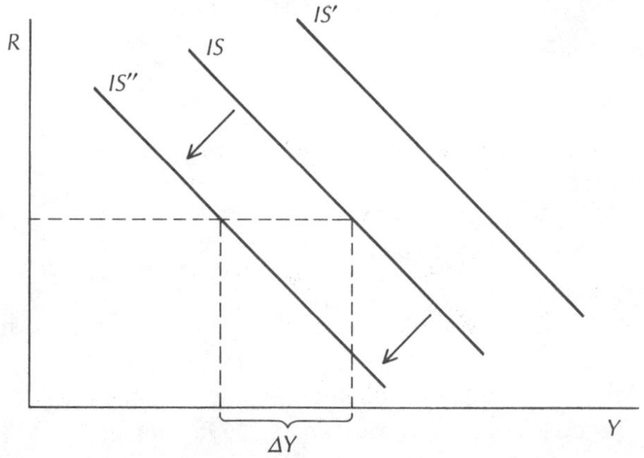

Figure 7–6.

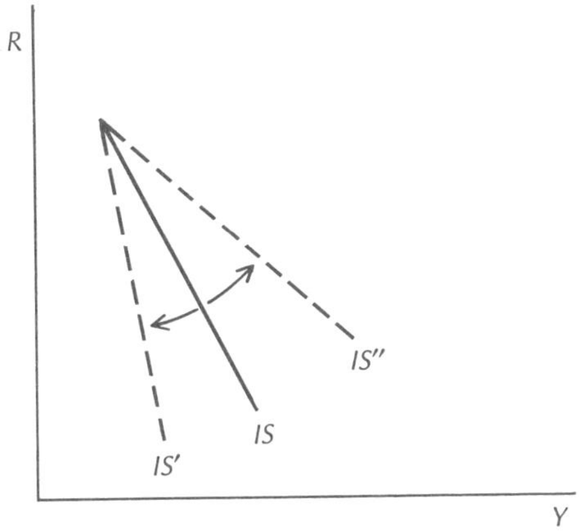

clockwise direction, as illustrated in Figure 7–6.[3] If *IS* represents the original set of commodity equilibria, those coefficient changes listed in the first column of Table 7–2 would serve to rotate *IS* toward *IS′*. The effect of each of these is to *decrease* the size of the income and consumption multipliers. The second column lists the factors that would alter the slope of *IS* in a counterclockwise direction.[4] The effect of these is to *increase* the size of the income and consumption multipliers.

Table 7–2.

Coefficient Changes Rotating IS Clockwise: Decreasing Multiplier	Coefficient Changes Rotating IS Counterclockwise: Increasing Multiplier
1. decrease in b	1. increase in b
2. increase in t	2. decrease in t
3. increase in m	3. decrease in m
4. decrease in h (h becomes more negative)	4. increase in h (h becomes less negative)
5. decrease in e	5. increase in e
6. decrease in d (d becomes more negative)	6. increase in d (d becomes less negative)

It is well to emphasize the policy implications of such a listing: When tax rates are lowered, the effect is to raise the equilibrium level of income associated with each rate of interest and level of investment spending. A decrease in tax rates moves output to a higher level. The transfer payment coefficient, *h*, may also be altered to bring about the desired direction of change in output and employment.

[3] The fixed point around which the curve rotates will depend on the values of the coefficients and on G and E_x.
[4] It is interesting to note that the multiplier will be indeterminate when $1 - b + bt - bh - e + m = 0$, and the *IS* curve will be horizontal.

It is desirable to stress again some matters concerning the use of taxation as an instrument for stabilization policy. Originally we were dealing with a lump-sum tax. Now our model contains an income tax, and rate changes may be used to achieve stabilization goals, but the previous arguments are still applicable. If the rate of taxation is increased to damp excess demand, it must be remembered that the private sector is being depressed and taxpayers are being asked to accept a fall in take-home pay in the full knowledge that neither the quantity nor the quality of public services is being improved. Taxpayers are required to surrender control over the purchase of goods and services in exchange for the indirect benefits of a more stable price level at full employment. On the other hand, as was true in the case of a lump-sum tax, a reduction in tax rates is much more easily accepted. When tax rates are lowered, more purchasing power is made available to households without any equivalent reduction in public services.

CONCLUSION

We have developed the behavior of transactor units in commodity markets to show the forces that determine capital expenditures by businessmen and influence households in allocating their income between current and future consumption. We have evaluated government expenditures and revenues singly and jointly as instruments of economic policy. And we have incorporated the influences on exports and imports into our model. The model itself has illustrated the fact that an economic system is one in which a large number of economic variables are simultaneously determined, and it has enabled us to state the conditions for equilibrium levels of income in the commodity markets.

Yet a difficulty remains and to its removal we must turn next. Unless a rate of interest is specified it is impossible to establish a unique level of income, output, and employment. So far we have resided in a moneyless world, or at least in one in which little or nothing has been said about the supply of money. It is time now to examine the monetary side of economic life and incorporate it into our model. In so doing we shall find that the rate of interest is determined simultaneously with income and the dependent variables in the system.

ADDITIONAL READINGS

Since this chapter serves to draw together the components of the model developed in earlier chapters, no special set of references is appropriate here. However, many other macroeconomics and money and banking texts contain both algebraic and graphical derivations of the *IS* curve. The interested student should find it rewarding to turn to one of these to see how other authors handle this topic.

QUESTIONS

1. What causes the *IS* curve to be downward sloping such that the equilibrium level of income in the commodity market is negatively related to

the rate of interest? In what situation would the *IS* curve be positively sloped?

2. The commodity market may be represented by the following model:

$$C = 20 + 0.5\,(Y - T + T_r)$$
$$I = 10 - 2R + 0.1Y$$
$$T = 0.2Y$$
$$T_r = 10 - 0.1Y$$
$$I_m = 0.1Y$$
$$G = 30$$
$$E_x = 15$$

Find the equation that represents the *IS* curve.
What changes in the above model will affect the slope of the *IS* curve?
Solve for all variables when $R = 4$.

3. What effect will the following have upon the *IS* curve?

(a) an upward shift in the investment schedule due to a technological change;
(b) a fall in exports;
(c) a fall in the marginal propensity to save;
(d) an increase in the marginal propensity to import;
(e) an increase in government expenditures on goods and services;
(f) an increase in the tax rate (t).

Identify whether the effect is to cause a shift in the position or the slope of the curve. Identify the nature of the shift. Identify those changes which affect the size of the multiplier.

4. (a) If the economy is at a level of income and a rate of interest to the right of the *IS* curve, what forces will move the economy to some point on the *IS* curve?
(b) If the economy is at a level of income and a rate of interest to the left of the *IS* curve, what forces will move the economy to some point on the *IS* curve?

Money in a Portfolio of Assets

8

Chapter

It is now time to complicate our simple model by introducing money and other financial assets. In Chapter 1 the role of financial assets in bringing real savings and real investment together was explained, and in Chapter 2 the problems of defining and measuring the money supply were detailed. Using currency plus demand deposits as our definition of money, we will now try to explain the demands for money on the part of individual decision-making units. To do this, we will try to show how the money supply of an economy is used, whether demands for money are related to the volume of output, and what connection there is between demands for money and demands for other types of assets, including both tangible and financial assets. We will thus emphasize the interdependence between the commodity-producing sector and the monetary sector and tie the concept of money into a general model of asset choice. Not until Chapters 9 and 10, however, will we bring together our analyses of money demand and supply and connect the monetary sector with our income-expenditure model.

THE BALANCE SHEETS OF DECISION-MAKING UNITS

To evaluate the impact of the monetary sector on changes in levels of output, it is first necessary to return to basic decision-making units, particularly to business firms and households. We cannot, however, use for this purpose the measures of income-expenditure flows developed in Chapter 1. Because we wish to examine money as an asset now, it is the balance sheet, or wealth position, that concerns us.

In contrast with the set of social accounts developed earlier to summarize income and payment *flows* over some time period, the balance sheet position of any decision-making unit represents his *stock* position at a specified point in time. This stock position is expressed in the accounting identity:

$$\text{Assets} = \text{Liabilities} + \text{Net worth (equity)}$$

Until now, we have considered money explicitly only as a unit of account whose purchasing power was unchanged up to the point of full employment. Business firms accumulated capital goods through real investment. Households also purchased capital goods in the form of durables and housing. Implicitly the asset holdings of both sets of decision-making units consisted of tangibles: plant, equipment, and inventories for the business firm; durables and housing for the household. Whatever change took place in the volume or value of these assets was assumed to have negligible influence on any of the macroeconomic flow variables.

Sectoral Balance Sheets

However, the real world is a deal more complicated in the range of alternative asset holdings open to these units and changes in these holdings may have significant effects. This is evident in the sectoral balance sheets reproduced in Table 8–1 for non-farm households and non-financial corporations. Estimated for the year 1956 by Goldsmith and Lipsey, these tables show assets as both "tangible" and "financial." Money in the form of currency and demand deposits is one of the entries under the "financial" category. There is, however, no formal inclusion of "human capital" as an asset in the household sector. The latter could be expressed as the sum of capitalized earnings over the working life of individual householders. Such assets represent the most important components of most household balance sheets.

Some Characteristics of Tangible and Financial Assets

If we take an orthodox point of view, thereby excluding human capital from the balance sheet of the household sector, we need pay attention only to tangible and financial assets. It is evident from Table 8–1 that the latter includes not only money, but also near-monies and securities which yield a stream of money income in the form of interest and dividend payments. To note the differing characteristics of tangible assets is to emphasize the alternatives open to transactor units and the choices they must make in terms of their preferences for asset holdings. The distinctions between tangible and financial assets may be summarized as follows:

Requirements for cooperating factors of production. Typically, tangible assets such as machinery and buildings must be combined with other factors of production in order to yield a return; financial assets require little, if anything, in the way of cooperating factors (a bondholder, for example, may need only a pair of scissors to clip his bond coupons).

Form of the return from assets. Typically, tangible assets produce a return in the form of specific commodities that must be priced and marketed for transformation into generalized purchasing power. An exception is where durable household goods yield a stream of services directly consumed by the

Table 8–1. Sectoral Balance Sheets (in billions of dollars).

Non-Farm Households, 1958			
Tangible Assets		Liabilities	
—Structures	373.0	—Consumer debt	44.8
—Land	92.2	—Other loans	14.6
—Durables	166.8	—Mortgages	117.0
Total	632.0	Total	176.4
Financial Assets		Net Worth	1425.5
—Currency and demand deposits	61.4		
—Claims against financial institutions	333.7		
—Bonds, notes, and other loans	97.7		
—Mortgages	27.2		
—Stocks and equity	449.9		
Total	969.9		
TOTAL ASSETS	1601.9	TOTAL LIABILITIES AND NET WORTH	1601.9
Non-Financial Corporations, 1958			
Tangible Assets		Liabilities	
—Structures	202.1	—Trade debt	68.8
—Land	63.5	—Loans	28.1
—Durables	145.5	—Bonds and notes	69.7
—Inventory	78.8	—Mortgages	29.7
Total	489.9	—Other liabilities	60.8
		Total	257.1
Financial Assets		Net Worth	508.4
—Currency and demand deposits	33.3		
—Claims against financial institutions	1.6		
—Bonds, notes, and other credits	113.5		
—Stocks and equity	127.2		
Total	275.6		
TOTAL ASSETS	1601.9	TOTAL LIABILITIES AND NET WORTH	1601.9

Source: Adapted from R. W. Goldsmith, R. E. Lipsey, and M. Mendelson, *Studies in the National Balance Sheet of the United States*, Vol. 2 (Princeton N.J.: National Bureau of Economic Research, Princeton University Press, 1963), pp. 68–69.

household (e.g., the transport services of the household car). In contrast, financial assets directly yield a stream of money income instead of a stream of specified goods and services.

Storage and carrying costs. Tangible assets entail storage and carrying costs. For financial assets these costs are negligible.

Creation and destruction. Tangible assets are created through real capital formation. Their life expectancy must be realized if their full yield is to be secured. Financial assets can be created instantaneously through an act of borrowing and can be destroyed instantaneously through an act of repayment or expenditure.

Liquidity. Financial assets as a general class possess a higher degree of marketability and capital certainty than do tangible assets. This follows from the first four characteristics stated above.

Returns from an Asset

An important question is how an individual comes to prefer one package of asset holdings to another, for each individual presumably has some optimum asset portfolio. In order to derive a normative rule for asset holdings, it is necessary first to define the nature of returns from assets.

The total return, TR, from an asset consists of (a) an explicit return in the form of money payments, MR, from which carrying charges and other costs, CC, must be subtracted to yield a net monetary return, NR, and (b) an implicit return provided by the asset's "liquidity," LL. Thus $TR = MR - CC + LL$, or $TR = NR + LL$.

Carrying or storage charges are of special significance for tangible assets, but for financial assets, CC is relatively unimportant. An investor's choice between the two types will thus be affected by the size of CC. Special interest attaches to LL, for it expresses a yield for liquidity which will be greatest for the subset of financial assets designated as money. The convenience yield of money derives from its general acceptability, i.e., from its medium-of-exchange function; the capital certainty yield of money arises from the fact that the only risk associated with holding it is that of inflation (rises in the general price level). Apart from such changes affecting purchasing power, there is no uncertainty that a dollar can be exchanged for its equivalent six months or a year from now.

If we designate the set of assets eligible for ownership as money, bonds, stocks, and tangibles and order these assets in terms of their characteristics, we find the sequence in Table 8–2. Explicit monetary yield generally increases as we move down the scale from money toward tangible assets. In achieving greater money returns, however, the asset holder trades off liquidity. If the decision-making unit holds only money, explicit returns would be zero (assuming no interest is paid on demand deposits), but yield, in the form of general acceptability and capital certainty, LL, would be at a maximum.

Table 8–2.

Asset Form	MR – CC	LL
(a) money	0	+
(b) bonds	│	↑
(c) stocks	↓	│
(d) tangibles	+	0

Asset Character: Expected Return and Risk

Since returns from asset ownership consist of both an explicit monetary yield and an implicit yield reflecting convenience and capital certainty, any asset may be evaluated by the individual in terms of its expected net return and the likelihood of that expected return. This implies a probability distribution of returns for each asset. The most probable, or expected, return is the mean of this probability distribution (indicated by the dotted lines in Figure 8–1). Likelihood is an indicator of the risk or uncertainty of return. This can be defined in terms of the variance of the distribution of expected returns.

In general, there is a positive relation between expected monetary returns and risk. We have seen that for money the expected return (apart from price level changes and negligible storage charges) is zero, and that the uncertainty of that return approaches zero. The monetary return of a government bond with ten years to maturity, on the other hand, will be positive, but there will be some uncertainty about the market value of the bond, and therefore about its effective yield six months from now. Any asset will have its own probability distribution of possible net monetary returns. The greater the variance of this distribution, the greater the risk and the smaller the degree of capital certainty in holding the asset; a government bond will have less uncertainty associated with it than a share of common stock in a titanium mine. The expected return on the mine's stock may be relatively great compared to that on government bonds, but the variance of the distribution will be large.

The marked contrasts between money, government bonds, and common stock in a titanium mine are illustrated in the three panels of Figure 8–1. In panel (a) the expected return from money is zero, but there is complete capital certainty since the probability of this return is 1.0. In panel (b) there is for government bonds a distribution of possible returns with the expected or mean return being 5 percent. In holding government bonds rather than money, it is apparent that the decision-making unit is trading off a reduction in capital certainty for an increase in expected monetary yield. Panel (c), however, shows that the asset holder can obtain a much higher expected return (10 percent), but only by trading this off against a further reduction in capital certainty. These examples are all drawn from the general set of financial assets, but tangible assets can also be ordered in terms of their expected returns and the probability of realizing them.[1]

Decision Rule of Asset Holders

To answer the question of how decision-making units select an optimum combination of assets, we can regard each decision-making unit as having a

[1] Courses in portfolio management devote considerable time to developing the concepts of risk and expected return. It would be inappropriate in a macroeconomics text to pursue this material in depth. Our purpose here is merely to draw out the important implications for macroeconomic theory and policy that stem from the theory of asset choice.

Figure 8–1.

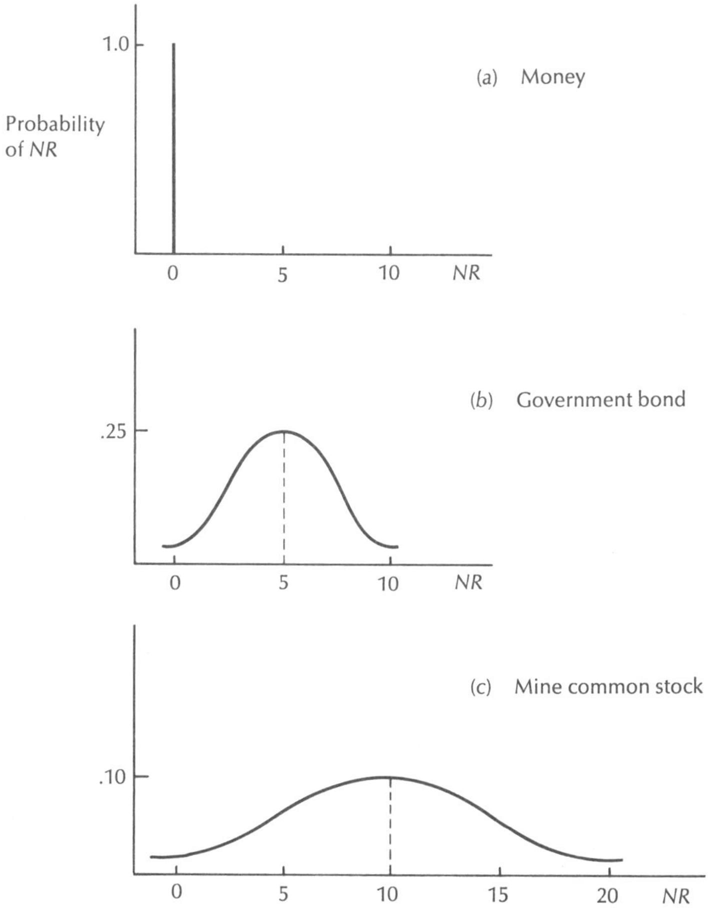

wealth preference function expressing his tastes and preferences for assets. The parameters of the function will be the set of social "norms" that exist in the society and the size of each unit's wealth holdings. The problem of asset choice is then one of maximizing this function subject to a wealth constraint.

Critical to the form of the preference function will be the decision-making unit's attitude toward risk. By this is meant the terms under which he is willing to accept increases in expected returns with increases in risk. We designate as *risk averters* those who receive diminishing marginal utility from increases in expected returns when those increases are accompanied by a reduction in the likelihood that they will be forthcoming. The risk averter does not feel that equiprobable large gains and large losses balance each other; the disutility of a large loss outweighs the utility of a large gain. As risk increases, it is necessary that he attain ever larger increments in expected returns if he is to remain indifferent to a choice between packages of assets.

Figure 8–2.

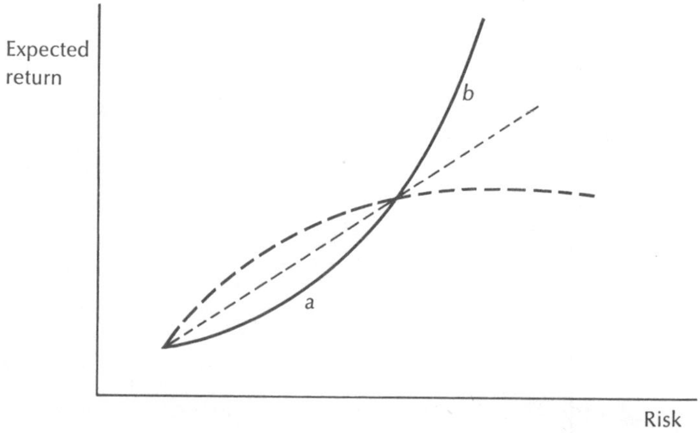

The type of preference function characteristic of the risk averter is illustratcd in Figure 8–2 (solid curve), where expected returns are plotted against risk. For this individual the curve represents all the points where return and risk are felt to be equal. His return is higher at point *b* than at point *a,* but so is risk, and as risk gets larger the change in expected rcturn necessary to compensate for a given change in risk becomes greater. Points to the left of the curve are preferred to points to the right. Except for those who enjoy the thrill of gambling, most decision-making units are risk averters, rather than *risk neutrals* (dotted line) or *risk lovers* (dashed curve). For the risk neutral, there is a constant marginal utility derived from added returns, while the risk lover enjoys increasing marginal utility of return.

A decision rule for choices among money, bonds, stocks, and tangibles can now be derived. It is clear that there will be a demand for money as an asset so long as decision-making units possess some degree of risk aversion and therefore attach utility to the capital certainty yield of money. At the same time, however, the returns they wish may be balanced with risk only by investing in some combination of assets. Accordingly, a wealth utility function may be written as:

$$U_W = U \text{ (money, bonds, stocks, tangibles)}$$

The constraint within which the choice must be made will be the sum of the value of the designated assets. This constraint may be written as follows:

$$W = P_M M + P_B B + P_S S + P_T T \qquad (8.1)$$

where W is the total wealth of the decision-making unit;

P_M is the "price" of a dollar, here equal to one;
P_B is the price of a bond;
P_S is the price of a stock;
P_T is the price of a unit of tangible asset;
M, B, S, and T are the quantities of money, bonds, stocks, and tangibles in the asset portfolio.

If a decision-making unit is to maximize the utility (where utility may be represented by TR, which allows for money return in NR and risk in LL) gained from his wealth holdings, he will distribute his wealth among the various assets in such a way that the last dollar devoted to each type of asset yields an equal amount of utility. This is the investor's decision rule. In the case where the marginal dollar invested in bonds yields more utility than the marginal dollar invested in stocks, the decision-making unit could increase the utility gained from his wealth holdings by shifting a dollar from stocks to bonds until the last dollar in each of the two asset forms yields equal utility. Therefore, the utility maximizing decision rule may be expressed as an equation:[2]

$$U_M/P_M = U_B/P_B = U_S/P_S = U_T/P_T \tag{8.2}$$

where U_M is the marginal utility of the last dollar held, $\Delta U/\Delta M$;
U_B is the marginal utility of the last bond held, $\Delta U/\Delta B$;
U_S is the marginal utility of the last stock held, $\Delta U/\Delta S$;
U_T is the marginal utility of the last unit of tangible asset held, $\Delta U/\Delta T$.

This says that a decision-making unit will tend to equate utilities at the margin from investments in each asset class. Because utility is equated with total returns, including both explicit and implicit returns, when we divide by the prices per unit of the relevant assets, then we have an expression for the return per dollar invested in each asset.

CONCLUSION

We have emphasized the differences in character between financial and tangible assets, and we have pointed out that each decision-making unit chooses among

[2] To derive a decision rule for asset holders we can now maximize U_W subject to the budget constraint. To do so we may use a Lagrange multiplier and form the Lagrangian function:

$$(1)\quad L(M,B,S,T,\gamma) = U(M,B,S,T) + \gamma[W - P_M M - P_B B - P_S S - P_T T]$$

where γ is the Lagrangian factor of proportionality. Then the first order conditions for constrained return maximization will be obtained by setting the first partial derivatives equal to zero:

$$(2)\quad \frac{\partial L}{\partial M} = \frac{\partial U}{\partial M} - \gamma P_M = 0$$

$$(3)\quad \frac{\partial L}{\partial B} = \frac{\partial U}{\partial B} - \gamma P_B = 0$$

$$(4)\quad \frac{\partial L}{\partial S} = \frac{\partial U}{\partial S} - \gamma P_S = 0$$

$$(5)\quad \frac{\partial L}{\partial T} = \frac{\partial U}{\partial T} - \gamma P_T = 0$$

$$(6)\quad \frac{\partial L}{\partial \gamma} = W - P_M M - P_B B - P_S S - P_T T$$

By combining equations (2)–(5) we obtain the decision rule:

$$\frac{\dfrac{\partial U}{\partial M}}{P_M} = \frac{\dfrac{\partial U}{\partial B}}{P_B} = \frac{\dfrac{\partial U}{\partial S}}{P_S} = \frac{\dfrac{\partial U}{\partial T}}{P_T} = \gamma$$

Maximum utility is thus obtained when returns at the margin are equal for the last dollar invested in each asset class.

the various types of assets according to a particular model. This model requires a wealth preference function in which the parameters are the attitude toward risk of the decision-making unit and the set of social norms that exist in the society. The optimum asset portfolio for each decision-making unit will then be the one in which he equates the rate of return at the margin of alternative asset holdings. We have also seen that returns from assets include explicit monetary yield, capital gains or losses, and implicit yields in the form of utility derived from convenience and capital certainty.

ADDITIONAL READINGS

Two excellent articles dealing with the demand for money as an asset are James Tobin's "Liquidity preference as behaviour towards risk," *Review of Economic Studies,* 25 (February 1958): 65–86, reprinted in *Readings in Macroeconomics,* M. G. Mueller (Ed.) (New York: Holt, Rinehart and Winston, 1966); and James S. Duesenberry's "The portfolio approach to the demand for money and other assets," *Review of Economics and Statistics,* 45 (February 1963): 1–31. A third relevant article is James Tobin's "An essay on principles of debt management," *Fiscal and Debt Management Policies,* Commission on Money and Credit (Englewood Cliffs, N.J.: Prentice-Hall, 1963).

QUESTIONS

1. What does it mean to say that one asset possesses less "liquidity" than another?
2. (a) How do you determine the yield of an asset? A tangible asset? A financial asset?
   (b) In what way is uncertainty incorporated into expected yield?
   (c) Must the yields of all assets be in explicit monetary form? Can you think of other forms in which a yield occurs?
3. Clearly distinguish between money and other assets, both tangible and financial.
4. Explain the following terms:
   (a) liquidity;
   (b) liquid asset;
   (c) capital certainty;
   (d) yield;
   (e) portfolio adjustment.
5. Distinguish between risk averters, risk lovers, and risk neutrals. Which do you think you are? What is the decision rule which all three follow when deciding upon the composition of the bundle of assets (portfolio) which they wish to hold?

6. Suppose assets may be held in the forms of money, bonds, equity shares, and tangibles. According to the decision rule reflecting rational behavior of asset holders, explain which of the following statements are true, and why.

   (a) Individuals will derive different utilities from assets because of differing attitudes to risk.
   (b) The same utility from assets would be derived by all individuals.
   (c) The change in utility would be measured by explicit money income alone.
   (d) The change in utility would include nonmonetary satisfactions as well as money income.
   (e) The maximization of utility from wealth is a general statement of rational behavior under uncertainty.
   (f) Maximization of expected utility rather than maximization of expected returns is preferred because asset holders are not indifferent to equiprobable large gains and losses.
   (g) The form of the function will have as parameters the set of social "norms" that exist in the society.

The Demand for Money

9
Chapter

The money-demand discussion developed in Chapter 8 places us in a position to develop a simple model of the monetary sector that will contain both money-supply and money-demand functions. The demand function comprises two parts, one a demand of the public for a medium of exchange and one a demand for liquidity. The first is sometimes called a *transactions* demand; the second, a *speculative* demand, an *asset* demand, or a demand for *capital certainty*.

THE DEMAND FOR A MEDIUM OF EXCHANGE

The demand for a medium of exchange is positively related to the output level of the economy and the price per unit of output (the price level). Continuing the convention of assuming the price level is constant up to the point of full employment, we can say that more money will be demanded for medium of exchange purposes as the volume of output increases. We may thus write an aggregate transactions demand for money, M_Y, as:

$$M_Y = M_Y(Y) \text{ and } \frac{\Delta M_Y}{\Delta Y} > 0 \tag{9.1}$$

The factors that determine the position and shape of the transactions demand function consist of both the customs or legal conventions regarding the typical pay and expenditure periods and the state of financial technology —the use of checks and credit cards, billing practices and the like—in the economy.

The nature of this function and its parameters may be illustrated by the medium of exchange demand of a hypothetical household. This is indicated in Figure 9–1, where money balances held for transactions are plotted against time. The time t represents the typical pay period over which income, Y, here equal to the sum $A - a$, is spent. On payday the medium of exchange balances held by the household will be $A - a$. The amount a is taken to represent a minimum balance held by the household to meet unforeseen contingencies.

Figure 9–1.

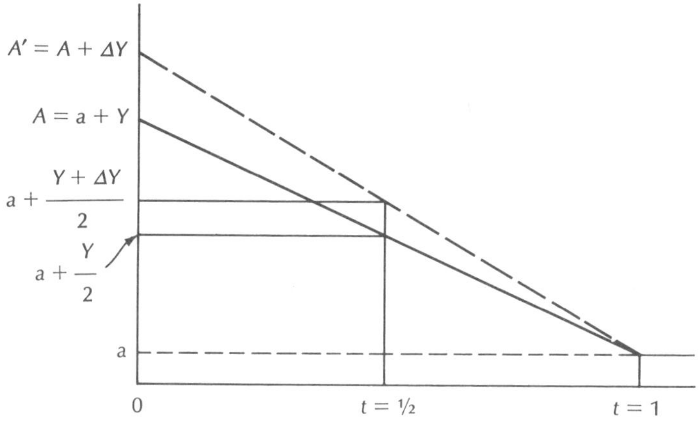

This may be termed a precautionary holding.[1] If expenditures are evenly distributed over the period t, the average balance held for medium of exchange purposes will be $Y/2$. Money balances decline over time as we move down the solid line. For the first half of the period, the household's money balance will exceed $a + Y/2$, and for the latter half it will be less than $a + Y/2$. If Y increases by ΔY, as might happen if output in the economy were to rise, with a consequent increase in the hours worked per week and hence in the paycheck of our representative household, the average balance over t will become $a + (Y + \Delta Y)/2$). Money balances will decline as we move along the dashed line.

The medium of exchange demand for money may also be illustrated for a representative business unit in the economy, as in Figure 9–2, where sales

Figure 9–2.

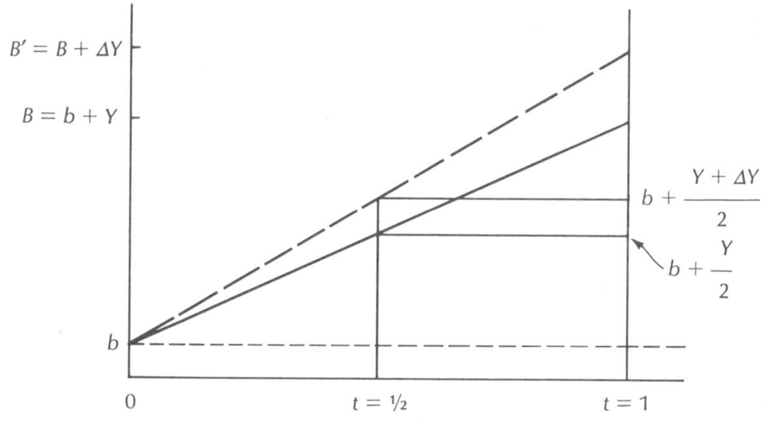

[1] Since precautionary holdings are believed to be small in amount and relatively insensitive to other important macroeconomic variables (such as the interest rate and income), we make the simplifying assumption that they are both small and fixed over time.

revenues, assumed to be received evenly over the period t, equal $B - b$, where b is the level of precautionary balances. Payments are made to the factors of production in a lump sum at the end of the period t. Money balances will rise along the solid line. In this case, the average balances held by the firm equal $b + Y/2$. If receipts rise by ΔY or B' as a result of increases in the output of the economy shared in by the producer unit, the dashed line indicates that average balances over t will increase to $b + (Y + \Delta Y)/2$.

To obtain our aggregate transactions money-demand function, we sum across all producing and consuming units and derive the specified medium of exchange money-demand function.

The student will observe that, under the conditions indicated in Figures 9–1 and 9–2, economic units hold balances in excess of their medium of exchange needs. Only on payday at the end of the expenditure (or receipt) period do holdings and needs coincide. If this is so, could not the decision-making unit get an equivalent convenience yield by holding smaller average balances, with the excess over requirement held in relatively liquid, income-yielding financial assets? The larger the explicit monetary yield, the greater the opportunity cost of holding unused transaction balances and the more likely it will be that decision-making units will conserve on these balances. Accordingly, we may add to pay and expenditure periods and financial technology, a third factor, interest rates (R), as another variable explaining the transactions demand for money. Then:

$$M_Y = M_Y(Y,R) \text{ and } \frac{\Delta M_Y}{\Delta Y} > 0, \frac{\Delta M_Y}{\Delta R} < 0 \tag{9.2}$$

Figure 9–3 shows the process by which transactions balances can be conserved by investing one half of income upon its receipt in government securities. Under these conditions there will be two transactions during the period t: an initial purchase and a conversion of securities to money at $t = ½$. In

Figure 9–3.

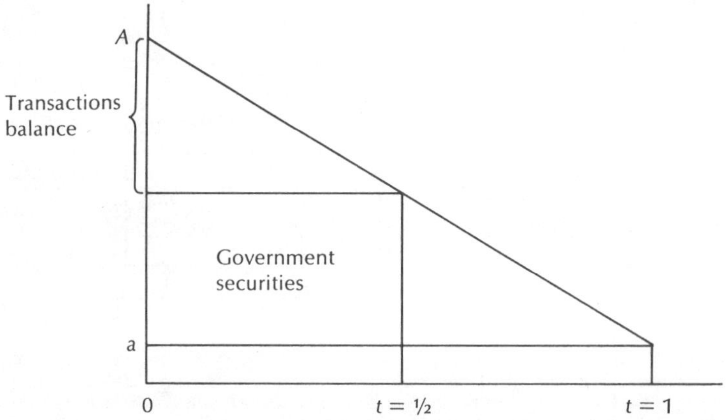

general, the proportion of income held by the economic unit in alternatives to money at $t = 0$ will determine the number of transactions in which he engages over t. Thus, if $(5/6)Y$ is invested initially, there will be one purchase and five sales during the period t. If his income were \$120 he would purchase \$100 of bonds at the outset and sell them off in \$20 amounts at five points in time so he will have \$20 to spend during each of the six periods. The transactor will then be holding at most $(1/6)Y$ in cash balances, \$20, and his average balance will be $(1/2)(1/6)Y = (1/12)Y = \$10$, plus his precautionary balance.

More generally, the transactor's optimum cash balance will be determined by maximization of the expression:

$$NR = GR - cn \tag{9.3}$$

where NR is the net interest revenue from income-yielding assets, GR is the gross interest revenue from these assets, c is the cost of transacting in these assets, and n is the number of transactions.

A more rigorous analysis allows us to determine the optimal number of purchases and sales of interest-earning assets that should be made. Taking R as the interest rate on assets and c as the cost of each transaction (we assume that c is fixed and does not depend on the size of the transaction), so that NR depends upon the number of transactions, then if one purchase is made and if 1/3 of the purchase is resold at the end of each of the first three quarters of the period, GR will be $(1/4)(3/4)RY + (1/4)(2/4)RY + (1/4)(1/4)RY$, or $(n - 1)\ RY/2n$. NR is thus $(n - 1)\ RY/2n - cn$, and the optimum number of transactions will exist when $\Delta NR/\Delta n = 0$, or when the net marginal revenue gained from an additional transaction is zero. It can be shown that this condition obtains when $n = \sqrt{RY/2c}$.[2] This indicates that the optimum number of transactions will increase with a rise in Y or R. The greater the number of transactions, the closer will be cash holdings to the medium of exchange needs, and the lower will be the amount of money held at any time for this purpose. Hence the medium of exchange demand for money will vary inversely with the interest rate.[3]

The function $M_Y = M_Y(Y,R)$ can be described by first assuming that R is fixed and observing the relation between M_Y and Y, and then assuming that Y is fixed and observing the relation between M_Y and R. If we were to plot M_Y on the horizontal axis of a graph and Y on the vertical axis, then a steep straight line out of the origin with a slope of about four would show us the approximate relation between M_Y and Y for a given R. That is, $Y = 4M_Y$ or $M_Y = (1/4)Y$. The coefficient, 1/4, is suggested only as a rough approximation for descriptive purposes in the text. It is thought to be a reasonable value because when U.S. income, as measured by gross national product, was near

[2] The student of calculus will recognize that to find a maximum the partial derivative of NR with respect to n must be equated to zero. Thus $\partial NR / \partial n = (1/2n^2)RY - c = 0$, and the optimum n is as specified.

[3] Refer to the article by James Tobin in the list of readings at the end of this chapter and to Chapter 8 of T. F. Dernburg and D. M. McDougall, *Macroeconomics*, 4th ed. (New York: McGraw-Hill, 1972).

Figure 9–4.

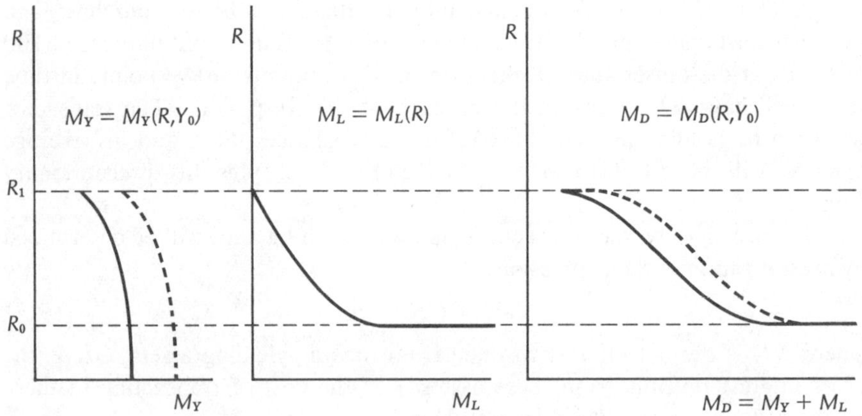

$1 trillion, the money supply, as measured by currency in circulation and demand deposits, was near $250 billion.

If we now assume that Y is constant and that R varies, we can see how interest rates affect the transactions demand for money. The panel on the left of Figure 9–4 shows a rough approximation of what economists think the shape of the curve should be. At low interest rates, the costs of moving into and out of securities to manage cash balances will exceed the value of any interest receipts. Therefore, R can vary considerably and have no effect on M_Y. Only when R is relatively high does it become profitable to invest temporarily in securities and incur the costs of managing transactions balances of money.

The position of the curve is clearly affected by the technology of transfer of funds. In the late 1960s interest rates rose and business firms and private individuals who had formerly ignored the issue began to manage their funds actively. They transferred funds out of checking deposits and into interest-earning time deposits. The movement along this curve, however, is not necessarily reversible, for if interest rates were to fall the skills acquired in cash management and the technology for rapid transfer of funds at low cost would still exist. Therefore, the curve may actually have shifted to the left as people have found ways to get along with less cash for transactions than before.

THE CAPITAL CERTAINTY OR ASSET DEMAND FOR MONEY

The asset, or liquidity, demand for money is the demand for its inclusion in the wealth portfolios of transactor units. In the preceding chapter we saw that the utility derived from the capital certainty of money constitutes its yield when held as an alternative to income-producing financial and tangible assets. The wealth owner evaluates the utility he gains from holding money against the explicit monetary yields of alternative assets.

This implies that one way of expressing the asset demand for money, M_L, is as:

$$M_L = M_L(R), \text{ and } \frac{\Delta M_L}{\Delta R} < 0. \tag{9.4}$$

The asset demand is inversely related to the opportunity cost of holding money, i.e., to the yield to be obtained on the next best alternative to money. This is illustrated in the middle panel of Figure 9–4, where M_L is plotted against the rate of interest. The quantity of money held as an asset increases as the interest rate falls. The curve becomes flatter at lower levels of R and eventually becomes parallel with the horizontal axis. The reason for drawing the curve with this shape can be understood if we alter our formulation slightly and introduce R^*, that interest rate believed by investors to be the "normal" or average interest rate over a long period of time. Then M_L may be formulated as:

$$M_L = M_L(R_a - R^*) \text{ and } \frac{\Delta M_L}{\Delta(R_a - R^*)} < 0 \tag{9.5}$$

where R_a is the actual rate of interest. Here the greater the difference, $R_a - R^*$, the smaller the asset demand for money, and the smaller the difference, the larger the asset demand for money.

Formulating the asset demand in this way introduces explicitly the consideration of *expected* capital gains or losses from the alternatives to holding money. If we assume that the asset holder has the alternative of holding money or government bonds, then at some high rate of interest, R_1, there is no asset demand for money because asset holders attribute a probability of 1.0 to a decrease in interest rates and an increase in the market value of government securities. The actual interest rate, R_a, is believed to be far above its normal level, and if it falls the market price of bonds will rise. Thus people hold bonds, not money, as an asset. As interest rates fall to lower levels, the probability of a further decrease diminishes until at R_0 the function becomes flat. At this point asset holders will universally expect an increase in interest rates (actual rates too far below normal) and a decline in the market value of government securities. Thus, R_0 is a "floor" below which interest rates on bonds will not fall. This floor is called the Keynesian "liquidity trap." It is a "trap" because at such low interest rates all increases in the money supply will be held in asset balances and will not be spent; they will not stimulate income and economic activity. The existence of such a trap is in dispute among economists but its theoretical possibility is real.

ADDING THE TRANSACTIONS AND ASSET DEMANDS FOR MONEY

By adding the horizontal distances in the first two panels of Figure 9–4, we arrive at the function for the total demand for money, $M_D = M_Y + M_L =$

$M_D(R,Y_0)$. This function is drawn for a *given* income level, Y_0. At some higher income level, say Y_1, there would be a larger demand for transactions balances and the curve in the left panel would shift to the right, as indicated by the dotted curve. This shift would also be reflected in the curve in the right panel showing the total money-demand function. Thus a family of demand functions exists, one function for each level of Y, and it is such a family of curves that represents the three-variable function $M_D = M_D(R,Y)$.

SHIFTS IN THE M_D FUNCTION

The M_D function of Figure 9–4 may also be shifted by other forces, such as changes in liquidity preference or financial technology. For example, in Chapter 8 we specified the probability distributions of expected returns on income-yielding assets. If the variance of these distributions (a measure of their spread) were to decrease, income-yielding assets would become more attractive relative to money. This change may be called the effect of differential capital certainty. An improvement in capital certainty, reflected in the reduced variance of the probability distribution of expected returns, would make bonds more attractive and money less attractive and would shift the asset demand function for money in the middle panel of Figure 9–4 to the left. This shift would also be reflected in a leftward shift in the M_D function and indicate a reduced demand for money.

Such a leftward shift might occur if, for some reason, a long period of economic stability were expected. Greater economic stability would lead investors to expect to receive earnings with greater certainty (reflected in narrower spreads in the probability distributions), and the demand for money would decrease. Of course, a period of disruption as with the energy crisis of 1973 and 1974 would lead to greater *un*certainty of returns and would lead to a rightward shift in the demand for money.

Technology can also have an effect on the position of the money-demand function, for advances in the financial technology for dealing with financial assets that are close income-yielding substitutes for money may shift the M_D function to the left. Shares in savings and loan associations, savings deposits, and certificates of deposit at commercial banks can be bought and sold (traded for demand deposits) with ease now that computers have taken over the task. An advance in financial technology could also occur through the introduction of such new financial instruments as the widely used negotiable certificate of deposit, introduced in the 1950s. This novel instrument is a highly marketable financial asset and its introduction did indeed reduce the demand for money; that is, it shifted the M_D function to the left.

Such shifting forces do not, however, arise with any regularity, and we have therefore not included them in our money-demand function. We have kept only R and Y as the variables upon which the quantity of money that people wish to hold depends, for the state of technology is quite constant over a short period of time and expectations about capital certainty in the financial marketplace are far from stable; the latter are, however, capable of causing sizable shifts in the demand for money in a short time. The exact stability of the money-demand function is the subject of much empirical study and debate; those economists who believe monetary policy is a powerful stabilization tool also generally believe that the money-demand function is stable.

THE MONEY SUPPLY

In Chapter 2 we developed a reserve availability description of the money supply in a fractional reserve banking system. Money supply, deposit, and credit multipliers were developed to show the effect of changes in the reserve availability of the commercial banking system. Reserve availability was discretionary on the part of the central bank, and therefore the money supply was determined exogenously by noneconomic forces so long as the reserve multipliers were constant. To assume that the multipliers *are* constant is a simplifying assumption that we make here for expository purposes. We believe that higher interest rates lead banks as well as individuals to economize on reserve balances and that this can increase the reserve multipliers and hence the money supply. Larger models of the economy, in fact, make explicit allowance for feedback effects such as this, but we will assume that the money supply, M_s, is given and that, in equilibrium, $M_s = M_D$.

Of course, our reserve availability explanation applied only to the *nominal* money supply. We will incorporate a price level component into our model later, but for now we can assume a stable price level and equate the *nominal* with the *real* money supply.

MODEL OF THE MONETARY SECTOR

We can now make a formal statement of our model of the monetary sector as follows:

$M_Y = M_Y(Y,R)$ is the transaction demand for money
$M_L = M_L(R)$ is the asset demand for money
$M_D = M_Y + M_L = M_D(R,Y)$ is the total demand for money
$M_s = M_D$ is an equilibrium condition

If we assume that M_s is exogenously determined by the central bank and that Y is given as Y_0, then this system of four equations contains but four variables, M_D, M_Y, M_L, and R, and can readily be solved for them.

A graphic illustration is found in Figure 9–5, where the equilibrium rate of interest is R_0. At this rate $M_D = M_s$, that is, R_0 is the rate of interest which equates the demand for and supply of money. Any rate other than R_0 is not sustainable, for if the prevailing rate is lower than R_0, say at R_1, the quantity of money demanded will exceed the available supply, $M_D > M_s$. In terms of asset choice, this means that at the margin the sum of the convenience and

Figure 9–5.

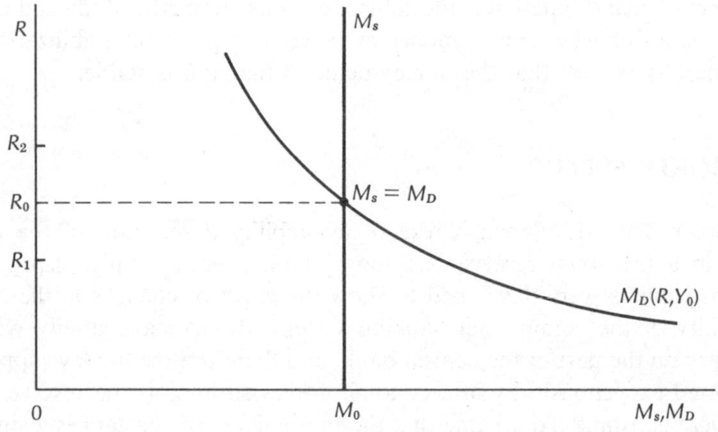

capital certainty returns from money will exceed the returns from income-producing assets. Accordingly, wealth owners will wish to reduce their holdings of these latter assets and will offer to sell them. The effect of these sales by wealth owners to convert income-earning assets into money will be to lower the market prices of these assets and increase their yields.[4] Interest rates will rise from R_1 to approach the equilibrium rate of R_0.

On the other hand, if the prevailing market rate is R_2, the supply of money will exceed the demand. Again, in terms of an analysis of asset choice, this means that wealth owners will find that returns at the margin from income-producing assets exceed the convenience and capital certainty yields from holding money. Portfolio adjustments will occur as asset holders transform some money holdings into alternative asset forms. The effect of this is to bid up the market price of these alternatives and lower their yield. Accordingly, interest rates will fall from R_2 toward the equilibrium rate of R_0.

One can interpret the effects upon R_0 of shifts in either the money-demand or money-supply functions similarly.

Connecting *R* with *Y* in Money Markets

In Chapter 7 we derived what we called the *IS* function to reveal the equilibrium levels of output associated with alternative rates of interest. Now we can develop an *LM* function to show the equilibrium levels of interest rates associated with specified alternative levels of income. Thus Figure 9–6 pictures a family of $M_D(R,Y)$ functions representing successively higher levels of income from Y_1 through Y_3. As Y rises, the increase in the transactions demand for

[4] There is an inverse relation between the price of a security and its yield. This can be seen in the discount formula of Chapter 6 on investment demand.

Figure 9–6.

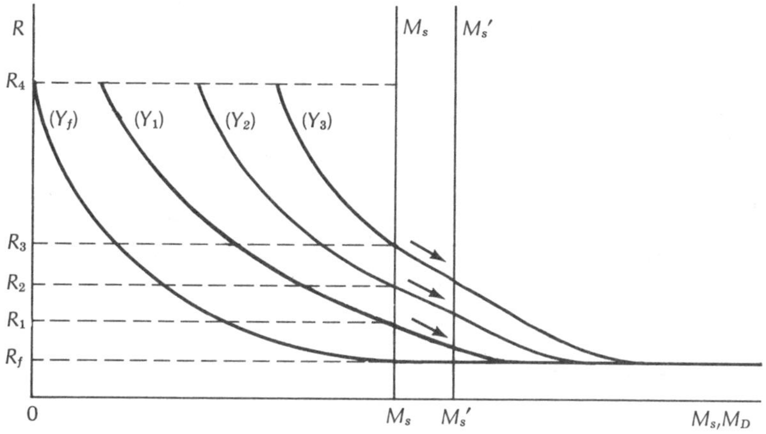

money causes the M_D function to shift to the right, although it does not affect the value of R_f, the liquidity trap, where interest rates have reached a floor level. The equilibrium interest rates are positively related to income levels. The arrows indicate that if the money supply increases to M_s' then the equilibrium level of R will fall for any given level of Y. Thus the figure shows the function $M_D(R,Y)$ for several Y's and we have equilibrium when $M_s = M_D$.

Another way to depict this three-variable function is to plot Y and R on the two axes and show the relation between them for a variety of different values for M_s. That is, we can form the implicit function $R = R(Y, M_0)$ from the money-demand function. This is the LM function.

Two LM functions are pictured in Figure 9–7. Each represents the appropriate function for a given money supply; if the money supply increases to M_s', the curve shifts to the right as indicated.

Figure 9–7.

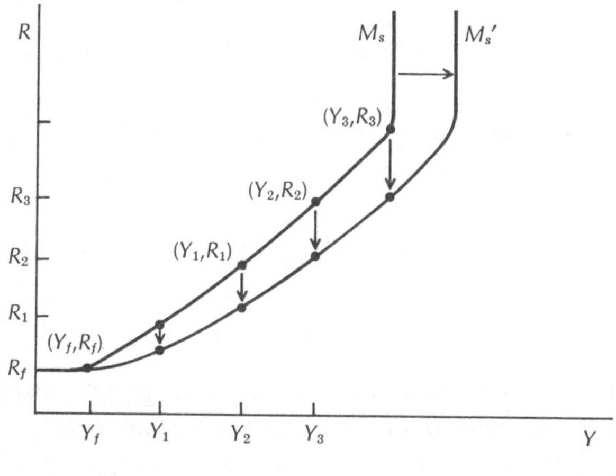

In Figure 9–7 the pairs of equilibrium values for Y and R indicated in Figure 9–6 are shown in parentheses. Thus the two figures show the same relationships and are merely plotted on different axes. Again, when the money supply increases, interest rates will fall for any given income level. Hence an increase in M_s will shift the *LM* curve rightward.

The horizontal section of the *LM* curve on its left is the result of the liquidity trap described earlier and appearing on the right of the money-demand function. Its interpretation is unchanged.

We have drawn the *LM* curve to be vertical at very high interest rates. At these rates, all money is presumably held for transactions purposes and none is held for asset purposes.

The *LM* Curve: A Linear and Numerical Model

The money market equilibrium curve (*LM* curve) may be depicted in an algebraic model of the money market in a manner similar to that used in Chapter 7 for the *IS* curve. Because we wish to put the *IS* and *LM* curves together in the next chapter, we must become familiar with the money market equations, assuming linear relations for simplicity (we ignore the vertical and horizontal portions of the *LM* curve for the purposes of our numerical example, as well as because the economy doubtless operates in the middle range rather than on these extremities).

The linear and numerical equations for the money market, where i, j, k, and l are coefficients, may be set forth as:

General Linear Model	*Numerical Model*	
$M_Y = jY + iR$, where $j > 0$ and $i < 0$	$M_Y = .2Y - R$	(9.6)
$M_L = k + lR$, where $k > 0$ and $l < 0$	$M_L = 40 - 3R$	(9.7)
$M_D = M_Y + M_L$	$M_D = M_Y + M_L$	(9.8)
M_s is given	$M_s = 20$	(9.9)
$M_D = M_s$	$M_D = M_s$	(9.10)

Substituting equations (9.6) and (9.7) into equations (9.8) and (9.10) yields:

$$jY + iR + k + lR = M_s \qquad .2Y - R + 40 - 3R = 20$$
$$\text{or: } jY + l'R + k = M_s, \qquad .2Y - 4R + 40 = 20$$
$$\text{where } l' = l + i$$

Solving for R in terms of Y yields the equation for the *LM* curve:

$$R = \frac{M_s - k}{l'} - \frac{jY}{l'} \qquad R = \frac{-20}{-4} - \frac{.2Y}{-4} = 5 + .05Y \tag{9.11}$$

Figure 9–7 showed that an increase in the supply of money would shift the *LM* curve to the right. If we now increase M_s, the money supply, in our numerical example from 20 to 30, the equation for the *LM* curve becomes $R = 2.5 + .05Y$. The *LM* curve has the same positive slope, but it now intersects the R axis at a lower point. In other words, the *LM* curve has shifted to the right.

An increase in the money supply has implications for the securities market that should be mentioned, for there are demand and supply curves for securities—a demand arises out of savings behavior by business and households, and a supply arises as business and government borrow funds. But a demand for securities also arises when the money supply increases as people attempt to unload their increased money holdings by buying securities. This pushes the prices of securities up and their interest yields down. Thus, although no explicit account of the securities market appears in the *LM* diagrams, we should remember that changes in the money supply and shifting *LM* curves will have their reflections in the demand curves of the securities market.

Four-Quadrant Derivation of the *LM* Curve

The *LM* curve, like the *IS* curve, can be given a four-quadrant graphical derivation. In so doing, it must be kept in mind that the money market is in equilibrium only when the supply of money equals the demand for money. In quadrant I is the asset money-demand function, M_L, which varies negatively with the rate of interest. At some low interest rate this demand for money becomes horizontal, representing the liquidity trap. Quadrant II is a representation of how the money supply is divided between money held for transactions purposes (as measured on the vertical axis) and money held for asset purposes (as measured on the horizontal axis; the total money supply, of amount M, must be held in these two forms). Quadrant III represents the transactions demand for money, M_Y, which we assume varies directly with the level of income, Y; for simplicity, in this graphical presentation we ignore the effect of interest rates on the transactions demand. In quadrant IV, the *LM* curve itself represents those interest rate and income level combinations at which the supply of money equals the demand for money.

Quadrant I indicates that for an interest rate of R_1 the quantity of money demanded for speculative purposes equals M_{L_1}. Moving from quadrant I to quadrant II we see that, with the quantity held for speculative purposes equal to M_{L_1}, the total money supply will be demanded only if the quantity of money demanded for transactions purposes is M_{Y_1}. Moving to quadrant III it becomes apparent that the transactions demand equals M_{Y_1} only at Y_1. Hence at R_1 the demand for money equals the supply of money only if income is at Y_1. Point C represents the combination R_1 and Y_1 for which the money market is in equilibrium, and this point is a point on the *LM* curve. A second point on the *LM* curve, point D, may be derived in the same manner. Quadrant I shows that at interest rate R_2 the quantity of money demanded for speculative purposes is M_{L_2}. With speculative demand equal to M_{L_2}, quadrant II shows that the demand for money will equal the total supply of money only if the quantity demanded

Figure 9–8.

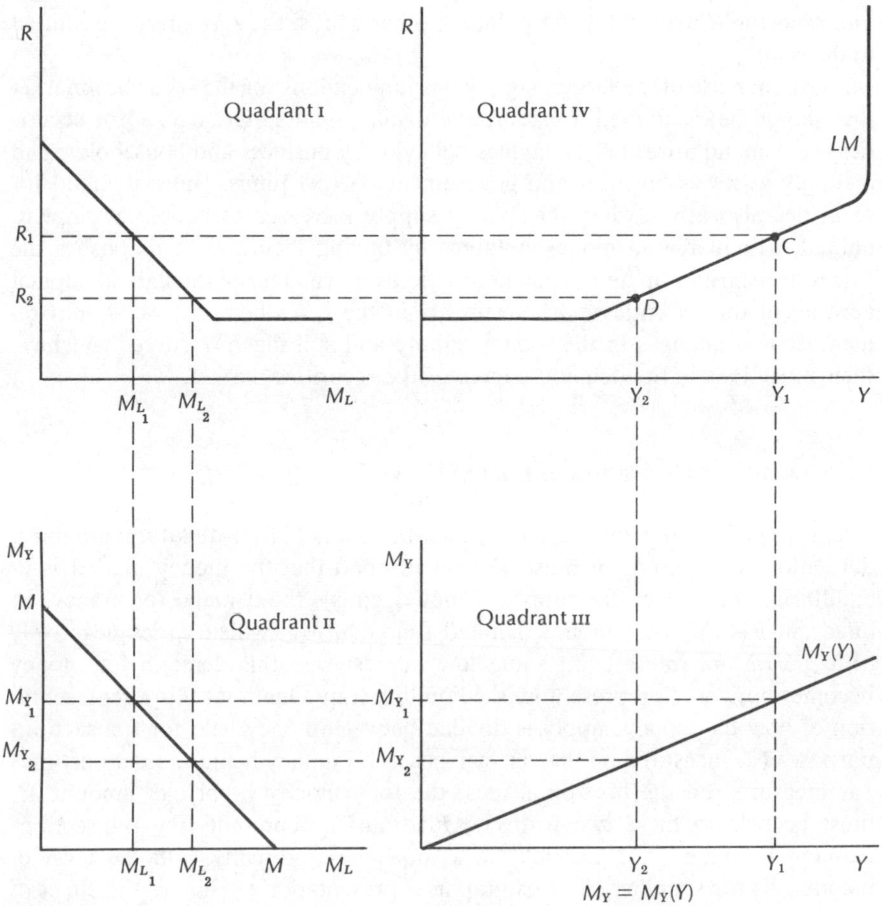

for transactions purposes equals M_{Y_2}. Quadrant III indicates that the transactions demand for money equals M_{Y_2} only at income level Y_2. Hence, at interest rate R_2 the money market will be in equilibrium only if the level of income is Y_2. Other points on the *LM* curve may be derived in similar fashion.

An increase in the money supply could be shown by drawing a new curve in quadrant II farther to the right and parallel to the old curve. This new curve would also show how this larger M_s could be divided among M_L and M_Y. Using it, a new *LM* curve could be derived as before. It would lie to the right of the existing *LM* curve.

CONCLUSION

Earlier chapters established that the level of aggregate demand is affected by the level of investment and that the level of investment is influenced by the interest rate. Output, therefore, is a function of the rate of interest, but without knowing the rate of interest we cannot determine what point on the *IS* curve is the equilibrium level of income.

In Chapters 8 and 9, we have examined the money market and seen that the interest rate may be considered the price that one has to pay to hold money, i.e., it is the opportunity cost of foregoing interest-earning assets. Similarly to other prices, interest rates are determined by forces of demand and supply. The supply of money is exogenously determined since it is assumed to be controlled by monetary authorities. Demand for money is determined by the length of pay periods, financial technology, differential capital certainty, and the level of output. Each of these factors, except for the level of output, is exogenously determined and taken to be given. Therefore, with the money supply also given, the equilibrium rate of interest (the price of money) will be determined by the level of output. This is indicated by the *LM* curve, where, for each level of output, there exists an interest rate that equates the supply and the demand for money.

To repeat, the *IS* curve indicates that output is a function of the rate of interest and the *LM* curve indicates that the interest rate is a function of the level of output. With two equations and two unknowns, we should thus be able to solve for the equilibrium levels of interest and income.

ADDITIONAL READINGS

A brief general discussion of the transactions demand for cash is presented in Gardner Ackley's *Macroeconomic Theory* (New York: Macmillan, 1961), pp. 113–119. The role that the interest rate plays in the transactions demand for cash is discussed in William Baumol's "The transactions demand for cash: An inventory theoretic approach," *Quarterly Journal of Economics,* 66 (1952): 545–556; and James Tobin's "The interest elasticity of the transactions demand for cash," *Review of Economics and Statistics*, 38 (1956): 241–247.

Three other studies examining the relationship between the interest rate and the demand for money are M. Bronfenbrenner and T. Mayer, "Liquidity functions in the American economy," *Econometrica*, 28 (1960): 810–834; T. H. Lee, "Interest rates and the demand for money," *American Economic Review*, 57 (December 1967): 1168–1181; and James Tobin, "Liquidity preference as behavior towards risk," *Review of Economic Studies*, 25 (February 1958): 65–86. The Bronfenbrenner-Mayer and Tobin articles are reprinted in M. G. Mueller (Ed.), *Readings in Macroeconomics*, 2nd ed. (New York: Holt, Rinehart and Winston, 1971). A time-series analysis of the demand for money is presented in Allan Meltzer, "The demand for money: The evidence from the time series," *Journal of Political Economy*, 71 (1963): 219–246.

Several more general studies of the demand for money may be of interest to the student: David E. W. Laidler, *The Demand for Money: Theories and*

Evidence (Scranton, Pa.: International Textbook Co., 1969); a useful bibliography is at the end of this short book; Milton Friedman, "The quantity theory of money—A restatement," in *Studies in the Quantity Theory of Money* (Chicago: University of Chicago Press, 1956); Milton Friedman, "The demand for money: Some theoretical and empirical results," *Journal of Political Economy*, 67 (June 1959): 327–351; in this study, Friedman presents empirical results which demonstrate no relationship between the demand for money and interest rates; and Ronald L. Teigen, "The demand for and supply of money," in W. L. Smith and R. L. Teigen (Eds.), *Readings in Money, National Income and Stabilization Policy* (Homewood, Ill.: Irwin, 1965), pp. 44–76.

QUESTIONS

1. List factors influencing the transactions demand for money and explain their effect.

2. Suppose that all individuals have the option of depositing their paychecks in time deposits earning interest and then withdrawing the money in lump amounts as cash is needed. With interest paid on the daily balance and a fixed cost per withdrawal, how should each individual decide on the number of withdrawals to make during the month to meet his transaction needs? If the interest rate rises, would you expect him to make more or fewer withdrawals? If the fixed cost per withdrawal increases would you expect each individual to make more or fewer withdrawals?

3. Suppose that all transactor units in an economy are in disequilibrium, i.e., the actual composition of their portfolios is insufficiently liquid. What effect on economic activity would you predict from this situation? What model could you use to analyze the effect?

4. Describe how the function $M_L = M_L(R)$ would shift if credit cards were introduced.

5. Suppose we specify that the asset demand for money is $M_L = 80 - 4R$ for all $R > 2$, and that when $R = 2$ the asset demand for money is horizontal.

   (a) In this formulation, why is the coefficient of R negative?
   (b) Changes in differential capital certainty are treated as parametric shifts. If capital certainty differentials increased or decreased, how would the M_L function shift?

6. The asset demand for money which we call M_L may be denoted $M_L(R)$, where R is the yield on the non-monetary holdings in transactors' asset portfolios and is defined as the dollar return of the asset less its carrying cost.

(a) In terms of the theory of asset choice, what is the yield of money holdings, and how does it differ from the yield of non-monetary assets?
(b) In terms of asset choice, is it correct to say that the asset demand for money is (i) positively related to the differential capital certainty yield, and (ii) inversely related to the expected income yield of non-monetary forms of wealth?

Be sure you understand what is meant by the capital certainty of an asset.

7. In early 1970, interest rates were high and many people expected them to fall. What effect would you expect this to have upon the demand for money as an asset? Upon the demand for bonds?

8. Let $M_Y = 0.25Y$ and $M_L = 80 - 4R$ for all $R > 2$.

   (a) What is the total demand for money when $Y = 200$ and $R = 3$? $R = 7$? $R = 12$? $R = 15$?
   (b) What is the total demand for money when $Y = 240$ and $R = 3$? $R = 7$? $R = 12$? $R = 15$?
   (c) Draw the aggregate demand for money at each of the above two income levels, and complete the drawing for when $R = 2$.

9. The following three equations represent the monetary sector of the economy:

   $$M_Y = 0.3Y - 2R$$
   $$M_L = 20 - R$$
   $$M_s = 30$$

   Find the equation that represents the *LM* curve.

10. Clearly explain what the *LM* curve represents. Why is it positively sloping over most of its range, but horizontal at very low rates and vertical at very high rates?

11. (a) What factors determine the position of the *LM* curve?
    (b) What factors determine the slope of the *LM* curve?

12. If a business' periodic income, Y, is \$80,000, $R = 0.04$, and the cost of a security purchase and sale, c, is \$4, how many transactions in interest earning securities should the business make each period in order to maximize NR? I.e., what is n?

Bringing the Commodity Market and Money Market Together

10
Chapter

We can now bring together the commodity market and the money market under conditions of a stable price level. In so doing it will be possible to observe the simultaneous determination of the variables in the economic system, identify the mechanisms by which developments in the two markets mutually influence one another, stress the policy options available for the maintenance of high levels of income and employment, and introduce what is called the "portfolio balance effect."

THE LINEAR AND NUMERICAL MODEL

The linear form of our income determination model can now be stated as:

Linear Form	*Numerical Example*
In the commodity market:	
Income:	
$Y = C + I + G + E_x - I_M$	$Y = C + I + G + E_x - I_M$
Consumption:	
$C = a + b\,(Y - T + T_r)$	$C = 25 + .5\,(Y - T + T_r)$
Income taxes:	
$T = tY$	$T = .3Y$
Transfer payments:	
$T_r = g + hY$	$T_r = 20 - .1Y$
Investments:	
$I = c + dR + cY$	$I = 20 - 4R + .1Y$
Imports:	
$I_m = mY$	$I_m = .2Y$
Government spending:	
G is given	$G = 30$

Exports:
E_x is given $\quad$ $E_x = 15$

In the money market:
Total demand for money:
$M_D = M_Y + M_L$ $\quad$ $M_D = M_Y + M_L$

Transactions demand for money:
$M_Y = jY + iR$ $\quad$ $M_Y = .2Y - R$

Asset demand for money:
$M_L = k + lR$ for all $R > R_f$ $\quad$ $M_L = 40 - 3R$

Money supply:
M_S is given $\quad$ $M_S = 20$
$M_D = M_S$ $\quad$ $M_D = M_S$

where $a, b, c, e, g, j, k, m, t > 0$ and $d, h, i, l < 0$ are coefficients. It should be noted that in this model investment, I, and the transactions demand for money, M_Y, are functions of the long-term interest rate, R, *and* income, Y.

The above model may be pictured as in Figure 10–1. *IS* illustrates the equilibrium relation of R to Y in commodity markets, where the equation for the *IS* curve is:

$$R = -\left[\frac{a + bg + c + G + E_x}{d}\right] + \left[\frac{1 - b + bt - bh - e + m}{d}\right] Y.$$

The equality of money demand and money supply is represented by the combinations of R and Y along the *LM* curve, whose equation is:

$$R = \frac{M_s - k}{l'} - \frac{jY,}{l'} \text{ where } l' = i + l < 0.$$

The factors determining the position and the shape of these functions have already been explored.

Figure 10–1.

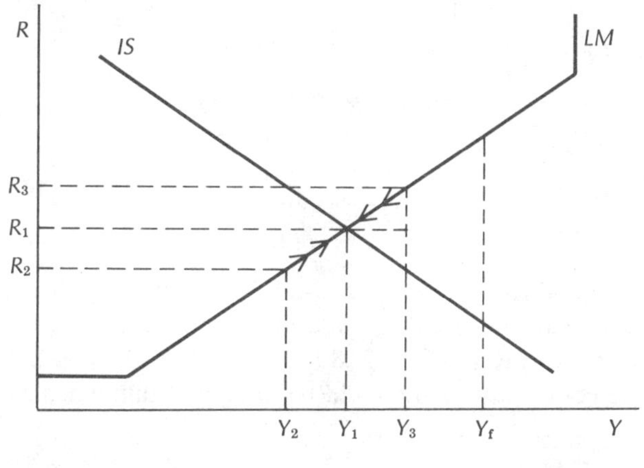

Figure 10–1 shows that, given the money supply, exports, and government spending, and the specified functional relationships in commodity and money markets, the point where the *IS* curve and the *LM* curve intersect, or where $IS = LM$, represents the equilibrium levels of real income and interest rates. At this point both the commodity market and the money market are in equilibrium, and the linear model may be solved for the equilibrium levels of income and interest rate by setting the equation representing the *IS* curve equal to that representing the *LM* curve and solving for *Y*.

Linear Form: IS = LM

for *IS*:

$$R = -\left[\frac{a + bg + c + G + E_x}{d}\right] + \left[\frac{1 - b + bt - bh - e + m}{d}\right] Y \tag{10.1}$$

for *LM*:

$$R = \frac{M_s - k}{l'} - \frac{jY}{l'} \tag{10.2}$$

and:

$$-\left[\frac{a + bg + c + G + E_x}{d}\right] + \left[\frac{1 - b + bt - bh - e + m}{d}\right] Y = \frac{M_s - k}{l'} - \frac{jY}{l'} \tag{10.3}$$

$$\left[1 - b + bt - bh - e + m + \frac{jd}{l'}\right] Y = a + bg + c + G + E_x + \frac{dM_s - dk}{l'} \tag{10.4}$$

$$Y = \left[\frac{1}{1 - b + bt - bh - e + m + \frac{jd}{l'}}\right] \left[a + bg + c + G + E_x + \frac{dM_s - dk}{l'}\right] \tag{10.5}$$

Numerical Example

for *IS*: $R = 25 - .2Y$
for *LM*: $R = 5 + .05Y$
and: $25 - .2Y = 5 + .05Y$

$$.25Y = 20$$
$$Y = 80$$

With the equilibrium level of *Y* established, the equilibrium level of *R* may be found by substituting this value of *Y* into either equation (10.1) or equation (10.2). Thus $R = 25 - .2(80) = 5 + .05(80) = 9$. Both the money market and the commodity market will be in equilibrium when $R = 9$ percent and $Y = 80$.

The equilibrium levels of consumption, savings, taxes, transfer payments, investment, imports, exports, the government's budget position, and the transactions and asset demands for money may also be determined by substituting into the appropriate equations the equilibrium values for R and Y.[1]

Four-Quadrant Graphical Derivations of the *IS* and *LM* Curves Combined

That the equilibrium interest rate and income level are determined by the intersection of the *IS* and *LM* curves can be shown by bringing together the graphs of *IS* and *LM* curves shown in Chapters 7 and 9, respectively. When this is done as in Figure 10–2, the equilibrium level of income, Y, and the equilibrium rate of interest, R, are shown to be consistent with the indicated values of the other variables.

To present the graphical solution to the model, we have had to simplify some of the functions—unlike the algebraic description of the theory of income determination, the graphs do not explicitly allow for taxes or transfer payments, for income as a variable in the investment demand function, or for the interest rate as a variable in the transactions demand function for money. Nevertheless, the graphical description is suggestive of the most important elements in the model.

Referring back to Figure 10–1, we can see that combinations of interest rate and income level other than R_1 and Y_1 would be unstable. When income is Y_2 and the interest rate is R_1, for instance, the supply of money will exceed the demand for money. In these circumstances, holders of money balances will exchange them for financial assets (such as government bonds), thus driving down the rate of interest. At R_2, the demands for and supply of money would be in equilibrium, but Y_2 is not a level of income where the spending plans of transactor units coincide with their production plans. At Y_2 and R_2, the interest rate is so low that aggregate demand exceeds aggregate supply. As producers try to raise production to meet demand requirements, output and income will rise. But an increase in income will also increase the demand for money for transactions purposes, thus raising interest rates above R_2 and toward R_1. And at R_1, both spending plans and production plans by transactor units are consistent with a level of output equal to Y_1. Income levels will then converge on Y_1.

Another unstable case is that of R_1 and Y_3, where the demands for money exceed the available supply. Transactors will therefore exchange other assets for money, thus raising the level of interest rates to R_3. But at R_3 there is a disequilibrium between the transactions demand and production plans of transactor units. More particularly, the level of investment spending and aggregate demand will not be sufficient to sustain an income level of Y_3. Income

[1] For example, $C = a + b(Y - T + T_r)$, where $T = .3Y$ and $T_r = 20 - .1Y$. Hence, $C = 25 + .5(Y - .3Y + 20 - .1Y) = 35 + .3Y$. Since $Y = 80$, $C = 35 + 24 = 59$.

Figure 10–2. The *IS* and *LM* Curves Brought Together.

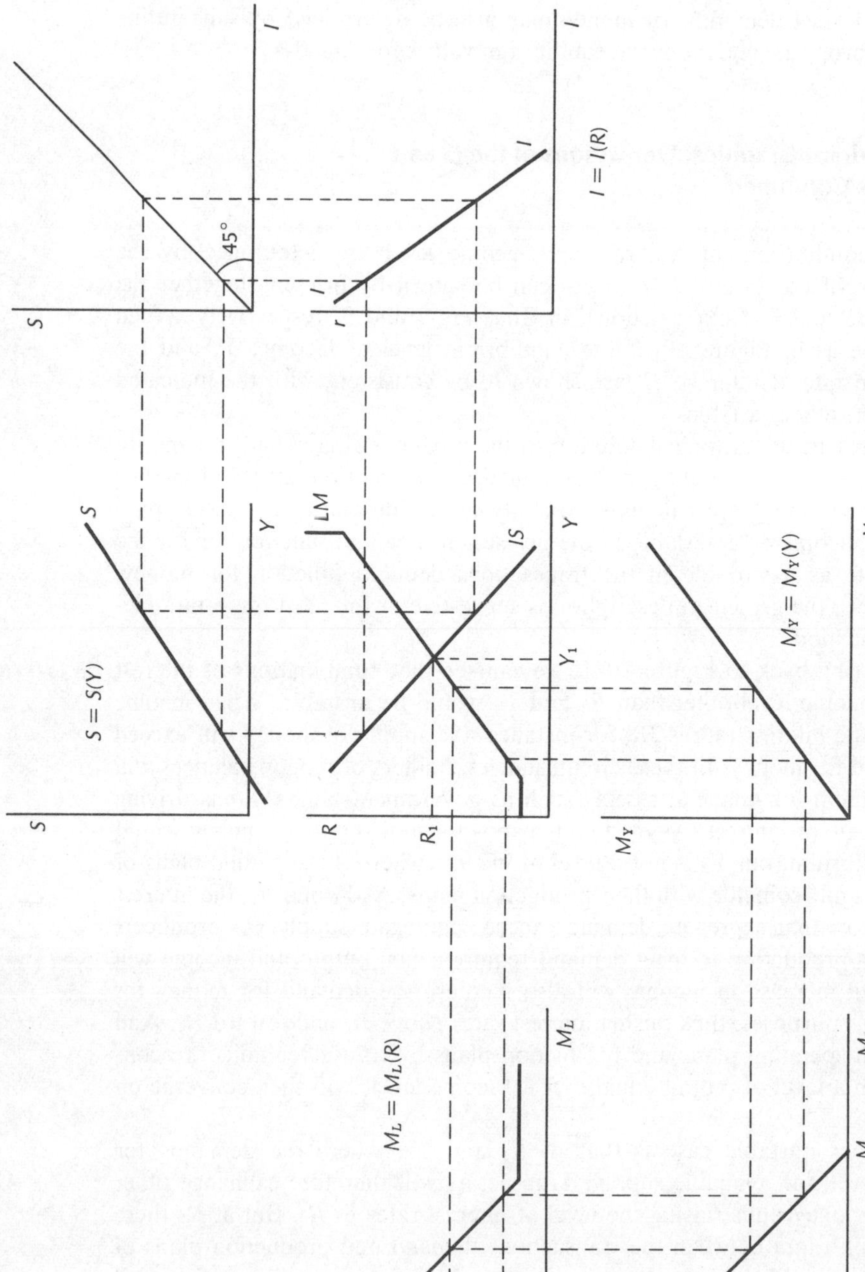

will fall and with it interest rates (in response to a decline in the transactions demand for money). Both R and Y will converge on R_1 and Y_1. That is, with a given level of government spending, a given volume of exports, and a given money supply, and with the specified consumption, investment, import, tax, transfer payment, asset demand, and transactions demand functions, R_1 and Y_1 represent respectively an equilibrium price in money markets and an equilibrium income in commodity markets.

Changing Equilibria

In Figure 10–1 Y_f can be taken to represent a full employment level of income. If the current level of income is Y_1, then the economic resources of the community are not being fully utilized and the people of the community have an income that is lower than it could be. To stimulate economic activity and raise income to its full employment potential there are two policy instruments available: fiscal policy and monetary policy.

Case I: An Increase in G

The effect of an increase in G will be to shift IS upwards and to the right from IS to IS' in Figure 10–3. Income will rise by more than ΔG, through the action of the multiplier, although the effect will also raise interest rates. If M_s remains unchanged, then the demand for money at Y_f will exceed that at Y_1 and R will rise. One important consequence of this is that I, the capital expenditures of business transactors, will be affected adversely by the rise in R. Hence, if the economy is pushed toward full employment by the rise of G alone, without a concurrent increase in the money supply, then if the positive effect on I of increasing income is insufficient to offset the negative effect of a rise in R, I may decline. This suggests that the desirable path in public policy may frequently be the use of policy alternatives in concert rather than singly.

Case II: A Decrease in the Tax Rate

The economy may also be moved to Y_f by a reduction in the tax rate, t. The effect in this case is to rotate IS in a counterclockwise direction from IS to IS'' in Figure 10–3, a change reflecting an increase in personal consumption and income. The same problem arises here as in the previous case, however. The increase in income and consumption may be at the expense of a decline in I if nothing is done to alter the money supply in order to maintain the existing rate of interest, R_1. In this instance,, the movement to Y_f is achieved through an increase in consumption and a possible decline in investment owing to the increase in R.

In Cases I and II, the behavior of investment spending depends upon both R and the level of income, Y, as Y increases from Y_1 to Y_f. The effect of the increase in interest rates upon I has to be offset against the increase in I

Figure 10–3.

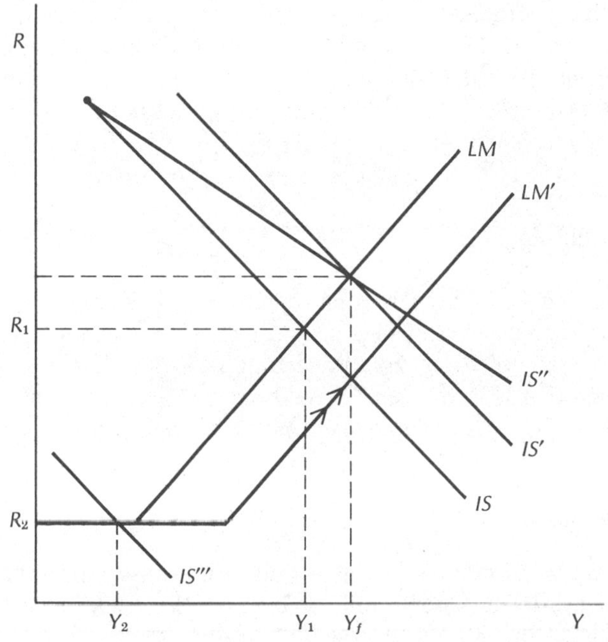

induced by the increase in Y. The net effect depends upon the coefficient relating I to Y, the slope of the investment demand function, and the slopes of LM and IS.

Case III: An Increase in M_s, the Money Supply

In each of the two cases above, the effort to move Y to full employment levels occurs directly via action in commodity markets, but similar effects can be achieved in the money market, for the range of the LM function with which we are dealing is one where monetary policy can be effective. If we were within the region of Figure 10–3 where LM is horizontal—in the region of IS'''—then no amount of action to increase the money supply, M_s, would be effective. This is the case of the "liquidity trap" obstacle to effective monetary policy. A shift of LM to LM' through an increase in M_s has no effect—income remains at Y_2 and the interest rate remains at R_2. However, if Y and R are in equilibrium at (Y_1, R_1), an increase in M_s will shift LM to LM' in Figure 10–3. The supply of money will exceed the demand for money at (Y_1, R_1), and decision-making units will consequently move from money to other financial assets, thus driving up the price of these assets and driving down the rate of interest. In an economy like that of the United States, where financial markets are highly developed, the initial impact of an increase in the money supply is thus an interest rate decline.

Now in order for these monetary developments to affect commodity markets, it is necessary to have some form of expenditure that is sensitive to interest rates. Investment is affected by the rate of interest and so will increase in response to the fall in R. The economy is then moved toward full employment by the increase in M_s acting on I through R. How large an increase in M_s will be necessary depends upon the slopes of *IS* and *LM*.

Slopes of the *IS* and *LM* Curves and Policy Implications

The slope of *IS* is, of course, affected by the slope of the investment demand function. As noted in Chapter 7, the slope of the *IS* curve is affected by the marginal propensities to consume, to tax, to make transfer payments, to invest, and to import, and by the sensitivity of investment to changes in the rate of interest. In other words, the coefficients $b, d, e, h, m,$ and t in our model determine the slope of the *IS* curve, and they therefore influence the effects of economic policies.

Case I: Where IS Is Negatively Sloping

If the *IS* curve has a negative slope and if the monetary authorities take an increase in the money supply as their policy tool, shifting *LM* to *LM′* in Figure 10–4, the effects of this corrective action are quickly felt in financial markets. Interest rates drop to R' from their initial level of R, but at R' intended investment will exceed intended savings, and activity levels in commodity markets will expand, interest rates will rise, and adjustment to a new equilibrium position will occur along the *LM′* curve. This is illustrated in Figure 10–4 by the arrows along *LM′* following the fall in rates from R to R'. As this figure indicates, the impact of an increase in M_s upon the level of output in the economy will depend upon the slope of the *IS* schedule. The steeper

Figure 10–4.

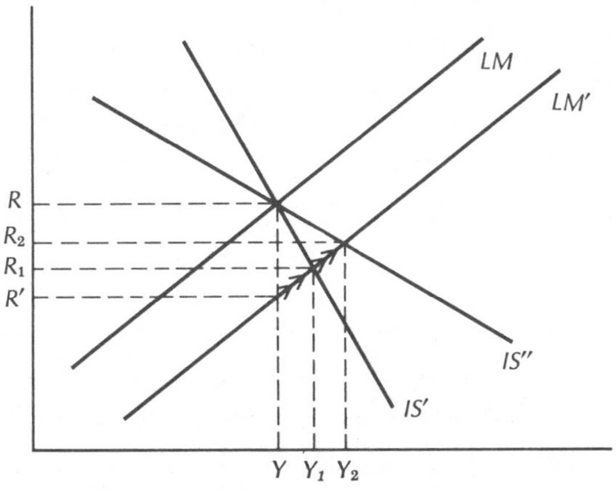

of the two schedules, *IS′*, indicates that income will increase to Y_1 and the interest rate will fall to R_1. With the flatter curve, *IS″*, income will expand to Y_2, a level somewhat greater than Y_1, and the interest rate will drop to R_2, somewhat above R_1. In terms of the above coefficients and their role in equation (10.1), the greater are *b, d, e,* and *h,*[2] the flatter is the *IS* curve and the greater is the impact of the change in the money supply upon the level of income. In other words, a number of discretionary policies or exogenous occurrences may flatten the *IS′* curve and stimulate economic activity; these include anything that increases the marginal propensities to consume or to spend on investment, reduces the sensitivity of transfer payments to changes in income, or increases the sensitivity of investment to changes in interest rates. On the other hand, a lower *t* and a lower *m* mean a flatter *IS* schedule. Therefore, past actions which have resulted in a lower tax rate and a lower marginal propensity to import have increased the impact that a change in the money supply will have upon the level of income.

The slope of the *LM* curve also significantly affects the impact of discretionary policy action. Two factors affecting the slope of this schedule are the sensitivity of the demand for money to changes in income (*j*) and to changes in the rate of interest (*i* and *l*). Since *i* and *l* are both negative, equation (10.2) indicates that as *j* increases (meaning that more dollars are needed for transactions purposes to support any given level of income), the slope of the *LM* schedule increases, while if the demand for money becomes less sensitive to changes in the interest rate (*i* and *l* become less negative and closer to zero), this also causes the *LM* schedule to become steeper.

Now if, when the level of income is at *Y* and the rate of interest is at *R* as in Figure 10–5, the government decides corrective action is necessary and pursues a more expansionary fiscal policy, then, through increased government

Figure 10–5.

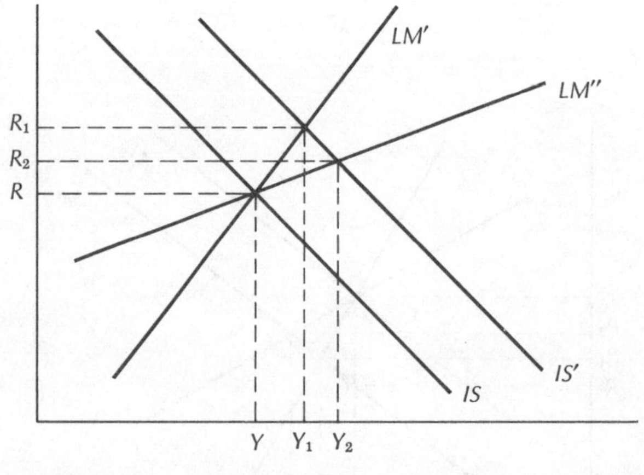

[2] Since *d* and *h* are negative, an increase in them means that they become less negative (move closer to zero).

spending and/or reduced taxes, the *IS* schedule will be shifted to the right. It can be seen that the impact of this policy will depend very much upon the slope of the *LM* curve. If *LM* is relatively steep, the expansionary fiscal policy will raise income to Y_1, and the interest rate will increase to R_1. In this case the increase in the transactions demand for money that accompanies the rise in *Y* causes the rate of interest to rise quite rapidly and to stifle investment. This prevents the fiscal policy from being more effective. If the money demand is fairly insensitive to changes in interest rates (i and l are close to zero), as interest rates rise the quantity of money demanded as an asset will fall only slightly and the upward pressures on the interest rate will be reduced but little. Investment is therefore stifled to a greater degree than would otherwise be the case. On the other hand, if *LM* is relatively flat, the expansionary fiscal policy will raise income to Y_2, but the interest rate will increase only to R_2. The flatter *LM* curve may mean that the quantity of money demanded for transactions is not particularly sensitive to changes in the interest rate (i is relatively small in absolute value), or it may mean that the quantity of cash demanded for speculative purposes is quite sensitive to changes in interest rates (l takes a large negative value).

Case II: Where IS Is Positively Sloping

The net effect of the relevant parameters in commodity markets can produce a positively sloping *IS* function, as was explained in Chapter 7, when e, the coefficient of *Y* in the investment demand function, is relatively large. One of the more important questions arising when the slope of the *IS* curve is positive is illustrated in Figure 10–6. In panel (a) the slope of *IS*, though positive, is less than the slope of *LM*, while in panel (b) the slope of *IS* exceeds that of *LM*.

Now if government tries to correct a case of underemployment through an increase in the money supply, so that *LM* shifts in both instances to *LM'*, the immediate impact of this attempt is to decrease interest rates from R_0 to R'.

Figure 10–6.

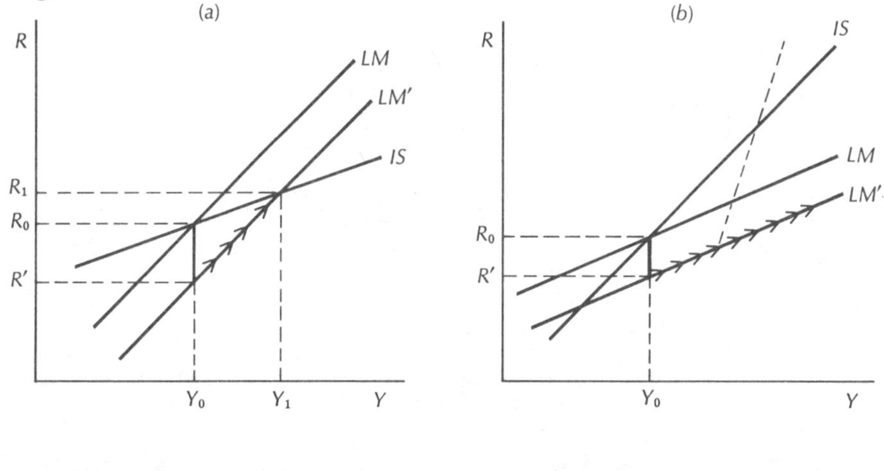

Again, this reflects the existence of highly developed financial institutions. At R′ the capital expenditure plans of businessmen exceed anticipated savings, and activity levels in commodity markets will increase. Adjustment to new equilibrium levels of R and Y occurs along the LM' function until, in panel (a), a new stable equilibrium is reached at R_1 and Y_1. Both interest rates and real output rise; in particular, the new interest rate, R_1, is above the old equilibrium level, R_0. The movement along LM' implies that an equilibrium condition (i.e., where the supply and demand for money are equal) exists in money markets throughout the adjustment process. The interest rates in money markets rise faster than the rates that maintain an equilibrating condition in commodity markets. Hence Y_1 represents a stable income level.

In contrast, if the slope of *IS* is greater than that of *LM*, as in panel (b), the increase in the money supply reflected in the rightward shift of *LM* to LM' will still lower interest rates in money markets to R', the investment plans of businessmen in the commodity markets will still exceed anticipated savings, and activity levels will still expand. But the intersection of LM' with *IS* at income and interest rate levels below R' and Y_0 means that there is no further equilibrium point along LM'. Panel (b), in fact, depicts an explosive system in which the gap between interest rates in money markets and the rates necessary to produce equilibrium in commodity markets is an ever-widening one. This is the case unless the *LM* curve turns upward, as indicated by the dashed line, until it intersects the *IS* curve. At this point of intersection, the *IS* curve cuts the *LM* curve from above and we have returned to the previous example.

Case III: Where IS Is Curved

In Chapter 7 we introduced the possibility that the *IS* curve could be negatively sloping over part of the output range and positively sloping once a threshold level of output had been attained. There, we drew the curve with kinks in it to dramatize the changes in the slope. Here, in Figure 10–7, we have

Figure 10–7.

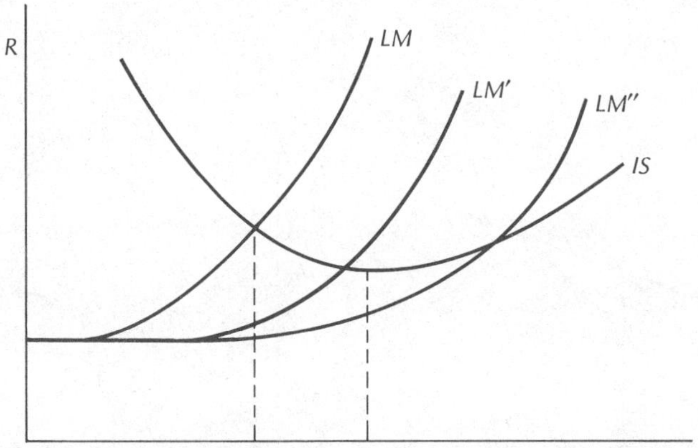

smoothed the kinks and drawn an *IS* curve with a parabolic shape. From earlier analysis we saw that if e, in the function $I = c + dR + eY$, were large enough, the *IS* curve would be positively sloped. We have been constrained by the linear form of our equations heretofore because they enable the use of simple numerical examples to illustrate the points we wish to make. But our theory should not be limited by this. The actual shapes taken by the curves will depend on empirical observation. If income is low we expect the coefficient e in the investment demand function to be small. Business firms have excess capacity and an increase in Y can be produced with little or no increase of investment in new capital goods. But if income is at a high level, e will be large—business firms will be pressing against their capacity and any increase in income will lead to an increase in demand for capital goods. Thus in this case e is not a constant, but is affected by Y. We could describe this effect by changing our investment demand function to $I = c + dR + e'Y + e''Y^2$. With the combined effect of Y and Y^2 in the function, higher levels of Y would be reflected in larger investment demands. Such a formulation would impart to the *IS* curve the general shape shown in Figure 10–7.

From the three *LM* curves it is clear that increases in the money supply might lead to reduced interest rates at first (moving from *LM* to *LM'*), but that eventually, as the *LM* curve shifts to a point of intersection with *IS* beyond Y_2, further increases in M_s lead to higher interest rates.

It is also clear that the variety of shapes assumed by the curves yield different implications about the effects of different policy acts. It is important, therefore, for policy makers and forecasters to have some idea of their shapes in the real world. For this we need empirical analysis, although the world of real data is unfortunately not as refined as the world of theory. Some rough and suggestive statistical estimates of *IS* and *LM* curves appear in the appendix to this chapter.

THE PORTFOLIO BALANCE EFFECT

We come now to a most important question concerning the interconnections between the real and the monetary sector. Our model is one of a rigid price level, an assumption that will shortly be modified, for there is reason to believe that the interest rate is not the only medium through which a change in the monetary sector can be carried over into the commodity-producing sector, and so influence the real behavior of transactor units. One reason for this is to be found in the portfolio balance effect of the increase in the "real" supply of money, or the money supply deflated by the price level.

In describing the consumption function, it was pointed out that the position of $C(Y)$ could be affected by the relationship between actual and desired holdings of durables, the latter expressed in terms of the allocation of household wealth among three forms of assets—money, financial assets, and durables. This became further evident in our consideration of the asset demand for money where a decision rule was presented for household and business transactor units, viz., that a desired portfolio could be defined in terms of the equality of the return at the margin of alternative forms of wealth holdings.

To see the effect of an increase in the real supply of money on households and business firms, we can begin by assuming that households are in a position of equilibrium where returns at the margin on money, on other financial assets, and on tangible goods are all equal. If the supply of real money balances held by households increases, this equilibrium will be disturbed. We would expect that, given a household utility function, returns of additional money holdings would decline, and that households would react by exchanging these money holdings for either financial assets or tangible goods, or for both. The process of establishing a new desired portfolio position would be under way. If money is exchanged for other financial assets, such as bonds and equities, the effect is to drive their prices up and their interest yields down. This is quite consistent with our earlier conclusion that a decline in interest rates can result from an increase in the real supply of money and that this fall in R would encourage investment expenditure. This may be viewed as a situation in which holdings of tangible assets are being readjusted in response to changes in financial asset prices and yields, and therefore to changes in the difference between returns on tangible and financial assets.

However, the household may also directly exchange money holdings for durable goods. This can occur simultaneously with interest rate changes rather than because of these changes, as households balance their portfolios by acquiring more tangibles. In this instance, the effect of the increase in the real money supply is to induce an upward move in the *IS* function resulting from asset imbalance.

In the case of business enterprises, it can likewise be argued that spending decisions will be influenced by the composition of the balance sheet. If we assume an equilibrium portfolio position for business firms, then if the money supply increases this equilibrium will be disturbed. Exchanges of money for other financial assets will occur, and as a result interest rates will decline in the manner outlined above. Such declines induce more investment spending as the business sector directly exchanges money for tangible assets in the effort to achieve a new portfolio equilibrium. Once again the effect is to move *IS* upwards, this time in response to a shift in the investment demand function.

CONCLUSION

In this chapter, we have completed our development of a comparative static model of income determination containing both a commodity and a monetary sector. It has been presented with the restrictive assumption of a stable price level up to the point of full employment levels of output. A statement has been made of equilibrium conditions in both commodity and money markets, and we have tried to show some of the interdependencies and complexities in the relationship of the commodity and monetary sectors of the economy. In developing this model, we have placed a good deal of stress upon the policy alternatives available to move the economy toward a position of full employment.

Our principal remaining task is to incorporate price level determination into the model. In so doing, it will be necessary to examine the conditions under which output is produced, particularly the nature of the labor market.

APPENDIX

Empirical Estimates of *IS* and *LM* Curves

The question of whether a theoretical model describes reality is the acid test of any theory, and, although the evidence is far from conclusive, several rough statistical studies do tend to confirm the existence of *IS* and *LM* curves of the general shape we have described.

There are many opportunities for error attached to every attempt to use statistical regression techniques on the data from economic time series to estimate equations, and these merely compound the many problems of measurement already alluded to in the chapters above. Nevertheless, data have been collected on government spending and on the money supply—exogenous variables determined by policy—and on income and the interest rate—dependent variables determined by the intersection of the *IS* and *LM* curves.

For the U.S. economy, the period from 1951 through 1964 was divided into high income and low income subperiods.[3] The statistically estimated equations for the *IS* and *LM* curves during low income periods were respectively:

$$Y = 755.02 - 631.25R + 21.31G \qquad (10.6)$$

$$R = 2.558 + .0204Y - .0400M_s \qquad (10.7)$$

Income, measured by gross national product in billions of dollars, is placed on the left-hand side of the equation for the *IS* curve in these estimates, unlike the convention we have used so far in which the rate of interest was on the left-hand side for both *IS* and *LM* curves. Here, the measure of the rate of interest is Moody's AAA corporate bond yield. Assuming $G = \$140$ billion and $M_s = \$300$ billion, the *IS* and *LM* curves can be graphed as in Figure 10–8, with the *IS* curve from equation (10.6) shown lying to the left of the *LM* curve.

The data for high income periods gave the following equations:

$$Y = 2099.8 - 1473.1R + 40.68G \qquad (10.8)$$

$$R = 2.156 + .0241Y - .0466M_s \qquad (10.9)$$

The *IS* curve from equation (10.8) lies to the right of the *LM* curve in Figure 10–8.

[3] These first four equations were taken from R. H. Scott, "Estimates of Hicksian IS and LM curves for the United States," *Journal of Finance* (September 1966): 479–487.

Figure 10–8.

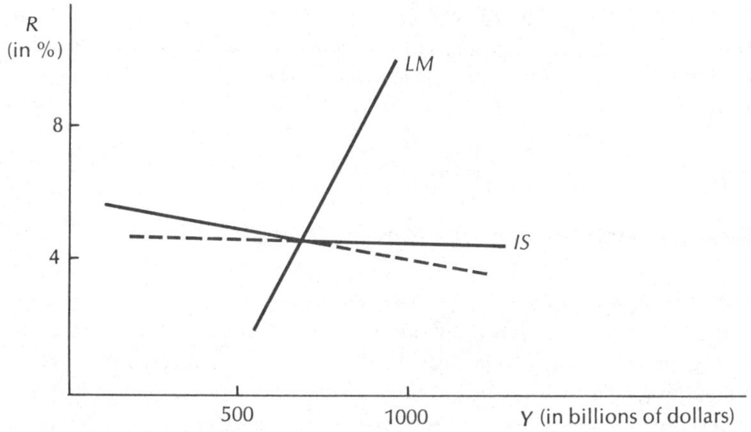

More recent estimates, using data covering the inflationary period beginning in 1964 with the onset of the escalation of hostilities in Vietnam and ending at the close of 1972, show an *IS* curve that is positively sloped. The estimates are not strictly comparable because here G is defined to include only federal government expenditures. The equations are:[4]

$$Y = -293.7 + 303.3R - 8.236G \qquad (10.10)$$

$$R = -4.034 + .0081Y + .0172M_s \qquad (10.11)$$

The curves are shown in Figure 10–9, assuming $G =$ \$100 billion and $M_s =$ \$250 billion.

The coefficient of R in equation (10.10) is positive, indicating a positive slope for the *IS* curve, while the coefficient of G is negative. By observing the respective curves in Figure 10–9, one can imagine that an increase in G would shift the *IS* curve *leftward,* leading to a higher R *and* higher Y. Thus when *IS* is positively sloped, a negative coefficient for G is required if an increase in G is to be expansionary.

Also, the positive relation between R and M_s in equation (10.11) suggests that an increase in M_s will shift the *LM* curve to the right, and the new point of intersection of *IS* and *LM* will record not only a higher Y, but also a higher R. When the *IS* curve is positively sloped, therefore, a higher M_s leads *not* to a reduction, but to an increase, in R.

Similar estimates are available for Canada.[5] The relatively slack income period from 1950 to 1962 gave:

[4] Equations (10.10) and (10.11) are taken from unpublished data recently processed with the assistance of Robert Mitchell.

Figure 10–9.

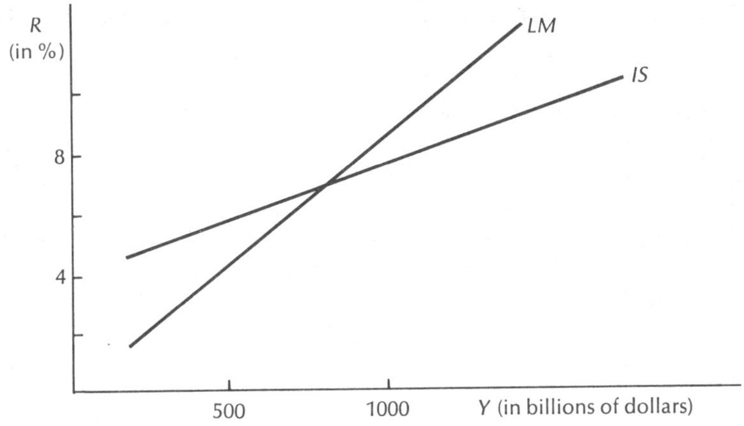

$$Y = 51{,}730 - 14{,}686R + 6.47G \qquad (10.12)$$

$$R = 5.140 + .000239Y - .0015M_s \qquad (10.13)$$

For the period of stronger expansion from 1962 to 1970, we again find the *IS* curve to be positively sloped:

$$Y = -74{,}610 + 36{,}846R = 5.34G \qquad (10.14)$$

$$R = 2.456 + .000186Y + .00088M_s \qquad (10.15)$$

The coefficients in these equations should not be accepted uncritically. They are beset with many statistical problems and they are presented here principally to indicate that, in a rough and general way, the forces described by the theoretical model for the macro economy do exist.

ADDITIONAL READINGS

An early formulation of the *IS* and *LM* curves may be found in J. R. Hicks, "Mr. Keynes and the 'classics': A suggested interpretation," *Econometrica,* 5 (1937): 147–159. The *IS* and *LM* curves are also developed by Alvin H. Hansen in Chapter 7 of *A Guide to Keynes* (New York: McGraw-Hill, 1953),

[5] R. H. Scott and Warren Thompson, "A note on estimates of Hicksian IS and LM curves for the Canadian economy, 1950–1970," *Journal of Business Administration*, 4, #2 (1973). The several equations presented above are not strictly comparable with one another because, for example, the money supply and government spending are measured differently in the equations. The results are presented merely to suggest that the *IS–LM* theoretical framework has some validity in real economies.

and in Chapters 4 and 5 of *Monetary Theory and Fiscal Policy* (New York: McGraw-Hill, 1949).

A concise textbook treatment of this same topic is presented by Joseph P. McKenna in *Aggregate Economic Analysis,* 3rd ed. (New York: Holt, Rinehart and Winston, 1969), Chapters 9–11.

An algebraic model of the commodity and money markets and numerical examples are contained in W. L. Smith and R. L. Teigen, *Readings in Money, National Income, and Stabilization Policy* (Homewood: Irwin, 1965), pp. 1–32.

An examination of kinked *IS* functions is found in H. R. Hudson, "A model of the trade cycle," *Economic Record*, 40 (March 1964): 78–85.

QUESTIONS

1. What factors determine "the" rate of interest?
   How would you explain the behavior of interest rates (assume they move together) during a "typical" business cycle?

2. What argument might be used against using the level or the movement of interest rates as an indicator of monetary policy?

3. Let $G = 12$ $M_s = 28$
   $C = 5 + 1/2\,(Y - T)$ $M_Y = (1/2)\,Y$
   $I = 53 - 5R$ $M_L = 20 - 2R$
   $T = (1/4)\,Y$

   (a) What is the formula for the *IS* curve?
   (b) What is the formula for the *LM* curve?
   (c) What are the equilibrium values of Y, C, I, R, M_Y, and T?

4. Take the following Keynesian model:

$$Y = C + I + G + E_x - I_m$$
$$C = 30 + 5/6\,(Y - T)$$
$$I = 120 - 6R$$
$$G = 80$$
$$E_x = 60$$
$$I_m = (1/10)Y$$
$$T = (1/5)Y$$
$$M_s = 120 + (3/20)Y$$
$$M_Y = (1/4)Y$$
$$M_L = 240 - 12R \text{ for all } R > 2,\ R = 2 \text{ for } M_L > 216$$
$$M_s = M_Y + M_L$$

   (a) What is the *IS* equation?
   (b) What is the *LM* equation?

(c) Find Y and R at equilibrium, and then find the corresponding values of I, T, M_Y, M_L, and M_s.
(d) Is the budget in balance, surplus, or deficit?
(e) What is Y if G rises to 100?

5. Historical data indicate that during times of expansion interest rates increase at the same time that the money supply increases. How do you reconcile this observation with the general proposition taught in courses in money and banking that a larger money supply, other things being equal, leads to lower interest rates?

6. Induced investment may lead to an upward sloping *IS* curve as mentioned in this chapter. In this case indicate the possible effects that an increase in the money supply might have on the equilibrium interest rate. Explain how this can come about.

7. Returning to Chapter 2, review those actions which may lead to a change in the money supply. How will these actions affect the rate of interest according to the model developed in this chapter?

8. A period of time in which long-term interest rates are high or rising is popularly called a period of *tight* money, and when rates are low or falling it is called a period of *easy* money. Examine data on the long-term interest rates over the past six or eight months in either the *Survey of Current Business* or the *Federal Reserve Bulletin.* Would you say monetary policy has been tight, easy, or neutral?

9. Assume the tax laws are changed to encourage business to depreciate new plant and equipment in half the period previously permitted. Consider in detail the effect of this on the present value of new investment and investment demand. Trace the probable effect of this tax change on interest rate, output, price, and employment levels.

Aggregate Supply: Output and the Price Level

11 Chapter

This chapter and Chapter 12 on the labor market provide the necessary background for our third and final approximation to the complete static income-determination model to be presented in Chapter 13.

So far, we have assumed that variations in demand in the range below the point of full employment result only in variations in real output and that prices are constant. However, we have also assumed that an increase in aggregate demand beyond the point of full employment will increase the price level only, that is, full employment gives the maximum real output for the economy by definition and, while monetary values for output can continue to rise, these merely reflect higher prices and not higher production levels. By evaluating supply, we can build a complete model in which real output and its composition, employment, and the price level are all simultaneously determined, along with levels of money income, interest rates, taxes, and so forth, as explained in Chapter 10.

As a first step we will develop a function that will describe how the number of jobs offered by producing units increases with expected sales revenues. We will start with the basic individual producing units in the economy, i.e., with business firms. Our approach is similar to that adopted in Chapter 1, where a set of social accounts was constructed. Our initial task then was to construct income and product statements for producing units. These measured, on the one hand, sources of revenue and, on the other, their allocations within the firm to factors of production. It is clear that each of these quantities can vary over time. We need then some workable model to show the effect that changes in prices and in the total receipts of producing units have upon the utilization of productive factors, particularly labor. The questions that need to be answered include: What increase in total receipts would be necessary for an enterprise to increase its job offers (employment) by, say, 10 percent? What increase in the price level would have to occur in order for an enterprise to increase its employment by 10 percent? Conversely, what would be the effect of a specified decrease in prices upon the number of available jobs offered by the business?

If a simple model of business behavior relating expected revenues and prices to job availability can be built, then through an aggregation process the relationship between factor earnings, output, employment, and prices can be conceptualized for the economy as a whole. This is a big task, but a very necessary one for an adequate understanding of macroeconomics.

DERIVATION OF THE MODEL

The following eight simplifying assumptions, necessary for any consideration of price effects, represent a combination of technological, behavioral, and institutional conditions:

(1) businessmen maximize profit;
(2) firms in the economy operate in a highly competitive market;
(3) there are two classes of factor inputs—labor and capital;
(4) labor is the variable factor;
(5) the state of technology, and the stock of capital, are both given;
(6) the labor force is homogeneous (i.e., one labor force unit is an hour's employment of ordinary labor; an hour's employment of special labor is taken as more than one unit in proportion to its relative remuneration, on the assumption that differences in productivity are reflected in differences in earning rates);
(7) business firms are vertically integrated (i.e., we can abstract from inter-firm transactions);
(8) the society is "closed," i.e., it has no foreign sector.

Within these assumptions we must develop for the firm an association between its revenues and offered employment. First, since total revenues are linked to employment through output, we need a production function, a technological condition that can be specified from assumptions (3), (5), and (7):

$$Q = Q(N, K, J) \tag{11.1}$$

where Q is the output of the firm;
N is the labor input of the firm;
K is the given capital input of the firm;
J is a general term introduced to represent the state of technology of the firm; J is given.

By fixing the stock of capital and technology, we are assuming the period of time we are concerned with is short enough that the stock of capital cannot be changed to any noticeable extent. Therefore, this is a short-run production function characterized, as output increases, by diminishing marginal physical productivity of labor. Because the firm's demand for labor is derived from the demand for the firm's output, we can approach the demand for labor by specifying a firm's optimal production level. Profit-maximizing businessmen will produce output up to the point where the cost of producing an additional unit is equal to the additional revenues derived from its sale. With labor as the only variable input, the cost of producing an added unit of the commodity, i.e., the marginal cost, will be the cost of the unit of labor required to produce the added output. Thus:

$$MC = W\Delta N \tag{11.2}$$

where MC is the marginal cost of production;
W is the hiring cost or wage rate;
ΔN is the additional units of labor required.

The revenue derived from added output, i.e., the marginal revenue, will be:

$$MR = P\Delta Q \tag{11.3}$$

where MR is the marginal revenue of the firm;
P is the price per unit of product produced by the firm;
ΔQ is the added units of output.

According to microeconomic theory, in a purely competitive market structure, the firm is a price taker, not a price maker. Therefore, the price is given and the marginal revenue from an added unit of output will be equal to price. Combining equations (11.2) and (11.3), our decision rule respecting output is therefore:

$$\overbrace{W\Delta N}^{\text{marginal cost}} = \overbrace{P\Delta Q}^{\text{marginal revenue}} \tag{11.4}$$

$$\text{or:}\quad P = W\frac{\Delta N}{\Delta Q} \tag{11.5}$$

$\Delta N/\Delta Q$ is the additional labor input required to produce an added unit of output, and from microeconomics we recall that its reciprocal, $\Delta Q/\Delta N$, is the marginal physical productivity of labor. From these equations we can see that the marginal cost to the entrepreneur for each planned level of output will vary directly with the wage rate and inversely with the marginal physical productivity of labor. Hence, in following the above decision rule for maximizing profits, the production of more product requires an increase in price to offset the higher marginal cost resulting from the diminishing marginal productivity of the variable input.

The demand for labor is derived from the entrepreneur's output plans, and equation (11.5) may be rewritten to emphasize labor demand. The cost of hiring an additional unit of input is the wage rate, W. The revenue derived from an additional hiring is the value of the marginal product of the input, i.e., the price of the product multiplied by the marginal physical product of labor. For a profit maximizer, hiring will occur up to the point where:

$$W = P\frac{\Delta Q}{\Delta N} \tag{11.6}$$

For now, we will take the wage rate as a given so that we can concentrate first on the relationship between the marginal physical productivity and the range of prices necessary to bring forth alternative planned levels of output. It should be understood, however, that this condition is subject to modification as we proceed.

Figure 11–1.

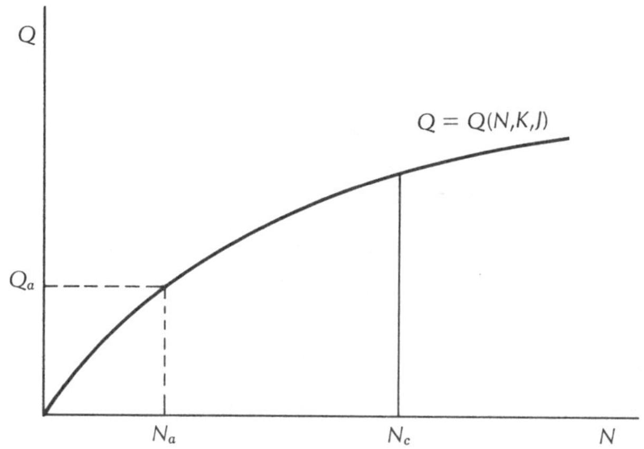

Combining the production function (11.1), the decision rule for output (11.4), and the statement about wage behavior (11.6), we are now in a position to determine a function for the firm relating total revenue to its demand for labor. Obviously, with a constant wage rate and a short-run production function subject to diminishing marginal productivity, profit-maximizing businessmen will increase planned output only in response to an expected rise in prices.

What has been described can be summarized graphically by considering Figure 11–1, a short-run production function with labor as the variable input and with both the stock of capital, *K*, and the state of technology, *J*, given; when labor input amounts to N_a, total output is Q_a.

If we then plot the slope of the curve in Figure 11–1 against the labor input, we obtain Figure 11–2. This function, $Q'(N)$, is the marginal produc-

Figure 11–2.

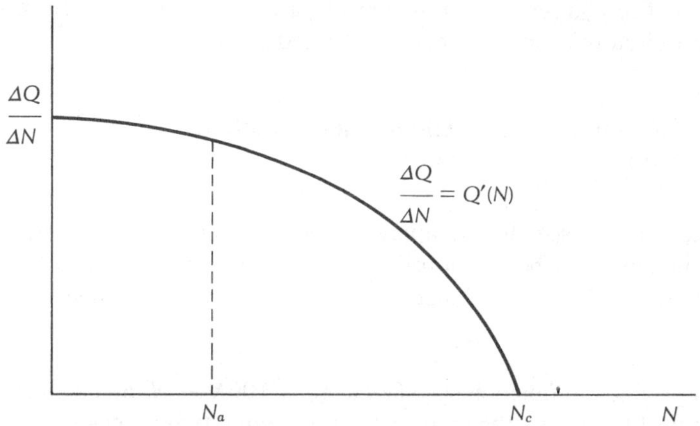

Figure 11–3.

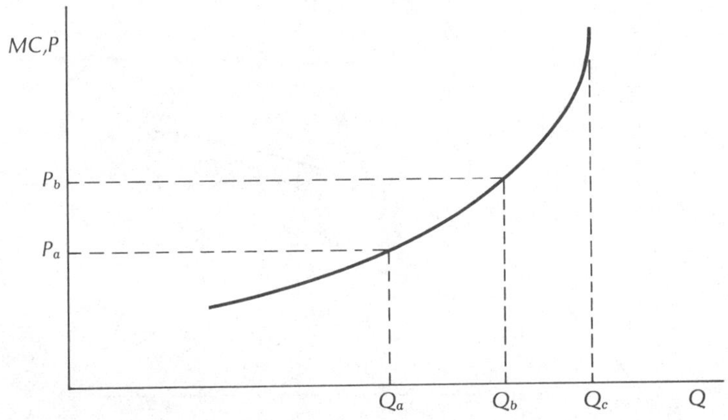

tivity function and its downward slope expresses the "law of diminishing returns."

Finally, Figure 11–3 indicates the behavior of marginal cost as output changes. The wage rate is constant and the production function is as specified in Figure 11–1. The curve is positively sloping because of the diminishing marginal productivity of labor. A fixed W and falling marginal product mean that the marginal cost rises as production rises, and hence the businessman's total revenues, PQ, also rise. Marginal cost approaches infinity as marginal productivity approaches zero. In these circumstances it is apparent that the anticipated price of output must rise as the planned output of businessmen increases. At an anticipated price of P_a planned output will be Q_a. However, were the planned level of output to rise to Q_b, then price would have to increase to P_b. A planned output of Q_b results in an increase in the quantity of labor demanded; the magnitude of the increase in quantity demanded will depend upon the slope of the marginal productivity function. It is also apparent from Figure 11–3 and equation (11.5) that an increase in the wage rate, W, would shift the entire marginal cost function upwards. The consequence would be a higher required price at *each* level of planned output.

Expected Revenue–Offered Employment Function for One Firm

The following two specific examples of how expected revenue–offered employment functions may be developed for a single-product firm involve different production functions and a range of hirings from 25 to 36 employees.

Case *I*

Given a production function specified as $Q = 100N - N^2$ and a constant wage rate, Table 11–1 shows the relation between input, output, costs, and revenues for one firm.[1] Column (f) indicates that the marginal cost per unit of output increases as the marginal productivity of labor in (c) decreases. With a decision rule of price = marginal cost, column (f) also reveals the increase in price per unit of output necessary for increases in output to be planned and for new hirings to occur. For example, our production function reveals that if 30 men are hired instead of 29, total output increases by 41 units. With a constant wage rate of $2.00 per hour, marginal cost rises from 4.7¢ to 4.9¢ per unit due to the declining $\Delta Q/\Delta N$. If the additional hiring is to occur, an increase in price equal to the increase in unit cost will be necessary.

An expected revenue–offered employment function is then derived by plotting column (a) (N) against column (h) (Total Revenue) in Figure 11–4. The production function gives us the amount of labor input required to produce a given level of output and, for any price level, given total revenues. If the firm expects a certain level of total revenues, then, it will hire the appropriate number of workers; but if the price level rises, the profit-maximizing level of output and the expected total revenues will rise too, and the firm will hire a larger number of employees. An increase in offered employment is thus associated with rising marginal costs. If the hirings are to take place, prices must increase to overcome the rise in marginal costs that results from declining marginal productivity. In Figure 11–4, the difference between the total wage bill and total expected revenues represents the earnings of factor inputs *other* than labor. Thus at $N = 29$, the wage bill is $58 and the income of other factors is $38.8. As offered employment increases, however, the return to labor relative to non-labor inputs *declines*; at $N = 33$, for instance, the wage bill, at $66, is *relatively* smaller and non-labor factor income, at $60, *relatively* larger. The decline in the share of labor in total income reflects the decline in the

Figure 11–4.

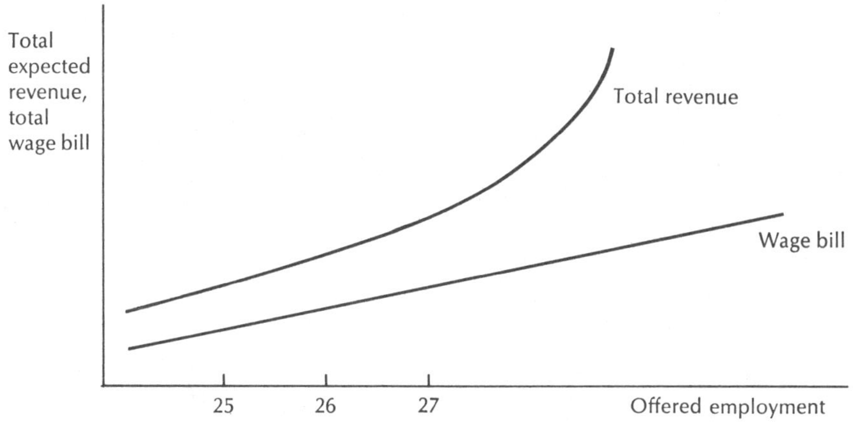

[1] This production function is a parabola that, if drawn, rises out of the origin and reaches a peak when $dQ/dN = 100 - 2N = 0$, or when $N = 50$ and marginal productivity is zero. Then it falls to the axis so that $Q = 0$ when $N = 100$. The firm will only operate freely in the range where the production function is rising and the marginal productivity is positive. It is, therefore, only the first half of this parabola that we are concerned with.

Table 11–1. Derivation of a Firm's Expected Revenue–Offered Employment Function.

(a) N	(b) Q	(c) ΔQ/ΔN	(d) Q/N (b) ÷ (a)	(e) W	(f) MC,P (e) ÷ (c)	(g) P(ΔQ/ΔN) (c) × (f)	(h) Total Revenue (b) × (f)	(i) Wage Bill (a) × (e)	(j) Total Revenue minus Wage Bill (h) − (i)	(k) Wage Bill as a Percent of Total Revenue (i) ÷ (h)
25	1875		75	2.00		2.00		50		
26	1924	49	74	2.00	.041	2.00	78.9	52	26.9	65.9
27	1971	47	73	2.00	.043	2.00	84.8	54	30.8	63.7
28	2016	45	72	2.00	.044	2.00	88.7	56	32.7	63.1
29	2059	43	71	2.00	.047	2.00	96.8	58	38.8	59.9
30	2100	41	70	2.00	.049	2.00	102.9	60	42.9	58.3
31	2139	39	69	2.00	.051	2.00	109.1	62	47.1	56.8
32	2176	37	68	2.00	.054	2.00	117.5	64	53.5	54.5
33	2211	35	67	2.00	.057	2.00	126.0	66	60.0	52.4
34	2244	33	66	2.00	.061	2.00	136.9	68	68.9	49.7
35	2275	31	65	2.00	.065	2.00	147.9	70	77.9	47.3
36	2304	29	64	2.00	.069	2.00	159.0	72	87.0	45.3

ratio of marginal to average physical product (ratio of column [c] to column [d]) as employment expands. Labor's share of the proceeds from the total output *declines* as output expands.

In Figure 11–4, the slope of W is determined by the money wage rate (W/N). The student should ask what would happen to the position of the expected revenue function if W/N were to increase from, say, $2.00 to $2.50.

Case II

One alternative production function is one in which a specified change in each and every input is accompanied by the same percentage change in output. In this type of production function, the shares of output going to the two factors of production, labor and capital, will be constant. This latter condition is consistent with conditions in the real world, for over the past quarter century the distribution of income between the wage and non-wage factors has been relatively stable. The sum of wages and salaries has generally been in the range of 65–70 percent of the national income. Therefore, the following example assumes more simply that shares in output are equally distributed between labor and capital.

The production function may be written as follows:[2]

$$Q = JN^{\alpha}\ K^{1-\alpha} \tag{11.7}$$

where Q is the output of the firm;
J is here a conversion coefficient, representing the state of technology, equal to ten;
K is a fixed quantity of capital, here equal to 25;
N is the input of labor, assumed to vary between 25 and 36;
α is the share of output going to labor; here $\alpha = 1/2$.

As in the preceding case it is assumed that the wage rate, W, is $2.00 and that the businessman follows the norm of profit maximization. Table 11–2 presents the input, output, costs, and revenues under the specified conditions. The columns are derived in the same manner as their counterparts in Table 11–1. The results of columns (i) and (j) are reproduced in Figure 11–5 and may be compared with Figure 11–4. The expected revenue function in this case is linear, and the wage bill is a constant share of total revenues. Table 11–2 shows that the ratio of marginal to average product is constant and determines the share of labor in total output. As with Case I, an expansion in offered employment is associated with rising marginal cost and, if entrepreneurial norms are followed, the price per unit must rise if the planned increase in output is to be realized and additional hiring is to occur. In both cases, the expected revenue function indicates the total revenues necessary for the offering of alternative levels of employment.

[2] This function is homogeneous of degree one. One property of such a function is that a proportional increase in each and every independent variable is accompanied by an equiproportional increase in the dependent variable. A function is said to be homogeneous of degree n whenever $\lambda^n Q = \lambda^n f(N,K) = f(\lambda N, \lambda K)$ for $\lambda \neq 0$. In equation (11.7) the exponents of N and K are α and $1 - \alpha$. The sum of these exponents is one. Therefore, because increasing both N and K by a factor λ gives $(\lambda N)^{\alpha}$ and $(\lambda K)^{1-\alpha}$, or $\lambda^1 N^{\alpha} K^{1-\alpha}$, the function is homogeneous of degree one.

Table 11–2. Derivation of an Alternative Expected Revenue–Offered Employment Function.

(a) K	(b) N	(c) Q	(d) $\Delta Q/\Delta N$	(e) Q/N (c) ÷ (b)	(f) W	(g) MC,P (f)/(d)	(h) $P(\Delta Q/\Delta N)$ (d) × (g)	(i) Total Revenue (c) × (g)	(j) Wage Bill (b) × (f)	(k) Wage Bill as a Percent of TR (j) ÷ (i)
25	25	250.00		10.00	2.00					
25	26	254.95	4.95	9.80	2.00	.404	2.00	103.00	52.00	50
25	27	259.80	4.85	9.62	2.00	.412	2.00	107.04	54.00	50
25	28	264.58	4.78	9.44	2.00	.418	2.00	110.59	56.00	50
25	29	269.26	4.68	9.28	2.00	.427	2.00	114.97	58.00	50
25	30	273.86	4.60	9.13	2.00	.435	2.00	119.13	60.00	50
25	31	278.39	4.53	8.98	2.00	.442	2.00	123.05	62.00	50
25	32	282.84	4.45	8.84	2.00	.449	2.00	127.00	64.00	50
25	33	287.23	4.39	8.70	2.00	.456	2.00	130.98	66.00	50
25	34	291.55	4.32	8.58	2.00	.463	2.00	134.99	68.00	50
25	35	295.80	4.25	8.45	2.00	.471	2.00	139.32	70.00	50
25	36	300.00	4.20	8.33	2.00	.476	2.00	142.80	72.00	50

Figure 11–5.

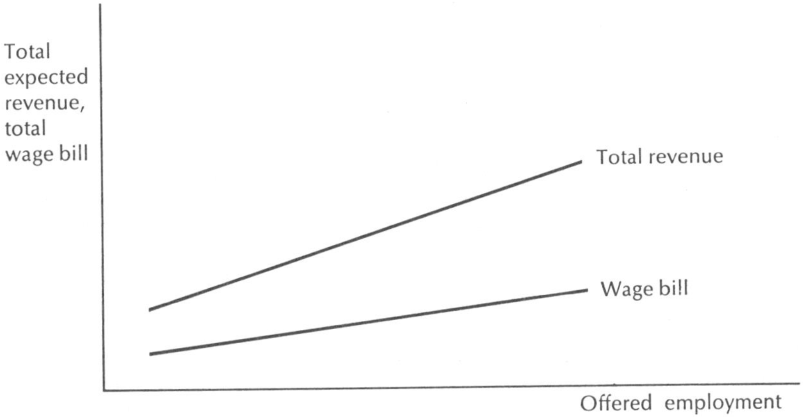

Expected Revenue–Offered Employment Functions for One Industry and for the Aggregate Economy

An industry's expected revenue–offered employment function relates the total expected revenues in the industry to job availability. To derive this function we need two pieces of information—an industry supply curve and a total product curve for the industry. These curves, if the production function for the firm can be regarded as characteristic of all firms in the industry, are of much the same form, and describe the same behavior, as the corresponding curves for the single firm shown in Figures 11–3 and 11–1, respectively. In the industry, as in the firm, an increase in expected prices will cause an increase in planned output and in offered employment. This aggregation process then permits us to construct an expected revenue–offered employment function for the industry as a whole. Should each firm have a production function equivalent to that of Case I, then Figure 11–6(a) would apply. Where each function

Figure 11–6.

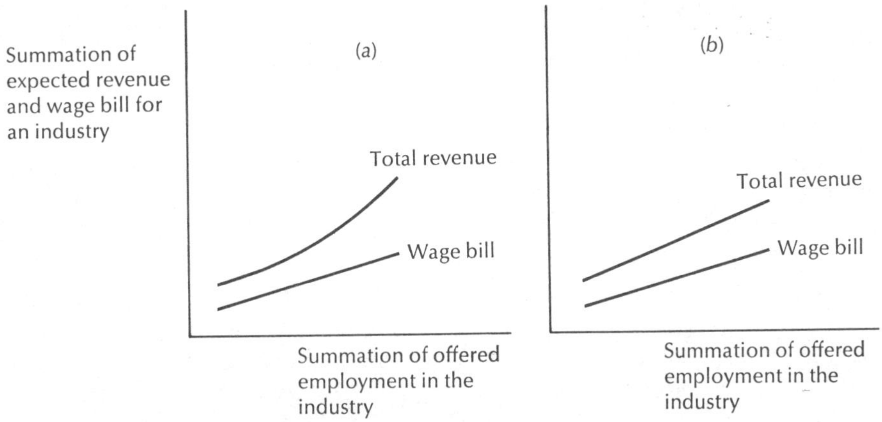

Figure 11–7.

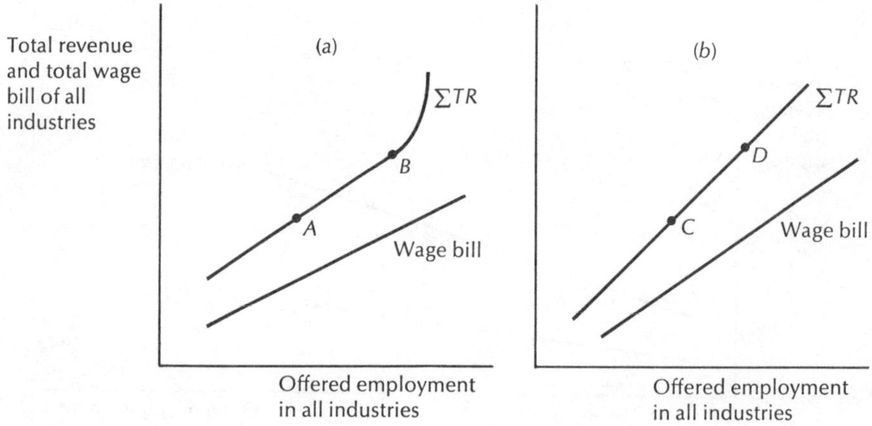

is of the type in Case II, then Figure 11–6(b) would approximate the situation.

If we assume that there are many industries in the economy and that as increases in output occur there are proportional increases in the output of each industry so that the composition of output is constant, then a unique expected revenue–offered employment function can be determined for the economy as a whole by aggregating similarly across the expected revenue–offered employment functions of all industries. The results of this aggregation process, where the underlying production functions are of the types described in Cases I and II, respectively, are illustrated in Figure 11–7(a) and (b). In view of the assumption of vertically integrated business firms, the summation of total expected revenues in all industries, $\sum TR$, will be equal to the contribution of the private business sector to the GNP as measured by the sectoral accounts of Chapter 1. $\sum TR$ also tells us the revenues necessary to induce businessmen to offer alternative levels of employment. The difference between total revenues and the wage bill represents returns to owners of property (nonlabor factor income).

The Employment–Supply Function and Aggregate Supply

For the businessman in pure competition an optimal level of output is that for which price equals marginal cost. We have seen that marginal cost equals $W/(\Delta Q/\Delta N)$, i.e., marginal cost varies directly with the wage rate and inversely with the marginal productivity of labor. Even with constant wage rates, instituting a planned increase in employment and in output will require an increase in prices to offset the accompanying rise in marginal cost when the marginal productivity of labor declines. In the production function $Q = Q(N,K)$, we see that output increases as employment increases; therefore *the price level must vary directly with offered employment and real output*. This was first seen in columns (a), (b), and (f) of Table 11–1, and as we aggregate

Figure 11–8.

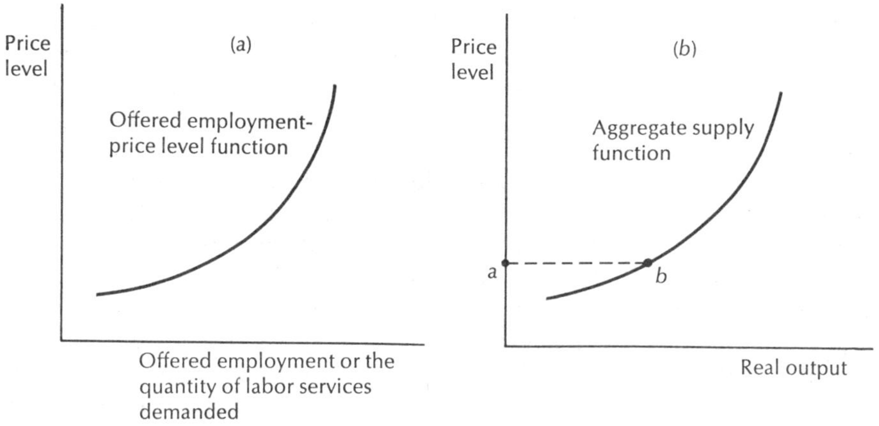

across firms and then across industries the same relations continue to hold. They are illustrated in Figure 11–8 (a) and (b), relating the price level of offered employment and real output. Figure 11–8 (a) explicitly illustrates what is implicit in Figure 11–7. In the latter, as we move up $\sum TR$ there is implicitly a higher price level at B than at A, and at D than at C, and as we move from A to B and C to D real output increases as employment increases. Hence Figure 11–8(b), which we call the *aggregate supply curve*, indicates that the price level varies directly with real output. This aggregate supply curve will be of particular importance in our analysis of inflation in Chapter 16. It perhaps deserves to be repeated that the functions in Figure 11–8 (a) and (b) rest on the condition of a constant wage rate, a short-run production function, and an unaltered composition of goods produced. In these circumstances, the extent of the increases in employment and planned output that accompany an increase in the price level will depend upon the marginal physical productivity of the variable input that in turn underlies marginal cost.

PREDICTING WITH THE MODEL

The model now shows the theoretical relation of output to the price level under some rigid assumptions. We will now change some of these assumptions, to see how aggregate supply is affected, by (a) introducing exogenous shifts in the wage rate, (b) dropping the assumption of a homogeneous labor force, (c) introducing a degree of monopoly in market structure, and (d) introducing changes in technology. We will consider the effect of each on the aggregate supply function which relates output to the price level.

Exogenous Shifts in the Wage Rate

If the money wage rate is no longer held constant, but allowed to shift upward discontinuously, as it does, for example, as a result of collective bargaining between labor and management, then as employment increases and the reservoir of unemployed labor is reduced, upward pressures on money wages will appear. Scarcities may develop in particular occupational groups and money wage rates will be raised. Further, continuously employed workers will observe that their real wage rate has declined as prices increase more rapidly than their money wage rate increases and they will seek to recoup their position through increased money wage demands.[3]

The effect of this on revenue-employment functions can be seen by recomputing the quantities in Tables 11–1 and 11–2 under the alternate production functions obtained by letting W rise to \$2.50 when more than 28 men are employed and to \$3.00 when more than 33 men are employed. The results, when summed across firms and industries to yield aggregate functions, are depicted in Figure 11–9(a) and (b).

It is evident that exogenous upward shifts in the wage rate serve only to increase the price level necessary to achieve given levels of employment and output. This causes the aggregate supply curve to shift upward too. Here, then, is a new source of price level changes to be considered in addition to the effects attributed to the presence of diminishing returns. It should be noted, however, that the wage increase does not necessarily alter the distributive shares of the economy between labor and non-labor factors, which, as mentioned earlier, has been around 65–70 percent for labor. The wage bill may remain the same proportion of total income (output) for given levels of employment after the wage increase as it was before, for the attempt by labor to bargain for an increase in its income share may be frustrated by management's response. Real wages may fail to change.

Pushing the implications of this analysis a bit further, there are some

Figure 11–9.

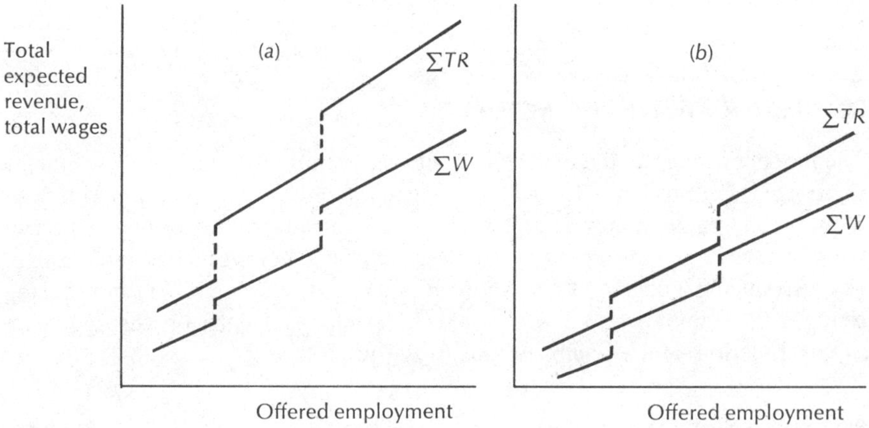

[3] This is true even if real output increases, at least in the Case I situation. There the share of wages in total output declines with increased employment, and the real wage rate of workers falls.

redistributive effects of the exogeneous shift in the wage rate even if the ratio of wage income to total income remains constant. Those who are on fixed incomes (pensioners and property owners drawing contractual income such as interest or rent) are worse off as a result of the wage-price hike. If we use a production function with constant shares, letting 50 percent of factor income go to owners of property, then profits are the residual. Rent and interest represent fixed-sum payments independent of output levels. As a result of the wage-price hike, profit recipients gain at the expense of rent and interest recipients. Those who remain unemployed as the economy expands also suffer ill effects from such an income redistribution. The actual cyclical swings in profits as measured in the national income accounts are roughly consistent with this theoretical view.

Non-Homogeneous Labor Force

The effect on our aggregate supply function if we modify the assumption of a homogeneous labor force can be seen by adopting the convention that businessmen will be forced to employ less effective workers at the margin as offered employment expands. This is not unrealistic because we can expect employers to use variation in labor effectiveness as a criterion in personnel selection. Less efficient workers (those with below average training, experience, and initiative) will tend to be in demand only when the pool of available workers is low. If each unit of labor is paid a wage that recognizes differentials in quality, then the money wage paid each unit will reflect these differences. To a large extent this does occur in competitive markets, but labor markets are rarely perfectly competitive. Workers in a given occupational class in a labor market receive the same money wage in spite of often distinct differences in productivity.

The existence of differences in worker quality will cause the revenue–employment function and the aggregate supply function in Figures 11–7 and 11–8(b) to rise at a sharper rate due to the added depressing effect of declines in quality on the marginal and average productivity of labor. The increase in the price level will be more pronounced than if the labor force were homogeneous.

Modification in Market Structure

The effect on the shape of the aggregate supply function if some degree of monopoly rather than pure competition characterizes the market structure of the economy can be seen by taking the extreme case where each industry consists of a single producer. Since each monopolist now faces the downward sloping industry demand curve rather than a fixed price, our profit-maximizing decision rule under the production function conditions previously outlined would be:[4]

$$MR = W/(\Delta Q/\Delta N) = MC$$

where MR is marginal revenue. This formula replaces $P = MC$. It can be shown that, in order to increase the volume of offered employment by a given amount, the price increase required in the case of profit-maximizing monopoly will be greater than if the market structure is purely competitive.[5]

It could be argued that firms in industries where monopoly exists might not wish to maximize short-run profits for various strategic reasons. For example, maximizing might serve simply to attract new entrants or to increase the likelihood of punitive government action. Hence a monopolistic firm might prefer the objective of maximizing revenues subject to the constraint of, say, a 15 percent return on invested capital. If firms operated with this decision rule under monopoly market conditions, the aggregate supply function would rise less steeply than would be the case under profit maximization.

Changes in Technology

The effect on the aggregate supply function of a change in technology can be examined with the function:

$$Q = JN^{\alpha}K^{1-\alpha}$$

An increase in engineering or managerial technology can for our purposes be represented by an increase in the value of J, the conversion coefficient, but could such a change occur independently of any net increase in the capital stock or replacement investment? If it did occur, it would imply that technical advance represents improved managerial know-how that can be incorporated into production processes without additions to capital. Alternatively, technical advance may entail "embodiment," a reflection of technology in continual improvements in the capital stock via investment.

In either case, the effect on the representative firm in Table 11–2 will be to raise the marginal and average product of labor, and, with a given wage rate, to lower the price of the product at each level of offered employment. Thus, if J changes from 10 to 11, the marginal physical product of the twenty-

[4] From microeconomics we know that this maximizing condition is the equivalent of $P(1 + 1/\varepsilon) = MC$ where P is the price per unit of the product of the monopoly industry and ε is the coefficient of elasticity, defined as $\varepsilon = (dQ/Q)/(dP/P) = P\ dQ/Q\ dP$, which is the ratio of the percentage change in quantity to the percentage change in price, a measure of the responsiveness of quantity to changes in price.

To show the equivalence, let TR be total revenue and MR be marginal revenue, then $TR = PQ$, $dPQ/dQ = MR$, and by the chain rule $MR = P + Q(dP/dQ)$, which can be changed to $MR = P(1 + QdP/PdQ) = P(1 + 1/\varepsilon) = MC$.

[5] From the previous footnote we see that when the demand curve has its usual downward slope, $-1 < \varepsilon < 0$. Since $P(1 + 1/\varepsilon) = MC$, a given increase in MC will require a larger increase in P for equilibrium, whereas under competition $P = MC$ and a given increase in MC is accompanied by an equal increase in price. Therefore, a larger increase in price is required in order to induce the monopolist to hire more labor.

seventh man will be 5.33 rather than 4.85 units, and with a wage rate of \$2.00, the profit-maximizing price will be approximately 37.5¢ rather than 41.2¢. If this is the outcome of productivity increases through technical advance, then the gains will be taken in the form of lower output prices and the functions relating the price level to offered employment and real output (Figure 11–8) will shift downward.

Lower prices, however, are not the only way in which the benefits of technical change may be distributed. In our society, where technical change results in more output for the same input, the benefits of technical advance are frequently captured by the factors of production directly involved, rather than being passed on to consumers via lower prices. That is, if producers can maintain existing prices in the face of a 10 percent increase in the productivity of all factors and can still sell all their output, the money wage rate can now rise to \$2.20, or by 10 percent, the amount of the productivity gain, without any change in the profit-maximizing price. The remainder of total revenues still goes to non-labor factors, and their return is also 10 percent greater, for the wage bill is still only one half of total revenues. Labor and non-labor factor inputs distribute among themselves the gains in productivity.

CONCLUSION

This chapter has focused on the derivation of aggregate supply expressing the relation between output and the price level. We have seen that the slope and position of the aggregate supply curve depend upon the nature of the underlying production function. Under conditions of a fixed capital stock and fixed wage rates (W), the production functions we have examined indicate that prices must rise if employment and output are to increase. This is because labor experiences diminishing marginal productivity. In other words, given that the profit maximizing condition is $P = W/(\Delta Q/\Delta N)$, if W is fixed and $\Delta Q/\Delta N$ is decreasing, P must rise. When we aggregate across firms and industries for the economy as a whole, we find that rising prices must accompany increasing output, i.e., the aggregate supply curve is upward sloping.

The latter part of the chapter discussed a number of factors which may alter the slope and position of the aggregate supply curve. If wages increase with employment or if the labor force is non-homogeneous, the aggregate supply curve becomes steeper. Monopoly power may lead to a flatter or a steeper supply curve depending upon how monopolists exercise their power in the market, and changes in technology may alter both the slope and the position of the supply curve.

ADDITIONAL READINGS

The concept of aggregate supply as a function of employment is presented in J. M. Keynes, *The General Theory of Employment, Interest and Money* (New

York: Harcourt Brace Jovanovich, Inc., 1936), Chapter 3. The following works build from and enhance Keynes' presentation of the concept of aggregate supply: F. J. De Jong, "Supply functions in Keynesian economics," *Economic Journal*, 64 (March 1954): 3–24; S. Weintraub, *An Approach to the Theory of Income Distribution* (Philadelphia: Chilton, 1958), Chapter 2; Paul Wells, "Keynes' aggregate supply function: A suggested interpretation," *Economic Journal*, 70 (September 1960): 536–542; Paul Davison, "More on the aggregate supply function," *Economic Journal*, 72 (June 1962): 452–457; and P. Davidson and E. Smolensky, *Aggregate Supply and Demand Analysis* (New York: Harper & Row, 1964), Chapter 9.

QUESTIONS

1. Compute a total revenue function for a representative firm where
   (a) its production function is $Q = 100N - N^3/3$; Q is the total product and N is the number of workers;
   (b) the wage rate is \$2.00;
   (c) the firm is a profit maximizer, $W = (P)(\Delta Q/\Delta N)$;
   (d) N ranges from 1 to 9.

2. (a) Compute the total product, marginal product, average product, price of the product, the wage bill, the expected total revenue, and the share of labor in the total revenue for the following production function:

$$Q = JN^{\alpha}K^{1-\alpha}$$

   where Q is the total output of the product;
   J is a conversion coefficient, here equal to 20;
   K is the fixed quantity of capital available, here equal to 36;
   N is the input of labor and is assumed to vary from 16 to 25 men;
   W is the wage rate and is assumed to be constant at \$2.00;
   $\alpha = 1/2$.

   Assume that businessmen will maximize profits such that

$$P = W(\Delta N/\Delta Q)$$

   (b) Now assume that W rises to \$2.50 when more than 20 men are employed. What happens to expected revenues and the wage bill? To P?
   (c) Assume that W increases to \$3.00 when more than 22 men are employed. What happens to expected revenues and the wage bill? To P?
   (d) Draw a graph relating expected revenues to employment incorporating the changes in W found in parts (b) and (c).
   (e) Draw a new graph relating P to employment incorporating the changes in W found in parts (b) and (c).

3. If the production function is $Q = 200N - 2N^2$, the share of income going to labor will fall as employment rises. If $Q = 25N^{.5}K^{.5}$ represents the production function, the share of income flowing to labor remains constant as employment rises. Explain. Assume that the wage rate is \$3.00 and $K = 100$. Develop a table indicating the necessary prices to ensure employment of 25, 36, 49, 64, and 81 workers for each of the production functions.

4. Would you expect both an increase in monopoly power and an increase in the heterogeneity of the labor force to lead to a more sharply rising aggregate supply curve? Explain your answer.

5. According to the analysis in this chapter, why will an increase in money wages *not* lead to an increase in real wages in general? However, for particular sectors of the economy, a rise in money wages may mean a rise in real wages. Explain.

6. Some firms practice average cost pricing rather than marginal cost pricing, where average cost equals total cost divided by Q. Assume fixed cost is a certain amount for all rates of output and let total cost equal fixed cost plus WN. Explain how the use of average cost pricing would affect the expected revenue–offered employment function for the firm in Table 11–1. How would the treatment of fixed costs differ from that in the marginal cost pricing case?

   Assume *all* firms practice average cost rather than marginal cost pricing. How will this affect the economy's aggregate supply curve if the production function of every firm is $Q = 100N - N^2$? Will the aggregate supply curve be affected if only a few firms use average cost pricing?

The Labor Market

12
Chapter

This chapter more thoroughly examines labor markets and considers the effects of alternative wage rates on the businessman's demand for labor and the quantity of labor supplied by the labor force. We will develop aggregate demand and supply functions for labor, present factors determining real and money wage rates, and clarify the terms voluntary and involuntary unemployment and full employment.

THE AGGREGATE DEMAND FOR LABOR

In Chapter 11 we saw that an output decision rule for entrepreneurs is:

$$W = P(\Delta Q/\Delta N) = MC$$

where P is the price per unit of output;
W is the money wage rate;
$\Delta Q/\Delta N$ is the marginal physical productivity of labor.

Now an aggregate production function in which labor is the only variable input, i.e., with constant technology and a fixed stock of capital, will show diminishing returns to the employment of labor. The relationship between P, W, and $\Delta Q/\Delta N$ can be rewritten as:

$$\Delta Q/\Delta N = W/P \tag{12.1}$$

In this form it emphasizes the derived demand for labor. New employees will be acquired up to the point where the marginal physical product is equal to the *real wage rate*, or the ratio of the money wage rate, W, to the price level of output, P.

The relationships summarized in this decision rule are illustrated in the three panels of Figure 12–1. In panel (a) is a short-run aggregate production function characterized by diminishing returns. $\Delta Q/\Delta N$, the slope of this function, is indicated in panel (b). Since marginal productivity falls as N increases, it is clear from the decision rule above that the amount of labor demanded varies negatively with the real wage rate. With a given production function,

Figure 12–1.

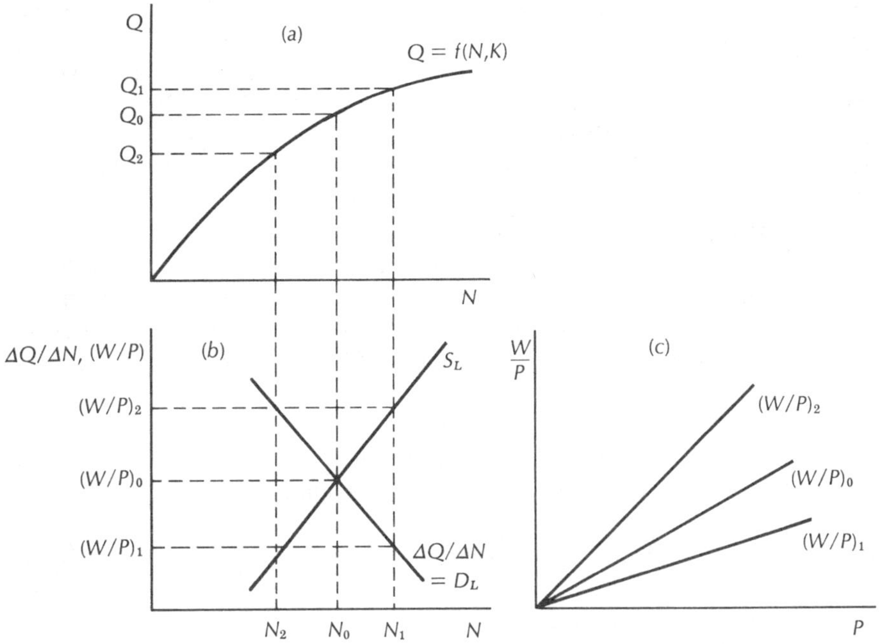

changes in employment are entirely dependent on the relationship of money wages to prices, i.e., on the real wage rate. The nature of the real wage rate is illustrated in panel (c). The line $(W/P)_0$ represents *all* combinations of money wage rates and price levels that result in a real wage of $(W/P)_0$, i.e., that maintain a constant wage-to-price level ratio. A steeper line, such as $(W/P)_2$, represents *all* combinations of money wage rates and price levels that result in a higher real wage. The steeper line means that the money wage rate has increased *relative* to the price level of output. A line with a flatter slope means the opposite.

Returning to panel (b) and reviewing the decision process that businessmen will make in determining the number of jobs to be offered, we can see that at a real wage of $(W/P)_0$, that is, at any combination of money wages and prices along the line $(W/P)_0$, the level of employment will be N_0. So long as changes in money wages and in prices maintain the relationship expressed in this graph there will be no change in the number of job offers, but an increase in the real wage rate, as to $(W/P)_2$, will reduce these offers. Such an increase may mean that labor costs have risen more than prices; the optimum level of output will therefore fall, and with it the quantity of labor demanded will fall to N_2. Should the real wage rate fall so far that the ratio of money wages to prices lies along the line $(W/P)_1$, there will be an increase in offered employment to N_1, for when prices rise relative to money wage rates, the optimum level of output rises and with it the derived demand for labor, D_L.

THE SUPPLY OF LABOR

An appendix to this chapter contains background information on some important statistical measures of the labor market—including working definitions of the labor force, the participation rate, employment, and unemployment. These are key measures not only in evaluating economic conditions but also in determining the effectiveness of policy and the choice of policy instruments required to secure full employment levels of output. Our task here is to indicate the most important influence, i.e., the numbers of people working or looking for work at a given time. As we did when we were considering employers in the last chapter, we will start with the individual worker and then aggregate our result to determine the hours of labor offered by the labor force as a whole.

The supply of labor (S_L) is taken as a positive function of the *real wage rate* (not the money wage rate). A simplified form of the relationship is found in the curve labeled S_L in panel (b) of Figure 12–1. The daily real wage rate can be described as the market basket of consumption commodities that can be purchased with a working day's money wages. A reasonable measurement of the real wage rate for most urban middle class families is:

$$w = \frac{W}{P} \tag{12.2}$$

where w is the real wage rate;
W is the money wage rate;
P is the consumer price index.

Some discussion is necessary of why the supply of labor is positively related to the real wage rate. It has been argued, for example, that over the last century the relationship has in fact been negative, with workers offering fewer hours of labor as the real wage rate has risen. We have seen the average work week for production workers decline from the twelve-hour day, six days per week, to the eight-hour day, five days per week, and we are likely to see it decline still further. These changes stress the growing importance of leisure time to most families as income levels have risen. But our interest is in the short run, not the long run, and it is the slope of the short-run function that must be considered.

Even in the short run, though, the influence of preferences for leisure cannot be ignored. Every individual enjoys or consumes leisure as well as other consumption goods such as housing, food, medical care, and personal services, to name just a few examples. From the viewpoint of the individual, leisure may be treated as one of many consumption goods. The market basket of commodities that a family consumes depends upon its tastes and preferences and relative market prices, and it is subject to the real income constraint. At a given real wage rate the number of hours worked sets the quantity of non-leisure goods that can be acquired and also the number of leisure hours left over. At issue in looking behind a short-run labor-supply function, then, is the choice that a person makes between leisure and other consumption goods. The bases of that choice involve two factors: (a) the relative price of leisure (this can be described as the opportunity cost of leisure, i.e., what the individual forgoes in the way of other goods; clearly the higher the real wage rate the greater the opportunity cost of leisure time); and (b) the sensitivity of leisure to income (it is clear from the evidence that the demand for leisure is positively related to income).

Point (a) involves both a substitution effect and an income effect. When the real wage rate rises, leisure becomes more expensive relative to other consumption goods. Workers can be expected to offer more hours of labor per day or per week as they substitute other consumption goods for leisure. An income effect arises because an increase in the real wage rate gives the worker a higher income and can be expected to lead members of the labor force to demand more leisure time. The slope of the short-run supply function depends upon the relative weights of the substitution and income effects. As drawn in Figure 12–1, S_L is assumed to be in a domain of the real wage rate where the substitution effect of rising real wage rates leading workers to offer more hours of employment outweighs the income effect of rising real wage rates leading them to offer fewer hours of employment. Were the income effect to become dominant, an extension of S_L in Figure 12–1 would turn upward.

EQUILIBRIUM LEVEL OF EMPLOYMENT

The demand and supply of labor are brought together in Figure 12–1(b) to show equilibrium levels of employment, output, and the real wage rate. In the figure, panel (a) indicates the production function and panel (b) the demand (D_L) and supply (S_L) of labor. In panel (b), S_L is drawn with a positive slope throughout. At a real wage rate of $(W/P)_0$, the equilibrium levels of output and employment are Q_0 and N_0, respectively. At this real wage rate, the hours of work sought by members of the labor force equal the hours of labor offered by employers. N_0 of labor is hired and N_0 of employment is offered. One can ask whether N_0 might be defined as a position of full employment since there is a matching of search with offer, for it can be so defined. To see why, it is desirable to indicate a condition of involuntary unemployment. For example, at a real wage rate of $(W/P)_2$, money wages are higher relative to the price level of output than at $(W/P)_0$. A higher established real wage rate induces labor to seek more hours of work so that the quantity of labor supplied will increase to N_2. On the other hand, a higher real wage rate also requires a reduction in the job offers of employers because the optimum level of output is now lower. At $(W/P)_2$, job availability will be N_2. The gap between N_2 and N_1 represents *involuntary* unemployment.

A condition of excess job availability is also possible, for at any real wage rate below $(W/P)_0$ the quantity of labor demanded will exceed the quantity supplied. This state of the labor market has existed in the past during periods of war.

This analysis of equilibrium levels of output, employment, and the real wage points to an adjustment mechanism that on first glance seems rather obvious. If the level of employment is below N_0, then a reduction in the real wage is called for. This will require a relative drop in money wages. If factor markets are characterized by worker competition, one can visualize those workers who are involuntarily unemployed offering their services at a lower money wage, and this will, assuming either no change in the price level of output or a smaller change in prices, drive down the real wage rate. With the given D_L and S_L functions, this process will continue until a condition of full employment is attained with the real wage of $(W/P)_0$ and job availability of N_0. A fall in the money wage rate may thus help to bring about a reduction in the real wage rate, and hence eliminate a labor market gap.

This analysis implies that workers can by their own competitive actions decrease involuntary unemployment by accepting a reduction in the real wage rate, and that a policy of money wage cuts is one possible means by which labor can, within limits, effect a cut in the real wage rate. For example, in Figure 12–1 if the real wage rate is at $(W/P)_2$, with the accompanying gap between jobs sought and jobs offered, then a policy of wage flexibility will mean labor acceptance of a need to reduce money wages sufficiently to lower the real wage rate to $(W/P)_0$.

Flexibility in the money wage rate is one policy option, but it is hardly a satisfactory alternative. In the first place, labor, usually through unions, negotiates over a money, rather than a real, wage rate. The functioning of the economic system, together with the set of existing legal and social institutions, results in collective bargaining between employer and employee over a money wage rate. In the second place, because real wages are a ratio of money wages to prices, a flexible wage policy, even if acceptable to labor, is not a sufficient condition for establishing the level of real wages. The impact of changes in the money wage rate upon the real wage is also affected by the price response of businessmen to lower monetary costs. If the response to a 10 percent across-the-board reduction in the money wage rate is an equivalent reduction in prices, then the real wage rate remains in our example at $(W/P)_2$. In the third place, given human attitudes and natural instincts, there is virtually no possibility in a democratic society of securing a voluntary across-the-board reduction of wages. In the fourth place, changes in money wages, even if they do bring about a fall in the real wage rate, will have an influence on the demand for labor inputs. We must remember that the demand for labor is a derived demand and that a very important question is the effect that changes in money wages have upon the components of real aggregate demand.

NEGOTIATED WAGE LEVELS

Bargaining between labor and management occurs over money wages rather than real wages. We cannot argue that labor and its union representatives are subject to short-sightedness simply because they settle for a money wage in a period of rising price levels. They may attempt to protect against declines in real wages through cost-of-living escalator clauses, or they may, through bargaining, anticipate changes in the price level that will occur during the contract period. The effective outcome of the collective bargaining process is the setting of a negotiated level of money wages. Such an institutionalized process and the conditions attendant thereto permit a reformulation of our S_L function, for once a negotiated level of wages has been set, none of the labor force offers itself for employment below that money (and real) wage.

Once struck, industrial agreements on wages—as well as the minimum wage laws—seem to establish the negotiated level of wages for the economy. For most individuals, it is a question of accepting or not accepting employment at the stipulated level of money wages resulting from the negotiation process. In many occupations, work is available only at the union scale—not at 10 percent above or 10 percent below it. In white-collar occupations, the effect of personnel classification systems is to produce a stratified set of wage levels. In less skilled occupations, employment is offered under conditions where minimum wage laws establish a floor.

The money wage rate may therefore be fixed over a wide range of employment levels. As full employment is approached, employers may increasingly have to rely upon somewhat more expensive labor—overtime and additional work shifts. Money wage rates are but one example of what are called "administered" prices. Wage rates are not set and reset in daily auctions in the manner of stock prices on the New York Stock Exchange, and they are therefore not continuously adjusting to excess supply or excess demand conditions in particular markets. Rather, they are "sticky" because they are set by contractual agreement and obtain for a finite time period.

This modified S_L function is shown in Figure 12–2, where N_f designates an index of full employment defined as all those who are either working or seeking employment at the negotiated level of the money wage rate, W_0. The supply curve of labor is then horizontal up to the point of full employment. Once this level of employment has been reached, money wages (and real wages) will have to rise if employers are to obtain more labor.

Figure 12–2.

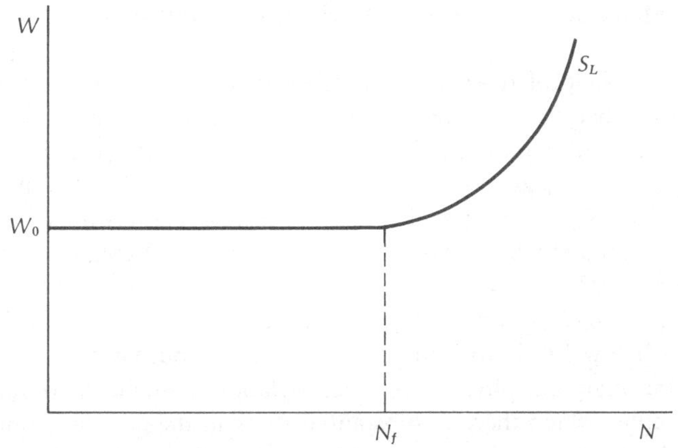

Figure 12–3.

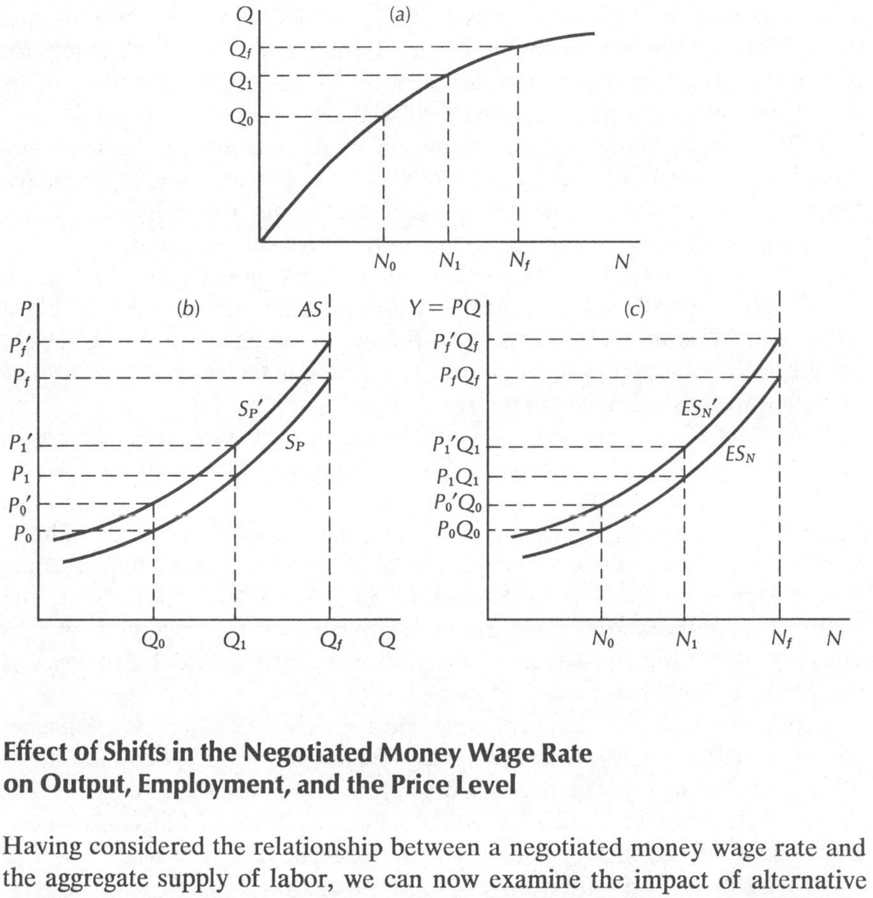

Effect of Shifts in the Negotiated Money Wage Rate on Output, Employment, and the Price Level

Having considered the relationship between a negotiated money wage rate and the aggregate supply of labor, we can now examine the impact of alternative negotiated wage levels on the revenue and price requirements for businessmen's production plans. After this we will consider the effect on the demand for labor of increases and decreases in the money wage rate. This will permit examination of the effect of money wage rate changes on our entire macroeconomic system.

First, it is helpful to restate the effect of alternative money wage rates on the relation between real output, its monetary value, and the price level. The three panels of Figure 12–3 illustrate this relationship under alternative money wage rates, W_0 and W_1, where $W_0 < W_1$. Panel (a) is the now familiar production function relating real output to employment with constant technology and a fixed stock of capital. Panel (b) is the aggregate supply curve. For a money wage W_0 the supply price of output is designated as S_P. In its lower range, S_P has a modest slope, which implies that when real output is significantly below full employment levels, then as output rises the extent of the fall in the marginal physical product of labor is small. As outlined in the previous chapter, when there is substantial slack in the economy only the best machines may be in use—and then only partially. As output expands, idle equipment can be combined with newly employed men so that only a slight fall in the marginal product of labor is evidenced. As output approaches the full employment level, the price level moves up more sharply as a fixed stock of capital combines with increasing quantities of labor.

When real output is Q_0, employment will be N_0 and the price level P_0. In panel (c), the employment level, N, is plotted against its monetary value PQ, and this curve is our aggregate expected revenue–offered employment curve, which we will henceforth call our *employment-supply function.* At Q_1, employment is N_1, the price level, P_1, and the monetary value of output, P_1Q_1. (In general $Y = PQ$, where Q is real output and Y is the monetary value of real output for a given price level.) With a money wage of W_0, the monetary value of full employment output is P_fY_f.

We can now consider an increase in the money wage rate to W_1. The aggregate supply function in (b) will shift up to S_P'. At real outputs of Q_0, Q_1, and Q_f, the price level will rise to P_0', P_1', and P_f', respectively. The higher price level will be required for businessmen to produce these outputs at the higher cost to them. As in Chapter 11, we see that upward shifts in the negotiated wage rate shift the supply price of output upward. Similarly, the employment-supply function in panel (c), relating the monetary value of output to employment, will also shift upwards from ES_N to ES_N'. Each level of employment will have an output of higher monetary value.

Effects of Money Wage Shifts on Aggregate Demand

The businessman's decision rule, $W = P\Delta Q/\Delta N$ may also be written as $w = W/P = \Delta Q/\Delta N$. It is apparent that the demand for labor can be stated in terms of either the money wage or the real wage rate. The rule states that, for any business firm, labor will be hired up to the point where the money wage rate equals the value of the marginal product, the price of the product times $\Delta Q/\Delta N$. In this instance it is obvious that an increase in the money wage rate serves to reduce job offers by the firm, that is, W is negatively related to N. This labor-demand function is shown in Figure 12–4. Its negative slope reflects the diminishing marginal productivity of labor. At a money wage rate of W_0, the amount of employment offered is N_0. The aggregate demand for labor will simply be the sum of all the firms' individual labor-demand functions like that in Figure 12–4. With a given technology, so that each firm's marginal physical productivity function is stable, and with a reasonably stable composition of output, then the aggregate demand for labor will have a similar negative slope.

In the preceding section the effect of increased money wage rates on aggregate output, its monetary value, and the price level was analyzed, and we saw then that an increase in the money wage rate results in an upward shift in the aggregate supply curve and in the employment-supply function. An exogenous increase in the money wage rate will also, however, affect aggregate demand, here expressed in monetary terms. For example, if the

Figure 12–4.

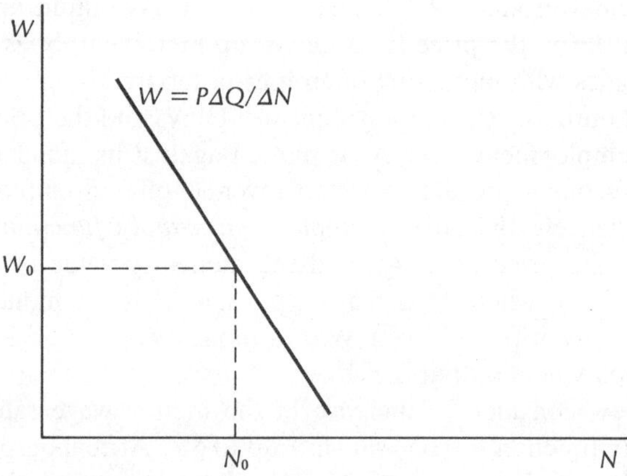

money wage rate rises, payments to labor and profit recipients increase and with them the monetary value of their consumption expenditures. The cost of producing a given volume of investment goods will rise also, and therefore the monetary value of planned expenditures on that volume of new capital goods will increase. With higher money wages, demand will be greater in monetary terms at each level of employment. The rise in the wage rate therefore produces a rise in both the employment-supply and the employment-demand functions.

This is illustrated in Figure 12–5, where ES_0, taken from Figure 12–3(c), represents employment supply at various employment levels and at a money wage rate of W_0. The employment demand function, ED_0, shows the relation between money income and the level of employment when the money wage rate is W_0. The equilibrium level of employment is then N_0. ES_1 and ED_1

Figure 12–5.

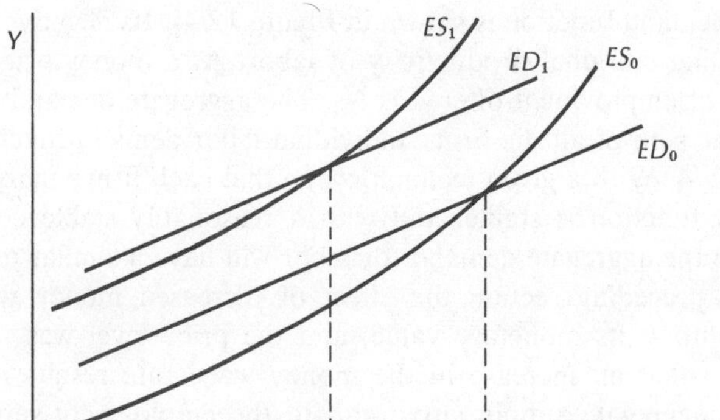

represent employment-supply and employment-demand functions at a higher money wage rate of W_1. The equilibrium level of employment indicated is N_1, which is lower than N_0. This decrease in employment with the rise in money wages is consistent with the labor-demand function in Figure 12–4 and follows from the fact that the increase in the money wage rate has shifted the employment-demand function upward less than the employment-supply function. Why is this the case? Why is this more likely than that a higher money wage rate would result in equal upward shifts in both functions? Why do we not see the higher money wage resulting in a greater than commensurate upward shift in *ED*?

To determine which of these is most likely, we must go back to the basics of our income-expenditure model and consider, for simplicity, a two-sector model with (a) a given consumption function; (b) a given investment demand function; (c) a given money supply; (d) given transactions and asset demands for money; (e) a specified money wage rate; and (f) a given production function with fixed capital stock. We wish to know the impact upon offered employment of an exogenous shift in the wage rate. We know the effect on aggregate supply. What is the effect on aggregate demand?

First of all, when the supply of money is held constant, the rise in wages and prices will cause a larger amount of the given money stock to be used for transactions purposes at each level of real output. With the supply of money fixed, interest rates will rise as money is withdrawn from asset into transactions uses. Higher interest rates will choke off some increment of investment demand, and, through the multiplier, a decline in output and employment will occur.

Second, if W_1 exceeds W_0 by 10 percent, we may generally expect that wage earners will maintain their level of real consumption. Though prices rise by 10 percent, their money wage increase of 10 percent has kept pace. Moreover, some economists have argued that wage earners may be subject to a "money illusion." [1] Wage earners would feel richer due to the increase in money income even though real income remains unchanged. This feeling of greater well-being may lead to the saving of a larger percentage of their income. Hence their level of real consumption falls. Though the "money illusion" effect will normally be small to the point of insignificance, it is one factor depressing aggregate demand as money wages rise.

Another and more significant factor that may serve to depress aggregate demand (a less than 10 percent rise in monetary aggregate demand) is the effect of the redistribution of income accompanying the wage increase. It was indicated earlier that wage earners, rentiers, and profit recipients participate in the factoral distribution of income. We have seen that the real income of wage earners remains roughly unchanged at between 65 and 70 percent of all income even though money wages rise. But all those living on fixed incomes experience a fall in real income as prices increase. Hence the real consumption of rentiers will fall as money wages rise, but offsetting this fall is the rise in the real income of profit recipients. Part of this increase will be retained in the

[1] See Gardner Ackley, *Macroeconomic Theory* (New York: Macmillan, 1961), pp. 228–230.

form of undistributed profits and will not result in increased consumption. Another part will flow in the form of increased dividends to firm owners. The effect of the undistributed profits, as well as of the fact that profit recipients in general have a lower propensity to consume than rentiers, also contributes to a fall in real consumption expenditures.

The net effect of these considerations is that the increase in money wages is likely to lead to a fall in real consumption. If adverse effects on employment are to be avoided, it will then be necessary that real investment or real public spending (when the government sector is included) rise to compensate. Our particular concern is with real investment. What, in fact, will happen to investment? Though in the example variable costs have risen by 10 percent, prices have also risen by 10 percent. This rise can be assumed to include the price of capital goods. Therefore, from the point of view of the firm, the proportionate increase in expected revenues and expected costs should lead to no change in investment plans. The rise in money wages should not affect the amount of real investment occurring at a *given* rate of interest.

Yet another factor which may lead to a fall in real aggregate demand as money wages rise is what is variously referred to as the *Pigou effect, wealth effect*, or *real balances effect*. The three terms are synonymous. They refer to the fact that as prices rise, holders of bonds or other debt instruments will feel poorer because at maturity the bonds will be paid off with money that will buy less than the money used to pay for them. In the case of private debt, though creditors feel poorer as they are repaid with dollars of lesser value, it is also true that the debtors feel better off. In the aggregate, the net effect of private debt on real consumption should cancel out as creditors reduce consumption and debtors increase consumption. But when we include the public sector, we see that the effect of public debt differs. Holders of public debt instruments—cash and government securities—will feel poorer as price levels rise with little or no offsetting effect of other individuals feeling richer. This should lead to some fall in the level of real consumption by those holding public debt. Empirical work done to ascertain the significance of the wealth effect indicates that the effect may be relatively unimportant,[2] but it is nevertheless a factor which can help explain why we may expect the labor-demand curve to be downward sloping, and the *ED* curve of Figure 12–5 to shift upward by a lesser amount than the *ES* curve.

Finally, we wish to note that the inclusion of the foreign sector in our model provides further reason for the demand curve to be downward sloping. The rise in domestic prices that would accompany a money wage increase would, under fixed exchange rates, lead to a fall in the real demand for domestic goods by foreigners and a rise in the real demand for imports. Both of these factors would contribute to a fall in real aggregate demand as prices rise.

As the preceding paragraphs indicate, we have strong reason to believe

[2] See Thomas Mayer, "Empirical significance of the real balance effect," *Quarterly Journal of Economics*, 73 (May 1959). For a valuable theoretical contribution on the real balance effect, see D. Patinkin, "Price flexibility and employment," *American Economic Review*, 38 (September 1948).

Figure 12–6.

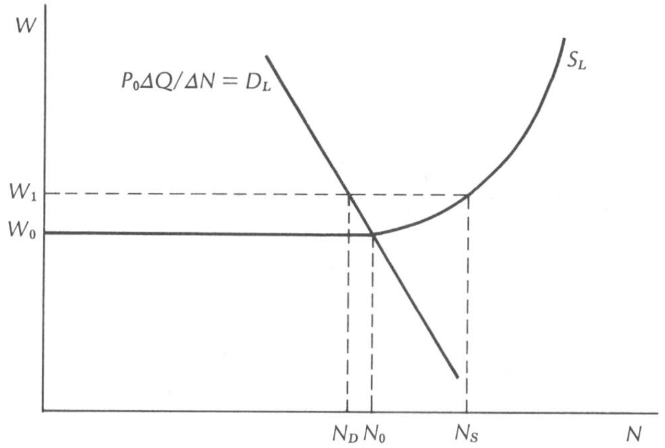

that the demand for labor varies negatively with the level of money wages. This is due to the possible existence of the money illusion, the effects of increasing money wages on income distribution, the wealth effect, the effect that increasing prices will have on imports and exports, and the effect of higher interest rates on investment demand (assuming the monetary authorities do not act to offset this effect).

BRINGING TOGETHER THE SUPPLY OF AND DEMAND FOR LABOR IN MONEY WAGE TERMS

Our aggregate labor-demand and labor-supply functions in terms of *money* wages may now be brought together as in Figure 12–6, where S_L represents the supply of labor. In this case the negotiated wage level is W_0. The labor-demand function is represented by $P_0\Delta Q/\Delta N$, where P_0 represents the prevailing price level. At the money wage rate W_0, the quantity of labor supplied and the level of offered employment is N_0 (N_0 and W_0 may be termed equilibrium levels of employment and the money wage rate). Employment can be increased only by a shift to the right in the demand for labor, arising from an increase in the aggregate demand for output. Should the negotiated money wage rate be shifted to W_1, so long as the demand for labor is unaffected, this would seem only to produce involuntary unemployment measured by the difference between N_S and N_D, as laborers offer an amount N_S of labor services to the market, but employers only offer to hire an amount N_D.

The implications of a negotiated money wage rate for attempts to correct involuntary unemployment in the labor market may be examined in Figure 12–7, which shows again the demand and supply of labor in money wage terms. If the negotiated wage level is W_0 and if with given labor-demand and labor-supply functions equilibrium employment and money wages are N_0 and W_0,

Figure 12–7.

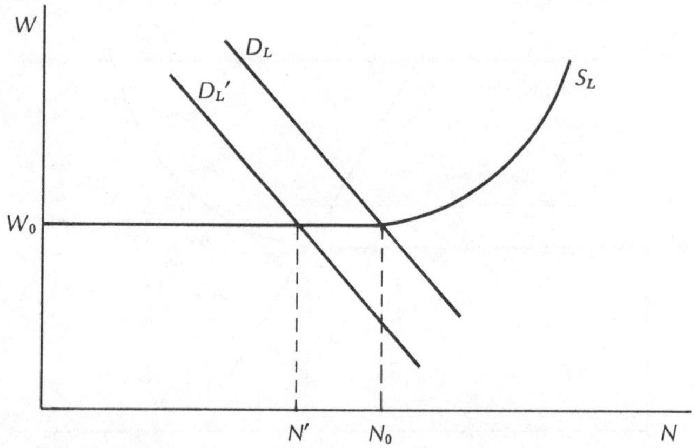

there exists no unemployment. Everyone willing to work at money wage W_0 can find a job. On the other hand, it is possible for aggregate demand to decline due to downward shifts in one of the commodity market functions. With the consequent fall in the employment-demand function from *ED* to *ED′*, illustrated in Figure 12–8, the price level will fall in the way indicated by the aggregate supply curve of Figure 12–3(b). At the same time, the aggregate demand for labor will fall from D_L to D_L' in Figure 12–7. If W_0 is a wage level that is inflexible downwards, then employment will decline from N_0 to N' along the horizontal W_0 line. Rigid wage floors thus force a drop in aggregate demand, accompanied by a given drop in the price level, to occasion a larger fall in employment than would be the case were S_L positively sloping throughout its range.

A possible upward shift in the employment-demand function in Figure 12–8 to *ED″*, as a result of an upward shift in the consumption function or

Figure 12–8.

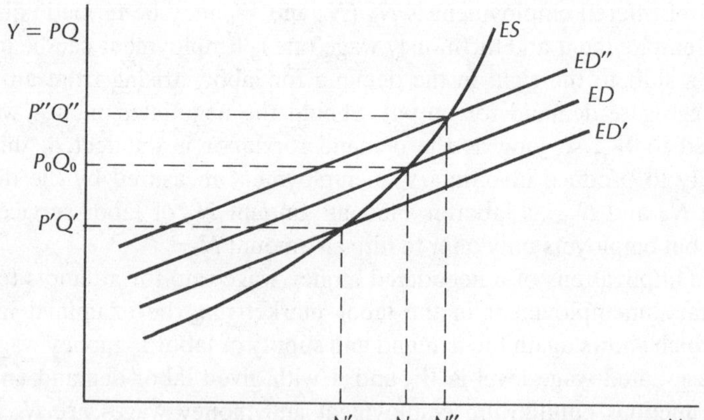

Figure 12–9

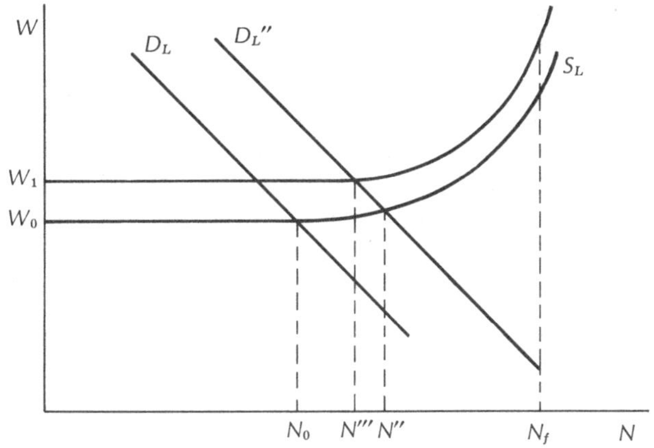

an exogenous change in government expenditures, is represented in a movement of the demand for labor in Figure 12–9 from its original position of D_L to D_L'' and an expansion of employment from N_0 to N''. This is unlikely to be the entire story, however, for the negotiated wage level will not be immune to labor market developments. Those originally employed, amounting to N_0, will be aware of a decline in their real wage as output expands and prices rise, and they will seek cost of living adjustments. Particular labor markets will show increasing shortages, and the probability will increase that the negotiated money wage level will increase to something more than W_0. As the labor pool dries up, employers will increase their employment by competitive bidding. That is, employers recognize that the members of any occupational group are not homogeneous. Rather, there are differences in capacity and skill within occupations. These are likely to become more evident as employers are forced to scrape the bottom of the barrel in labor markets. The search process becomes expensive and the returns unrewarding. Accordingly the optimum course is to buy away labor from other employers, although this course does bid up wage rates. Keynes himself emphasized that, prior to the point where involuntary unemployment is eliminated, there would be a number of positions of "semi-inflation" where wage increases would be bargained for and granted. There would be, in effect, a *ratchet effect* serving to increase the money wage rate as the quantity of employment increased.

The actual result is indicated in Figure 12–9 where the negotiated money wage level now shifts upward from W_0 to W_1. When the economy is recovering from a period of significant unemployment, the completely elastic (horizontal) portion of the labor supply curve may well shift upward before the point of full employment is reached. Employment then increases not from N_0 to N'', but rather by something less, from N_0 to N'''. When wages are flexible upward, a given price level increase causes a smaller increase in N than would be true with wage rigidity.

THE ASYMMETRY OF PRICE LEVEL BEHAVIOR

We know that the price level will be higher at full employment than at lower levels of output owing to (a) the presence of diminishing returns to the variable factor (labor); (b) the likelihood that there will be exogenous upward shifts in the wage rate as the point of full employment is reached; and (c) the influence of heterogeneity in quality among particular occupational groupings. But is the price level as flexible downward as it is upward to the point of full employment? Is the behavior of the price level symmetrical in the face of increases and decreases in effective demand?

The answer to this question depends primarily upon whether and how much money wages decrease in the face of a decline in effective demand. There are good reasons, rooted in institutional relationships and in the instinctive resistance of individuals to pay cuts, for believing that, as D_L'' shifts back to D_L in Figure 12–9, the negotiated wage level will not fall far below W_1, certainly not back to W_0. This means that in the face of a decline in effective demand the increase in unemployment will be greater than it would be if wages were in fact flexible downward.

There is an important lesson to be drawn from this analysis for policy. One approach to full employment would be through the adoption of policies designed to assure greater flexibility of wages and prices. However, though it may be possible, this is not a viable alternative in a world of uncertainty where major institutional and legal obstacles to wage flexibility exist. We are therefore back to the alternatives of fiscal and monetary policy as a means of ensuring adequate levels of effective demand.

CONCLUSION

In this chapter, we first examined the factors which determine the equilibrium real wage rate in order to reinforce our earlier point that upward shifts in money wages lead to upward shifts in the aggregate supply curve. We then turned to the effects of money wage changes upon the level of output and employment in the economy to show that a rise in money wages, other things being equal, leads to a fall in the level of employment and output. This is because the following factors cause a rise in money wages to be accompanied by a fall in real aggregate demand: (a) the possible existence of the money illusion; (b) the effects of increasing money wages on income distribution; (c) the wealth effect; (d) the effect of price increases on imports and exports; and (e) the effect of a rise in interest rates on investment.

We have also seen that negotiated money wages may lead to a number of problems in a dynamic economy in which the demand and supply of labor are continually changing. We analyzed the cases where (a) an increase in the negotiated wage, and (b) a fall in the demand for labor accompanied by downward rigidity in the negotiated wage lead to a significant increase in involuntary unemployment. The asymmetry of price and wage behavior increases the difficulty of maintaining output at a full employment level.

This chapter completes our basic model of the economy. The commodity, money, and labor markets have now all been examined. In the following chapter, we extend the analysis developed in Chapter 10 by incorporating the labor market and its effect on prices.

APPENDIX

Measuring Employment, Unemployment, and Wages

In 1961 President John F. Kennedy appointed a committee to appraise employment and unemployment statistics.[3] This was in clear recognition of the importance, from both a political and a policy-making point of view, of the monthly employment statistics issued by the Labor Department. The purpose of this appendix is to examine how the unemployment rate—considered by many to be the most important statistic published by the federal government is estimated. We will examine the limitations of this statistic as well as what it includes.

Methods of Estimating Employment and Unemployment

Employment estimates of the Labor Department are based upon a weekly *household survey* conducted by the Bureau of the Census. The sample relied upon is one of about 50,000 households scientifically chosen from 863 counties and independent cities in 449 areas representing all 50 states and the District of Columbia in order to reflect as closely as possible true conditions for the nation as a whole. Each of the 50,000 households is questioned by a trained interviewer to ascertain which members of the household are in the labor force, and if so, whether they are employed or unemployed. Making the household survey statistically reliable for the country as a whole is the size of the sample. Unfortunately, to get equally reliable statistics for each state would require a sample of around 50,000 for each of the states. The cost of this would be prohibitive.

Two other sources of employment information are an *establishment survey* and the *administrative records of unemployment insurance systems.* The establishment survey is conducted through mail questionnaires by the Bureau of Labor Statistics (BLS) and is concerned with nonagricultural wage and salary employment, average weekly hours, average hourly and weekly earnings, and job vacancies. The sample covers establishments employing about 30 million nonagricultural wage and salary workers and is compiled for states and local areas as well as for the nation as a whole. The unemployment insurance records include only those workers insured under the system. This

[3] The findings of the President's Committee to Appraise Employment and Unemployment Statistics are reported in *Measuring Employment and Unemployment* (Washington, D.C.: Government Printing Office, 1962).

covers only about 60 percent of the civilian labor force and excludes many of the workers included in the household survey—farm workers, domestic servants, and self-employed persons, as well as others who are not insured.

Definitions

The household survey data are those most heavily relied upon by the BLS. For this reason it is important to understand the definitions upon which the survey is based.

Employed persons are those 16 years old and over who, during the week of the survey, did any work as paid employees, in their own business or farm, or as unpaid employees for 15 or more hours per week in an enterprise operated by a member of the family; or were temporarily absent from a job or business due to illness, bad weather, vacation, labor management disputes, or personal reasons.

Unemployed persons are all those 16 years old and over who did not work during the survey week, who made specific efforts (e.g., applying to an employer, answering a want-ad, being on a union or professional register) to find a job sometime in the last four weeks, and who were available during the survey week. People waiting to be recalled to a job from which they have been laid off or waiting to report to a new wage or salary job within 30 days are also included among the unemployed.

The *civilian labor force* is composed of those classified above as either employed or unemployed. This is less than the total labor force by the number of members of the Armed Forces.

The *unemployment rate* which is so frequently referred to is the number of unemployed as a percentage of the civilian labor force.

There is no question but that the definitions employed in the household survey are to some degree arbitrary. For example, some of the problems arising from these definitions are that an unpaid individual working ten hours for a family-operated enterprise will be considered as neither in the work force nor employed, while another individual receiving a wage for one hour of work during the week of the survey is considered both in the work force and employed; that a skilled machinist who cannot find work in his regular occupation but works several hours a week as a gas station attendant is classified as employed; that a 16-year-old high school student who is actively and unsuccessfully searching for baby-sitting jobs, though he suffers from no economic hardship, is classified as unemployed; and that the lower age limit for inclusion in the labor force was changed from 14 to 16 in 1967—why not 18? Though each of these problems is well recognized by the government agencies, it is believed that equally arbitrary changes in the definitions would not increase the usefulness of the unemployment statistics.

Table 12–1 illustrates in aggregate form the type of information collected by the Bureau of the Census. A Labor Department monthly report, *Employment and Earnings*, also includes breakdowns of this information by age, sex, marital status, race, industry, and occupation.

Table 12–1. Employment Status of Noninstitutional Population in June 1971 (in thousands).

Total noninstitutional population*		142,482	
Total labor force		87,784	
Not in labor force		54,698	
Civilian labor force		84,968	
Total employed		79,478	
Agriculture	3920		
Non-agriculture industries	75,559		
Unemployed		5490	
Percent of civilian labor force unemployed			
Not seasonally adjusted			6.5
Seasonally adjusted			5.6

* This excludes inmates of institutions and persons under 16 years of age.
Source: U.S. Department of Labor, *Employment and Earnings*, Vol 18, No. 1 (July 1971), p. 21.

One other major problem with respect to measuring unemployment is also worth mentioning. Since unemployment rates are expressed as a percentage of the labor force, it is important that the labor force be measured accurately. Economists have demonstrated that the size of the labor force varies inversely with the level of employment. As the unemployment rate drops, individuals previously out of the labor force become optimistic about finding a desirable job and begin to look actively. By actively looking for jobs they increase the size of the labor force. T. F. Dernburg and K. T. Strand found in 1962 that if the labor force is 71.8 million when unemployment is 5.6 percent, it will increase to 74.2 million if unemployment falls to 4 percent.[4] Dernberg and Strand concluded that with this "hidden unemployment" included the unemployment rate is 8.5 percent rather than 5.6 percent. For 1962, a U.S. Senate subcommittee guessed significantly lower—estimating that hidden unemployment was somewhere between 800,000 and 1,500,000 persons.[5] Therefore, to achieve "full" employment (say 4 percent unemployment), the number of jobs created will have to exceed the number of unemployed, because as unemployment falls the labor force grows. The current unemployment rates as derived from the household survey do not include "hidden" unemployment, although until 1967 hidden unemployment was at least partially included; individuals who volunteered that they would have been looking for work, if they had believed work to be available, were included in the labor force and considered to be unemployed. A major shortcoming of this practice was that individuals had to *volunteer* the information and the practice was terminated in January 1967.

[4] T. F. Dernburg and K. T. Strand, "Hidden unemployment, 1953–1962: A quantitative analysis by age and sex," *American Economic Review,* 56 (March 1966).

[5] Subcommittee on Employment and Manpower Policy of the Senate Committee on Labor and Public Welfare, *Toward Full Employment: Proposals for a Comprehensive Employment and Manpower Policy in the United States* (Washington, D.C.: Government Printing Office, 1964), p. 32. For an evaluation of the literature on the subject of "hidden unemployment," see Jacob Mincer, "Labor force participation and unemployment: A review of recent evidence," in R. A. Gordon and Margaret S. Gordon (Eds.), *Prosperity and Unemployment* (New York: John Wiley and Sons, 1966).

Table 12–2. Unadjusted and Seasonally Adjusted Unemployment Rates for the Period October 1970 to June 1971.

Month	Unadjusted	Seasonally Adjusted
October 1970	5.1	5.5
November	5.5	5.9
December	5.6	6.2
January 1971	6.6	6.0
February	6.6	5.8
March	6.3	6.0
April	5.7	6.1
May	5.3	6.2
June	6.5	5.6

Source: U.S. Department of Labor, Employment and Earnings, Vol. 18, No. 1 (July 1971), p. 21.

Seasonal Adjustment of Unemployment Statistics

Table 12–1 contains both the seasonally adjusted unemployment rate and the unadjusted rate. For policy purposes, the adjusted rate is the more important. For example, as is shown in Table 12–2, from December 1970 to January 1971 the unadjusted unemployment rate *rose* from 5.6 percent to 6.6 percent, while the seasonally adjusted rate *fell* from 6.2 percent to 6.0 percent in the same period. This movement in the adjusted rate indicated that the Nixon Administration's expansionary economic policy may have been causing the level of employment to increase, as desired, even though the unadjusted rate of unemployment rose.

Under both expanding and depressed conditions, it is normal for the unadjusted unemployment rate to rise from December to January. Each year business activity expands to a peak around Christmas and falls off in the following months. This is reflected in our unadjusted rates as unemployment rose one whole point to 6.6 percent. Seasonal adjustment is an attempt to deflate the January unemployment rate, for instance, by an amount that reflects how much higher unemployment generally is on the average in January due to seasonal factors than during the rest of the year; the adjustment of the December rate is an inflation intended to reflect how much lower unemployment usually is in December than for the year as a whole. If after such an adjustment we find that the adjusted rate for January is higher than for December, this might indicate that economic policy is having an adverse effect on employment. This was not the case at the end of 1970 and the beginning of 1971.[6]

[6] The seasonally adjusted figures, being subject to errors in the adjustment process, are more subject to error than the unadjusted figures. The seasonal adjustment process now being utilized by the Labor Department is an adaptation of the standard ratio-to-moving-average method. The method is fully described in the booklet *The BLS Seasonal Factor Method* (U.S. Department of Labor, 1966).

International Comparisons of Unemployment Rates

Japan and Canada also rely upon sample surveys as the source of official employment data, but only the Canadian statistics can be compared with the U.S. statistics on an unadjusted basis. Japan's cannot, for Japan includes in the labor force unpaid family workers working less than 15 hours in a family establishment, the Special Defense Force, and certain residents of institutions, while the American survey excludes such groups. Many European countries, including France, Germany, Great Britain, and Italy, rely upon registration figures at government employment offices. Sweden depends primarily upon unemployment statistics maintained by the trade unions. Australia relies both on monthly statistics of unemployed persons registered with their Commonwealth Employment Service and upon quarterly population surveys made by the Commonwealth Bureau of Census and Statistics. Simply on the basis that it is possible to seek work without registering at government employment offices, unemployment rates based on employment office registrations are not comparable to U.S. rates.[7]

Types of Unemployment

We have already noted that unemployment rates generated by the Bureau of Labor Statistics of the Labor Department do not reflect the extent to which hidden unemployment exists. The BLS statistics also, however, tend to lump together several types of unemployment which may have different causes, and therefore different solutions, and to exclude still others.

Frictional unemployment refers to individuals who are unemployed because they are in the process of moving from one job to another, because they have given up a job specifically to search for another more to their liking, or because they are temporarily out of work due to seasonal factors. This type of unemployment exists even when an economy is operating at what might be considered the full employment level. In a market economy, some percentage of persons will be moving from job to job as they search for new opportunities. Frictional unemployment is considered to be a natural phenomenon and is generally set at a level of between 3 and 4 percent of the labor force in the U.S. When this level of unemployment is achieved the American economy is considered to be at a level of full employment.

Unemployment due to insufficient aggregate demand, also called *cyclical unemployment*, is due to the continuing inability to eliminate the business

[7] In order to facilitate international comparisons of employment and unemployment rates, staff members of the Bureau of Labor Statistics have attempted to adjust foreign series. For a discussion of the necessary adjustments and the comparative figures, see R. J. Myers and J. H. Chandler, "International comparisons of unemployment," *Monthly Labor Review*, 85 (August 1962): 857–864; A. F. Neef, "International unemployment rates, 1960–1964," *Monthly Labor Review*, 88 (March 1965): 250–259; and A. F. Neef and Rosa A. Holland, "Comparative unemployment rates, 1964–1966," *Monthly Labor Review*, 90 (April 1967): 18–20. The article by Myers and Chandler is a summary of "Comparative levels of unemployment in industrial countries," Appendix A of *Measuring Employment and Unemployment*, a report by the President's Committee to Appraise Employment and Unemployment Statistics (Washington, D.C.: 1962).

cycle (fluctuations in business activity). Were monetary and fiscal policy perfect instruments, and were there no other considerations such as stable prices and the balance of payments, cyclical unemployment could be eliminated. As long as periods of slack can continue to develop in our economy, some cyclical unemployment will exist.

Structural unemployment exists when individuals looking for jobs cannot match the available job vacancies. It also exists when the number of unemployed in a certain region exceeds the number of job vacancies in that region, though this situation does not exist for the economy as a whole. This form of unemployment may arise for several reasons. First, labor may be immobile due to regional attachments, lack of education, or lack of information concerning job opportunities. The rapid exodus of industries from certain regions and unemployment caused by technological changes in production processes are perhaps our clearest causes of structural unemployment. The New England textile or shoe worker may be attached to his community and unwilling to move even if he feels certain he could find a job in New York City. Likewise, the West Virginia coal miner may be unwilling to move from his rural environment even though he has learned of job opportunities for the unskilled in nearby cities. There may even be opportunities for skilled workers in his home community for which he is unqualified, and this, too, is a form of structural unemployment. While a partial answer to both hidden and cyclical unemployment may be expansionary monetary and fiscal policies, similar actions may be of little value if most unemployment is due to structural causes. Policies which facilitate mobility within the labor force and provide retraining for the unemployed, such as the Job Corps and other training programs for the unemployed, are more appropriate.

The extent to which structural unemployment exists is partially reflected in the Labor Department statistics as the household survey breaks down unemployment by broad industry categories. In addition unemployment broken down by region is reported monthly by the Labor Department in the insured unemployment data and in the establishment survey data included in *Employment and Earnings*.

Disguised unemployment is a term most frequently used in discussions of low income countries. This form of unemployment exists when the marginal productivity of a worker is close to zero in the activity in which he is engaged. For example, some economists claim that in peasant economies the movement of one family member from the farm to the city would lead to no fall in farm output. If this is true, a large labor force can be made available for the construction of social overhead capital—roads, canals, dams, etc.—or for industrial job training without experiencing a reduction in agricultural production. The widespread existence of disguised unemployment would mean that economic development could move at a rapid rate as the disguised unemployed were put to productive purposes. Unfortunately, other studies have disclosed that disguised unemployment is close to nonexistent in many low-income countries—as workers move from the agricultural sector, production does fall.

Disguised unemployment also exists in the high-income countries. Though workers may not have zero marginal product, they may be employed at work in which they are relatively unproductive. An example is our previously mentioned skilled mechanic who is pumping gas. Immobility created either by regional attachments or by lack of information may prevent workers from moving to jobs in which they could be much more productive. The extent to which disguised unemployment exists in our economy is not identified in the unemployment statistics developed by the Labor Department.

Finally, we wish to mention *involuntary part-time unemployment.* Many individuals working part time and considered as employed members of the labor force are, at best, only partially employed. For example, in June 1971, 2.9 million workers were involuntarily working on a part-time basis. The average number of hours worked per week by this group was 20.6, or about half of a 40-hour week.[8] This is roughly the equivalent of another 1.4 million workers being fully unemployed. Adding this number to the other unemployed would raise the Labor Department's unadjusted unemployment rate from 6.5 percent to 8.1 percent. Though details on part-time labor are reported by the Labor Department, fluctuations in involuntary part-time unemployment are not reflected in the commonly quoted unemployment rate. Though greatly complicating the data gathering process, this problem could be overcome by measuring unemployment in hours rather than in persons.

Measuring Money and Real Wages

In Chapters 12 and 13, we refer to both money wages and real wages. The *money wage* is the monetary remuneration given to the worker for his labor. Increases or decreases in it indicate nothing about the purchasing power of the worker's earnings. If money wages rise more slowly than the consumer price index, the worker may experience a reduction in his purchasing power. If they rise more rapidly than the consumer price index his purchasing power increases. For the purpose of examining the real value of the worker's earnings, it is necessary to look at his *real wage*, which may be defined as the money wage divided by the consumer price index.

The establishment survey, as earlier mentioned, collects data on wages and salaries of the private sector of the economy as well as on employment. In 1967, hours and earnings data were collected on about 45 million wage and salary workers. Table 12–3 summarizes the growth in money and real wages for these workers over the past two decades. Column (2) indicates that average money wages in the private sector rose 56 percent from 1950 to 1960 and 55 percent from 1960 to 1970. During these same periods real wages rose only 27 and 18 per cent, respectively. The contrast between the rate of change in money wages and real wages can be very great and will vary directly with the rate of change in prices. Hopefully, the evidence provided in Table 12–3 will clarify the need to distinguish between the two.

[8] U.S. Department of Labor, *Employment and Earnings,* Vol. 18, No. 1 (July 1971), p. 38.

Table 12–3. Money and Real Wages.

(1) Year	(2) Average Hourly Money Earnings*	(3) Consumer Price Index	(4) Average Hourly Real Earnings (2) ÷ (3)
1950	1.34	72.1	1.86
1951	1.45	77.8	1.85
1952	1.52	79.5	1.91
1953	1.61	80.1	2.01
1954	1.65	80.5	2.05
1955	1.71	80.2	2.13
1956	1.80	81.4	2.21
1957	1.89	84.3	2.24
1958	1.95	86.6	2.25
1959	2.02	87.3	2.31
1960	2.09	88.7	2.36
1961	2.14	89.6	2.39
1962	2.22	90.6	2.45
1963	2.28	91.7	2.49
1964	2.36	92.9	2.54
1965	2.45	94.5	2.59
1966	2.56	97.2	2.63
1967	2.68	100.0	2.68
1968	2.85	104.2	2.74
1969	3.04	109.8	2.77
1970	3.23	116.1	2.78

* This is an average of earnings of production workers in mining and manufacturing, construction workers in contract construction, nonsupervisory workers in wholesale and retail trade, workers in finance, insurance, and real estate, and workers in transportation, public utilities, and services. The average hourly earnings are on a "gross" basis, reflecting factors such as the premium paid for overtime and late shifts. The average hourly earnings do not include irregular bonuses, retroactive items, payments of various welfare benefits, or payroll taxes paid by the employers.

Source: U.S. Department of Labor, *Employment and Earnings*, Vol. 18, No. 1 (July 1971), Table C–1; *Economic Report of the President*, 1971 (Washington, D.C.: U.S. Government Printing Office, 1971).

ADDITIONAL READINGS

For a similar presentation of the material in this chapter, see P. Davidson and E. Smolensky, *Aggregate Supply and Demand Analysis* (New York: Harper & Row, 1964), Chapter 11. Much of this material was first developed by Sidney Weintraub, "A macroeconomic approach to the theory of wages," *American Economic Review*, 46 (December 1956): 836–856.

Factors contributing to the rigidities of wages are discussed by Albert Rees in "Wage determination and involuntary unemployment," *Journal of Political Economy*, 59 (April 1951) (particularly pp. 148–153). For some additional insight into factors affecting wage rigidities, see Paul Sultan, *Labor Economics* (New York: Holt, Rinehart & Winston, 1957), pp. 536–541.

On the matter of the labor-supply function, see J. M. Keynes, *The General Theory of Employment, Interest and Money* (New York: Harcourt Brace

Jovanovich, Inc., 1936), Chapter 2; and James Tobin, "Inflation and unemployment," *American Economic Review*, 62 (March 1972): 1–18 (especially pp. 1–5).

Informative discussions of the limitations on weekly earnings series published by the Bureau of Labor Statistics are found in G. L. Perry, "Real spendable weekly earnings," *Brookings Papers on Economic Activity*, No. 3 (1972): 779–787; and T. W. Gavett, "Measures of changes in real wages and earnings," *Monthly Labor Review*, 95 (February 1972): 48–53. For an interesting analysis suggesting a new index of Employment and Earnings Inadequacy, see the article by S. A. Levitan and Robert Taggart, "Employment and earnings inadequacy: A new social indicator," *Challenge*, 16 (January-February 1974): 22–29.

QUESTIONS

1. What evidence have you observed to indicate that money wages will not remain constant? From the *Survey of Current Business* find how much money wages in manufacturing have increased during the past five years. How much have they risen during the past year?
2. J. M. Keynes believed that the level of money wages would have little effect on the demand for labor. Fully explain why you do or do not agree with this position.
3. For the individual firm, the lower the money wage rate, the larger will be the quantity of labor demanded. Why, if this is true for the firm, is it not so obviously true for the economy as a whole?
4. Nevertheless, aggregate demand for labor is inversely related to the money wage rate. What factors account for this? Explain.
5. An increase in the demand for labor with respect to money wages leads to a decrease in the supply of labor. Can you account for this?
6. Explain the relationship between wage rigidities and involuntary unemployment.
7. Using Figure 12–1, work through the effects of technical change (which shifts the production function upward) and an increase in S_L (due perhaps to growth in the labor force). What are the effects on real wages, output, and employment? By what mechanism do these effects occur?

Labor, Commodity, and Money Markets Combined

Chapter 13

We have examined commodity markets, money markets, and the labor market and the conditions under which businessmen are willing to produce the output of the economy. The first two were brought together in a preliminary fashion in Chapter 10. The labor market was developed by itself in Chapter 12, and it is now our task to bring the three markets together into a comprehensive model of short-run income determination. In Chapter 10, we adopted the convention of a stable price level and related the demands of decision-making units to the level of output to enable us to equate output with the money income of the economy, and therefore to make demand a function of money income. However, now that we have a statement of production conditions in the economy, namely a production function, it is possible to relate the level of output to the volume of employment. After all, in pursuit of a policy of full employment, an explicit statement of labor market conditions is both necessary and desirable. This statement may be obtained by restructuring our model of income determination to give explicit recognition to both the price level and employment. P and N will now become dependent variables in our expanded system.

PUTTING THE MODEL TOGETHER

We will deal with the parts of the model in the following sequence: (a) the labor market and the conditions under which output is produced; (b) demands for goods and services in the commodity market; and (c) the money market.

The Labor Market and Production

We begin with the underlying aggregate production function first presented in Chapter 11, in which technology, or the state of the art, is constant, and capital is the fixed factor. Labor is the variable factor subject to diminishing returns. Output, Q, is then:

$$Q = JN^{\alpha} K^{1-\alpha} \qquad (13.1)$$

where N is employment, now expressed in hours worked per week by the labor force;
K is the constant stock of capital;
J is the constant conversion coefficient whose value depends upon the state of technology;
α is a constant representing labor's share of the output;
$1 - \alpha$ is the share of the output going to owners of capital.

The next step is to develop aggregate supply from the underlying production function by obtaining the employment-supply function (which gives the gross revenue that businessmen would have to have to offer employment) and the money wage rate, W. Then aggregate supply will be obtained as follows:

$$\alpha Z = WN$$

$$\text{or: } Z = \gamma WN \qquad (13.2)$$

where Z is aggregate supply;
$\gamma = 1/\alpha$.
We will see shortly that Z may be substituted for Y in our earlier models. Since our aim here is to describe the distribution of income and aggregate supply as a function of the price level, we will use this different notation temporarily.

The final step is to incorporate the price level, P, which, as we saw in Chapter 11, is directly related to the wage rate and inversely related to the marginal productivity of the variable factor, labor, $\Delta Q/\Delta N$. Thus:

$$P = W/(\Delta Q/\Delta N) \qquad (13.3)$$

The wage rate can be brought into the model in two ways, each consistent with the analysis of Chapters 11 and 12. We can assume that it is a constant, or, more realistically, we can assume that the money wage rate is an increasing function of the volume of employment and that the relationship is nonlinear:

$$W = u + vN^2 \qquad (13.4)$$

where u is a minimum or floor level of wages;
v is a positive coefficient.

This chapter will consider only the effects of a constant wage rate. Those of the variable rate are reserved for Chapter 14.

Effective Demand in Commodity Markets

The simplest case is a closed economy in which aggregate demand is composed of consumption, investment, and government purchases of goods and services. For the sake of further simplicity, we shall also ignore transfer payments in the consumption function.

Consumption is first and foremost a function of household behavior, and in Chapter 11, in which an aggregate supply function was developed, it became apparent that households should be divided into three groups: wage earners, those on fixed incomes, and profit recipients. Accordingly, we shall modify our initial statement of household behavior by broadening it to include separate consideration of these three groups.

The consumption of wage and salary earners, C_1, is dependent upon disposable money income:

$$C_1 = b_1 (WN - tWN) \tag{13.5}$$

where b_1 is a coefficient representing the marginal propensity to consume of wage and salary earners;
t is a tax coefficient.

The difference between wages and direct taxes, $WN - tWN$, is the disposable money income of this group. The savings, S_1, of wage and salary earners can also be defined as:

$$S_1 = (WN - tWN) - C_1 \tag{13.6}$$

C_1 and S_1 may be transformed into *real* consumption and savings by dividing by the price level, P.

Rentiers are those households in the economy that are living on fixed incomes representing the contractual payments of business enterprises that must be met even if output is zero. Their consumption, C_2, is dependent upon disposable income, which in turn is determined by their fixed receipts:

$$C_2 = b_2 (F - tF) \tag{13.7}$$

where b_2 is the propensity to consume of rentiers;
F is the fixed money income of rentiers.

Again, the disposable money income of rentiers is defined as $F - tF$ and the savings of this group, S_2, is:

$$S_2 = (F - tF) - C_2 \tag{13.8}$$

C_2 and S_2 may also be divided by P to obtain their real equivalents.

Profit recipients are those households with an equity participation in the business sector of the economy. Their consumption also depends upon their disposable income, and under our constant-output-share production function their disposable income is determined by the money wage rate. Money profits, ϕ, are derived by letting:

$$Z = WN + F + \phi$$

where WN is wages and salaries;
F is the income of rentiers;
ϕ is the profit residual.

Since $Z = \gamma WN$ under the constant-shares assumption:

$$\phi = (\gamma - 1)\, WN - F$$

The consumption function for profit-recipient households is then:

$$C_3 = b_3 (\phi - t\phi) \tag{13.9}$$

where C_3 is the consumption of profit recipients;
b_3 is the marginal propensity to consume of profit recipients.

The disposable money income of rentiers is $\phi - t\phi$, and the savings, S_3, of rentiers is:

$$S_3 = (\phi - t\phi) - C_3 \tag{13.10}$$

Again, dividing by the price level transforms C_3 and S_3 into the real consumption and savings of profit recipients.

As we have seen, the classic formulation of investment demand is to treat it as a function of the rate of interest. Given technology, the state of expectations, and a set of risk preferences, investment spending depends upon the relation of the expected marginal rate of return to the rate of interest. If we follow this formulation and put it in linear terms, then:

$$I = c + dR \tag{13.11}$$

where I is investment;
R is the rate of interest;
c and d are, respectively, positive and negative coefficients; c represents the intercept of the investment demand curve and d its slope.

Alternatively, we can make investment also dependent upon levels of income, as developed in Chapters 5 and 10, where doing so introduced an availability of funds concept into investment demand. Investment would then be written as:

$$I = c + dR + e\gamma WN \tag{13.12}$$

where e is the negative coefficient of income.

Real investment is obtained simply by dividing I by P.

Government expenditures may be treated as exogenously determined, for since such expenditures result from a sociopolitical process, it is more satisfying to think of them in terms of some target level of monetary outlays. That is:

$$g = \frac{G}{P} \tag{13.13}$$

where g is real government expenditures;
G is a given monetary level of government outlays on goods and services.

We continue the convention of the previous model that all factor income is paid to households and that the latter are therefore the transactor units subject to a tax levied as a proportion t of their income. Taxes are therefore a function of monetary income:

$$T = t\gamma WN \tag{13.14}$$

where T is the monetary value of taxes;
t is the tax coefficient.

Definitional relationships in commodity markets are formed when we take a total and define it as a sum of a set of mutually exclusive parts. Perhaps the most important one of these that we have encountered so far is the equilibrium condition that aggregate supply must equal aggregate demand. In the earlier and preliminary model, under the assumption of a constant price level, the equality of aggregate demand and aggregate supply was expressed as $Y = C + I + G$. Now that supply conditions are incorporated, however, Z, or γWN, is substituted for Y, and because aggregate supply is in *money* terms, aggregate demand must also be in money terms. Hence the equilibrium condition is that:

$$\gamma WN = Z = C_1 + C_2 + C_3 + I + G$$

$$\text{or: } Z = b_1(WN - tWN) + b_2(F - tF) + b_3(\phi - t\phi) + c + dR + e\gamma WN + G \quad (13.15)$$

Another definitional relationship in which we were previously interested is the government's budget position, $G - T$. Since $T = t(WN + F + \phi)$, the budget position is:

$$G - T = G - t(WN + F + \phi) \quad (13.16)$$

Demand and Supply in Money Markets

Turning from the commodity markets to the money markets, we wish to make the appropriate substitutions to integrate aggregate demand and aggregate supply into the model.

We recall that the transactions, or medium of exchange, demand for money is determined by the volume of transactions, the price level at which they occur, and the interest rate. Earlier we wrote:

$$M_Y = M_Y(Y, R) = jY + iR$$

Now we substitute to form:

$$M_Y = M_Y(\gamma WN, R) = j\gamma WN + iR \quad (13.17)$$

The asset demand for money is determined by the rate of return on tangible assets and a wealth-holding preference function. Hence:

$$M_L = M_L(R)$$

or, in linear form:

$$M_L = k + lR \quad (13.18)$$

where $k > 0$ and $l < 0$.
This equation is familiar from our discussion of the money market in Chapter 9. This equation, of course, does not hold in the area of the liquidity trap, where there is a floor below which the interest rate cannot fall.

With the money supply, M_s, set at the discretion of the monetary authority, and the equilibrium condition that the demand and supply of money be equal, then:

$$M_Y + M_L = M_s \qquad (13.19)$$

This completes the alterations of the model under the assumption of an exogenously determined money wage rate.

SUMMARY OF THE MODEL

Table 13–1 summarizes our model in terms of its component parts for the labor, commodity, and money markets. The basic conditions, exogenous variables, coefficients, and simultaneously determined variables are presented in columns (1) through (4). In Part I of the table it is assumed that the money wage rate is given. In Part II, the only change is to make W an increasing function of the level of employment, thus adding two more coefficients: u, representing the floor level of money wages, is both a legal and an institutional coefficient; while v, representing the manner in which the wage rate increases with the square of employment, is best characterized as an institutional coefficient representing the response of labor to varying labor market conditions.

We can now examine a diagrammatic presentation of the model when *the money wage rate is exogenous.* We will then be able to review the factors, including those directly subject to public policy, which will change levels of employment.

Diagrammatic Presentation of the Model with a Given Money Wage Rate

The full income determination model may be reduced to basic commodity and labor market relationships on the one hand, and money market relations on the other. With a given money wage rate, equations (13.1) through (13.15) reduce to one equation in two unknowns, N and R,[1] as do equations (13.17) through (13.19), representing the money market. This allows us to express commodity-labor market and money market equilibria in terms similar to those we previously called *IS* and *LM* functions. Our axes are now N (employment) and R (the interest rate), and linear approximations of the two new functions are found in Figure 13–1. To distinguish the commodity-labor market relationship from the commodity market relationship in the simpler model, where supply conditions in commodity markets were suppressed, we have relabeled the *IS* curve the *YZ* curve. This curve represents all pairs of R and N for which aggregate demand (Y) and aggregate supply (Z) are equal in the

[1] This can be seen by substituting equations (13.1) through (13.14) into (13.15) and solving for R. We obtain: $R = ([1 - b + bt]/d)\ (JN^{\alpha}K^{1-\alpha}) - (c + G)/d$, where b, a weighted average of b_1, b_2, and b_3, is positive, $t > 0$, and $d < 0$. Similarly, equations (13.17) through (13.19), representing the money market, reduce to one equation in the same two unknowns when we substitute (13.17) and (13.18) into (13.19) to obtain: $R = (M_s - k)/(i + l) - j\gamma WN/(i + l)$, where $k > 0$ and $l < 0$.

Table 13–1. Summary of Full Income Determination Model with Exogenously Determined Wage Rate.

Market	Basic Conditions (1)	Exogenous Variables (2)	Coefficients (3)	sign	technical	behavioral	legal	Institutional	Simultaneously Determined Variables (4)
I. Labor market	Given technology	W, the wage rate	γ	+					$\Delta Q/\Delta N$, the marginal product of labor
	Given stock of capital		α	+				√	P, the price level
	Aggregate production function								N, the volume of employment in terms of hours worked
									Aggregate real and monetary factor incomes
	Profit maximizing entrepreneurs in pure competition								Real and monetary consumption of households
									Real and monetary investment
Commodity market	Equilibrium condition: aggregate demand equal to aggregate supply	F, the money income of rentiers	b_1	+		√			Real and monetary savings
		G, government expenditure in money terms	b_2	+		√			Tax revenues
	Given state of expectations		b_3	+		√			The government's budget position; G − T
			t	+			√		The transactions demand for money

Market	Basic Conditions (1)	Exogenous Variables (2)	Coefficients (3)						Simultaneously Determined Variables (4)
				sign	technical	behavioral	legal	Institutional	
			c	+		√			The asset demand for money
			d	−		√			The interest rate
			e	+		√			
Money market	Discretionary monetary authority	M_s, the money supply	j	+				√	
	Equilibrating condition: demand for money equal to the supply		i	−				√	
	Given wealth preference function		k	+			√		
	The possible existence of a "liquidity trap"		l	−			√		
II. A labor market in which W is a function of the volume of employment	No exogenous variables								W is added to the list of simultaneously determined variables
			u	+			√	√	
			v	+				√	

Figure 13–1.

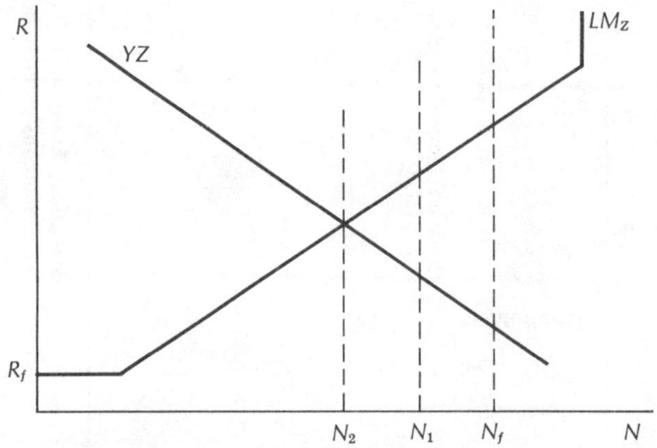

commodity markets, hence the label *YZ*. To distinguish the money-labor market relationship, we have renamed the *LM* curve the LM_Z curve.

The meaning of this diagram is that in the commodity-labor market with a given production function, with profit-maximizing entrepreneurs operating under conditions approximating pure competition, with a given money wage rate, with given consumption and investment demand functions, and with a given level of government purchases of goods and services, *YZ* represents all combinations of the interest rate and employment that equate aggregate demand and aggregate supply. Put differently, these combinations equate the expenditure plans of transactors with the revenue-employment requirements of businessmen, for levels of employment are uniquely related to real and monetary income through the production and aggregate supply functions. Further, as we move down *YZ* we have an increase in employment. Although the level of *P* does not appear in the graph, we know from our analysis in Chapters 11 and 12 that higher levels of *N* can only be achieved with higher price levels. The extent of the increase in prices depends upon the significance of diminishing returns. If we let N_f represent a position of full employment, then at that point the price level will be higher than at an employment level of N_1, and at N_1 the price level will be higher than at N_2. We also know that as employment rises real income will rise, but since the money wage rate is fixed and the price level rises, the real wage *rate* will fall.[2]

The LM_Z function is drawn under the assumption that the money supply is given. The horizontal portion of the curve on the left of the figure is included

[2] Since a rise in employment usually means that previously unemployed persons are now at work, their production is added to the stream of income and their wage rate has, in a sense, risen from zero to some positive level. But those who were previously employed now find their money wage will buy less because of higher prices. Thus an expansion of employment and income in this manner involves a partial redistribution of income away from the presently employed in favor of the new workers. In one sense, however, the real wage of all is raised by increasing the level of employment because per capita income (the ultimate measure of a "wage") will rise as employment and income increase until full employment is reached.

to suggest the possible existence of a liquidity trap. Because changes in the price level accompanying increases in employment are built into the transactions demand for money, LM_Z represents all combinations of N and R where the supply of money is equal to the demand for money.

Factors Shifting *YZ* and LM_Z

Given the money wage rate, a shift in YZ will result from those changes in the demands of transactor units that were examined in Chapter 7. Thus an upward shift in the consumption function, a shift in the investment demand function owing to more favorable expectations or to a change in technology, or an exogenous rise in G will shift YZ to the right. The LM_Z function will shift to the right if M_s increases or if the wealth preference function changes so that money is less desired as an asset at each rate of interest.

The Slope of *YZ* and a New Multiplier

We have already learned from the earlier form of our model that the slope of IS increases with the value of the income multiplier, which in turn depends upon the marginal propensities to consume, tax, import, and pay transfer payments. Now that supply conditions are included in the model, however, we must reexamine the nature of the multiplier. By so doing, we will be able to draw some important contrasts between the multipliers of this full model and those previously developed. We do this in two stages, developing first money income multipliers, and then employment multipliers.

Income Multipliers

From equation (13.1), labor's share in total output is α, while claims of profit recipients are $1 - \alpha$.[3] A weighted average of the wage-earners' and profit recipients' marginal propensities to consume is then:

$$B = b_1(\alpha) + b_3(1 - \alpha) \qquad (13.20)$$

If we now stipulate an increase in G, government purchases of goods and services, and that monetary authorities act to keep the interest rate unchanged so that there will be no second-order impact upon investment spending (through money markets) as a result of this commodity market action, then, using equation (13.15), substituting Y for Z, and looking at changes in variables, the anticipated increase in income from the change in G will be:

$$\Delta Y = \Delta C + \Delta G$$

$$\text{or: } \Delta Y = B(\Delta Y - t\Delta Y) + \Delta G$$

[3] It is assumed here, for purposes of simplification, that no income goes to rentiers, i.e., we are neglecting the C_2 term in equation (13.15).

Collecting terms, we have:

$$\Delta Y - B\Delta Y + Bt\Delta Y = \Delta G$$

$$\Delta Y(1 - B + Bt) = \Delta G$$

$$\Delta Y = \frac{1}{1 - B + Bt} \Delta G \tag{13.21}$$

and the income multiplier, $\Delta Y/\Delta G$, attributable to the increase in government spending is:

$$\frac{1}{1 - B + Bt}$$

That is, for every $1 increase in government spending, income will rise by:

$$\frac{1}{1 - B + Bt}$$

Under equivalent conditions the same multiplier coefficient would apply to an increase in investment spending.

This income multiplier depends upon the weighted average of the marginal propensities to consume, B, and the tax coefficient, t. B *in its turn depends upon the distribution of income between wage earners and profit recipients.*

Employment Multiplier

The conversion of the income multiplier into employment terms can be accomplished by recalling that $Z = \gamma WN$, and hence $\Delta Z = \gamma W\Delta N$. This expression, when simplified by multiplying both sides by $1/\gamma W$, allows us to see that the increase in employment accompanying an increase in expected receipts can be expressed as:

$$\Delta N = \frac{\Delta Z}{\gamma W} \tag{13.22}$$

$1/\gamma W$ is a conversion factor relating any given level of expected receipts to employment. The relation of employment to expected receipts depends upon the wage rate and income shares. Thus to hire one additional worker an employer must pay the going wage rate, W, and he must have expected receipts amounting to γW, where γ is the reciprocal of labor's share in output.

Now, to derive an employment multiplier, we can assume as before an increase in government spending, ΔG, impose the condition that monetary authorities act to keep interest rates unchanged, and use $\Delta Z = \gamma W\Delta N$ and equation (13.21) to give:

$$\gamma W\Delta N = \frac{\Delta G}{1 - B + Bt}$$

$$\text{or: } \Delta N = \frac{\Delta G}{\gamma W(1 - B + Bt)} \tag{13.23}$$

And the change in employment, ΔN, for every \$1 increase in government spending, is:

$$\frac{1}{\gamma W(1 - B + Bt)}$$

The employment multiplier, like the income multiplier, depends upon the weighted marginal propensity to consume, B, and the tax coefficient, t, but it also depends upon the money wage rate, W, and the distribution of income between wage earners and profit recipients reflected in γ. Since W is, in this analysis, taken as given, it is apparent that with an exogenously determined wage rate *the larger the labor content of each dollar's worth of output, the greater the increase in employment.*

As before, the tax coefficient, t, plays an important role in the multiplier. A reduction in t will still flatten the YZ curve by increasing its slope and an increase in t will do the opposite, or turn YZ in a clockwise direction. The value of this multiplier, however, also depends upon changes in the distribution of income. This is a matter that we have not directly encountered before. There is no a priori reason to assume that wage earners and profit recipients have equivalent consumption propensities, although there are good empirical grounds for believing that profit recipients have the higher propensity to save. Hence, if a redistribution of income occurs toward profit recipients, γ will become larger and B, the weighted marginal propensity to consume, will become smaller. The income and employment multipliers will fall in size, which is equivalent to saying that YZ will become steeper.

CONCLUSION

This chapter has assembled commodity, money, and labor markets into the full income determination model summarized in Table 13–1. This model differs from that in Chapter 10 because it specifically states supply conditions and because its consideration of labor markets permits the distinction of wage, profit, and rental sources of household income.

YZ and LM_Z functions were derived on the assumption of a constant money wage rate. The YZ curve, then, represents all combinations of interest rates and employment that equate aggregate demand and supply. Along it, the expenditure plans of decision-making units are equated with the revenue-employment requirements of businessmen. The LM_Z curve assumes a constant money wage rate, a given money stock, and a liquidity trap, and represents all combinations of employment and interest rates where the supply and demand for money are equal. We briefly considered the elements in commodity and money markets that can bring about shifts in either YZ or LM_Z. These forces were previously considered at length in Chapters 7, 9, and 10.

Finally, income and employment multipliers were derived under the assumption of a fixed money wage rate. The size of the income multiplier was shown to depend upon the weighted marginal propensity to consume and the tax coefficient. The size of the employment multiplier depends upon these, but also upon the wage rate and the share of labor in total output.

ADDITIONAL READINGS

Since this chapter summarizes the model to this point and since the model is discussed further in Chapter 14, see the references at the ends of the previous chapters and at the end of Chapter 14.

QUESTIONS

1. List all of the variables in the model in equations (13.1) to (13.19). From the annual data in the appendix to Chapter 1, record values of all of the variables in the model for which measurements are provided. Do these data permit you to calculate any of the parameters of the model?

2. In which direction would the *YZ* curve of Figure 13–1 shift in response to:

   (a) an increase in the propensity to consume?
   (b) an increase in the income tax rate?
   (c) an improvement in technology?
   (d) a decline in *G*?

3. In which direction would the LM_Z function of Figure 13–1 shift in response to:

   (a) an increase in the money supply?
   (b) an increase in the desire to hold wealth?

4. What is the equation for the employment multiplier, $\Delta N/\Delta G$? Define each of the terms in the equation.

5. How would a redistribution of income in favor of profit recipients affect the terms in the income and employment multipliers? How would these multipliers change?

Further Complications: A Variable Wage Rate and Wealth Effects

Chapter 14

In Chapter 13, our model of income determination was constructed assuming a constant money wage rate, although we did mention that it could also incorporate a wage rate that is a positive function of employment. This chapter will examine two examples of such a variable wage rate: The first is the more simplistic case in which a money wage rate increase is expected to be a once-and-for-all situation; the second is the more realistic one that an inflationary psychology exists and each increase in money wages and in prices is expected to lead to a further increase. We consider these in turn, proceeding step by step to analyze the influence of the variable money wage rate on the YZ and LM_Z functions, and therefore on employment and the rate of interest.

The second portion of this chapter concerns the nature and significance of what is called the wealth effect, sometimes referred to as the real balance or Pigou effect. Our approach will be, first, to derive a suitable definition of wealth and, second, to consider the avenues through which changes in wealth might be expected to influence aggregate economic activity. The question may be put this way: What effect will changes in wealth exert upon the flow of expenditures?

THE MONEY WAGE RATE AS A FUNCTION OF EMPLOYMENT

Case A: Continuous Wage Increase Without an Inflationary Psychology

The first effect of the variable money wage rate on the labor-commodity market relationships of decision-making units may be seen best if we begin simply with a once-and-for-all wage increase. Only when we have examined the changes associated with this static situation will it be possible to extend our conclusions to the continuous case.

If, at an employment level of N_1, the money wage rate increases by 10 percent, the increase in the wage rate has no effect on the production function, so that the ratio of marginal to average product is unchanged at each employment level. In response to the wage increase, and assuming no redistribution effects on the composition of output, the employment-supply and aggregate supply functions will shift upward by 10 percent. That is, the expected receipts of businessmen must rise by 10 percent if they are to continue to offer a quantity of employment equal to N_1.

Since money wages and prices rise proportionately at each level of employment, however, the real consumption of wage-earners is unchanged. The real income, and therefore the real consumption, of those on fixed money incomes will decline at each level of employment. In fact, non-labor incomes will be redistributed from rentiers to profit recipients, and an increasing absolute and relative amount of the non-labor share of income will go to profit recipients. The effect of this redistribution of income on consumption will depend upon two factors: (a) the dividend policies of business firms; and (b) the propensity to consume of profit recipients compared with rentiers. With respect to dividend policies, the question is what proportion of increased profits is held as retained earnings. If, for example, the increase in dividends does not match the increase in profits, then the decreased real consumption of rentiers is not likely to be matched by equivalent increases in consumption on the part of profit-recipient households. As for (b), there is little reason to believe that the consumption propensities of profit recipients and rentiers are identical. There is instead good empirical evidence that profit recipients have a higher propensity to save than either wage earners or those on fixed incomes. Hence, a redistribution from rentiers to profit recipients should shift the consumption function downward.

The effect of the rise in the wage rate and prices on investment demand is determined by the influence of the wage increase on the marginal efficiency of capital. An increase in the wage rate will affect, besides operating costs, the supply price of capital and the stream of future earnings, both of which we can expect to increase by 10 percent. Since costs and earnings are affected equally, and *if the monetary authorities take action to maintain a constant* R, there will be no reason for businessmen to alter their investment program on this account, and hence there will be no effect on investment spending.

It is also necessary to consider the effect of the wage increase on the liquidity of the business sector. Thus the process of redistribution occurs under the aegis of the business firm. If retained earnings increase more rapidly than dividends, the liquidity of the business sector increases and a source of portfolio imbalance is introduced. The availability of funds to the firm increases, and, to the extent that investment is functionally related to the internal availability of funds, real investment rises.

Finally, because government expenditures on goods and services are of a fixed monetary amount, G, the increase in wages and prices will serve to reduce real government spending, g.

The reduction in consumption will probably not be offset by the rise in

Figure 14–1.

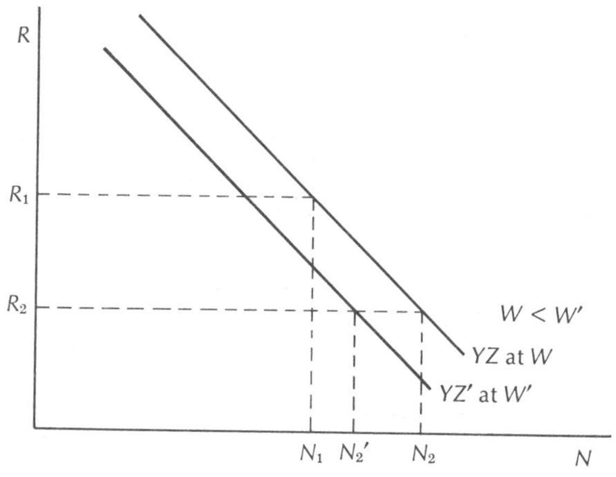

investment, so that the net effect of these countervailing influences will shift the YZ curve downward. As in Chapter 12, at the new higher wage rate, W', the volume of employment will be less than at the original wage rate, W. This situation is illustrated for YZ in Figure 14–1. At each alternative rate of interest, we should expect a smaller volume of employment at the higher wage rate, W'.

The analysis in labor-commodity markets from this simplest of cases can readily be extended to the case of continuous increases in the wage rate. If YZ, in Figure 14–1, expresses commodity-labor market equilibria at alternative rates of interest and wage rate W, then at R_1 the equilibrium level of employment will be N_1; at R_2 it will be N_2. However, since W is a function of employment, in moving from N_1 to N_2 there will be a higher level of money wages, W', and consequently a lower level of aggregate demand at any given R. Hence, we draw a new YZ function, YZ', associated with wage rate W'. YZ' will be to the left of YZ. The volume of employment consistent with R_2 is then $N_2' < N_2$. And so it would be for each level of employment greater than N_2'. That is, if R were to fall below R_2, we would not move down YZ' in order to find the new level of employment. Rather, we would have a new YZ function representing the higher money wage rate. The new level of employment would be read from this function.

Should we now take a wage rate $W'' > W'$, a further shift to the left in YZ would take place so that YZ'' (associated with W'') would be to the left of YZ'. The reasoning is identical to that previously outlined.

To sum up, the effect of a variable money wage rate (without an inflationary psychology) can be seen in Figure 14–2. YZ represents a fixed money wage rate of W. YZ', YZ'', and YZ''' represent money wage rates of W', W'', and W''', respectively, where $W < W' < W'' < W'''$. The effect on YZ of a *continuous* upward variation in the wage rate is to form the new function YZ_v.

Figure 14–2.

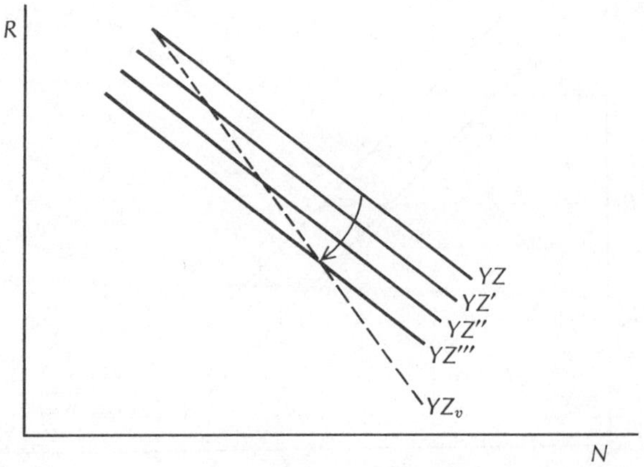

Commodity Market Multipliers with a Variable Wage Rate

We developed earlier money and employment multipliers for the constant wage rate; we will now develop these multipliers for the variable wage rate. To obtain the income multiplier for an increase in, say, government spending, we observe changes in Y using equation (13.15) in precisely the same fashion as we derived equation (13.21):

$$\Delta Y = B(\Delta Y - t\Delta Y) + \Delta G$$

$$\frac{\Delta Y}{\Delta G} = \frac{1}{1 - B + Bt} \tag{14.1}$$

This is the same result as in the case of the fixed wage rate.

For the employment multiplier, however, the conversion factor previously presented changing the wage bill into total receipts must now be applied not only to the wage rate but also to the rate of change in the wage rate. If the wage function is specified for illustration as in equation (13.4):

$$W = u + vN^2$$

Then:

$$\frac{\Delta N}{\Delta G} = \frac{1}{\gamma(u + vN^2)(1 - B + Bt)} \qquad (14.2)^1$$

In this case, the size of the employment multiplier depends upon the weighted marginal propensity to consume, the tax coefficient, the distribution of in-

[1] This equation is derived from equations (13.2) and (13.15) by setting $\gamma WN = \gamma B(WN - tWN) + G$, which, since $W = u + vN^2$, is identical to: $\gamma N(u + vN^2) = \gamma BN(u + vN^2)(1 - t) + G$, or $\gamma N(u + vN^2)(1 - B + Bt) = G$. Hence,

$$N = \frac{G}{\gamma(u + vN^2)(1 - B + Bt)} \quad \text{and} \quad \frac{\partial N}{\partial G} = \frac{1}{\gamma(u + vN^2)(1 - B + Bt)}.$$

Figure 14–3.

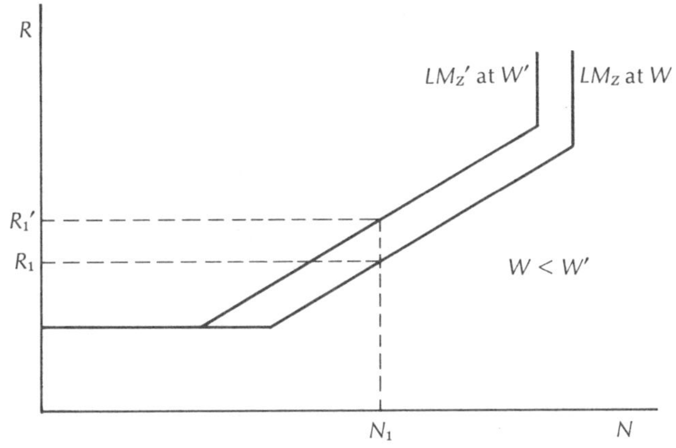

come, and the initial level of employment. The higher the level of employment when an increase in government spending occurs, the smaller the increase in employment and therefore in real income. More of the expenditure is siphoned off into bidding up the wage rate and the price level, and less is reflected in an increase in real income.

The Effect of the Variable Wage Rate on the Money Market

The effect of the variable wage rate on the LM_Z curve can be evaluated by using the same step-by-step procedure followed with YZ. With a given money supply, the effect of the one-time increase in the wage rate from W to W' is to increase the transactions demand for money. The same real output is now evaluated at the 10 percent higher level of prices, and as money income is higher, more nominal units of money are required for transactions. In their attempt to acquire more money, people sell securities, and prices of securities fall while interest yields rise. With a given set of wealth preferences on the part of decision-making units, there should be no change in the asset demand for money. Thus the effect of the increased demand for money for transactions purposes would shift the LM_Z curve to the left as in Figure 14–3, which shows that at N_1 the effect of the wage increase is to raise the rate of interest from R_1 to R_1'. This is a clear example of the influence that labor market conditions can exert upon interest rates in financial markets.

The case of continuous wage increases can be seen by looking at LM_Z in Figure 14–4, which expresses the equilibrium rates of interest equating the demand and supply of money at alternative levels of employment. At N_1 the equilibrium level of interest rates is R_1; at N_2 it is R_2; and so on. However, as we have seen, LM_Z is drawn assuming a fixed wage rate, and in moving from N_1 to N_2 here, there is an increase in the wage rate. This will result in an increased demand for money at each level of employment, so that LM_Z will shift

Figure 14–4.

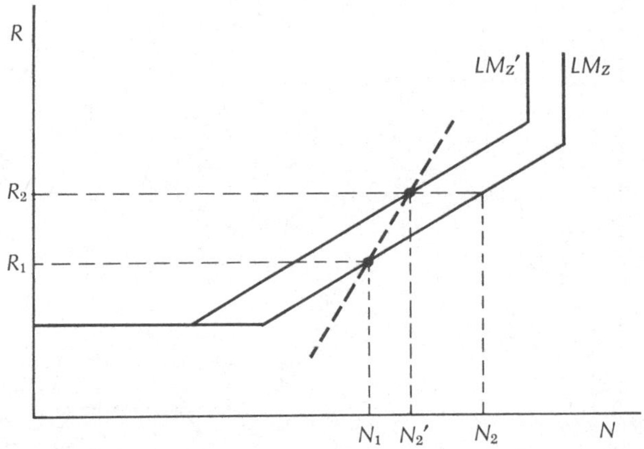

back to LM_Z', which represents the new set of money market equilibria at the higher wage rate W'. The volume of employment consistent with R_2 is now really N_2' rather than N_2. Further, if we were to move levels of employment above N_2', we would not move up LM_Z'. Rather, there would be a set of LM functions drawn to the left of LM_Z' made necessary by the fact that the money wage rate was rising continuously from W'. In sum, the effect of a variable money wage rate is as illustrated in Figure 14–4 by the dashed line connecting the equilibrium points.

Case B: Continuous Wage Increases With an Inflationary Psychology

A more realistic case is seen where the continuous rise in wages and prices creates expectations of further increases in wages and prices. This is the inflationary psychology case and it is the most difficult of all to examine.

In commodity markets, businessmen's investment demands and expectations of a continuous rise in prices will move the investment demand curve to the right. The reason, as is apparent from the present value formula,

$$V = \sum_{j=1}^{n} \frac{NR_j}{(1 + i)^j}$$

(where NR_j is the net interest revenue in year j and i is the discount rate), is that the current prices of capital goods are given and do not reflect expectations of future wage and price increases. On the other hand, expected future net revenues in the present value formula rise because they include higher expected prices and present value will also rise. As present value comes to exceed the current price of capital goods, investment is expected to be profitable and businessmen elect to expand. There are two sets of price levels: the lower

Figure 14–5.

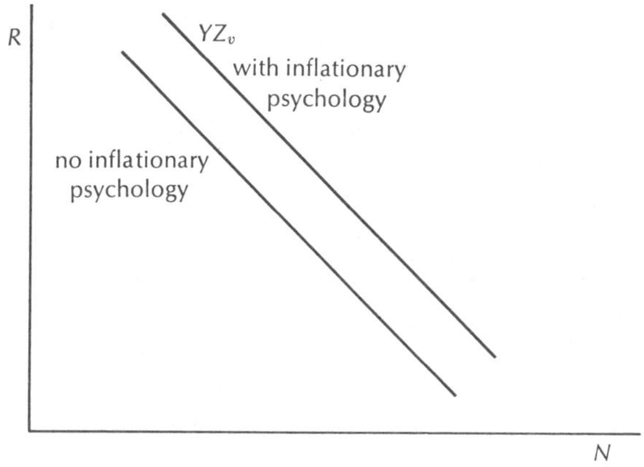

applied to the current supply prices of capital goods, and the expected higher prices applied to the expected future net revenues.

As far as household demand is concerned, changes in income distribution occasioned by the continuous rise in prices are still present. However, with an inflationary psychology would normally lead to an increase in spending; incomes, may decide to increase real consumption at each level of real income. At issue here is the strength of upward shifts in the consumption function because of price expectations as opposed to downward shifts owing to income redistribution.[2]

We also must consider how legislators and the executive branch plan government spending under an inflationary psychology. On the one hand, we could expect that expectations of wage and price increases would tend to raise G, particularly if legislators had some notion of a target level of expenditures in terms of the share of output devoted to public use. But, on the other hand, it is clear that in recent years legislators have argued that government expenditures should be reduced in order to damp inflationary psychology.

Taking commodity markets as a whole, therefore, we conclude that an inflationary psychology would normally lead to an increase in investment spending and, perhaps, to increases in consumer and government spending; it would therefore shift YZ_v to the right of its position in Figure 14–2. This is illustrated in Figure 14–5, where the position of YZ_v under the two alternative sets of expectations accompanying a variable wage rate is indicated.

[2] A recent empirical investigation into the impact of inflation on household expenditures concludes that a significant factor is whether the rising price level is anticipated or unanticipated. The study of Thomas Juster and Paul Wachtel, "Inflation and the consumer," *Brookings Papers on Economic Activity*, No. 1, 1972, pp. 71–114, draws upon consumer survey data on expenditures for durables, nondurables, and services during the late 1960s and early 1970s. The authors conclude that the estimated effects of inflation are not entirely unambiguous and consistent, but they do find that anticipated inflation tends to depress spending on durables while encouraging spending on nondurables and services, while the unanticipated component of inflation tends to depress spending on nondurables and services, has no effect on durable spending, and therefore serves to increase rates of saving.

In the money market, the quantity of money demanded for transactions will increase. Each level of employment will be associated with a higher level of money income, and as the economy moves toward full employment, the price level will rise due both to diminishing returns and to the continuous rise in the money wage rate.

The asset demand for money, however, is more difficult to analyze, for it is essential to do the analysis within a full asset choice framework. If we return for a moment to our original wealth preference function, in which holding money was seen as an alternative to holding bonds, equities, or tangibles, we see that the effect of an expected wage-price spiral will be to disturb the old equilibrium. The purchasing power of the money used to pay off the bondholder at maturity will fall, and the risk of loss from holding such assets will increase. However, expected returns will increase (relatively) on equities and tangibles because they will be expected to rise in price. A process of adjustment will be set in motion and will lead to a fall in the price of bonds and a rise in the prices of equities and tangibles as people unload both money and bonds in exchange for equities and tangible goods and property until a new equilibrium is reached. In this new equilibrium, the price of bonds must have fallen sufficiently that their yield will compensate bond holders for their expectations of inflation and that the differential between returns on bonds, equities, and tangibles will be an adequate reflection of their respective expected yields in terms of real purchasing power.

Putting these monetary factors together with the fact that the central bank will surely pursue an active anti-inflationary policy by reducing the money supply (restricting its growth), it is almost certain that LM_Z will shift even further to the left than in Figure 14–3. The central bank's restraint will push LM_Z to the left, the increase in Y will also push it leftward, and although the reduction in the asset demand for money will be reduced and would be expected to shift the LM_Z curve to the right, this money will be spent on equities and real assets rather than on bonds, so the net effect we would expect would be a leftward shift in LM_Z.

Bringing together YZ_v and LM_Z for Case B, as opposed to Case A, our conclusion with respect to interest rates on financial assets is clear-cut: They will be higher as the YZ_v curve shifts rightward and the LM_Z curve shifts leftward, and both shifts lead to higher interest rates. The net effect upon employment, N, depends upon the order of magnitude of the respective shifts in YZ_v and LM_Z, which have offsetting effects on employment.

Policy Instruments Once Again

By bringing together the labor, commodity, and money markets to develop one full model, we have devised a more realistic—though more complicated—model than that which we explored when supply conditions were suppressed. Price and wage movements as well as changes in real output and its composition are now an integral part of the machinery, and it is appropriate to pause and consider once again the policy instruments available for attaining and maintaining acceptable levels of employment.

In our earlier analysis, public policy could be either fiscal or monetary in nature. Government expenditures, an exogenous variable, could be increased to raise the commodity market equilibria. The propensity to tax could be altered to change the size of the commodity market multiplier. The money supply could be increased to shift the *LM* curve to the right by increasing the liquidity of the economy; this affected commodity markets through reduced interest rates and through the process of wealth portfolio adjustments. These policy instruments, used either singly or in concert, are no less relevant to our full model.

The importance of the slopes of the *IS* and *LM* curves to policy choice was emphasized in Chapter 10 and the issues raised then are no less important for the YZ and LM_Z curves.

Asymmetrical Wage-Price Behavior

We have learned why—with a constant wage rate—the price level will increase as we approach full employment. When the wage rate is an increasing function of employment, price increases will be even greater. There is thus no doubt that, as unemployed labor is drawn into productive use, the price level will be flexible upward. Also, some downward flexibility in prices is to be expected with diminishing employment, as marginal productivity increases, although, empirically, this has not been too significant in the past. But what of the more realistic case when the money wage rate and prices do not vary together? When effective demand declines and prices fall, does the money wage rate also fall? If it does not, then we have a situation of asymmetrical wage-price behavior.

That wages and prices are indeed subject to a kind of ratchet effect, increasing with increases in effective demand, but refusing to decline significantly in the face of a fall in aggregate demand and real output, may be seen by considering that as output rises with an increase in effective demand, wages and prices also rise. Scarcities appear in the labor and commodity markets and lead to union demands for and management acceptance of upward shifts in the money wage rate. Once the economy approximates a position of full employment, the level of wages and prices that prevails becomes a kind of floor. In the case of a decline in effective demand, however, this floor is not significantly modified by flexibility in a downward direction, for no one readily accepts a cut in his money wages; indeed, his reaction is to resist strongly any effort at scaling them down. The increase in money wages is eagerly sought after; the decrease in money wages is stoutly resisted; and any serious effort in our society to make money wages flexible downward would bring on massive social unrest. Thus our formula relating W to N is overly simple. It holds when N increases, but not when N falls. As each new higher level of employment is reached it becomes a floor.

This complicates the use of policy instruments. They no longer have the easy simplicity previously outlined. When the economy is operating at less than full employment, some increases in effective demand generated by the use of the policy instrument—be it fiscal or monetary—are dissipated through increases in the money wage rate and in the price level. The effect is to increase wages and prices simultaneously with the increase in employment. In contrast, if policy instruments are used to restrict effective demand, the effect is virtually entirely on the level of employment. The money wage rate holds its level, the decline in expenditures is felt entirely in the numbers employed, and policy instruments therefore exert an asymmetrical effect in labor markets.

Conclusion on Variable Money Wages

The most important objective of this first part of Chapter 14 has been to identify the effects of wage movements and changes in the labor market on the equilibrium levels of output, prices, and interest and on various multipliers. The following conclusions may be derived from the analysis:

(1) Continuous money wage increases, when not accompanied by an inflationary psychology, are likely to lead to lower levels of real output and employment at a given rate of interest as the YZ curve shifts leftward.

(2) With the money wage rate increasing with the level of employment, the YZ curve becomes steeper, indicating that both the employment and real output multipliers for a change in government spending have decreased.

(3) A money wage rate increasing with employment as compared to a constant money wage rate also causes the LM_Z curve to become steeper, indicating that a given shift in the YZ curve caused by expenditure changes leads to a smaller change in real output and employment and a larger change in interest rates.

(4) If continuous upward shifts in money wages and prices are expected (inflationary psychology), the YZ curve shifts upward. The level of real output and employment increases for a given rate of interest compared to the situation of no inflationary psychology. This upward shift of the YZ curve is likely to be accompanied by a leftward shift of the LM_Z curve as the transactions demand for money increases at each level of output and the monetary authorities pursue an anti-inflationary policy. These shifts indicate that higher interest rates will accompany an inflationary psychology.

The policy implications of this analysis are significant. As both the YZ and the LM_Z curves become steeper, multipliers become smaller and levels of output and employment become less responsive to changes in government expenditures, taxes, or the money supply. Therefore, to reach or maintain appropriate levels of output and employment requires that countercyclical monetary and fiscal policies be exercised relatively aggressively.

THE WEALTH EFFECT

We have already, in Chapters 3, 8, and 10, discussed the portfolio balance effect—the influence upon expenditures when a discrepancy exists between the desired and the actual composition of the wealth held by decision-making units. The matter before us now, as in Chapter 12, is the effect of changes in the price level upon wealth, whether the resulting shift in wealth positions affects the behavior of decision-making units, and, if so, in what manner. What is the relation between wealth and income? Does a change in real wealth affect the income-expenditure behavior of decision-making units?

Up to now, with the exception of the portfolio balance effect, we have treated real wealth as a parameter in the analysis. We can no longer do this, however, for if real wealth increases households will increase their expenditures at all levels of income and business enterprises will increase the level of their investments, or their investment demand.

Definition of Wealth

We must first define the real wealth position of a society. *Human wealth* is the present value of the earning power of a laborer. When a laborer spends money to train himself to become skilled so he can earn more, he is said to invest in human capital (wealth). This is contrasted with *material wealth,* in the form of productive machines or land and buildings capable of providing an income stream, and with *financial wealth,* in the form of securities. We could lump all forms of wealth into one all-inclusive definition, but for the purposes of this text it is best to take the more restrictive approach of ignoring human wealth and explicitly considering only nonhuman forms of wealth.[3]

The real wealth position of a society then consists of the sum of: (1) the quantity of money, in real terms, held by decision-making units; (2) the present value of the expected stream of real non-labor income (profits and rents, but not wages and salaries); and (3) the present real value of interest payments to be made on the public debt.[4] Wealth may thus be summarized as:

$$A = \frac{M_s}{P} + \frac{Y_n}{R_n} + \frac{G_R}{R_g} \tag{14.3}$$

where A is real wealth, or net assets;

P is the price level;

M_s is the nominal money supply;

Y_n is real non-labor income;

G_R is real interest payments on the public debt;

R_n and R_g represent capitalization rates applied to real non-labor income and real interest payments on the public debt respectively.

[3] The concept of human wealth is more relevant to the analysis of long-term trends in output and productivity—economic growth—than it is for short-term stabilization policy.

[4] The value of private debt cancels out because what is an asset to one person is a claim on another person's income. New wealth is not created by a transfer of claims.

The same considerations apply to the choice of an appropriate capitalization rate for R_n and R_g as were developed in our analysis of investment demand in Chapter 5.

Significance of the Wealth Effect

M_s, the nominal supply of money, is the policy variable subject to determination by the central bank. (In our full income determination model, it was made clear that an increase in M_s would shift LM_Z downward, thus lowering interest rates in money markets.) The extent of the effect of changes in M_s on commodity markets will depend upon the shape of the investment demand function and the size of the multiplier. The influence of changes in M_s upon wealth depend upon whether there is complete wage price flexibility or whether wages and prices are flexible upward, but inflexible downward.

In the face of falling levels of output and employment, if the price level, P, stays constant and the central bank increases the money supply, M_s, the effect is to improve wealth positions and therefore provoke increased expenditures.[5] If, under conditions of rising employment and output, the central bank reduces M_s, an action which would be reinforced by a rising price level, the monetary component of real wealth will be reduced and expenditures will tend to decrease if other things remain unchanged.

Even if the central bank holds M_s constant in the face of increases or decreases in employment, there would, if prices are flexible, be an automatic wealth effect because of changes in the ratio of M_s to P. Since P is simultaneously determined with output and employment in our most general model, and since it rises with increases in output, the monetary component of real wealth would vary inversely with output changes.

If wages and prices are inflexible downward in the face of a decline in effective demand, then P cannot fall and an increase in the nominal money supply is essential for any increase in monetary wealth, while under conditions of increasing effective demand where wages and prices are flexible upward, a refusal by the central bank to alter M_s will still result in a fall in monetary wealth as a result of increases in P. Clearly, this automatic wealth effect can be reinforced by implementing a monetary policy of active restriction (i.e., reducing M_s), but the active intervention by the central bank is not essential. Only when wage-price behavior is asymmetrical and effective demand is falling will it be a necessary condition for the wealth effect to become operative that the central bank increase M_s.

R_n and R_g, on the other hand, represent interest rates used in the present value formula to relate net revenues from an income stream to their present value. They are also called discount rates and capitalization rates. The level of these rates will be simultaneously determined with employment and output.

[5] To the extent that the price level does have some slight downward flexibility a decrease in prices accompanying the decline in output and employment would improve the wealth position of money holders.

Changes in them will be positively related to changes in output and employment; when output increases, capitalization rates will rise; when output falls they will decline. There is then an interest rate-induced wealth effect; as these rates rise, A will fall according to equation (14.3).

In sum, we can say that changes in the money supply, coupled with changes in the price level (the extent of which will depend upon the degree of price flexibility that reality allows) and changes in interest rates, will alter the wealth positions of society and the individual. An increase in wealth is expansionary and a decrease is contractionary. Therefore, higher interest rates not only inhibit investment but also lead to contractionary declines in wealth. Also, a rising price level reduces wealth as M_s/P declines and again the net effect is contractionary.

Since we expect P, R_n, and R_g to rise in an economic boom, they bring about an automatic reduction in wealth and this acts as an "automatic stabilizer." The importance of the wealth effect as an "automatic stabilizer" depends upon the degree of wage-price flexibility present in the economy. The more nearly we approach complete wage-price flexibility, the greater the automatic stabilization associated with the wealth effect. However, if wage-price rigidities exist, then exogenous—or policy directed—changes in M_s will have an important influence on the wealth equation. The closer we approximate complete wage-price rigidity the greater the effect upon wealth of changes in M_s.

Finally, and most critically, we come to the question of the empirical strength of the wealth effect. We must ask how significant is the combination of the portfolio adjustment effect, the real balance effect, and the interest rate-induced wealth effect in the expenditure plans of transactors. This is currently a matter of much controversy among economists, and so far the studies undertaken have resulted in conflicting evidence. At this point only one thing is certain: Before we can evaluate the real-world significance of the wealth effect, we must understand much more fully both the chain of causation by which money creation leads to changes in commodity market behavior and the relative strengths of the linkages in that chain.[6]

ADDITIONAL READINGS

The foundations for part of the multiplier analysis presented in this chapter and in Chapter 13 may be found in Chapter 20 of Keynes' *The General Theory of Employment, Interest and Money* (New York: Harcourt Brace Jovanovich, Inc., 1936). The development of multipliers incorporating aggregate supply concepts may also be found in P. Davidson and E. Smolensky, *Aggregate Supply and Demand Analysis* (New York: Harper & Row, 1964), pp. 146–155, and P. Davidson, "Income and employment multipliers, and the price level," *American Economic Review*, 52 (September 1962): 738–752.

[6] See Thomas Mayer, "Empirical significance of the real balance effect," *Quarterly Journal of Economics*, 73 (May 1959). For a valuable theoretical contribution on the real balance effect, see D. Patinkin, "Price flexibility and employment," *American Economic Review*, 38 (September 1948).

QUESTIONS

1. The comprehensive model presented in this chapter illustrates that labor unions share with the monetary authorities the responsibility for the interest rate. Explain how the wage policies of unions influence the interest rate.

2. In an environment free of offsetting policy actions:

   (a) Steadily increasing wage rates without inflationary psychology will lead to a fall in the levels of employment;
   (b) In a situation with an inflationary psychology and steadily rising wages, employment may either rise or fall.

   Discuss.

3. In Chapters 11 and 12, the fact that money wages tend to rise with employment was discussed. If wages rise at an increasing rate as employment increases, rather than at a constant rate, how will this affect the slope of the *YZ* curve?

4. How would the following changes affect the employment multiplier?

   (a) a fall in the money wage rate;
   (b) a rise in the share of income going to labor;
   (c) a fall in the marginal propensity to consume of profit recipients.

   How would each of these changes affect the steepness of the *YZ* curve?

5. What are the assumptions underlying the conclusion that continuous wage increases without an inflationary psychology would lead to a leftward shift in the *YZ* curve? How realistic do you believe these assumptions to be?

6. Remembering the wealth effect and starting with Chapter 3, trace through the likely effects of an increase in the money supply on:

   (a) consumption; (b) investment; (c) the budget position; (d) imports; (e) exports; (f) interest rates; (g) employment; (h) output; and (i) prices.

7. Since Keynes wrote his *General Theory of Employment, Interest and Money,* many economists have believed that changes in the money supply would have their primary effect upon the economy through interest rate changes. The wealth effect suggests that the linkage between the money supply and economic activity is more direct. Explain.

8. Can you think of any conditions under which a falling money supply might coincide with falling interest rates? Under such conditions would you expect the wealth effect to have a positive or a negative effect upon the level of real aggregate demand?

9. The wealth effect suggests that the existing stock of outstanding government debt acts as a built-in stabilizer. Explain.

Income and the Balance of Payments

15
Chapter

With the rapid expansion in world trade and the increasing economic power of European and Asian countries, the continued growth and stability of American exports has been challenged by foreign imports. This challenge has focused increasing attention on the foreign sector of our economy. Though exports compose only about 7 percent of total U.S. production, changes in even a small demand sector of the economy may, as we have seen, have widespread repercussions through the multiplier. Thus, a shift from domestically produced goods to imports may have widespread effects. Because of the comparative advantages that different countries have in production of different goods, substantial gains in welfare for all countries can be achieved through expanded trade. For these reasons, any changes, autonomous or discretionary, which lead to a disruption in trade can have a significant impact on the living standard of a country.

This chapter adds to the discussion of Chapter 6 by indicating the types of problems the foreign sector account may create for government policy makers as well as the options available for the solutions to these problems. The first two sections of the chapter incorporate the foreign sector more formally into the model under the assumption of fixed exchange rates. The third section of the chapter concerns the international balance of payments and how it may be used to evaluate a country's external position. In the fourth section, the balance of payments equilibrium under fixed exchange rates is reconciled with equilibrium conditions in commodity and money markets. The fifth section discusses flexible exchange rates, and the sixth examines fiscal and monetary policy as stabilization instruments under fixed and flexible exchange rates.

THE FOREIGN SECTOR: EFFECT ON AGGREGATE SUPPLY

In Chapter 6 the effects of foreign purchases of domestic goods and domestic purchases of foreign goods were incorporated into our model of the commodity-producing sector. It was relatively easy to see the effect of the foreign sector on aggregate demand and to indicate the changes that occur in a nation's trade balance with fluctuations in aggregate demand. However, the foreign sector must be incorporated into aggregate supply as well, and to do so considerably complicates the model.

The basic theorem of international trade is the *law of comparative advantage*, which states that under free trade, businessmen (producers) in each trading nation will find it profitable to specialize in the production of those goods and services in which their relative advantage is greatest. They will exchange with producers abroad any surplus over domestic requirements for those products which they are relatively less efficient in producing. The structure of *relative prices* in one country compared with that in another reflects, in addition to comparative advantage, differences in such matters as tax laws (including tariffs), the degree of monopoly in product and factor markets, and the prevailing set of tastes and preferences. Relative prices differ across nations and it is to these differences that businessmen respond.

The *exchange rate* represents the value of one nation's currency in terms of another and can be interpreted as representing some kind of average relationship between price levels in the two countries. In the analysis which follows it will be assumed that exchange rates are fixed.

The shape and position of the aggregate supply function in an open economy will differ from that in a closed economy. Because of the law of comparative advantage, the composition of output will be altered simply because businessmen will be specializing in the output of those commodities that can be produced relatively efficiently. In deriving the aggregate supply function for an open economy there will therefore be a summation across a different set of industries than for a closed economy.

It is also important to stress that not only does aggregate supply in an open economy differ from that in a closed economy, but also that there may be no unique slope or position for the aggregate supply function in an open economy. The reason may be seen by considering the admittedly unrealistic case where there is no interdependence among the output levels of nations. When any country moves from lower to higher levels of output (as a result of increases in aggregate demand) diminishing returns will push the price level upward. Price levels in other nations will remain unchanged, and therefore with fixed exchange rates there will be a deterioration in the competitive position of the expanding country. Given profit-maximizing entrepreneurs there will be a substitution of imports for domestically produced goods. Put otherwise, the composition of output will change at each level of employment because of both domestic conditions of supply and demand and the effects of changes in domestic prices relative to those abroad. The expanding country's propensity to import should increase.

THE FOREIGN SECTOR: FEEDBACK EFFECTS ON AGGREGATE DEMAND

Retaining the condition of fixed exchange rates and assuming constant money wage rates, but replacing the restrictive assumption of independent output levels with one of interdependence, we can see that if output in country *A* expands, both output and the price level will rise. However, the rise in output will induce an increase in aggregate demand in *A*'s trading partners, for the rise in *A*'s income and in *A*'s price level will induce additional imports. These added sales by foreigners to *A* (increase in foreign exports to *A*) will raise output and also prices abroad, although, if diminishing returns proceed at about the same pace abroad as at home, *A*'s prices will rise more than those abroad. Direct expansion in *A* will normally have a greater effect on *A*'s output, employment, and price levels than the induced effects of *A*'s expansion on the output and price levels of foreigners. Country *A* will find its prices rising *relative* to foreign prices; foreigners will find their own products becoming relatively cheaper. The desire of *A* to import will thus rise and that of foreigners will fall, for the change in relative prices favors the sale of goods by foreigners. There will be some partially offsetting increase in foreign imports (*A*'s exports) as foreign income rises, but this effect will be only partially offsetting.

If the condition of constant money wage rates is relaxed and in its place the money wage rate is made a positive function of employment, the effects developed in the preceding paragraphs are only intensified.

The results of such a domestically created expansion in *A*'s aggregate demand may be summarized as follows:

(1) Since the effects of the expansion in domestic output will in an open economy spill over to foreign nations, the impact on output will normally be less than in the case of a closed economy.[1]

(2) In an open economy, because of the continuing upward shifts in the propensity to import, there may be no unique aggregate supply function. This means that with rising prices even more of the expansion in aggregate demand will be met by commodity purchases abroad (imports).

(3) Since in the normal case imports will rise more than the induced increase in exports, the external trade position will deteriorate, other things being equal.

THE BALANCE OF INTERNATIONAL PAYMENTS

Definition

It is possible for a nation's economic relationships with the rest of the world to change, but economies are not tied to one another only by commodity trade. There are other ways, too, which we need to understand in order to establish more precisely the manner in which policies aimed at securing internal equilibrium (i.e., at maintaining high and expanding levels of output and employment) may affect the degree of external equilibrium that an economy is

[1] In a closed economy $Y = C + I + G$ and an increase in G will lead to an expansion of Y by some multiple. But in an open economy $Y = C + I + G + E_x - I_m$ and the increase in imports that follows an increase in G will mean that Y will not increase as much as it would in the closed economy.

capable of achieving. It is one thing to talk about stabilization policies in a closed economy; it is another to assess their impact in an open economy.

In Chapter 1 we derived an output measure for an economy, the gross national product, which, rooted in double-entry bookkeeping, results in a measure of transactions based upon either value-added, if approached from the sources side, or expenditures, if recorded on the uses side. Now it is necessary to outline another widely used type of social account that provides a record of commodity and financial transactions between the residents of one country and the residents of all others for some stipulated period of time. Such a record is called a *balance of international payments.*

It is important to note at the outset that because this record too is based upon the principles of double-entry bookkeeping it will always balance in an *ex post facto* sense. *Ex post facto* balance, however, must not be confused with meaningful economic balance. In the GNP accounts, because the income side is always equal to the payments side, the balance tells us nothing about the adequacy of a particular recorded level of GNP. It may or may not be optimal, depending upon the set of objective criteria that define optimality. Similarly, the balance of international payments will always balance. Whether the economic criteria of balance are met is quite another matter, for *ex post facto* balance can obviously include unsustainable economic behavior.

The balance of international payments for a country may be defined as:

$$X = X_r - X_p \tag{15.1}$$

where X_r is aggregate receipts by residents from foreigners and X_p is aggregate payments to foreigners by residents.

Since the balance of payment must always balance, $X = 0$ and $X_r = X_p$, but to discuss economic balance in any meaningful fashion, we must define X' as the net balance from exchange of goods and services, X'' as the net balance from international capital flows, and X''' as "accommodating" changes in financial reserves necessary to finance any surplus or deficiency arising from trading goods and services and from autonomous investments abroad. Thus if X''' is zero we have meaningful economic "balance" in our international exchanges. If X''' is positive, net accommodating payments are necessary and we have a "deficit" in our balance of payments. And if X''' is negative we have accepted net accommodating receipts and we have a "surplus" in our balance of payments.

Before examining these measures in greater detail we will examine a statement of the balance of payments.

Composition

From Table 15–1, a summary statement of the 1970 United States Balance of International Payments, it is evident that transactions involving American residents and those in the rest of the world can be divided into four categories: *goods and services; private capital; government;* and *other.*

Goods and Services

These include exports and imports of merchandise and the providing of services by Americans to foreigners as well as the sale of services by foreigners to Americans. The receipts column shows the dollar value of claims on foreigners created by the sale of goods or services by Americans. In the payments column is the dollar value of foreigners' claims on Americans resulting from the sale of commodities to Americans.

Private Capital

The receipts and payments columns in this category state changes in stock positions rather than expenditure flows. "Portfolio investment" covers changes in the ownership of financial assets; "direct investment" covers the operation of American subsidiary firms abroad or foreign subsidiaries in the United States. Long-term capital, including direct investment and portfolio investment, represents changes in United States privately owned assets. The payments column includes such cases as portfolio investment, when an American resident acquires the equities of an American corporation from a foreign resident, the foreigner receiving a dollar claim in exchange. In the receipts column are changes in United States assets sold to foreign residents, as when a foreigner purchases a share of common stock in an American corporation from a U.S. resident, providing the latter with dollars in exchange, that is, with a dollar claim against foreign currencies. The payments column under direct investment represents an expansion in investment abroad.

Short-term capital movements are defined arbitrarily to cover financial assets, such as Treasury bills or bonds, certificates of deposit, commercial paper, and bank loans, having a term-to-maturity of one year or less. The payments column represents changes in all assets privately held by residents of the United States. Payments mean that claims are created against dollars by the transfer of assets held by foreigners to American ownership. The receipts column means that claims are created against foreign currencies by the transfer of assets to foreign ownership.

Government

This covers loans, grants, and transfers. If, for example, a foreign government sells a bond issue in the New York capital market to raise funds, this will appear in the payments column. The foreign government has been given claims against U.S. dollars.

Other

This category includes private transfers such as gifts and remittances from American residents to those abroad. "Errors and omissions" constitutes a statistical discrepancy between all identifiable receipts and payments. "Changes in

U.S. reserve assets" represents official transactions of the U.S. government with foreign governments and the International Monetary Fund. "Changes in U.S. liquid liabilities" represents changes in foreign holdings of the liquid dollar liabilities of American banks and the Treasury.

Table 15–1. United States Balance of Payments, 1970* (in billions of dollars).

Transaction	Balance of Payments Accounts: Receipts	Payments	Balance	Liquidity Balance: Net Balance	Financing of Net Balance
I. Goods and Services	63.0	59.3	+3.7	+3.7	
1. Goods	42.0	39.9	+2.2		
2. Services	21.0	19.4	+1.6		
a. Military	1.5	4.8	−3.4		
b. Investment income	9.6	5.1	+4.5		
c. Travel	2.3	3.9	−1.6		
d. Other	7.5	5.6	+1.9		
II. Private Capital	3.8	6.4	−2.6	−2.6	
1. Long term	3.1	5.3	−2.2		
a. Direct investment	.9	4.0	−3.1		
b. Portfolio investment	2.2	.9	+1.3		
c. Bank and other loans	.0	.4	− .4		
2. Short term	.7	1.1	− .4		
III. Government	1.8	5.4	−3.6	−3.6	
1. Loans	1.3	3.3	−2.0		
2. Special liabilities	.5	—	+ .5		
3. Grants and transfers	—	2.1	−2.1		
IV. Other					
1. Private transfers	—	.9	− .9	− .9	
2. Allocation of SDR†	.9	—	+ .9	+ .9	
3. Errors and omissions	—	1.3	−1.3	−1.3	
4. Changes in U.S. reserve assets	3.4	.9	+2.5		+2.5
a. Gold (outflow is receipt)	.8	—	+ .8		
b. SDR†	—	.9	− .9		
c. Convertible currencies	2.2	—	+2.2		
d. IMF‡ gold tranche	.4	—	+ .4		
5. Changes in U.S. liquid liabilities	7.8	6.4	+1.4		+1.4
a. Foreign official holdings	7.6	—	+7.6		
b. Private foreign holdings	—	6.4	−6.4		
c. International organization other than IMF	.2	—	+ .2		
TOTAL	80.6	80.6	.0	−3.8	+3.8§

* Figures are preliminary. Source: Federal Reserve Bank of St. Louis, *Review*, 53 (April 1971): 29.
† Special Drawing Rights—a form of "paper" gold accepted by international agreement.
‡ International Monetary Fund—net change in U.S. deposits of gold held by the Fund.
§ Does not add due to rounding.

The Balance

The balance column of Table 15–1 does two things: (a) It shows the source of the aggregate deficit or surplus, and (b) it shows how the deficit is financed or the surplus disposed of. The total of items I, II, and III, and parts 1, 2, and 3 of item IV will leave a net balance, either deficit or surplus, which must be financed. Items IV.4 and IV.5 *taken together* serve to explain how the deficit is financed. IV.4 represents the change in the official international reserve assets of the United States. If these reserves fall, the amount of the decline is entered here with a positive sign to indicate that dollars are received in payment for these reserve assets. Additional financing is indicated under item IV.5, which shows the willingness of foreign governments, central banks, and international organizations to increase dollar balances with the excess of payments over receipts. Increases in foreign holdings are treated as receipts and decreases are recorded as payments. The net change, if positive, represents one means of financing a deficit; if negative, it shows the use to which a surplus is devoted.

Table 15–1 shows that the balance of payments does in fact balance. However, a bookkeeping balance differs from equilibrium. Balance can result from transactions whose magnitude and direction are not economically sustainable over a long period of time. For example, IV.4 represents changes in the official reserve assets of the United States, and IV.5 represents changes in dollar liabilities to foreigners, mainly by the commercial banking system. Large unidirectional changes in these categories may not be sustainable indefinitely.

Returning to our definition of balance of payments, $X = X_r - X_p = 0$, we can let the balance on the goods and services account be:

$$X' = X_r' - X_p' \tag{15.2}$$

the balance on capital account (including government, etc.) be:

$$X'' = X_r'' - X_p'' \tag{15.3}$$

and the net balance of necessary accommodating payments be:

$$X''' = X_r''' - X_p''' \tag{15.4}$$

Therefore:

$$X = X_r - X_p = (X_r' - X_p') + (X_r'' - X_p'') + (X_r''' - X_p''') \tag{15.5}$$

Now we can recognize the economic issues in the balance of payments. We know $X = 0$ by our accounting principle, but since $X = X' + X'' + X''' = 0$, $-X''' = X' + X''$. Thus, if $X''' = 0$, which means no net accommodating changes in accounts are necessary because $X' = -X''$, then the "balance of payments" is balanced. If $X' + X'' > 0$, then receipts are greater than payments on these accounts and accommodating balances rise; $X''' = X_r''' - X_p'''$ is negative and we have a surplus in the balance of payments. If $X' + X'' < 0$, X''' is positive and we have a deficit. To remedy a deficit some action must thus be taken to increase receipts from foreigners and reduce payments to foreigners, or to increase receipts more than payments, or reduce payments more than receipts. The converse, of course, must occur with a surplus.

SOME KEY FUNCTIONAL RELATIONSHIPS

A close study of the major components of the balance of payments in Table 15–1 will let us establish some of the key functional relationships necessary to integrate the foreign sector into our model.

The goods and services account was introduced into our analysis in Chapter 6 to show how commodity exports—given relative prices—are determined by output levels abroad and can therefore be treated as exogenous to the domestic economy. On the other hand, imports (which bring about payments to foreigners) are a positive function of output and employment levels, and the net balance on the goods and services account is therefore a negative function of output levels.[2] If the net balance on the goods and services account is $X' = X_r' - X_p'$, where X_r' represents receipts from foreigners for goods and services and X_p' represents payments to foreigners for goods and services, the following behavioral relationships will prevail:

$$X' = X'(Y) \text{ and } \frac{\Delta X'}{\Delta Y} < 0 \qquad (15.6)$$

The size of the government account is determined by congressional directive as an instrument of foreign policy, as when X' is, in fact, adjusted for the net payments made available to foreigners via loans and grants in the government account. We therefore accept the net balance in the government account as given.

If the exchange rate is fixed, the position of the goods and services account balance, also referred to as the "current account balance," will be determined by the same factors that determine the structure of relative prices. Thus, for example, a shift in tastes and preferences toward domestic and away from foreign-produced goods would tend to reduce imports and "improve" the current account balance.

Category II in Table 15–1 represents movements of private long- and short-term capital in response to international differentials in rates of return. Thus, if U.S. interest rates are low relative to those abroad, then Americans would be encouraged to purchase foreign securities or to engage in direct investment abroad. Payments to foreigners on "capital account" would rise. On the other hand, if American interest rates rise relative to rates abroad, U.S. residents will be less interested in investment opportunities abroad or in the purchase of foreign assets, while foreigners will be expected to step up their acquisition of U.S. assets. We can thus designate the balance on private capital account as $X'' = X_r'' - X_p''$, where X_r'' represents receipts from foreigners on capital account and X_p'' represents payments to foreigners on capital account.

[2] We examine only the first effects and ignore the feedback effects from foreign reactions in the short-run analysis.

The value of X'' is clearly a positive function of the level of interest rates in the U.S., so we can also write:

$$X'' = X''(R) \text{ and } \frac{\Delta X''}{\Delta R} > 0 \qquad (15.7)$$

When a net deficit (or surplus) on the goods and services account, X', is offset by a surplus (or deficit) on the capital account, X'', then no change in a country's international reserve assets will be necessary in order to balance payments with receipts. That is, $-X''' = X' + X''$ and if $X' = -X''$, then $X''' = 0$. This case is one of external equilibrium, or external balance.

Deriving an External Equilibrium (*EE*) Function

With a given rate of exchange, the surplus (excess of receipts) on goods and services is negatively related to output. This is illustrated in Figure 15–1. Quadrant I shows the functional relationship between output, Y, and the balance on current account (including government). The current account balance, X', varies negatively with Y, for an increase in Y will increase payments to foreigners on current account without any significant change in receipts in the short run.

Quadrant III shows X'', the balance on capital account, as a positive function of the rate of interest. A positive change in the interest rate is expected to reduce the domestic investment of funds in a foreign economy (X_p'' falls), and expand the foreign economies' investment of funds in the domestic economy (X_r'' rises), therefore X'' rises. A revision in the international value of the domestic currency either upward or downward would not be expected to shift the X'' function. If the domestic currency is devalued, the dollar price of foreign assets to domestic residents will rise but so will the dollar returns on those assets. Similarly, the foreign currency price of domestic assets will fall, but so will the returns in foreign currency on these domestic assets.[3]

Quadrant II merely connects quadrants I and III which show the two functional relations. Thus, the negatively sloped 45-degree line connects all points for which $X' = -X''$, or $X' + X'' = 0$, that is, for which $X''' = 0$, so that the balance of payments is in balance and not in surplus or deficit.

To find one point on the *EE* curve, we can take income as Y_1. Quadrant I then indicates that the current account is in surplus as X' is at X_1'. For external balance to exist, the capital account deficit must offset the current account surplus. Quadrant II shows that this capital account deficit equals X_1''. Quadrant III indicates that this capital account deficit exists only when the rate of interest equals R_1. Therefore, with income equal to Y_1, the only interest rate consistent with the achievement of external balance is R_1. Such a point is represented by E_1 in quadrant IV, and E_2 and E_3 represent other points of external balance when income has risen to Y_2 and Y_3, respectively.

[3] Of course, any action to impede the international movement of capital, or any change in the conventions affecting tax liabilities of foreign or domestic assets, will shift X''. Similarly, if risk and uncertainty parameters shift, there will be changes in the slope and position of X''.

Figure 15–1.

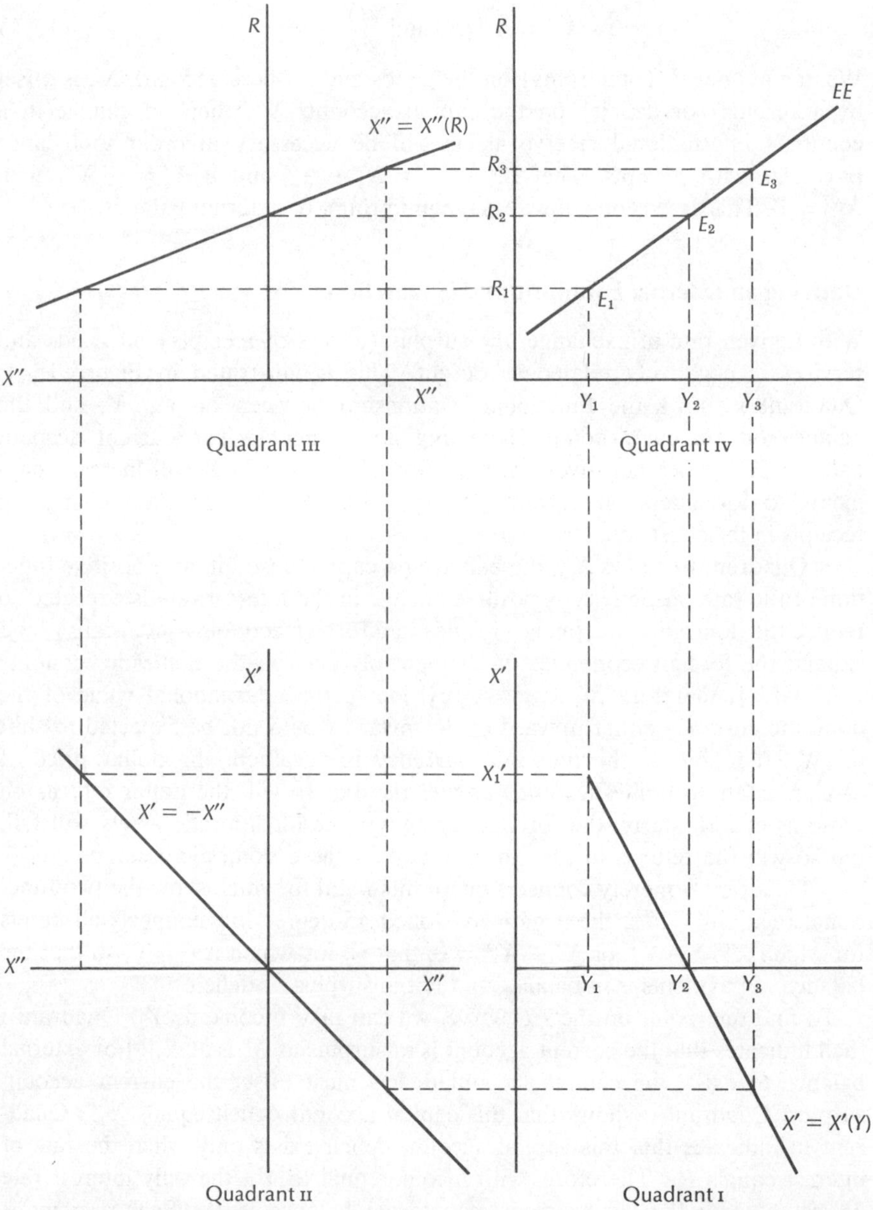

Were a change in the value of the exchange rate to occur, $X'(Y)$ would shift. Thus, if the domestic currency is devalued internationally, $X'(Y)$ will shift to the right because at each level of income exports will increase and imports will decrease if domestically produced goods carry a lower price tag internationally. The basic assumption here, of course, is that no countervailing price quotation adjustments are made by either domestic or foreign producers to overcome the impact of the exchange rate change.[4] Exchange rate devaluation, therefore, means that the *EE* curve will also shift to the right. In contrast, if under fixed exchange rates an appreciation or upward valuation occurs, $X'(Y)$ will shift to the left and so will the *EE* curve.

The first thing to observe about the *EE* curve is the positive slope. The economic explanation for this is simple. A higher Y will result in a smaller net receipts balance on the goods and services account. To maintain external balance, R must rise in order to make capital outflow (payments to foreigners) less attractive and capital inflow (receipts from foreigners) more attractive.

We have noted in Chapter 9 that *LM* will also be positively sloping, at least over much of its range, and how the slope of the *EE* curve compares with combinations of Y and R that preserve equilibrium in money markets is shown in Figure 15–2, which brings the *EE* and *LM* functions together (the *IS* function, also drawn in the figure, will be discussed shortly). The intersection at A means that there is some positive R, here R_1, and some level of Y, here Y_1, which simultaneously satisfy the demand for and the supply of money *and* external equilibrium. As a consequence, then, of any expansion in the economy, money demanders will adjust their balances rapidly, drawing money from asset into transactions uses so that the higher R-Y combination will still be on the *LM* curve. But the point (R_2, Y_2), or B, representing the new market equilibrium is not a point that satisfies external balance. The income effect on imports (payments to foreigners) will then outweigh the interest rate effect on discouraging domestic capital outflows and encouraging foreign capital inflows. Y is too large and R is not high enough for external equilibrium. The point B will thus be associated with a payments deficit. Payments to foreigners will exceed receipts from foreigners, and the difference will have to be made up by a change in the international reserve asset position of the country, in

Figure 15–2.

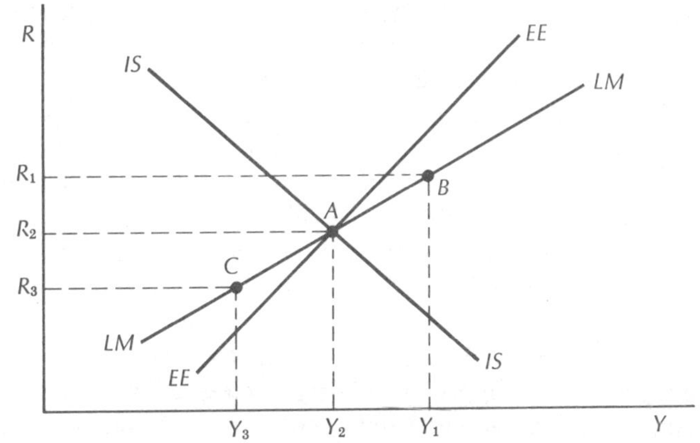

[4] As, for example, if Japanese automobile producers offset a 10 percent appreciation of the yen by reducing quoted prices on their cars by 10 percent.

terms, as we have seen, of either a drawing down of official reserves or a willingness of foreigners to accept dollars, in which case future drafts on official reserves have been created.

The opposite situation is created if a decline in economic activity occurs from point *A* to point *C*. Here, as before, money markets will adjust rapidly as money demanders shift their portfolios. The income effects on the current account balance will again outweigh the effect of a falling interest rate on the capital account, and external disequilibrium will occur. The balance of payments will be in surplus with receipts from foreigners exceeding payments to foreigners. An increase in the international reserve asset position of the country will be the means by which receipts and payments are equalized.

Combining External Balance with Money Market and Commodity Market Equilibrium

To combine external balance with both commodity markets and money markets we will now consider an open economy trading with the rest of the world under fixed exchange rates. The *EE* and *LM* functions are as previously described. The commodity market, the money market, and the balance of payments are in full equilibrium when the three functions have a common value of R and Y, as at the intersection of the *EE*, *LM*, and *IS* curves in Figure 15–2. If Y_1, the equilibrium value of Y, represents a level of output that is less than the full employment level, then there is slack in the economy even though the balance of payments is in equilibrium. On the other hand, if Y_1 represents an "over-full employment" level of output, then Y_1 will be associated with inflation.

If full employment, stable prices, and balance of payments equilibria cannot be simultaneously attained, a choice must be made among the three by policy planners. In the United States, where foreign trade is small relative to the size of the domestic economy, the stress will be on internal balance, and planners must strive for employment and price stability at the possible expense of the balance of payments. The foreign sector does not have as great an influence on either output or interest rates as the commodity and money sectors. No country, however, can long sustain a position of external imbalance without having to take corrective action. Certainly it has not been possible for the United Kingdom, France, West Germany, or Canada to experience external imbalance indefinitely. In all these cases, changes have occurred in the external values of their currencies. The case of the United States, however, differs in one important respect. The dollar has been the international unit of account, and that very fact enabled America to reap the benefits of external deficits for 25 years after World War II. The dollar enjoyed a special status, and in the 1960s, rather than disturb unduly the international monetary system by threatening the dollar's value through attempts to exchange excess dollars for gold or other currencies, other nations adopted different courses of action. Central banks and other holders of official foreign exchange reserves permitted dollar holdings to accumulate rather than exchange them for gold; foreign individuals, including commercial banks, allowed their holdings of dollars to increase; and some countries, such as West Germany and Canada, revalued their currencies upward.

By August of 1971, however, it had become apparent that the United States could no longer continue to finance its deficits in this manner. The inevitable limit to the willingness of central bankers, commercial bankers, and individuals to increase their dollar holdings had been reached, and the increased pressure to convert dollars into gold or other currencies forced the United States to seek a realignment of currencies—essentially the devaluation of the dollar. This, however, was not the first move by the United States to achieve a better balance in its external accounts. Pressures resulting from increased foreign holdings of dollars accompanied by the drain of gold from the U.S. had been felt for some time. The Interest Equalization Tax (IET) of 1962 and the "voluntary restraint" program of 1965 were also efforts to improve the balance of payments by keeping money at home. The IET, by reducing the return on investment abroad, reduced the attractiveness of foreign investments. Under the "voluntary restraint" program, the government asked large corporations active in international investment and trade to increase exports, repatriate earnings, and reduce their capital outflows to developed countries. The United States also attempted to increase the participation of Western Europe in NATO and in other mutual defense expenditures. Therefore, the developments of August 1971—the devaluation of the dollar, a temporary 10 percent import surcharge, and the subsidization of exports—should be viewed as part of a trend toward increasing concern for the position of the United States' balance of payments.

If the domestic economy is underemployed, then an expansionary fiscal policy leading to an increase in income is appropriate. But if the balance of payments is also in deficit, the expansion of income can only make the deficit worse. Thus policies to stimulate the economy may serve the goal of increased employment but conflict with the goal of balance of payments equilibrium. In the examples below we describe the various packages of policies that might be used to overcome conflicts that arise in pursuing multiple goals.

Some Case Illustrations of *IS*, *LM*, and *EE*

We can clarify the kinds of policy adjustments necessary to resolve some disequilibrium situations by examining specific cases involving alternative external and internal economic conditions.

Underemployment with a Payments Surplus

This condition is illustrated by Figure 15–3, where the vertical designated as Y_f represents a full employment level of output—the objective of domestic economic policy. At point A, the economy is operating at less than full employ-

Figure 15–3.

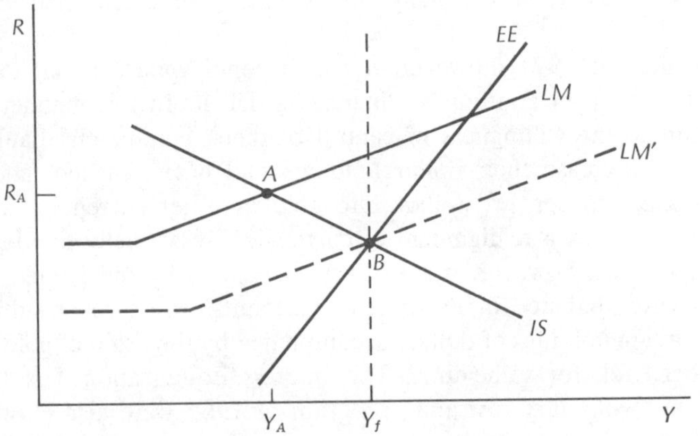

ment since the actual Y at this point is less than Y_f. (Actual income and the actual interest rate level in this graph and in those that follow will always be indicated by the point where the *IS* and *LM* curves intersect). Since the *EE* curve lies below point *A* there is a balance of payments surplus with R_A too high and Y_A too low for external balance. It is possible, however, to take a simple corrective action to secure simultaneously external and internal balance, for, as the figure is drawn, an increase in the money supply will shift *LM* to the right to *LM′*, where *IS*, *EE*, and *LM* intersect in the point *B*, the point of external equilibrium and full employment. In this case, given the slopes and positions of *IS*, *LM′*, and *EE*, it is at least possible to achieve internal and balance of payments equilibria.

Underemployment with a Payments Deficit

The combination of *R* and *Y* represented by point *A* in Figure 15–4 indicates too low an *R* for external balance since the *EE* curve lies above point *A*. There is a deficit in the balance of payments because the actual level of *R* is not high enough to encourage sufficient capital inflow. This example illustrates the need for selectivity in the use of monetary and fiscal programs, for if the goal of policy were to achieve simultaneously full employment and balance of payments equilibrium, it would be necessary to assign fiscal policy the task of securing an output level of Y_f. Either an increase in government expenditures to shift *IS* to the right or a tax rate reduction to rotate it in a counterclockwise direction could be adopted. At the same time, *LM* would have to be moved to the left; this would mean a contractionary monetary policy designed to reduce the money supply and consequently to raise interest rates. With these two shifts the equilibrium point *B* could be reached. At *B* we have both full employment and external balance.

Figure 15–4.

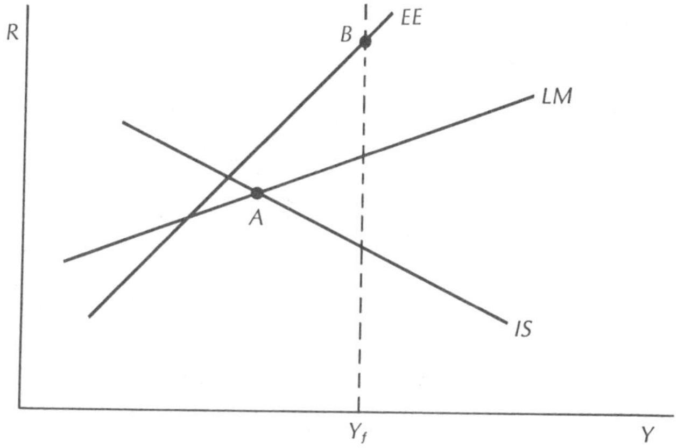

An alternative to exclusive reliance on monetary and fiscal policies would be the devaluation of the currency. This would shift the *EE* curve downward and mean that only smaller shifts in the *IS* and *LM* curves would be required to reach full employment and have external balance as well.

This example of underemployment with a payments deficit allows us to see more clearly the implications of the difference in slopes of the *EE* and *LM* curves. If, in fact, *EE* is less steep than *LM*, so that it cuts *LM* from above rather than from below,[5] the policy prescription is not so clear. Indeed, depending on where *EE* cuts *LM* in relation to the full employment level of income, either expansionary fiscal and restrictive monetary policies or expansionary fiscal and monetary policies may be required to achieve both internal and external balance. The interested reader might examine the policies necessary to achieve full employment income levels when *EE* cuts *LM* from above in the other cases described in this section.

Full Employment with a Surplus

Figure 15–5 illustrates the case of full employment with a balance of payments surplus. Point *A* represents a full employment combination of *R* and *Y*, but at this level of *Y* the rate of interest is too high for external balance since the *EE* curve showing the appropriate levels of *R* for external balance lies below point *A*. If these circumstances remain unchanged, the country will continue to accumulate exchange reserves (i.e., claims on foreigners). The policy alternatives open to the country are a contractionary fiscal policy shifting *IS* to the left combined with an expansionary monetary policy shifting *LM* to the right

[5] That the *EE* curve need not always slope upward as in these figures may be seen by considering that if world capital markets were perfect, capital would flow into the country in large volume with the slightest rise in domestic interest rates and the *EE* curve would be roughly horizontal. On the other hand, if the international flow of capital were totally unaffected by interest rates, the *EE* curve would be vertical.

Figure 15–5.

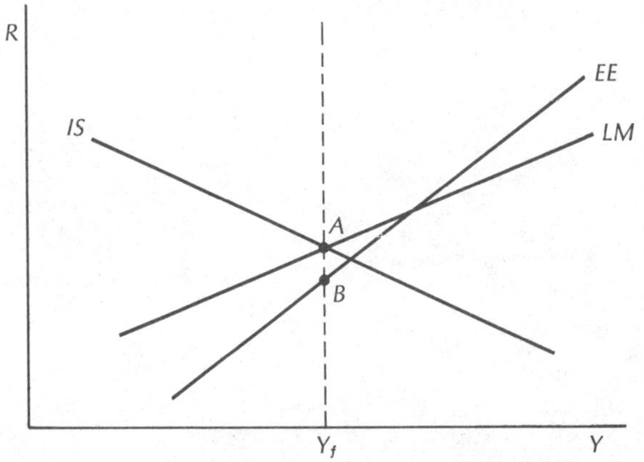

until point *B* is reached, and an increase in the exchange rate (an upward revaluation rather than a devaluation) to shift the *EE* function upward. The exchange rate appreciation would probably have some minor effects on the position and slope of *IS* because of changes in the composition of imports and exports, but, at least in the case of the United States, only minor compensating adjustments in fiscal or monetary policy would be required.

Full Employment with a Deficit

In Figure 15–6 point *A* involves too low an *R*, while Y_f is too high for external balance. In this case monetary policies could set external equilibrating forces in motion through higher interest rates. For example, if the deficit continued it would be accompanied by a deterioration of the country's international

Figure 15–6.

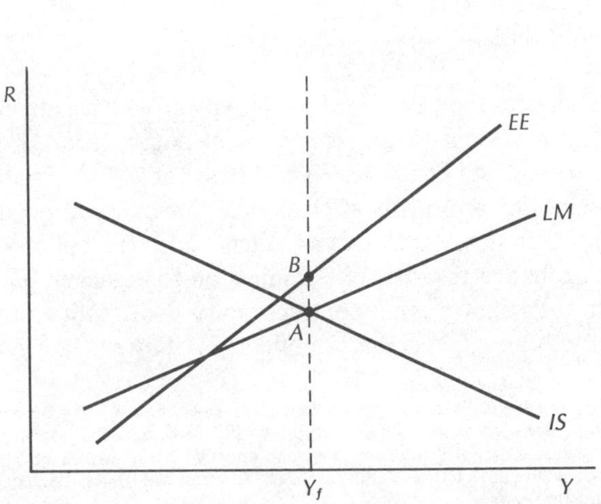

reserve asset position. If gold provided part of the country's monetary base and if the country lost gold, then a contraction in the monetary base would reduce the money supply and would shift *LM* to the left. In the absence of compensating policy (e.g., fiscal action to shift *IS*) income would fall below Y_f and domestic employment would be sacrificed to achieve external balance. But by combining an expansionary fiscal policy shifting *IS* to the right with the contractionary monetary policy, point *B* could be reached.

Inflation and a Deficit

This case is illustrated by Figure 15–7. Inflationary conditions are represented by the intersection of the *IS* and *LM* functions at *A*. Demand pressure is too great at Y_A and interest rates too low for external equilibrium. For the policy maker, this is a relatively simple case with which to deal, for both monetary and fiscal policy should be contractionary with reductions in *G* and M_s shifting both *IS* and *LM* to the left toward intersection at point *B*. If the deficit itself leads to a loss of gold and a reduction in M_s, the contractionary monetary policy will arise without overt action on the part of the monetary authorities. Some combination of orthodox and mutually reinforcing fiscal and monetary instruments gives promise of accommodating both internal and external balance in this case.

Inflation and External Surplus

In Figure 15–8 an inflationary situation is again represented by the intersection of *A* of *IS* and *LM* to the right of the Y_f target. Interest rates are too high for external balance since *A* is above the *EE* curve. In this case restrictive monetary action that would shift *LM* to the left, desirable from the viewpoint of restricting excess demand, would only intensify the balance of pay-

Figure 15–7.

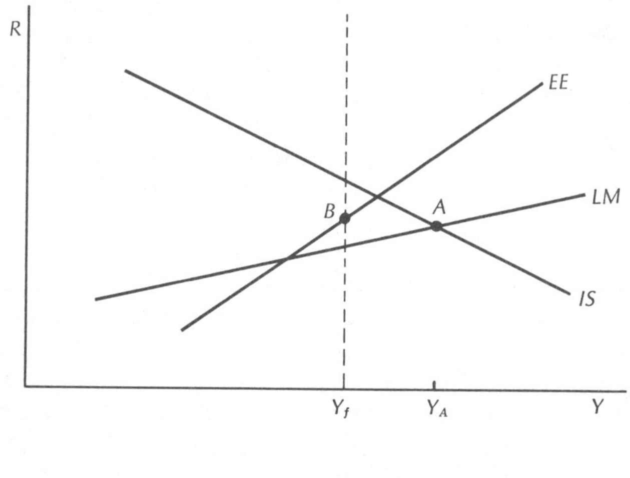

ments disequilibrium. An equilibrating force appears, however, when inflation occurs. With a given money supply a higher price level will then raise the transactions demand for money at all outputs and shift *LM* upward. *IS* will also shift downward as higher prices reduce wealth—the wealth effect—and *EE* will shift upward because higher-priced exports will be less attractive and commodity imports relatively more attractive.

If there exists an inflationary psychology, however, the situation is more difficult, for then the direction of change in *IS* depends upon a weighing of the wealth effect against the impact of price expectations. *LM* and *EE* will probably both shift upward, but there is no certainty that the net effect of these forces will be in favor of equilibrium.

Concluding Comments on Internal and External Balance Under Fixed Exchange Rates

Close examination of the graphical model presented in the preceding section indicates that, theoretically, internal and external balance can be simultaneously achieved if the proper combination of policy tools is employed. Because of the sensitivity of capital flows to interest rate changes, this means applying monetary policy to the problem of external balance and fiscal policy to the problem of internal balance. The proper tools for use in the preceding cases may be summarized as follows:

Problem	*Proper Policy with a Fixed Exchange Rate*
(1) Underemployment and payments surplus	Expansionary fiscal policy and expansionary monetary policy
(2) Underemployment and payments deficit	Expansionary fiscal policy and restrictive monetary policy
(3) Full employment and payments surplus	Restrictive fiscal policy and expansionary monetary policy
(4) Full employment and payments deficit	Expansionary fiscal policy and restrictive monetary policy
(5) Inflation and payments deficit	Restrictive fiscal policy and restrictive monetary policy
(6) Inflation and payments surplus	Restrictive fiscal policy and expansionary monetary policy

Though these are the actions which the theoretical model would suggest, the above discussion has stressed the fact that in particular circumstances a revaluation of currencies is more likely to occur than the implementation of the policy combination.

At this point we must briefly mention several other problems which make it clear that the solution to the external-internal balance problem may not be

Figure 15–8.

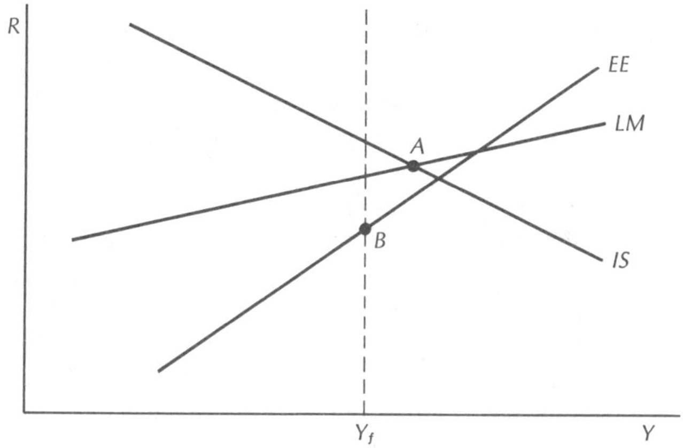

as simple as our model suggests. In assuming that monetary policies can be used to achieve external balance, our model rests heavily upon the beliefs that capital flows are very sensitive to changes in interest rates and that the desired interest rate changes can be achieved. Hence, by raising interest rates sufficiently, external balance may be achieved. However, the continual reliance upon such a policy may either be impossible or lead to undesirable effects for any of the following reasons. First, due to usury laws and internal political pressures, there may exist a limit on how far interest rates may be raised to achieve external balance. Second, investment is a function of both interest rates and income. If low interest rates may lead to an expanding economy and rising income there will be opportunities for real investments which may lead to a large inflow of capital. This relationship between capital inflows and economic expansion may be more pertinent to a country such as Canada than to the United States. Third, the maintenance of external balance by continual reliance on capital inflows may have a limited lifespan because if foreign portfolios reach a desired level of holdings in any one country, interest rate reductions will lead to little additional investment, and because if gross foreign capital inflow remains constant, as interest payments on debt increase, net inflows will shrink. Finally, continued use of high interest rates to achieve external balance may, by stifling investment, reduce export capacity over the long run and help to perpetuate balance of payments problems.

The model presented in this chapter more fully integrates the foreign sector into our model of the commodity and money markets. It also represents an important step in understanding the problem of simultaneously achieving external and internal balance. As our concluding comments have indicated, the problem is complex and economists are continuing their efforts towards finding a solution. One solution to external imbalance referred to previously is through exchange rate adjustments. This solution is relied upon most heavily under the flexible exchange rate system discussed in the following section.

FLEXIBLE EXCHANGE RATES

Under the theory of flexible exchange rates, external balance is achieved solely through the working of market forces and without overt policy actions. If United States imports of goods and services and capital outflows increase relative to exports of goods and services and capital inflows, the demand for foreign currencies will grow relative to the willingness of foreigners to supply their currencies. It is through the purchase by foreigners of goods and services produced in the United States and of financial or real assets from U.S. citizens or institutions that foreign currencies are supplied to U.S. citizens. If this supply falls relative to demand, the price of the foreign currencies rises in terms of dollars, and the dollar is effectively devalued. So long as market forces are allowed to operate, there will be a market clearing price at which the demand for foreign currency just equals the supply of the currency—point *A* in Figure 15–9. In this way international reserves need not be used to support the price of any currency. Deficits, indicated by a reduction in international monetary reserves, no longer occur. External balance is automatically achieved through the market forces of demand and supply.

Figure 15–9 depicts a demand and supply curve for a foreign currency in terms of dollars; in this example the foreign currency is British pounds sterling. As the price of pounds sterling decreases from P_A to P_B, the quantity demanded increases from Q_A to Q_C as British goods become more attractive to individuals holding dollars. It is also normally the case that, as the price of pounds sterling in terms of dollars increases (from P_B to P_A), the quantity of pounds sterling supplied will increase (from Q_B to Q_A) as foreign goods become more attractive to holders of pounds sterling.[6] Under a system of flexible exchange rates,

Figure 15–9.

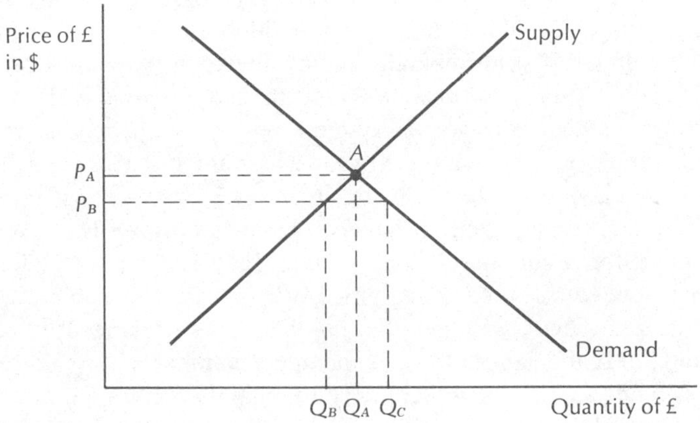

[6] A backward-bending supply curve may exist and, depending on whether the supply curve cuts the demand curve from above or below, flexible rates may have a destabilizing rather than stabilizing effect because the equilibrium itself is unstable. Existing empirical evidence suggests that this has not been a problem and is unlikely to be one.

demand and supply curves for each currency will exist in terms of every other currency, and a market clearing price will exist in each case. This point *A* is the point of external balance.

FISCAL AND MONETARY POLICY FOR STABILIZATION UNDER FIXED AND FLEXIBLE EXCHANGE RATES

When we assumed fixed exchange rates, we concluded that, when conflicting goals exist, monetary policy could be used to achieve external balance and fiscal policy could be used for internal balance. This correctly implies that monetary policy under fixed exchange rates has limited usefulness when it comes to achieving internal balance. With the introduction of flexible rates and the elimination of external balance as a problem, monetary policy can be more effectively employed to supplement fiscal policy as a stabilization tool.

Fixed Rates

Fiscal Policy

In Figure 15–10, Y_f represents full employment. In this case the point of equilibrium in the money and commodity markets, *A*, lies at a level below that of full employment, and hence expansionary fiscal and monetary policies would appear to be the appropriate means of achieving full employment. Expansionary fiscal policy (a cut in taxes or an increase in government expenditures) causes the *IS* curve to shift up to *IS′*. At the new higher level of income, imports have increased and, to pay for these imports, importers have converted their U.S. demand deposits into foreign exchange. This leads to some slight upward shift in the *LM* curve to, say, *LM′*. However, there is likely to be a more than compensating downward shift since international capital movements are sen-

Figure 15–10.

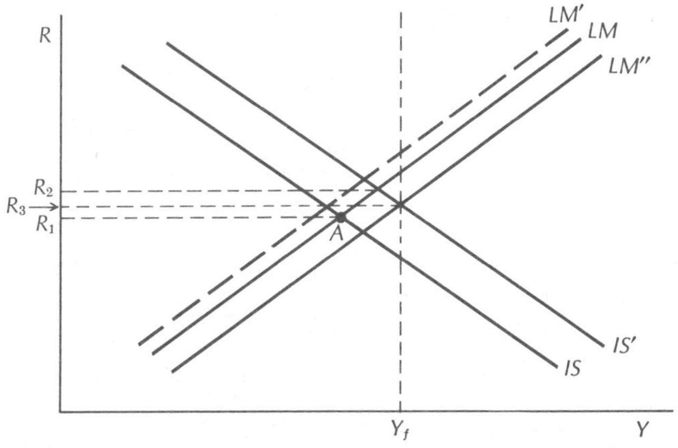

sitive to interest rate changes. The interest rate rises from R_1 to R_2, due to the *IS* shift leading to an increase in the transactions demand for cash. This rise in *R* increases the attractiveness of investment in the country relative to other countries, leading to a reduction in investment abroad by residents and an increase in investment by foreigners. This change in the flow of funds will continue until the interest rate differential is reduced to achieve a new equilibrium. In order to maintain the fixed exchange rate, the monetary authorities must stand ready to sell sufficient domestic currency to prevent the increased demand for dollars from raising their price. This action by the monetary authorities has the same effect as if they were pursuing an expansionary monetary policy through the purchase of government securities. The purchase of foreign currencies (sale of the domestic currency) creates new demand deposits, increasing the money supply as well as the potential of the commercial banks to make additional loans. These actions lead to a downward shift in the *LM* curve to *LM″*. In a world where capital movements have proved very sensitive to interest rate differentials, the capital flow is likely to more than offset the upward shift that had been created by the increase in imports. Hence, if the monetary authorities pursue no policy other than the maintenance of the fixed exchange rate, the new equilibrium is at Y_f and R_3. R_3 is somewhat higher than R_1, as it must be if there is to be no differential between U.S. interest rates and the increased foreign interest rates generated by the outflow of funds from foreign countries. Fiscal stabilization policy under fixed rates may be effective, but its effectiveness is definitely complemented by the induced increase in the money supply.

Monetary Policy

In the alternative case in which the government relies on an expansionary monetary policy to move to full employment—a shift from *LM* to *LM′* in Figure 15–11—income rises and the interest rate falls. The rise in income

Figure 15–11.

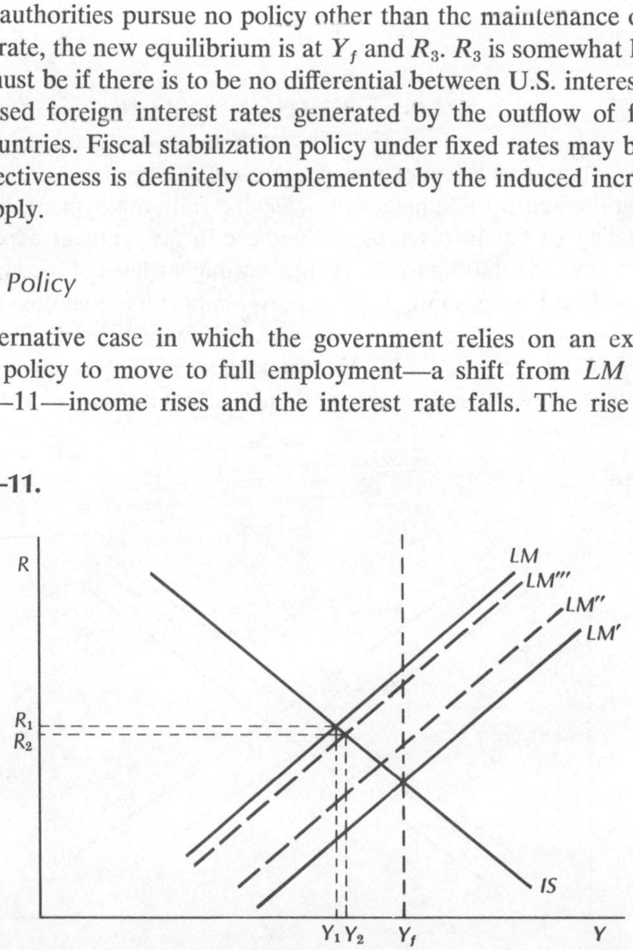

leads to a rise in imports, again to be paid for by the sale of foreign currency to importers and a reduction in their demand deposits. This causes *LM′* to shift slightly back to *LM″*. The fall in interest rates accompanying the shift to *LM′* or *LM″* leads to a capital outflow as investment becomes relatively more attractive in foreign countries. As more individuals wish to sell dollars and purchase other currencies in order to invest abroad, downward pressure is exerted on the dollar in foreign exchange markets. The monetary authorities must then support the price of the dollar by the purchase of dollars and the sale of other currencies. This has the same effect as a contractionary open market policy in which the monetary authorities sell securities to the general public. Only, in this case, demand deposits are used to purchase foreign exchange rather than government securities. As demand deposits fall, the money supply shrinks. This capital outflow continues until the interest differential is eliminated, and this occurs when the money supply is nearly as it was before the expansionary monetary policy was implemented. In other words, the *LM* curve has nearly returned to its original position with interest rate R_2 and income level Y_2. The final interest rate is somewhat lower than the original rate. The capital outflow has led to a fall in rates abroad (unless foreign authorities take offsetting action), and this means the rate at which the differential is eliminated is less than R_1. Monetary policy is an *ineffective* stabilization instrument under fixed exchange rates.

Since capital is not perfectly mobile in the real world, monetary authorities are able to take some (though strictly limited) discretionary action without it being negated by international capital movements. William H. Branson estimated that U.S. domestic interest rates may move within a range of 0.36 percent without international repercussions in the form of U.S.-Canadian and U.S.-U.K. short-term capital movements.[7] This limited freedom of interest rate movements can exist due to the minimum transaction costs in switching investments and the fact that foreign assets are imperfect substitutes for domestic assets.

Flexible Rates

A switch to flexible exchange rates would reduce the usefulness of fiscal policy as a stabilization tool, although it would make monetary policy a much more effective stabilization device.

Fiscal Policy

Point *A* in Figure 15–12 again represents a position of less than full employment. As expansionary fiscal policy shifts *IS* to *IS′*, both the level of income and the interest rate rise. The increase in imports induced by the rise in income causes the demand for foreign currencies to rise, and their prices rise accord-

[7] William H. Branson, "The minimum covered interest differential needed for international arbitrage activity," *Journal of Political Economy*, 77 (November-December 1969): 1028–1035.

Figure 15–12.

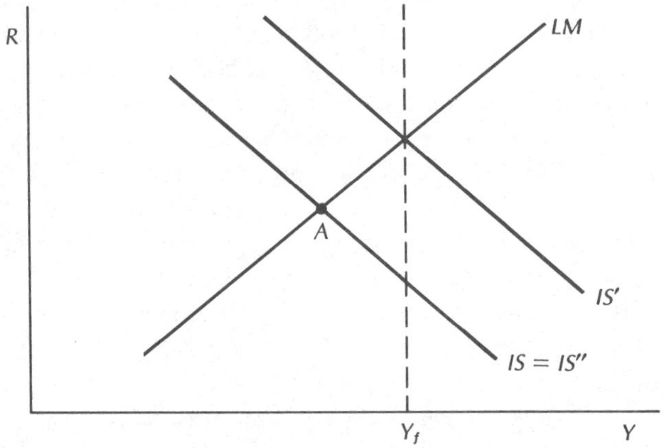

ingly. With the higher price of foreign currencies, exports rise and imports fall, leading *IS* to shift somewhat further to the right. However, this import-induced rise in the price of foreign currencies is unlikely to occur due to capital movements. The higher interest rate will lead to an increase in the inflow of foreign capital and a reduction in the outflow of domestic capital, or an increase in the supply of foreign currencies relative to their demand. People will wish to sell their foreign currencies in order to buy the dollars which allow them to invest in the United States. As their supply increases, the price of foreign currencies will fall, and this in turn will lead to a rise in imports and a fall in exports, shifting *IS′* back to a final position of *IS″*. This relative appreciation of the dollar has reduced the effectiveness of the fiscal policy action; in this case its effectiveness has been eliminated.

Monetary authorities under flexible rates do not have to buy foreign currency in order to keep its price pegged relative to the domestic currency. Rather than create new demand deposits through the purchase of foreign currencies, the monetary authorities need only encourage the use of private demand deposits or excess reserves to buy the foreign currencies. The process is more a change in the ownership of demand deposits than a creation of new demand deposits. Hence the *LM* curve in Figure 15–12 may not shift at all compared to the shift to *LM″* with fixed exchange rates in Figure 15–10. If the monetary authorities remain passive with respect to stabilization policy, the induced change in the money supply will no longer complement fiscal policy as it did under fixed rates. In fact, if the money supply remains constant, government action shifting *IS* upward will lead to a higher interest rate, and the consequent interest rate differential will exist until the inflow of foreign capital is sufficient to raise the price of the dollar to the point where the fall in exports and the rise in imports cause *IS* to return to its original position. Where monetary policy is relatively *in*effective under fixed rates, fiscal policy is *in*effective under flexible rates.

Monetary Policy

Monetary policy, in contrast, is an effective stabilization instrument under flexible rates. In Figure 15–13 an expansionary monetary policy moves the economy from underemployment (point *A*) to a higher level of employment (point *B*). The rise in income induces an increase in imports, increasing the demand for foreign currencies. The lower interest rates also lead to a flow of capital out of the country, meaning a further increase in the demand for foreign currencies. However, in this case, as opposed to the fixed rate situation, the monetary authorities do not have to support the price of the dollar. Therefore, they do not have to sell other currencies and buy dollars—an action which would be the antithesis of the desired expansionary monetary policy.

The falling value of the dollar has an impact on the competitive position of U.S. producers vis-à-vis foreign producers. U.S. products become more attractive to foreigners and foreign products become less attractive to buyers in the United States. The fall in imports and increase in exports caused by the devaluation of the dollar shift the *IS* curve upward, complementing the expansionary monetary policy and eliminating the interest rate differential originally created by that policy (point *C* in Figure 15–13).

CONCLUSION

The two basic exchange rate systems are those of fixed and flexible rates. Under a fixed rate system the external account is not automatically kept in balance. In other words, governments may have to initiate discretionary actions to achieve the desired balance. This chapter has indicated the optimal combinations of monetary and fiscal policy under various conditions of imbalance. One of the major shortcomings of the fixed rate system is that countries frequently conclude that additional policy actions—such as tariffs, quotas, export sub-

Figure 15–13.

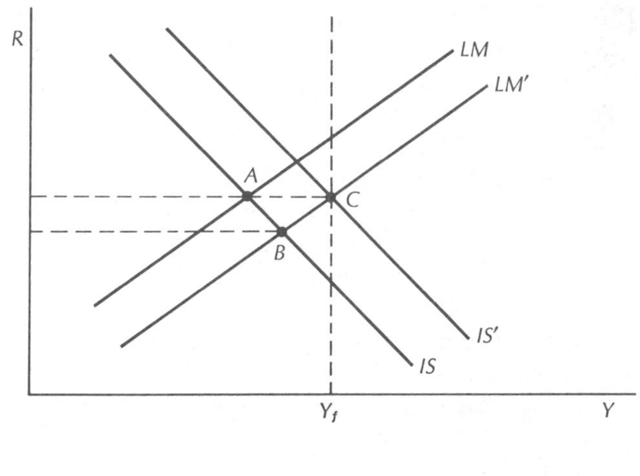

sidies, foreign exchange controls, and restrictions on capital flows—are needed to correct the imbalance. Such actions may lead to retaliatory measures and result in a significant disruption of the flow of trade. Alternatively, under the fixed rate system a major disruption may occur when a supposedly "once-and-for-all" devaluation occurs and a major currency is pegged at a new "fixed" rate.

Flexible exchange rates are seen as an alternative to disruptions created by trade imbalances. Under such a system monetary policy is relatively *more* effective and fiscal policy relatively *less* effective than under a system of fixed rates. Both monetary and fiscal authorities can act with less concern for the balance of payments. To date, the uncertainties generated by day-to-day fluctuations in exchange rates are something which many businessmen and central bankers have been unwilling to accept. Whether these uncertainties are great enough to justify the retaining of a fixed exchange rate system is a much debated matter.

ADDITIONAL READINGS

A thorough discussion of the imbalance of payments can be found in any standard international economics textbook. Two such texts are C. P. Kindleberger's *International Economics*, 4th ed. (Homewood, Ill.: Irwin, 1968), Part VI; and J. E. Meade's *The Balance of Payments* (London: Oxford University Press, 1951), Part I. See also the Federal Reserve Bank of Boston's "Accounting for the balance of payments," *New England Economic Review* (May-June 1971).

An article along lines similar to those of this chapter is Dwayne Wrightsman's "*IS*, *LM*, and external equilibrium: A graphical analysis," *American Economic Review*, 60 (March 1970): 203–208.

The appropriate policies for simultaneously achieving both internal and external balance were first discussed by R. A. Mundell in "The appropriate use of monetary and fiscal policy for internal and external stability," *I.M.F. Staff Papers*, 9 (1962): 70–79, and "Capital mobility and stabilization policy under fixed and flexible exchange rates," *Canadian Journal of Economics and Political Science*, 30 (1963): 475–485. Much work on this issue has appeared since Mundell's, and to some extent it has been pulled together in H. G. Johnson's "Some aspects of the theory of economic policy in a world of capital mobility," in T. Bagiotti (Ed.), *Essays in Honour of Marco Fanno* (Padua: Cedam, 1966), pp. 345–359; and in J. Helliwell's "Monetary and fiscal policies for an open economy," *Oxford Economic Papers*, 31 (March 1969). See also Anne O. Kreuger's "Balance-of-payments theory," *Journal of Economic Literature*, 7 (March 1969): 1–26.

For discussions of monetary and fiscal policy under fixed and flexible exchange rate systems see R. M. Dunn, Jr., *Canada's Experience with Fixed and Flexible Exchange Rates in a North American Capital Market* (Washington, D.C.: Canadian-American Committee, 1971); and G. W. McKenzie, "International monetary reform and the crawling peg," Federal Reserve Bank of St. Louis, *Review*, 51 (February 1969).

For an excellent discussion of the problems of using the dollar as an international currency, see Michael H. Keran's "An appropriate international currency—Gold, dollars, or SDRs?" Federal Reserve Bank of St. Louis, *Review*, 54 (August 1972).

QUESTIONS

1. How is it possible for the balance of payments to actually be in balance and yet not be in equilibrium? Explain carefully!
2. Why were countries willing to help finance United States balance of payments deficits by holding United States dollars when they would not do the same for other countries? Why could this situation not continue indefinitely?
3. It is generally believed that monetary policy can be used more effectively to achieve full employment in a situation of flexible exchange rates than in a situation of fixed rates. Can you explain why this is true?
4. In a situation of unemployment and a balance of payments deficit, what policy actions should be taken to achieve internal and external balance simultaneously? Why might it be difficult to implement such a policy combination?
5. If a country attempts to accelerate growth by stimulating investment, it may end with a sizable balance of payments deficit. What policies can a country then pursue to correct the balance of payments deficit? Could such policies have undesirable effects?
6. In a situation of unemployment and a balance of payments deficit, thoroughly explain how monetary and fiscal policy can be used jointly to achieve external and internal balance simultaneously. What problems may be involved in using monetary policy to achieve external balance?
7. Under a system of fixed exchange rates, many Canadians claimed that the United States was exporting inflation to Canada. What if any validity do you see in this claim? How would the floating of the Canadian dollar in foreign exchange markets alter the situation?

III

Part

INFLATION AND GROWTH

In Part II we developed a comprehensive model of the commodity, money, and labor sectors of the economy. In doing so, we saw that changes in policy variables affect the price and output levels and interest rates. However, the control of the price level during the postwar period has been a sufficiently intractable problem to deserve more of our attention. We are therefore devoting Chapter 16 to the discussion of changes in the price level.

Among professional economists there has been wide disagreement concerning those factors that contribute most to inflation. We therefore examine the various theories of inflation in order to better understand those factors that can lead to changes in the price level and why professional economists may differ in their opinions regarding these factors contributing to inflation.

We will then turn to the question of a price-incomes policy. Many policy makers and professional economists believe that the monetary and fiscal policies discussed in Part II are insufficient for the purpose of adequately controlling the price level and that they must be supplemented by such additional tools as some form of price-incomes policy. The purpose of such a policy is to influence the labor-management role in price level determination. This may range from moral suasion through the mobilization of public opinion to direct interference in the setting of wages and prices. Though controversial, a price-incomes policy has been implemented, as in the 1960s and 1970s, for varying periods by countries in Western Europe as well as by the United States. We have included a careful evaluation of the strengths and shortcomings of this tool for controlling price level movements.

During the postwar period, the rate of economic growth has been another major concern of economic policy makers. In Part II we were primarily concerned with ensuring that the existing production capacity of the economy is fully utilized. Economic growth is concerned with the expansion of production capacity over time. In Chapter 17 we examine those conditions necessary for steady expansion of a nation's production capacity. We also examine some of the problems which have accompanied growth. In doing so, we see that policy makers can influence the rate of economic growth and the seriousness of problems accompanying growth by the manipulation of policy variables.

Inflation

16
Chapter

Our short-run comparative static model has shown us that the price level will be higher at full than at less-than-full employment because of diminishing marginal physical productivity, the behavior of the money wage rate relative to the real wage rate, and the continuing struggle between labor and management over the functional distribution of income. There is, however, another kind of price level behavior that is less dependent upon change in economic forces. This is the problem of inflation, defined as a *continuous* increase in the price level over time, which has been so evident during the past quarter century in the United States and other developed countries. Not all of these nations have experienced precisely the same rate of increase in their price levels, but not one of them is a stranger to this phenomenon. Table 16–1 presents rates of inflation experienced by selected countries for the period from 1959 to 1972. The nature of secular inflation in the United States can be seen from Figure 16–1, which summarizes the behavior of the price level over the years since 1948. With the exception of 1949 and 1954, the price level has risen in every year since the end of World War II, and during the decade of the sixties the price level showed a steadily accelerating rate of increase.

This chapter begins by outlining the association between rates of unemployment and the annual rates of change in the price level. A fact of contemporary economic life is the trade-off (inverse relationship) between unemployment rates and price level changes—a trade-off that poses a dilemma for those who make and execute policy. We then proceed to outline two alternate theories of inflationary movements in the price level, one emphasizing demand management, the other the roles of industry and labor in initiating upward shifts in the price-cost structure. We then turn to a treatment of inflation as a monetary phenomenon, showing that the monetary-fiscal authorities have the power to restrain the price-cost actions of private decision-makers, though admittedly there may be great reluctance to exercise that power fully. Next, we consider the costs of both anti-inflationary policy and increases in the price level that exceed a socially tolerable rate. The chapter concludes with an outline and evaluation of price-incomes policies, emphasizing some difficulties in implementing these programs as an anti-inflationary tactic.

Table 16–1. Rise of Consumer Prices (percentage change at annual rate).

	Average 1959–60 to 1970–71	1964 to 1965	1965 to 1966	1966 to 1967	1967 to 1968	1968 to 1969	1969 to 1970	1970 to 1971	1971 to 1972
United States	2.8	1.7	2.9	2.8	4.2	5.4	6.1	4.3	3.3
Canada	2.6	2.5	3.7	3.5	4.2	4.5	4.2	2.9	4.8
Japan	5.7	6.6	5.1	4.0	5.4	5.2	7.9	6.1	4.5
France	4.1	2.5	2.7	2.7	4.6*	6.4	5.7	5.5	5.9
Germany	2.8	3.4	3.5	1.5	1.8*	2.7	3.7	5.2	5.8
Italy	3.9	4.5	2.3	3.2	1.4	2.6	4.9	4.8	5.7
United Kingdom	4.2	4.7	3.9	2.5	4.7*	5.5*	5.4*	9.4	7.1
Austria	3.6	5.0	2.2	3.9	2.8	3.0	4.1	4.7	6.3
Belgium	3.0	4.0	4.2	2.9	2.7	3.8	4.2	4.3	5.5
Denmark	5.7	6.1	6.9	7.7	8.0	3.3	5.6	5.8	6.6
Finland	5.0	5.3	3.6	5.5	8.5*	2.4	2.6	6.1	7.4
Netherlands	4.4	4.9	5.8	3.4	3.7	7.5*	3.5	7.6	7.8
Norway	4.4	4.3	3.3	4.4	3.5	3.1	9.4*	6.2	7.2
Sweden	4.2	5.0	6.4	4.3	2.0	2.7	6.3	7.4	6.0

* These price increases are influenced by indirect tax changes. The upward effect of some of these changes on the price level is estimated as follows: France, 1968, about 1 percent; Germany, 1968, 0.4 percent; United Kingdom, 1968, 1–1.5 percent; 1969, 2.5 percent; 1970, 0.5–1 percent; Denmark, 1968, 2.5 percent; Netherlands, 1969, 1.5 percent; Norway, 1970, 5.8 percent.

Source: Organization for Economic Cooperation and Development (OECD), *Economic Outlook* **(Paris: December 1973), p. 35; and OECD,** *Inflation: The Present Problem* **(Paris: 1970), p. 59.**

Figure 16–1.

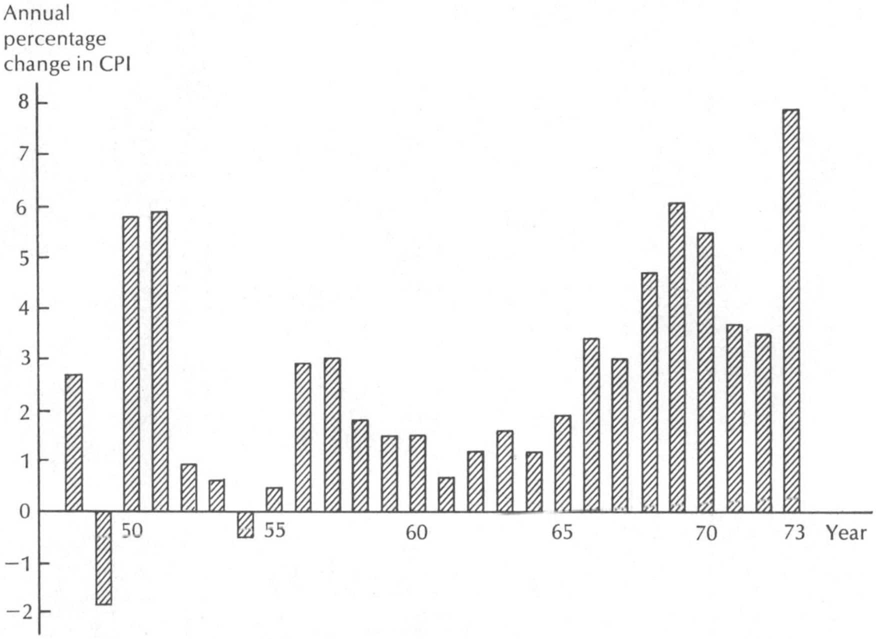

Source: U.S. Bureau of Labor Statistics. Data based on December to December figures.

THE TRADE-OFF BETWEEN THE RATE OF CHANGE IN THE PRICE LEVEL AND THE RATE OF UNEMPLOYMENT

Figure 16–1 shows the annual percentage change in the consumer price index (CPI) for the years 1948–1973, while Figure 16–2 depicts the aggregate unemployment rate for the same years.[1] The data from Figures 16–1 and 16–2 are brought together in Figure 16–3 where the *LL* curve roughly approximates American experience over the past two and a half decades. This curve is generally known as the "trade-off" or "Phillips curve" [2] because of the way

[1] The CPI is a proxy for the commodity price level. Even more comprehensive than the CPI, though not used in our analysis, is the implicit GNP deflator, a weighted measure of the prices of all commodities entering into final demand, whether from households, business, government, or the foreign sector. Price indices must be used with caution because they are adjusted neither for quality change nor for the effect of changes in *relative* prices upon allocation of expenditures to available commodities. (From the viewpoint of the consumer it is worth recognizing that improvements in efficiency—technical change—may be made available by producers either as the same quality of product or service at a lower price, or as a higher quality product at the same price.) Hence the usual measures of price level change tend to overstate price increases.

[2] The original Phillips curve represented a trade-off between the unemployment rate and the rate of change in wages and first appeared in the article by A. W. Phillips, "The relation between unemployment and the rate of change in money wage rates in the United Kingdom, 1861–1957," *Economica*, 25 (November 1958): 283–299.

the rate of increase in the price level grows as the unemployment rate decreases. There have, however, been some substantial departures from this evident trade-off. Most evident are the years 1950, 1952, and 1953, where significant distortions were induced by the Korean War.

As an approximation of American experience over the past quarter century, *LL* suggests that the unemployment rate would have to exceed 6 percent of the labor force for price level stability. Such a level of unemployment is not socially acceptable. However, a summary of experience over 25 years obscures the fact that the trade-off function itself may be subject to drift. In the late 1960s and early 1970s, with the advent of simultaneously high unemployment and inflation, it became apparent that the trade-off between inflation and unemployment may change from year to year, and policy options may not always be particularly attractive. For example, in 1970 the average unemployment rate was 4.9 percent and the CPI had risen by 5.9 percent since 1969. When unemployment was held at 4.1 percent in 1956, the change in the CPI from 1955 to 1956 was only 1.5 percent. It would appear that the "short-run" trade-off curve had drifted to the right. The dashed lines in Figure 16–3, *SS* and *S′S′*, represent two short-run trade-off curves which approximate the experience of both specified subperiods. It appears that the trade-off of the late 1960s and early 1970s was significantly less attractive than in the late 1950s.

Figure 16–2.

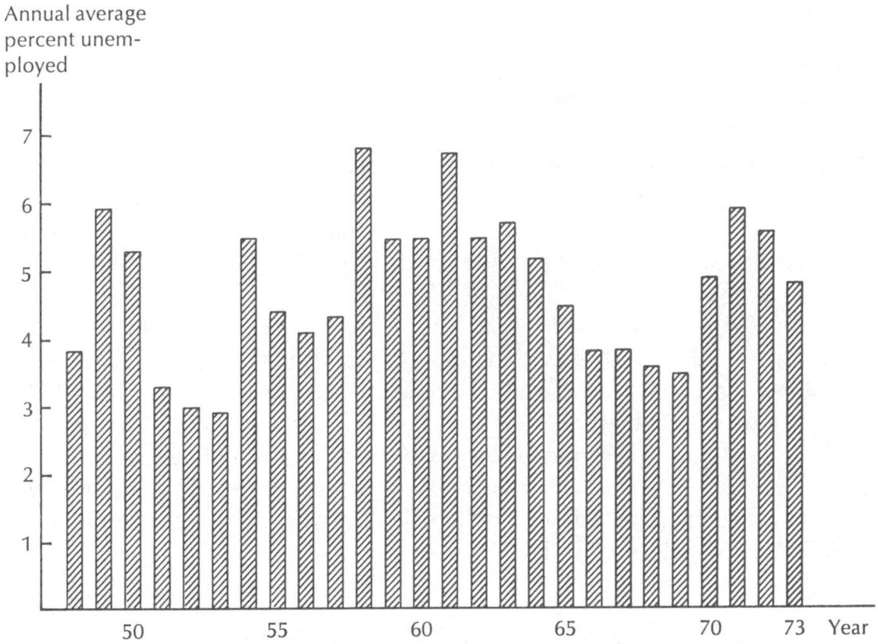

Source: Economic Report of the President, **January 1972 (U.S. Government Printing Office, Washington: 1973), p. 233.**

Figure 16–3.

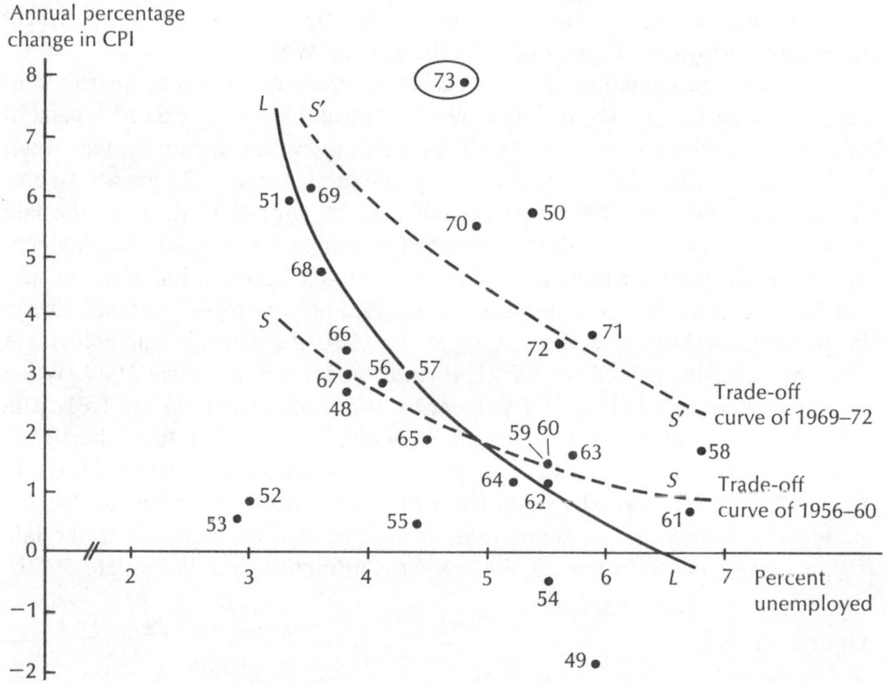

This condition has been associated with changes in the demographic composition of the labor force. A study by Perry points out that:

> "A given unemployment rate is associated with a tighter over-all labor market today than it was ten or twenty years ago. . . . Today a given unemployment rate is associated with a more inflationary rate of wage change than it was in the earlier periods." [3]

The point is that those groups in the labor force with relatively high unemployment rates—particularly those under 24 years old—have in recent years accounted for a larger share of the labor force than they did in the late 1950s. Perry estimated that had the labor force had the same hypothetical composition in 1969 as it had in 1956, and assuming the same unemployment rates prevailed for each subsector, then unemployment in 1969 would have been 3.1 percent rather than the 3.5 percent actually recorded. Hence the actual figure was not really indicative of the degree of tightness then prevailing when compared with earlier periods.

[3] George L. Perry, "Changing labor markets and inflation," *Brookings Papers on Economic Activity*, No. 3, 1970, pp. 411–412. On the question of shifting short-term trade-off functions, see also Charles L. Schultze, "Has the Phillips curve shifted? Some additional evidence," *Brookings Papers on Economic Activity*, No. 2, 1971.

Others, such as Otto Eckstein and Roger Brinner, have emphasized that differing price expectations may also cause the position of the trade-off curve to differ from year to year.[4] They pointed out that, following a period of price stability, the short-run trade-off curves are relatively near the origin in the unemployment-inflation graph. But as the rate of inflation increases, the trade-off curves shift upward year by year. This being the case, the price increases illustrated in Figure 16–1 suggest that the trade-off curve was shifting up in the 1960s. Based on their empirical evidence demonstrating the importance of changing prices and price expectations on the position of the short-run trade-off curve, Eckstein and Brinner believe the wage-price freeze of 1971 (which we discuss later) was necessary to stem the inflationary tide and prevent the trade-off options from becoming increasingly unattractive. However, the point in the graph representing 1973—circled for emphasis—indicates the problem has not been solved.

The price change-unemployment rate experience since the late sixties and, in particular, the evidence showing the coexistence of excess labor demand in particular markets with stronger inflationary expectations have led to still other interpretations of the contemporary condition of the Phillips curve. For example, it has been suggested that the trade-off function is kinked at some rate of unemployment, perhaps in the 4–5 percent zone.[5] The shape of the function is conceived as resembling that shown in Figure 16–4.

Figure 16–4.

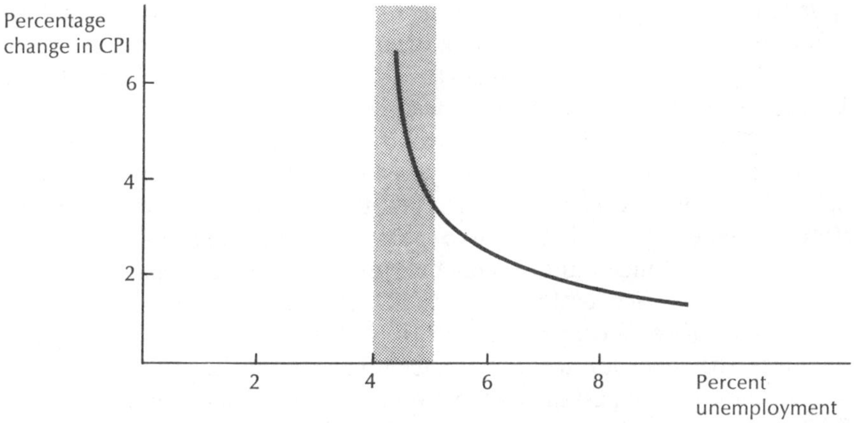

[4] Otto Eckstein and Roger Brinner, "The inflation process in the United States," a study prepared for the use of the Joint Economic Committee, Congress of the United States, February 22, 1972 (Washington, D.C.: U.S. Government Printing Office, 1972). See also S. J. Turnovsky and M. L. Wachter, "A test of the 'expectation hypothesis' using directly observed wage and price expectations," *Review of Economics and Statistics*, 54 (February 1972): 47–54.

[5] See James Tobin, "Inflation and unemployment," *American Economic Review*, 62 (March 1972): 1–18; R. J. Gordon, "Wage-price controls and the shifting Phillips curve," *Brookings Papers on Economic Activity* No. 3, 1972, pp. 385–421; and Edmund Phelps, et al., *Microeconomic Foundations of Employment and Inflation Theory* (New York: Norton, 1970).

Moving down the curve to the right of the shaded critical zone, the flatness of the function is explained by the resistance to downward wage adjustments. In many labor markets, the employee has come to expect that wages and terms of employment steadily improve in return for his own commitment, including greater learning and experience. At higher levels of unemployment, inflationary expectations are not especially strong. Related to this is the fact that at levels of aggregate unemployment considerably above 5 percent, there will be relatively few labor markets in which the number of job vacancies exceeds the number of those seeking new positions, i.e., where excess labor demands exist.

Moving back to the left along the relatively horizontal portion of the curve, we see that with a decline in the aggregate unemployment rate some changes will occur in the balance between job vacancies and unemployment in specific labor markets. A small increase in inflation secures a relatively large number of jobs. However, as expansion continues and the aggregate unemployment rate declines, there will be relatively more markets characterized by excess labor demand; i.e., job vacancies will exceed the number of unemployed, even though the number of those seeking employment will exceed the number of job vacancies overall. Vacancies will become harder to fill, and employers in markets where excess labor demands exist will become much more willing to make wage and working condition concessions in the hope of luring workers from their present jobs.

As we approach the shaded zone, further increases in the inflation rate will have less and less effect in creating new jobs. Wage adjustments will reflect excess demand conditions in particular labor markets and will disturb the relative real wage position of workers. The response will be pressure for wage adjustments sufficient to restore the former structure of relative wages, and the result of this will not be a reduction in unemployment, but largely an increase in the cost-price structure. In this area, further increases in the inflation rate will have negligible effects in reducing unemployment.

The discussion of the trade-off curve does point to the existence of a conflict between two important policy goals—high employment and stable prices. The empirical evidence indicates that there is a trade-off. However, this brief examination of the Phillips curve should suggest the dangers in using this function as an instrument for setting policy objectives or selecting from policy options. Thus the price level-unemployment behavior of recent years alerts us to the naivety of confident predictions that a 4 percent rate of unemployment would be associated with, say, a 3.5 percent increase in the price level. While it is true that over the past quarter century in this and other countries a trade-off has been observed, we can say much less about either its stability or its shape.

THEORIES OF INFLATION

Our short-run income determination model can be of some assistance in understanding the problem of inflation, for even though it is a short-run model, it indicates the significant role that three groups play in the performance of the economy. One of these is the fiscal-monetary authority whose primary objective is to select and implement those policies that maintain a socially acceptable rate of resource utilization. But while the fiscal-monetary authority can use the levers of taxation, government expenditure, and the money supply to secure full employment, it does not possess sovereignty over both employment and the price level. There is a tripartite division of power with respect to the price level. To the fiscal-monetary authority must be added two other groups: industry and labor. Both are strong pressure groups with substantial reservoirs of power. Their actions with respect to prices, wages, and the distribution of income help to determine the level of prices. Even though our model does not explain continuous rises in the price level over time, at least it provides insights into why they might occur.

More useful for purposes of explanation is a classification that places the initiation of price level change in either demand conditions or the cost functions of producers. The sources of inflation are then classified as demand induced and as cost induced.

The Excess Aggregate Demand Theory of Inflation (Demand-Pull)

One widely held explanation of inflation is that it arises from excess aggregate demand, frequently referred to as the "demand-pull" theory of inflation. In the simple schematic illustration given in Figure 16–5, *SS* represents an aggregate supply function presumed to become vertical at a full employment level of real income, Y_f. An aggregate demand level of D_1 is sufficient to maintain full employment at a price level P_1. However, should aggregate demand rise to D_2, then the price level would rise to P_2.

Aggregate demand could rise because the expenditures desired by transactor units exceed the aggregate capacity of the economy to produce. In this

Figure 16–5.

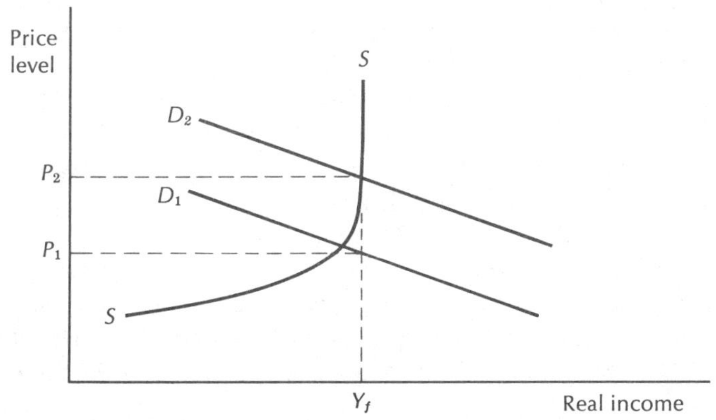

case, planned expenditures at the existing price level exceed the capacity of the economy; they are equated to capacity again by an increase in the price level. Figure 16–5 is the extreme case of demand inflation, for it assumes no effect on the aggregate supply function as a result of the upward shift in aggregate demand. However, given the interdependencies between commodity and factor markets, it is almost certain that the aggregate supply function will shift upward as interest groups in the economy seek to "protect" themselves against anticipated declines in their real incomes. For example, the initial rise in commodity prices will be accompanied by a rise in profits, quickly followed by an increase in wages and salaries. In a tight labor market, employers will increase the rates of income they offer to attract labor and prevent their present labor force from drifting away. The rise in profits which reflects excess aggregate demand is quickly transmitted to increases in costs through a rise in the wage component.

The problem of demand inflation is more fully illustrated in Figure 16–6. Here the price level is plotted against money income, Y, and real expenditures, Q. The diagonal line OO' represents a relationship between full employment income and the price level. Thus any point on OO' is a full employment level of output and real income. The monetary value of GNP at (Y_1, P_1) will be less than at (Y_3, P_3), owing to the higher price level. However, real income at (Y_1, P_1) is equal to real income at (Y_3, P_3). Full employment output is, of course, determined by the capacity of the economy to produce, but the higher the price level the higher the monetary value of full employment output and real income. Q' is a desired or planned real expenditure function. This expenditure function is, as we should expect, a positive function of real income. Desired real expenditure at full employment is then determined by full employment real income. If desired real expenditures are also a function of the price level, then at a monetary value of full employment (Y_1, P_1), desired real expenditures exceed the capacity of the economy to produce by the distance AB. This can be labeled an inflationary gap. Desired real expenditures can exceed full employment output because of destabilizing fiscal-monetary policy, i.e., a federal government deficit at full employment financed by monetary expansion as in the 1966–1969 period. Another source might be the existence of a major discrepancy between the actual and desired wealth positions of transactor units; i.e., household and business firms may possess more liquid and fewer tangible assets than they desire, as after World War II.

In Figure 16–5 it is assumed that real expenditures are negatively related to the price level (a relationship consistent with that in Figure 16–4). This assumption determines the slope of Q' in Figure 16–6. For example, if real desired expenditures were independent of the price level, increases in the latter would not serve to eliminate the AB gap, or if they were positively related to the price level this gap would continuously widen with increases in the price level. With planned expenditures negatively related to the price level, the effect of increases in the nominal value of full employment output is to diminish AB and finally to eliminate it altogether. At C, then, any inflationary gap is

Figure 16–6.

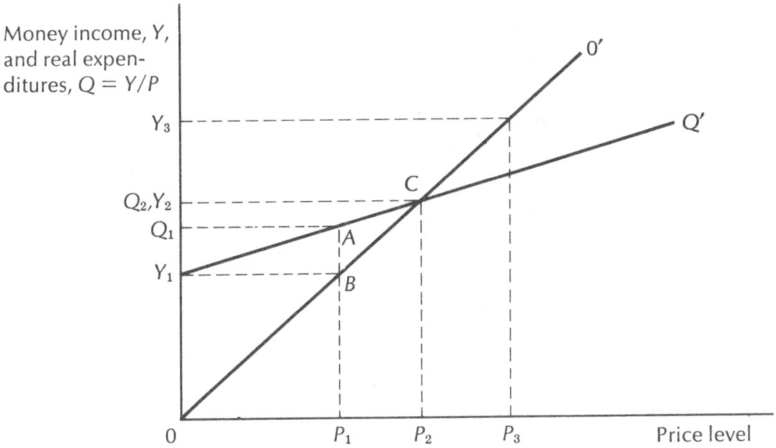

eliminated as rising prices reduce the amount by which the real demands of transactor units exceed the potential of the economy to produce.[6]

The Supply Theory of Inflation (Cost-Push)

The statistical fact of a trade-off between the unemployment rate and the rate of change in the price level has led many economists to doubt that a continuously rising price level can be explained entirely in terms of excess demand. Thus postwar experience has demonstrated that even in years when labor market slack has existed, indices of the price level have risen at a rate greater than could be explained by any biases in their construction. Alternative models of inflation which stress continuous upward shifts in the aggregate supply function have therefore been offered. These shifts, as we know, reflect rising money wage rates and prices. The struggle by the factors of production over the distribution of income results in steadily rising prices in commodity markets, and what is emphasized in these models is the active role played by industry and labor in determining the general price level. Monetary-fiscal policy plays a distinct role in expanding monetary demand to accommodate the new and higher level of costs and prices, and this reaction on the part of the monetary-fiscal authority is what distinguishes the sophisticated from the crude versions of cost-induced inflation.

To state this model of inflation more fully, Figure 16–7 illustrates the extreme case of supply inflation; it may be contrasted with Figure 16–5. S_1, S_2, and S_3 here represent aggregate supply functions, each of which, as we move from S_1 to S_3, represents a successively higher set of costs and prices. The

[6] In drawing Figure 16–6 we have assumed that full employment real income is independent of the price level.

Figure 16–7.

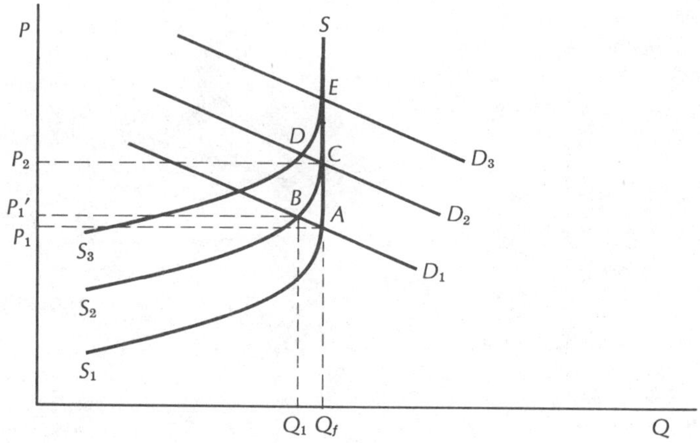

aggregate supply curve shifts upward from S_1 as a result of pressures exerted by unions, as well as by oligopolistic and near-monopolistic market structures in many producing industries. There is then a reservoir of monopoly power that can be exercised in industry and labor in the struggle over the distribution of income.

If Q_f represents a full employment level of real income, aggregate demand is D_1, the price level is P_1, and S_1 is shifted upward to S_2 as a result of this exercise of power by industry and labor, there will be a new price level at P_1' achieved at the cost of some unemployment, represented by the difference between Q_f and Q_1. What is implied here is that prices and wages rise as a result of explicit managerial decisions reflecting agreement between industry and labor over the money wage rate and the factoral distribution of income. Now in the absence of compensating action by the monetary-fiscal authority, the cost-price structure then becomes high relative to demand so that inventories accumulate, production is cut, and labor market layoffs occur.

The more sophisticated version of cost-push inflation theory assumes a reaction on the part of the monetary authorities to the upward shift in costs and prices. If there is a commitment to full employment, even though it may not be a completely rigid and inflexible one (by which we mean that there is some degree of concern with other economic objectives), the authorities will probably validate the higher cost-price level through the use of monetary-fiscal measures to expand aggregate demand to, say, D_2. In this case, full employment is restored with an increase in prices from P_1 to P_2. The economy has moved from *A* to *B* to *C*.

If S_2 should again shift upward, as to S_3, for reasons similar to those previously developed, then it would be even more necessary for the monetary-fiscal authority to intervene by raising D_2 to D_3 in order to maintain a socially acceptable rate of resource utilization. The economy would now move from *C* to *D* to *E*.

Further clarification of supply inflation as validated by the monetary-fiscal authority is found in Figure 16–8. This figure emphasizes some of the sociological dimensions of inflation by illustrating the conflict between groups reflected in a "struggle" over the distribution of income. Given the models we have developed in this book covering output, employment, and prices, it is impossible to ignore questions of income distribution and relative claims. Many of the institutional changes achieved in part by the use of political instruments were designed to alter the distribution of income. When these actions are taken in the context of a commitment to acceptably high levels of employment, then their potential impact on the price level cannot be dismissed. This is to say that wage and salary earners, profit recipients, and those on fixed incomes are not willing to accept any specified distribution of claims as optimal. In a society where group conflict does exist, they are quite likely to bring to bear a combination of economic and noneconomic forces in order to secure a more favorable income distribution from their own viewpoint.

The axes of Figure 16–8 are the same as those in Figure 16–6 except that on the vertical axis we measure not only income but also the shares of income going to labor, WN, to business profits, ϕ, and to rentiers, F. We can then let F be a fixed amount, as indicated by the horizontal line labeled F, and WN and ϕ be positively related to the price level as labor and business attempt (perhaps with some lag) to raise or maintain their real income by raising their money incomes when prices rise.

If a money income Y_1 is then associated with a price level P_1, but total claims amount to Y_2 and exceed the real income available at (Y_1, P_1), factor prices will rise as a result, and commodity prices will move up to P_2, at which level money income and claims are equal. The struggle over the distribution of income and the search for a larger real income by the groups of income recipients will be resolved by the rise in prices as everyone adapts to the new monetary arrangements. Another resolution of the problem would be if real income were sufficiently redistributed away from the rentiers, or fixed income groups, to satisfy the desired claims on real income of wage earners and profit recipients.

In Figure 16–8 the fact that the total claims function intersects the diagonal ray OO' from above means that an equilibrium price level, one reconciling money income and claims, exists. However, there is no guarantee that this will be the case. The total claims function might fail to converge on OO', as when, for example, fixed income recipients also insist on cost of living adjustments in their contractual payments. Such adjustments have been made, in part reflecting price level changes, in Social Security benefits; the Federal Civil Service Retirement System has a cost-of-living escalator; and bondholders may adjust to rising price levels by incorporating a cost-of-living factor into a lending rate they are willing to accept. These patterns have become very apparent during the past decade.

The doubts of convergence of the total claims function on OO' may also involve the wage share, WN. In some sense, this may be considered to represent either the aggregate of wage claims by all occupational groups in the

Figure 16–8.

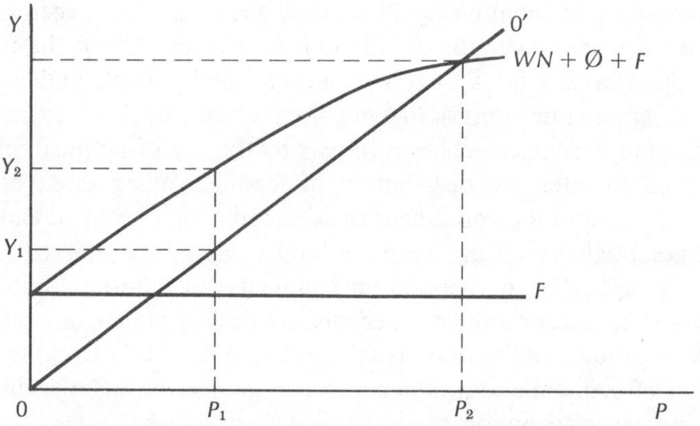

economy, or, alternatively, the summation of wage and salary claims on an industry classification basis. Viewed in either way, this part of the claims function may be subject to steady upward drift throughout its range. This is because one of the most important factors in labor negotiations over contract terms is the question of *comparative* wages. Those who work in manufacturing or in the service industries, or, for that matter, in the public sector, and the union leaders who bargain for them are quite aware of wage settlements negotiated in the construction industry, for example, and will strive to emulate them. Experience during the sixties has shown the tenacity with which existing wage differentials are defended. And only one indication of this is the increased organization and militancy of white-collar workers—including those in the public sector. The scenario of Figure 16–8 is not one of free, self-interested men bargaining for their wage claims in a relatively independent competitive atmosphere; rather it emphasizes that those who make up any occupational group in any industrial setting follow closely the wage increases received by their fellow workers and make sure, at the very least, that their own position in the occupational wage hierarchy does not deteriorate. By this means they protect their relative living standards.

The conflict over claims on income and its effect on output and employment depends upon the response of the monetary-fiscal authority. Validation of the struggle through expansion of monetary demand to meet the higher cost-price structure will leave the price level free to increase indefinitely.

Inflationary Theories and the Trade-off

The contrast between demand-pull inflation and cost-push inflation, as well as some problems for policy selection and implementation, can be illustrated through Figure 16–9. On the horizontal axis is the rate of unemployment, where *A* is the target rate or maximum level that is socially acceptable. On the vertical axis is the annual percentage change in the money wage rate, where *B* is the maximum annual rate of change in the money wage rate consistent with a stable price level and the existing factoral distribution of income. It is obvious, then, that the value of *B* depends upon the rate of growth of factor productivity in the economy. This is, of course, an adaption of Figure 16–3, except that here the vertical axis, instead of reflecting commodity prices, now measures the rate of change in one component of the costs of production; we already know how these costs are related to the price level through the aggregate supply function. In an expanding economy, productivity gains may be distributed as higher wage incomes, higher property incomes, or lower commodity prices. Thus *B* stands for the increase in money wages consistent with the allocation of productivity gains between labor and property so that the existing distribution of income is maintained.

If the trade-off function is represented by curve I, a portion of which passes within the bounded area of *OBCA*, conventional monetary and fiscal policy should be able to move the economy to some combination of wage increases and unemployment that assures both a stable price level and an acceptable rate of resource utilization. However, the position of the trade-off function may be represented by curve II rather than curve I. In this case, price level stability and full employment are inconsistent, for the parameters of the trade-off function, which are largely institutional in nature and are present in the basic income determination model through industry and labor, are such that *either* price level stability *or* the goal of full employment must be sacrificed to the other. None of the three factors determining the price level—the monetary-fiscal authority, industry, and labor—can reconcile these goals. The sovereign power of the monetary-fiscal authority is not really sovereign with respect to the economic goals of price level stability and full employment, for its actions are subject to constraints of labor-management relationships, and these force the monetary-fiscal authority to guarantee full employment only by validating successively higher price levels.

Figure 16–9.

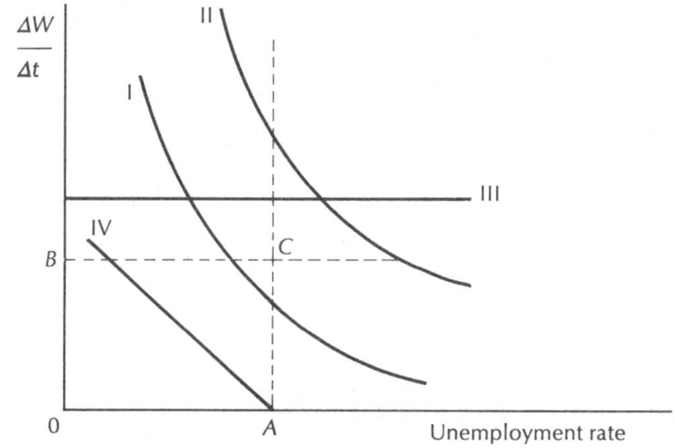

Of the two other cases also shown in Figure 16–9, the horizontal line III represents pure supply inflation. Here there is no trade-off between unemployment and the price level. The rate of change in the money wage rate is completely independent of labor market conditions. This case is neither conceptually interesting nor empirically relevant to the experience of the last quarter century. Line IV illustrates pure demand inflation. There is no increase in the money wage rate until full employment at A is reached. The more quickly the labor market reacts at full employment, the steeper the negative slope of line IV.

Inflation as a Monetary Phenomenon

The price level at which society provides a full employment guarantee is jointly determined by the monetary-fiscal authority, industry, and labor. We have considered the meaning of excess aggregate demand inflation and supply or cost-push inflation, but from what has been outlined we might also choose to regard inflation as essentially a monetary phenomenon. According to the simple definitional relationship:

$$GNP = MV$$

the monetary value of output (GNP) is equal to the product of the stock of money (M) and the velocity of circulation (V). For a given stock of money, V will increase as the output of the economy rises, and with it the price level.[7] V rises then with the monetary value of output, while M is increasingly used for transactions purposes, but V is not indefinitely expansible. Although, as the interest rate increases, the opportunity cost of holding money becomes too great for it to be held as an alternative to either financial or tangible assets and it is therefore used more and more for transactions purposes. There are physical and technological constraints on the efficiency with which each unit of the money stock can be used as a unit of exchange. At some point it becomes impossible to stretch the existing stock any further in order to complete exchange. Money substitutes, such as credit cards, may emerge, but their general use and acceptance will come only after some period of time.

If we assume that the economy is at a position of full employment equilibrium and that the existing money stock is being used entirely and optimally for transactions purposes, there is then no way in which each dollar can be used in more transactions. Now, if there should be an increase in aggregate demand as a result, say, of an increase in loan-financed government spending, the money supply would be increased through an expansion in the reserves of the banking system. This is the classic case of demand inflation. The desired level of transactor expenditures exceeds the capacity of the economy to produce and a rising price level results.

[7] In the model of Chapter 10, money demand was labeled M_D and was the sum of both income (M_Y) and liquidity (M_L) demands. Also, $M_D = M_s$. Here, we do not explicitly break out the two parts of money demand but simply let M refer to both the supply and the demand for money.

If, on the other hand, labor and management should agree to increases in factor payments that exceed the growth in factor productivity, the money wage rate and prices would rise. This is bound to be the case unless either labor or management is altruistic enough to surrender some of its share of income to the other. The issue is, then, one of whether the monetary authority is willing to validate the increase in the cost-price structure by increasing the stock of money. An increase in *M* is necessary, under these postulated circumstances, to avoid unemployment. Monetary GNP will grow (as capacity output is valued at the higher price level), but monetary outlays cannot rise with a given *M* because velocity has reached a physical limit. Full employment simply cannot be sustained at the new higher level of costs and prices. Should production continue at the same physical rate as that recorded under the former cost-price structure, inventories will accumulate, goods remain unsold, and layoffs ensue. Should *M* remain constant, what will happen is that the monetary authority will refuse to endorse automatically the new and higher price level.

This is the heart of the price level dilemma under conditions of full employment. If the monetary-fiscal sovereign authority is always ready to validate the actions of industry and labor in order to sustain full employment levels of output, then it can exercise no effective check on the behavior of the price level. Given the current practices of management and labor, an approach to the price level dilemma requires some flexibility in the pursuit of alternative objectives by the monetary-fiscal authority. The latter must be willing to state that it will not automatically validate any and every upward shift in the cost-price structure by private interest groups in the economy. Responsible behavior by government is also required, in particular a refusal to use inflation as a means of taxation to support increases in public outlays at full employment.

But when all this is said, we still confront the possibility that our theoretical examination is too simplistic for factor markets as presently constituted. The measures that have been developed in this book as means of regulating effective demand may also influence wage claims and profit margins and so have effects on cost-price levels.[8] Generalizations about responsible monetary-fiscal behavior have to be made operational, and this means that the cost-inflationary effects of orthodox monetary-fiscal actions have to be considered when a policy mix for restraining aggregate demand is selected. To illustrate this problem, we can consider a world in which union policies are aimed at securing a stated standard of living rather than a certain money or real wage before taxes. If, under these circumstances, a policy decision is made to restrain effective demand by increasing personal income taxes, or even by increasing interest rates, the reaction may well be to trigger wage claims that compensate for the reduction in perceived living standards. This is a case where conven-

[8] On these questions a considerable literature has recently developed: See G. Robert Eisner, "Fiscal and monetary policy reconsidered," *American Economic Review*, 59 (December 1969): 897–905, and Bent Hansen's comment on this article in *American Economic Review*, 61 (June 1971): 444–447; G. Brennan and D. A. L. Auld, "The tax cut as an anti-inflationary measure," *Economic Record*, 44 (December 1968): 520–525; and Sir Roy Harrod, "Reassessment of Keynes' views on money," *Journal of Political Economy*, 78 (July-August 1970): 617–625.

tional monetary-fiscal devices have cost-push effects with the gain on the demand side offset by the loss on the cost side.

What has been posed in this evaluation is the problem of human behavior —action and reaction—in a complex institutional setting. The human factor raises doubts about the use of taxation as a device for "fine tuning" the economy. It might bc argued that a more appropriate alternative would be reductions in government expenditures as an anti-inflationary agent. While this may be so, the answer is hardly clear cut. Government expenditures are hardly ever reduced across the board. Rather, there are selective changes, and by their very nature these raise serious questions of equity. Why one program and not another? Why an impact in one region and not in others?

The question is: What mix of monetary-fiscal measures to curtail aggregate demand will have the smallest cost-increasing effect on the wage claims of employees and the profit margins of employers, and is that mix equitable in its impact?

The Costs of Anti-Inflationary Policy vs. the Costs of Inflation

In exploring the problems of inflation, an important question is that of the costs of anti-inflationary policy versus the costs of inflation at a socially acceptable rate of, say, 3 percent annually.

Some Costs of Anti-Inflationary Policy

Assuming that the orthodox, traditional monetary-fiscal tools are employed to keep the price level increase to a tolerable rate, the use of monetary-fiscal policy means, as our model has shown us, that aggregate demand will be depressed. This will affect output and serve to reduce the upward pressure both on prices in commodity and factor markets and on profits. Our discussion of growth will emphasize that the capability of the economy to produce goods and services expands each year because of increases in productivity and in factor inputs. A monetary-fiscal policy of restraint in a growing economy by no means necessitates an absolute decline in levels of output, but it does imply the opening up of a gap between what output might potentially be and what it actually is.

To consider the costs of anti-inflationary policy, we can take as an example that an unemployment rate of 4 percent prevails and that policy makers adopt as a target an increase in the unemployment rate to 5 percent of the labor force as a means of alleviating inflationary pressures. In terms of the early 1970s labor force, this would mean an increase of about 800,000 in the number of unemployed. We also know, however, that this is not the end of the matter. Studies suggest that for every 10 unemployed there are perhaps 6 who drop out of the labor force, i.e., people who no longer actively seek work.[9] This then con-

[9] G. L. Perry, "Labor force structure, potential output, and productivity," *Brookings Papers on Economic Activity*, No. 3, 1971, pp. 541–542.

stitutes an additional 480,000 (.6 × 800,000). Further, an increase in unemployment would be accompanied by a reduction in the average length of the work week. Labor would be kept on the payroll, but it would be less intensively utilized. Estimates suggest that a 1 percent increase in the unemployment rate would be accompanied by a reduction of 0.4 percent in the average work week. Simple arithmetic then suggests that the costs of the increase in the unemployment rate from 4 percent to 5 percent could be stated in terms of the percent change in labor inputs as in Table 16–2. Since in the American economy labor inputs claim about three fourths of output, a reduction of 2.06 percent in labor inputs would serve to decrease output by (2.06) (.75) or 1.54 percent. When the annual current dollar value of GNP amounts to $1.5 trillion, the loss in output amounts to approximately $23 billion per year.

But the costs of anti-inflationary policy also have to be considered in terms of impact across the demographic and occupational component parts of the labor force. It is important to inquire into the impact of unemployment in these terms and Table 16–3 shows the effect on segments of the labor force resulting from an increase of 1 percentage point in the aggregate unemployment rate (in this case, from 3.7 to 4.7 percent). The table indicates that the major burden of unemployment is borne by production workers, especially the semiskilled and the unskilled, and by blacks. For adult male blacks, the effect is more than 2.5 times as great as on whites in the same age-sex group; in the case of adult black women, the impact is almost twice what it is on white women; and the impact on blue-collar workers as a whole is more than four times as great as that on white-collar workers. Given the evidence of this differential impact, it is difficult to ignore its implications for exacerbating an already pervasive social tension.

The Costs of Inflation

In a sense, what we are considering here is the cost of a permissive monetary-fiscal policy that validates the cost-price standard set by the actions of industry and labor. When full employment prevails and there is no firm attempt to limit the increase in the price level to what general consensus would regard as an acceptable rate, the costs of inflation can then be analyzed in terms of their income and wealth effects.

Table 16–2.

Factor	Percent change
Reduction in jobs for the employed as a result of increase in the unemployment rate to 5% from 4% (1/96)	− 1.04
Reduction in length of the work week	− .40
Reduction in labor force participation (.6 × −1.04)	− .62
Total reduction in labor inputs	− 2.06

Table 16–3. Average Change in Unemployment Rates for Labor Force Groups Accompanying a 1 Percent Change in the Aggregate Unemployment Rate (1959–1968).

By age, sex, and color		By occupation	
Aggregate rate	1.0	Aggregate rate	1.0
Men, 20 and over	1.2	White-collar workers	0.4
Women, 20 and over	0.8	Professional and technical	0.3
Teenagers, 16 to 19	1.4	Managers, officials, proprietors	0.3
For whites	0.9	Clerical	0.5
Men, 20 and over	1.0	Sales	0.6
Women, 20 and over	0.7	Blue-collar workers	1.7
Teenagers, 16 to 19	1.5	Craftsmen and foremen	1.3
For blacks	1.8	Operatives	1.7
Men, 20 and over	2.6	Nonfarm laborers	2.6
Women, 20 and over	1.3	Service workers	0.9
Teenagers, 16 to 19	0.8	Farm workers	0.2

Source: Paul M. Ryscavage, "Impact of higher unemployment on major labor force groups," Monthly Labor Review, 93 (March 1970): 21–25.

The income costs of the type of inflationary conditions specified may be considered by seeing that families may perceive differently the relation, on the one hand, of inflation to increases in income and, on the other, of inflation to the prices they pay for goods and services. To the extent that this is the case, inflation may contribute to social tension. Thus if a family experiences an increase in wage and salary earnings, this may be attributed to deserving performance or increased productivity on the job, rather than as an adjustment of wage levels to living costs. While increases in income are perceived as earned, however, increases in the price level may be understood as caused by the selfish actions of other members of society—price gouging by producers or the selfish actions of trade unions. The view may well be: "My increase was earned, but it is being eroded by the greedy actions of others."

It is also clear that one major cost of inflation is borne by one particular group—the retired aged. To some degree, this may be compensated for by automatic living cost adjustments in Social Security benefits and by tying pension payments to changes in living costs. So far, few pension schemes incorporate the latter provision, and even the Social Security adjustments that have taken place may be interpreted as a desire to share national improvements in productivity with this particular group.

Finally, we might take the late sixties as a period characterized by permissive monetary-fiscal policy validating the actions of industry and labor over prices and costs. A substantial realignment of real incomes with wages and salaries occurred, and where this takes place, questions of justice and equity are certain to be raised. Such matters received overt expression, for example, in the increased militancy of public sector employees during this period. In the private sector, some evidence on the realignment of incomes is apparent in Table 16–4, where wage and benefit changes for the three years 1967–1969 are summarized by industry. The 5.1 percent figure for manufacturing in 1967 refers to annual increases averaged over the life of the contracts negotiated in 1967. In looking at the table, we might ask whether the changes that did occur, and that widened wage differentials, did in fact create incentives for a desirable movement of resources and for the reallocation of productive endeavor. One might also ask whether the abandonment of the price level to determination by the actions of industry and labor is not also a guarantee of an accelerating rate of increase in the price-cost structure.

In considering the costs of inflation in terms of wealth effects, one important matter is that in the absence of a firm commitment by the monetary-fiscal authority to a tolerable rate of price increase, there is little predictability about the course of inflation. The freedom of industry and labor to set the cost-price structure increases uncertainty about the course of the price level. To a degree, this difficulty could be surmounted if there were some asset which showed a high correlation on a year-to-year basis with rates of change in the price level. There are no such assets, however, not even equities—in 1968 and 1969 the stock market averages actually declined by about 25 percent at the same time that the price level was rising by 5 percent per annum. When price level change is unpredictable, those who save can no longer specify their command over commodities at some future time. There are no simple rules that will let investors cope with the uncertainties of an unpredictable price level.

A further consideration, also of great importance, is the effect on the entire financial system of unpredictable inflation. This system is in large measure designed to allow those in savings surplus positions to acquire financial claims against those in savings deficit positions. The system serves to allocate savings among alternative investment opportunities after evaluation. Investment decisions can be assessed by estimating the present value of future income streams. A price level risk accompanies any investment, but this risk becomes great relative to those other risks enumerated in Chapter 8 when the rate of price increase may be both unpredictable and large. Investment decisions in these circumstances become distorted. The search for inflation-proof assets is intensified, producing an allocation of capital expenditures that can create significant gaps between private and social needs. In effect, then, the efficiency of the financial system deteriorates as it becomes preoccupied with ways of hedging against price level risks.

Table 16–4. Summary of Industry Wage and Benefit Changes Negotiated in 1967, 1968, and 1969 Spread over Life of the Contracts.

	Percent change averaged over contract life		
	1967	1968	1969
Manufacturing	5.1	4.9	5.8
Nonmanufacturing	5.0	5.9	8.9
Construction	7.2	8.6	12.9

Source: J. E. Talbot, Jr., "Analysis of changes in wages and benefits, 1969," *Monthly Labor Review*, 93 (June 1970): 45–50.

Finally, in a society such as our own, concerned with questions of equity and justice, special emphasis might be given to the impact of inflation upon the poor, those, say, in the lowest fifth of income recipients. In the case of this group, relatively small net gains or losses in wealth and income may have a significant effect on personal welfare. A few empirical studies, summarized in the additional readings at the end of this chapter, have been undertaken, but their results are inconclusive. This is a subject that warrants much more systematic investigation, particularly of the impact of inflation on the distribution of the real rather than the nominal tax burden, on the real as opposed to the nominal level of public expenditures, and on the real level of transfer payments.

PRICE-INCOMES POLICY

Price-incomes policy is the term applied to the set of actions directed specifically at influencing the labor-management role in price level determination. These actions can vary all the way along a spectrum from moral suasion or "jaw-boning," through the mobilization of public opinion, to direct interference in the setting of price and wage levels. These approaches are not unique to the United States but have in fact been applied in most developed countries. In a very real sense, they recognize the determining role in the price level played by labor and management when the monetary-fiscal authority is inalterably committed in demand management to the maintenance of full employment. There is no suggestion that these policies are designed to replace the conventional monetary-fiscal actions already examined. Rather they are regarded as subsidiary instruments that can be harnessed to responsible demand management.

A price-incomes policy for the United States was first specifically stated in the 1962 *Annual Report* of the President's Council of Economic Advisors. The rule of reason with respect to prices was stated as:

> "The general guide for noninflationary price behavior calls for price reduction if the industry's rate of productivity increase exceeds the over-all rate for this would mean declining unit labor costs; it calls for an appropriate increase in price if the opposite relationship prevails; and it calls for stable prices if the two rates of productivity increase are equal." [10]

What is implied is a markup or markdown theory of pricing based upon labor costs per unit of output. The guidepost for wages was stated as:

> "The general guide for noninflationary wage behavior is that the rate of increase in wage rates (including fringe benefits) in each industry be equal to the trend rate of over-all productivity increase. General acceptance of this guide would maintain stability of labor cost per unit of output for the economy as a whole—though not of course for individual industries." [11]

[10] *Economic Report of the President* (January 1962), together with the *Annual Report of the Council of Economic Advisors* (Washington, D.C.: U.S. Government Printing Office, 1962), p. 189.
[11] *Ibid.*, p. 189.

This says that, in the case of wage policy, the percent change in money wages should match the trend increase in factor productivity for the nation. Under these circumstances the product price level can remain stable in an aggregative, or index, sense, as a simple arithmetic example will illustrate:

If product per man-year is 10,000 units × \$1, or \$10,000, \$7500 of which is the wage component and \$2500 of which is property income, and if the productivity gain this year is 4 percent, then total product is now \$10,400 (10,400 units × \$1), of which \$7800 is wage and \$2600 property income. Productivity gains have gone into factor incomes and there has been no change in price.

This price-incomes policy was not suggested as the basis for detailed government intervention either at the collective bargaining table or in establishing prices. Rather, it was proposed as a standard against which the conformity to the national interest of key wage and price decisions could be judged. Key decisions were:

> "Individual wage and price decisions assume national importance when they involve large numbers of workers and large amounts of output directly, or when they are regarded by large segments of the economy as setting a pattern." [12]

And, as originally outlined, price-incomes policy was primarily an exercise in public understanding:

> "An informed public aware of the significance of major wage bargains and price decisions, and equipped to judge for itself their comparability with the national interest, can help to create an atmosphere in which the parties to such decisions will exercise their powers responsibly." [13]

The effectiveness of the price-incomes policy which lasted from 1962 to 1966 is still being debated. Though the evidence is not conclusive, it appears that by focusing on key wage and price decisions within the economy the Administration was able to reduce the overall rate of change in wages and prices below what it otherwise would have been.[14]

[12] *Ibid.*, p. 185.

[13] *Ibid.*, p. 185.

[14] Econometric evidence supporting the use of the guideposts may be found in the following G. L. Perry, "Wages and the guideposts," *American Economic Review*, 57 (September 1967): 897–904, and "Wages and the guideposts: Reply," *American Economic Review*, 59 (June 1969): 365–369; Gail Pierson, "The effect of union strength on the U.S. 'Phillips curve,'" *American Economic Review*, 58 (June 1968): 456–677; and Otto Eckstein and Roger Brinner, "The inflation process in the United States." A more general case in support of the guideposts is made by Robert M. Solow, "The case against the case against the guideposts," in *Guidelines: Informal Controls and the Market Place*, G. P. Schultz and R. Z. Aliber (Eds.) (Chicago: University of Chicago Press, 1966), pp. 40–54. P. S. Anderson, M. L. Wachter, and A. W. Throop all take issue with some of the econometric evidence used to support the guideposts in "Wages and the guideposts: Comment," *American Economic Review*, 59 (June 1969): 351–365. A general argument against the usefulness of guideposts is made by Milton Friedman in "What price guideposts?" in Schultz and Aliber, *Guidelines: Informal Controls*, pp. 17–39.

In late 1969 and 1970 the economy experienced a decline during which unemployment increased while the rate of price level change failed to slow significantly. (This was indicated in Figure 16–3 as a rightward drift in the trade-off function.) Recovery from this decline was quite slow by postwar standards and in 1971 the rate of price increase still gave little evidence of abating. Against this background the Nixon Administration chose to institute a mandatory price-incomes policy. For the first time direct economic controls were imposed on the American economy in peacetime. Effective in mid-August and for 90 days thereafter, the so-called Phase I froze all prices, wages, salaries, and rents. During this 90-day period the CPI rose at an annual rate of 1.7 percent and average hourly earnings increased at roughly the same rate.[15]

Following the direct freeze on prices and wages, the Administration set about the task of executing a price-incomes program. The road followed was a rocky one. In sequence from the Phase I wage-price freeze (August to November 1971), there followed:

Phase II: a period of mandatory controls from November 1971 through January 1973;

Phase III: a period with primary emphasis on voluntary compliance from January 1973 through June 1973;

A price freeze from mid-June to early August of 1973; and

Phase IV: a period of mandatory controls following the temporary price freeze and ending April 30, 1974.

The Price-Unemployment Record: 1970–1973

The period since August 1971 provides a good case study of the approaches possible in implementing a stabilization program aimed at the aggregate price level. To place the matter in some perspective, it is appropriate to present the price level-unemployment record from the beginning of 1970 through the end of 1973. In Table 16–5 movements in the all-item CPI and in its major components are summarized for specific intervals during these years. In the table, price level movements are converted to annual rates of increase for comparability. The first two intervals are prior to the institution of the program, and the final four are those coinciding with the various stages from Phase I to Phase IV.

The evidence bearing directly on the price level-unemployment trade-off suggests that the program had some success through the beginning of 1973 in slowing the rate of price level increase during a period of relatively sharp economic expansion. But it should also be noted that in the initial part of Phase II there was a considerable degree of slack, not only in the labor force, but also in underutilization of plant capacity in many industries. The striking rise in the CPI in Phases III and IV is due principally to increases in food prices. In a very real sense the behavior of food prices became of dominant importance to the entire program.

[15] *Economic Report of the President, 1972* (Washington, D.C.: U.S. Government Printing Office, 1972), pp. 81–82.

Table 16–5. Annual Rates of Change in the CPI and Main Components and the Average Rate of Unemployment for Designated Periods, 1970–1973.

	CPI all items	CPI food	CPI nonfood commodities	CPI services	Average unemployment rate
Jan 70–Dec 70	5.1	2.2	4.8	8.2	5.0
Jan 71–Aug 71	3.8	4.8	2.9	4.5	6.0
Sept 71–Nov 71 Phase I	2.0	1.7	0.3	3.1	5.9
Nov 71–Jan 73 Phase II	3.6	6.5	2.4	3.5	5.6
Jan 73–June 73 Phase III	8.3	20.3	5.2	4.3	5.0
July 73–Dec 73 Phase IV	10.6	20.2	6.0	9.4	4.7

Source: U.S. Department of Commerce, *Business Conditions Digest*, and Bureau of Labor Statistics, *The Consumer Price Index*.

Implementing a Price-Incomes Policy

In the evaluations that follow, stress will be placed on Phases II and IV of the program, during both of which mandatory controls were in operation. The experiences of these periods serve to illustrate difficulties both in execution and in the manner in which unanticipated pitfalls can intrude upon the policy maker. Our approach is to pose a number of questions that must be addressed in the search for a working control over the entire price level. And it must be remembered that the object of the exercise is control over the entire price level, by which is meant reduction of the rate of increase to an acceptable standard. The list of questions below is by no means exhaustive, but it will help in bringing the issues into focus.

(1) Can a price-incomes program strike an acceptable balance between compulsion and voluntary compliance?

(2) Are controls to be administered on a sectoral basis? If so, will they be flexible enough to recognize the existence of differing market, technical, and institutional conditions?

(3) Under what criteria are price increases justified?

(4) Since the attempt is to control the aggregate price level, how, if at all, are controls to be applied to raw agricultural products whose prices are determined in significant degree by growing conditions and their effect on supply?

(5) How do foreign suppliers and foreign trading conditions impinge on a price stabilization program?

(6) Are guidelines or controls provided for rates of increase in money wages and in fringe benefits?

(7) Are similar guidelines applied to non-wage sources of income?
(8) What are the economic implications of coupling disaggregated estimates of productivity increases with an aggregative wage guidepost?

We will deal with each of these questions in sequence.

(1) The American program represented an attempt to control the entire price level through a combination of compulsion and voluntary compliance. Singled out for special attention were the approximately 1700 large producers with annual sales greater than $100 million. They included the giants of American industry, the so-called center firms or price makers that may be expected to have substantial amounts of unexercised market power. Firms in this category were subject to mandatory controls and were required to file notice one month in advance of any proposed price increases with the administering agency for the program, the Cost of Living Council (CLC). During the 30-day notice period, the CLC could take action either to approve or to disapprove the proposed price increase. Disapproval involved three possible options: modification; suspension; or deferment. The criteria for disapproval were (a) failure to meet the terms of the cost increase formula (discussed below), or (b) an impact on the economy deemed harmful to the objectives of the price stabilization program.

Medium-sized firms were subject to a reporting, but not to a prenotification, provision. Such firms were defined as those with sales between $50 and $100 million (some 3100 in number) and were required to file with the CLC quarterly reports on costs and on commodity prices. Firms with sales of less than $50 million were required to file the same information annually. Small firms with less than 60 employees were exempt from the control system.

In Phases II and IV of the price-incomes program, a staff varying from 2500 to 4000 was required for administration. The number included individuals working for the CLC, the Internal Revenue Service, and the Justice Department. The latter two agencies were primarily concerned with enforcement procedures.

(2) A price-incomes policy should be sufficiently flexible to accommodate differing technical and institutional circumstances between sectors of the economy and to adapt to changing market conditions. The American program did adopt a sectoral approach and so accepted the need for flexibility.

Flexibility, however, runs the risk of extreme pragmatism, i.e., of expediency, and it is no secret that ad hoc programs require careful monitoring and evaluation to minimize the inconsistencies and inequities that almost surely creep in. Yet once the decision has been taken to institute a price-incomes program, sectoral differences have to be taken into account if the program is to have any chance of retaining a large measure of public support. There is really no choice but to proceed with the jigsaw puzzle of the economy on a piecemeal basis. To do otherwise is to place the economic system in a straitjacket and run the risk of fostering serious distortions correctable by neither the administering agency nor the market place.

Special regulations covering calculations of costs, revenues, and operating margins were promulgated for each of a number of sectors, including manufacturing, most services, wholesalers, retailers, insurance carriers, providers of health services, and general contractors. Flexibility in approach was also evident in other ways. The regulations of Phase IV applicable to the petroleum industry provided special incentives in the form of exemption from ceiling prices on that volume of domestically produced crude oil which exceeded 1972 levels. Here supply shortages were used as the basis for special incentives to the producing industry. Adequacy of supply was also used as a criterion for releasing or exempting other industries from mandatory controls. Thus in Phase IV lumber and plywood were exempted because of a lowering of market prices. Special provisions also applied to the construction industry. In particular there were close surveillance of labor contracts and regulation of the degree to which increases in labor costs were eligible for inclusion in the base upon which price adjustments were allowable.

(3) Central to a price-incomes program are the conditions under which requests for price increases will be granted. What will the criteria be? The general principle is that price increases may be based on allowable "cost pass-through." This means that increases in price may be granted to compensate for increases in "adjusted" costs, involving productivity offset and an operating margin limit.

In implementing the criteria for price increases, the American program's regulations provided basic rules for the calculation of baseline cost levels for labor, direct materials, and other costs. A baseline price per unit was also computed (in the case of multi-product firms this was a unit weighted average price). Comparison of baseline unit prices and costs established a baseline operating margin which became a constraint on the pass-through of cost increases.

The productivity adjustments were specified by subsector within each major sector subject to controls. A producer wishing a price increase had to first calculate the increases in his costs per unit over those prevailing in the baseline period, and then adjust this increase in unit costs by incorporating the estimated increase in productivity experienced by his industry since the baseline period. If the adjusted costs after these calculations exceeded baseline costs and the producer's baseline operating margin was impaired, then the pass-through to prices could be either a percentage increase or a dollar for dollar increase. In the example in Table 16–6 column (1) summarizes the baseline experience

Table 16–6.

	Base period condition	Percentage adjustment	Dollar for dollar adjustment
Unit price	$1050.00	$1102.50	$1100.00
Unit cost	1000.00	1050.00	1050.00
Operating margin	50.00	52.50	50.00

of the producer. His unit cost is $1000, his weighted average unit price is $1050, and his operating margin is $50. Now after a period of time, his adjusted costs increase to $1050 and notification of a price increase is posted. In column (2) a price adjustment to $1102.50 per unit is based on maintenance of a specified percentage operating margin. If cost pass-throughs are limited to a dollar for dollar or absolute basis as in column (3), then the new ceiling price is $1100 which maintains the $50 operating margin.

It may be of some interest that Phase II of the American program provided for cost pass-through on a percentage basis, while Phase IV restricted pass-through to absolute dollar amounts.

(4) The objective of the American price-incomes program was to limit the increase in the aggregate price level to a socially acceptable rate. Such an objective underscores the need to subject all the component parts of the price level to scrutiny and control as requirements dictate. However, raw agricultural commodities were specifically exempted from the stabilization program. This decision was political, but it also reflected the previous decade's experience that food prices contributed relatively little to increases in the aggregate price level. Yet 1973 was to demonstrate the manner in which random events can intrude unexpectedly upon stabilization objectives.

These events took the form of dramatic increases in food prices that eroded the effectiveness of the entire program. Supply shortages in agriculture (equivalent to a leftward shift in the supply function) due to unfavorable growing conditions were the main difficulty. Prices of some agricultural commodities rose several-fold. Though food processors and distributors were subject to the same controls as other manufacturers, wholesalers, and retailers, there was an immediate pass-through of these increases in raw material costs to food prices. The result was that from the fall of 1972 to the fall of 1973 food prices rose by 20 percent and accounted for half the increase in the all-item CPI, while in the previous decade less than one quarter of the annual increase in the price level was accounted for, on the average, by the food component. No price-incomes program is designed to cope with such agricultural supply shifts. Because increases in food prices were general, they affected all families. Put otherwise, the principle of substitutability in expenditure was not particularly applicable. Other elements in the stabilization package were therefore thrown into doubt. Among the more important were the guidelines for wage increases, for when food prices are rising rapidly, added pressures arise for upward adjustments in these guidelines, if only from the standpoint of equity.

(5) Between 1971 and late 1973 the average value of the dollar, relative to other major currencies, declined by about 15 percent. One way to consider the impact of this is in aggregative terms. An aggregative evaluation would suggest that the effect of such a decline of the currency would be slight, but even though imports of goods and services are a relatively small fraction of output amounting to about 4 percent of GNP, this kind of analysis ignores the way rises in the price of a specific commodity may permeate the economy and so affect a price stabilization program.

An example of the impact of a price increase in a single commodity is provided by crude petroleum, the price of which rose markedly as a result of direct action by the oil exporting countries to achieve political ends. The price increase was not primarily a result of altered supply-demand relationships. The response within the framework of the price-incomes program was to offer price incentives for increased domestic production through the set of regulations previously mentioned. Obviously, fuel is an essential, widely used commodity to the extent that one tenth of the 1973 increase in the all-item CPI has been attributed to this source. It is apparent, then, that in the absence of a subsidy to users designed to insulate the domestic market from the international economy, a price-incomes program must be subject to international influences whose behavior cannot be predicted with any degree of certainty.

In sum it is noteworthy that about three fifths of the price level increase in 1973 occurred as a result of developments outside the generally accepted boundaries of a price-incomes program.

(6) The price-incomes program provided a guidepost for wage increases: 5.5 percent plus 0.7 percent for fringe benefits. As previously pointed out in this book, changes in money wages affect price through their impact on unit labor costs, i.e., on monetary costs per unit of output. In general, an increase in wages will increase unit labor costs by an amount equal to the increase in wages less any increase in productivity. Thus if productivity is rising by 3 percent annually, a wage guideline of 5.5 percent implies an increase in unit labor costs and in prices of 2.5 percent.

The special price control provisions applied to firms with sales in excess of $100 million, with prior notification and the basis for price increases mandatory, permitted the effect of newly negotiated wage increases on requested price adjustments to be assessed. Hence one avenue available for indirect pressure on wage negotiations was the reception that the CLC might give to a producer's potential request for a compensating price increase. Where the labor contract adhered closely to the guideposts, a producer could be reasonably sure of an adjusted cost pass-through. There was even the possibility that the particular industry might be decontrolled, as was the automobile industry in December 1973.

The wage guidepost side of the program contained a heavy emphasis on moral suasion and "jaw boning" of union leadership in the high-wage, highly unionized price making industries where trend setting contracts are generally struck. Thus the singling out of large firms had its counterpart on the labor side. Courting of union leadership was held to be an effective means of soliciting public support.

Evidence of the success of this approach is found in Table 16–7 containing a quarterly all-industry summary of negotiated wage and benefit agreements. The figures are annual average changes in wage rates and fringe benefits over the life of contracts negotiated in each quarter. The notable feature of the table is the clear downward movement in the rate of wage increase after the first quarter of 1972.

Table 16–7. Annual Rate of Change in Wage and Fringe Benefits over the Life of Labor Contracts Negotiated in Designated Quarters, 1970–1973.

	Percent increase		Percent increase
1970 1st	8.0	1972 1st	8.2
2nd	10.9	2nd	7.3
3rd	11.6	3rd	7.3
4th	7.5	4th	6.6
1971 1st	8.5	1973 1st	5.5
2nd	8.2	2nd	6.6
3rd	8.7	3rd	6.4
4th	10.6	4th	5.6

Source: U.S. Department of Commerce, *Business Conditions Digest.*

Further very special provisions in the price-incomes program were directed at the construction industry and unions. We saw in Table 16–4 the accelerating rate of pay increase recorded in this industry during the late sixties. The stabilization program provided, however, that there would be no authorization for the pass-through of wage increases in excess of the guideposts for any construction project receiving federal funding. Support for this was elicited from the unions through a complex process of negotiation, bargaining, and, on occasion, some arm twisting. The outcome was that in the early seventies annual rates of wage increase in this industry were quite well contained within the guidepost range.

The wage guideposts raise some major questions of equity, however. Perception of fairness is obviously a major factor in public support and acceptance of a price-incomes program. One issue affecting equity is the difficulty that arises when the behavior of food and fuel prices, as in 1973, indicates that control of the aggregate price level may be beyond the scope of the program. The question then becomes one of what is an equitable wage guidepost in the face of substantial rises in food and fuel prices, rises whose incidence falls most heavily on lower income groups. Equity requires that the hard and fast standard of 5.5 percent be modified to allow for escalator clauses, or at least for some partial adjustment (of a living cost nature) to cover increases in food prices. For example, if fairness points to a 7.5 rather than a 5.5 percent wage increase, though this change might be necessary to preserve equity it could also be interpreted as clear evidence that changes in food prices were driving the entire stabilization program. In other words, a 7.5 percent wage guidepost would be inconsistent with price goals in the non-food sector.

A second question is the degree to which any program is flexible enough on the wage side to recognize the peculiar circumstances of specific occupational groups. This again is to a significant extent a matter of equity. Are there some occupations whose pay by some agreed set of criteria is clearly out of line? Can correction of this condition occur without eroding the program? This was not a widely apparent problem in the American program, but it most certainly has arisen elsewhere. In the United Kingdom, for example, in 1972 and again in 1974 special adjustments were demanded and received by coal miners. These demands were based on a concept of "relativity," i.e., on the bases of the position of this group in the total wage alignment, given the high risk factors in mining, and of the importance of the industry to the national welfare. Application of relativity to a particular occupation requires general acceptance that an inequity exists and should be corrected. In the absence of this consensus so-called "leapfrogging" arguments may be advanced by other unions as they seek in their wage claims to restore the preadjustment wage alignment. The potential accelerating effect of this on guideposts is readily evident.

(7) A necessary condition for the successful implementation of any price-incomes program is that labor and union leadership not feel they are being singled out for guideposts and controls while the remuneration of other factors of production is left relatively free from regulation and public attention. Again the question is one of equity. Though this problem was not of serious import in the United States from 1971 through 1973, it has been important in the income programs of other countries. For example, in the United Kingdom labor unions have never supported government attempts to carry through a price stabilization program. In Canada an effort at a voluntary program floundered in 1971 because union leaders believed that wage earners were being asked to bear a disproportionate share of the burden.

The American program relied on voluntary compliance with controls over dividends and interest. Corporations were requested not to increase dividend payments per share, while moral suasion was exerted by the Federal Reserve Board to restrict increases in the prime lending rates of commercial banks. Farm incomes and rents were exempted from the program.

In putting the guidelines for wage and non-wage income into perspective, it is readily apparent that a price-incomes policy involves, among other things, economics by exhortation, and the difficulties with moral suasion are no less evident in this situation than in any other. Moral suasion carries with it neither the threat of punishment nor the promise of reward. The issue of the common interest might be supported on the propositions that production is a cooperative effort and that matters of common concern should be reflected in the efforts of labor and management in mutual cooperation with the government. But though it might be argued that, since inflation is now a serious social problem, a shift must occur so that more account is taken of the general welfare in making price and income decisions, we are here in the realm of political economics, and the realm of the political is the realm of power and authority relationships among people. As groups, labor and management pursue the self-interest of their constituents, and the leaders of these groups are chosen on the basis of their ability in this regard. Support of an income guideline with regard to wages may raise serious problems for union leadership, for it is likely to present the union leader with a conflict situation. If he advocates that his membership follow guidelines based on the trend in national average productivity when bargaining with management, he can be accused of not sufficiently representing his membership. And corresponding statements can be made about business leaders contemplating the extent of a price increase.

(8) The factors that contribute to increases in factor productivity are discussed in Chapter 17. However, it is appropriate now to consider some of the economic implications of coupling sectoral rather than aggregative measures of productivity with an aggregative wage guidepost. If we take two industries, *A* and *B*, and examine the increase in productivity that takes place over a five-year interval beginning and ending in periods of full utilization of capacity, we should not be surprised if we determine that the rate of productivity increase in *A* is double that in *B*. Empirical evidence clearly demonstrates that there is substantial interindustry variation in annual rates of productivity increase.

We saw in answering question (3) above that sectoral productivity estimates entered into the calculation of adjusted costs, while in answering question (6) it was apparent that a national standard wage guidepost was adopted. The effect of this is to make the need for and the extent of price adjustments greater in those industries with relatively low rates of productivity increase. Since uniformity in wage increases is fostered, interindustry variation in productivity is likely to be reflected in differential price movements. This arrangement over time would maximize relative price flexibility in commodity markets. Were an opposite policy adopted of encouraging wage increases to reflect variation in factor productivity the effect would be to widen differentials in factor prices (incomes) and so stress incentives for factors to shift from less to more "progressive" industries.

Certainly a price-incomes policy should not interfere with the efficacy of the price system in shifting resources and reallocating output, and hence policy makers must ask whether maximizing commodity price differentials or factor price differentials best serves the allocation role. The answer to this question will determine whether an aggregative or a disaggregative approach to guidelines is preferred. Economists have approached this problem by attempting to describe the effect of changes in relative wages on the reallocation of labor between different industries and occupations. Though these descriptions were far from conclusive, they suggest that on the whole labor mobility has been rather insensitive to changes in relative wages.[16] Where linked with the desire to avoid detailed government intervention in the price-incomes area, these findings, however tentative, have served to foster the use of the trend in national average productivity, with its aggregative application, as a guideline. A subsidiary problem that arises from use of a longer-term trend in factor productivity to calculate adjusted unit cost is that year-to-year changes in factor productivity may differ from the long-term trend. In the United States, the

[16] See OECD, *Wages and Labor Mobility* (Paris: 1965); L. A. Dicks-Mireaux and J. R. Shepherd, "Wages structure and some implications for incomes policy," *National Institute Economic Review* (November 1962): 38–48; and Lloyd Ulman, "Labor mobility and industrial wage structure in the postwar United States," *Quarterly Journal of Economics*, 79 (February 1965): 73–97.

secular rate of increase in productivity has been about 3.2 percent. On the other hand, between 1965 and 1970 the short-term trend was distinctly downward.

Whenever the annual gain is substantially different from the long-term trend, shifts in the factoral distribution of income occur. Depending upon the nature of the discrepancy, either union or management leaders may be subjected to substantial *ex post facto* criticism for acceptance of the long-term guideline. It is a well recognized fact, for example, that the 1968 breakdown in West German price-incomes policy resulted from acceptance by union leadership of a forecast of slower economic recovery than was actually achieved. Actual growth was on the order of 7 percent, while the norm agreed to by the unions for wage adjustments was 4 percent. The result was a cooling of union enthusiasm for the entire program.[17] One must recognize that though complex criteria are more economically defensible, they are also more difficult to make operational.

CONCLUSION

This chapter has indicated the limitations of conventional monetary-fiscal policies in controlling inflation. Such policies are blunt instruments for securing price stability, for their primary and most useful role is in responsible demand management targeted at full utilization of sources. Once it is recognized that control over the price level is shared by the three factors of the monetary-fiscal authority, labor, and management, then complications in the apparent trade-off between stable prices and unemployment become readily apparent. These suggest that demand management alone cannot harness the actions of these factors to force price stability to accompany full utilization. Organizational rigidity, economic power blocs, the distribution of political clout, and socio-psychological influences, including perceptions of fairness and equity, all increase the difficulty of finding an acceptable answer in the search for stable prices.

These realities have led the United States and other countries into the use of supplementary policy tools directed at unit costs and prices. These are aimed at supply conditions and at factor prices and incomes, and we have seen how complex a price-incomes policy can be in its implementation. Nevertheless, many governments have concluded that actions to maintain aggregate demand can be more effective when supplemented by a price-incomes program, and that such a program will be a continuing part of their efforts to stabilize prices.

Yet the limitations of the policy tools available for fighting inflation are severe. Increased cooperation between the economic power blocs—unions, management, and government—*could* improve the chance of stable prices, but such cooperation implies a reduction in freedom in the market place. Price pressures might also be lessened by reducing union power and stepping up antitrust actions against business, but such measures would, of course, involve

[17] OECD, *Inflation: The Present Problem* (Paris: 1970), p. 81.

high political costs. The one clear thing is that inflation is a difficult and costly problem to solve.

ADDITIONAL READINGS

The original work concerning the trade-off between the rate of change in the money wage rate and the unemployment level is A. W. Phillips' "The relation between unemployment and the rate of change in money wage rates in the United Kingdom, 1861–1957," *Economica*, 25 (1958): 283–300. P. A. Samuelson and R. M. Solow examine the trade-off for the United States in "Analytical aspects of anti-inflation policy," *American Economic Review*, 50 (May 1960): 177–194. Both articles are reprinted in M. G. Mueller's *Readings in Macroeconomics*, 2nd ed. (New York: Holt, Rinehart and Winston, 1971). For more recent work on the trade-off in the United States, see G. L. Perry's *Unemployment, Money Wage Rates, and Inflation* (Cambridge, Mass.: The M.I.T. Press, 1966), and the references cited in footnotes 3 and 4. A number of models which do not provide for the possibility of a long-run Phillips curve are found in E. S. Phelps (Ed.), *Microeconomic Foundations of Employment and Inflation Theory* (New York: Norton, 1970). Some emphasize that it is only through faulty expectations (a generally rising wage and price level is mistaken for an improvement in relative wages) that inflation can increase employment. Other models emphasize the costs of acquiring good information about the job market. This is especially costly to collect for those presently employed, and so an individual who becomes voluntarily unemployed can be regarded as investing in himself to allow better use of his talents.

For a thorough survey of inflation theory see M. Bronfenbrenner and F. D. Holzman, "Survey of inflation theory," *American Economic Review*, 53 (September 1963): 593–661 (reprinted in the American Economic Association and Royal Economic Society's *Surveys of Economic Theory*, Vol. 1 [New York: St. Martin's Press, 1965]). A valuable contribution to inflation theory was made by Charles L. Schultze in "Recent inflation in the United States," in *Study of Employment, Growth, and Price Levels*, Joint Economic Committee, 86th Congress, 1st Session (Washington, D.C.: 1959), pp. 4–16 (reprinted in J. Lindauer's *Macroeconomic Readings* [New York: The Free Press, 1968]). For a discussion of the relationship between money and inflation, see R. J. Ball's *Inflation and the Theory of Money* (Chicago: Aldine, 1964).

The relationship between administered prices and inflation is discussed in the following four articles: G. Ackley, "Administered prices and the inflationary process," *American Economic Review*, 49 (May 1959): 419–430; M. A. Adelman, "Steel, administered prices, and inflation," *Quarterly Journal of Economics*, 75 (1961): 16–40; H. J. Depodwin and R. T. Selden, "Business pricing policies and inflation," *Journal of Political Economy*, 71 (1963): 116–126; and L. Weiss, "Business pricing policies and inflation reconsidered," *Journal of Political Economy*, 74 (1966): 177–187.

The costs and benefits of inflation versus unemployment are examined by

Tibor and Anne Scitovsky in "Inflation versus unemployment: An examination of their effects," in the Commission on Money and Credit's *Inflation, Growth, and Employment* (Englewood Cliffs, N.J.: Prentice-Hall, 1961), pp. 429–470. Articles dealing specifically with the issue of the effect of inflation on the distribution of income include G. L. Bach and A. Ando, "The redistributional effects of inflation," *Review of Economics and Statistics*, 39 (February 1957): 1–13; A. F. Brimmer, "Inflation and income distribution in the United States," *Review of Economics and Statistics*, 52 (November 1970): 37–48; A. E. Burger, "The effects of inflation (1960–68)," Federal Reserve Bank of St. Louis, *Review*, 59 (November 1969): 24–36; and Edward Foster, *Costs and Benefits of Inflation*, Federal Reserve Bank of Minneapolis Studies in Monetary Economics, 1972.

Attempts to evaluate the effects of inflation on the poor are found in R. G. Hollister and J. L. Palmer, "The impact of inflation on the poor," Discussion Paper No. 40–69 (Institute for Research on Poverty, University of Wisconsin, 1969); E. D. Budd and D. F. Seiders, "The impact of inflation on the distribution of income and wealth," *American Economic Review*, 61 (May 1971): 128–138; Louis De Allessi, "The redistribution of wealth by inflation: An empirical test with United Kingdom data," *Southern Economic Journal*, 30 (October 1963): 113–127; and R. A. Kessel, "Inflation caused wealth redistribution: A test of a hypothesis," *American Economic Review*, 46 (March 1956): 128–141.

The recent experiences of a number of countries with income policies are discussed in the OECD's *Inflation: The Present Problem* (Paris: 1970) and in David C. Smith, *Incomes Policies* (Ottawa: Economic Council of Canada, Special Study No. 4, 1966), and Lloyd Ulman and Robert J. Flanagan, *Wage Restraint: A Study of Incomes Policies in Western Europe* (Berkeley: University of California Press, 1971).

For econometric evidence on the success or lack thereof of the 1962–1966 U.S. wage and price guideposts, see the references cited in footnote 14. The *Economic Report of the President, 1972* provides a background for, as well as the structure of, the incomes policy implemented by the United States in 1971.

QUESTIONS

1. J. M. Keynes stated that a "change in the value of money, that is to say in the level of prices, is important to Society only in so far as its incidence is unequal" (*Monetary Reform* [New York: 1924], p. 3). Carefully explain why you agree or disagree.

2. The curve portraying the relation between the rate of unemployment and the rate of increase in wages is called the "Phillips curve." A version of this curve occurs in Figure 16–3. What factors might cause this modified Phillips curve to be much closer to the origin (further to the left) for countries such as Great Britain and Germany than for the United States?

3. Using the analysis developed in this chapter, explain how an economy can experience rising unemployment and inflation at the same time.

4. Incomes policies have frequently emphasized that wages should not be increased by more than increases in productivity. In some cases, national leaders have appealed to business and labor groups to voluntarily show "statesmanship" and hold their wage demands and price policies to these guidelines. In other cases, upper bounds have been rigidly set on wage and price increases. Both actions may be considered an attempt to move the Phillips curve toward the origin.
   Evaluate the past success of these actions and their probable success in future years.

5. If wage rates rise faster than labor productivity during a period of inflation, this proves that the inflation is the cost-push type. Explain why you agree or disagree.

6. To what extent are economic growth and stable prices compatible objectives? Explain.

7. Distinguish between cost-push and demand-pull inflation. Explain why it may be difficult for economists to identify clearly which one of these types is responsible for an existing inflationary bout.

8. Unemployment is a major cost of anti-inflationary policy. Moreover, in several ways, the changes in the unemployment rates do not fully reflect the cost of anti-inflationary policies. Explain.

9. (a) What do we mean by a "price-incomes policy?"
   (b) Explain the problems encountered when (i) wages in each sector are allowed to rise by the rate of productivity increase for the economy as a whole while (ii) interindustry variations in productivity are reflected in differential price movements.
   (c) What are the implications of most price-incomes policies with respect to income distribution?

10. One criticism of a price-incomes program is that price increases are simply delayed until the mandatory controls are removed, so that the price level 6 months, say, after the end of the controls is what it would have been in the absence of a program. Based on recent American experience, do you believe this a valid criticism?

Economic Growth

17 Chapter

Economic growth is the primary goal of all present economies. However, the idea that growth is inherently good is coming increasingly under attack. No longer is the question "Is growth good?" answered with an automatic "Yes!" The answering economist will first want to know what the questioner means by "growth."

Economic growth can be defined in many ways. Most commonly, it is referred to as an increase in the real aggregate output of goods and services in a country. This may be the relevant concern if one is interested in the military capacity of a country. The rate of increase in per capita output is another common way of viewing growth, and this way is more appropriate to one interested in the goods and services available to each individual or the standard of living in a country. Finally, one may wish to view positive growth as an increase in a country's general well-being, or welfare—either aggregate welfare or per capita welfare, although welfare is not a concept which the economist is well equipped to handle. Increases in aggregate and per capita output of goods and services as measured by GNP need not be accompanied by increasing welfare, as has become increasingly apparent as our cities have become congested with traffic, our landscapes unsightly, and our air and water unfit for consumption. Economists and others have recognized that increased output of goods and services may be accompanied by an increasing number of *ills*, which must, in order to examine the overall effect on welfare, be offset against the *goods*. Increased air traffic cannot be valued in welfare terms without examining the increase in noise and air pollution. The value to society of growing industrial production and automobile transportation cannot be measured without adjusting for air and water pollution.

The problems, such as pollution, that accompany the increasing output of goods and services are referred to as either "spillovers" or "external diseconomies." Spillovers or external diseconomies are those costs of production (or consumption) which are not fully met by the producer (or consumer). For example, the industry that pollutes a river inflicts a cost on other users of the river who now find it less suitable for recreational purposes or for drinking. Similarly, the driver entering traffic at the rush hour adds to the congestion and by slowing traffic inflicts a cost on others driving in the vicinity at that time. If society's welfare is to rise with the growing output of goods and services, these types of costs must be fully accounted for before it is decided that industrial output or traffic congestion should be allowed to increase.

The British economist, E. J. Mishan, devoted much of a book[1] to the issue of spillovers. Mishan believes that *amenity rights* similar to the currently existing rights of private property must be established. Laws must ensure that every individual has a right to clean air, clean water, and peace and quiet. Should someone wish to build an airport or a factory, steps should be taken to eliminate noise, air, and water pollution, or the airport authority or factory owner should have to compensate individuals affected by the pollution. Mishan believes that this compensation can be adequate only if the amenity rights of individuals are firmly established by law. In this way, the full costs of producing a given product or service will be considered before production is undertaken.

Economists, with the help of other scientists, have also devised means of dealing with the problem of traffic congestion. Estimates have been made of the extent to which an additional car will slow the movement of traffic at different times of the day, and, after placing a value on the time of other drivers, the spillover inflicted by driving at the rush hour may be roughly calculated. A mechanism, such as the two electronic systems currently being tested by 5000 London motorists, can be inserted in an automobile to measure the extent to which spillovers are being inflicted.

> "In one a black box is fitted underneath the vehicle which transmits an impulse on to recording devices activated when the vehicle passes over a strip in the road. Such strips could be placed at the entry to congested areas and crossing them might cost more than 50p a day. Each journey would be recorded in a centre, in the same way that telephone calls are registered, and accounts would be sent out periodically.
>
> "The second system also involves an activating device under the vehicle but would have a recording meter fitted near the wind-screen as well. Wire loops would be let into the road to act on the meter each time the vehicle crossed them. The disadvantage is that vehicle owners would have to take their meters somewhere to be read. The equipment for road pricing has been quietly developed almost to perfection." [2]

The external diseconomies of water, air, and noise pollution could be largely ignored when industrialization, material wealth, and population densities were all at significantly lower levels, but this is no longer true. As clear air, clean water, and peace and quiet have become increasingly scarce, material goods and services have become increasingly plentiful. We have reached the

[1] E. J. Mishan, *The Costs of Economic Growth* (London: Staples Press, 1967).
[2] *The Economist* (March 27, 1971), p. xiii.

point where the marginal value to society of a few more units of clean air may be greater than that of a few more industrial goods. The establishment of a system of amenity rights, though a legal nightmare, would result in a market value for amenities. This would facilitate decision-making through the market place as to whether we should have more (or less) pollution and less (or more) industrial production, and in the process the direction and speed of our economic growth would be affected.

As pointed out in Chapter 1 and in the preceding paragraphs, we fully recognize the inadequacies of using the current measure of GNP as an indicator of welfare. If spillovers can be eliminated or costed by the establishment of a system such as Mishan's amenity rights, GNP may become a more accurate reflection of welfare. However, though we would like to concentrate on growth in the welfare of people, problems of measurement and available data make this extremely difficult, and in the following sections of this chapter we have chosen to concentrate on growth in GNP. We will be focusing on growth in the aggregate output of goods and services in the economy as measured by national income accountants, while recognizing that a better picture of individual well-being is given by per capita output.

A large number of economic growth models have been developed during the past few decades.[3] This chapter will attempt to deal at some length with two of the most important contributions to economic growth theory, the Domar and neoclassical growth theories, each of which is concerned with the maintenance of an equilibrium rate of growth. In earlier chapters, we have been concerned with the conditions necessary to achieve an equilibrium level of income at a point in time. In other words, we have been dealing with a "static" economy. In this chapter, we examine the conditions necessary to maintain equilibrium in a steadily changing or "dynamic" economy.

DOMAR'S THEORY OF ECONOMIC GROWTH

In 1947, Evsey Domar published a theory of economic growth conceptually similar to one developed in England by R. F. Harrod in the late 1930s and early 1940s.[4] Domar's theory of growth, however, was solidly based on the belief that investment plays a dual role: *First*, investment increases aggregate demand, which has been made clear in the preceding chapters; *second*, investment, by adding to the stock of capital, simultaneously adds to the capacity of the economy to produce goods and services. Since Domar was interested in a growing economy, he was primarily interested in net investment and the rate at which net investment must grow in order for aggregate demand to grow rapidly enough to justify past increases in capacity created by the larger stock

[3] For a thorough survey of economic growth theory, see F. H. Hahn and R. C. O. Matthews, "The theory of economic growth: A survey," in *Surveys of Economic Theory*, Vol. 2, edited by the American Economic Association and the Royal Economic Society (New York: St. Martin's Press, 1965).

[4] E. D. Domar, "Expansion and employment," *American Economic Review*, 37 (March 1947): 34–55; R. F Harrod, "An essay in dynamic theory," *Economic Journal*, 49 (March 1939): 14–33.

of capital. In traditional Keynesian fashion, Domar pointed out the role played by adequate aggregate demand in the growth process. But, in addition, he emphasized the impact that net investment would have upon aggregate supply.

The simplified Domar model is based on the following assumptions:

Assumption 1. The level of output (Y) that an economy is capable of producing is proportional to the stock of capital (K). Hence output grows at least as rapidly as capital. This relationship is set forth as:

$$Y_t = (1/\hat{a})K_t$$

where Y_t is net national product in year t, $\hat{a}$ is the capital-to-output ratio, and K_t is the stock of capital in year t. If $\hat{a} = 4$, this means that \$4 of capital are used in the annual production of \$1 of goods and services. This proportional relationship between output and capital is fixed.

Clearly, $Y_t = (1/\hat{a})K_t$ may be viewed as an oversimplified production function, as output appears to be solely dependent upon the stock of capital in the economy. While this is true and is a problem partly overcome both in Harrod's similar model and in the neoclassical model, the Domar model does usefully highlight the important role that investment can play in the growth process.

Assumption 2. The economy remains on an equilibrium growth path with the equilibrating condition that savings (S) equals investment (I).

Assumption 3. Consumption (C) is proportional to income:

$$C = bY$$

where b is the average propensity to consume and equal to the marginal propensity to consume.

$$Y = C + S.$$

Therefore: $S = (1 - b)Y$

or: $S = sY$

where $s = (1 - b)$ is the marginal and average propensity to save.

The second assumption excludes the government and foreign sectors for purposes of simplification. The third is consistent with our earlier empirical findings with regard to the long-run consumption function.

Figure 17–1 indicates that if the consumption function in period 1 is C, and investment is equal to I_1, the equilibrium level of income is Y_1. At this point aggregate demand, $C_1 + I_1$, just equals aggregate supply. Since I_1 represents *net* investment, the capacity to produce goods in the following period will have increased. Therefore, I will equal the change in capital stock. If the capital stock is increased by I_1 and the capital-to-output ratio is $\hat{a}$, the capacity of the economy in period 2 will be larger by $(1/\hat{a})I_1$. $(1/\hat{a})I_1 + Y_1$ will equal

Figure 17–1.

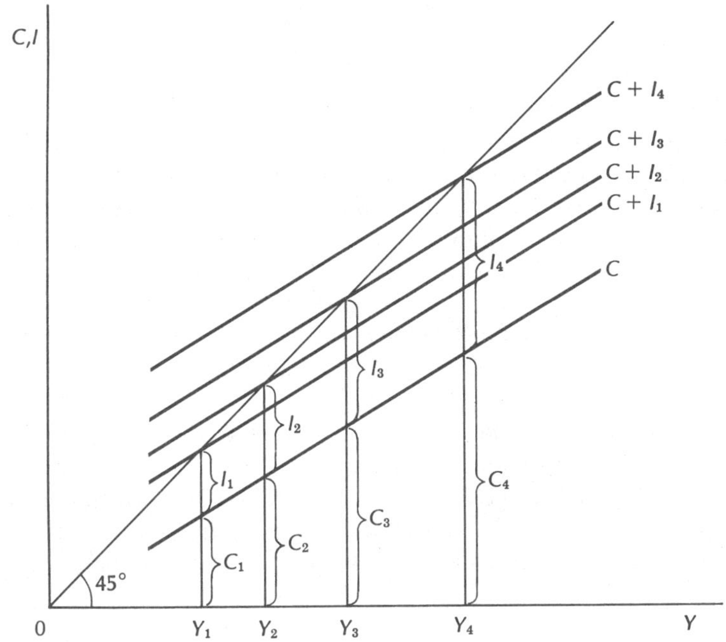

aggregate supply in period 2. And $\Delta Y = Y_2 - Y_1 = (1/\hat{a})I_1$ represents the *change in aggregate supply.*

If this new level of output is to be purchased, then aggregate demand must increase by a like amount. Any change in demand will be made up of the change in consumption and the change in investment. This theory can be summarized in the following set of equations:

$$\Delta Y = \Delta C + \Delta I \tag{17.1}$$

From assumption 3:

$$\Delta C = b\Delta Y \tag{17.2}$$

$$\Delta Y = b\Delta Y + \Delta I \tag{17.3}$$

$$\Delta I = (1 - b)\,\Delta Y \tag{17.4}$$

$$s = 1 - b$$

$$\Delta I = s\Delta Y \tag{17.5}$$

The *change in aggregate demand* may be viewed as an increase in investment times its multiplier:

$$\Delta Y = \Delta I/s \tag{17.6}$$

The equilibrium condition is equality of the changes in aggregate demand and aggregate supply:

$$\Delta I/s = I_1/\hat{a} \tag{17.7}$$

$$\text{or: } \Delta I/I_1 = s/\hat{a} \tag{17.8}$$

Equation (17.4) indicates the necessary change in current investment if past investment is to be justified. *Equation (17.8) indicates the rate at which investment must grow* (s/â) *if the economy is to maintain equilibrium growth.*

It can also be shown that the equilibrium rate of growth in investment will be the same as the equilibrium rate of growth in income. Assumption 2 specified that for the economy to be in equilibrium, savings must equal investment. By assumption 3, $S = sY$. Therefore $I = sY$. The change in income will equal the output-to-capital ratio multiplied by the increase in investment, $\Delta Y = (1/\hat{a})I$. Therefore, $\Delta Y = (1/\hat{a})I = (1/\hat{a})sY$ and $\Delta Y/Y = s/\hat{a}$.

Figure 17–1 helps illustrate the point that investment must continue to grow. If investment of I_1 in period 1 leads to an output of Y_2 in period 2, then investment must grow to I_2 in period 2 to justify the new and higher level of output. Similarly, if I_2 leads to output of Y_3 in period 3, investment must grow to I_3 in period 3 to justify the new level of output. The same process leads to the need for increasingly larger amounts of investment in later periods.

A Numerical Example

Perhaps a brief numerical example may help clarify Domar's growth theory. Beginning at an equilibrium level of income equal to $1000 billion, with net investment equal to $100 billion, the capital-to-output ratio ($\hat{a}$) at 2.5, and the propensity to save (both marginal and average) at .10, the net investment of $100 billion in period 1 will lead to an increase in productive capacity of $100 billion/2.5, or $40 billion. Therefore, demand will have to expand by $40 billion in period 2 if it is to justify the rise in output to $1040 billion.

How much then will net investment have to increase to lead to a sufficient increase in demand? Two approaches yield the same answer. First, at the new level of output ($1040 billion) consumption will equal $.9Y$, or $936 billion. Investment must fill the gap between consumption and output. Therefore investment must grow to $104 billion (by 4 percent) if aggregate demand is to equal aggregate supply. Second, in this simple two-sector model the multiplier is the reciprocal of the marginal propensity to save ($1/[1 - b] = 1/s = 10$), and again we see that in order to increase aggregate demand by $40 billion net investment must rise by $4 billion, or 4 percent.

Domar's formulation of the equilibrium rate of growth in net investment leads to this same conclusion:

$$\Delta I/I = s/\hat{a} = .10/2.5 = .04$$

Net investment in period 2 must therefore equal $104 billion. This level of

Table 17–1.

			s = 0.1; â = 2.5			
Period	Y	C	S	I	$I_t - I_{t-1}$ (ΔI)	$\Delta I / I_{t-1}$
1	1000	900	100	100		
2	1040	936	104	104	4	.04
3	1081.6	973.44	108.16	108.16	4.16	.04
4	1124.9	1012.41	112.49	112.49	4.33	.04
5	1169.9	1052.91	116.99	116.99	4.50	.04
6	1216.7	1095.03	121.67	121.67	4.68	.04

investment will cause capacity to grow by $41.6 billion (104/2.5) to a level of $1081.6 billion in period 3. If the multiplier is 10, this means that net investment must grow by $4.16 billion. And if the Domar formulation is correct then $s/\hat{a} = 4.16/104 = .04$. We find, in fact, that investment must grow constantly at a 4 percent rate if the economy is to stay on the equilibrium growth path. In Table 17–1 the necessary levels of investment are indicated for several additional periods.

The Domar Growth Model and Economic Instability

The Domar type of growth model helps us focus on instability that may exist within a market economy when investment grows at either too fast or too slow a rate. The model does not identify forces that would ensure an adequate rate of growth in investment.[5] For example, if investment were to grow at 2 percent in the second period rather than at the equilibrium rate of 4 percent, Figure 17–2 illustrates what could happen. Investment in period 1 is sufficient to raise capacity from $1000 to $1040 billion, but the 2 percent current increase in investment raises aggregate demand only to $1020 billion ($Y_2'$). Aggregate supply exceeds aggregate demand and excess capacity exists due to the shortfall in demand. Unsold stocks of goods accumulate and a deflationary gap is created. Too little investment creates an atmosphere in which further investment looks unwise. Should investment in fact grow at a more rapid rate of 4 percent in the second period, additional investment would look attractive.

On the other hand, if investment were to grow at 6 percent rather than the previous rate of 4 percent, this would create an inflationary gap. This situation is illustrated in Figure 17–3, in which productive capacity has grown only from $1000 billion ($Y_1$) to $1040 billion ($Y_2$) although aggregate demand has grown to $1060 billion ($Y_2'$). With aggregate demand exceeding aggregate supply, inventories are depleted and the atmosphere appears ripe for even larger percentage increases in investment in subsequent periods, which will cause the inflationary gap to become larger.

[5] R. F. Harrod, in developing his similar model, linked investment through a non-lagged accelerator to current changes in income. In this way he provided the motivating force for investment.

Figure 17–2.

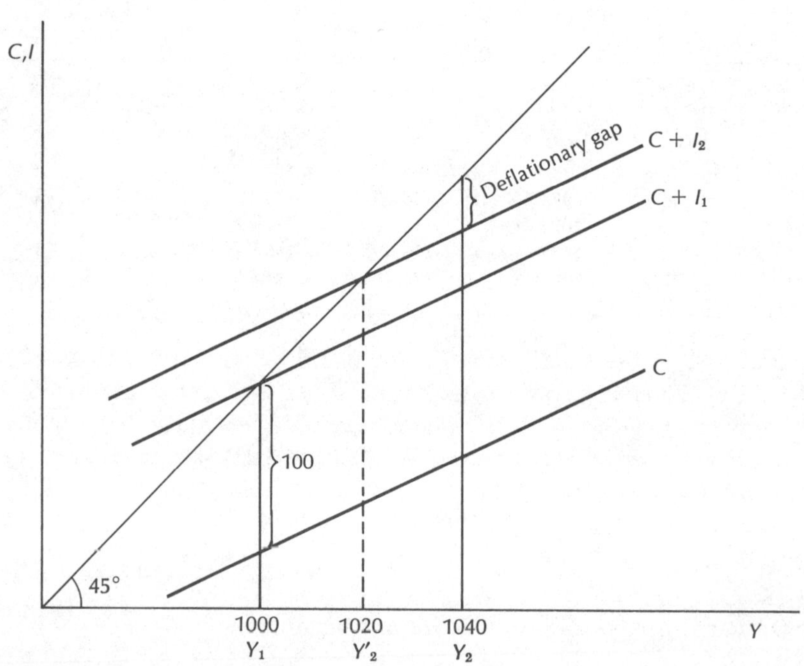

The above represents the paradox in the Domar growth model. When business invests too little, excess capacity exists and it appears that business has in fact invested too much, so businessmen are led to cut back on investment even further. And when net investment grows more rapidly than the equilibrium rate, inventories diminish and it appears that more investment is needed to expand productive capacity even more. Once the rate of change in investment diverges from the equilibrium growth path, in other words, business incentives carry investment further and further from that path.

Stability in the Domar model is based on the belief that *if past investment has been justified by sufficient growth in aggregate demand, business will increase investment by the same percentage this year as it did last year.* On the other hand, should aggregate demand exceed aggregate supply this year, investment will grow by a larger percentage next year than it did this year. And should aggregate demand fall short of aggregate supply this year, investment will increase by a smaller percentage next year.

Investment activities are based upon the expectations of growth in aggregate demand, and, as we have seen, the equilibrium rates of growth of income and net investment are equal. When output and net investment have both been moving along the equilibrium growth path at a 4 percent rate, business may then expect aggregate demand to continue to grow at 4 percent. If the propensity to save, *s*, now rises significantly, aggregate demand will grow by less than 4 percent, by, say, 3 percent, and productive capacity based upon past investment will exceed aggregate demand. Past investment, based on the expectation of a 4 percent rate of growth in aggregate demand, proves excessive, and business must revise its expectations. The increase in *s* has left a larger gap between output capacity and consumption to be filled by investment. Simultaneously, it has caused businessmen to revise their investment plans downward, and business may now expect aggregate demand to continue to grow at only a 3 percent rate. But to achieve this, investment must grow at 3 percent, and this will not occur. Due to the redundancy of capital in the past period, business recognizes that it needs to increase investment by less than 3 percent to meet the expected rise of 3 percent in aggregate demand. It is precisely the fact that business does not raise net investment by 3 percent that causes its expectations of a rise in aggregate demand of 3 percent not to be met. Again, investment plans are revised downward, and again, for the same reason, these new plans will appear unjustified. Output continues to diverge further and further from the original equilibrium growth path.

This continual fall is caused by aggregate demand not meeting expectations. The fall can be reversed or halted by any occurrence which causes the aggregate demand curve to shift upward sufficiently to at least justify the most recent level of net investment.

Similarly, we can explain an upward divergence in output from the equilibrium growth path. In this case, the propensity to save may fall, causing demand to rise by more than the equilibrium rate of 4 percent, by, say, 5 per-

Figure 17–3.

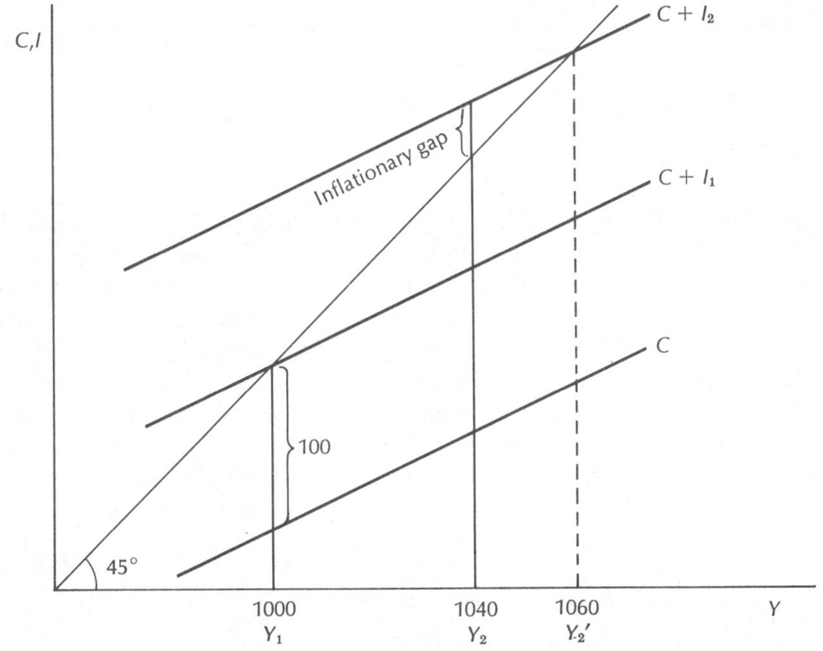

cent. Past growth rates in investment, based on an expected 4 percent rise in demand, now appear insufficient. A shortage of capacity exists, and businessmen revise their investment plans to meet a 5 percent rate of growth in aggregate demand. In order to compensate for the temporary deficiency, however, investment will initially rise by more than 5 percent, but this rise in investment will cause a greater than 5 percent rise in demand and investment will again appear to be insufficient. Plans are again revised upward as aggregate demand is expected to continue to grow at more than a 5 percent rate. Net investment must grow faster than the expected growth in aggregate demand to make up for past capital deficiencies, as well as to add the necessary capital to meet levels of aggregate demand expected in the future. This again causes aggregate demand to grow faster than expected and the upward divergence from the equilibrium growth path gets larger and larger.

The upward divergence, however, cannot continue indefinitely. Capacity limitations exist in any economy. At some point limited quantities of natural resources and/or labor will prevent output and investment from continuing to grow. This will lead to a downturn as past investment appears redundant, and the growth rate will decrease as in the previous case when capital became redundant.

Domar's equilibrium rate of growth is dependent upon two factors—the capital-to-output ratio ($\hat{a}$), and the propensity to save (s). Quite possibly, the rate of growth determined by these factors may be insufficient to ensure full employment. If, in fact, the equilibrium rate of growth is slower than growth in the labor force and in the population as a whole, policies that would increase the equilibrium rate of growth would appear appropriate. This might involve actions that would either raise s or lower $\hat{a}$. As the capital-to-output ratio is dependent upon the state of technology, s could be most readily altered through tax or other government policies offering disincentives for saving.

Some Limitations

The Domar growth model is subject to several major limitations. First, the stock of capital is assumed to grow in a manner which keeps the capital-to-output ratio constant, but, in reality, investment will vary in its response to changes in demand. Business will sometimes meet increases in demand by using the existing capital stock more intensively, through additional work shifts or overtime work. At other times, investment may grow faster than expected demand as an attempt is made to reduce shifts or overtime. Second, the model gives little attention to the possible influences of monetary and fiscal policy. And third, the roles played by growth in the labor force and changes in technology are inadequately treated.[6] Attempts to alter the model to overcome these shortcomings may make it more realistic, but they almost invariably reduce

[6] Technological changes and money supply changes will both be essential to ensure that investment can continue to grow at the equilibrium rate. See W. Fellner, *Trends and Cycles in Economic Activity* (New York: Holt, Rinehart & Winston, 1956).

its usefulness as a pedagogical tool. As they stand, limitations and all, the Domar model and other similar models make an important contribution to the understanding of the growth process.

The neoclassical model of economic growth to which we now turn explicitly recognizes the important role that changes in the labor force and technology can play in the growth process. However, this model does not recognize that growing productive capacity and growing aggregate demand play equally important roles in the growth process, for the focus of the neoclassical model is on the supply side. As with earlier classical models, it is assumed that demand will always be sufficient to ensure full employment.

A NEOCLASSICAL MODEL OF ECONOMIC GROWTH

A basic feature of Domar's growth model is the fixed relationship between the stock of capital and the production capacity, for it was based on the concept of fixed factor proportions. If labor grew faster than the capital stock, this would, since each unit of capital can work effectively with only a fixed amount of labor, lead to an increase in unemployment or disguised unemployment. The Domar model eliminates the possibility of altering the labor-capital combination per unit of output.

Two basic differences of the neoclassical growth model are that it allows for (a) the varying of the capital-to-output ratio, and (b) the impact of technological change. If labor should grow more rapidly than capital it is always possible to increase output and yet maintain full employment simply by combining more and more units of labor services used in production with each unit of capital. Combined with the neoclassical assumption of adequate demand, this ensures that both labor and capital will be fully utilized at all times.

The simplest of the neoclassical models is based on a long list of assumptions, which can be relaxed with varying effects on the model.[7] The following assumptions are part of the model that we will examine:

Assumption 1. No foreign or government sector exists.

Assumption 2. A perfectly competitive economy exists.

Assumption 3. The production process is one in which given percentage increases in inputs result in equivalent percentage increases in output; i.e., the production function is homogeneous of degree one.

Assumption 4. Prices are constant.

Assumption 5. Full employment exists.

Assumption 6. Machinery is completely malleable; i.e., it can be combined in an unlimited number of ways with labor.

[7] For a thorough and detailed analysis of the neoclassical model, see J. E. Meade, *A Neo-Classical Theory of Economic Growth* (London: George Allen and Unwin, 1961).

Assumption 7. There are only two factors of production—labor and capital.
Assumption 8. Each factor is paid the value of its marginal product.

The neoclassical production function may then be written as:

$$Y = f(J, N, K) \tag{17.9}$$

The output (Y) of the economy will depend on the state of technology (J), the size of the work force (N), and the stock of capital (K).

There are three ways in which growth in output can be achieved: (a) A change in technology makes it possible to produce more with the same amount of labor and capital; (b) with fixed capital and technology, a growth in the labor supply makes possible an increase in output; (c) with fixed technology and an unchanged labor supply, a growth in the capital stock also permits an increase in output.

To be somewhat more explicit we will examine a production function that is homogeneous of degree one (introduced in Chapter 11):

$$Y = J N^{\alpha} K^{1-\alpha} \tag{17.10}$$

where $0 < \alpha < 1$.
This particular production function can meet all of the requirements of assumptions 1–8.

First, let us look at the effect that a change in the labor supply will have upon output. This can most easily be seen by first looking at $\Delta Y / \Delta N$:

$$\Delta Y/\Delta N \approx J\alpha N^{\alpha-1}K^{1-\alpha} \tag{17.11}$$

$\Delta Y/\Delta N$ is the marginal product of labor.[8] Therefore a small change in $N(\Delta N)$ would cause the following change in $Y(\Delta Y)$:

$$\Delta Y \approx J\alpha N^{\alpha-1}K^{1-\alpha}\,\Delta N \tag{17.12}$$

Similarly, a small change in $K(\Delta K)$would result in a change in $Y(\Delta Y)$ equal to:

$$\Delta Y \approx J(1-\alpha)N^{\alpha}K^{-\alpha}\,\Delta K \tag{17.13}$$

And a change in output due to a change in technology may be viewed as:

$$\Delta Y \approx N^{\alpha}K^{1-\alpha}\Delta J \tag{17.14}$$

We may then write the total effect on output of changes in technology, labor, and capital as:

$$\Delta Y \approx N^{\alpha}K^{1-\alpha}\Delta J + J\alpha N^{\alpha-1}K^{1-\alpha}\Delta N + J(1-\alpha)N^{\alpha}K^{-\alpha}\Delta K \tag{17.15}$$

Using equation (17.10) and dividing through by Y, we find that the percentage change in output is equal to:

$$\frac{\Delta Y}{Y} \approx \frac{\Delta J}{J} + \frac{\alpha\Delta N}{N} + \frac{(1-\alpha)\Delta K}{K} \tag{17.16}$$

[8] The student of calculus will recognize that the marginal product of labor is the partial derivative of Y with respect to N; thus, if $Y = JN^{\alpha}K^{1-\alpha}$, $\partial Y/\partial N = J\alpha N^{\alpha-1}K^{1-\alpha}$

In the equation above we have used $\Delta Y/\Delta N$ to represent $\partial Y/\partial N$ and since ΔN is discrete we have let the sign for approximation replace the sign for equality. In equation (17.13) we have approximated the marginal productivity of capital in a similar fashion.

The growth in output depends upon the growth in technology plus the weighted averages of the growth in the labor supply and the capital stock.

The weights of labor growth (α) and capital growth ($1 - \alpha$) are in fact the shares of total output going to labor and capital, respectively. In our perfectly competitive system, both labor and capital are paid amounts equal to the value of their marginal product. Any change in income will therefore be composed of the change in labor supply (ΔN) times the value of the marginal product of labor ($P\Delta Q/\Delta N = W$), plus the change in capital stock (ΔK) times the value of its marginal product ($P\Delta Q/\Delta K = P_K$, where P_K represents the price of capital), plus the share of the change in income which is due to technological advances (ΔY_J), or:

$$\Delta Y \approx W\Delta N + P_K\Delta K + \Delta Y_J \tag{17.17}$$

Dividing through by Y we can rewrite this as:

$$\frac{\Delta Y}{Y} \approx \frac{WN}{Y}\frac{\Delta N}{N} + \frac{P_K K}{Y}\frac{\Delta K}{K} + \frac{\Delta Y_J}{Y} \tag{17.18}$$

where $WN/Y = \alpha$, the share of income going to labor,
$P_K K/Y = 1 - \alpha$, the share of income going to capital;
$\Delta Y_J/Y = \Delta J/J$, the growth in output due to technological advance.

Letting small letters represent proportional changes in the variables, and letting $\beta = 1 - \alpha$, we may now rewrite equation (17.18) in its final form:

$$y \approx \alpha n + \beta k + j \tag{17.19}$$

where $y = \Delta Y/Y$, the growth in output;
$n = \Delta N/N$, the growth in labor force;
$k = \Delta K/K$, the growth in the capital stock;
$j = \Delta J/J$, the growth in output due to technological progress that is not accounted for by increases in inputs.

Growth Without Technological Progress in the Neoclassical Model

In the case where no technological progress exists, the change in output will depend solely upon changes in the labor force and in the stock of capital:

$$y \approx \alpha n + \beta k \tag{17.20}$$

As a numerical example, we can take the share of income going to labor as $\alpha = .75$ and the share going to capital as $\beta = .25$. With capital stock growth at 4 percent and labor unchanged, then, there will be a 1 percent growth in output, while with labor force growth at only 1⅓ percent and capital unchanged, the same 1 percent growth in output occurs. If both labor and capital grow at a 4 percent rate, output will grow at 4 percent.

The importance of increasing per capita income as a measure of growth was indicated earlier in this chapter. We can assume that the labor force and the population grow at roughly similar rates, and we can gain an intuitive understanding of how per capita income will respond to changes in labor, capital, and technology. For example, as long as the capital stock grows more rapidly than the labor force ($k > n$) each worker will have more capital with which to work and the marginal product of labor and output per capita will rise. If, on the other hand, labor grows more rapidly than capital ($k < n$) each worker will be combined with less capital and the marginal productivity of labor and output per capita will fall. In the case of constant technology, living standards can rise only if the capital stock is growing more rapidly than the labor force.

The growth process will also have effects upon the productivity of capital, for potential investors will be interested in the returns to capital investment. If capital grows more rapidly than labor, the marginal productivity of capital will fall, and as output per unit of capital falls it will only be a matter of time before returns to investment in capital stock will appear insufficient to justify further investments. Why, in fact, has the capital stock continued to grow more rapidly than the labor force in many areas? A major reason has been the continual improvement in technology.

Growth with Technological Progress in the Neoclassical Model

If we allow for technological progress, then $y = \alpha n + \beta k + j$, and of course j is no longer equal to zero. This has important consequences for growth in both output per capita and output per unit of capital. It is now possible for the labor force to grow more rapidly than the stock of capital ($n > k$) and still experience an increase in output per capita. The fact that each worker now has less capital to work with may be more than offset by an improvement in technology. So long as j is positive, it is quite possible for the stock of capital to grow more rapidly than the labor force and still result in an increase in output per unit of capital. In this manner, technological change can more than offset a fall in the productivity of new capital which would lead to a stifling of investment.

The Equilibrium Rate of Growth in the Neoclassical Model

J. E. Meade has pointed out that, under certain conditions, the neoclassical model that we have been examining will also tend toward an equilibrium rate of growth. Given the rate of change in income as in equation (17.19) and adding three assumptions to this model, that as income grows savings will remain a constant proportion (s) of income, that the labor force grows at a constant rate (n), and that technology also progresses at a constant rate (j), we may rewrite equation (17.19) as:

$$y = \alpha n + \beta sY/K + j \qquad (17.21)$$

where sY is the amount of savings in any given year, and therefore the amount of capital (ΔK) that is formed during that year.

Since there are five constants in equation (17.21) (α, n, β, s, and j), y will be a constant only if Y/K is constant, and Y/K will be constant only if the stock of capital and the level of income are growing at equal rates, i.e., only if $k = y$. Setting y equal to k and solving for this constant growth rate yields:

$$y = \alpha n + \beta y + j$$

$$\text{or: } y = (\alpha n + j)/(1 - \beta) \qquad (17.22)$$

Though equation (17.22) gives us a constant rate of growth, we have not yet shown that it is an equilibrium rate of growth. This can be done by taking the case where the capital stock growth rate temporarily diverges from the rate $(\alpha n + j)/(1 - \beta)$ due to an increased desire to save. This causes $sY/K = k$ to be larger than y. This in turn will cause K to grow more rapidly than Y, and k will begin to fall as a result. This fall in k will continue so long as k exceeds y, so that if k temporarily exceeds y, market forces will cause it to fall toward y. Similarly, if k falls below y due to a decreased desire to save, sY/K will tend to rise as Y increases faster than K with s constant. Hence, if k is less than y, market forces will cause k to rise toward y.

The above paragraphs indicate that the economy will always tend toward some steady-state growth rate, y. This does *not* preclude the possibility of an increased rate of savings leading to a higher level of output due to increased capital accumulation. The increased rate of capital accumulation will cause income to rise more rapidly, but this will only be a temporary phenomenon. From equation (17.21) we can see that a rise in the proportion of income saved, s, will lead to an increase in the growth rate, y. But the increase in s eventually leads to a rise in the stock of capital, K, which offsets the rise in s and returns us to the equilibrium growth rate. An increase in s causes only a temporary increase in the growth rate. This is illustrated in Figure 17–4, in which the logarithm of Y is plotted against time. (A straight-line curve on semilogarithmic axes shows a constant rate of change of income over time.) At time t, a rise in the propensity to save increases the growth rate. By time t', if the propensity to save had remained unchanged, the income level would have been at Y, but with the change in the propensity to save the income level rises to Y' at time t'. However, though the income in period t' is higher, by this time income has returned to its equilibrium growth rate. In other words the slope of the new growth path is equal to that of the old.

Shifts in the propensity to save can lead to a temporary increase in the growth rate, but the effect of even sizable shifts is likely to be small. A numerical example can illustrate this point, for if we take the case where the growths of labor and of technological progress are both zero, equation (17.21) becomes $y = \beta sY/K$. If $\beta = .25$, as earlier suggested, and the capital-to-output ratio is 2.5, a propensity to save equal to .10 will lead to a growth rate of 1 percent. A doubling of the savings propensity to .20 will raise the growth rate to 2 percent. The temporary increase in the growth rate caused by a doubling of savings would be 1 percentage point. Truly major shifts in saving would then be required in order to have a significant impact on the growth rate.

Figure 17–4.

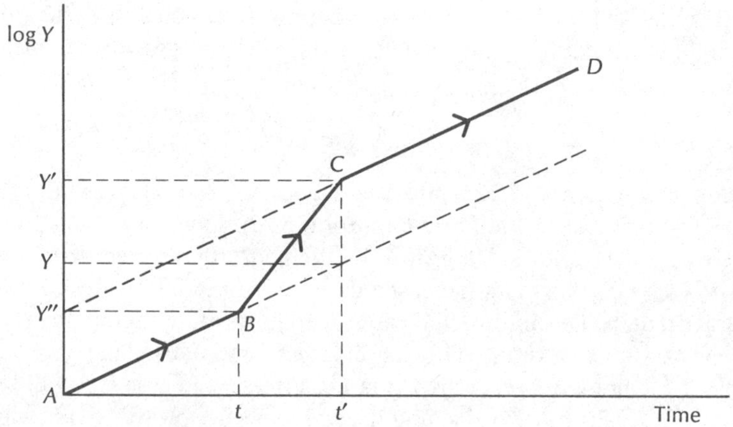

EMPIRICAL EVIDENCE

Several empirical studies, the best known of which are E. F. Denison's *The Sources of Economic Growth in the United States* and *Why Growth Rates Differ*, have been done in an attempt to identify the contributions that improved technology and growing supplies of labor and capital have made to growth. Denison divides the contributions to economic growth into two broad categories: (a) growth due to increased factor inputs such as labor and capital; and (b) growth due to the improved use of inputs. He finds that the improved use of inputs in the United States is basically due to three factors, advances in knowledge, improved allocation of resources as factors shift away from agriculture and self-employment and trade barriers are reduced, and economies of scale as incomes rise and markets grow. He estimates that increased labor and capital inputs accounted for 1.46 percent of the 3.32 percent average growth rate between 1950 and 1962 in the United States, while improved education and better use of resources accounted for the remaining 1.86 percent, or about 56 percent of the growth rate.[9] His estimates for Northwest Europe as a whole

[9] Many of Denison's computation techniques are complicated and cannot be related here. However, with regard to growth due to increased factor inputs, his heavy reliance on income shares allows us to quickly demonstrate as examples his calculation of growth due to (a) a growing labor force, and (b) increasing nonresidential structures and equipment. Denison asks "what fraction of the increase in real national income that would result from a 1 percent increase in all factors of production is obtained from a 1 percent increase in only one factor or group of factors?" His answer is "The fraction is the same as the fraction of total national income that is earned by the factor or group of factors that increases." For example, the share of national income in the U.S. going to labor from 1950 to 1962 averaged 78.6 percent. Employment over this period grew at 1.1 percent. The contribution of growing employment to the growth rate was then 0.786×0.011, or .86 percent. Likewise, the average share of income going to nonresidential structures and equipment from 1950 to 1962 was 11.2 percent. Growth in the supply of nonresidential structures and equipment averaged 3.8 percent. The contribution of this element to overall growth was 0.112×0.038, or .43 percent. See E. F. Denison, *The Sources of Economic Growth in the United States*, Supplementary Paper No. 13 (New York: Committee for Economic Development, 1962), and *Why Growth Rates Differ* (Washington, D.C.: Brookings Institution, 1967).

for this same period indicate that increased labor and capital accounted for 31 percent of the growth experienced and better use of resources and improved education accounted for the remaining 69 percent. Careful examination of Table 17–2, which summarizes Denison's findings, indicates that increased factor inputs were relatively more important for growth in the United States and Canada than in Europe. Northwest Europeans gained relatively more from improved resource allocation and economies of scale.

Careful examination of the neoclassical growth model presented earlier, which is the model used in Denison's measurements, reveals a basic shortcoming, namely that the growth in capital stock, the growth in the labor force, and technical progress are presumed factorable and independent of one another. Reflection indicates the difficulty of separating growth due to the increase in capital stock from that due to the improvement in technology embodied in newly installed capital equipment and also, for example, the problem of distinguishing improvements in the quality of the labor force due to education from advances in technology.

One aspect of Denison's estimates that has thus been understandably subjected to severe criticism is his estimate of the contribution of advances in technological and managerial knowledge to growth. After estimating the contribution of all other identifiable factors, Denison assigns the residuum to this category. This residuum does not fully reflect the contribution to growth that is made by technological progress (referred to as "advances of knowledge" in Table 17–2). The basic shortcoming is that interdependence does exist between the variables that Denison assumes to be independent. Three points well illustrate this: (a) Net investment not only increases capital stock, it also raises the level of technology in the economy since much of any advance in technology is actually embodied in the new capital goods being installed; (b) part of the return to increased education is due to improved technology that is combined with the better trained workers; and (c) improved allocation of resources, such as the movement out of agriculture, is not independent of technological advances. To allocate growth explicitly to other factors, leaving the residuum to advances in knowledge, is to understate the contribution of advances in knowledge.

Professor Harvey Leibenstein has shed some further light on the problem of estimating the contribution of technological change to growth.[10] He points out that the increase in output may be due more to knowledge dissemination or the adoption of existing techniques than to invention and that lags in these factors ("X-inefficiency") exist in the economies of both industrialized and low-income countries because: (a) Individual workers are not adequately motivated; (b) people do not work at the tasks at which they would be most proficient; (c) available improvements in production techniques are not utilized; and (d) there are few competitive pressures forcing the use of already

[10] Harvey Leibenstein, "Allocative efficiency vs. 'X-efficiency'," *American Economic Review*, 56 (June 1966): 392–415, and "Organizational or frictional equilibrium, X-efficiency, and the rate of innovation," *Quarterly Journal of Economics*, 83 (November 1969): 600–624.

Table 17–2. Contributions of Factor Inputs and Output Per Unit of Input to Growth Rates of Total National Incomes (in percentage points).

Sources of growth 1950–1962	United States	Northwest Europe	Belgium	Denmark	France	Germany	Nether-lands	Norway	United Kingdom	Italy	Canada
National income	3.32	4.76	3.20	3.51	4.92	7.26	4.73	3.45	2.29	5.96	3.8
Total factor input	1.95	1.69	1.17	1.55	1.24	2.78	1.91	1.04	1.11	1.66	2.7
Labor	1.12	.83	.76	.59	.45	1.37	.87	.15	.60	.96	1.4
Employment	.90	.71	.40	.70	.08	1.49	.78	.13	.50	.42	1.5
Hours of work	−.17	−.14	−.15	−.18	−.02	−.27	−.16	−.15	−.15	.05	−.2
Age-sex composition	−.10	.03	.08	−.07	.10	.04	.01	−.07	−.04	.09	−.1
Education	.49	.23	.43	.14	.29	.11	.24	.24	.29	.40	.2
Capital	.83	.86	.41	.96	.79	1.41	1.04	.89	.51	.70	1.3
Dwellings	.25	.07	.02	.13	.02	.14	.06	.04	.04	.07	.3
International assets	.05	−.03	−.06	.02	.02	−.08	.10	−.07	−.05	−.03	—
Nonresidential structures and equipment	.43	.64	.39	.66	.56	1.02	.66	.79	.43	.54	.8
Inventories	.10	.18	.06	.15	.19	.33	.22	.13	.09	.12	.2
Land	.00	.00	.00	.00	.00	.00	.00	.00	.00	.00	—
Output per unit of input	1.37	3.07	2.03	1.96	3.68	4.48	2.82	2.41	1.18	4.30	1.1
Advances of knowledge	.76	.76	.76	.76	.76	.76	.76	.76	.76	.76	.5
Changes in the lag in the application of knowledge, general efficiency, and errors and omissions											
Reduction in age of capital		.02	.00	.04	.00	.04	.00	.04	.00	.00	.0
Other		.54	.08	−.32	.75	.80	.44	.14	.03	.89	−.2

Sources of growth 1950–1962	United States	Northwest Europe	Belgium	Denmark	France	Germany	Netherlands	Norway	United Kingdom	Italy	Canada
Improved allocation of resources											
Contraction of agricultural inputs	.25	.46	.20	.41	.65	.77	.21	.54	.06	1.04	.5
Contraction of nonagricultural self-employment	.04	.14	.15	.18	.23	.14	.26	.23	.04	.22	.1
Reduction of international trade barriers	.00	.08	.16	.09	.07	.10	.16	.15	.02	.16	—
Balancing of the capital stock		.08				.26					
Deflation procedures		.07	.17		.23						
Economies of scale											
Growth of national market measured in U.S. prices	.30	.41	.33	.35	.44	.63	.48	.38	.22	.55	.4
Income elasticities		.46	.11	.23	.49	.91	.23	.12	.09	.60	—
Independent growth of local markets	.06	.06	.07	.07	.07	.07	.07	.07	.05	.07	.1
Irregularities in pressure of demand	−.04	−.01		.22			.19		−.09		−.4
Irregularities in agricultural output	.00	.00		−.07	−.01		.02	−.02		.01	.1

Sources: E. F. Denison (assisted by J.-P. Pouillier), *Why Growth Rates Differ*, (Washington, D.C., Brookings Institution, 1967), pp. 192, 298–316. © 1967 by the Brookings Institution, Washington, D.C. The Canadian figures are from Dorothy Walters, *Canadian Income Levels and Growth: An International Perspective*, Economic Council of Canada Staff Study No. 23 (Ottawa: Queen's Printer, 1967).

developed techniques. Compared to any loss of welfare due to allocative inefficiency created by monopoly power, Leibenstein believes that loss due to X-inefficiency is impressively large, and he believes that it can be corrected by appropriate and currently feasible improvements in materials handling, plant organization, waste controls, work methods, etc. In other words, much of the growth due to *j* in our neoclassical model may be due to the increased use of previously discovered production techniques. The data in Table 17–3, collected by the International Labor Organization and presented by Leibenstein, are primarily based on experiences in low-income countries. They impressively indicate the increases in output that can be achieved without increasing labor inputs, capital inputs, or new inventions.

Clearly it would be difficult to measure the aggregate contribution of any increase in "X-efficiency" to the rate of economic growth. Leibenstein puts it well when he states that:

> "People normally operate within the bounds of a great deal of intellectual slack. Unlike underutilized capital, this is an element that is very difficult to observe."

This, of course, has made it more difficult for those such as Denison who have attempted to measure the contribution of technological change to economic growth. It also demonstrates that changes in the lag between invention and implementation can have a significant impact upon the growth rate.

Denison's work has received the professional attention that it deserves. Major strides have been made toward identifying the factors that have contributed to economic growth in Northwest Europe and in North America. Shortcomings, inevitable in such extensive research, have been identified and attempts to resolve them have resulted in and will continue to result in additional constructive research.[11]

POLICY IMPLICATIONS

We have presented two basic models of economic growth and described attempted empirical investigation within the framework of one of them, the neoclassical. One model is demand-oriented, stressing the importance to the growth process of sustaining a high rate of resource utilization. The other model emphasizes the dependence of growth upon increases in the availability and improvements in the quality of factor inputs, including technical progress. The contrast is quite striking; one approach largely dismisses the potential problems of the availability of more inputs, while the other assumes that high levels of demand are automatically present.

[11] The interested student is referred to R. R. Nelson, "Aggregate production functions and medium range growth projections." *American Economic Review*, 54 (September 1964): 575–606.

Table 17–3. ILO Productivity Mission Results.

Factory or Operation	Method*	Increase in Labor Productivity %	Impact on the Firm (Unit Cost Reduction)	
			Labor Savings %	Capital† Savings %
India				
Seven textile mills	n.a.	5–250	5–71	5–71
Engineering firms				
All operations	F,B,	102	50	50
One operation	F	385	79	79
One operation	F	500	83	83
Burma				
Molding railroad brake shoes	A,F,B	100	50	50
Smithy	A	40	29	29
Chair assembly	A,B	100	50	50
Match manufacture	A,F	24	19	—
Indonesia				
Knitting	A,B	15	13	—
Radio assembly	A,F	40	29	29
Printing	A,F	30	23	—
Enamel ware	F	30	23	—
Malaya				
Furniture	A,D	10	9	9
Engineering workshop	A,D	10	9	9
Pottery	A,B	20	17	17
Thailand				
Locomotive maintenance	A,F	44	31	31
Saucepan polishing	E,D	50	33	—
Saucepan assembly	B,F	42	30	—
Cigarettes	A,B	5	5	—
Pakistan				
Textile plants	C,H,G			
Weaving		50	33	33
Weaving		10	9	9
Bleaching		59	37	37
Weaving		141	29	29
Israel				
Locomotive repair	F,B,G	30	23	23
Diamond cutting and polishing	C,B,G	45	31	—
Refrigerator assembly	F,B,G	75	43	43
Orange picking	F	91	47	—

*A = plant layout reorganized
B = machine utilization and flow
C = simple technical alterations
D = materials handling
E = waste control
F = work method
G = payment by results
H = worker training and supervision

† Limited to plant and equipment, excluding increased depreciation costs.

Source: Harvey Liebenstein, "Allocative efficiency vs. 'X-efficiency,'" *American Economic Review*, 56 (June 1966): 400. This data first appeared in this form in Peter Kilby, "Organization and productivity in backward economies," *Quarterly Journal of Economics*, 76 (May 1962): 306–307.

Considering these alternative approaches, the implications for economic policy lead logically to a quite different emphasis. In the demand-oriented Domar model, the effort of the policy maker is concentrated on the maintenance of an aggregate demand sufficient to ensure that the equilibrium rate of growth will be secured. Tax, government expenditure, and monetary policies can all be manipulated in a manner such that aggregate demand grows neither too slowly nor too rapidly. On the supply side of this model, only the stock of capital is considered to have an important effect on economic growth. Only by influencing the level of investment or by attempting to alter the capital-to-output ratio through research expenditures can authorities change the equilibrium rate of growth itself. It can easily be understood how this somewhat myopic view of the predominant importance of aggregate demand came to dominate the world of the 1930s and 1940s, for it was during this period that the economic theories stressing the danger of inadequate demand became more generally known and accepted. Through the 1930s, much of the industrialized world had experienced unemployment as high as 25 percent of the work force, and only the growing demands of war proved sufficient to reverse this situation.

With the end of World War II, the situation changed. The Employment Act of 1946 committed the United States government to the continual promotion of maximum employment. Other industrialized nations followed suit, and the periods of inflationary demand experienced at the end of the 1940s and again in the 1950s and 1960s indicated that a stable growth policy can only be achieved if growing supply consistently satisfies growing demand. In this atmosphere of government commitment to full employment, the neoclassical model with its focus on the supply side becomes a particularly relevant and useful model of the economy.

The empirical studies of Denison and others have provided estimates of the contributions of labor, capital, technological progress, and the improved use of resources to the growth rates of various nations, and alternative policies based on these estimates have been proposed. Denison has suggested several possible means of increasing the growth rate. For example, a 0.1 percentage point increase in the growth rate between 1960 and 1980 could be achieved by (a) increasing the standard work week by one hour over what it would otherwise be, (b) adding one and a half years to the time that would otherwise be spent in school by everyone completing school between 1960 and 1980, (c) raising the amount of annual private net investment by 1.4 percent of national income, and (d) doubling the rate of net immigration. Unfortunately, problems such as disentangling the contribution of technological progress from other factors contributing to growth and the limitations of the data make the original estimates and the policy conclusions flowing from them subject to a sizable margin of error. Denison's estimates would indicate that advances in technological and managerial knowledge are relatively unimportant to economic growth. If these estimates are accurate the government might (a) devote few resources to research and development (R&D) and eliminate existing tax incentives for private investment in R&D, and (b) provide incentives for investment in new plant and equipment[12] and allocate additional resources to education. If, on the other hand, it is believed that technological improvements are embodied in new plant and equipment and that returns to additional education are in large part due to improved technology, the contribution of "advances in knowledge" to growth is larger than Denison's estimates indicate. In this case, it might be wise for the government to increase its expenditures on R&D and to do more to stimulate private R&D. Professor Leibenstein has clearly pointed to the gains that may be achieved by, for instance, improving communications to reduce the lag between the development and implementation of new techniques.

But growth also has other implications for the policy maker. As national output has grown, it has become obvious that though the process of growth improves the material terms of existence and adds to the alternatives open to human beings, it creates problems as well. Many were alluded to at the beginning of this chapter, but one more illustration—the way economic growth has generated budgetary pressures for urban areas—may be in order. The difficulties that arise in this situation stem from the facts that economic activities may be categorized as either progressive or nonprogressive and that wages paid to workers in these activities, whether progressive or nonprogressive, tend to move together despite disparities in productivity experience. In technologically progressive industries, such as aerospace and electronics, output per employee will increase rapidly so that wages can increase commensurately without any rise in either labor costs per unit of output or in selling prices. The so-called nonproductive sectors include many of the services that cities provide or support, including police, fire protection, hospitals, social services, inspection services, recreation facilities, libraries, and the arts—in them, productivity increases have occurred slowly. As labor productivity in other activities has increased much more rapidly, the per unit cost of urban services has risen both in large absolute amounts and relative to the cost of many other goods and services. Equally troublesome is the fact that many urban services will by their very natures remain technologically nonprogressive and their relative per unit cost will continue to rise. This pressure on the urban budget, a by-product of economic growth, has contributed significantly to the increasing revolt of the local property tax payers who have to meet the rising costs.[13]

Finally, it is good to remember that, with the increased recognition of environmental problems, increasing GNP no longer has the same welfare implications that it once had. If the problem of continuing economic growth is to receive the attention that it richly deserves, the normal measurements of economic growth will have to become more closely identified with the improved welfare of the population.

[12] This can be done, for example, by allowing a faster depreciation write-off for new investment or by using an investment tax credit of the type implemented in the U.S. in 1962.

[13] The points made here are drawn from a much more rigorous and complete theoretical treatment of the issue by William J. Baumol in "Macroeconomics of unbalanced growth: The anatomy of urban crisis," *American Economic Review*, 57 (June 1967): 415–426. Empirical evidence supporting Baumol may be found in D. F. Bradford, R. A. Malt, and W. E. Oates, "The rising cost of local public services: Some evidence and reflections," *National Tax Journal* (June 1969): 185–202.

CONCLUSION

The relevance and policy implications of economic growth theories change with the times. The demand-oriented and neoclassical theories discussed in this chapter and their refinements have contributed much to the understanding of the economic growth phenomenon. These theoretical developments and increasing empirical research have provided better information upon which to base decisions. This in no way, however, denies the limitations of past work and the need for research in the future, for economic growth will long remain a fertile field for investigators.

ADDITIONAL READINGS

One of the earliest statements of demand-oriented theories of growth is found in R. F. Harrod's "An essay in dynamic theory," *Economic Journal*, 49 (March 1939): 14–33. A more complete statement of the Harrod model is found in *Toward a Dynamic Economics* (London: Macmillan, 1948). The Domar model can be consulted by the student in E. D. Domar's "Expansion and employment," *American Economic Review*, 37 (March 1947): 34–55.

Two important statements of the neoclassical approach to growth are found in two articles by Robert M. Solow. These are "Technical progress and the aggregate production function," *Review of Economics and Statistics*, 39 (August 1957): 312–320, and "Technical progress, capital formation and economic growth," *American Economic Review*, 52 (May 1962): 76–86. Difficulties in treating the determinants of growth as independent of one another are well summarized at the end of the article by R. R. Nelson, "Aggregate production functions and medium range growth projections," *American Economic Review*, 54 (September 1964): 575–606. A further statement of neoclassical growth theory is found in J. E. Meade's *A Neo-Classical Theory of Economic Growth* (London: George Allen and Unwin, 1961).

A valuable survey of growth theory literature up to 1964 is found in F. H. Hahn and R. C. O. Matthews, "The theory of economic growth: A survey," in *Surveys in Economic Theory*, Vol. 2, edited by the American Economic Association and the Royal Economic Society (New York: St. Martin's Press, 1965). This article contains a detailed bibliography at its end.

The attempts at measuring the contribution of the various components of growth in the U.S. economy are found in E. F. Denison's *The Sources of Economic Growth in the United States* (New York: Committee for Economic Development, 1962). An excellent review of the Denison work is found in M. Abramovitz' "Economic growth in the United States," *American Economic Review*, 52 (September 1962): 762–782. Denison's attempt at measuring the importance of growth factors in the case of a number of European countries is in E. F. Denison's *Why Growth Rates Differ*, (Washington, D.C.: Brookings Institution, 1967). The student will find that *Long Term Economic Growth, 1860–1970* (Washington, D.C.: U.S. Government Printing Office, 1973) provides approximately 1200 annual time series bearing on national and regional growth in the United States. This publication also includes an excellent introduction to the problems of measuring economic growth.

Two articles that stress the importance of knowledge dissemination and the removal of market and other impediments in moving from inefficient to efficient production frontiers are found in H. Liebenstein's "Allocative efficiency vs. 'X-efficiency,'" *American Economic Review*, 56 (June 1966): 392–415, and "Organizational or frictional equilibria, X-efficiency, and the rate of innovation," *Quarterly Journal of Economics*, 83 (November 1969): 600–624.

A good statement of the undesirable effects of growth is found in E. J. Mishan's *The Costs of Economic Growth* (London: Staples Press, 1967). Mishan presents the same arguments in slightly simplified form in *Growth: The Price we Pay* (London: Staples Press, 1969).

QUESTIONS

1. Explain the role that each of the following plays in the Domar growth model:
   (a) the propensity to save;
   (b) the supply of labor;
   (c) the capital-to-output ratio;
   (d) the rate of interest;
   (e) the rate of technological change;
   (f) business expectations.
2. Carefully consider the limitations of both the Domar and the neoclassical growth models with respect to policy formulation. For the types of problems faced by the United States economy today, which model do you feel can help most in policy making? Why?
3. (a) According to the neoclassical theory of economic growth, how will an increase in the rate of saving affect the rate of growth in the long run and in the short run? Explain.
   (b) How will an increase in the savings rate affect the equilibrium rate of growth in the Domar growth model?
4. Under certain circumstances, output per laborer and output per capita may fall.
   (a) With respect to the neoclassical model, under what conditions could this occur?
   (b) Do you think that this would now be unlikely to occur in the American economy? Why or why not?
5. In the neoclassical model that we have examined, the equilibrium rate of growth is independent of the rate of saving. How can this be possible?

6. What factors have contributed most to growth in the United States for the 1950–1962 period according to Denison? How does this differ from the Northwest European experience? Can you think of reasons why you might expect these differences to exist?
7. Explain the dual role that investment plays in the growth process. Discuss those policies that could be employed to bring the economy back into equilibrium if investment were growing too slowly.
8. Identify and discuss the problems related to estimating the contribution that technological change makes to the growth process.
9. Discuss the problems inherent in equating the level of national output with the level of national welfare.

IV
Part

PREDICTION

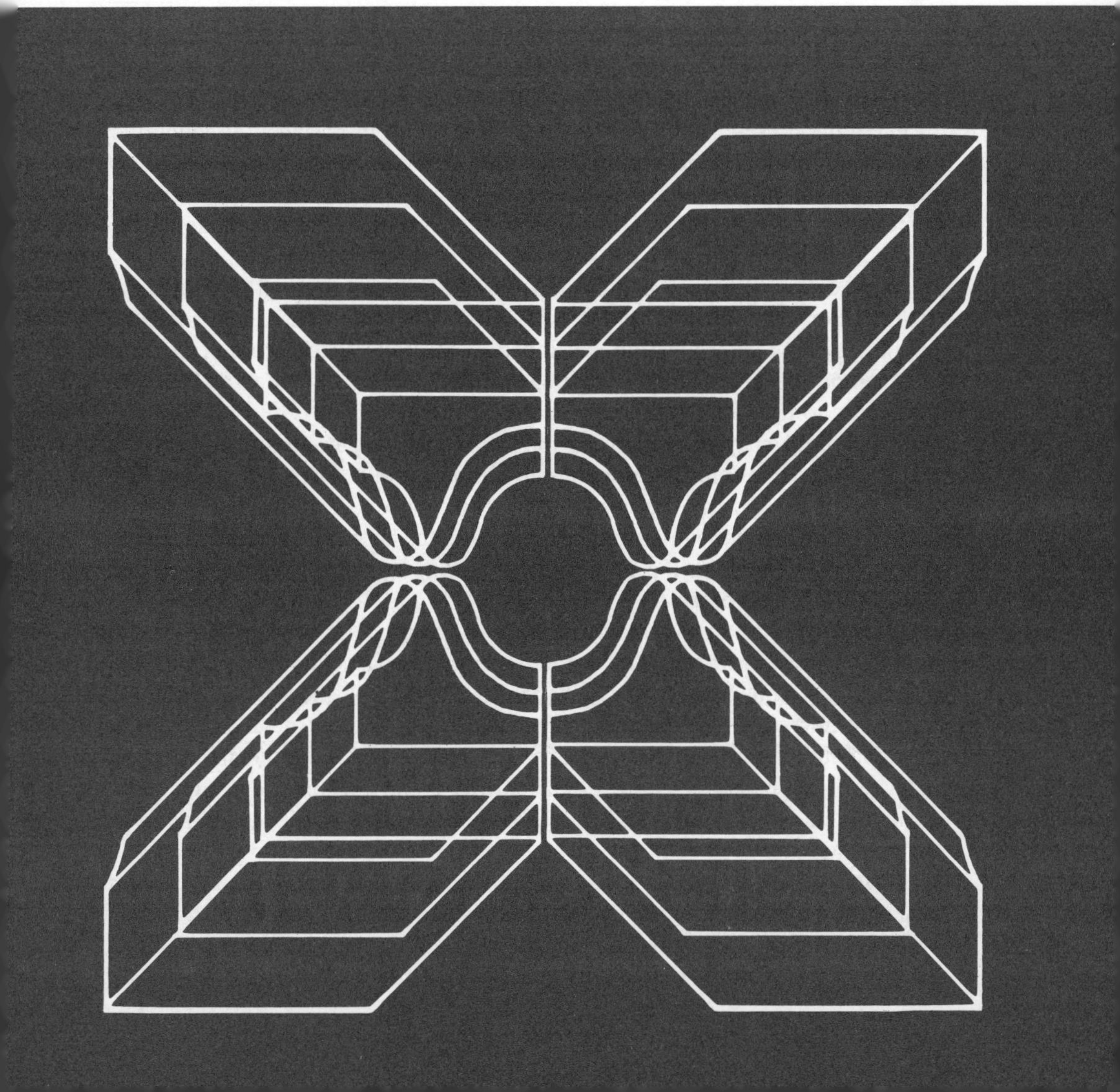

We begin Part IV with a brief discussion of selected business cycle theories and of the measurement and forecasting tools developed by the National Bureau of Economic Research. These tools are widely used in business, although they have been developed more out of historical observation than from theoretical reasoning. But the measurement of business fluctuations is crucial to our understanding of current fluctuations and our forecasting of future economic behavior. We need to know what happens when business fluctuates.

The second chapter in this part is about forecasting with econometric models. For our examples we draw directly upon the theoretical model of national income determination developed in the previous chapters of this text. We then provide very brief descriptions of more elaborate models to introduce the reader to the world of large econometric models.

The final chapter introduces the concept of input-output analysis that describes the interindustry relations in the economy. These lie behind, and are covered up by, the aggregation of income into consumption, investment, etc. To break down the industrial structure and see how it is affected by changes in aggregate demand is the purpose of this chapter. It concludes our all-too-brief discussion of forecasting.

Short-run prediction or forecasting is, simply, the construction of an operational statement regarding future events. It is particularly concerned with the direction and magnitude of change in certain specified target variables. Target variables for the macroeconomic policy maker may include the level of unemployment, the rate of change in the price level, and the international balance of payments position. For a participant in the private sector of the economy, they may include a firm's sales volume, its cash flow, and its profit performance.

Models for short-range forecasting may or may not have a causal content, or contain a systematic statement of the cause and effect relationships between variables. A model that does contain such a causal statement is usually based on both theory and experience; that is, it combines deductive logic with empirical observation. The previous sections of this book have been devoted to articulating a macro model that has been widely used retrospectively, that is, to describe or explain past short-term fluctuations in the aggregate economy. That model describes the interrelations between exogenous variables, policy instruments, and the endogenous variables of the economy. Within the constructs of that model, history has yielded a series of observations on the functional relationships expressing household and investment demand, the transactions and asset demands for money, costs, and output. The past is the basis for estimating coefficient values. To the extent that historical experience displays regularity and remains valid in the future, then such a model is predictive. However, large obstacles to the use of a forecasting model are introduced by irregularities in the past or by the relative novelty of a future event. Notwithstanding these considerations it is evident in the social sciences that interest in forecasting models with causal content has recently gained impetus. This is despite the fact that forecasting on a "scientific basis" remains in a very early stage of development.

Of course making a prediction does not require an elaborate scientific model. The alternative is usually described as "naive" forecasting. This approach is characterized by the application of simple mathematical rules and by the absence of a concise systematic view of the subject. Forecasts may be based on constant absolute increases, on a constant rate of growth in output, or on a rate of growth in output during period $t + 1$ assumed to be the same as that recorded for period t. Despite their simplicity, naive models *may* perform quite adequately.

It should be apparent by now that in our society certain variables are of prime concern to the policy maker. Among these the rate of unemployment and the rate of change in the price level rank high. But in dealing with these target variables the policy maker has to make decisions under conditions of uncertainty. Indeed, the presence of uncertainty is precisely the reason that forecasts are a necessary condition for making and executing policy decisions.

For policy making to be rational—in the sense that it contributes to and facilitates the attainment of social goals—the policy maker must consider the role of forecasting in the decision-making process. This role involves several steps.

(1) Prediction begins with the world as it now is and so requires knowledge of the present values of the relevant variables. In practice this requires the forecaster not only to know their current quantitative magnitudes, but also to evaluate currently relevant qualitative factors. Consideration of the qualitative is a means of probing for a rounded picture of the forces, including random disturbances, that determine the level of any variable. It is where judgment enters into forecasting, for knowledge of the present state of things is never perfect; it is inevitably incomplete and therefore characterized by a degree of uncertainty.

(2) For purposes of prediction, it is of key importance to divide the set of variables considered relevant for the task into those that the policy maker cannot control, but can only indirectly influence, and those over which he can

exert a direct control. For example, expenditures by households, the investment demand of private firms, and the level of interest rates can only be influenced indirectly by the policy maker. Our model has shown us that the primary policy variables are the monetary-fiscal levers: government expenditure, the rate of taxation, and the money supply. These are variables through which policy is exercised.

(3) Using a model, the policy maker can then proceed to make predictions regarding the course of the economy under alternative sets of assumptions regarding his own behavior. Thus he may assume no change in the currently recorded levels of the policy variables or he may alter these variables in several ways. In each instance he observes the course of the noncontrolled variables. A range of outcomes results showing changes in the controlled variables, and the accompanying changes in the noncontrolled, including the target, variables. Policy requires that a choice be made among all the available alternatives.

Business Fluctuations

18
Chapter

Recurrent periods of economic boom and depression have damaged economies throughout history. In preindustrial periods, of course, prosperity and poverty depended more upon good weather and good crops than upon the internal workings of the economy. After the Industrial Revolution, it became apparent that economies were repeatedly victimized by alternate periods of rapid economic expansion and severe economic depression just as agricultural economies before them had been buffeted by bumper crops and famine, although the causes of these fluctuations were much less easy to observe. Indeed, economists today still find that the best of their explanations are less than satisfactory.

The modern national income analysis developed throughout this book is essentially static; that is, it seeks to explain the determination of national income, but it does not describe the path of income as it varies over time. Monetary and fiscal policies may reverse the trend of inflation or depression, but they do not tell us what initiated these adverse phenomena.

Having found, from the complete Keynesian model, that monetary and fiscal authorities have the power to stabilize economic activity and avoid severe depression and inflation, many economists have lost interest in studying the more fundamental question of why such phenomena occur.[1] Economists are like medical men who, having found a simple remedy for the gout, lack interest in pursuing the reasons for the malfunctioning of the organs of the body that control the production and disposal of uric acid in the blood. There is a difference between a remedy for a malady and a cure for it, and if the remedy is easy to apply, interest in the malady subsides. Courses in the study of business cycles, formerly required for all students of economics, are now elective in most academic institutions if they are offered at all.

[1] "Monetarists," for instance, believe that all significant business cycles, other than "mild" variations in income, have been caused by variations in the money supply.

BUSINESS CYCLE THEORIES

Modern economic forecasters rely extensively not only upon elaborate econometric models of the sort to be described in Chapter 19, but also upon statistical indicators and indices that owe their origin to various theories of the business cycle.[2] Thus brief mention of the various types of business cycle theories is in order to set the stage for the description of cycle indicators. We will not offer detailed examinations of business cycle theories. Our purpose here is merely to introduce the subject of cycle theory and to suggest that forecasters are often greatly influenced by their beliefs in such theories. This influence is reflected in their forecasts.

Business cycle theories may be classified as (a) monetary vs. "real," (b) exogenous vs. endogenous, (c) overinvestment vs. underconsumption, (d) psychological, and (e) mixed. Category (e), of course, includes most theories of the complete cycle, for most of them draw upon a variety of forces in describing economic fluctuations.

A Monetary Explanation of the Cycle

One monetary theory of the cycle was put forward by R. G. Hawtrey, who argued that increases in short-term interest rates would trigger a chain reaction leading to recession. At any point in time, "traders" or "merchants" hold sizable inventories. The principal cost of holding these is the short-term interest charges that traders must pay the banks. If interest rates rise, the charge for holding inventories rises and this leads merchants to allow sales without replacement in order to let inventories decrease. But this means new orders decline too, and this is followed by a decline in manufacturing activity, an increase in unemployment, and a decline in factor incomes. With declining income, sales fall off and inventories build up, which leads to further reduction of new orders and further cutbacks in production. According to Hawtrey, the process is reversed only when interest rates become low enough to encourage traders to expand orders leading to resurgence of activity.

The Hawtrey cycle is sometimes called an "inventory" cycle. The reason short-term interest rates rise initially is that banks are fully-loaned. Thus the monetary system is the culprit, and Hawtrey's view is classed as a monetary theory explaining the cycle in inventories.

Does an inventory cycle exist? The data clearly do show periodic fluctuations in inventories. The "change in inventories" is a category under the heading of investment spending in the national product accounts. Insofar as inventories increased last quarter, output was produced but was not consumed;

[2] The interested student should examine the relevant literature: Edward J. Chambers, *Economic Fluctuations and Forecasting* (Englewood Cliffs, N.J.: Prentice-Hall, 1963); Alvin H. Hansen, *Business Cycles and National Income* (New York: Norton, 1951); Louis A. Dow, *Business Fluctuations in a Dynamic Economy* (Columbus, Ohio: Charles E. Merrill, 1968); Carl A. Dauten, *Business Cycles and Forecasting*, 2nd ed. (Cincinnati: South-Western, 1961); Robert A. Gordon, *Business Fluctuations*, 2nd ed. (New York: Harper & Row. 1961); and Gottfried Haberler, *Prosperity and Depression*, 3rd ed. (United Nations, 1946).

instead, it was added to the stock of wealth. Hence increased inventories are part of investment spending. Over the past several years the change in inventories in the U.S. has fluctuated between minus two and plus ten billion dollars annually. On occasion, when additions to inventories have declined by, say, four billion dollars and GNP has also declined by four billion dollars, analysts say "We're in an inventory recession." Then they note that expansion can be expected to follow the period of inventory decline.

But while the data clearly show an inventory cycle, the *origin* of the cycle is not clear. Hawtrey contended that changing short-term interest rates cause the inventory oscillation, but alternative explanations are just as reasonable—or more so. If long-term investment spending falls, then employment falls as wage-earners' income is down, consumption spending falls, and inventories build up on the supermarket shelves. This leads merchants to cut back on new orders and allow inventories to decline so as to be commensurate with the new and lower level of expected sales. Hence inventories rise at first but eventually fall as a result of a cutback in long-term investment spending; what appears as an inventory recession is in fact a "fixed-investment" recession.[3]

Keynes did not articulate a cycle theory, although he did devote a chapter of his *General Theory* to "Notes on the Trade Cycle." He indicated that he attributed most oscillation in income to the instability in long-term business investment spending, and he felt that the long-term interest rate, not the short-term rate, was the more relevant rate to observe in analyzing business fluctuations. Thus Hawtrey's explanation of the cycle may be criticized.

The important point to note here, however, is that series of data on *new orders* are used in forecasting economic activity. Upswings in new orders are typically followed by upswings in general economic activity. The consistency with which this has been true over many cycles in the past suggests that economic forecasters can ignore a changing pattern of new orders only with trepidation.

Over-Investment Cycle Theories

In contrast with the readily observable fluctuations in inventory levels, we sometimes find that fixed investment spending by business fluctuates widely. For example, the economic boom of 1956–1957 in the United States was called an "investment" boom by most analysts. That is, investment spending by businessmen led to over-full employment. Data on macroeconomic events during the period clearly show that investment spending on construction, plant, and equipment exceeded normal values.

Keynes felt that businessmen were subject to waves of optimism and pessimism that set off the chain reactions in spending and employment that give rise to booms and depressions. Keynes did not develop a theory of the cycle based on over-investment. Indeed, he criticized those who did by arguing

[3] For a complete discussion of this point, see Hansen, *Business Cycles and National Income.*

that if excess capacity were created by over-investment, the simple solution to the matter would be to promote expansionary monetary and fiscal policy, so that excess capacity would shortly disappear. In arguing this, he responded in essence to over-investment theories such as those articulated by Hayek and Schumpeter.

F. A. Hayek developed an elaborate and complicated explanation of the business cycle. At the base of his reasoning was the recognition that businessmen make investment decisions and that consumers make savings decisions. These are two entirely different groups of people. Yet, in the end, the amount of real saving that is done must equal the amount of investment that takes place. His analysis, then, concerned the structural problems that arise in the economy when savings decisions differ widely from investment decisions. If businessmen decide to expand their plant capacity, and if consumers do not increase their savings rate, then both business and consumers are competing for scarce resources. Prices rise and society is "forced" to save because consumers' incomes will simply not command the delivery of goods at higher prices. Banks continue to offer funds to expanding businesses and more capital is constructed. "Capital deepening" of the processes of production takes place. But this elongation of the structure of production is not sustainable. The additional investment spending causes money incomes to rise, accompanied by a rise in consumption expenditures. This rise in the demand for consumption goods increases the need for scarce resources and drives up the cost of capital goods production. In addition, the rate of bank credit expansion cannot be maintained indefinitely. In Hayek's view, the rising cost of capital goods and the reduction in the rate of credit expansion inevitably lead to a collapse as businessmen find their investment is not sustainable.

This is the most cursory treatment of Hayek's thesis and hardly does it justice. The point to note is simply that business investment spending plans are closely watched by economic forecasters. These plans may foreshadow a boom or a recession, for a rapid upswing in investment spending may lead to an upward spiral in economic activity, and a decline in investment may lead to a downward spiral.

Joseph A. Schumpeter was the author of another "over-investment" theory of the business cycle. The key actor in his theory was the entrepreneur, who, in his view, is not just a business manager; he is rather an innovator who introduces new inventions, new products, and new organizational schemes or develops new markets or new deposits of natural resources. He is, in other words, the one primarily responsible for economic growth. Many entrepreneurs may fail in their risky ventures, but often enough a winner appears. He makes huge profits, the lure of which draws a continuous stream of would-be entrepreneurial talent. This incentive mechanism, according to Schumpeter, is the key to economic growth and without it development will wane to the detriment of the average citizen whose standard of living will then stagnate.

The business cycle, in Schumpeter's view, is the natural result of a world with strong entrepreneurial incentive. It is an unavoidable by-product of an economy that grows and prospers. A "host of imitators" are drawn to a successful innovation. They are attracted to profits like moths to a candle. The result is excessive investment. Profits are driven out as excess capacity is created and this leads to a period of business failure and depression.

Schumpeter examined economic history in detail to cast light on his views. In the United States, the 1870s and 1880s were undoubtedly the golden age of railroads; a few entrepreneurs became very wealthy and imitators built railroads all over the country; but in the end many railroad companies failed from overexpansion. The 1910s and 1920s saw the development of the automobile; Ford, Olds, and others became rich, but countless others failed in the 1930s and 1940s. The 1950s and 1960s could be called the golden age of electronics and the computer, and so on. The "innovator" theory of cycles has thus stimulated economists to search for developments in particular industries and segments of the economy. Active forecasters try to keep abreast of new markets and new methods and the magnitude of the impact they make when introduced.

The Acceleration Principle and Multiplier-Accelerator Interaction

No discussion of business cycle theories would be complete without some mention of the acceleration principle. This principle, described as a stock-adjustment model in Chapter 5, concerns the relation between the demand for consumers' goods and the demand for the producers' equipment used in the production of consumers' goods. It may be best seen if we consider a situation where 10 machines operating at capacity each produce 1000 units of cloth each year, for a total output of 10,000 units, and in the normal course of events one of the 10 machines wears out each year and must be replaced. Thus the normal demand for cloth is 10,000 units and the normal demand for machines is 1 unit. An increase in consumer demand of 10 percent, to 11,000 units of cloth, would require the capacity operation of 11 machines. Therefore, in the year that consumer demand increased 10 percent, the producer would purchase one machine for replacement and one to add to his stock of 10 machines. The producer of *machines* would find the demand for his output increased by 100 percent. If consumer demand returned to its previous level the following year, then in that year it would not be necessary even to replace a worn-out machine, let alone purchase a new one. Thus the producer of machines would close his shop for lack of orders. Economic activity in the capital goods industries oscillates widely in response to relatively small changes in demand expressed in the consumers' goods industries. This is, in essence, the "acceleration principle."

The conceptual framework of the acceleration principle is intuitively pleasing. It also fits one's casual observation that capital goods industries are less stable than consumers' goods industries, which is to say that investment spending fluctuates with greater amplitude over a cycle than consumer spending does.

In equation form the principle may be expressed as $I_t = a(C_t - C_{t-1})$, where I_t represents the investment spending in the current period that is induced by the accelerator, a, the coefficient of the change in consumption spending, C, from the previous period to the current period.

This accelerator can be combined with the simple multiplier to reveal an interaction between the two.[4] If $C_t = b(Y_{t-1})$ we say that current consumption is some fixed proportion of income in the previous period. By substituting this consumption function in the formula for the accelerator we have:

$$I_t = a(bY_{t-1} - bY_{t-2}) \qquad (18.1)$$

Therefore, since $Y_t = C_t + I_t + G_t$ it follows that $Y_t = (1 + a)bY_{t-1} - abY_{t-2} + G_t$. If government spending is set at a given level, then current income can be determined by the incomes recorded in the two previous periods. A change in G will stimulate oscillations in Y which may be explosive, constant, or damped, according to the sizes of the coefficients b and a. If one imagines an economy subjected to a variety of random shocks, then this multiplier-accelerator model can help explain why a cyclical pattern in income may follow.

The model can be criticized on a number of different grounds: It must be set in motion by unexplained exogenous shocks to the system; it contains no allowance for adjustments in interest rates or prices of consumers' goods and investment goods that would reduce the sensitivity of investment to changes in the strength of consumer demand; it has consumption as a function of lagged income instead of current income, permanent income, or relative income; and, finally, it is surely oversimplified, for economic fluctuations never follow the symmetrical pattern suggested by the model. Accordingly, it cannot and should not be used as a forecasting tool by itself, although insight into the forces described can furnish more of the understanding necessary for effective forecasting.

CYCLE FORECASTING AND MEASUREMENT

Business cycles were first described in the late nineteenth century by Joseph Clement Juglar, a French physician who turned his attention from the wave-like patterns of population, births, and marriages to the similar wave-like patterns of certain financial data on prices and interest rates. He concluded that a business cycle of about 10 years duration existed and that the cause of any depression is to be found in the preceding prosperity.

Subsequently, in 1923, Joseph Kitchin published the results of a closer look at the data and noted the appearance of a 40-month cycle. He concluded that the "major" or "Juglar" cycle consisted of two or three "minor" cycles. Later still, Nicolas Kondratieff, a Russian economist, collected and analyzed—using a nine-year moving average—data that seemed to establish the existence of a cycle with a duration of about 50 years. These have been called "long

[4] See Paul A. Samuelson, "Interaction between the multiplier analysis and the principle of acceleration," *Review of Economic Statistics*, 21 (May 1939): 75–78.

waves" in business activity, and he believed they were inherent in the capitalistic system. His data have been challenged, however, and in any case the time period covered is too long to be of serious interest to the economic forecaster.

There is, however, another type of cycle, or "sub-cycle," of great interest to forecasters. These are cycles that are related to particular industries and that seem to run out of phase with the general cycle reported by the National Bureau of Economic Research (NBER). For example, the cotton textile industry seems to have a cycle lasting about 18 months. In contrast, the construction industry appeared to have a cycle of 15 to 20 years in the period between 1850 and 1945. Since World War II, however, financial regulation in the U.S., under the control of the Federal Reserve Bank (Regulation Q), has tended to cut off the flow of funds into mortgage construction in boom periods and then make them available in recessions, so that building has tended to show a countercyclical pattern. The point is that the evidence on general business activity may not help one to forecast specific business activity. It is the job of the business forecaster to examine the evidence to see whether his business pattern is, or is not, closely aligned with that of the general business indicators.

Measurement of the Business Cycle

In the 1920s and 1930s, under the stewardship of Wesley Clair Mitchell, the NBER set itself a monumental task—that of recording the events that accompany business fluctuations in order to uncover, if possible, systematic tendencies that would be useful in forecasting. With no clear theoretical understanding of the causes of business fluctuations, it was hoped that by careful examination of what happens in business cycles some light could be cast upon this complex subject. Reasoning by induction, rather than deduction, was the scientific frame of reference.

Someone once suggested that astronomers could plot the stars forever and yet fail to discover the laws of motion that Newton constructed. Perhaps plotting the business cycle is fruitless too, and this criticism has been leveled at this part of the work of the NBER.[5] The criticism is well taken, but one does not throw away well-digested information solely on the grounds that it is not likely ever to generate a comprehensive theoretical explanation of economic events. Forecasters today, therefore, look to the NBER for information about developing business cycles and for announcements that past periods constituted recession periods by their definition in terms of their unique manner of recording economic events.

Our brief description below concerns (a) measurement techniques, (b) leading indicators, and (c) diffusion indices. These three topics hardly reflect all the extensive efforts of the NBER's researchers, but they do introduce the

[5] Wesley C. Mitchell, *What Happens During Business Cycles* (New York: National Bureau of Economic Research, 1951); Arthur F. Burns and W. C. Mitchell, *Measuring Business Cycles* (New York: NBER, 1946); Geoffrey H. Moore (Ed.), *Business Cycle Indicators* (Princeton, N.J.: Princeton University Press, 1961); Julius Shiskin, "Signals of recession and recovery," NBER Occasional Paper No. 77 (October 1961); and "Business cycle indicators, the known and the unknown," *Review*, International Statistical Institute, Ottawa, Canada, Vol. 31, No. 3.

student to some important and widely known topics of concern to economists engaged in forecasting.

Measurement Techniques

The research staff of the NBER carefully examined over one thousand economic time series for evidence of cyclical behavior. These series were smoothed by moving averages in order to damp the random fluctuations and clarify the patterns of movement over time. Approximately four hundred series were found to have cyclical patterns that correspond roughly with variations in general economic activity, some of which appear to match the Juglar and Kitchin cycles.[6]

After dividing the year into quarters, each series was examined to see if it reached a peak or a trough in a particular quarter. In this way the percentage of series reaching a peak and the percentage of series reaching a trough was recorded for each quarter by plotting the percentages in a histogram, as in the hypothetical one of Figure 18–1. The bunching of peaks and troughs then becomes evident, and most of the time it is easy to choose a period (or quarter) that approximately can be called a peak period and another that can be called a trough period. Thus, the essence of NBER cycle measurement is the *timing* or dating of the cycle. Economic forecasters routinely plot time series data with the period between the peak and the trough shaded in order to indicate a period of economic recession.

Having chosen the peaks and troughs, the period for a complete cycle is divided arbitrarily into nine stages, as depicted in Figure 18–2. Stage I is the trough period, stage II the period of increasing expansion, stage III the period

Figure 18–1.

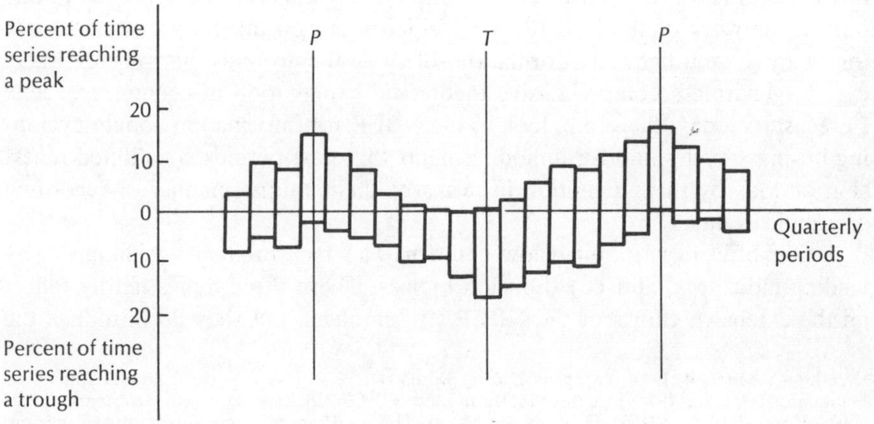

[6] For a description of the chronology of business cycles in five countries, see E. J. Chambers, *Economic Fluctuations and Forecasting*, pp. 42–43.

Figure 18–2.

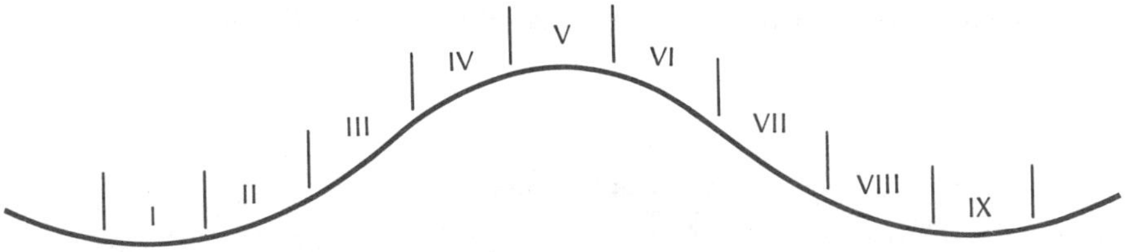

in which the rate of expansion is greatest, and stage IV the period in which the rate of expansion begins to slow just prior to the peaking-out indicated in stage V. A similar series of developments occur in the downswing culminating in the trough of stage IX which also, of course, is stage I of the subsequent cycle.[7]

As depicted, the stages appear uniform, but unfortunately actual business conditions do not oscillate in a smooth rhythm over time. While conditions vary from good to bad, they do not vary with constant periodicity. Most economists would agree that it is more accurate to speak of "business fluctuations" than it is to speak of "business cycles" because of the rhythmic motion implied in the latter term.

The timing of booms and recessions gives no indication of the severity of the recession or strength of the boom. That is, cycles have amplitudes as well as durations. A so-called boom may last a very long time but be weak over the entire period. Thus from the trough of the first quarter of 1961, business expanded into 1970, but the rate of unemployment remained above 4 percent from 1961 through 1965—five full years.

Leading Indicators

Having designated the turning points, the peaks and troughs of business activity, NBER analysts set about the task of examining the hundreds of series to see if they could find any series that consistently turned down before the peak and consistently turned up before the trough. Their search bore fruit. Today some 36 such series are kept up to date and reported in *Business Conditions Digest*, a publication of the Bureau of Economic Analysis in the U.S. Department of Commerce under the direction of a committee whose members are drawn from the Departments of the Treasury, Labor, and Commerce, the Federal Reserve Board, and the Council of Economic Advisors.

By "eyeballing" the patterns of the twelve series shown in Figure 18–3, one can note that these series tend to show downturns prior to the recording of a peak in general economic activity (indicated by the beginning of each shaded area; the shaded areas themselves denote periods of recession). These twelve series also have a tendency to turn up prior to the trough.

[7] The student of calculus will recognize that the stages can be identified in terms of the signs of first and second derivatives.

Figure 18–3. The NBER Short List of Leading Indicators.

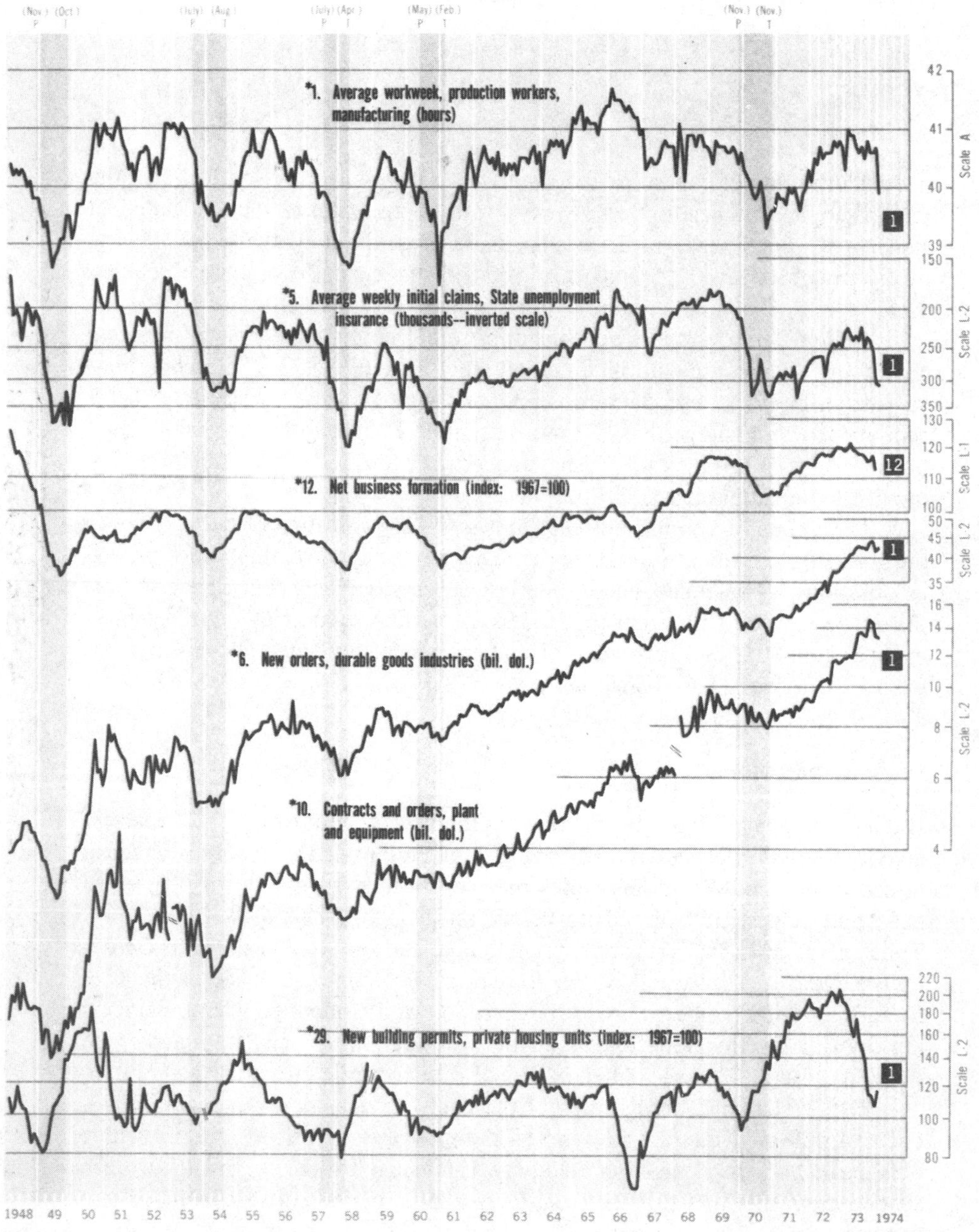

Source: Reprinted from Business Conditions Digest (February 1974), pp. 39–40.

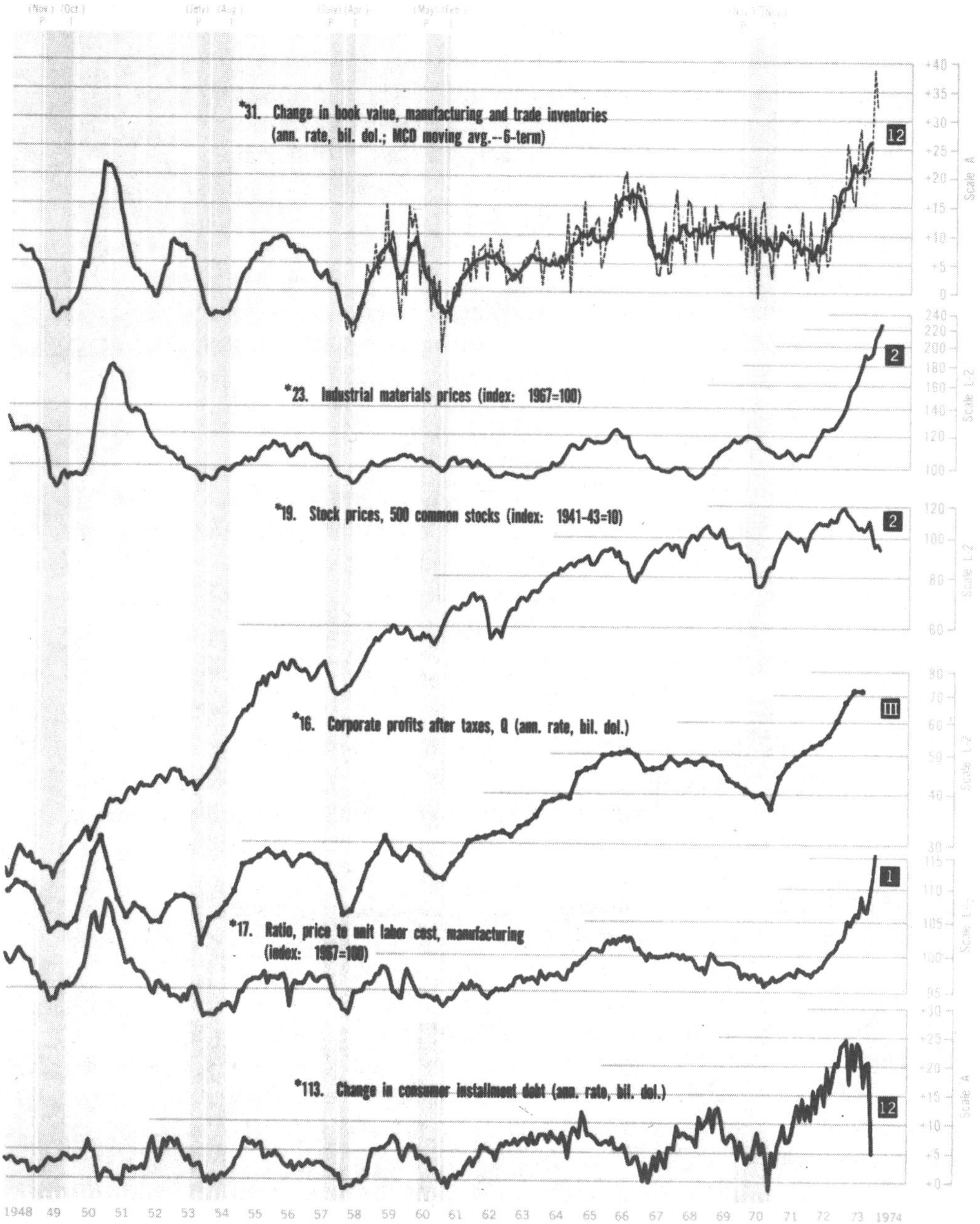
(Nov.) (Oct.)
P T
(July) (Aug.)
P T
(July) (Apr.)
P T
(May) (Feb.)
P T
(Nov.) (Nov.)
P T
*31. Change in book value, manufacturing and trade inventories
(ann. rate, bil. dol.; MCD moving avg.--6-term)
12
Scale A
*23. Industrial materials prices (index: 1967=100)
2
Scale L-2
*19. Stock prices, 500 common stocks (index: 1941-43=10)
2
Scale L-2
*16. Corporate profits after taxes, Q (ann. rate, bil. dol.)
III
Scale L-2
*17. Ratio, price to unit labor cost, manufacturing
(index: 1967=100)
1
*113. Change in consumer installment debt (ann. rate, bil. dol.)
12
Scale A
1948 49 50 51 52 53 54 55 56 57 58 59 60 61 62 63 64 65 66 67 68 69 70 71 72 73 1974

The indicators come from diverse sectors of the economy. The first two listed, the records of the average work week of production workers and the average weekly initial claims for state unemployment insurance, relate to employment. The next series is an index of net new business formation. Three more series concern new investment: new orders for durable goods, contracts and orders for plant and equipment, and new building permits for private housing units. The seventh series relates to manufacturing and trade inventories and the change in their book value. The next four series relate to prices, costs, and profits and include the index of prices of 500 common stocks. The final series is chosen from the category of money and credit and depicts the pattern of changes in consumer installment debt. (*Business Conditions Digest* also contains a single composite index—Chart B7—derived by pooling these twelve indicators.)

The figures show that the leading indicators begin to decline several periods before the peak is registered, although they have also signaled downturns when no peak followed, as in 1951, 1956, 1959, 1962, and 1966. Thus they appear to have signaled recession in these five years when no recession followed as well as signaling recession prior to the five that did occur. But the consistency of the leading indicators is better than this record seems to suggest because, while no recession occurred in the five listed years as measured by the NBER, these declining indicators *did* lead either declines or slow-downs in the *rate of increase* of such general measures of the level of economic activity as GNP and the industrial production index. According to the NBER techniques, real GNP must decline for at least two quarters (close, but not necessarily sequential, quarters) before a recession is declared (other factors, and their severity, are also considered). Thus, if it fails to *grow*, this is not a recession in some technical sense, although it may mean unutilized resources exist. Perhaps a period in which the rate of growth of GNP is below some long-term trend rate should be called a recession period in the sense that potential output is not being achieved. If this criterion were established for the leading indicators, their record of consistently accurate predictions would be truly astounding.

Besides the leading indicators, the analysts have also spotlighted "coincident" and "lagging" indicators. The broad indicators such as GNP, retail sales in industrial production, employment, wholesale prices, and bond yields are all classified under the heading of roughly coincident indicators. These series, of course, represent the important variables of income, employment, price levels, and interest rates that played the crucial roles in the theory of macroeconomics developed throughout the early chapters of this book. (The series measuring a six-month moving average of changes in the money supply has been listed as one of the 36 leading indicators.)

Diffusion Indices

Figure 18–4 contains four "diffusion" indices, each of which records the percent of the total number of components of a series that is rising. For example,

Figure 18–4. Four NBER Diffusion Indicators.

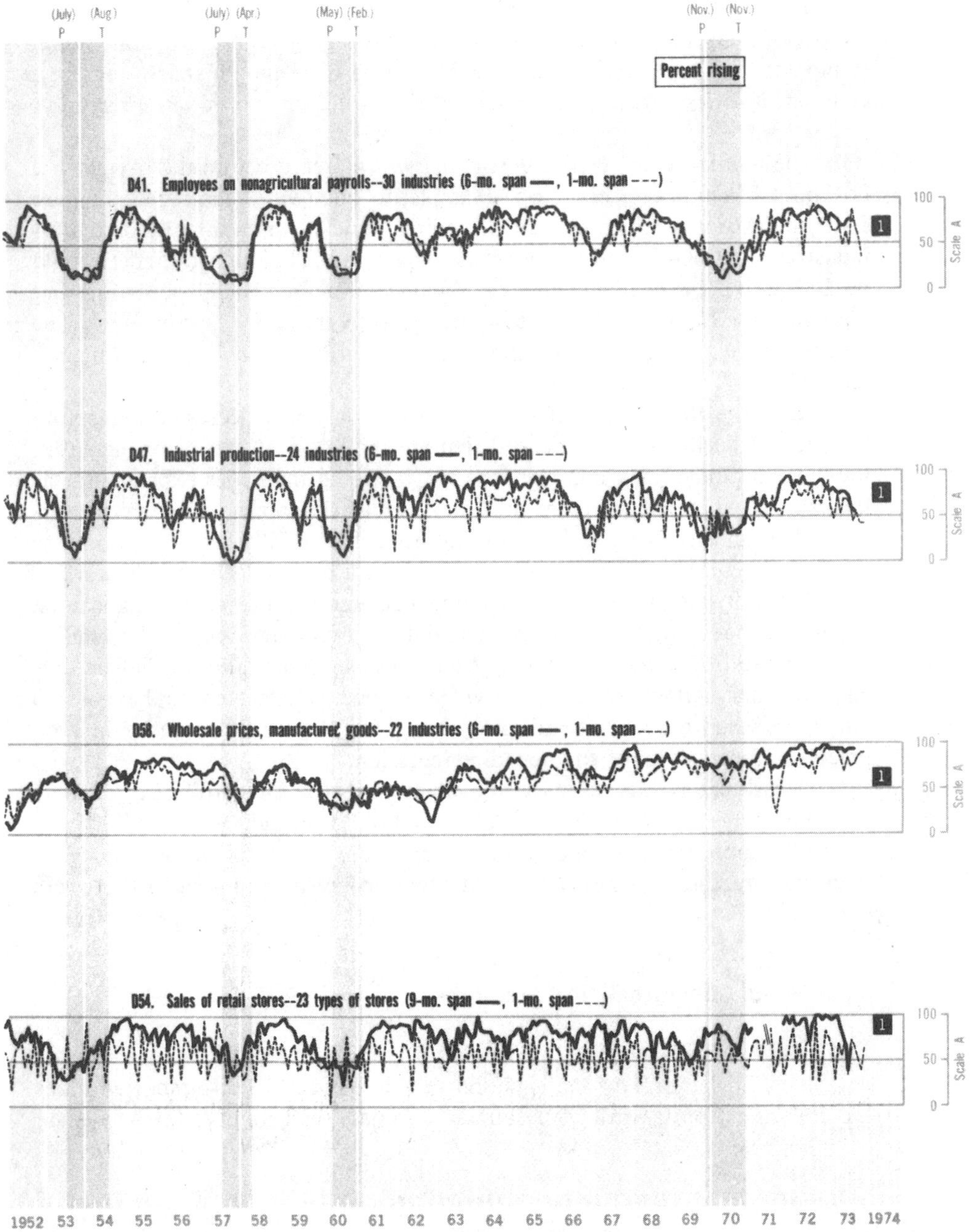

Source: Reprinted from Business Conditions Digest (February 1974), p. 64.

the second series, D47, shows the industrial production index, made up by averaging the indices of 24 separate industries. To compute a diffusion index, one notes how many of the 24 individual series increased from the last period to the current period. If 12 rose, then the diffusion index would show 50 percent rising; if 18 rose, it would show 75 percent rising; and so forth. Diffusion indices calculated in this manner tend to be very jagged if observed from month to month; they are therefore smoothed by using a six-month span—that is, a component series is recorded as "rising" if it is higher than it was six months previously.[8]

The number of industries expanding will increase before the trough in a downturn is actually reached. For example, in stage VII of the cycle in Figure 18–2, industrial production may be falling rapidly, with, say, 18 of the 24 industries contracting and the other six expanding. The diffusion index would be 25. As the cycle moves into stage VIII, contraction is still occurring, but perhaps only 16 of the 24 are contracting, with the other 8 expanding. The diffusion index is then 33, and the index has turned up before the trough is reached.

Similarly, the number of industries expanding will decrease well before the peak in business is experienced. During the midst of expansion, stage III, the diffusion index may register close to 100 as all industries expand. But as the peak is approached, more and more industries realize they have overexpanded, and as they cut back the diffusion index falls before the peak is reached. Therefore, diffusion indices tend to be a type of leading indicator.[9]

The diffusion indices illustrated are calculated from coincident indicators. Again, they recorded downturns in about the same fashion as the leading indicators did. *Business Conditions Digest* also presents diffusion indices calculated from certain indicators. Evidently, one is expected to be able to anticipate when the leading indicators are going to turn down and gain even greater advance notice of an impending recession.

Unfortunately it is not easy to evaluate the "track record" of forecasters who have relied upon leading indicators and diffusion indices. Indeed, if forecasters became proficient and effective steps were taken to iron out the cycle, then the forecasters themselves would prove to be in error—when they were perfect!

Surveys and Other Analytical Measures

Business Conditions Digest also contains a number of series of data from surveys, including several on "anticipations and intentions." These reported series are collected from a variety of sources. business expenditures for new plant

[8] See E. J. Chambers, *Economic Fluctuations and Forecasting,* Chapter 13.

[9] The percent rising tends to resemble the rate of change. Thus in calculus, if a smooth cycle is examined, the rate of increase begins to diminish and becomes zero as the function slows its increase and reaches a peak. Calculating a diffusion index is like taking the first derivative of the aggregate function, and diffusion index construction seems to reflect belief in a business "cycle."

and equipment from the Securities and Exchange Commission; contracts and orders for plant and equipment from the McGraw-Hill Information Systems Company; newly approved capital appropriations from the National Industrial Conference Board (now known as The Conference Board); indices of consumer sentiment from the Survey Research Center, University of Michigan; freight carloadings from the Association of American Railroads; new orders in manufacturing from Dun and Bradstreet, Inc.; and so forth.

The attention paid to survey data and their widespread use in major news media indicate that an economic forecaster can hardly ignore their existence. Their acceptance among the lay public means that if he disagrees with the outlook they suggest he must explain away their importance.

CONCLUSION

The data we examine today—provided to us because of their relevance to forecasting economic conditions—are offered by the agencies that compile them largely because in years past some economic theorist offered the profession a cycle theory that suggested certain data be collected. To understand the relevance of such data, therefore, it is important to have at least a passing acquaintance with the sort of theories that produced them. This we have attempted to provide in this chapter.

We also examined two of the forecasting methods that were developed by the National Bureau of Economic Research—leading indicators and diffusion indices. Forecasters often use these indicators either as the basis for their forecasts or to verify or support their forecasts derived by other techniques. No discussion of economic forecasting would be complete without some mention of business cycle theory and measurement and the techniques used by the NBER.

ADDITIONAL READINGS

Business Economics, a quarterly publication of the National Association of Business Economists, contains regular reviews of forecasts and discussions of measurement and forecasting techniques.

Widely used texts and references include Alvin H. Hansen, *Business Cycles and National Income* (New York: Norton, 1951); *Business Cycles and Their Causes* (Berkeley: University of California Press, 1941); Carl A. Dauten and Lloyd M. Valentine, *Business Cycles and Forecasting*, 3rd ed. (Smith-Weston Publishing Co., 1968); John P. Lewis, *Business Conditions Analysis* (New York: McGraw-Hill, 1959); Robert A. Gordon, *Business Fluctuations*, 2nd ed. (New York: Harper & Row, 1961); E. J. Chambers, *Economic Fluctuations and Forecasting* (Englewood Cliffs, N.J.: Prentice-Hall, 1961); and Louis A. Dow, *Business Fluctuations in a Dynamic Economy* (Columbus, Ohio: Charles E. Merrill, 1968).

QUESTIONS

1. Briefly outline the sequence of events in (a) Hawtrey's theory of the business cycle, (b) Hayek's theory, and (c) Schumpeter's theory.
2. Describe the construction of the NBER's "reference cycle."
3. What is a diffusion index? Give an example.
4. Obtain a recent issue of *Business Conditions Digest* from the library and interpret the current status of the leading indicators.

Forecasting with Econometric Models

19
Chapter

The better we understand the interrelations between economic variables, the better we can forecast or predict the impact of changes in the economic environment that follow exogenous shocks to the system. Ability to forecast is highly desirable if man is to improve his control over his own economic destiny. Government economists must forecast income and income tax receipts in order to make up the budget for the coming year; and budgets are necessary if national priorities are to be given expression and social and political programs are to be pursued in the public interest. Business economists must forecast economic conditions so that business management can minimize costs of production by arranging production to meet demand. Both business and government economists must thus collect and analyze data on economic conditions on a continuous basis.

Not only is forecasting important for routine planning by business and government, but it is also crucial for the exercise of effective monetary and fiscal policies. Most of this book has focused upon our understanding of macroeconomic relations. In the previous chapter we saw that our economy is subject to fluctuations in business activity and employment, and it is the avowed purpose of policy makers to introduce policies that will stabilize the economy. Policy makers can, of course, wait until a downturn is clearly under way and then respond with expansionary policies, but only to the extent that they can forecast accurately will they be able to halt the downturn. Instead of correcting a bad situation they wish to prevent it from occurring. If a forecast is good, they want to act so to make it come true, but if it is bad, they want to make it false.

If we begin from a position of relatively full employment and money income, Y, rises sharply, this will result mostly in inflation—the sharper the rise in Y the worse the inflation, and, since inflation is clearly undesirable, the greater the public's unhappiness. We can call this unhappiness the public's *disutility*. Similarly, a fall in money income will lead to unemployment—and again the public will suffer disutility—the larger the fall in Y the greater the unemployment and the greater the public's disutility. Thus the greater the swings in money income (the greater their amplitude over time), the worse off the people will be.

Swings in government spending also have their disadvantages. Large cuts in G may require some desirable social services to be halted, and large increases in G in a short period of time are likely to result in costly and wasteful programs.

Therefore, if we wish to stabilize Y and if we use changes in G to bring about a more stable Y, it is important to have accurate forecasts of Y. If we simply let Y fall and after the fact try to counter the fall with a large increase in G, then the amplitude of both G and Y will be larger and will result in more social disutility than would be the case if we forecast the change in Y and then use smaller changes in G to stabilize the economy. A similar argument holds for monetary policy as well. Therefore, forecasting is important if our stabilization policies are to be pursued in an efficient manner—one that avoids disruptions.[1]

ECONOMETRIC MODELS

In recent years, economists have placed increasing emphasis on the use of econometric models in their analyses of economic conditions. Therefore, this chapter is devoted principally to a description of a very oversimplified econometric model so that the reader may gain an intuitive grasp of what the technique involves. An econometric model consists of a set of empirically estimated functional relations—estimates of the theoretical equations we have specified in our model of income determination.

Econometric forecasts are scientific forecasts; that is, they are defined in terms of a long list of assumptions and conditions, few of which ever appear when the press reports the "meat" of a forecast. For example, most forecasts assume implicitly that no war will break out to disturb the economy, or that a war will continue at a particular level, or that major labor disputes resulting in strikes in, say, the automobile or steel industry will not occur. Often, if the threat of a strike or war is real, alternative forecasts will be presented to the public—one conditional upon its absence. Except for major events such as wars or strikes, the all-inclusive conditional clause, "*If the economy operates as it has done in the past*, then . . . ," is implicit. By collecting and analyzing statistical evidence from previous periods and observing how statistical series fit together, economists project the data into future periods.

The *IS-LM* Model

The *IS* curve, described in Chapter 7, was formed by combining a consumption function, an investment demand function, a tax function, and an import func-

[1] C. C. Holt articulates the above proposition in his paper "Linear decision rules for economic stabilization and growth," *Quarterly Journal of Economics*, 76 (February 1962): 20–45.

tion into one equation relating income to government spending, exports, and the interest rate. In linear form that *IS* function may be written as:

$$Y = \alpha + \beta R + \gamma G \tag{19.1}$$

where G stands here for the sum of government spending and exports.

The *LM* curve, described in Chapters 8 and 9, is composed of the transactions demand and liquidity demand for money. In linear form it may be written as:

$$R = \alpha' + \beta' Y + \gamma' M_s \tag{19.2}$$

In this two-equation model of the economy there are two dependent variables, Y and R, and two exogenous or independent variables, M_s and G.[2] By examining historical data on Y, R, M_s and G, statistical estimates of the coefficients, α, β, etc., can be obtained, as outlined in Chapter 10. The first step in the process consists of putting the two equations into "reduced form." This means that, by substitution, each dependent variable is made a function of exogenous variables only. By substituting equation (19.2) into equation (19.1), we get:

$$Y = \alpha + \beta(\alpha' + \beta' Y + \gamma' M_s) + \gamma G \tag{19.3}$$

$$Y = \frac{\alpha + \beta\alpha'}{1 - \beta\beta'} + \frac{\beta\gamma' M_s}{1 - \beta\beta'} + \frac{\gamma}{1 - \beta\beta'} G \tag{19.4}$$

Similarly, by substituting equation (19.1) into (19.2):

$$R = \alpha' + \beta'(\alpha + \beta R + \gamma G) + \gamma' M_s \tag{19.5}$$

$$R = \frac{\alpha' + \beta'\alpha}{1 - \beta\beta'} + \frac{\beta'\gamma}{1 - \beta\beta'} G + \frac{\gamma'}{1 - \beta\beta'} M_s \tag{19.6}$$

The coefficients in equations (19.4) and (19.6) can then be simplified:

$$Y = A + BM_s + CG \tag{19.7}$$

$$R = A' + B'G + C'M_s \tag{19.8}$$

From equation (19.7) the dependent variable, income, is a linear function of the two exogenous variables M_s and G, and from equation (19.8) the interest rate is also a function of these two exogenous variables. This is the form of the model appropriate for forecasting.

By least squares multiple regression techniques, the following formulas were estimated from data on the U.S. economy.[3]

[2] We are making the a priori assumption that M_s and G are exogenous and not dependent variables. Of course, some parts of G are functionally related to income, and M_s is not completely independent of the interest rate. But for expository purposes our assumption of exogenous G and M_s is useful.

[3] Quarterly data from 1951 through 1967, seasonally adjusted, were used. Income is gross national product; the money supply includes currency in circulation, demand deposits, and time deposits; the interest rate used was the AAA corporate bond yield and G stands for all government spending plus exports of goods and services. See R. H. Scott, "The marginal propensity to import: Estimates derived from a Hicksian model," *Malayan Economic Review*, 15 (April 1970): 120–125.

$$Y = 2.692 + \underset{(.225)}{1.352M_s} + \underset{(.319)}{1.525G} \tag{19.9}$$

$$R = 2.117 + \underset{(.006)}{.038G} - \underset{(.004)}{.014M_s} \tag{19.10}$$

These formulas are used here for expository purposes only, for not only are the data they contain out of date, but other variables and other regression forms give better forecasting results. An intuitive grasp of what is involved in the *process* of forecasting, however, can be gained by working through this brief example.

The numbers in parentheses beneath the regression coefficients are called "standard errors." Statisticians often use a rule of thumb to interpret the "significance" of coefficients with these "standard errors." In general, if the absolute value of the standard error is less than half the size of the coefficient itself then the coefficient is "significant." Here, all standard errors are one-fourth or less. However, other statistical problems are involved and one should not rigidly interpret the results in this fashion.

Exogenous variables, M_s and G, are thought of as policy variables in a Keynesian system. They may be increased or decreased to expand or contract economic activity. The coefficients of M_s and G in equation (19.9) indicate how much change in Y will result from changes in M_s and G, respectively. This equation may be written as:

$$\Delta Y = 1.352\Delta M_s + 1.525\Delta G. \tag{19.11}$$

If we then consider the change in Y from quarter to quarter, writing Y_t for the present quarter and Y_{t-1} for the previous quarter (and similarly for M_s and G), we can write:

$$Y_t - Y_{t-1} = 1.352(M_{s_t} - M_{s_{t-1}}) + 1.525(G_t - G_{t-1}) \tag{19.12}$$

If we know the actual values for Y_{t-1}, $M_{s_{t-1}}$ and G_{t-1} as they are reported by the Department of Commerce and the Federal Reserve System, these values can be inserted in the appropriate slots in equation (19.12). We can thus let $Y_{t-1} = \$1000$ billion, $M_{s_{t-1}} = \$400$ billion, and $G_{t-1} = \$200$ billion.

The next step is crucial. What values will M_s and G assume during quarter t? To answer this, one must make a forecast. If we assume that M_s will increase at an annual rate of 4 percent, so that in this quarter it will increase roughly 1 percent, then $\Delta M_s = M_{s_t} - M_{s_{t-1}} = \$4$ billion or 1 percent of \$400 billion. Furthermore, if G is expected to increase by \$5 billion (G and Y are both expressed in terms of annual rates), then $\Delta G = \$5$ billion. Substituting the values for ΔM_s and ΔG into equation (19.11) we obtain: $\Delta Y = 1.352(4) + 1.525(5)$, and $\Delta Y = 12.033$.

Since we began with $Y = \$1000$ billion and we find $\Delta Y = \$12.033$ billion, we expect that $Y_t = \$1012$ billion. This is our forecast of the income for quarter t.

To obtain a forecast for R, we simply observe the value of R_{t-1} and incorporate projected values for M_s and G in analogous fashion.

To forecast further into the future, we must project values for M_s and G further into the future as well.

This example will surely appear mechanistic to the reader. We took some statistical equations, plugged in values for exogenous variables, and ground out our answer in just the way one might expect a mechanical engineer to use a formula to calculate the force needed to lift a certain weight. Unfortunately for economists, though, what appears to be precise and mechanical lacks sufficient accuracy for most uses. The standard errors attached to the coefficients in these equations mean that our forecast would be better expressed in terms of a degree of confidence, or a "confidence interval." We might say that although we expect Y to be, for example \$1012 billion, we are "95 percent confident" that Y will be somewhere between \$1006 and \$1018 billion. The larger the standard error attached to the coefficients the larger will be the interval within which we are 95 percent confident that the value of Y will fall.

Simple econometric models usually have relatively large standard errors. Because of this, economists are continually searching the theories and the data for better models that will have lower standard errors and will provide narrower confidence intervals for their forecasts. Many models that have been developed are elaborate and would require an entire book to describe them. But in each, the procedure we have outlined is essentially the procedure that is followed. We will mention but a few of the other models now in use.

Other "Simple" Forecasting Models

Professor Milton Friedman sometimes bases forecasts on a very simple model that is of slightly different form. He does not offer quantitative estimates of future business conditions, but he does make qualitative and comparative statements about business activity in a future period on the basis of a one-equation model. According to Professor Friedman, nominal gross national product will respond to changes in the rate of growth of the money supply occurring roughly three quarters earlier. Thus, one might write $\Delta Y_t = f(M_{s_{t-3}})$ to express in a very general way the relation that Professor Friedman has argued is most pertinent to forecasts of general business activity.

Professor Friedman is the principal spokesman for the so-called "monetarist" position. The "monetarists" feel that changes in the money supply have paramount influence on nominal gross national product and that changes in G have little effect on Y. This is in sharp contrast with the "fiscalist" position that G is important but that M_s is relatively unimportant. Of course, when both M_s and G appear in the forecasting equation, both the monetarist and the fiscalist positions are accommodated, but the relative strength given M_s and G in the equations is still a matter for debate.

Following in the monetarist tradition, economists working at the Federal Reserve Bank of St. Louis have constructed another "simple" forecasting model.[4] It also has one equation to forecast GNP and one equation for a long-term interest rate. However, each equation contains an entire system of "distributed lags." One of the early forms of the GNP predicting equation is:

$$\begin{aligned}\Delta Y_t = {} & 2.67 + 1.22\Delta M_{s_t} + 1.80\Delta M_{s_{t-1}} + 1.62\Delta M_{s_{t-2}} + .87\Delta M_{s_{t-3}} \\ & + .06\Delta M_{s_{t-4}} + .56\Delta E_t + .45\Delta E_{t-1} + .01\Delta E_{t-2} \\ & - .43\Delta E_{t-3} - .54\Delta E_{t-4} \end{aligned} \tag{19.13}$$

Here, Y is measured by GNP, M_s represents the money supply defined to include currency and demand deposits (but not including time deposits as in our example above), and E represents, not all government spending and exports, but rather what is called "high employment" federal government spending only, that is, the level of government spending that would have occurred if the economy were running at full employment. Essentially, high employment expenditures are actual expenditures less unemployment compensation payments that would not be paid if full employment existed.[5]

In order to forecast one period into the future, one must project a value for the next period's money supply and the next period's expenditure; to forecast two periods, one needs M_s and E for two future periods, and so forth.

The coefficients of current and lagged values of ΔM_s are believed to indicate the pattern of the impacts of changes in the money supply on nominal GNP over five periods consisting of four previous periods and the current period. These impacts remain positive over each of the five periods. In contrast, the coefficients of ΔE represent the estimated extent of the current lagged impacts of this variable over time; thus the positive effects of ΔE in the first three quarters change to negative effects in the last two, so that the net effect of a given ΔE over a five-quarter period approximates zero. This suggests that monetary policy has powerful and permanent effects on GNP while fiscal policy has only weak and transitory effects, so that the model's authors classify themselves as monetarists and offer their model in support of this stance.

However, other econometric models treat fiscal policy as of equal or greater importance than monetary policy. Of course, although the simplest Keynesian model excludes the monetary sector, the complete Keynesian position is that *both* monetary and fiscal policies are important.

Besides the forecasting equation (19.13) used for predicting income, the St. Louis economists have another equation that is used to predict long-term AAA corporate bond yields from the rate of change of the money supply and the rate of change of real income (the independent variables) and several

[4] L. C. Anderson and J. L. Jordan, "Monetary and fiscal actions: A test of their relative importance in economic stabilization," Federal Reserve Bank of St. Louis, *Review*, 50 (November 1968): 11–24, Reprint Series #34; "Comment" by F. De Leeuw and J. Kalchbrenner, and "Reply," same *Review*, 51 (April 1969): 6–16, Reprint series #37. For the model described above, see L. C. Anderson and K. M. Carlson, "A monetarist model for economic stabilization," same *Review*, 52 (April 1970): 7–25, Reprint series #55. Also see M. G. Corrigan, "The measurement and relative importance of fiscal policy," Federal Reserve Bank of New York, *Monthly Review*, 52 (June 1970): 133–145; and Stephen M. Goldfield and Alan S. Blinder, "Some implications of endogenous stabilization policy," *Brookings Papers on Economic Activity*, No. 3, 1972, pp. 585–644.

[5] For definitions, see K. M. Carlson, "Estimation of the high employment budget: 1947–1967," Federal Reserve Bank of St. Louis, *Review* 49 (June 1967): 6–14, Reprint Series #23, and the references cited therein.

lagged variables purporting to measure the expectation of inflation and the rate of unemployment. Three other equations (giving a total of five predicting equations altogether) predict short-term interest rates, unemployment, and inflation. By predicting inflation and nominal GNP from the forecasting equations, one can also derive an estimate of "real" GNP from the St. Louis model.

Another simple model in the monetarist tradition was constructed by Laffer and Ranson, who used logarithms of non-seasonally adjusted quarterly data.[6] The coefficients in their equations indicated that the impact of changes in the money supply occurs principally in the current quarter, and that money may not really have the lengthy influence suggested by the St. Louis group.

Research economists at the First National City Bank of New York also utilize a monetarist model similar to those just described. RCA Corporation officials have a model that resembles the St. Louis model in that GNP is related to monetary and fiscal factors (altogether, their model has 13 equations, 6 identities, and a price expectation equation), and many other business firms construct their own simple models with equations adjusted to suit their own private interests.[7]

A Glance at Some Equations from Large Models

Professor Lawrence R. Klein, a noted pioneer in the construction of econometric forecasting models for the United States,[8] established the Wharton econometric forecasting model at the University of Pennsylvania—the first large model of its type. Over the years this model has been continuously developed and improved; its coefficients and variables are routinely updated to take into account the most recently available information, and its size has varied over the years; for example, in 1970 it contained 47 equations and 29 identities, only two representative members of which will be presented here in order to give the "flavor" of their content:[9]

$$C_n = 27.7 + .259\,\frac{Y-T}{P_n} + 8.88\,\frac{P}{W} + (1.91)\,\frac{1}{8}\sum_{i=1}^{8}(C_n)_{-i} + .00056\,\frac{L}{(P_n)_{-1}} \tag{19.14}$$

$$h = .721 + 320(X/X_c) + .00217\,(X - X_{-1}) - .00026t \tag{19.15}$$

where C_n is expenditures on consumer nondurables;

[6] See Arthur B. Laffer and R. David Ranson, "A formal model of the economy," prepared for the Office of Management and Budget, Executive Office of the President, dated February 26, 1971, mimeographed.

[7] For a brief description of five models, see F. R. Strobel and W. D. Toal, "Econometric models: What they are and what they say for 1971," Federal Reserve Bank of Atlanta, *Monthly Review* (March 1971), available in reprint form.

[8] L. R. Klein, *Economic Fluctuations in the United States, 1921–1941* (New York: John Wiley & Sons, 1950). One of the first simultaneous equation Keynesian models of the U.S. economy is described in L. R. Klein and A. S. Goldberger, *An Econometric Model of the United States, 1929–1952* (Amsterdam: North-Holland, 1955).

[9] These equations were taken from pp. 13–19 of L. R. Klein, "A postwar quarterly model: Descriptions and applications," in *Models of Income Determination* (Washington, D.C.: National Bureau of Economic Research, 1964). Also see M. K. Evans and L. R. Klein, *The Wharton Econometric Forecasting Model* (Economics Research Unit, University of Pennsylvania, 1967).

$Y\text{–}T$ is disposable personal income;
P is non-labor personal income in billions of current dollars;
W is wages, salaries, and other labor income in billions of current dollars;
P_n is the implicit price deflator for consumer nondurables;
L is end of quarter cash balances in billions of current dollars;
h is hours worked per week, an index;
X is private gross national product (GNP less government spending representing "public" product) in billions of 1954 dollars;
X_c is private gross national product at full capacity in billions of 1954 dollars.

Equation (19.14) is the predicting equation for spending on consumer nondurables. It is considerably more complicated than the one we have dealt with in our theoretical treatment, for in it C_n depends upon real disposable income (disposable income divided by the price index for consumer nondurables), upon the ratio of personal income to labor income, upon the average level of consumer nondurable spending during eight previous periods, and upon the real value of cash balances that consumers held as the quarter began. Values of C_n are estimated jointly with values of other elements of consumption, investment, and income.

The variable h stands for labor hours worked. It is related to the ratio of actual to potential gross product and also to the recent change in private gross product. Hours worked increases as full capacity is approached and as private gross product increases. However, a small negative time trend indicates that the work-week is subject to gradual shortening. This is expected if leisure is a "luxury" good—if as incomes rise people prefer more leisure time.

Another pioneer in the construction of larger econometric models is Professor Daniel Suits. Under his supervision in the 1960s, the Economic Research Seminar at the University of Michigan constructed a model with about 35 equations and eight identities. This model too has been altered and updated periodically in a continuing search for a version that will yield better forecasts. Unlike the Wharton model, the Michigan model is expressed in first differences; that is, period-to-period *changes* in activity levels are estimated from data on previous changes in other variables. A representative equation taken from one early version used to forecast the economic outlook is:

$$\Delta HS = .47\Delta HF + .55\Delta Y - .1886(HS - HF)_{-1} + 2.8J - 2.5 \quad (19.16)$$

where HS is housing starts (in thousands of units per month);
HF is household formations;
Y is disposable income in 1958 constant dollars;
J is estimated change in mortgage lending by financial institutions.

Here, an economic variable in the construction industry depends upon other economic factors such as income and financial lending activity. But it also depends upon a demographic factor—household formations. The third term on the right-hand side of the equation indicates that if housing starts increased more than household formations did last year, this year's housing starts will be lower than otherwise. This is called a "stock adjustment" element in the model.

These few equations from the Klein and Suits models fail to do justice to their elegance and the reader should look to the references for comprehensive descriptions that cannot be presented here.[10] Other prominent large econometric models include the Brookings Institution–Social Science Research Council model (Brookings–SSRC), the Federal Reserve Board–Massachusetts Institute of Technology model (FRB–MIT), the U.S. Department of Commerce, Bureau of Economic Analysis model (BEA), the Data Resources, Inc., model (DRI), the one constructed at Chase Econometrics, Inc., under the supervision of Michael K. Evans, who formerly worked closely with Professor Klein on the Wharton model, and Ray C. Fair's model, maintained by the Department of Economics at Princeton University.

ALTERNATIVE PROJECTIONS AND MODEL RELIABILITY

We have focused on the projections that econometric models generate for the broad aggregative variables, for these are the variables that attract the most public attention. But it is also true that the models have predicted the broad aggregates more closely (in a relative sense) than they have predicted their component parts. In other words, it appears that offsetting errors among the estimates of component parts of a model lead to a closer estimate of the aggregate itself.

Model forecasts are often provided in threes or fours—that is, model operators may choose three alternative values of a crucial exogenous variable and run three alternative sets of projections. In our example above we assumed a 4 percent annual growth rate in the money supply. Alternatives could have been 2 percent or 6 percent growth rates. It is all too clear that what is put into the model affects what comes out of it. In simple models it is easy to see the impact of various alternatives without working through the model. In larger models it is not so easy to follow through all of the ramifications of a given alternative, although some are so computerized that variables can be changed at will to obtain special-purpose forecasts (the DRI model allows private businessmen to "consult" via telephone in just this way).

Econometric models, when originally published, were expected by some to replace the variety of other forecasting techniques in use. (The scientific aura of the complicated formula was impressive—"Omne ignotum pro magnifico est." [11] But as experience has been gained in working with them it has

[10] D. B. Suits, "Forecasting with an econometric model," *American Economic Review*, 52 (March 1962): 104–132; L. R. Klein and G. Fromm, "The Brookings–S.S.R.C. econometric model of the United States," *American Economic Review*, 55 (May 1965): 348–361.

[11] "That which is unknown appears to be magnificent" (*Tacitus*)

become more and more evident that judgment is a necessary adjunct to the formal model. To project the money supply one must forecast Federal Reserve policy. To project the budget one must forecast the fiscal policy of the President and the Congress. To project foreign trade one must forecast foreign economic activity and the policies of foreign governments. Consumers may change their spending attitudes so that a different savings ratio must be introduced as an "add-factor." Business investment intentions may be amended and, again, an "add-factor" is required.

Those who use econometric models to forecast do not, however, always have a better batting average than other forecasters. In a recent survey one econometric model user did "best" on the average over 1959–1970, but was closely followed by a traditional forecaster; and a second econometric model user did only fair.[12] Of a sample of 13 forecasters one showed an average error of 2.4 percent of GNP, while another's error was only 1.9 percent. "For all forecasters the average error was about 2.2 percent," [13] but if GNP is $1000 billion, a 2 percent error is $20 billion—a rather sizable sum. There is much room for improvement, and economists will continue to search for better forecasting techniques.[14]

CONCLUSION

The macroeconomic model developed in this book is used implicitly in broad policy decisions regarding the establishment of institutions to carry out countercyclical monetary and fiscal policies. But it also provides the basic framework for the construction of econometric models for use in forecasting the level of economic activity.

The development of econometric models has been actively supported by both business and government. The sizable financial contributions made by one group of business firms to the development of the Wharton model indicate the strength of their interest in developing effective forecasting tools. Both the DRI and the Chase Econometrics modelers sell the use of their forecasting techniques to private business firms. And the government of the United States, with its FRB-sponsored and BEA models, and the governments of other nations, including the Soviet Union, and of many states and regions within each nation, have their own descriptive econometric models and actively support the ongoing search for improved forecasting techniques.

The pitfalls of relying on statistical data and statistical estimating procedures are known, but one attractive feature of any econometric model is that

[12] Ira Kaminow, "How well do economists forecast?" Federal Reserve Bank of Philadelphia, *Business Review* (May 1971): 9–19. Also see W. V. Bussmann and M. S. Margolis. "Large models aid GNP forecasters," Federal Reserve Bank of Dallas, *Business Review* (June 1973): 1–7.

[13] Kaminow, "How well do economists forecast?" p. 11.

[14] See Gary Fromm and Lawrence Klein, "A comparison of eleven econometric models of the U.S.," *American Economic Review*, 63 (May 1973): 385–393; and "Forecasts from the Fair model and a comparison of the recent forecasting records of seven forecasters," Economic Research Program, Department of Economics, Princeton University, January 22, 1973.

differences in forecasts can, in theory, be resolved. One who disagrees with the model's forecast must be able to specify just which part of the model he disagrees with. In this way differences can be reconciled; if not, at least the user of the forecasts can be told the precise reason for the difference of opinions.

ADDITIONAL READINGS

Perhaps the most comprehensive treatment of macroeconomic models, including a detailed theoretical analysis of individual sectors and equations is Michael K. Evans' *Macroeconomic Activity: Theory, Forecasting, and Control* (New York: Harper & Row, 1969). The step-by-step development of a medium-sized econometric model appropriate for student use has been provided by Edwin Kuh and Richard L. Schmalensee in their book, *An Introduction to Applied Macroeconomics* (New York: American Elsevier, 1973).

The papers presented at the second Australian Conference of Econometricians, held at Monash University on August 9–13, 1971, cover the econometric models developed for Australia, Canada, and New Zealand. A few of these papers deal specifically with the monetary sector. They have been published in a volume edited by Alan A. Powell and Ross A. Williams and titled *Econometric Studies of Macro and Monetary Relations* (New York, American Elsevier, 1973).

QUESTIONS

1. What does it mean to put a system of equations into "reduced form"?
2. Explain why it is necessary in using econometric models for forecasting to begin with a forecast of exogenous variables. Discuss whether this procedure renders econometric model forecasting "unscientific" or not.
3. Describe how "big" (number of equations, number of variables) some econometric models are, and discuss how big they "ought" to be.
4. Using the most recent information available for Y, M_s, G, and R, fill in equation (19.12). Then make projections for M_s and G and obtain a forecast for the current quarter's Y. Using the appropriate equation for R, make a forecast for R as well.

Forecasting with Input-Output Tables*

20
Chapter

In a highly diversified economy characterized by industrial specialization in the provision of goods and services to meet the wants of consumers, raw materials move through many stages of production. Direct consumer sales represent only a portion of the sales of many industries and some industries never sell to consumers, but only to other industries. Many producers are so remote from consumer markets that a direct analysis of consumer demand tells us very little about their basic industrial market. Only after a circuitous route of processing and exchange does their output reach the consumer. To forecast sales, one must therefore predict industrial market demand as a very indirect function of the demands of final users.

Input-output tables both record the sources of the materials and services used by all the industries in an economy and describe the markets for the products of these industries. They provide a framework for displaying the transactions that occur among the participants in the economic process. And they permit us to analyze the chain reaction created among linked industries by any change in final demand, a chain reaction often called the "ripple effect."

Input-output tables, whose use was pioneered by Wassily Leontief of Harvard University, provide a quantitative picture of the linkages that bind together the activities of the many different industries in a complex interrelated economy. In recent years economists have increased their application of input-output tables to economic forecasting. Since they describe the purchases-sales relationships among industries, they are particularly useful in forecasting industrial sales. In this chapter, we will also see how the sales of individual industries are tied in with the broad aggregates of final demand—consumption, investment, and the components of gross national product. In this way, forecasting with input-output tables is linked with other macroeconomic forecasts.

* The author of this chapter is Philip J. Bourque, Professor of Business Economics at the University of Washington Graduate School of Business Administration. An earlier version of this chapter was published as Business Studies #5 by the University of Washington Graduate School of Business Administration.

THE INPUT-OUTPUT ACCOUNTING FRAMEWORK

Before discussing the forecasting uses of input-output tables, we should consider the information contained in the accounting framework. Our discussion runs in terms of an *interindustry* input-output model, but *the techniques to be described are applicable to the study of other types of interdependencies and have predictive implications as long as the feedbacks among units occur in a fixed pattern.*

The total dollar value of the output of any industry can be traced to the markets in which it is sold. That portion of the ouput of an industry sold to another industry for further processing is called "intermediate product," for it is used by the purchasers as a current input in their production processes. The output of an industry not sold to another industry as current input is, by definition, sold to final demand. Final demand is conventionally defined for input-output purposes in the same way as it is in the GNP accounts. It includes spending by consumers, government, and investors (capital formation and net inventory accumulation) and sales to export markets (GNP = final demand less imports). This definition of final demand has the advantage of relating industrial output to the GNP accounting framework. But the definitions of final sales and intermediate sales may be varied, and in principle the distinction separates those areas of activity for which the investigator believes he can successfully establish the existence of invariance between input and output from those for which he cannot. In the language of econometrics, intermediate transactions are the endogenous variables of the system, while the final demand components are exogenous.

The flows of goods and services among and between industries and final users may be notationally described:

If X_i is the sales of any industry, $i = 1, \ldots, n$ industries;

x_{ij} is the sales of the ith industry to the jth industrial user, $j = l, \ldots, n$ industries;

Y_i is the sales to consumers, investors, government, and exports;

then:

$$X_i = x_{i1} + x_{i2} + \ldots + x_{in} + Y_i \qquad (20.1)$$

Equation (20.1) is a balanced equation defining the output of any industry as equal to the sum of its sales to all industrial customers and all final users.

A balanced equation may be written for each industry, and when the equations for all of the n industries are placed in order they provide a system of n equations. This system of equations is called a transactions matrix, and it appears as follows:

$$\begin{array}{lcccccccccc}
\textit{Out-} & & & & \textit{Intermediate} & & & & & & \textit{Final} \\
\textit{put} & & & & \textit{Demands} & & & & & & \textit{Demand} \\
X_1 & = & x_{11} & + & x_{12} & + & \cdots & + & x_{1n} & + & Y_1 \\
X_2 & = & x_{21} & + & x_{22} & + & \cdots & + & x_{2n} & + & Y_2 \\
\vdots & & \vdots & & \vdots & & & & \vdots & & \vdots \\
X_n & = & x_{n1} & + & x_{n2} & + & \cdots & + & x_{nn} & + & Y_n
\end{array} \qquad (20.2)$$

Each of the *row* variables on the right side of each equation of the matrix, after values have been estimated for them, describes the value of the output of the *i*th industry sold to each *j*th industry customer (x_{ij}) or sold to final users (Y_i). Each sale is also a purchase, so the *columns* of the intermediate sector show how much the *j*th industry purchased as an input from each supplier. Since the transactions matrix describes the sales-purchase network in a selected period, it is an "input-output" table. Entries in the table may be estimated either by measuring the inputs purchased by each industry from each of the others, or by measuring the distribution of the output of each industry to others (a row versus a column approach). The conceptual and empirical problems of quantifying this matrix are quite involved, but benchmark input-output tables are available for the United States for the years 1947, 1958, 1963, and 1967.[1]

These accounts of industrial flows are useful in marketing analysis. Comparisons of successive tables show the changing importance of markets over time. An individual producer, by comparing his sales patterns with those of his industry, can appraise the extent to which he shares in supplying the input requirements of various industrial and final markets for his product. By reading down the column for his industry, he can compare his purchases (costs) with those of his competitors.

Table 20–3 illustrates the basic structure of input-output tables. Producers sell to one another, in transactions called intermediate flows, and to final markets, the elements of the GNP expenditure categories. Reading across a row shows the disposition of the output of an industry, and reading down a column shows the inputs used by the industry to produce its output. At the bottom of the table are the value-added components of an industry's expenditures; the reader should recall that the gross national income originating in all industries combined equals the gross national product produced.

Several caveats are important in analyzing input-output tables of this kind. One is that the definition of "industries" consolidates establishments producing different products, and hence the "mix" of output of the industry named in the input-output table may be different from that of a particular firm. Mix differences also mean that the inputs used by a particular business may be different from those of the industry. After all, industries are pragmatically identified as establishments producing "related" products or using "similar" processes; this means that *an industry's statistics conceal a good deal of heterogeneity among the establishments which compose it.* In making interpretations from input-output tables, one should carefully consider the conventions in respect to valuation and classification—a practice appropriate in the interpretation of any accounting framework.[2]

[1] The dimensions of U.S. tables vary in size. The 1947 table was prepared for approximately 450 industries, but published in collapsed versions of 210 and 50 sectors. The 1958 table was initially published with 85 sectors, with some additional detail published separately. The 1963 and 1967 tables have nearly 370 industries, with 85-sector versions comparable to the 1958 table.
[2] We have side-stepped any discussion of the numerous accounting conventions, such as the valuation of output, the handling of competitive and noncompetitive imports, the use of margins as measures of activity in certain industries, and the transfer or redefinition of activity from one sector to another Such considerations are beyond the scope of an introductory discussion.

INPUT-OUTPUT COEFFICIENTS

The discussion thus far has been limited to the framework for tracing the actual flows of goods and services among industries. Having determined the historical network of interindustry transaction, how can we use this pattern to forecast future levels of industry activity? More specifically, what determines the values X_i and x_{ij}?

Economic theory offers a hypothesis to explain the relationship between the purchases by industry *j* from industry *i*. The magnitude of the sales of the *i*th industry to the *j*th industry, x_{ij}, depends on the level of output of the *j*th industry. Increases or decreases in the output of an industry are accompanied by increases or decreases in the various current inputs absorbed by the industry. This proposition is merely a statement of the law of costs—larger outputs require larger inputs—and may be described generally as follows:

$$x_{ij} = F(X_j) \tag{20.3}$$

This form does not specify the exact character of the relationship. The law of costs requires merely that this relationship be restricted to make the function a monotonically increasing one. Under these conditions the ratio of x_{ij} to X_j need not be constant. It is usual, however, to write this relationship in the more restricted form:

$$x_{ij} = a_{ij}\, X_j \tag{20.4}$$

where a_{ij} is a constant coefficient of production termed a "flow coefficient." It implies a linear homogeneous relationship between the output of an industry and the various industrial supplies and services the industry must purchase to produce that output. This form of production coefficient is not a theoretically valid generalization, but it is an approximation. Its chief appeal lies in its simplicity for both estimation and subsequent computations. It is important to note that this linear relationship is not, in theory, a necessary condition for the use of input-output tables and need not be adhered to if a variable rather than a constant coefficient of production is important enough to warrant additional complications. In practice, however, it is costly to introduce variability into the coefficient of production.

Substituting equation (20.4) into equation (20.1) yields:

$$X_i = a_{i1} X_1 + a_{i2} X_2 + \ldots + a_{in} X_n + Y_i \tag{20.5}$$

Each of the a_{ij} values is estimated from past ratios of x_{ij}/X_j. A complete set of flow coefficients for an input-output model of n industries forms a square matrix:

$$\begin{matrix} a_{11}, a_{12}, \ldots, a_{1n} \\ a_{21}, a_{22}, \ldots, a_{2n} \\ \vdots \qquad\qquad \vdots \\ a_{n1}, a_{n2}, \ldots, a_{nn} \end{matrix}$$

in which *each column describes the cents' worth of each kind of material, energy, and service required from other industries by a given industry per dollar of its output*. In Leontief's words, each *column* describes the "menu" or "recipe" followed by the column industry when it purchases goods and services to be used as operating inputs in producing a dollar's worth of output.

Can the matrix of flow coefficients, derived from past experience, be used to forecast the input requirements of industry for some future period? This depends upon its stability over time. Practitioners of input-output analysis view the coefficients matrix as primarily determined by the technological structure of production. Since technology changes but slowly over time, they argue, the flow coefficients will often have a degree of stability useful for forecasting purposes.

If the pattern of inputs required by an industry to produce its output exhibits strong elements of stability, observations from recent experience may be used to infer the distribution of procurement for some interval of time beyond that of the observations. Coupled with the assumption that the distribution of inputs is not significantly affected by the level of output, the coefficient matrix becomes a constant useful for prediction.

> "In other words, and in rather oversimplified form, a basic concept of input-output approach is that in many cases the pattern of goods and services needed to carry on a given productive activity is identifiable through empirical research, exhibits strong elements of stability, and hence is useful for a variety of analytical purposes."[3]

By treating flow coefficients (a_{ij}) as independent structural parameters in the system of equations (20.5), substitution effects that might be caused by relative price changes are ruled out. Since all current inputs are assumed to be utilized in fixed proportions regardless of possible variations in their relative prices, the model may be considered theoretically incomplete.

Leontief has argued that the importance of substitution due to changes in relative prices has been exaggerated in production economics. In his view, the degree of complementariness among inputs is often so high that even quite wide variation in their relative prices may only slightly affect the combination of inputs that would be used. Moreover, insofar as relative price changes are important to particular industries, such changes themselves are in large part the consequences of technological changes. That is, changes in the technology of production alter the industrial demand for inputs and, through this impact upon markets, lead to relative price variations. If this is so, perhaps changes in the coefficient structure of production affect prices more than changes in relative prices affect the coefficient structure. However, the issue is not so much a matter of basic theory as one of emphasis; the assumption of fixed coefficients within a given technology is a pragmatic simplification.

[3] W. Duane Evans and Marvin Hoffenberg, "The nature and uses of interindustry data and methods," in *Input-Output: An Appraisal, Studies in Income and Wealth*, Vol. 18, by the Conference on Research in Income and Wealth (Princeton, N.J.: Princeton University Press, 1955).

Since the coefficients that express the input structures of industries are taken from observations of past experience, to what extent can that experience be projected into the future? The assumption that technology changes but slowly over time is not necessarily valid. Innovations reported in production processes in both the popular and engineering literature and the obvious development of new products certainly lend the impression that the pace of technological advance is very rapid indeed. However, technological change within a nation has not yet been subjected to the kind of independent measurement that would make possible an evaluation of this assumption. Even when remarkable new innovations in production appear, they are introduced marginally and the carry-over of existing techniques is likely to dominate an industry's input pattern for some time. Indeed, the empirical investigations conducted to measure input-output coefficients are increasing our knowledge of the technological structure of industry, and the pattern of change over time is the subject of current research by several investigators.[4] How long it takes before an input-output table becomes outmoded is difficult to say since this depends upon the purposes to which it is put and the precision expected. It has been suggested that input-output tables have a useful life of up to a decade from their date of construction, and it is always possible to alter historical coefficients where new information indicates these have changed. Engineering studies and operating cost projections for new or proposed plants are sometimes available to advance the input coefficients into the period of the projection.

The development of the flow coefficient matrix is central to the input-output concept because it sets the behavioral pattern for translating the implications of a set of final demands (Y) into levels of industry activity (X) required to achieve those final demands. Equation (20.5) says that the level of output of the ith industry (X_i) depends upon (a) the levels of output of each of its industrial customers (X_j), (b) these customers' dependence upon the ith industry for inputs (a_{ij}), and (c) the levels of final demand for the ith product (Y_i). Since there are as many equations of the form of equation (20.5) as there are industries, the production levels of each of these industries is determinate. In other words, given a column vector of n final demands and the matrix of flow coefficients, the X_i terms may be solved simultaneously.

The economic significance of the calculation is that both the direct and indirect production requirements implied by any level of final demand are solved. For example, if the demand for automobiles changes by \$1.00, the coefficient column for automobiles describes the direct inputs the automobile industry needs in order to increase its deliveries to final users by that amount. Its purchases of steel, glass, paper, paints, electrical parts, fuel, and so forth

[4] Comparison of coefficient matrices over time or between countries is one method for quantifying the notion of technological change. See Ann P. Carter, "Changes in the structure of the American economy, 1947 to 1958 and 1962," *Review of Economics and Statistics*, 49 (May 1967): 209–224; Beatrice H. Vaccara, "Changes over time in input-output coefficients for the United States," *Applications of Input-Output Analysis*, Vol. 2, *Proceedings of the Fourth International Conference on Input-Output Techniques*, A. P. Carter and A. Brody (Eds.) (Amsterdam: North-Holland, 1970).

are described by its column in the coefficient matrix. Suppliers of these products, in order to make deliveries to the automobile industry, must purchase inputs from other industries, whose amounts per dollar of their sales likewise are described by their column coefficients. These suppliers in turn place orders with other suppliers. The demands upon the outputs of each industry to support the production of $1.00 of automobiles may be accumulated to show how much production must take place in each industry to supply the automobile industry, its suppliers, their suppliers' suppliers, etc.

This computation is analogous to the Keynesian investment multiplier which measures the direct effect of a change in investment expenditure upon income plus the indirect effect of induced expenditures for consumption upon income. In the input-output framework, the induced spending effects for intermediate inputs are accumulated and it is the output (or sales) of each industry that is measured.

A more convenient, and certainly more compact, way of representing a system of input-output equations is in vector and matrix notation. If **X** represents a vector of outputs whose values are to be determined for each of n industries, **Y** represents a vector of final demands, and **A** represents the matrix of flow coefficients, then:

$$\mathbf{X} = \mathbf{AX} - \mathbf{Y} \tag{20.6}$$

which states that the outputs of different industries depend upon the demands for inputs by industry and demands for inputs by final users. Since the **A** matrix is a constant and the **Y** vector is independently determined, the solution of the **X** vector is obtained as follows:

$$\mathbf{X} - \mathbf{AX} = \mathbf{Y} \tag{20.7}$$

$$(\mathbf{I} - \mathbf{A})\mathbf{X} = \mathbf{Y} \tag{20.8}$$

where **I** is an identity matrix playing the role in matrix algebra that the number 1 plays in ordinary algebra. Dividing both sides by $(\mathbf{I} - \mathbf{A})$, we obtain:

$$\mathbf{X} = \left(\frac{\mathbf{I}}{\mathbf{I} - \mathbf{A}}\right)\mathbf{Y} \qquad \text{or} \qquad \mathbf{X} = (\mathbf{I} - \mathbf{A})^{-1}\,\mathbf{Y}. \tag{20.9}$$

The expression $(\mathbf{I} - \mathbf{A})^{-1}$ is called the inverse matrix. Such a table constitutes the focus of an input-output study for impact analysis since it indicates both the direct and indirect effects upon the output of *every* industry per dollar's worth of final demand for the output of any *one* industry. It is a table of *industrial* output multipliers.

These ideas can be illustrated by a simple numerical example if we consider an economy composed of three industries ($i = 1,2,3$), with production coefficients (a_{ij}) and final demands (Y_i) as follows:

$$\mathbf{A} = \begin{vmatrix} .20 & .00 & .25 \\ .20 & .33 & .00 \\ .00 & .33 & .50 \end{vmatrix} \qquad \mathbf{Y} = \begin{vmatrix} 35 \\ 10 \\ 0 \end{vmatrix}$$

We wish to determine the levels of output each industry must produce if the final demands are to be met, that is, the magnitudes of X_1, X_2, and X_3. The direct impact of final demands upon the outputs of these industries is 35, 10, and 0, since these are the amounts specified for delivery to final users. For industry 1 to deliver that output, it must purchase 7 units of input from itself (.20)(35) and 7 units of input from industry 2. Similarly, for industry 2 to deliver 10 units of output to final demand it must purchase 3.33 units of supply from itself and from industry 3. There are no final demands for industry 3, so it has no outputs to produce on this account and therefore no input requirement. The first round industrial support requirements therefore generate intermediate demands of 7.00, 10.33, and 3.33 for the outputs of industries 1, 2, and 3, respectively.

In order to meet these intermediate demands for output, each industry must purchase additional inputs, creating second round supporting industry outputs, and this in turn requires still more intermediate inputs. This scenario is spelled out for several steps in Table 20–1.

After several rounds the necessary supporting requirements trail off into rather small magnitudes and their sum approaches a limit of accumulated impacts as indicated in Table 20–2.

Our particular focus of attention is upon the total levels of output each industry must produce if the final demands are to be met. If producers in each industry had forecast the demands for their products based only on a GNP forecast of final demands, they would have seriously underestimated the demands indirectly generated for their products. Consumer demands for potatoes create, indirectly, demands for gasoline and cotton cloth and many other goods and services!

The reader should not interpret the succession of supporting industry

Table 20–1. Supporting Requirements for Deliveries to Final Demand.

		Industry 1	Industry 2	Industry 3	Indirect demands for output
Final demand for output		35	10	0	—
First round indirect demands for the outputs of industry	1	7.00	0	0	7.00
	2	7.00	3.33	0	10.33
	3	0	3.33	0	3.33
Indirect demand generated by first round		7.00	10.33	3.33	—
Second round indirect demands for the outputs of industry	1	1.40	0	0.84	2.24
	2	1.40	3.44	0	4.84
	3	0	3.44	1.68	5.12
Indirect demand generated by second round		2.24	4.84	5.12	—
Third round indirect demands for the outputs of industry	1	0.44	0	1.28	1.72
	2	0.44	1.61	0	2.05
	3	0	1.61	2.56	4.17

Table 20–2. Accumulated Impacts upon Output.

Industry	1	2	3
Direct	35.00	10.00	0
First round	7.00	10.33	3.33
Second round	2.24	4.84	5.12
Third round	1.72	2.05	4.17
Fourth round	1.38	1.02	2.76
Fifth round	0.97	0.62	1.72
$D + \sum_{1}^{5}$	= 48.31	28.86	17.10
$D + \sum_{1}^{\infty}$	= 50.00	30.00	20.00

requirements generated by the example as a sequence related to a particular time dimension. Operating in a static framework, input-output as yet lacks a temporal dimension; some of the adjustments that take place in industrial production as final demands change undoubtedly involve lags, but there may also be anticipatory adjustments.

Our example has employed an iterative technique to solve for the total demands placed upon industry as a consequence of a given bill of final demand. A mathematical treatment is readily adaptable to computer solution even for very large systems of equations. The general system of equations (20.2) for the input-output model is:

$$\begin{aligned} X_1 &= a_{11}X_1 + a_{12}X_2 + \cdots + a_{1n}X_n + Y_1 \\ X_2 &= a_{21}X_1 + a_{22}X_2 + \cdots + a_{2n}X_n + Y_2 \\ &\vdots \\ X_n &= a_{n1}X_1 + a_{n2}X_2 + \cdots + a_{nn}X_n + Y_n \end{aligned}$$

For the **A** matrix in our example, this may be written:

$$\begin{aligned} -.80X_1 + .00X_2 + .25X_3 + Y_1 &= 0 \\ .20X_1 + (-.67X_2) + .00X_3 + Y_2 &= 0 \\ .00X_1 + .33X_2 + (-.50X_3) + Y_3 &= 0 \end{aligned}$$

These simultaneous equations may be solved for X_1, X_2, and X_3 as functions of Y_1, Y_2, and Y_3. Ordinarily this is done by matrix inversion. In matrix notation:

$$\mathbf{X} = (\mathbf{I} - \mathbf{A})^{-1}\mathbf{Y}$$

so that in our particular problem:

$$\begin{vmatrix} X_1 \\ X_2 \\ X_3 \end{vmatrix} = \frac{\begin{vmatrix} 1 & 0 & 0 \\ 0 & 1 & 0 \\ 0 & 0 & 1 \end{vmatrix}}{\begin{vmatrix} 1 & 0 & 0 \\ 0 & 1 & 0 \\ 0 & 0 & 1 \end{vmatrix} - \begin{vmatrix} .20 & 0 & .25 \\ .20 & .33 & 0 \\ 0 & .33 & .50 \end{vmatrix}} \begin{vmatrix} Y_1 \\ Y_2 \\ Y_3 \end{vmatrix}$$

The middle term of this expression is the solution of the inverse matrix, which the computer will tell us is:

$$(\mathbf{I} - \mathbf{A})^{-1} = \begin{vmatrix} 1.33 & 0.32 & 0.67 \\ 0.40 & 1.59 & 0.20 \\ 0.27 & 1.06 & 2.13 \end{vmatrix}$$

This is a table of inverse coefficients. Reading down the columns this table tells us that for each dollar of final demand for the output of industry 1, that industry's own output must increase by a total of 1.33 units, the output of industry 2 must expand by .40 units, and the output of industry 3 must expand by .27 units. Industry 1 must produce more than is directly required of it by final users since it must also supply its suppliers; and although industry 3 sells none of its output directly to industry 1, indirect supporting requirements dictate that it expand its output by .27 units for every unit of output industry 1 delivers to final demand. Such a table is a valuable guide to forecasters in a particular industry in trying to assess the impact of changes in final demands for products or services to which they may be only distantly related.

Carrying our hypothetical example further, we may substitute the values in this inverse matrix into equation (20.9):

$$\begin{aligned} X_1 &= 1.33Y_1 + 0.32Y_2 + 0.67Y_3 \\ X_2 &= 0.40Y_1 + 1.59Y_2 + 0.20Y_3 \\ X_3 &= 0.27Y_1 + 1.06Y_2 + 2.13Y_3 \end{aligned}$$

Given that the final demands for Y_1, Y_2, and Y_3 are respectively 35, 10, and 0, the levels of output this combination of demands will impose upon each industry are:

$$\begin{aligned} X_1 &= 47 + 3 + 0 = 50 \\ X_2 &= 14 + 16 + 0 = 30 \\ X_3 &= 9 + 11 + 0 = 20 \end{aligned}$$

Since the output levels of each industry have been determined, the input coefficients (**A** matrix) can be applied to indicate the amounts of the output of each industry which will be deliverable to each other industry. In the illustration, industry 1 produces 10 units of output ($a_{11}X_1$) for its own consumption and sells 5 units ($a_{13}X_3$) to industry 3 and none to industry 2; these sales, combined with a delivery of 35 units to final demand, describe the markets in which industry 1 will dispose of its total output under the stipulated final demand conditions. Of course, by applying its input coefficients to the predicted level of output, the level of its purchases (inputs) of goods and services from suppliers is also described.

The preceding discussion of input-output tables has been abstract. As a more concrete expression of these ideas, a portion of the 1967 dollar flow table for the United States is reproduced from the *Survey of Current Business* (February 1974) in Table 20–3. Reading across the rows of the Interindustry Transactions table shows the dollar flows from each industry to each user, while reading down the columns reveals the operating expenditures of each

Table 20–3. Interindustry Transactions 1967 (in millions of dollars at producers' prices).

Industry No.	For the distribution of output of an industry, read the row for that industry. For the composition of inputs to an industry, read the column for that industry.	Livestock and livestock products	Other agricultural products	Forestry and fishery products	Agricultural, forestry and fishery services	•••	Rest of the world industry	Household industry	Inventory valuation adjustment
		1	2	3	4		85	86	87
1	Livestock and livestock products	5,610	1,448	96	169		....	....	....
2	Other agricultural products	8,379	905	105	507		....	....	....
3	Forestry and fishery products	....	....	34	....		....	....	....
4	Agricultural, forestry and fishery services	603	1,335	45	....		....	....	....
5	Iron and ferroalloy ores mining	....	....	....	....		....	....	....
6	Nonferrous metal ores mining	....	....	....	....		....	....	....
7	Coal mining	4	1	....	(*)		....	....	....
8	Crude petroleum and natural gas	....	....	....	....		....	....	....
9	Stone and clay mining and quarrying	2	119	....	....		....	....	....
10	Chemical and fertilizer mineral mining	....	12	....	....		....	....	....
11	New construction	....	....	....	....		....	....	....
12	Maintenance and repair construction	233	370	....	....		....	....	....
13	Ordnance and accessories	....	....	....	....		....	....	....
14	Food and kindred products	3,694	....	24	44		....	....	....
15	Tobacco manufactures	....	....	....	....		....	....	....
16	Broad and narrow fabrics, yarn and thread mills	....	9	....	....		....	....	....
17	Miscellaneous textile goods and floor coverings	10	29	59	46		....	....	....
18	Apparel	....	....	....	....		....	....	....
19	Miscellaneous fabricated textile products	(*)	43	(*)	5		....	....	....
20	Lumber and wood products, except containers	3	3	....	....	•••	....	....	....
⋮						⋮			
68	Electric, gas, water and sanitary services	97	205	1	2	•••	....	....	....
69	Wholesale and retail trade	1,333	1,527	48	28		....	....	....
70	Finance and insurance	257	314	16	2		....	....	....
71	Real estate and rental	475	2,062	13	79		....	....	....
72	Hotels; personal and repair services except auto	7	....	....	....		....	....	....
73	Business services	76	1,231	(*)	(*)		....	....	....
75	Automobile repair and services	124	132	5	1		....	....	....
76	Amusements	....	....	....	....		....	....	....
77	Medical, educational services and nonprofit organizations	183	17	....	....		....	....	....
78	Federal Government enterprises	3	4	(*)	(*)		....	....	....
79	State and local government enterprises	2	....	....	....		....	....	....
80A	Directly allocated imports	....	....	....	36		....	....	....
80B	Transferred imports	182	333	505	5		1,763	....	....
81	Business travel, entertainment and gifts	28	40	15	13		....	....	....
82	Office supplies	1	1	1	1		....	....	....
83	Scrap, used and secondhand goods	....	....	....	....		....	....	....
84	Government industry	....	....	....	....		....	....	....
85	Rest of the world industry	....	....	....	....		....	....	....
86	Household industry	....	....	....	....		....	....	....
87	Inventory valuation adjustment	....	....	....	....		....	....	....
I.	Intermediate inputs, total	22,552	14,587	1,126	1,146		1,763	....	....
V.A.	Value added	8,086	13,953	819	1,524		4,517	4,701	-1,843
E.C.	*Employee compensation*	*1,211*	*2,169*	*112*	*718*		*45*	*4,701*	....
I.B.T.	*Indirect business taxes*	*768*	*937*	*11*	*62*		....	....	....
P.T.I.	*Property-type income*	*6,108*	*10,847*	*695*	*744*		*4,472*	....	*-1,843*
T.	Total	30,638	28,540	1,945	2,670		6,280	4,701	-1,843
TR.	*Transfers*	*228*	*408*	*750*	*500*	•••	*1,763*	....	....

Source: *Survey of Current Business* (February 1974), pp. 38–43.

Intermediate outputs, total	Final Demand												
					Federal Government Purchases			State & Local Government Purchases					
	Personal consumption expenditures	Gross private fixed capital formation	Net inventory change	Net exports	Total	Defense	Nondefense	Total	Education	Other	Total final demand	Total	Transfers
28,620	1,811	....	129	55	8	5	4	15	1	13	2,018	30,638	2,453
21,691	3,756	....	1,031	3,184	-1,195	7	-1,202	73	16	57	6,849	28,540	2,182
1,696	449	....	2	47	-255	5	-260	5	1	4	249	1,945	52
2,486	136	....	....	14	11	10	1	24	17	7	185	2,670	14
1,662	....	....	25	122	-66	-65	(*)	....	....	....	82	1,744	10
1,467	....	....	12	35	126	58	67	....	....	....	173	1,640	36
2,545	121	....	125	306	43	36	7	22	15	7	618	3,163	42
14,692	....	....	257	82	....	....	....	....	....	....	339	15,031	1,138
2,304	4	....	12	84	-2	-1	-1	-47	....	-47	51	2,355	95
838	2	....	8	149	(*)	(*)	....	31	....	31	189	1,027	237
....	....	54,338	....	15	3,475	975	2,501	22,061	6,176	15,885	79,889	79,889	....
17,696	....	....	....	....	1,453	973	480	4,241	772	3,470	5,695	23,391	....
1,657	322	25	147	309	8,266	6,432	1,834	7	....	7	9,076	10,734	825
24,540	60,974	....	899	1,906	655	207	448	477	68	409	64,911	89,451	4,181
1,881	5,270	....	189	601	....	....	....	-1	....	-1	6,059	7,940	217
14,908	592	....	114	250	74	73	1	27	9	18	1,058	15,966	980
2,958	1,406	89	107	89	20	14	6	(*)	(*)	-1	1,710	4,668	282
5,698	16,247	....	281	169	127	96	31	43	2	41	16,867	22,566	289
1,824	1,983	....	49	74	336	323	13	17	5	12	2,459	4,283	171
12,118	259	7	121	367	30	22	8	4	3	1	787	12,905	254
21,370	13,935	....	....	74	344	295	49	1,599	1,054	545	15,952	37,321	188
42,551	109,367	6,544	508	2,615	1,397	1,142	255	384	-88	472	120,815	163,365	3,431
21,934	25,267	4	-1	90	54	17	37	403	173	231	25,818	47,711	1,772
38,798	70,868	2,100	....	577	292	129	163	618	168	450	74,456	113,253	....
4,640	15,472	....	....	3	616	511	105	74	-159	234	16,165	20,805	2,197
47,156	4,590	....	....	458	2,689	1,866	824	1,551	631	920	9,289	56,444	909
6,471	8,069	....	....	....	64	55	9	152	43	110	8,285	14,756	89
3,587	5,571	....	-57	332	189	196	-7	23	24	-1	6,057	9,644	555
2,688	41,112	....	....	....	2,227	1,085	1,142	2,480	138	2,342	45,819	48,507	141
5,840	1,223	....	....	106	281	225	57	230	27	203	1,841	7,691	1,805
8,414	925	....	....	....	286	6	280	23	14	9	1,233	9,647	7,962
3,826	9,870	658	-100	-18,221	3,964	2,877	1,087	3	(*)	3	-3,826	....	....
22,570	....	....	....	-22,570	....	....	....	....	....	....	-22,570	....	22,570
11,206	....	....	....	....	....	....	....	....	....	....	....	11,206	....
2,137	....	....	....	....	176	99	77	294	143	151	470	2,607	....
2,613	1,287	-2,921	-121	580	-304	-219	-85	857	22	835	-622	1,991	....
....	....	....	....	....	35,205	27,126	8,080	46,449	26,982	19,467	81,654	81,654	....
....	-2,047	....	....	9,188	-861	....	-861	....	....	....	6,280	6,280	....
....	4,701	....	....	....	....	....	....	....	....	....	4,701	4,701	....
....	....	....	-1,843	....	....	....	....	....	....	....	-1,843	-1,843	....
....	....	....	....	....	....	....	....	....	....	....	....	....	....
....	....	....	....	....	....	....	....	....	....	....	....	795,388	....
....	....	....	....	....	....	....	....	....	....	....	....	*471,090*	....
....	....	....	....	....	....	....	....	....	....	....	....	*70,239*	....
....	....	....	....	....	....	....	....	....	....	....	....	*254.060*	....
....	490,660	110,443	10,034	5,132	90,804	71,333	19,471	88,315	39,512	48,803	795,388	....	....
....	....	....	....	....	....	....	....	....	....	....	....	....	....

industry. Near the bottom of the table is a row called "value added." This represents expenditures by the industry at the top in the form of wages, property income, and taxes, and is therefore the GNP originating in the named industry.

From the transactions table the input coefficient matrix for the U.S. economy is derived by expressing each industry's expenditure for each kind of input as a percentage of total output. The transposed inverse of the **A** matrix is then computed to obtain the Total Requirements matrix, $(\mathbf{I} - \mathbf{A})^{-1}$, which displays the direct and indirect output generated in each industry per dollar of final demands in the economy. The three sets of tables—the transactions table, the coefficient table, and the inverse matrix—are usually published as companion tables so that for many uses it is unnecessary for the analyst to depend on his own computer resources.

Sets of input-output tables have been constructed for the American economy for the years 1947, 1958, 1963, and 1967, and it is expected that benchmark tables will be prepared in the future at five-year intervals. In addition, estimated versions are available for some intervening years. Input-output tables are also available for a number of areas within the United States and for many other countries as well.

INDUSTRIAL MULTIPLIERS AND KEYNESIAN INCOME MULTIPLIERS

The Leontief input-output model bears a formal resemblance to the Keynesian model of income determination. While both models are capable of expansion to introduce additional variables, their basic properties bear striking similarities. Expressing the Keynesian model in its usual simplified form, letting Z represent government plus investment expenditures, and using **S** to represent intermediate transactions in the Leontief model, we obtain:

	Leontief input-output	*Keynesian national income*
Definitional equation	$\mathbf{X} = \mathbf{S} + \mathbf{Y}$	$Y = C + Z$
Behavioral relation	$\mathbf{S} = \mathbf{AX}$	$C = MPC \cdot Y$
Reduced form	$\mathbf{X} = (\mathbf{I} - \mathbf{A})^{-1}\,\mathbf{Y}$	$Y = (1 - MPC)^{-1}\,Z$

The Keynesian model describes the determination of the level of aggregate final demand, given autonomous investment and government expenditures; the Leontief model describes the determination of the structure of industrial production, given a level of final demand. The behavioral relationships of Keynesian economics turn mainly on a fixed psychological relationship between consumption and income. In the Leontief model, the posited behavior is a fixed technical relationship between intermediate inputs and industrial output. The multiplier relationship of the Keynesian model runs in terms of the multiple change in final demand (via consumption) associated with autonomous income; the multiplier relationship of the Leontief model is the multiple change in industrial output (via intermediate input) generated by any change in sale to final demand.

Since a Keynesian income-expenditure model provides a technique for determining the level of final demand, while the Leontief input-output model provides a way of determining the implications of that level of final demand upon industrial output, the complementary features of the two models should be apparent.

There are, of course, differences between the two models. The usual version of the Keynesian model is highly aggregative, while an input-output model is disaggregated by industry. The units of measurement in the Keynesian system are stated in terms of net expenditure (GNP), while those of the input-output system measure gross shipments (sales). By means of an input-output system, the **Y** values of the Keynesian system, which represent net final demand, can be translated into gross industrial shipments. Because of the industrially disaggregated character of the input-output model, it employs a system of equations usually expressed by matrix algebra; the Keynesian model can usually be expressed in a few equations. In order to restate a final demand obtained from a GNP forecast in terms capable of being used in an input-output model, aggregate demand must be divided according to delivering industry. That is, GNP projections must be converted into a vector showing the distribution of total expenditures according to producing industries (the equivalents of $Y_1, Y_2, \ldots, Y_n$).

The relationships between the national income determination model and the input-output model may be sketched graphically:

$$\mathbf{X} = \mathbf{AX} + \mathbf{Y} \longleftarrow Y = MPC \cdot Y + Z.$$

The arrows indicate the direction of the spending flows, with the loop between **X** and **AX**, and between Y and $MPC \cdot Y$ representing the feedbacks associated with the input-output inverse and the investment-income multiplier, respectively.

USE OF INPUT-OUTPUT IN IMPACT ANALYSIS

One of the basic uses of input-output, certainly up to this time its most frequent application, has been for appraising the industrial impact of changes in final demands. The simplest impact analysis can be made directly by a reading of the computed inverse—the $(\mathbf{I} - \mathbf{A})^{-1}$ matrix—since each column of this matrix describes the direct and indirect output changes required of each of the industries in the economy per unit change in final demand for the output of any given industry. For example, paper manufacturing firms can size up the implications of shifting demands in seemingly distant and unrelated markets to determine how much paper will be needed in total and by each using industry. Each industry can learn a great deal about its markets by a careful scrutiny of the tables.

More elaborate computations requiring the use of a computer make it possible to assess the impact of changing technology in one industry upon the demand for output of others. A paper container manufacturer, for example, may be interested in estimating how deeply a trend toward utilizing metal containers (by food processors or tobacco manufacturers, or by other industries) will cut into demand for paper containers. The **A** matrix may be altered to reflect an anticipated substitution in which inputs of one kind are displaced by another, and an alternative inverse matrix may be computed. These matrices can then be compared to contrast the total requirements for paper containers under the two technologies.

THE ECONOMIC IMPACT OF DISARMAMENT

An interesting and illuminating application of input-output analysis was made by Leontief and Hoffenberg,[5] who examined the industrial consequences of a transfer of national expenditures from military to civilian purchases. They asked what would happen to output and employment in different industries if the level of government defense expenditures were reduced and some other category of final demand increased by the same amount. Since the shopping list of the Defense Department is quiet different from that of the housewife, a conversion from military to civilian markets would create substantial shifts in the levels of output of different industries.

In order to evaluate both the direct and indirect industrial consequences of alternative spending packages (**Y** vectors), they expressed each bill of final demand—military, investment, consumption, and exports—in amounts directly spent for particular goods per $100 million of each alternative. They then multiplied each bill of final demand by the inverse matrix to obtain estimates of the dollar flows required directly or indirectly by each industry in order to produce each final demand alternative. The differences between the inverse weighted by a $100 million military package and the inverse weighted by each alternative civilian use of $100 million showed the net industrial effect of a change in that amount of spending from military to each set of civilian demands.[6]

They emphasized the *net* effects per $100 million of expenditure because virtually every industry, directly or indirectly, is affected by a shift in final demands—but each package of final demands affects them in different degrees. A table of differences indicates that a cutback of military spending reduces the demand for the products of some industries by a smaller amount than the induced rise in demand for their products caused by an offsetting expenditure for nonmilitary purposes. In the case of apparel and textile mill products, for instance, a shift of $100 million of military spending to nonmilitary govern-

[5] Wassily W. Leontief and Marvin Hoffenberg, "The economics of disarmament," *Scientific American*, 204 (April 1961): 47–55.

[6] That is, $(\mathbf{I}-\mathbf{A})^{-1}\,\mathbf{Y}'-(\mathbf{I}-\mathbf{A})^{-1}\,\mathbf{Y}''=\mathbf{X}'-\mathbf{X}''$, where $\mathbf{Y}'$ is the military spending vector; $\mathbf{Y}''$ is an alternative; and $\mathbf{X}'$ and $\mathbf{X}''$ are output vectors under each condition.

Table 20–4. Net Change in Output and Employment in Apparel and Textile Mill Products Industries Caused by a Shift in Final Demand from a $100 Million Military Procurement Package to an Alternative.

Alternative demands which could be served	Net change in output (in thousands of dollars)	Net change in employment (man-years)
Government, nonmilitary	−300	−20
Residential construction	−100	−14
Personal consumption	7700	572
Business investment	0	− 6
Exports (except military)	7400	416
Exports to India (nonfood)	8500	473

Source: Wassily W. Leontief and Marvin Hoffenberg, "The economics of disarmament," *Scientific American*, 204 (April 1961): 47–55.

ment spending or to residential construction would lead to a net decrease in demand for that industry's output. A shift to investment would have negligible effects. A shift to either personal consumption expenditure or exports would increase demand for apparel and textile mill products by much more than the decreases in demand associated with the reduction in military spending. The net changes in output and employment in apparel and textiles that would occur as spending shifts from military to some other forms of final demand are illustrated in Table 20–4.

The implications of disarmament for industrial output can readily be seen from this type of analysis. It is important to understand that these predictions take account of the indirect as well as the direct industrial requirements needed to produce each bill of final demand. Simply looking at the direct military and alternative demands will not provide a measure of impact on an industry since the largest buyers served by industry are often other industries. Even though final demands constitute the raison d'être of production, the means for their fulfillment are indirect.

INPUT-OUTPUT PROJECTIONS

Perspectives on the growth and composition of the American economy in future years are essential in evaluating prospective market trends. But broad aggregates, such as forecasts of GNP, employment, and population, conceal the crosscurrents of change that underlie the process of growth. Furthermore, for marketing and various other planning purposes, we would like to know not only how much the nation will produce and how many people will be employed, but also the kinds of goods that will be consumed and what type of work people will engage in. It should be apparent that there is a connection between the distribution of consumers' expenditures and the rates of production and employment in industries. As noted earlier, input-output matrices help one translate changes in final demand into their implications for industrial output. Thus input-output analysis constitutes a bridge between the rather aggregative GNP-type forecasting framework usually employed in making projections of output and the disaggregation needed to trace its implications for detailed activities. The two comprehensive studies of industrial growth described below will illustrate the application of input-output analysis to forecasting.

The Interagency Growth Study

The U.S. Economy in 1980, prepared by the U.S. Bureau of Labor Statistics (BLS), is a study of the potential demand, interindustry relationships, and employment in the United States under alternative growth rate assumptions.[7] In basic outline, the BLS initially made projections of the growth of the labor force, hours of work, and productivity to 1980. Given alternative assumptions concerning unemployment rates, these elements determine the GNP, or potential output. The mix of final demand for this potential output was then estimated for each of the major demand components of GNP; this involved extensive studies of consumer, investor, and government spending. The composition of spending, disaggregated into expenditures on the products of 86 supplying industries, was projected to 1980 on the basis of past trends and other factors. These studies provided a basic projection of final demand as a vector for forecasting industry activity.

The projected final demand vector, $\mathbf{Y}$, was then multiplied by an inverse matrix $(\mathbf{I} - \mathbf{A})^{-1}$ for 1980 to obtain the projection of each industry's output level. Technological change is difficult to predict, but values in the 1980 $\mathbf{A}$ matrix were estimated on the basis of past trends and judgment. Employment changes in each industry were related to the projected output levels, taking into account trends in productivity and hours of work. Supporting studies, of course, were also required to include changes in techniques of production, productivity changes, and other factors influencing the direct employment requirements in each industry. Since there are many uncertainties in each component of the projection—final demands, the coefficient matrix, and employment-output relationships—the projections for 1980 should be regarded as the result of extended assumptions about the structure of economic growth rather than as a forecast.

It is not appropriate here to discuss the substantive results of *The U.S. Economy in 1980*, but its implications for market forecasting are important. Of major significance is the linking of projections of industrial activity to final sales so that intermediate transactions are determined. While the projections

[7] U.S. Department of Labor, Bureau of Labor Statistics, *The U.S. Economy in 1980*, Bulletin No. 1673 (Washington, D.C.: U.S. Government Printing Office, 1970).

are primarily oriented toward an analysis of the industrial distribution of employment, it is rather easy to adjust them to a "dollar-flows" basis that shows the dollar sales and purchases by industries to and from each other. From these projections, the relative growth of each market served by each industry can be calculated. Further, projections of spending by consumers, investors, government, and each industrial sector are specified in unusual detail. This feature will be especially helpful to market forecasters who have found the familiar GNP expenditure categories far too broad for most commercial purposes. Of course, neither emphasis on causal interdependencies nor disaggregation by themselves guarantee a projection, but the framework within which these projections have been made provides a significant advance in forecasting technique.

The Almon Model

Professor Clopper Almon, Jr., an economist with the Maryland Research Center, has made projections of American economic growth using an input-output model, and his initial projections for 1975 have been periodically extended. The Almon models have somewhat more dynamic properties than the Interagency Growth model discussed above, and, because consumer and investment spending as well as interindustry activities are mutually interdependent, the system he uses is essentially an integration of a dynamic Keynesian demand model and the Leontief input-output model. In Professor Almon's words:

> ". . . the keynote of the system is that it builds checks and balances into the forecasts, assuring a fivefold *consistency* between:
> (1) The sales projected for an industry and the purchases of its products by all its customers;
> (2) The output of an industry and the materials it purchases and the labor it employs;
> (3) The growth of each industry's sales and its capital investment;
> (4) Consumers' after-tax income and their spending on the products of each industry;
> (5) Total employment and the expected future labor force." [8]

The Almon model is discussed by reference to the schematic diagram of Figure 20–1, which is not an exact representation of his system but conveys its broad features. Government spending, exports, and those components of consumption and investment functions which are related neither to income nor output are exogenous; these are independently forecast either by assumption or from past trends. This demand (G, E, Z) vector gives rise to direct demand

[8] Clopper Almon, Jr., *The American Economy to 1975* (New York: Harper & Row, 1966).

for industry output, $X_1, \cdots, X_n$. To produce these outputs, industries purchase from suppliers in successive rounds (in amounts as shown by the inverse matrix). Industrial output gives rise not only to interindustry transactions but also to payments to factors of production or value-added (VA_i). Leakages in the form of imports (M_i), taxes, and savings take place, but the income generated affects spending by consumers. Their response to income changes depends upon disaggregated marginal propensities to consume outputs produced in different industries so that consumer demands for industrial output rise, though not in strict proportion to the income of consumers. Consumer spending leads to a higher level of interindustry transactions, income, and consumption in a familiar output multiplier and income multiplier fashion.

At the same time, another feedback relationship is also at work. Changes in the level of industry demand may require increases in productive capacity if demand presses on capacity. Thus, either simultaneously or with some lag, each industry responds to increased demand for its output by requiring more capital inputs as well as current inputs. The amount of capital additions required depends upon capital requirements per unit of capacity change. These are described by a matrix of capital coefficients (**B**) which shows the amount of investment goods required by each industry from each producer

Figure 20–1. Diagrammatic Representation of the Interindustry Model.

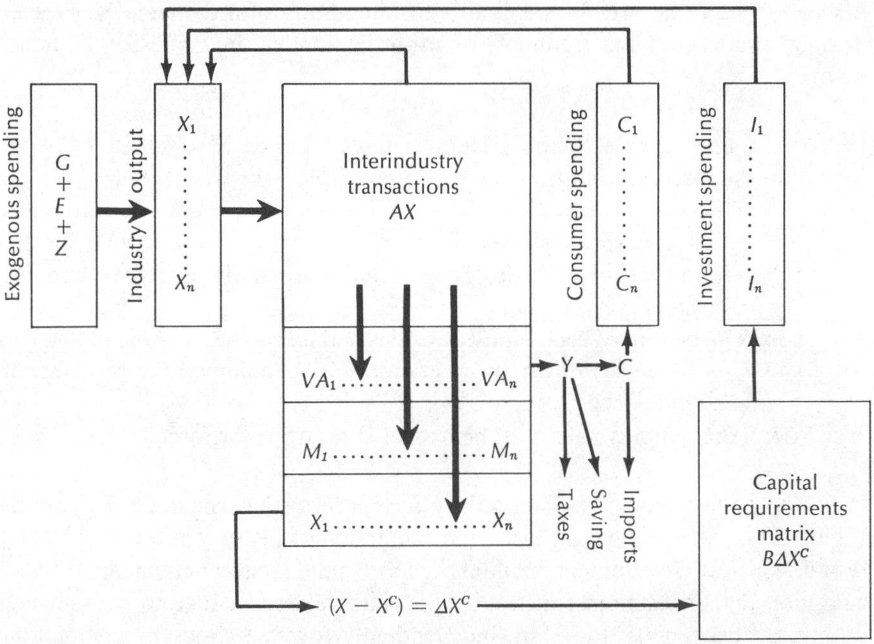

This is a partially closed, dynamic interindustry model. Exogenous expenditures create a demand for industry output generating interindustry transactions and value-added (GNP); incomes affect the level of consumer spending, creating further demand for industry output. If output levels of industry exceed X^c, capacity output, then ΔX^c, required increments in capacity, create investment demand by amounts and kinds indicated by the capital coefficients matrix, B.

of capital for each unit of change in its capacity. In this way, changes in industrial output generate additional demands for output from industry in the form of capital goods. This is depicted by the arrow from the investment vector to the output vector. This, of course, now has further effects on both consumption and investment. Hence, the consumption sector and the investment sector are internally dependent upon income and output as in the Hicksian-type multiplier-accelerator model.

The especially interesting features of this model for forecasting are: (a) the linking of a dynamic income-expenditure model to an input-output system so that industry-level activity results from the analysis; (b) the disaggregation of industrial and final demands that permits introduction into the analysis of large amounts of detailed factual information as well as particularized behavioral relationships; and (c) the opportunity the model gives for incorporating new information or positing varying situations whose implications may be explored.

Among its drawbacks—aside from quantitative problems related to data accuracy—are problems of incomplete or incorrect specifications of behavioral relationships and the large number of side forecasts which are necessary inputs into the system. For short-term projections, the coefficient structure should be time-phased to reflect the lags necessarily entailed in the linkages. Adjustments for price changes are exogenously determined if they are considered at all.

It must be recognized that a good deal of judgment is required to make input-output models operational, for their users must analyze data and interpret causal linkages. Their great benefit is that while they remind us of our limited knowledge, they also organize in a meaningful way the knowledge we possess. The Almon model is an attempt to construct a quantified model of the inner workings of the economy and provide a more coherent picture of the *whole* economy in much greater detail than we have ever had before.

APPLICATIONS OF INPUT-OUTPUT AT THE FIRM LEVEL

From a practical viewpoint, input-output forecasts provide individual industries with estimates of their probable future growth, of the industrial markets that account for that growth, and of the inputs each industry will require from others if that growth is to be achieved. While it is traditional for a company's projections to be prepared in the light of its own industry's probable growth, many business firms are not a part of a single industry but produce products classified in several industrial categories. Moreover, because of market specialization, a given firm may selectively service certain types of users, or users in certain regions. It is then necessary for such companies to split industries as identified in the input-output tables into subcategories that engage their special interests.

The absence of highly detailed industrial sectors has been one of the recurring criticisms of input-output by company economists. In part, this criticism has been met by the detailed 1963 input-output study (approximately 350 industries) prepared by the Bureau of Economic Analysis. For even greater detail, it is possible to relate the industrial sectors of input-output to product components by using commodity information available in census reports.[9]

Another way of adapting input-output tables to the needs of a particular firm has been suggested by Charles Tiebout. In essence, he has said that a firm can better use interindustry tables by adding itself as a separate row in the available tables. The marketing department of a firm can estimate its own sales to the sectors specified in the input-output study, and from this it can calculate how much each industry acquires from it per dollar of output. Other row coefficients are appropriately adjusted to accommodate the company row. The firm may also add itself as an additional column in the coefficient matrix simply by entering its own cost experience. A new inverse is then computed as a basis for individual company input-output forecasting. If an added conditional assumption is made in the enlarged inverse to the effect that the individual firm will hold a stipulated relative share as a supplier in each of the markets in which it sells, the company can estimate how much it should produce as changes take place in final demand, and how each market it serves will change.[10] Simulations may be run assuming different degrees of market penetration or combinations of market shares that are needed to assure a specified growth in total sales.

A rather novel use of input-output has been developed by one company particularly concerned about the ability of its suppliers to meet delivery schedules. Initially the analysis was made by finding out the union contract expiration dates of its direct suppliers. Then, in order to catch strike threats in earlier stages of the production chain, the inverse table was used to determine important "back-up" industries, and collective bargaining difficulties were appraised at still earlier stages. In this way, the firm was forewarned not only of work stoppages that might directly affect its own suppliers, but also of stoppages in earlier stages that might indirectly affect its suppliers' ability to meet commitments.

It has been suggested that input-output be applied to the internal operations of companies with several interrelated divisions. Hubbell and Ekey have designed a variant of the Leontief model in which intracompany transactions are projected by substituting "departments" for the usual industrial sectors.[11]

[9] As an illustration, see the discussion in *Sales Management* (November 5, 1965).

[10] Charles M. Tiebout, "Input-output and the firm: A technique for using national and regional tables," *Review of Economics and Statistics,* 44 (May 1967): 260–262. Tiebout suggests that only a desk calculator is necessary provided an original inverse is available, but full advantage of "inserting yourself" into the matrix is gained by rather conventional input-output computer programs.

[11] J. Paul Hubbell and David C. Ekey, "The application of input-output theory to industrial planning and forecasting," *Journal of Industrial Engineering,* 14 (January-February 1963): 49–56.

Several companies are experimenting with this type of model for use in facilities planning, budgeting, and manpower planning.

APPLICATIONS IN REGIONAL ANALYSIS

Input-output has also been extensively applied in the study of regional economies, where the emphasis shifts from the analysis of technologically-grounded input-output dependencies to assumed fixed trading patterns among industries within a region.[12] Because the dependence of a region on imports is much greater than that of a large national economy, the feedback effects upon a local economy of changes in its final demands are more difficult to predict. Nevertheless, input-output analysis has filled a significant void in the ability of economists to assess regional linkages.

The most useful application of regional input-output models has been the appraisal of the consequences of changes in exports (e.g., out-of-state sales) upon the activity levels of regional industries, recognizing that within regions there is considerable interdependence between export-oriented industries and those serving local markets. Policymakers use input-output tables as a framework for regional planning—especially for evaluating the effects of alternative regional policies upon the output of industries and income earned in the area. Regional input-output tables, when available, portray the existing industrial linkages and serve as a framework for regional income and product accounting. However, the lack of uniformity in design and the infrequency of preparation mean that the commercial application of regional input-output tables is sporadic.[13]

CONCLUDING COMMENTS

Input-output analysis focuses upon the interdependencies of industrial activity. Its most promising feature is that it can be used as a technique for analyzing the productive process as a single and complete economic system. Since many variables not specified in the model are functionally related to industrial activity, the value of the model is enhanced by its capacity to be related to a large variety of decision problems. It can be useful as a part of the forecaster's tool kit, but it is not a forecaster's panacea. Input-output analysis rests on simplified assumptions concerning economic behavior, and its utility in any particular application must be judged in the light of the compromises with reality that make the model operational.

[12] For an extended discussion of regional input-output models and their forecasting applications, see Harry W. Richardson, *Input-Output and Regional Economics* (New York: John Wiley & Sons, 1972).

[13] See also *An Inventory of Regional Input-Output Studies in the United States*, by Philip J. Bourque and Millicent Cox, Occasional Paper No. 22, Graduate School of Business Administration, University of Washington, 1970.

ADDITIONAL READINGS

The following publications contain essential treatments of the nature and applications of input-output analysis:

Clopper Almon, Jr., *The American Economy to 1975—An Interindustry Forecast* (New York: Harper & Row, 1966).

Anne P. Carter, *Structural Change in the American Economy* (Cambridge, Mass.: Harvard University Press, 1970).

Hollis B. Chenery and Paul G. Clark, *Interindustry Economics* (New York: John Wiley & Sons, 1962).

Input-Output Analysis: An Appraisal, Studies in Income and Wealth, Vol. 18, Conference of Research in Income and Wealth, a report of the National Bureau of Economic Research (Princeton, N.J.: Princeton University Press, 1955).

Interindustry Economics Division, "The input-output structure of the U.S. Economy: 1967," *Survey of Current Business*, 54 (February 1974): 24–56.

Wassily W. Leontief, *The Structure of the American Economy 1919–1939* (New York: Oxford University Press, 1951).

Wassily W. Leontief, et al., *Studies in the Structure of the American Economy* (New York: Oxford University Press, 1953).

William H. Miernyk, *Elements of Input-Output Analysis* (New York: Random House, 1965).

Office of Business Economics, *Input-Output Structure of the U.S. Economy: 1963*, Vol. 1–3 (a supplement to the *Survey of Current Business*) (1969).

Harry W. Richardson, *Input-Output and Regional Economics* (New York: John Wiley & Sons, 1972).

U.S. Department of Labor, Bureau of Labor Statistics, *The American Economy in 1980*, Bulletin No. 1673 (Washington, D.C.: U.S. Government Printing Office, 1970).

QUESTIONS

1. Given the following transactions table showing the dollar value of sales by the row industry to the column industry:

Industry Producing	Industry Purchasing				
	Intermediate use			Final use	Gross
	Agriculture	Manufacturing	Services	Households	output
Agriculture	10	30	20	40	100
Manufacturing	10	60	30	200	300
Services	0	30	10	60	100
Households	80	180	40	0	300
Gross input	100	300	100	300	800

calculate the following:[14]

(a) The direct requirements per dollar of gross output table.
(b) The direct and indirect requirements table.
(c) The total output of the agriculture, manufacturing, and services sectors needed to produce simultaneously $1 of output for final use by each of the three sectors.
(d) The total output of each of the three sectors needed to provide $30 of agricultural goods, $220 of manufactured goods, and $70 of services for final use (instead of the $40, $200, and $60 in the table).

2. What information is provided by the number in a cell of a transactions table? Of a direct requirements table? Of a total requirements table?

3. Perhaps the most telling criticism leveled at input-output analysis concerns the assumption of constant coefficients of production. Write a paragraph or two describing the nature of the problem, and another supporting the assumption.

4. What is an income multiplier in the framework of input-output?

5. Describe how an input-output table may help one forecast the impact of disarmament on the structure of industry.

6. The Almon model ensures consistency in its forecasts in five ways. What are these ways?

7. How might individual firms use input-output analysis?

[14] See W. H. Miernyk, *Elements of Input-Output Analysis* (New York: Random House, 1965), Chapter 7, for a review of the necessary matrix algebra.

INDEX

A

Abramovitz, M. 338
Absolute income hypothesis 75–76
Accelerator 129,
  and multiplier 349–350, 391
  See also Capital stock adjustment
Ackley, G. 27, 70, 161, 209 n, 312
Adelman, M. A. 312
Aliber, R. Z. 301 n
Almon, Clopper, Jr. 389–391, 394
Anderson, J. 48 n
Anderson, L. C. 366 n
Anderson, P. S. 45 n, 301 n
Ando, A. 81, 83, 312
Angevine, G. E. 64 n
APC. *See* Average propensity to consume
APS. *See* Average propensity to save
Asset account 44
Assets
  financial 139–141
  tangible 139–141
  and risk 142
  See also Interest rate; Money; and Wealth
Auld, D. A. L. 295 n
Automatic stabilizers 127, 249
Average propensity to consume
  defined 57
  and income distribution 66–68
  See also Consumption
Average propensity to save 61, 72

B

Bach, G. L. 312
Bagiotti, T. 276
Balanced budget multiplier 111–112
Balance of international payments
  bookkeeping balance 257–278
  components of 254–258
  defined 253–254
  and policy 263
Balance of trade. *See* Balance of international payments
Balance sheet 138
  sectoral 139–140
Balancing item 7
Ball, R. J. 312
Baumol, W. 161, 337 n
Behavioral coefficients 116
Bell, G. 46 n
Blinder, A. S. 366 n
Bodkin, R. 82, 84
Boulding, Kenneth 46
Bourque, Philip J. 272 n, 393 n
Bradford, D. F. 337 n
Brady, D. 81–82
Branson, W. H. 273
Brennan, G. 295 n
Brimmer, A. F. 312
Brinner, R. 285, 301 n
Brody, A. 377 n
Bronfenbrenner, M. 161, 312
Brookings Institution 369
Brumber, R. 83
Budd, E. D. 313
Budget
  balanced 110
  deficits and surpluses in 118–120
Bureau of Census 216
Bureau of Economic Advisors
  econometric model of 369, 370
  and leading indicators 353–356
  1963 input-output study by 392
Bureau of Labor Statistics 388
Burger, A. E. 312
Burns, Arthur F. 351 n
Business cycle theory
  and accelerator theory 349–350
  and coincident indicators 356
  and diffusion indices 356–358
  and forecasting 346
  Hawtry theory 346–347
  Hayek theory 347
  innovator theory 348–349
  and lagging indicators 356
  and leading indicators 352–356
  and long waves 350–351
  measures of 351–353, 358–359
  monetary theory 346–347
  over-investment theory 347–349
  Schumpeter theory 347–349
Bussmann, W. V. 370 n
Butters, J. K. 123

C

Capital
  human 139
  private 254
  short term 255
  See also Capital stock; Investment
Capital account 4
Capital coefficients 390–391
Capital spending rule 16–17
Capital stock 94
  adjustment 129
  optimum level of 96
Capital structure 90
Capital-to-output ratio 318
Carlson, K. M. 366 n

Carrying charges 140, 141
Carter, A. P. 377 n, 394
Chambers, E. J. 346 n, 352 n, 358 n, 359
Chandler, J. H. 219 n
Chandler, L. V. 50
Checkbook float 45 n
Check kiting 44–45
Chenery, H. B. 394
Clark, J. M. 99
Clark, P. G. 394
Closed economy 225–226
Commodity market equilibrium 166
 See also IS
Commodity-labor market 229–232
 See also LM_Z; *YZ*
Comparative statics 53
Compensating balances 45 n
Confidence interval 365
Consumer price index 281
 See also Price index
Consumption
 absolute income hypothesis of 75–76
 in basic model 225–228
 and consumer durables 68–69
 and credit 63–64
 and demography 65–66
 and demonstration effect 77
 determinants of 62–70
 in Domar growth model 318
 and expectations 63–64
 function 56–57, 117
  empirical evidence for 81–82
 and income 54
 and income distribution 66–68
 and inflation 243 n
 and interest rate 63–64
 and liquidity 63
 measurement of 69–70
 and permanent income hypothesis 79–82
 of profit recipients 226–227
 real 110, 237–238
 and relative income hypothesis 76–79, 81–82
 of rentiers 226
 of wage earners 226
 and wages 110, 237–238
 and wealth 62–63
Corrigan, M. G. 366 n
Cost of capital 90
 See also Discount rate
Cost of living 291
 clause 204, 213
 index 18
Cost pass-through 305
Council of Economic Advisors 119, 123
Cox, M. 393 n
Credit 63–64
Credit money 30
 creation of 32–41
 sources of 31
Currency 42
Currency devaluation 263
Currency ratio 33
Current account balance 4, 258
Cycle theory 347–349
 See also Business cycle theory

D

Dauten, C. A. 346 n, 359
Davison, Paul 198, 222, 249
DCE. *See* Domestic Credit Expansion
De Allessi, L. 313
Decision rule 145
Deflationary gap 321
de Gyor, P. G. Gschwindt 46 n
De Jong, F. J. 198
De Leeuw, F. 366 n
Demand
 aggregate
  in foreign sector 252–253
  and real balance effect 210
 final
  effect on industries of 385–386
  in input-output table 373
 for labor 207
Demand deposit 43
Demography and consumption 65–66
Demonstration effect 77
Denison, E. F. 27, 330–331, 338
 policy implications of 336–337
Depodwin, H. J. 312
Dernburg, T. F. 151 n, 217
Devaluation
 and investment 95
 and price-incomes policy 306–307
Dicks-Mireaux, L. A. 310 n
Diffusion index 356–358
Diminishing returns 186
Disarmament 386–387
Discount rate
 approximations to 88–91
 defined 87
 and market rate of interest 88–91
 and risk 88–89
Discretionary operations 37
Discretionary policy
 and slope of *IS* 172, 175
 and slope of *LM* 172–175

Disposable income 13
Domar, E. D. 317, 338
See also Growth and Domar model
Domestic Credit Expansion 46
Dow, L. A. 346 n, 359
Duesenberry, James S. 65 n, 76, 81, 83, 89 n, 99, 146
Dunn, R. M., Jr. 276

E

Eckstein, O. 285, 301 n
Econometric models 361–371
See also Forecasting; Input-output models
EE curve
defined 259
and exchange rate 259–262
and *LM* 261
See also Balance of international payments
Eilbott, P. 123
Eisner, R. 99, 295 n
Employment
and balance of payments 265–267
defined 216
equilibrium 203–211
and money wage 208–210
full 217
defined 219
in full model 265–267
in industry 191–192
measures of 215
seasonal adjustment of 218
See also Phillips curve; Trade-off; Unemployment
Employment-supply function 225
defined 207
Entine, A. D. 50
Equilibrium
basic model 228
changes in 168–175
in commodity market 166
in Domar growth model 318, 320
of *IS* and *LM* 166
in neoclassical model 329
See also IS; LM; LM_Z*; YZ*
Eurodollar float 44 n
Evans, M. K. 62–63, 83, 89 n, 99, 367 n, 369, 371
Evans, W. D. 376 n
Excess reserves 39
Exchange rate 252
and *EE* curve 259–262
Expectations
and consumption 64–65
and investment 95
Exports 120
External diseconomies 315–317
External equilibrium 259
See also Balance of international payments; *EE* curve

F

Fair, R. C. 369
Federal Reserve Bank
Boston 276
St. Louis 313
forecasting model 366–367
Federal Reserve operations 37
Fellner, W. 324 n
Ferber, R. 83
Fine tuning 296
See also Fiscal policy; Monetary policy; Policy
Finance sources 15
Firms
input-output analysis 391–392
national income accounting 4
Financial technology 154
Financing costs 89–91
Fiscal policy
in basic model 244–245
discretionary 134
in Domar growth model 324
and fixed exchange rates 268–269
and flexible exchange rates 273–274
and government expenditures 105
and inflation 293–294
and *IS* 135–136
lags in 114
and lump-sum taxes 107–108
and unemployment 220
Flanagan, R. J. 313
Flexible exchange rates 270–271
and policy 273–275
Flow coefficient 375, 376
matrix 377–378
Forecasting
Almon model 391
and business cycles 346, 350–359
defined 342
with econometric models 361–371
with input-output projections 387–391
and judgment 369–370
models
Keynesian 366–367
Klein 367–368

monetarist 366–367
Suits 368–369
Wharton 367–368
naive 343
predictive ability of 369–370
See also Input-output analysis
Foreign sector
and aggregate demand 252–253
and aggregate supply 251–252
and wages 253
See also Balance of international payments
Foster, E. 313
Fractional reserves 32
FRB-MIT model 369, 370
Friedman, M. 46 n, 79, 83, 162, 301 n
econometric model 365–366
as monetarist 365–366
Friedman, R. 81–82
Friend, I. 84
Fromm, G. 369 n, 370 n
Full-employment budget 119

G

Gaines, T. C. 45 n
Galbraith, J. K. 69
Gavett, T. W. 223
General linear model 131
Goldberger, A. S. 63 n, 367 n
Goldfield, S. M. 366 n
Goldsmith, R. W. 139
Gordon, M. S. 217 n
Gordon, R. A. 123, 217 n, 346 n, 359
Gordon, R. J. 285 n
Government function 7
Government expenditures
in basic model 227
in commodity market model 102
determinants of 101–102
and high employment 366
and *IS* 168
and multiplier 103–104
and policy implications 104–105
Government production 12–13
GNP. *See* Gross national product
Gross national cost 19
Gross national product
defined 11, 12
implicit deflator of 282 n
measurement problems with 20–21
social costs of 19
and welfare 19, 377
Gross savings and investment account 14–17
Growth
causes of 330–334
defined 315
and Domar model 317–325
equilibrium 318, 320
instability 321
limitations 324–325
empirical evidence of 330–334
and input-output projections 388–391
measures of 327–328
and neoclassical model
assumptions 325–326, 327–328
equilibrium 328–329
stability 329
and technological progress 327–328
policy implications of 334–337
and technological progress 331
policy implications 336–337
and X-inefficiency 331–334
Guideposts 301 n

H

Haberler, G. 346 n
Hagen, E. E. 83
Hahn, F. H. 317 n, 338
Hall, C. W. 45 n
Hansen, A. H. 179, 346, 347 n, 359
Hansen, B. 295 n
Harrod, Sir Roy 295 n, 317, 321 n, 338
Hart, A. G. 50
Hawtry, R. G. 346–347
Hayek, F. A. 347
Heller, W. W. 123
Helliwell, J. 276
Hicks, Sir John 128 n, 179
Hicksian model
and Almon model 391
and *IS* 128
Hirshliefer, J. 99
Hoffenberg, M. 376 n, 386
Holland, R. A. 219 n
Hollister, R. G. 313
Holt, C. C. 362 n
Holzman, F. D. 312
Homogeneity 189 n
Housewives' services 10
Hubbell, J. P. 392 n
Hudson, H. R. 180
Human capital 139
Humphrey, T. M. 48 n

I

Impact analysis 385–386
Imports 120–124

Imputed rent 10
Imputed sales 9
Income
  disposable 13
  full-employment level of 168
  and interest rate 156–158
  permanent 79–82
  personal 12
  present value of 86
  real disposable 54
  transitory 79–82
Income and product
  account 6
  gross 7
  net 7
  statement
    firm 5
    foreign sector 13
    government unit 9
    households 10
Income determination 127–128
  See also IS; LM; LM_Z*; YZ*
Income distribution
  and consumption 66–68
  defined 66
  and employment multiplier 235
  and income multiplier 234
  and inflation 290, 300
  and production function 187–188
  and supply of labor 202–203
  and wages 194–195, 209–210
    and inflationary psychology 243
    without inflationary psychology, 237–238
Income statement 4
Incomes policy. *See* Prices-incomes policy
Inflation
  and balance of trade 267–268
  and comparative wages 292
  and consumption 243 n
  cost-push 289–292
  costs of validation 297–300
  defined 280
  demand-pull 287–288
  and financial system 299
  and income distribution 290, 300
  and job vacancies 286
  and labor markets 286
  as monetary policy 294–296
  predictability of 299
  and resource allocation 299
  semi- 213
  validation of 290, 295
Inflationary gap 288
  in Domar growth model 321
Input-output analysis
  Almon model 389–391
  on firm level 391–393
  and impact analysis 365, 366
  and Keynesian model 384–385
  and regional analysis 393
  and time 380
Input-output coefficients 375–384
Input-output table
  defined 374
  estimation 374
  stability 376–377
Institutional coefficients 116–117
Interbank deposits 43
Interest Equalization Tax 263
Interest rate
  and consumption 63–64
  and demand for money 150–173
  and discount rate 88–91, 127
  and government 8
  and income 155–158
  and investment 98–99, 127
  and money supply 171
  normal 153
  and slope of *LM* 173
  and wealth effect 248–249
  See also Internal rate of return; Cost of capital
Internal rate of return 91
  and aggregate investment 92–93
  See also Interest rate; Marginal efficiency of capital
International Labor Organization 334
International Monetary Fund 256
International unit of account 262
Inventory
  defined 4
  and saving 60
Inventory cycle. *See* Business cycle, monetary theory of
Investment
  in balance of international payments 254
  in basic model 227
  and capital stock 94, 96
  and capital stock adjustment 96–97
  direct 254
  in Domar growth model 317–318, 322–324
  and expectations 95
  and financing 98
  function 92–98
  gross 96
  and interest rate 98–99
  and internal rate of return 92–93

net 96
foreign 121
portfolio 245
and rate of income growth 72–74
real 210
shifts in 94
and technological change 94–95
and time 97–98
See also Business cycle theory
IS function 131
in econometric models 362–365
and equilibrium 166
and exchange rate 271–272
and government expenditures 168
graph of 127, 132
Hicksian 128
kinked 130
and *LM*
empirical estimates 177–179
graphical derivation 167–169
and monetary policy 171–172
and money supply 176
shifts in 133–134
slope 134–136, 171–175
and taxes 168
See also LM; YZ

J

Job vacancies 286
Johnson, H. G. 276
Jordan, J. L. 48 n, 366 n
Juglar, J. C. 350
Juglar cycles 352
Juster, F. T. 27, 243 n

K

Kahn, R. F. 70
Kalchbrenner, J. 366 n
Kamenow, I. 370 n
Katona, G. 64 n, 70
Kenen, P. 50
Kennedy, J. F. 215
Keran, M. H. 277
Kern, D. 46 n
Kessel, R. A. 313
Keynes, Sir John M. 63, 70, 72, 197, 213, 222, 249
and consumption function, 56, 74–76
and cycle theory 347
Keynesian model
and econometric model 364–365
and input-output model 384–385
Kindleberger, C. P. 124, 276
Kitchin, Joseph 350
Kitchin cycles 352
Kiting checks 44–45
Klein, L. R. 63 n, 123, 367–369, 370 n
econometric model 367–368
Kondratieff, N. 350–351
Kravis, I. 84
Kreuger, A. O. 276
Kuh, E. 99, 371
Kurihara, K. 83
Kuznets, Simon 74, 80, 83

L

Labor
demand for 184–186
aggregate 200–201
and real wage 200–202
mobility 310
search for 213
supply of 202–203
and real wage 202
Labor Department 215–218
Labor force
defined 216
impact of unemployment on 297
non-homogeneity of 195
size of 217
Labor market
adjustment in 211–213
basic model of 224–225
and inflation 286
Laffer, A. B. 367
Laidler, D. E. 47 n, 161
Law of comparative advantage 252
Lee, T. H. 161
Leibenstein, H. 331–334, 339
policy implications of 337
Leontief, W. 372, 376, 386, 394
model. *See* Input-output model
Lerner, A. P. 123
Levitan, S. A. 223
Lewis, J. P. 359
Lindnauer, J. 123, 312
Lindsay, J. R. 89
Lipsey, R. E. 139
Liquidity 41
of assets 141
and consumption 63
trap 153, 158, 170, 229
LM curve 156–157
in econometric models 362–365
and *EE* function 261
and equilibrium 166
and exchange rates 271–272
graphical derivation of 160

in linear model 158–159
and money supply 170–171
shifts in 156–158, 170–171, 271–272
slope of 172–175
See also IS; LM_Z
LM_Z curve
defined 232
and money wage 241–242
shifts in 244
Lump-sum tax 105

M

McDougall, D. M. 151 n
McKenna, J. P. 180
McKenzie, G. W. 277
Malchup, F. 123
Malt, R. A. 337 n
Marginal cost 183–184
Marginal efficiency of investment 92–93
defined 93
shifts in 94
and wages 238
See also Investment
Marginal productivity function 185–186
Marginal propensity to consume 57
and income distribution 66–68
Marginal propensity to import 120
Marginal propensity to save 61
Marginal revenue 184
Margolis, M. S. 370 n
Market valuation
for firms 5
for government 7
Marx, Karl 74
Matrix
of capital coefficients 390–391
of flow coefficients 377
inverse 378
of total requirements, 384
Matthews, R. C. O. 317 n, 338
Mayer, T. 82, 84, 161, 210 n, 249 n
MC. See Marginal cost
Meade, J. E. 124, 276, 325, 338
on growth 328
Measure of economic welfare 20
Mendelson, M. 140
Metzles, A. 161
Meyer, J. R. 99
Miernyk, W. H. 394
Miller, M. H. 90 n
Mincer, J. 217 n
Mishan, E. J. 27, 316, 339
Mitchell, R. 178
Mitchell, W. C. 351
Modigliani, F. 81, 83, 90 n
Monetarists 345 n
and econometric model 365-367
Monetary base 48 n
Monetary policy
and fixed exchange rates 268–269, 271–273
and flexible exchange rates 275–276
in full model 244–245
in growth model 324
and inflation 293–294
and inflationary gap 288
and inflationary psychology 244
and *IS* 171–172
and unemployment 220
and wealth effect 248–249
See also Fiscal Policy; *LM*; LM_Z; Policy
Monetary sector 155–160
Money
as asset 138–139
defined 30–31
demand
as asset 138–139
function 153–154
and interest rate 151, 173
and precautionary balances 149
shifts in 154–155
stability of 155
total 153–154
for transactions 148–152
liquidity of 4
and *LM* 174
market 228–229
as medium of exchange 148–152
supply
and compensating balances 45
as currency 42
defined 33, 41, 45
in equilibrium 155
Federal Reserve definition of 41
and interest rate 171
and *LM* 170–171
real 175–176
and securities 159
See also Credit money; Federal Reserve operations
Money illusion 210
Money market
equilibrium 166
in commodity-labor market 232–233
and wage rate 241–242, 244
Money substitutes 294
Moore, G. H. 351 n
Moral suasion 300
Morris, F. E. 45 n

MPC. See Marginal propensity to consume
MPS. See Marginal propensity to save
Mueller, E. 64 n, 65 n
Mueller, M. G. 62 n, 146, 161, 312
Multiplier
  and accelerator 391
  balanced budget 111–112
  consumption 135–136
  defined 60
  deposit 39
  employment
    in commodity-labor market 234–235
    and income distribution 235
    and wages 240–241
  in expanded model 116–117
  export 122
  government expenditure 103–104
  import 122
  income 135–136
    in commodity-labor market 233–234
    and wages 240
  industrial output 378
  and input-output model 384–385
  interaction with accelerator 349–350
  investment 60
    and input-output model 378
  Keynesian model 384–385
  lump-sum tax 106–107
  matrix 113, 126
  super- 129
  and tax coefficients 234–235
Mumey, G. A. 89 n, 99
Mundell, R. A. 276
Musgrave, R. A. 123
Mutual savings banks 43 n
Myers, R. J. 219 n

N

National Bureau of Economic Research 27, 342, 351, 352, 359
National income 12
Neef, A. F. 219
Nelson, R. R. 334 n, 338
Net national product 12
Net foreign investment 121
Net revenues 86
Newman, H. E. 123
NNP. See Net national product
Nordhaus, W. 20, 27

O

Oates, W. E. 337 n
OECD 310 n, 313
Office of Business Economics 27
Okun, A. M. 119 n, 123
Open market operations 37, 41
  See also Federal Reserve operations

P

Palmer, J. L. 313
Patinkin, D. 62 n, 210 n, 249 n
Perry, G. L. 223, 296 n, 301 n, 312
  and labor force 284
Personal income 12
Pesek, B. P. 50
Phelps, E. 285 n, 312
Phillips, A. W. 311
Phillips curve 282–283, 284, 285
  policy instrument 286
  See also Trade-off curve
Pierson, G. 301 n
Pigou, A. C. 62
Pigou effect 210–211
  See also Wealth effect
Policy
  anti-inflationary 296–297
  and balance of payments 263
  and economic growth 334–337
  and forecasting 343–344
  for full employment 204
  and goal choice 262–263
  and inflation 293–294
  and price flexibility 214
  problems under full employment 295–296
  and wage flexibility 214
Policy instruments
  in basic model 244–245
  government expenditures as 104–105
  trade-off 286
  and wage-price flexibility 246
Portfolio adjustment 63, 68–69
Portfolio balance effect 175–176
  and *IS* 176
  See also Money supply, real
Powell, A. A. 371
Prell, M. J. 119 n
Present value 87, 242–243
  See also Discount rate
Price-incomes policy 300–310
  and controls 303–304
  and devalution 306–307
  effectiveness of 301–302
  and equity 308–309
  flexibility of 304–305, 308–309
  and guideposts 307
  and involuntary controls 309
  and productivity 309–310

and resource allocation 310
in U.S. 300–303
Price deflator 18
Price flexibility 214
Price index 17–19
problems of 282 n
Price level
and aggregate supply 192–193
determinants of 287
flexibility of 214
and market structure 289–290
and ratchet effect 245–246
and wages 193–194
Product 8–9
Production function 183
and income distribution 187–188
neoclassical 326
Production statement 4, 9
Productivity
and price-incomes policy 309–310
and technological change 196–197
Profits 184
Public goods 3

R

Ratchet effect
in consumption 78
and prices and wages 245
and wages 213
Ranson, R. D. 367 n
Real balance effect 210–211
See also Wealth effect
Recession
fixed-investment 347
inventory 346–347
Rees, A. 222
Regional analysis 393
Reserve requirements
and demand deposits 43
and notes payable 46
Reserves
defined 32
excess 39–41
and Federal Reserve actions 34–39
and general public 33–34
leakages 40–41
time dimension 40
and Treasury actions 34–37
Resource allocation 310
Richardson, H. W. 393 n, 394
Ripple effect 372
Risk
and assets 141, 142
averter 143
and discount rate 88–89
and expected returns 142
lover 144
neutral 144
Ruggles, N. 27
Ruggles, R. 27

S

Salant, W. A. 123
Sales
on capital account 4
on current account 373–374
Sametz, A. W. 89 n
Samuelson, Paul A. 99, 312, 350 n
Saving, T. R. 50
Savings
and consumption 65
and income 60
and inventories 60
and investment 60
Schmalensee, R. L. 371
Schultz, G. P. 301 n
Schultze, C. L. 284, 312
Schumpeter, J. A. 347–349
Schwartz, A. J. 46 n
Scitovsky, A. 312
Scitovsky, T. 312
Scott, R. H. 177 n, 179 n, 363 n.
Seasonal adjustment 218
Securities 159
Seiders, D. F. 313
Selten, R. T. 312
Semi-inflation 213
Shapiro, E. 50
Shapiro, H. T. 64 n
Shepherd, J. R. 310 n
Shiskin, J. 351 n
Smith, D. C. 313
Smith, H. M. 50
Smith, W. L. 162, 180
Smithies, A. 75–76, 83, 123
Smyth, D. J. 123
Smolensky, E. 198, 222, 249
Social costs 19
Social Security 291
Solomon, E. 50
Solow, R. M. 301 n, 312, 338
Spillovers 315–317
Sprenkle, C. M. 47 n
Stabilization policy 136
Stabilizers 113–114
Standard errors 364
Stock adjustment 369
Strand, K. T. 217

Strobel, F. R. 367 n
Strotz, R. 99
Studenski, Paul 27
Subsidies
  direct 5
  indirect 5 n
Substitution effect 202–203
Suits, D. B. 64 n, 69
  econometric model 368, 369
Sultan, P. 222
Super-multiplier 129
Supply
  aggregate 192–193
    assumptions 183
    and foreign trade 251–252
    in full model 224
    and market structure 195–196
    and technological change 196–197
    and wages 193–194
Supply price 87
Sweezy, P. M. 74 n

T

T-account 33
Taggart, R. 223
Tax coefficient 234–235
Tax cut of 1964 111
Tax rate 118
Taxes
  in basic model 227
  as function of income 114
  and *IS* 168
Technological change
  and aggregate supply 196–197
  embodied 196
  and input-output tables 376–377
  and investment 94–95
Teeters, N. H. 119 n
Teigen, R. L. 47 n, 162, 180
Thompson, W. 179 n
Throop, A. W. 301 n
Tiebout, C. 392
Toal, W. D. 367 n
Tobin, J. 20, 27, 81, 83, 146, 151 n, 161, 223, 285 n
Trade-off curve 282–283
  and expectations, 285–286
  and inflation 292–294
  kinked 285
  and labor force 283–284
Transfer payments 8
  in commodity-labor market 112
  as function of income 115
Turnovsky, S. J. 285 n

U

Ulman, L. 310 n, 313
Underemployment 174
Unemployment
  cyclical 219–220
  defined 216
  disguised 220–221
  frictional 219
  hidden 217
  in full model 263–265
  involuntary
    defined 203
    and negotiated wage 211–213
    part-time 221
  and labor force groups 297
  measures of 215
  rate of 216
    and employment 282–284
    in other nations 219
  seasonally adjusted 218
  structural 219
  See also Employment; Trade-off curve

V

Vaccara, B. H. 377 n
Valentine, L. M. 359
Value-added 5, 381
Vanek, J. 124
Van Horn, C. 90 n
Vertical integration 192
Voluntary restraint program 263

W

Wachtel, P. 243 n
Wachter, M. L. 285 n, 301 n
Wage-price flexibility 249
Wage-price spiral 244
Wages
  flexible 214
  minimum 205
  money 221
    and employment 206–207
    and involuntary unemployment 211–213
    negotiated levels 204–213
  and price level 193–194
  ratchet effect 245
  real 202, 221
    and demand for labor 200–201
    and involuntary unemployment 204
    and supply of labor 202–203
  variable 246
    and employment 237–246

and foreign sector 246
and inflationary psychology 242–245
policy implications 246
Wealth
and consumption 62–63
defined 247
financial 247
human 247
material 247
and money supply 248–249
real 247
Wealth effect 62, 210–211, 247–249
as automatic stabilizer 249
and monetary policy 248–249
See also Pigou effect; Real balance effect
Wealth preference function 142–144
Wealth utility function 144
Weintraub, S. 198, 222
Weiss, L. 312
Wells, P. 198
White, W. L. 50
White, W. H. 99
Witte, J. G., Jr. 99
Wrightsman, D. 276

X

X-inefficiency 331, 334

Y

YZ curve
defined 229–232
and inflationary psychology 243
shifts in 233–239
slope 233–235
See also IS

Z

Zellner, A. 63 n

1 2 3 4 5 6 7 8 9 10 –CP– 80 79 78 77 76 75 74